# THE EARL, THE KINGS, AND THE CHRONICLER

**Frontispiece.** Earl Robert and Countess Mabel of Gloucester as Monastic Patrons s.xvi[in].
The Bodleian Libraries, The University of Oxford, MS Top. Glouc. d. 2, fol. 15r.

# The Earl, the Kings, and the Chronicler

*Robert Earl of Gloucester and the Reigns of Henry I and Stephen*

ROBERT B. PATTERSON

Great Clarendon Street, Oxford, OX2 6DP,
United Kingdom

Oxford University Press is a department of the University of Oxford.
It furthers the University's objective of excellence in research, scholarship,
and education by publishing worldwide. Oxford is a registered trade mark of
Oxford University Press in the UK and in certain other countries

© Robert B. Patterson 2019

The moral rights of the author have been asserted

First Edition published in 2019

Impression: 1

All rights reserved. No part of this publication may be reproduced, stored in
a retrieval system, or transmitted, in any form or by any means, without the
prior permission in writing of Oxford University Press, or as expressly permitted
by law, by licence or under terms agreed with the appropriate reprographics
rights organization. Enquiries concerning reproduction outside the scope of the
above should be sent to the Rights Department, Oxford University Press, at the
address above

You must not circulate this work in any other form
and you must impose this same condition on any acquirer

Published in the United States of America by Oxford University Press
198 Madison Avenue, New York, NY 10016, United States of America

British Library Cataloguing in Publication Data
Data available

Library of Congress Control Number: 2018946763

ISBN 978–0–19–879781–4

Printed and bound by
CPI Group (UK) Ltd, Croydon, CR0 4YY

To Robert and Denise, Duncan,
Josiah, and Ruth Patterson

## *Preface*

This book has emerged from a doctoral dissertation initially directed by Professor Sidney Painter at The Johns Hopkins University and completed in 1962 after his death under the supervision of his successor, Professor John W. Baldwin, with the assistance of Professor Joseph R. Strayer of Princeton University. I put the idea of a book aside to pursue interests in scribal administrations and their generated business documents, but continued to hunt for Robert and earldom of Gloucester material. I was encouraged in these efforts over the years by Professor R. H. C. Davis of Merton College, whom I first met in Oxford when he was preparing his edition of King Stephen's, the Empress Matilda's, and Henry fitz Empress's charters. I also never came away from discussions of my work with my friend James Campbell of Worcester College without some new idea and question to ask of my material. I profited from the advice of Richard Sharpe about Tewkesbury Abbey's charters and am particularly indebted to David Bates, Nicholas Vincent, and Daniel Power for documentary transcriptions. The virtual explosion of literary and documentary editions along with scholarly studies of King Henry I's and Stephen reigns and of allied subjects from the 1970s along with my accumulated data has made a full study of Robert an obvious opportunity. Furthermore, some of David Crouch's studies have raised some challenging issues about Robert and the testimony of the *Historia Novella* about certain Robert-related subjects. Edmund King's new edition of the *Historia* highlighted the Gloucester family's role, including possibly Robert's, in creating its version of the text.

My efforts have been aided by the staffs of the Thomas Cooper Library, University of South Carolina; The British Library; Department of Coins and Medals, The British Museum; The National Archives (formerly The Public Record Office); The Bodleian Library; The Bibliothèque Nationale; the Archives Départmentales du Calvados; The Wiltshire Record Office; The Bristol Record Office, and The Gloucestershire Record Office. In particular I am indebted to Michael A. Williams and Amanda Saville, Queen's College Library, Oxford; D. J. McKitterick and Joanna Ball, the Wren Library, Trinity College, Cambridge; Paul Zutshi and Frank Bowles, Cambridge University Library; Irvine Gray, Brian Smith, and David J. H. Smith of the Gloucestershire Record Office; Gwyn Jenkins, Daniel Huws, Rhydian Davies, and Rhianydd Davies of the National Library of Wales; Zoe Stansell of the Department of Manuscripts, the British Library, Tamsin Mallett of the Cornwall Record Office; Gaye Morgan of the Codrington Library, All Souls College, Oxford; and Michael Riordan, Archivist, St. John's College, Oxford. Funding for my research trips has been provided by the Research and Productive Scholarship Committee, University of South Carolina; the National Endowment for the Humanities; and from the Southern Region Education Board. Periodic hospitality was provided by H. G. Pitt, David Bates, John and Frances Walsh, James and Baerbel Brodt Campbell, Robert and Amanda Simpson, Brian and Alison Smith, Christopher and Jean Elrington; Sir James Holt, Joseph P. Funke, and the Fellows of Merton and of Worcester Colleges. Robert Faber, Terka Acton, Stephanie Ireland, Cathryn Steele, Manikandan Chandrasekaran, Donald Watt, and Edwin Pritchard all have helped me get this project to press. Lastly, no acknowledgment can do justice to the many contributions my wife, Ruth Weider Patterson, has made to this book through her keen interest, encouragement, productive questions, and suggestions.

*Columbia, South Carolina*
*June 2018*

# Contents

| | |
|---|---|
| *List of Figures and Acknowledgments* | xi |
| *Table of Abbreviations* | xiii |
| *Introduction* | xv |
| *Genealogical Chart: Robert of Gloucester and the Norman Ducal-Royal Family* | xxi |

| | |
|---|---|
| 1. A King's Illegitimate Son | 1 |
| 2. A Second Career: Royal Counselor and Official: *c*.1121–1135 | 29 |
| 3. The Making of a Super-Magnate | 57 |
| 4. Feudal Baron | 82 |
| 5. The Empress's Champion | 126 |
| 6. The Earl and the Chronicler | 178 |

| | |
|---|---|
| *Bibliography* | 207 |
| *Maps* | |
|   1. Robert earl of Gloucester and Normandy | 239 |
|   2. Significant Anglo-Welsh Demesne and Military Actions Involving Earl Robert of Gloucester | 240 |
| *Index* | 241 |

# List of Figures and Acknowledgments

Frontispiece. Earl Robert and Countess Mabel of Gloucester as Monastic
Patrons s.xvi[in].     ii
The Bodleian Libraries, The University of Oxford, MS Top. Glouc. d. 2, fol. 15r.

1.1. Evidence of Robert earl of Gloucester's hand from the first-person
subscription in his name at the foot of Richard de Grainville's foundation
charter for Neath Abbey in 1130: The charter's text and subscription are
in different hands.     10
© WGAS, GB0216 A/N 1, ll. 31–5.

4.1. Seal of Robert earl of Gloucester altered and used by his son and successor
William (1147–83). NLW, Penrice and Margam Estate Record, no. 20.     113
© by permission of Llyfrgell Genedlaethol Cymru/The National Library of Wales.

5.1. a–d: Obverse and reverse of silver pennies issued in the name of Robert earl
of Gloucester at Bristol by local moneyers c.1143–c.1147: a–b, by Farthegn;
c–d, by Iordan. BM, CMB 394387; CMB 394388.     172
© The Trustees of the British Museum.

6.1. The rubricated Prologue of Margam Abbey's copy in an unidentified
hand of William of Malmesbury's *Historia Novella* sent to Robert earl
of Gloucester. BL, MS Royal 13 D.ii, fol. 110r, col. a, ll. 30–2; partial
text of dedication to the earl, ll. 30–41.     179
© British Library/Granger.

6.2. *Ex libris* inscription in an unidentified hand of Margam Abbey's codex
containing copies of William of Malmesbury's *Gesta Regum Anglorum* and
*Historia Novella* and Geoffrey of Monmouth's *Historia Regum Britanniae
(De Gestis Britonum)*. BL, MS Royal 13 D.ii, fol. 173v, col. b.     187
© British Library/Granger.

# Table of Abbreviations

| | |
|---|---|
| AD | Archives Départmentales |
| *ANS* | *Anglo-Norman Studies*: Proceedings of the Battle Conferences |
| *BGAS/BGAST* | *Bristol and Gloucestershire Archaeological Society Transactions* |
| *BIHR/HR* | *Bulletin of the Institute of Historical Research/Historical Research* |
| BL | British Library |
| BM | British Museum |
| BN | Bibliothèque Nationale |
| *BNJ* | *British Numismatic Journal* |
| Bodl. | Bodleian Library |
| BRS | Bristol Record Society Publications |
| *BSAN* | *Bulletin de la Société des Antiquaires de Normandie.* |
| *EHR* | *English Historical Review* |
| *HSJ* | *The Haskins Society Journal. Studies in Medieval History.* |
| *MSAN* | *Mémoires de la Société des Antiquaires de Normandie* |
| NA | National Archives (formerly Public Record Office) |
| NLW | National Library of Wales |
| PRO | Public Record Office (now National Archives) |
| PRS | Pipe Roll Society |
| SRS | Somerset Record Society |
| TCD | Library, Trinity College, Dublin |
| *TRHS* | *Transactions of the Royal Historical Society* |
| WGAS | West Glamorgan Archive Service |

Abbreviated titles for sources and secondary works can be found in the Bibliography. Lower-case Roman numerals following 's.' indicate paleographical dating.

# *Introduction*

Robert (*c*.1088 × 90; d. 1147), grandson of William the Conqueror and eldest son of the future King Henry I of England (1100–35), could not succeed his father because he was a bastard. Instead, as the earl of Gloucester, he helped change the course of English history by keeping alive the prospects for an Angevin succession through his leadership of its sympathizers against his father's successor, King Stephen (1135–54), in the civil war known as the Anarchy. Although, with England as a prime example of the dynastic instability plaguing western European monarchies in the twelfth century, the period more than fulfilled what the term implies, it also witnessed great cultural developments, in which Robert participated.[1] He is one of the great figures of Anglo-Norman history (1066–1154) and for his many-faceted links to it occupies important niches in the era's historiography, from comprehensive political studies of Henry I's and Stephen's reigns to the "Brother Cadfael" novels of Ellis Peters.[2] The breadth of his activities has earned him places in the literature of modern history's allied fields such as studies of Norman or Anglo-Norman England;[3] government and law;[4] art and architecture;[5] the Church,[6] literacy, literature, and education,[7] urban geography,[8] social and

---

[1] Bisson, *The Crisis of the Twelfth Century*, 60, 182–91, 269–88.

[2] Hollister, *Henry I*; Green, *Henry I*; Round, *Geoffrey de Mandeville*; Davis, *King Stephen*; Chibnall, *The Empress Matilda*; Bradbury, *Stephen and Matilda*; Crouch, *The Reign of King Stephen*; Stringer, *The Reign of Stephen*; King, *King Stephen*; *The Anarchy of King Stephen's Reign*; e.g., Pargeter (alias Peters), *Brother Cadfael's Penance*.

[3] Chibnall, *Anglo-Norman England*; Chibnall, *The World of Orderic Vitalis*; Le Patourel, *The Norman Empire*; Bates, *The Normans and Empire*; Bartlett, *England under the Norman and Angevin Kings 1075–1225*; Garnett, *Conquered England*.

[4] Warren, *The Governance of Norman and Angevin England 1086–1272*; GOE; Painter, *Studies in the History of the English Feudal Barony*; Haskins, *Norman Institutions*; Richardson and Sayles, *The Governance of Medieval England*; Kealey, *Roger of Salisbury: Viceroy of England*; MMI; *Law and Government in Medieval England and Normandy*.

[5] Boase, *English Romanesque Art 1100–1216*; *Tewkesbury Abbey: History, Art & Architecture*; Renn, *Norman Castles in Britain*, 118; Grant, *Cardiff Castle*; Brown, *English Castles*, 70. Fernie, *The Architecture of Norman England*.

[6] Cheney, *Roger, Bishop of Worcester,1164–1179*; Cownie, *Religious Patronage in Anglo-Norman England 1066–1135*; Cowley, *The Monastic Order in South Wales 1066–1349*; Cowley, "The Church in Medieval Glamorgan"; Williams, *The Welsh Cistercians*, 2 vols.; Saltman, *Theobald, Archbishop of Canterbury*.

[7] Clanchy, *From Memory to Written Record*; Dutton, "*Ad Erudiendum Tradidit*: The Upbringing of Angevin Comital Children"; Short, "Patrons and Polyglots: French Literature in Twelfth-Century England"; Thomson, *William of Malmesbury*, 2nd edn.; Damian-Grint, *The New Historians of the Twelfth-Century Renaissance*; *Anglo-Norman Political Culture and the Twelfth-Century Renaissance*, 13, 33–4. Haskins, "Adelard of Bath and Henry Plantagenet."

[8] Beresford, *New Towns of the Middle Ages*; *Bristol*; Tait, *The English Medieval Borough*; Hemmeon, *Burgage Tenure in Medieval England*; Brooke and Keir, *London 800–1216: The Shaping of a City*; *Winchester in the Early Middle Ages: An Edition and Discussion of the Winton Domesday*.

economic history,[9] numismatics,[10] and military history and the chivalric code.[11] Indeed, Robert of Gloucester was a twelfth-century Renaissance man.

As part of his plan to make war on King Stephen on behalf of his half-sister's claim to the Anglo-Norman throne, Earl Robert added a weapon to appeal to the *litterati* by commissioning the great Benedictine scholar William of Malmesbury to write a history of their times. The result was the *Historia Novella*, which is an apologia for the Empress Matilda's right to the throne and for the earl of Gloucester's sponsorship. Anyone attempting a biography of Robert is confronted by the political persona Malmesbury created of the high-minded baron who, although at heart loyal to Matilda, had to perform a conditional homage to Stephen out of necessity until the king gave him grounds to rebel and champion the empress. On top of that, there is the challenge of dealing with the inherent contradiction of the *Historia*'s case for the earl and then of sorting out fact from varieties of distortion in a mostly reliable work to create a more accurate political Robert.

Malmesbury's version of current events never became a major part of the corpus of medieval historical knowledge because for centuries his chief literary successors mostly ignored the *Historia*. The major exception, thirteenth-century Matthew Paris of St. Albans, gave Robert's so-called conditional oath of fealty to Stephen a classical flourish: "As long as you shall maintain me as senator I will support you as emperor."[12]

The chronicler's account of Robert's career during the Anarchy became a force in English historiography during the nineteenth century when history was becoming established as an academic subject. The first critical edition of the *Historia* appeared in 1840, the work of Thomas Duffus Hardy, but it was its successor, edited with commentary for the Rolls Series and published in 1887–9 by the extremely influential Oxford scholar William Stubbs, ultimately bishop of Oxford, which exerted the most influence. Stubbs gave the work his complete endorsement, although he recognized its limitations.[13] Key elements of the work appear in

---

[9] Stenton, *The First Century of English Feudalism 1066–1166*; Green, *The Aristocracy of Norman England*; Newman, *The Anglo-Norman Nobility in the Reign of Henry I: The Second Generation*; Crouch, *The Image of Aristocracy in Britain 1000–1300*; Crouch, *The English Aristocracy 1070–1272: A Social Transformation*; Le Patourel, *The Norman Empire*; Bates, *The Normans and Empire*.

[10] Blackburn, "Coinage and Currency under Henry I: A Review"; Boone, *Coins of the Anarchy*; Archibald, "The Lion Coinage of Robert Earl of Gloucester and William Earl of Gloucester."

[11] Beeler, *Warfare in England 1066–1189*; Hollister, *The Military Organization of Norman England*; Morillo, *Warfare under the Anglo-Norman Kings 1066–1135*; Gillingham, "Conquering the Barbarians: War and Chivalry in Twelfth-Century Britain"; Strickland, *War and Chivalry: The Conduct and Perception of War in England and Normandy 1066–1217*; *War and Society in Medieval and Early Modern Britain*.

[12] Among annals, Winchester's, which did use the *Historia Novella*, contradicted its representation of Earl Robert's oath to King Stephen: "Ann. Winchester," 50; Matthew Paris, *Chronica Majora* ii. 164 (transl., mine); King, *HN* (1998), lxviii–lxix, xcv–cvii; see also Chapt. 6, 203. Scribe 24, the author of the "Margam Annals," barely used the *Historia Novella* or mentioned little concerning Robert even though the abbey possessed a copy and was the earl's foundation: Patterson, "The Author of the 'Margam Annals': Early Thirteenth-Century Margam Abbey's Compleat Scribe," 198–9; Patterson, *The Scriptorium of Margam Abbey and the Scribes of Early Angevin Glamorgan*, 92–3; see also Chapt. 6, 203 and Figure 6.1.

[13] See, e.g., Maitland, "William Stubbs, Bishop of Oxford," 420; Patterson, "William of Malmesbury's Robert of Gloucester," 983–4.

Kate Norgate's mainly chronicle-based *England under the Angevin Kings*, and in the entry for Robert she contributed to *The Dictionary of National Biography*.[14] And the *Historia* achieved an enhanced standing through document-verified accounts used by John Horace Round, the apostle of the new methodology, in his *Geoffrey de Mandeville*, even though he found some of Malmesbury's passages questionable and partisan.[15]

For over half of the twentieth century scholars recognized some of Malmesbury's faults as a historian, but saw little to criticize in the *Historia Novella* except bias.[16] However, I was moved to probe the text further by H. W. C. Davis's remark that "no doubt we receive from William of Malmesbury the version of events Robert of Gloucester desired to be set before posterity." That led in part to a severely critical assessment of the *Historia* and its author in a 1965 article, "William of Malmesbury's Robert of Gloucester: A Reevaluation of the *Historia Novella*," and a follow-up piece in 1968 and ultimately to this book.[17]

Before the year was out, the first publication of Stephen's, Matilda's, her husband's and son's *acta* in *Regesta Regum Anglo-Normannorum*, volume three, edited by R. H. C. Davis challenged me to rethink some of my former positions.[18] David Crouch's full-length study of the Anarchy, *The Reign of King Stephen* (1970), a full-scale revisionist piece by Joe Leedom, "William of Malmesbury and Robert of Gloucester Reconsidered" (1974), and Crouch's partly supportive, partly critical essay of 1985, "Robert of Gloucester and the Daughter of Zelophehad," gave added impetus. Warren Hollister's 1975 article, "The Anglo-Norman Succession Debate of 1126: Prelude to Stephen's Anarchy," enhanced the image of Earl Robert as a Matilda loyalist during the late 1120s. And then you could not read Rodney Thomson's *William of Malmesbury* (1970) and not wonder how my vintage 1965 image of the historian could exist side by side with the scholarly polymath of 1970. Marjorie Chibnall's *The Empress Matilda* (1991) showed model subtlety in handling both criticism and implicit endorsement of the *Historia Novella*'s testimony on a case-by-case basis. Several interpretations of passages particularly benefiting Robert's image by David Crouch in *The Reign of King Stephen* and Edmund King in his new edition, *William of Malmesbury Historia Novella: The Contemporary History* (1998), were encouragements to expand the topic of Robert's literary patronage to include his likely direct or indirect role as one of Malmesbury's sources. King's Introduction also was both resource and foil for my thinking about the alteration of the text of

---

[14] Stubbs, William of Malmesbury, *GR* i and ii. cxli–cxlii; Gordon-Keltner & Millican, "Norgate, Kate," 9; Norgate, *England under the Angevin Kings* i. 270–1 & n., 274, 294 & n. Norgate, "Robert, Earl of Gloucester," 1242–4.

[15] Round, *Geoffrey de Mandeville*, e.g., 11, 61, versus 22, 69, 115.

[16] Galbraith, "Historical Research in Medieval England," 17, 23; Darlington, *Anglo-Norman Historians*, 9; Southern, "Aspects of the European Tradition of Historical Writing: The Sense of the Past," 253–6; Gransden, *Historical Writing* i. 183.

[17] Davis, "Henry of Blois and Brian Fitz Count," 297; Patterson, "William of Malmesbury's Robert of Gloucester: A Reevaluation of the *Historia Novella*," 983–97; Patterson, "Stephen's Shaftesbury Charter: Another Case against William of Malmesbury," 487–92.

[18] *Regesta* iii, esp. no. 898.

the *Historia* Earl Robert received and production of the codex containing a copy of the work later sent to Margam Abbey.[19]

Contrary to my former views, Robert *was* loyal to Matilda during the last decade of his father's reign, but certainly not immediately following the king's death. The earl also may have had grounds before late May 1138 for believing that Stephen was attempting to seize at least some of his estates.[20] Furthermore, evidence of Robert's involvement with the Angevins before he led Matilda to England in 1139 is even stronger than I formerly claimed.[21] Malmesbury, however, is still open to criticism for omitting Robert's abandonment of his oath to Matilda and recognition of Stephen as king in the winter of 1135.[22] Nor did William mention the loss of the earl's place at court to Waleran of Meulan and the king's favoritism toward his family, which were motives for Robert's retraction of fealty to Stephen.[23] William is accountable to some degree for publishing a disingenuous explanation of Robert's homage to Stephen. The chronicler falsely claimed that his patron's service to Matilda was completely unselfish.[24] Some dubious stories like Henry I's deathbed concession of Normandy and England to Matilda in Robert's presence and Stephen's attempted abduction of him are more valuable as evidence of the earl's literary collusion with Malmesbury than grist for indictments other than for his gullibility. Malmesbury's failure to publish the papal injunction Robert conjured up to justify his denial of fealty may not be William's fault but Robert's or a member of his household.[25] His willingness to accept possibly promised material and failure to correct his manuscript might be excusable because of his failing health.[26]

William of Malmesbury's *Historia Novella* reveals an unabashed propagandist, but also, as readers of this book will find, a valuable resource for the study of the Anarchy, reflecting a range of virtues found in his other works. Malmesbury also deserves credit for what may be considered the only contemporary biography of his patron and special respect for striving to complete his commission under adverse conditions.[27]

My findings in these topical categories are reorganized in the six following chapters containing aspects of three major phases of Robert of Gloucester's life, which I refer to as careers, and of his baronial modus operandi: his youthful grooming (Chapt. 1); promotion to favored royal counselor, servant, and a specially designed

---

[19] King, "Introduction," *HN* (1998), xvii–cvii; see Chapt. 6, e.g., 191, 198–202.
[20] Patterson, "William of Malmesbury's Robert of Gloucester," 986; *Regesta* iii. no. 898; see also Robert's foundation of St. James's Bristol and possibly his grant to the abbey of Tiron as complimentary gestures toward Matilda: see Chapt. 4, 118–19; also Chapt. 2, 44.
[21] Patterson, "William of Malmesbury's Robert of Gloucester," 991–2; see Chapt. 5, 143–4.
[22] Patterson, "William of Malmesbury's Robert of Gloucester," 985–6, 987–8; see also Chapt. 5, 131.
[23] Patterson, "William of Malmesbury's Robert of Gloucester," 990–1; Crouch, *Reign of King Stephen*, 68, generously acknowledged my introduction of this reason for Robert's rebellion; see Chapt. 5, 137–8.
[24] Patterson, "William of Malmesbury's Robert of Gloucester," 993–5, 998–9; Gransden, "Prologues in the Historiography of Twelfth-Century England," 74–5; see Chapt. 5, 169–70; Chapt. 6, 197.
[25] *HN* (1998), 24–5; Patterson, "William of Gloucester's Robert of Gloucester," 989, 992–3.
[26] Farmer, "William of Malmesbury's Life and Works," 53; See Chapt. 6, 197–8.
[27] Chapt. 6, 197–8. For an assessment of Malmesbury and his *Historia* embodying the preceding points, see Bradbury, *Stephen and Matilda*, 125.

earldom (Chapt. 2); aspects of his baronial life (Chapts. 3–4); and his military, political, and literary sponsorship of Matilda's succession (Chapts. 5–6).

From all of this material emerges an exemplary post-Conquest baron. In pursuit of traditional aristocratic goals, Robert and Mabel fitz Hamon more than rectified her parents' dynastic failure, which had brought her to the king's son as her family's heiress. Socially and politically enhancing marriages were obtained for several of their children. But a failure in this regard and in providing an appanage led in part to Robert's facing military rebellion from at least one son.[28]

Robert reveals a range of jurisdictional powers enjoyed by only a tiny minority of the Anglo-Norman aristocracy. As a Marcher lord in his Welsh honor of Glamorgan his courts exercised almost complete viceregal powers. Elsewhere, he enjoyed most major prerogatives of ordinary lordship over tenants. His earldom of Gloucester, with overlordship of the constable of Gloucester castle, who also was the county's sheriff, made him politically dominant in the demesne heartland of his most valuable English honor of Gloucester.[29] To rule and exploit his Norman, English, and Welsh honors Robert developed an administrative system resembling the king's, including a writing-office and staff which Robert's nephew later as Henry II found advantageous to raid for his own administration.[30] Evidence about his best-illustrated English honor of Gloucester confounds some long-held notions about feudal lords and honorial society. The honor was socially and tenurially diverse. Tenants by knight-service like Richard Foliot and Osbert Eightpence might be considered burgesses; some of the honor's barons, holders of multiple knights' fees, were themselves barons of their own lordships and vassals of lords other than Robert, including the king.[31] Armies Robert mustered also were not limited to tenants by knight-service.[32] The apex of his power was reached not just by being lord of military tenants, but as leader of an affinity made up of independent lords who were in some way under his orders. At least during the 1140s independent lords were minting pennies in Robert's name on their lands with dies supplied by his administration.[33]

As a demesne landlord, Earl Robert was exceptional for the extent of his urban holdings in England, for his burghal development, and for his patronage of the merchant class. Urban unrest fueled by the increasing wealth and the de facto power it gave conflicted with the old social order in Western Europe. Robert appreciated the economic potential of boroughs and gave personal and economic privileges in return for rents and other revenues and with political savvy made members of his boroughs' patriciates trusted councilors like Robert fitz Harding of Bristol.[34]

Robert of Gloucester, who was at least bilingual in Anglo-Norman French and Latin, was very much a part of a realm and culture that was in many ways more

[28] See Chapt. 4, 87–8.
[29] White, "Earls and Earldoms during King Stephen's Reign," 78–9; see Chapt. 2, 33. Appendix 2.1.
[30] Chapt 1, 11; Chapt. 4, esp. 108–17.  [31] Chapt. 4, 100, 104–5.
[32] Chapt. 5, 139–41, 151, 154, 168–9, 173; Chapt. 4, 97.
[33] Chapt. 4, 96–7; Chapt. 5, 139, 191.
[34] Chapt. 4, 100–5. On the symbiotic relationship between urban landlords and burgess-tenants, see Dyer, *Lords and Peasants in a Changing Society: The Estates of the Bishopric of Worcester 680–1540*, 32, 61, 86; Postan, *The Medieval Economy and Society*, 212.

extensive than the label Anglo-Norman implies.[35] Wales provides perhaps the best examples of his cultural involvement beyond the kingdom and duchy. His trans-Channel barony included honors there as well as in England and Normandy. Some of his military tenants held land in the honor of Glamorgan as well as in England. The earl's mercenaries included Welshmen and Flemings.[36] A vernacular history Robert personally commissioned to be adapted from Welsh histories about the ancient kings of Britain became one of the sources of Geoffrey Gaimar's *Estoire des Engleis* and illustrates how the power the earl achieved in South Wales by marriage, conquest, and treaty could lead to literary assimilation and then reincarnation in another form.[37]

This example of Robert's taste for romanticized history and his role in its transmission are just some of the reasons for his deserved prominence in what Charles Homer Haskins dubbed "The Renaissance of the Twelfth Century." The king's son was raised to be a fully literate knight (a *miles litteratus*), educated in the Liberal Arts, and thus prepared for a notable participation in the increasingly literate culture of his father's court. Robert became a dedicated reader with a taste, I believe, for Latin classics and for history, including the just-mentioned new romance type, and even maintained a library to support his tastes. His membership in the royal family and reputation for learning attracted patronage-seeking authors representing each of his historical tastes, William of Malmesbury with traditional Suetonian and Carolingian roots and Geoffrey of Monmouth still composing in Latin but recording a romanticized version of the past. Robert's just-mentioned sponsored vernacular adaptation of Welsh histories and patronage of Geoffrey earn the earl of Gloucester some credit as a promoter of the Arthurian legend. The Cluniac Gilbert Foliot, abbot of St. Peter's Abbey Gloucester, the poet Serlo of Wilton, and the distinguished scholar of Arabic science and philosophy, Adelard of Bath, moved in the earl's circle. He also belonged to a literary network which may have begun in either his court or his father's and led to Lincolnshire and possibly Yorkshire. But rivaling even the Gaimar details is the fact that this Renaissance man who fought for Matilda and against Stephen had the supreme self-confidence to commission a self-serving apologia of his politics and influence the verdict of future generations.[38]

---

[35] Short, "Patrons and Polyglots: French Literature in Twelfth-Century England," 242; Bates, *The Normans and Empire*, e.g., 62, 74, 86, 120–6, 186–7.
[36] Chapt. 3, 57–8; Chapt. 4, 106; Chapt. 5, 134, 152, e.g., 154; Bates, *The Normans and Empire*, e.g., 17, 37–8, 54, 73–4, 96, 117–18, 189.
[37] Chapt. 1, 11; Chapt. 2, 50; Chapt. 6, 178–80.
[38] Haskins, *The Renaissance of the Twelfth Century*; Gransden, *Historical Writing*, 186–7; Short, "Gaimar's Epilogue and Geoffrey of Monmouth's *Liber vetustissimus*," 338 & n.; Damien-Grint, *The New Historians of the Twelfth-Century Renaissance*, 43–4; see also Hanning, *The Vision of History in Early Britain*, 135–37, 71–2; see Chapt. 1, 10–11; Chapt. 2, 49–50; Chapt. 6, 178–80, 183.

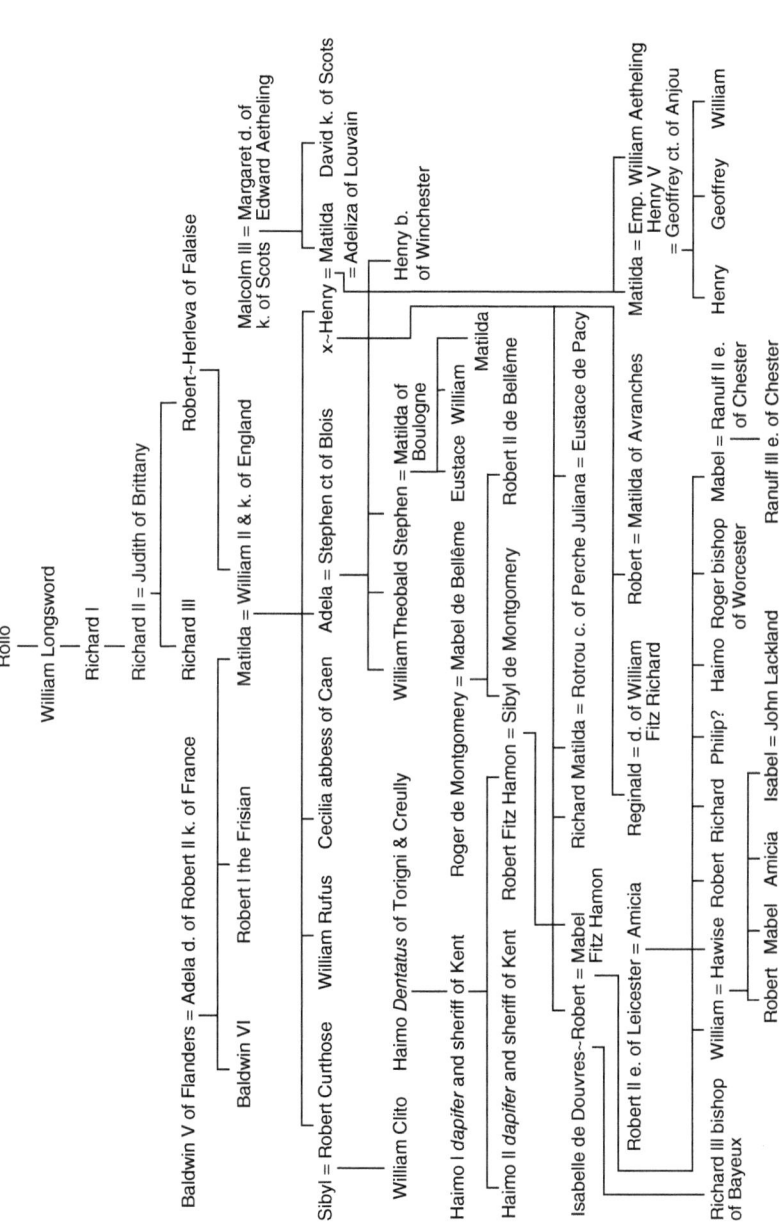

# Genealogical Chart
## Robert of Gloucester and the Norman Ducal-Royal Family

# 1
# A King's Illegitimate Son

On September 30, 1139, in the fourth year of King Stephen of Blois's reign (1135–54), King Henry I's only living legitimate child and designated heiress, the Empress Matilda, landed in England to claim her father's throne from Stephen, her paternal first cousin. Her sponsor and military escort was her half-brother, Robert earl of Gloucester, one of the mightiest barons of the Anglo-Norman realm, backed up by a force of some 140 knights.[1] Thus began the leadership role in England Robert would play in Matilda's and the Angevins' dynastic war over the royal succession until his death in 1147, a major political example of the challenges traditional western European cultural institutions and patterns of power faced during what has been called the Crisis of the Twelfth Century.[2]

To begin with, in an earlier age, Robert, eldest and firstborn son of King Henry I (1100–35), might well have become king of England on his father's death in 1135.[3] Instead, Henry first groomed him for a baronial career, then later elevated him to the rank of earl and made him one of his most intimate counselors and trusted agents. Robert's political ambitions remained baronial throughout his public life; when given the opportunity later to lay claim to his father's throne, he declined because he considered his nephew Henry the rightful heir. William of Malmesbury's *Historia Novella*, which Robert commissioned, portrayed him in large part as a betrayed baron. The reason for Robert's apparently paradoxical career was stated simply by the anonymous author of the *Gesta Stephani*: "Robert... [was] King Henry's son, but a bastard."[4]

Robert was one of several of his father's pre-accession and premarital progeny.[5] They were the early products of Henry's prodigious sexual drive, which the Anglo-Norman historian Orderic Vitalis colorfully described as "lasciviousness like any horse or mule which is without reason" and which the king's marriage to Edith-Matilda, daughter of King Malcolm III of Scotland, was supposed to curb, but failed to accomplish.[6] William of Malmesbury excused Henry's womanizing as his

---

[1] *HN* (1998), 60–1. Stephen was the son of Henry I's sister Countess Adela of Blois and her Crusader husband, Count Stephen-Henry, who perished at the battle of Ramla in May 1102: LoPrete, *Adela of Blois Countess and Lord (c.1067–1137)*, 4; Runciman, *A History of the Crusades* i. 76–8.

[2] Bisson, *The Crisis of the Twelfth Century*, 17–18, Chapts. 3–4.

[3] *GND* ii. 248–9. For Robert's familial relationships, see Genealogical Chart, xxi.

[4] *GS* (2004), 12–15; see also Chapt. 6, 185, 189.

[5] *GND* ii. 248–9. On Henry's illegitimate children, see *CP* v. 683; xi, Appendix D, 105–21; Given-Wilson and Curteis, *Royal Bastards*, 60–73; the most recent study is Thompson, "Affairs of State," 129–51, esp. 134.

[6] *OV* v. 298–9; *GR* i. 714–17. See also Henry of Huntingdon (1996), 700–1.

desire to obtain a plentiful supply of royal offspring;[7] if that was his motive, one can only observe that for Henry this must have been a labor of love. Following Robert and before 1100, Henry's various sexual liaisons produced first Richard and then, in uncertain order of birth, possibly William de Tracy, but at least a Sibyl, and probably Juliana and Matilda; after Henry became king, the list continued to grow until the grand total reached about twenty-five. So far as can be determined, Robert shared no mother with any of this illegitimate brood, although some others like Richard and Juliana did.[8]

Henry's illegitimate first offspring was born between *c*.1082, when his father would have reached puberty, and Henry's acknowledgment of him as his son, sometime before his accession to the Anglo-Norman throne on August 5, 1100.[9] The mother's name is unknown. Robert's first place in the order of his father's five or six bastards' births before 1100 suggests a natal date for the future *filius regis* well back from then. Also, Henry's premarital sexual liaisons may only have begun after he became a knight in 1086 and joined the permissive culture of bachelor knighthood in which beguiling or intimidating women into sexual relationships was part of common behavior.[10] Furthermore, if Robert's own illegitimate son Richard was regarded as ageworthy (30) to be a bishop *c*.1135, as seems very likely, his necessarily pubescent father must have been born no later than about forty-four years earlier, or *c*.1091. About 1088–90 seems to be the most likely.[11]

Considering these chronological calculations about Robert and his father, Henry's known itinerary during the 1080s makes England, *c*.1081–*c*.1087 and part of 1088, to have been the likely place for his sexual encounter with Robert's mother.[12] Henry only crossed the Channel to the duchy in late 1086. He was with his father when the Conqueror died at Rouen (Seine-Inf.) on September 9, 1087 and was the only son in attendance at the funeral in Caen.[13] After this the young prince remained in Normandy and only returned to England before 1091 in an attempt during July 1088 and several months following to receive from his royal brother William Rufus extensive estates left him by their mother.[14] At his death

---

[7] *GR* i. 744–5.

[8] Ansfrida probably was not the mother of Richard, born *c*.1094 × 1100, and Robert; the *Chronicon Monasterii de Abingdon*, ii. 122, which mentions her maternal relationship to Richard, does not mention Robert; *GR* i. 760–1. Thompson, "Affairs of State," 133–4; Appendix A., 141–51.

[9] *HN* (1998), 8–9; Brooke, *Medieval Idea of Marriage*, 138n., reports the age for girls was 12 and for boys 14. Henry was born in 1068/9.

[10] The five most likely pre-1100 children are Robert, Richard, Matilda of Perche, Juliana, and Sibyl; William de Tracy may be another: Thompson, "Affairs of State," 134, 138; Duby, "Youth in Aristocratic Society," 112–22.

[11] 3rd Lateran Council, c. iii: Mansi, *Concilia* xxii, cols. 218–19; Cheney, *Roger, Bishop of Worcester*, 7n.; for Bishop Richard, see also Chapt. 4, 86. Against John of Worcester and the "Gloucester Chronicle," *JW* iii. 178–9, see *HN* (1998), esp. 8–9, even 112–13; King, *King Stephen*, 5.

[12] *OV* iv. 148 & n., 149; *Regesta* i (1998), nos. 39, 60 & n., 146, 193, 253, 266 III, 301; *OV* iv. 148–9; *Regesta* ii. pp. 393, 397; Hollister, *Henry I*, 36, 48, 61, 68; Bates, *William the Conqueror*, 129.

[13] *OV* iv. 80–1, 94–7; *ASC a*.1086, 1087; Thompson, "Affairs of State," 138.

[14] *OV* iv. 148 & n., 149; *GR* i. 510–13, 710–13; Aird, *Robert Curthose*, 115; Green, *Henry I*, 29, believes Henry made another visit to England *c*.1089 based on the *GR*'s reference to one (i. 712–13); Hollister, *Henry I*, 68, I believe, more correctly interprets the passage as a recapitulation of Henry's previous visit.

in 1087 William the Conqueror left his Anglo-Norman realm divided, with his Continental domain to be under the rule of his eldest but alienated son Robert Curthose and England positioned to become Rufus's. The Conqueror provided no land for Henry, only a legacy of £5,000.[15] Queen Matilda (d. 1083) had intended for him to receive a major portion of the appanage created for her from estates confiscated from an Anglo-Saxon thane, but after her death Henry's father retained them as royal demesne and William Rufus (1087–1100) quickly had other plans for them.[16]

Professor David Crouch has argued that a nameless, hypothetical sister of an Oxfordshire landlord, Stephen Gay, was Henry's partner in fathering Robert during one or more of his visits to the area in 1084 or soon after.[17] An original charter in the muniments of St. John's College, Oxford, in favor of St. Mary's Kirtlington (Oxon.), a dependency of Norman Aunay Priory, establishes that the donor, Philip Gay, was the son of Stephen Gay.[18] And the Gloucester Chronicle contained in the Chronicle of John of Worcester refers to a Philip Gay as the *cognatus* of Earl Robert of Gloucester.[19] Since in Crouch's experience with charters *cognatus* has mostly stood for first cousins, he deduces that with Philip Gay as Robert's first cousin, Philip's father Stephen would be the earl's maternal uncle and a sister of Stephen, Robert's mother. Furthermore, Henry can be placed at least once in the 1080s in the Oxfordshire area, where the Gay family held land, during a visit to Abingdon Abbey (Berks.) in 1084, and at least one of Henry's known mistresses, Ansfrida, belonged to a local family.[20]

There are, however, several problems with this theory of Robert–Gay lineage and its later influence in Anarchy politics. Aside from the fact that there is no evidence that the Stephen Gay of the St. John's College charter had a sister, the term for Philip Gay's affinity to Robert, *cognatus*, does not necessarily mean first cousin, as Crouch himself admits; it is commonly used to designate a kinsman of some sort, as in Orderic Vitalis's *Historia Ecclesiastica*. William the Conqueror referred to his second cousin Edward the Confessor as his *cognatus*.[21] Charter evidence of Robert's son and successor, Earl William of Gloucester (1147–83),

---

[15] Holt, "Politics and Property in Early Medieval England," 17–19, 45–8, revising Le Patourel, "The Anglo-Norman Succession 996–1135," 225–34; Le Patourel, "Normandy and England 1066–1144," 4–5. William's division has generated considerable scholarly debate; for an illustrative bibliography, see Aird, *Robert Curthose*, 99n.

[16] *GR* i. 510–13; *OV* iv. 220–1.

[17] Crouch, "Robert of Gloucester's Mother," 323–33; see Genealogical Chart, xxi.

[18] Transcr. in Crouch, "Robert of Gloucester's Mother," 331–2 from St. John's College Oxford, Mun. XXI (1); Crouch, *Reign of King Stephen*, 215 & n., is more cautious. For the connection between Kirtlington and Aunay, see *VCH Oxfordshire* vi. 41 & n., 228–9.

[19] *JW* iii. 249–50; Crouch, "Robert of Gloucester's Mother," 324, 333; Crouch and Trafford, "The Forgotten Family in Twelfth-Century England," 48 & n. Philip *was* first cousin of Reginald Gay, an Oxfordshire tenant of the honor of Gloucester: *Cart. Thame* i. no. 5, grant by Reginald of land with consent of the earl of Gloucester (Robert) *c*.1138; *VCH Oxfordshire* vi. 153, 155, 279.

[20] *VCH Oxfordshire* vi. 327 & n.

[21] *Regesta* i (1998), e.g., nos. 139, 181; a *cognatio* can mean a society of some kind: DuCange, *Glossarium* ii. 392. For another possibility for Bishop Jocelin's and Earl William's *association*, see Barlow, *Thomas Becket*, 111–12; was Philip Gay a *cognatus* of Earl Robert because his uncle was one of the earl's Oxfordshire tenants?: *Cart. Thame* i. no. 5; see also Crouch, *Reign of King Stephen*, 215n.

addressing Bishop Jocelin de Bohun of Salisbury (1142–84) as his *cognatus* expressed an affinity that to date has defied discovery.²²

Kathleen Thompson also has pointed out that Philip Gay's particular affinity to Earl Robert could also have come about if Stephen Gay's wife was the sister of Robert's mother. And there is even the remote possibility that Philip Gay, Robert's "kinsman," was his son Philip, because descriptions of the atrocious behavior attributed to each during the Anarchy are similar.²³ Finally there is evidence that Robert's mother may not have been English, but Continental and Norman.

The historian Orderic Vitalis may well have referred to Robert's Norman birthplace by using a Norman toponymic, "of Caen" (Calvados), together with his English title, "earl of Gloucester," to identify him. Norman provenance also is supported by an Anglo-Norman verse chronicle of Anglo-Saxon and post-Conquest kings which states that Henry produced Robert "en Normandie de une damisele sa amie." Although this is a late Anglo-Norman *Brut*, it also correctly credits Robert with the construction of castles and priories, respectively, at Bristol and at Cardiff.²⁴ Kathleen Thompson has pointed out other suggestive indicators of Robert's Norman origins: William of Malmesbury's citation of Robert's ancestral Continental personal features without English ones; Robert's arguably being named for his ducal uncle, Robert Curthose; his kinship with the Fécamp family-based Nigel fitz William; his early Norman mistress Isabelle de Douvres (Calvados); and his devotion to the Norman saint Ewen, expressed in the church he founded at Bristol, his baronial capital.²⁵

The itinerary of Robert's father before Robert's birth also adds some support for the duchy as his birthplace.²⁶ Except for his 1088 visit to England, Henry remained on the Continent at least through 1093. In March 1088 he became the vassal of his cash-strapped brother Duke Robert as count of the Cotentin, with a great fee in western Lower Normandy in return for £3,000 of his father's £5,000 legacy. The count's holdings included a string of castles and lands in the Cotentin and Avranchin, notably Coutances, Avranches, the fortress-monastery of Mont Saint-Michel, and the extensive fee of Hugh of Avranches earl of Chester. Orderic Vitalis characterized the swath of Henry's power as encompassing one-third of the duchy.²⁷

---

²² Patterson, *EGC*, no. 263; note the comment of Kemp, "Bohun, Jocelin de," 446–7.

²³ Patterson, *EGC*, no. 263; Kemp, "Bohun, Jocelin de," 445–6; Thompson, "Affairs of State," 143. Compare the description of Philip's behavior in *GS* (2004), 186–7 with *JW* iii. 248–51, 270–3; John of Worcester's editor, Patrick McGurk, translates *cognatus* as "kinsman," *JW* iii. 251, but *s.v.* Philip Gai in the index adds "son (?) of Robert earl of Gloucester."

²⁴ *OV* vi. 534; *Cont. Wace*, 102, 105 (edited from BL, MS Cotton Vitellius A.x, fol. 128r, dated by Ker s.xiii [*MLGB*, 88]; but BL, "Catalogue of Cotton Manuscripts," s.xiii[ex] x s.xiv[in]); *Anglo-Norman Literature: A Guide to Texts and Manuscripts*, no. 24, s.xiii[ex]; the chronicle also mentions Henry I's wooing of Mabel fitz Hamon for his son: *Cont. Wace*, 103–4; see n. 98; Round, *Family Origins*, 214; Thompson, "Affairs of State," 138.

²⁵ *Regesta* ii. no. CCXI (cal. no. 1562); Thompson, "Affairs of State," 141–2; Nigel was Robert's nephew.

²⁶ *Regesta* i (1998), nos. 65, 176, 261. Note Judith Green's comment, *Henry I*, 26 n. 33.

²⁷ *OV* iv. 118–21; *GND* ii. 204–5; Haskins, *Norman Institutions*, Appendix E, nos. 1, 4a, 6; *Regesta* i. nos. 297, 324; Hollister, *Henry I*, 48–66, esp. 54–6, for rights in the Bessin; for estimates of limitations on Henry's authority, see Thompson, "From the Thames to Tinchebray," 19–20, and Davies, "The Count of the Cotentin: Western Normandy, William of Mortain, and the Career of Henry I," 130–4.

Then, as already noted, Henry visited England later in 1088 and upon failing to accomplish his purpose, angrily returned to Normandy. However, his approach to William Rufus cost him imprisonment by Curthose on suspicion of disloyalty for some months in 1088 and early 1089. After his release the count remained outwardly loyal to the duke, including famously helping in 1090 to suppress an uprising intended to seize Rouen (Seine-Maritime) for William Rufus. Henry also involved himself with his own Norman administration, particularly strengthening his castles, according to Orderic Vitalis, out of a distrust of both of his brothers.[28] It was well founded.

Henry apparently next left the duchy in 1191, when his brothers drove him from his lordship into exile. After Rufus successfully put down a rebellion in 1088 by a coalition of trans-Channel magnates led by Bishop Odo of Bayeux, earl of Kent, on behalf of Robert Curthose's claim to England, William Rufus first counterattacked against his elder brother by successfully wooing some of his key vassals in Upper Normandy and then forced him to accept a treaty at Rouen in February 1091, granting each, inter alia, territorial concessions in the other's realm to the total exclusion of their brother Henry. Cheerfully making war on him (as Sidney Painter would have put it), the two allies by early April 1091 drove the count of the Cotentin from the final bastion of his Norman lordship, Mont Saint-Michel (Manche), and into an exile in Brittany, the Vexin, and France.[29]

Only around mid-1092 was the vagrant prince able to return and gain a foothold for recovering his former Norman fee, when supporters within the fortified hilltop town of Domfront (Orne), by some unknown tactic, overthrew the governance of the mighty house of Montgomery-Bellême heir, Robert de Bellême, and made Henry their lord.[30] Over approximately the next two years Henry fought to re-establish his former position in western Lower Normandy with the help of allies such as Richard de Redvers, Hugh I of Avranches earl of Chester, and ultimately King William.[31] Robert is unlikely to have been born by the mid-1090s, given the previously discussed evidence for the event.

Advancement for Robert and Henry's other non-*porphyrogeniti* children, as for other illegitimate children of the aristocracy in this period, depended entirely upon their father's recognitions and choices about promoting them.[32] That crucial step for Robert came at least before August 1100, when Henry staged a successful coup and became king.[33] However, because the newborn was christened Robert, which

---

[28] *OV* iv. 220–7; Haskins, *Norman Institutions*, 63–4; Barlow, *William Rufus*, 265–8; Thompson, "From the Thames to Tinchebray," 18–21.

[29] *ASC a*.1088, 1090, 1091; *OV* iv. 120–35, 250–3; *GR* i. 544–53, 714–15; Henry of Huntingdon (1996), 412–17; *JW* iii. 46–59; Wace, *Le Roman de Rou*, ii. ll. 9380–96; *GND* ii. 204–7; Barlow, *William Rufus*, 273–88; Hollister, *Henry I*, 70–85.

[30] *OV* iv. 256–9; *ASC* a.1094; *GND* ii. 206–7; Hollister, *Henry I*, 85–90; Le Patourel, "Norman Barons," VI, 18–20.

[31] *OV* v. 26–7; Robert of Torigny, "Interpolations," 271; *GND* ii. 208–9; *ASC a*.1094, 1095; Hollister, *Henry I*, 88–90.

[32] Newman, *Anglo-Norman Nobility*, 55–7; Hollister, *Henry I*, 44.

[33] *HN* (1998), 8–9; *GND* ii. 248–9.

arguably was a political compliment to his father's brother, I suspect that the recognition occurred early in Henry's vassalage to the duke. After that, whether or not the child was taken immediately into Henry's domestic household (the *domus*) to be reared, his father had taken responsibility for seeing his rearing through. Henry's acknowledgment should not be viewed as necessarily routine: Curthose had to be persuaded by the results of an ordeal of hot iron before doing the same thing for two sons by a beautiful concubine.[34] When Robert acquired a recorded voice, he never stopped proclaiming his royal lineage.[35]

The later mighty trans-Channel baron and earl of Gloucester more than anything else was the product of his father's unpredictable and gradual metamorphosis from landless youngest son of King William I to his successor in both England and Normandy. As just seen, having established himself as a force in Anglo-Norman politics in 1088, he not only survived potential political annihilation three years later, but recovered, even possibly improved, the extent of his Norman lordship. By 1094–5 Henry's and William's shared interests in Normandy made them allies and won Henry Rufus's confirmation of his Cotentin fee. Henry's fortuitous membership in his brother's hunting party in the New Forest on August 2, 1100, when Walter Tirel's errant arrow killed the king, provided the count with the opportunity to seize the throne. Curthose's absence on the First Crusade enabled Henry to accomplish this without the duke's challenge.[36] When he did return, the reluctance of the king's and the duke's invasion forces to engage in battle led in 1101 to the peace treaty of Alton between the brothers which recognized Henry's title to England and only promised financial compensation to Curthose.[37] Henry next proceeded to win Normandy: first by extension of his overlordship in the duchy as Rufus had done, then by conquest due to his victory at the battle of Tinchebrai, possibly forty years to the day after his father had landed at Pevensey. The king also succeeded in defending his Continental acquisition in two wars, 1111–13 and 1117–19, against coalitions of Norman barons and neighboring princes who supported his nephew William Clito's claims to be rightful ruler of Normandy, if not England as well.[38]

What limited the new king's eldest son's future was his birth. During the late eleventh and early twelfth centuries, ecclesiastical reforms in both Normandy and England more closely defined canonically lawful marriages and in time affected customs regarding inheritance to the patrimonies of kindreds and on a larger scale to political entities.[39] The standardization of aristocratic family surnames and the structure of inheritance assumed by Henry I's Charter of Liberties or Coronation Charter of 1100, as Sir James Holt shrewdly noted, seems evidence of this

---

[34] *OV* v. 282–3.  [35] e.g., Patterson, *EGC*, nos. 166, 82.
[36] Green, *Henry I*, 34–41.  [37] See 8.  [38] See 20–1, 25; Green, *Henry I*, 93.
[39] Brooke, *Medieval Idea of Marriage*, 56–60, Chapt. 2, 29, 39, 41; Esmein, *Le Mariage en droit canonique* i, Chapt. 1; Newman, *Anglo-Norman Nobility*, 39, 49–50, 55–9, 197–201; Holt, "Feudal Society and the Family in Early Medieval England I: The Revolution of 1066," 198, 201, 204. For the intricacies and contradictions involved, see esp. Chibnall, *The World of Orderic Vitalis*, 128–32.

influence.[40] While it is true that illegitimacy was not yet a bar to inheritance, the tide of influential opinion was running in favor of lawful offspring.[41]

Bastardy had not prevented Robert's grandfather William from becoming duke of Normandy, but a charter of his grandmother Queen Matilda proclaiming herself as William's *legalis coniunx* echoes the new trend.[42] However, in the decade or so after Robert was born, legitimate birth and marriage emerged for the first time as criteria in Anglo-Norman dynastic politics. The already mentioned Treaty of Rouen between Henry's brothers William and Robert provided that in the event either of them died without a surviving heir born of lawful wedlock, the other would be sole heir to the deceased's lands.[43] Such a condition has added significance because at the time neither brother had such a son.

The principle surfaced again after Henry received coronation on August 5, 1100. A number of measures he took to solidify his position and gain needed support against the impending claim to his throne from absent Crusading Robert Curthose included, on the advice of his friends and especially his bishops, entering into a *conubium legitimum*, so as to live together lawfully, Robert of Torigny later observed.[44]

Henry's intended spouse, Edith or more commonly Matilda, daughter of King Malcolm III Canmore and Queen Margaret of Scotland, great-grandniece of Edward the Confessor, was seen to add dynastic legitimacy (in a different sense) to the new king's shaky title.[45] Matilda's upbringing in nunneries particularly at Romsey under the tutelage of her formidable aunt Christina and at Wilton (Wilts.) caused *conubium legitimum* to be the central issue of their marriage. Some alleged that the girl had worn the veil as a professed nun during her monastic residence. Archbishop Anselm's personal view was that Matilda's previous convent status barred her from marriage. However, possibly to avoid adding another dispute with Henry to an already existing one over lay investiture, he agreed to have the marital issue decided by a council. The council held at Lambeth (Surrey), with Anselm absenting himself from its final deliberations, supported Matilda's vociferous denial of any monastic vows; and, as a consequence, Henry's and Matilda's *conubium legitimum* was celebrated in Westminster Abbey by Anselm on November 11, 1100, after which the archbishop anointed and crowned the new bride queen of England.[46]

---

[40] Holt, "Politics and Property in Early Medieval England," 7–9. For the text, *Regesta* ii. no. 488; *Die Gesetze* i. 521; transl. in *EHD* ii. no. 19, 400–2; for current analysis, Green, "A Lasting Memorial," 53–69.

[41] Norman custom regarding inheritance, although unwritten, was developing: Tabuteau, *Transfers of Property in Eleventh-Century Norman Law*, 24–5 & nn. 110, 114–15; 178 & n.; 223; Garnett, "'Ducal' Succession in Early Normandy," 85, 108 & n., for Dudo of Saint-Quentin's obliviousness to ducal wives married *Danico more* or *Christiano more*, but William of Jumièges's awareness of them.

[42] *Regesta* i (1998), no. 193. On attitudes to William's bastardy, see esp. Bates, "The Conqueror's Adolescence," 1–6.

[43] See 5.

[44] *GND* ii. 216–17; *JW* iii. 96–7; *ASC a.*1100; *GND* ii. 216–17; *GR* i. 714–15 (for *legitimum... conubium*); Hollister, *Henry I*, 126–7.

[45] *GR* i. 714–17; Eadmer, 121; Southern, *Saint Anselm and his Biographer*, 188; Brooke, *Medieval Idea of Marriage*, 75.

[46] *GR* i. 470; *ASC a.*1100; Eadmer, 121–5; Southern, *Saint Anselm and his Biographer*, 188–91.

Within a year legitimate birth again came into play in a resumption of civil war over succession to the partitioned Anglo-Norman realm. In late August or September 1100 Henry's brother Robert returned to Normandy from the fledgling Crusader states he had helped to establish. Heirs of much the same baronial faction that had supported his challenge to William Rufus in 1088 now rebelled on his behalf against Henry. Curthose appealed to Pope Paschal II, claiming that Henry had unjustly seized the throne in violation of an oath apparently taken when he had become the duke's vassal for the Cotentin in 1088.

The duke landed at Portsmouth (Hants.) at the head of an invading force on July 20, 1101 to claim the kingdom by the judgment of God. Curthose never got the chance to do so, because, when Henry met him with his own army at Alton in Surrey, neither side had an appetite for the uncertain outcome of a pitched battle. Under pressure from the two brothers' baronial supporters and from Archbishop Anselm of Canterbury, a peace was brokered and later ratified by oaths by Henry and Robert and twelve barons of each side at Winchester on August 2, 1101. Among the treaty's provisions, Robert surrendered his claim to England in return for an annuity of 3,000 marks, as reported by most sources, and renounced the homage Henry had performed to him for the Cotentin; furthermore, the earlier plan for succession to the king's and duke's realms, with the qualification of legitimate birth to be a successor, was reiterated. And just as at the earlier Rouen pact, when this one was formally ratified, neither brother had a lawful male heir.[47] Since Henry already had acknowledged his bastard Robert as his son, the king's agreement to the treaty implicitly declared the boy's exclusion from the royal succession. The Latin translation of Anglo-Saxon law, the "Instituta Cnuti," made between 1066 and 1123/4, reserved the title aetheling to a king's son who was a *filius a legali coniuge* (son of a legal wife).[48]

Further reducing Robert's potential as an heir, Henry's *conubium legitimum* first produced a daughter, Matilda, around February 7, 1102. To forge an alliance with the Empire against King Louis VI of France, Henry betrothed her at the tender age of 8 to the future Emperor Henry V; and the two were married in January 1114. King Henry got his lawful male heir with the birth of William Aetheling or Adelin around August, 1103.[49] William Clito (Aetheling), only legitimate offspring of Robert Curthose and Sibyl of Conversano, was born on October 25, 1102. The infant might have entered the world earlier. His father and mother had married in Apulia in 1101 during the duke's homeward travel from the East. However, they

---

[47] *ASC* a.1100, 1101; Henry of Huntingdon (1996), 448–51; Wace, *Le Roman de Rou* ii. ll. 10319–472, esp. ll. 10451–72; *GR* i. 704–5; *OV* v. 306–21, and 318–19: £3,000, and *GND* ii. 220–1: 4,000 marks, plus Robert's gift of the same amount to Queen Matilda, are the major exceptions; Hollister, "The Anglo-Norman Civil War: 1101," 330–1; David, *Robert Curthose*, 130–6, 157; Green, "Robert Curthose Reconsidered," 112; Aird, *Robert Curthose*, 197–9, 206 & n. 95, 207–11; Strevett, "Anglo-Norman Civil War of 1101," esp. 164, 168–74.

[48] "Instituta Cnuti," III, 56.2, *Die Gesetze* i. 615; Liebermann, "On the Instituta Cnuti Aliorumque Regum Anglorum," 82, 92; O'Brien, "The *Instituta Cnuti* and the Translation of English Law," 177–86, esp. 182–8, 196; Patterson, "Anarchy in England," 192.

[49] Chibnall, *Empress Matilda*, 9, 14, 24, 26, 31–3, 39–40, 50–1; Leyser, "England and the Empire in the Early Twelfth Century," 63–70; see Genealogical Chart, xxi.

refrained from intercourse until they made a pilgrimage to Mont Saint-Michel in thanksgiving for the duke's safe return from the Crusade.[50]

King Henry's response to the promotional limitations imposed by his firstborn son's illegitimacy was to create a great baronial career for him, the first of three Robert ultimately would enjoy. Major steps Henry took to groom Robert for such a life have no recorded dates, but they follow a certain logical sequence.

Formal education involving Latin studies, which, for aristocratic boys, occupied them between roughly the years 5 to 10, came first. Robert already would have acquired the lingua franca of the Anglo-Norman Francophone elite, possibly English too, depending on the circumstances and environments of his earliest years. Bible stories and saints' lives—even observations of religious practices and imagery—likely introduced the very young "Fitz Count" to elements of Latin Christian belief.[51] Traditionally the nobles of the Norman Conquest, in the words of V. H. Galbraith, "lived for hunting and the greater game of war"; and their early years were spent in honing the skills necessary for these pursuits. When lay lords sought the information or inspiration books contained, they could be read to; when they needed the fruits of literacy for their fledgling seigniorial administrations, they obtained the services of literate clerks. Literacy and education in the arts had been mostly been intended for, and cultivated by, monks and diocesan clergy. But in the age into which Robert was born, dubbed culturally "The Renaissance of the Twelfth Century," some members of the greatest aristocratic houses were beginning to add a literary education to their list of skills. Robert and his later political rivals, the Beaumont twins Waleran and Robert, came to be prime examples.[52]

The vogue in the ducal-royal house began in the eleventh century. By the beginning of the century the conquering and colonizing Norsemen had long been assimilated into West Frankish culture. Duke Richard II (996–1026) was largely responsible for patronizing the monastic revival upon so much of which Normandy's initial literary revival depended; the future conqueror of England, William II (1035–66), presided over its flowering.[53] By his accession, his family had begun pursuing some rudiments of a Christian literary education. William was instructed during his minority by one of his guardians, a *pedagogus* named Turold, and later into his adolescence by a master William and Ralph the monk. The duke and Conqueror himself employed household tutors and external teachers for his children, male and female alike. Robert fitz Henry's uncle Robert Curthose was taught by several teachers, the most famous of whom was a certain household tutor Ilger. Robert's uncle William Rufus and aunt Cecilia studied with Arnulf of Chocques,

---

[50] *OV* v. 300–1; Aird, *Robert Curthose*, 200 & n.
[51] Bartlett, *England under the Norman and Angevin Kings*, 486–508; Orme, *From Childhood to Chivalry*, 119–25, 128–33; Chibnall, *Anglo-Norman England*, 211–12; Wogan-Browne, "General Introduction: The 'French' of England," 1, 12.
[52] Galbraith, "Literacy of Medieval English Kings," 201, 228; Crouch, *The Beaumont Twins*, 7, 207–11; Haskins, *The Renaissance of the Twelfth Century*; Clanchy, *From Memory to Written Record*, 224–52; Damian-Grint, *The New Historians of the Twelfth-Century Renaissance*, 32–6.
[53] Douglas, *William the Conqueror*, 105–32; Le Patourel, *The Norman Empire*, 13; Musset, "La Naissance de la Normandie," 111, 120–1, 131; Musset, "Actes inédits du xi$^e$ siècle vi," 119, 122–6; Leblond, *L'Accession des Normands de Neustrie à la culture occidentale*, 179–243.

a chaplain and chancellor of Curthose and the future controversial patriarch of Jerusalem. Rufus also was under the tutelage of the Conqueror's archbishop of Canterbury, Lanfranc, who knighted him.[54] It is not known how the young Henry was educated, but scholars, having cut through the rhetoric of his contemporary literary admirers, have salvaged a cautious claim of limited literacy for him—not only able to read Latin from youth, but exposed to likely samplings from the Arts curriculum, Christian writers, and the Bible.[55] Robert's education had similar characteristics, but there is more evidence about the future earl than for his father and more indicative of a higher level of learning. Certain of its elements may have been the roots of his later political, military, and cultural behavior.

Robert emerged from the process very possibly fully literate in the modern sense.[56] His first-person subscription in a contemporary semi-cursive business hand, "Et ego Rob(er)t(us) Gloecestrensis Comes has Om(ne)s res in meo patrocinio. Custodia. et defensione suscipio. et abbas ibidem Canonice Constituatur," at the foot of his vassal Richard de Grainville's original foundation charter for Neath Abbey of 1130 may be a sample of his handwriting (Figure 1.1).[57] Robert

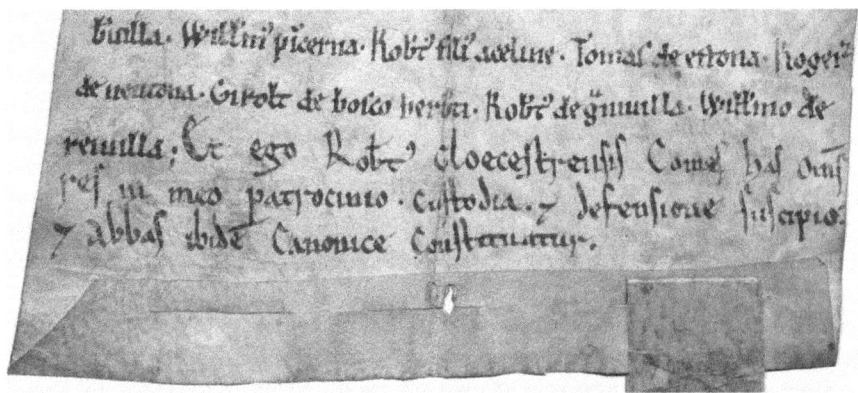

**Figure 1.1.** Evidence of Robert earl of Gloucester's hand from the first-person subscription in his name at the foot of Richard de Grainville's foundation charter for Neath Abbey in 1130: The charter's text and subscription are in different hands.
© WGAS, GB0216 A/N 1, ll. 31–5.

---

[54] *GR* i. 542–3; Douglas, *William the Conqueror*, 37; Legge, "L'Influence littéraire de la cour d'Henri Beauclerc," 679–80; Barlow, *William Rufus*, 12–13, 20–1; Aird, *Robert Curthose*, 36–7. For Arnulf, see Hamilton, *Latin Church in the Crusader States*, 12–16, 61–4.

[55] e.g., *OV* iv. 120–1; *GR* i. 708–11; David, "The Claim of King Henry I to Be Called Learned," 45–56; esp. Hollister, *Henry I*, 33–7; Barlow, *William Rufus*, 12–13, 20–1; Green, *Henry I*, 22–3; Clanchy, *From Memory to Written Record*, 161, 228, 235, esp. 232–4.

[56] On lay literacy, see Clanchy, *From Memory to Written Record*, 8, 10, 186, 232–4.

[57] WGAS, GB0216 A/N 1: Clark, *Cartae et alia* i. no. lxvii; Patterson, *The Scriptorium of Margam Abbey*, 30–1, Appendix III, no. 271; Patterson *EGC*, 22–3; a first-person subscription may not be in that individual's hand: Warner & Ellis, no. 67 & n.; while *consul* was the title Robert preferred for the address clauses of his *acta* and seals' legends, *comes* appears in some address clauses and in his coins' legends; the adjectival form of Gloucester, *Gloecestrensis*, which suggests episcopal influence, also was

also reputedly enjoyed reading and being read to, the upshot being that, for example, copies of the *Gesta Regum Anglorum* and the *Historia Novella* that William of Malmesbury later sent him arguably got his personal attention.[58]

Advanced education involved the boy's exposure to elements of the trivium. Geoffrey of Monmouth's original dedication of his *Historia Regum Britanniae* (*De Gestis Britonum*) to the then earl states that he was trained in the liberal arts and William of Malmesbury and Walter Map imply as much.[59] His studies may have included works by Cicero (for rhetoric) and Virgil (for grammar). The deceased earl was eulogized by the contemporary poet Serlo of Wilton as a personification of the two. It is even possible that Virgil's *Aeneid* was one of Robert's Classical Latin favorites, judging by the overwhelming number of references to the work William of Malmesbury put in the *Historia Novella* which he later wrote under the then earl's commission.[60] This patronage was just one aspect of the penchant for Histhory, including the romance variety, Robert developed over the years.[61]

Even so, book-learning probably was not the sole inspiration behind Robert's behavioral *savoir faire*. As a member of the royal household, he enjoyed a bird's-eye view of the mechanics of court administration and politics. Doubtless there were also opportunities to learn from his father's and uncle Robert's experiences about the perils of survival in Anglo-Norman power politics and the fragility of agreements, even when secured by oaths. And as will be seen, training in the use of arms could inculcate chivalric ideals.

Put all of this together and you get the later lionized intellectual prince. Walter Map considered that the earl's learning and prudence were his defining qualities. But a political enemy could be made to see the *festina lente* by-product of this intellectualism as a man given to more talk than action; in the translated words Henry of Huntingdon attributed to Baldwin fitz Gilbert of Clare, "Robert…usually threatens much and does little, with the mouth of a lion and the heart of a rabbit, famous for his eloquence, notorious for his idleness."[62]

Where Robert was educated is completely conjectural. Grooming in an episcopal or a monastic household is a definite possibility. Robert's half-brother Richard was placed by his father in the elegant household of the jovial and reputedly lecherous royal *curialis* Robert Bloet bishop of Lincoln (1094–1123) sometime after 1100.[63] Robert's own studies may have begun before 1105 during his presence in

---

one of the forms the foundation charter's scribe used: Cheney, *English Bishops' Chanceries*, 62–3. *Regesta* ii contains no examples of this form for the earl.

[58] *GR* i. 10–13, 798–9, §447; see also §446; King, *HN* (1998), xxiii, xxxvi; see also Chapt. 6, 198–9; see Figure 6.1.

[59] *HRB*, ix, 4–5; *GR* i. Letter III, 10–11, 798–9; *De Nugis Curialium*, 426–7; *LCGF*, no. 26, pp. 61–2. On the title *De Gestis Britonum*, see Reeve, *HRB*, vii, lix. I will continue to employ the work's traditional title.

[60] *GR* i. 10–11, 798–9; King, *HN* (1998), 134; Öberg, *Serlon de Wilton: Poèmes latins*, no. 15, l.13; "Plangite…Marcum [Cicero], clere, Maronem [Virgil]"; Solan, "Study of the Life and Works of Serlo of Wilton," 144; Damian-Grint, *New Historians of the Twelfth-Century Renaissance*, 32–6. Virgil and Cicero were Malmesbury's favorite authors: Thomson, *William of Malmesbury*, rev. edn. 48–9.

[61] See Chapt. 6, 179–80.

[62] For Walter Map's comment, see n. 59; Henry of Huntingdon (1996), 734–5.

[63] Henry of Huntingdon (1996), 594–5; *GP*, 474–5. For the term *curialis*, see Chapt. 2, n. 33.

12 *The Earl, the Kings, and the Chronicler*

the Bayeux–Caen area. Sources of potential instruction ranged from some clerk or literate priest to the school of Bayeux Cathedral or even Benedictine Saint-Étienne Caen.[64] The former count's son likely completed his education in the royal household under the tutelage of Othuer, bastard son of Hugh earl of Chester, as his sibling William Aetheling did.[65]

Robert's presence in the Bessin for study before 1105, about the time he achieved the age of puberty, is strengthened by an extracurricular sexual liaison which probably occurred about then. The king's illegitimate son fathered his own, named Richard, who, although illegitimate, in 1135 was considered canonically suitable for consecration as a bishop by having reached the required age of 30. Richard was not, I suspect, the product of a casual relationship, but the product of the kind of longer-term extramarital relationships which custom allowed young aristocrats.[66] The lady, Isabelle de Douvres, belonged to a local family of high-profile ecclesiastical careerists closely associated with Bayeux Cathedral and traditional beneficiaries of royal patronage. Her father Samson and uncle Thomas, sons of a married priest Osbert and his wife Muriel, attracted the patronage of Bishop Odo of Bayeux (1049–97), who had them both educated at Liège, and they then in turn served as canons and treasurers of the cathedral chapter. Each went on to royal chaplaincies and to important English bishoprics under the first two Anglo-Norman kings, Thomas (I) to York (1070–1100) and Samson to Worcester (1096–1112).[67]

It is tempting to see this relationship as somehow associated with study connected to the Bayeux chapter. However, it may have been simply a collateral interlude of concubinage involving a favored local family at least allowed by Henry and acceptable to Isabelle's family. Henry I continued his brother's and father's support by granting bishoprics to Isabelle's brothers, Bayeux in 1107 to Richard (II) and the archbishopric of York to Thomas (II) in 1108 (cons. 1109). When Richard II died in 1133, Henry gave the bishopric to Robert's and Isabelle's son Richard (III: 1135–42). He remembered his paternal link with pride. An original charter of his proclaims, "RICARD(US) DEI GR(ATI)A BAIOC(EN)SIS EP(IS)C(OPUS), ROB(ER)TI COMITIS Gloc(estrie) FILII REGIS ANGLIE FILI(US)"; and at some point his mother's relationship with his father was memorialized at the cathedral.[68]

---

[64] *OV* vi. 428–9, 442–9; *Gallia Christiana* xi. 353–4; *Regesta* ii. nos. 1909, 1917. For the issue of Richard's age worthiness, see Chapt. 4, 86. Legge, "Influence littéraire de la cour d'Henri Beauclerc," 685; Bates, "The Character and Career of Odo, Bishop of Bayeux," 6, 13; Speer, "William Bona Anima," 56–7; Spear, "The School of Caen Revisited," 56, rules out Saint-Étienne's maintenance of a school after 1100.

[65] In *OV* vi. 304–5, Othuer is *tutor regiae prolis et pedagogus*, but in *GR* i. 760–1, he is *nutritius et magister filii Regis*; see also Dutton, "*Ad erudiendum tradidit*: The Upbringing of Angevin Comital Children," 27–8; for application of the collective meaning of *prolis* here, see Hollister, "Henry I and the Anglo-Norman Magnates," in *MMI*, 183, and Richardson and Sayles, *Governance*, 272–3. Othuer attested the king's transactions from at least 1108, but possibly 1107: *Regesta* ii. nos. 828? & n., 875. For Master Picard see Chapt. 4, esp. 108.

[66] Bates, "The Conqueror's Adolescence," 4–5.

[67] *Gallia Christiana* xi. 361; Navel, "L'Enquête de 1133 sur les fiefs de l'évêché de Bayeux," 23 n. 2; Brooke, *Medieval Church and Society*, 84, 86 & n. 39.

[68] See Chapt. 4, 86–7; see also AD du Calvados, H.1: *Gallia Christiana* xi. Instrumenta IX, p. 78; "24 die mensis Aprilis, Obitus Isabellis, matris Ricardi Episcopi Baiocensis, filii Comitis Glocestriae": *Journal de Verdun*, Oct. 1760, p. 276; *Neustria Pia*, 743; see Genealogical Chart, xxi.

## A King's Illegitimate Son

Henry I further enhanced Robert's acknowledged position as his son and nudged him toward a secular career by knighting him. At the time, this could be accomplished by ritualized dubbing or conferral of arms. Either one conveyed membership in a developing elite fellowship of mounted warriors, *militia*, to which Robert belonged. Martial behavior of its *milites* or *chevalers* by his day was becoming influenced by various Germanic, feudal, and ecclesiastical concepts.[69] Knights were the shock troops of contemporary armies, accurately portrayed by the twelfth-century ivory Lewis chess pieces in the British Museum, mounted and fully equipped with the customary helmet, hauberk, lance, sword, and shield; but they were not always tactically deployed on battlefields.[70]

Especially among the upper echelons of society, it was common for young men to receive training in horsemanship and appropriate weaponry in lords' households, the most prized of which were kings'. Robert's grandfather, uncle, and father were notable sponsors of the practice and participants in it. William I not only supported, trained, and knighted youths sent to his court, but he also had his sons made knights. Henry I did the same; furthermore, Geoffrey of Monmouth's depiction of post-prandial martial games at King Arthur's courts in his *Historia Regum Britanniae* may have been meant to conjure up in readers' minds images of Henry I's practice. The king's chivalric protégés included, besides Robert, his future curial associate and ally Brian fitz Count and his later political enemies Stephen of Blois and the Beaumont twin brothers Waleran of Meulan and Robert of Leicester.[71]

Like the rest of Robert's grooming his military training is undocumented. However, adolescents typically undertook this regime from age 14 or 15 to their twenties in royal and baronial households amidst the martial exercises of their corps of household knights (the *familiae*) maintained as guards, escorts, castle garrisons, and battlefield forces.[72] William of Malmesbury describes how William Rufus, once his boyhood was over, spent his adolescence in various military exercises and competitions with older household knights; and motives Rufus exhibited in these activities hint of his practice of several chivalric ideals such as bravery, prowess, and honor. Wherever and how Henry's son was trained, contemporary historians called him a distinguished knight (*miles egregius*) and a model of knighthood.[73] For Robert, the most important aspect of his progression to knighthood was that his father the king had conferred it upon him.[74]

---

[69] Painter, *French Chivalry*, 28–94; Keen, *Chivalry*, Chapt. 4, esp. 66–71; Duby, *Chivalrous Society*, 174–5; Green, *Aristocracy of Norman England*, 9–12; Chibnall, *The World of Orderic Vitalis*, 132–45; Crouch, *Image of Aristocracy in Britain*, 136–8; Gillingham, "1066 and the Introduction of Chivalry into England," 31–55.

[70] Strickland, *War and Chivalry*, 143–9, esp. 143; Morillo, *Warfare under the Anglo-Norman Kings*, 152, 154; Peirce, "The Knight, his Arms and Armour in the Eleventh and Twelfth Centuries," 153–6; Lasko, "Ivory Carvings," in *English Romanesque Art*, no. 212 and illustr. p. 72.

[71] *OV* iii. 110–13; *De Nugis Curialium*, 470–1; *HRB*, ix, ll. 392–8; Aird, *Robert Curthose*, 55–8; for Stephen and the others, see n. 78.

[72] *De Nugis Curialium*, 166 n. 3.; Barlow, *William Rufus*, 22–4; p. 23 for an earlier date for advanced military training; Stenton, *English Feudalism*, 132; Keen, *Chivalry*, 26; for knights' further training, see also Duby, *Chivalrous Society*, 114.

[73] *GR* i. 542–3, 798–9; *OV* vi. xviii, 236–7.

[74] *Serlon de Wilton: Poèmes latins*, no. 15, l.29; Barber, "When is a Knight not a Knight?," 2, 10–15, sees investiture with arms as only related to celebrating a prince's coming of age. However, terms

The sole source of the investiture event is an elegy to Robert written soon after his death in 1147 by the Paris-trained Anglo-Norman poet and rhetorician Serlo of Wilton, possibly clerk of Henry I's second queen Adeliza and tenant of churches in Berkeley Hernesse (Glos.) near Bristol. He later taught at Oxford and finally became abbot (1168 × 73) of Cistercian L'Aumône (Val-d'Oise).[75]

One of the poem's lines begins *Rex pater arma dedit...*[76] Unfortunately there is no way of knowing whether this passage is a complete description of the king's action or just a cryptic poetic allusion to a more elaborate ceremony; but there is no reason to doubt Serlo's testimony insofar as it goes. William of Malmesbury described the knighting of Robert's father in similar wording, even though a more elaborate account by Orderic Vitalis states that Henry was clothed with hauberk and helmet, and girded with the belt of knighthood.[77] Furthermore, the kind of phraseology Serlo used, conferral of arms, was one of several ways the knighting of major aristocratic families' sons was described, by Orderic among others, during the late eleventh and early twelfth centuries. Henry I's knighting of his nephew Stephen of Blois, the Beaumont twins Waleran and Robert, and Brian fitz Count are prime examples.[78]

Henry I's immediate reason for knighting Robert could have been to celebrate such life passages as completion of his education, official coming of age, impending marriage, or some combination of them.[79] Whatever the knighting marked, there are grounds for placing the occasion at least prior to the marriage the king arranged for his son. Henry recognized the chivalric rite as a preliminary step to marriage in a charter recording his gift of Matilda, daughter of Geoffrey Ridel, in marriage to Richard Basset. Along with the bride, the groom also received custody of her father's lands until Robert Ridel, Matilda's brother, could be a knight and marry a granddaughter of Ralph Basset.[80] There were years between Henry's knighting of Stephen of Blois and his nuptials; and chronological separation in varying degrees was not exceptional.[81]

A marriage King Henry arranged for Robert definitively set the course for the baronial life the king intended for him. Henry must have recognized that attitudes toward children born of canonically illicit unions probably ruled out his firstborn's

---

signifying investiture such as *dare arma* also were used to describe elevation to knighthood: *GR* i. 710–11 uses a variation in reference to the knighting of Robert's father: *sumpsit arma a patre;* Keen, *Chivalry*, 64–71; Crouch, *Birth of Nobility*, 84, 212; see n. 75.

[75] On Serlo, Edward William Solan, "A Study of the Life and Works of Serlo of Wilton"; Thomson, 'Serlo of Wilton and the Schools of Oxford,' 1–12, esp. 5–6; Rigg, "Serlo of Wilton: Biographical Notes," 96; *De Nugiis Curialium*, 136 n. 4; *Cart. Reading* i. no. 270, for the charter evidence connecting Serlo with the queen; Barlow, *The English Church*, 265–6 & n.

[76] *Serlon de Wilton: Poèmes latins*, no. 15, l. 29.

[77] *OV* iv. 120 & n. I have altered the wording of Orderic's description slightly. See also Barlow, *William Rufus*, 24–5.

[78] *OV* vi. 42–3, 328–9; Davis, "Henry of Blois and Brian Fitz Count," 303; *Serlon de Wilton: Poèmes latins*, no. 15, ll. 11, 13; Bartlett, *England under the Norman and Angevin Kings*, 232–5, esp. 233, for some other terms used to describe knighting.

[79] Keen, *Chivalry*, 66–7; Boulton, "Classic Knighthood as Nobiliary Dignity," 45–9, considers the likely era of Robert's knighting "Middle to Late Pre-Classic" in the development of the institution.

[80] Reedy, *Basset Charters*, no. 47.    [81] Crouch, *Reign of King Stephen*, 17, 21, & n. 20.

chances of succeeding him as king. Such nuptial aims were part of Henry's developing policy of politically ensnaring the heirs and heiresses of strategic lordships through marriages to his illegitimate daughters and sons and at the same time providing for them. The practice began as one of the tactics Henry I employed to expand his influence in Normandy at the expense of his brother Duke Robert following the truce he made with him at Alton in 1101 ending his invasion to claim the throne of England.

Around 1102 Henry tried to lure into his political web Ralph III de Tosny, lord of Conches, Tosny, Portes, and Acquigny (Eure), by granting him marriage to Adeliza, heiress to half of the extremely valuable former honor of Waltheof earl of Northampton and Huntingdon. Then, he began to make particular use of his own illegitimate offspring in such political gambits. Henry made sons-in-law of Eustace de Pacy, lord of the great honor of Breteuil in 1103, and of Rotrou count of Perche shortly after, by granting them marriages to, respectively, his daughters Juliana and Matilda.[82]

Initially, the de Pacy marriage gave Henry I the opportunity to strengthen his political hold on the lord of Breteuil (Eure), who was embroiled in a war over his succession at the time with his two first cousins. While death removed one of them, the surviving rival, Reginald de Grancey, attracted powerful regional allies: William count of Évreux (Eure), Ralph III of Conches and Tosny (Eure), and William's nephew Amaury of Montfort-l'Amauri. Eustace may well have trolled for recognition from both Duke Robert and King Henry as his father William of Breteuil's heir before his death in January of 1103. In any case, having seized Breteuil and under attack, he appealed to Henry for military aid rather than to Curthose. Henry more than obliged and dispatched his most trusted *familiaris*, Robert count of Meulan and lord of nearby Beaumont (Eure), to reinforce Eustace. To further cement their relationship Henry, as already noted, also gave Juliana to Eustace in marriage.[83] The king even went so far as to order his brother and those loyal to him not to intervene on the side of his son-in-law's enemies or face the consequences of his rage. Eustace and Juliana survived, in large part because of Count Robert's efforts.[84] The next year Henry's dominion over the Évrecin became complete when the king forced his brother to grant him the county of Évreux and surrender fealty of Count William and all his men in order to win a restoration of peace between them.[85]

Rotrou of Perche's marriage to Matilda followed sometime in 1103–4. It expanded Henry I's influence over a key lord in the Corbonnais and Chartrain just

---

[82] *OV* vi. 40–1 & nn.; *GND* ii. 250–1; Thompson, "Affairs of State," 132, 147–8; the betrothal of the king's son Richard to Amice daughter of Ralph de Gael may have been at Ralph's initiative: *OV* vi. 294–5.

[83] See n. 82; *OV* vi. 40–1, 44–7; Thompson, "Thames to Tinchebray," 24–5. For William fitz Osbern's family and Breteuil, see Le Patourel, "Norman Barons," VI, 5–9. For the Tosny family, see Musset, "Aux origines d'une classe dirigeante: les Tosny," 45–80, and genealogical table, p. 57, and for Ralph III, pp. 62–3. For the term *familiaris*, see Chapt. 2, n. 79.

[84] *OV* vi. 40 & nn., 41; 44–7; David, *Robert Curthose*, 144–5; Hollister, *Henry I*, 179; see also Aird, *Robert Curthose*, 221–3.

[85] *OV* vi. 56 & n., 57–61; Aird, *Robert Curthose*, 224–5.

beyond Normandy's southern frontier. Rotrou's predecessors were vassals of the counts of Chartres (Eure-et-Loir), which made him a potential ally against the count of Anjou, the Thibaudian counts' traditional enemy.[86] Henry's son-in-law also could be expected to take his side against Robert de Bellême since Rotrou's and Robert's families had a history of warring over disputed territories. While fighting against Robert for his late father Geoffrey count of Mortagne (d. 1100), Rotrou even had endured captivity at Bellême's hands. At the same time, his father had fought for the Conqueror at the battle of Hastings.[87] But a tie to the ever stronger Henry probably was welcomed by Rotrou given the increasing aggressiveness of Robert de Bellême from 1102 on and the military impotence of Duke Robert. In 1103, prompted by Henry's demand, Duke Robert had waged war on Robert de Bellême and had been defeated ignominiously at Exmes and forced into an alliance with him. In response, Henry led a well-equipped army to Normandy in 1104, where Orderic informs us he was met and entertained in royal fashion by his magnates. Rotrou was one of them, either already or about to be Matilda's husband.[88]

King Henry's most important marital maneuver with one of his illegitimate offspring was the one he arranged for his son Robert with Mabel fitz Hamon sometime after her father Robert's death on the Ides of March 1107. Fitz Hamon had been heir to his father Haimo I *dapifer* and sheriff of Kent's patrimonial lands mostly held of the bishop of Bayeux in Lower Normandy, but he was originally landless elsewhere in the Anglo-Norman realm until the reign of William Rufus. Robert's apparent younger sibling Haimo II inherited their father's English lordship of considerable value concentrated in Kent, Essex, and Surrey. Support for William Rufus by Haimo I and his two sons during the English rebellion of 1088 won for Robert curial ranking as Rufus's trusted adviser and favorite as well as major elements of what became the English honor of Gloucester, concentrated in six southwestern shires. Its strategic and economic jewel was the lower Severn river fortified port of Bristol (Glos.).[89]

During the 1090s, with Rufus's blessing, Fitz Hamon used his heavily Severn Valley-based honor as a springboard to conquer strategically important lands in South Wales which became the Marcher lordships of Gwynllŵg and the county and honor of Glamorgan. Both of these holdings had as administrative and military centers (*capita*) ports, respectively, at Newport (Monm.) and Cardiff (Glam.), from which there was easy connection by sea and the Severn estuary with Bristol.

Robert fitz Hamon was in the ill-fated hunting party of William Rufus along with his brother Henry on August 2, 1100 when the king was accidentally killed.

---

[86] *OV* vi. 398–9; Thompson, *Power and Border Lordship in Medieval France*, 52–4, 56; for the dowry given Rotrou with Matilda, see Thompson, "Dowry and Inheritance Patterns: Some Examples from the Descendants of King Henry I of England," 53.

[87] *OV* iv. 160–1 & n., 252–3, 298–300 & n., 301; William of Poitiers, 132–5; *OV* ii. 174–5, 266 & n., 267; see also 356 & n. 3, 357, 360 n. 1, 361.

[88] *OV* vi. 32–7, 56–7, 394 & n., 395–9.

[89] Fitz Hamon's grandfather Haimo the Toothed was lord of Torigni, Évrecy, and Creully: Wace, *Le Roman de Rou* ii. ll. 4027–8, 11073–6; Douglas, *Domesday Monachorum*, 55 & n.; see also Chapt. 3, 57; see Genealogical Chart, xxi.

Robert quickly transferred his loyalty to Henry and retained his previous prominence at court. Fitz Hamon was one of the few who witnessed King Henry's Coronation Charter and he attested Henry's recall of Archbishop Anselm from his self-imposed exile. According to Wace, Robert acted as one of Henry's three emissaries to several of the baronial leaders of Curthose's 1101 invasion at Alton, William of Mortain and Robert de Bellême. Fitz Hamon sided with the Norman baronage which welcomed Henry to the duchy in 1104. During the following year he campaigned for the king in the Bessin, endured captivity for him, and, after being rescued by Henry with his invading army, was rewarded for his service with the bailliage of Caen. His death resulted from wounds incurred during King Henry's siege of Falaise in 1106 prior to the battle of Tinchebrai. He was laid to rest in the choir of the Benedictine abbey he had founded in 1102 at Tewkesbury (Glos.).[90] What Robert's posthumous son-in-law gained *iure uxoris* transformed him from a landless royal bastard into a great baronial trans-Channel magnate with "imperial" connections from Ireland to Normandy and beyond, one of the Anglo-Norman aristocracy's *optimates*, in Orderic Vitalis's judgment.[91]

Mabel fitz Hamon's status as an unmarried daughter of a royal tenant-in-chief made this marital transformation of the king's son possible. Mabel was subject to feudal prerogatives Henry claimed over widows, minor heirs, and unmarried heiresses, and he controlled the disposition of such vassals' estates.[92] Fitz Hamon and his wife Sibyl, in spite of seeking spiritual assistance, had produced no son, only three or four daughters. Mabel's special prominence as her father's heiress may be why the monks of Tewkesbury listed her as present with her father and mother in the *actum* recording the establishment of the abbey's obedientiary system in 1105, allegedly with Robert's advice and counsel as lord and founder. Henry I certainly treated her as Robert's sole heiress; and at some point he had enhanced that status by placing Mabel's sisters in nunneries and marrying one of them, Amicia, to a Breton count.[93] By such tactics, Henry was following the well-established Norman and Anglo-Norman custom traced by Sir James Holt of descent to a single heiress. The king's motive according to Tewkesbury Abbey tradition was to keep the Fitz Hamon conglomeration of lordships from being divided.[94]

---

[90] William of Malmesbury believed that a blow to the head from a pike rendered Robert mentally incapacitated for some time before his death: *GR* i. 722–3; Wace, *Le Roman de Rou* ii, ll.11233–4; BL, Add. MS 36985, fol. 12b; *Mon. Angl.* ii. 81; Green, "Robert fitz Haimon," 118; Hollister, "The Anglo-Norman Civil War: 1101," 90.

[91] BL, Add. MS 36985, fol. 12b; *OV* vi. 174–5; *GND* ii. 248–9 (where Mabel is called Sibyl); Green, "Robert fitz Haimon," 117–19; for aspects of Fitz Hamon's career, see Barlow, *William Rufus*, 73, 77, 85, 93–4, 173, 192, 321, 360, 419–21, 427, 436; and Green, "William Rufus, Henry I and the Royal Demesne," 341 & n. For an Irish connection, see Bates, *The Normans and Empire*, 88, and n. 163.

[92] *GND* ii. 248–9; *Mon. Angl.* ii. 81; *Die Gesetze* i. 521, cls. 2–4; *Select Charters*, "Charter of Liberties," cls. 2–4, pp. 100–1; *EHD* ii. no. 19, cls. 2–4, p. 401; Holt, "Politics and Property in Early Medieval England," 3, 6–9.

[93] BL, Add. MS 36985, fol. 14b; Bodl., MS Top. Glouc. d.2, fol. 14v; *Mon. Angl.* ii. 81; Knowles, *HRH*, 219, 222, and Knowles, *MOE*, 431–9, for monasteries' departments and endowments. The dates for these maneuvers are unknown, as is the name of the Breton count.

[94] Bodl., MS Top. Glouc. d.2, fol. 14v; this of Tewkesbury provenance and a close copy, BL, Additional MS 36985, respectively, s.xvi[in] and s.xvi[ex] and extramural BL, MS Cotton Cleopatra C.iii

We know nothing of any royal wardship of Fitz Hamon's widow Sibyl;[95] but it is quite possible that Mabel spent some years in this state. In 1109 her father's donations to Tewkesbury Abbey were confirmed not by Mabel or her husband Robert in right of his wife, but by the king's chief justiciar, Bishop Roger of Salisbury, apparently acting in a viceregal capacity.[96]

In his Coronation Charter of 1100 Henry I had promised to consult his barons about his use of the marriage prerogative, but we hear of no such consultation about his giving nuptials with Mabel to Robert; as Eleanor Searle pointed out, any promises made in his charter were just pledges.[97]

By the late thirteenth to fourteenth century the mechanics of the process were transformed into an entertaining romance tale. Henry, with bastard son Robert in tow, did the courting for him; Mabel, knowing full well her position and the king's real aims, rejected the royal advances until Henry declared for his son and remedied his two disabilities, namelessness and lack of a title. First, Henry recognized Robert to be "Robert fitz Roy" and then, to be earl of Gloucester. Finally satisfied, the lady gave her consent.[98] More than likely, the prospects of a Fitz Hamon bride would have been no surprise to the king's son given his early presence in the area where Mabel's father had been so prominent as the king's protagonist.

The exact date of the marriage may be beyond reach, but a reasonable estimate is important because it helps to distinguish between phases of the baronial career Henry I intended for Robert as well as the king's possible political motives. The nuptials certainly occurred after the death of Mabel's father in 1107, but how long afterwards? A tradition preserved at Bristol, Robert's headquarters, could support a date later in the year; however, that evidence is three centuries later and its exact description of the tenure Robert held at the time is inaccurate.[99] On the other hand, a passage from a later text of William of Malmesbury's *Historia Novella* has been taken to associate the dates of the marriage and the conferral of the earldom of Gloucester upon Robert;[100] and this chronological linkage is supported by a

---

(s.xvi[med]), contain biographical information concerning the abbey's founders; Luxford, "'Secundum originale examinatum': The Refashioning of a Benedictine Historical Manuscript," 163–79; Luxford, "The Founder's Book," 53–6; see also Holt, "Feudal Society and the Family in Medieval England: IV: The Heiress and the Alien," 8–10.

[95] Sibyl, noted as the mother of the countess of Gloucester (Mabel), gave a "just" in the shape of a cock to Ramsey Abbey which was among the church's ornaments alienated by Abbot Walter (1133–60) during Stephen's reign: *Cart. Ramsey* ii. 274; Knowles, *HRH*, 62.

[96] Kealey, *Roger of Salisbury*, Appendix 2, no. 2. Tewkesbury was in the diocese of Worcester, not in Roger's diocese, so he could not have been acting in his ecclesiastical capacity.

[97] *Die Gesetze* i. 521; cl. 3; *Select Charters*, "Charter of Liberties," cl. 3, pp. 100–1: *EHD* ii., no. 19, cl. 3, p. 401; Green, "A Lasting Memorial," 61; Searle, "Seignorial Control of Women's Marriage," 12.

[98] The *Histoire des ducs de Normandie et des rois d'Angleterre* dating from early s.xiii mentions neither the courtship of Mabel nor the grant of a name or title to Robert; the stories are in the Anglo-Norman *Brut.*, BL, MS Cotton Vitellius A.x, fols. 135–135v: *Cont. Wace*, 103–4, and in the *Metrical Chronicle* ii. 633–5, which its editor dates *c*.1300, considers an English translation from a French work, and with the Cotton text descended from a common source: *Metrical Chronicle* i. xi, xiv, xxvii; see n. 24.

[99] *The Maire of Bristowe Is Kalendar*, 19.

[100] "Mox Rotbertus filius regis, quem ante regnum susceperat, et comitem Gloecestre fecerat, data ei in matrimonium Mabilia," *HN* (1998), 8–9 & n. Note however that with the use of the perfect

tradition preserved at Tewkesbury Abbey, whose patrons were Fitz Hamon and his Gloucester successors.[101] Nevertheless, John Horace Round demonstrated long ago that at least Henry I's conferral of the earldom occurred in 1121/2 *following* a period when Robert as simply the king's son and not yet an earl disposed of Fitz Hamon land as Mabel fitz Hamon's husband.[102]

The king's son probably achieved that status sometime between 1109/10 and *c*.1115, with the best estimate being *c*.1113. The Lindsey Survey of Lincolnshire estates shows that six bovates at Aisthorpe in Lawress wapentake had passed to Robert, almost certainly because of his marriage to Mabel. Robert, as the king's son, is recorded as being the undertenant of William Turniant there. Trevor Foulds has persuasively dated the survey, long thought to date from 1115 × 1118, to have been drawn up after mid-July 1115 and before April–May 1116—more likely late summer or autumn 1115.[103]

A *c*.1113 date for the nuptials is suggested by the historian Orderic Vitalis's association of Robert with magnates (*optimates*) who were called upon by Henry I at Rouen in that year to corroborate grants to the abbey of Saint-Évroul (Eure): a tenurial transformation which logically would have been accomplished by then by his marriage to Mabel fitz Hamon.[104] Earlier than 1109–10 is unlikely. A survey of Winchester (Hants.) of *c*.1110, referring to a tenement held of Fitz Hamon's fee, may establish that the land had not yet passed by marriage to the king's son;[105] and, as already seen, there is strong evidence that an unmarried Mabel was in her royal future father-in-law's wardship in 1109.[106]

Before arranging the fitz Hamon marriage, circumstances moved the king from the defense of his throne to Normandy's conquest. His success in achieving that helped to secure his son's trans-Channel future. The Treaty of Alton of 1101 was in effect a truce between King Henry and Duke Robert. Over the next few years, Henry dealt with real or perceived enemies in England by banishment and confiscation of estates, which culminated in his treatment of his first cousin William count of

---

passive participle *data* with *Mabilia* to form an ablative absolute clause, a translation could read "after Mabel had been given to him in marriage."

[101] Bodl., MS Top. Gloucs. d.2, fol. 14v; BL, MS Cotton Cleopatra C.iii, fol. 352r: *Mon. Angl.* ii. 60–1; BL, Additional MS 36985, fol. 14b; *The Metrical Chronicle* ii, ll. 8876–905. Robert of Torigny separated the two events, but not in specific chronological order: *GND* ii. 248–9.

[102] Round, *Geoffrey de Mandeville*, "Excursus: The Creation of the Earldom of Gloucester," 422–33, esp. 422: "Let us first observe that there is no evidence for the belief that Robert received his earldom at the time of his marriage to the heiress of Robert fitz Hamon." See also Patterson, *EGC*, no. 166 & n.

[103] *The Lincolnshire Domesday and Lindsey Survey*, L3/18, p. 242; Round, "The Lindsey Survey (1115–18)," 181–95, esp. 189; Foulds, "The Lindsey Survey and an Unknown Precept of King Henry I," 13–14. The Northamptonshire Survey provides no clue to the marriage's date, but by attributing tenure of Raunds to Robert fitz Roy it may reveal another nuptials-related grant: Round, "Northamptonsire Survey," 377 & n. A writ of Henry I dated 1110 × 23, if genuine, suggests that Malvern (Worcs.), which had belonged to Robert fitz Hamon, had not yet passed to the king's son by marriage: *Regesta* ii. no. 1413 [no. CLXIX]. See also Chapt. 3, 64.

[104] *OV* vi. 174–5; *Regesta* ii. no. 1019. All the witnesses, except for Robert, are known holders of land; for Nigel d'Albigny: *Charters of the Honour of Mowbray*, xvii–xxv; Roger of Thibouville: Loyd, *Anglo-Norman Families*, 102.

[105] *Winchester*, "Survey I," no. 96.   [106] Kealey, *Roger of Salisbury*, Appendix 2, no. 2.

Mortain.[107] Like William Rufus, the king also advanced his influence in the duchy by increasing the number of Norman lords owing allegiance to him over and above those already loyal to him such as Richard de Redvers and Hugh of Avranches in the Cotentin, Robert fitz Hamon in the Bessin, and Robert count of Meulan in the Évrecin. Henry's expeditions of 1104 and 1105 yielded the allegiance of William count of Évreux and the towns of Bayeux and Caen. Whatever the king's intentions had been prior to 1104, by about this time he was now bent on disinheriting his brother. When Curthose visited Henry at Northampton in February of 1106 and asked as a brother for the acquisitions' restoration, Henry refused.[108]

Ultimately, this creeping conquest led to the military showdown between the king and duke at the battle of Tinchebrai about October 28, 1106 which resulted in Robert Curthose's defeat and imprisonment for life and Henry's conquest of the duchy. Nevertheless, Henry had to deal with significant residual baronial resistance and to fight two defensive wars, c.1111–13 and 1117–19, against coalitions of neighboring princes at times in league with Norman rebels before his tenure of Normandy was secure. Even then, the king faced one last rebellion in the duchy during 1123–4.[109]

Norman rebels were driven by a range of motives, sometimes combinations, such as kinship and proprietary complaints against King Henry, and, especially for the frontier barons, additional ties to external princes with their own agendas.[110] King Louis's motive between 1109 and 1113 originated from his accession in 1108, when Henry evidently refused to perform homage for Normandy and to surrender or destroy two Vexin castles. Henry also actively supported his nephew Count Theobald IV of Blois (1107–52) in a war with Louis from about 1111.[111] Counts Robert II and his successor Baldwin VII of Flanders feared Anglo-Normandy's growing strength. After Fulk V of Anjou inherited the intermediate county of Maine *iure uxoris* in 1110, he fought to nullify Henry's claimed overlordship of it.[112]

William Clito's claim to the duchy as his father's rightful heir also emerged as the *casus belli* for both baronial rebels and their foreign allies. His cause gained momentum after 1109, when the boy, whom King Henry had placed after Tinchebrai in the guardianship of a son-in-law of Curthose, was spirited from Normandy before he could be arrested on Henry's orders. The guardian Helias de Saint-Saens then promoted Clito's case with Louis VI of France and other regional princes. Robert de Bellême, who had abandoned his allegiance to King Henry c.1110,

---

[107] Davies, "The Count of the Cotentin: Western Normandy, William of Mortain, and the Career of Henry I," esp. 123–32.
[108] *OV* vi. 56–61, 78–83; *ASC a.*1105, 1106; *GR* i. 722–3; Henry of Huntingdon (1996), 452–3; *JW* iii. 106–9; Robert of Torigny, "Chronica," 84–5.
[109] *JW* iii. 108–11; *OV* vi. 82–91; *Warenne Chronicle*, 53–5; Green, *Henry I*, 89–95.
[110] Green, "King Henry I and the Aristocracy of Normandy," 162–5; Hollister, *Henry I*, 224–8, 244–74.
[111] *GR* i. 758–9; *Warenne Chronicle*, 56–63, 66–81; Suger, *Vie de Louis VI le Gros*, esp. 102–7, 150–5, 170–3, 182–7; *ASC a.*1116, also *a.*1111, 1112, 1113; Henry of Huntingdon (1996), 460–1; *OV* vi. 158–63, 176–81; Green, *Henry I*, 118–19; Hollister, *Henry I*, 229–30, 244, 246; LoPrete, *Adela of Blois*, Chapts. 6 & 7.
[112] Le Patourel, *Norman Empire*, 17–18, 73, 79–80, 85–7. Hollister, *Henry I*, 224–5; LoPrete, *Adela of Blois*, 315–17, 325.

acted similarly with sympathetic elements of the Norman baronage.[113] Fulk of Anjou took up the cause in 1111; Baldwin VII, possibly three years years later.[114] After Henry I preemptively had the Norman baronage swear fealty to William Aetheling's succession in 1114, Louis VI, reminded of his prior support for Clito, refused Henry I's offer of his son's profession of fealty and pushed Clito's succession agenda forward. He and the two counts swore to replace Henry with his nephew in 1117.[115]

It may be no coincidence that in the rising support for Clito King Henry's scribes began to record the presence of his sons at court. Robert's name appears in the witness-lists of two confirmation charters his father issued in 1113, one at Rouen for the abbey of Saint-Évroul (Seine-Maritime) sometime after 3 February and the other for the abbey of Bec (Eure) mentioning among the witnesses his half-brother William Aetheling's name for the first time.[116] Within a year Robert's younger half-brother and fellow bastard Richard also made his curial debut of record.[117]

On the other hand, the catalyst for publicly recognizing the royal sons' presence at court could very well have been Henry's decision to betroth William to Count Fulk V of Anjou's daughter Matilda. It was part of several peace-making agreements the king made with the count in February 1113 which helped to end his first post-Tinchebrai defensive war.[118]

William's special ranking at court is evident in the placement of his name in the witness-lists of royal *acta* immediately after the king's or the queen's.[119] And King Henry formalized William's status as heir to Normandy in early 1115 and to England in 1116, when his barons swore fealty to the young man's succession. As Warren Hollister pointed out, the Aetheling was referred to as *rex et dux designatus* and may have held the title *Dei gratia rex designatus*. Toward the end of the decade he even acted as regent in his father's absence.[120]

Robert's image which datable evidence has left of him in the early years of his public life is that of an emerging curial baron. Marriage, as already noted, made him a major and politically important tenant-in-chief; and there survives at least a glimpse of him administering a portion of his vast trans-Channel barony.[121] Invisible to us are two interrelated institutions Robert had begun to employ which were integral to his new seigniorial life but are only known to us from evidence deriving long after his death: his domestic household (*domus*) and his administrative and social hall (*aula*). The two are mentioned in a briefly recorded encounter

---

[113] *OV* vi. 162–5, 176 & n., 177–9;, 184–7; *GR* i. 730–1; *Warenne Chronicle*, 54–61; Hollister, *Henry I*, 206, 227–8, 234, 244–8. For Robert de Bellême's shifting loyalties, see esp. Thompson, "Robert of Bellême Reconsidered," 276–9.

[114] *OV* vi. 166–7, 256–7; *ASC a.* 1117, *a.*1118; Eadmer, 248; Henry of Huntingdon (1996), 460–1; *JW* iii. 142–3; Hollister, *Henry I*, 244.

[115] Henry of Huntingdon (1996), 460–1.

[116] *OV* vi. 174–5; *Regesta* ii. no. 1019; see also no. 1015a.   [117] *Regesta* ii. no. 1062.

[118] *OV* vi. 180–1; Green, *Henry I*, 126.

[119] *Regesta* ii., e.g., nos. 1015a, 1091–2, 1098a, 1102, 1108, 1131.

[120] Green, *Henry I*, 135 & nn.; Hollister, "Rise of Administrative Kingship," 229 & n. 19. On the charter evidence, see *Regesta* ii, nos. 1074 & n., 1204 & n., and Round, *Geoffrey de Mandeville*, 423–7.

[121] Patterson, *EGC*, no. 166; see Map 1, 239; Map 2, 240.

between Richard of Ilchester, who had served Robert as a notary in his *aula*, and Ralph, the earl's former pelterer and member of his *domus*, on a pilgrimage *c.*1155 × 1174 to the shrine of St. James at Compostella.[122]

It is fair to assume that the time gaps between sightings of Fitz Roy at his father's court were due in part to visitation of his estates. Otherwise, Robert periodically joined his father as the king itinerated through his trans-Channnel realm, according to common practice, accompanied by a variable roster of his family and administrative household members, assorted tenants-in-chief, and other invited parties.[123] He was with his father in Normandy at Rouen in 1113, in England at Westbourne (Sussex) in 1114, at Westminster (Middlesex) at a great council on September 16, 1115, at Reading (Berks.) sometime between 1113 and 1116, in Normandy at Arganchy (Calvados) in 1118, and at Rouen again in 1119.[124]

At court, Robert enjoyed a place of honor.[125] His designation *filius regis* identified him as a member of the royal family, but he was not grouped in witness-lists of his father's *acta* with such members of the immediate royal family, Henry, Queen Matilda, William Aetheling, as they were recorded. Robert's place in these listings varied. But in clearly hierarchically arranged ones, he could appear first before other laymen, following the earls who themselves were preceded in ascending order upwards by members of the royal household and sometimes *curiales*, archbishops, bishops, and the immediate royal family. His half-brother Richard was similarly treated.[126] Court protocol assigned the two to a category separate from their legitimately born siblings—what we would call extended family. To use a wildly anachronistic analogy, when group pictures were taken at official gatherings of the court, the official photographer would place the king, queen, and legitimate heir in the center, flanked by their archbishops, bishops, and abbots, with Robert and Richard off to the side, in turn flanked by as many tenants-in-chief as could be fitted into the picture.

Robert's average annual rate of court appearances, less than once per year, was statistically paltry. Like other attendees he could be called upon to witness his father's *acta* and be prepared to testify that the recorded transactions agreed with the actual proceedings.[127] Nevertheless, on occasion, he was deemed important enough to be included with those, such as the king, queen, aetheling, royal officials, and current clerical and lay favorites, to confirm with their *signa* certain transactions assigned special dignity. A single extant example in which Robert's name appears among its list of signatories rather than its witnesses drives the point

---

[122] "Inventio S. Nectani Martyris," 411.
[123] White, "The Household of the Norman Kings," 127–55; Chibnall, "Mercenaries and the *Familia Regis* under Henry I," 15–23. See also, e.g., Hugh the Chanter, 126–7.
[124] *OV* vi. 174; *Regesta* ii. nos. 1019, 1062, 1091, 1128, 1183, 1204.
[125] For Robert's standing at court, see 28 & n. His brother Richard was even less a presence at court: *Regesta* ii., nos. 1062, 1204. William in the same period attested 9 *acta*: nos. 1015a, 1091, 1092, 1098a, 1102, 1108, 1131, 1204, 1224; he also issued 5 *acta* as regent: nos. 1189, 1191, 1192, 1201, 1202. For the Aetheling's viceregal function, see West, *Justiciarship*, 14–15; Bates, "Origins of the Justiciarship," 10; Hollister, "Rise of Administrative Kingship," 875 & n., 876 & n.
[126] See n. 125.
[127] *HN* (1998), 8–9; *Regesta* ii. nos. 1015a, 1019, 1062, 1091, 1128, 1183, 1204.

home. He even could be assigned this role at a plenary meeting of his father's court when the available pool of such *familiares* was at its greatest level.[128]

These curial functions gave Robert associations with key figures of his father's English and Norman central administrations.[129] Understandably, the two most frequently encountered were the chancellor, the obscure Ranulf (1107–22), and Roger bishop (1107–39) of Salisbury (Wilts.). The chancellor, as head of the royal chapel, had authority over its chaplains, the royal seal, and chancery scribes, although the chancellor's assistant, the keeper of the seal, supervised its use and members of the royal writing office.[130] Roger was King Henry's rising untitled administrative chief of staff for England and head of the kingdom's Treasury and Exchequer court at Winchester (Hants.). His curial influence had been earned from his record of continuous service to Henry; and during his early years in Normandy Robert may have met Roger. The priest of Avranches was then manager of Henry's comital household. After Henry's accession, Roger became successively a royal chaplain, chancellor (1101–2), and then bishop of Salisbury.[131] Also notable among the royal son's bureaucratic associates were several high-ranking *curiales* who served under Bishop Roger at the Exchequer court and on viceregency councils for Queen Matilda and then William Aetheling, William Rufus's chancellor Bishop Robert Bloet of Lincoln (1094–1123), dubbed by William of Malmesbury worldly, but second to none in his knowledge of secular affairs,[132] the royal justice Ralph Basset (d. 1129 × 30),[133] and the former important household knight Nigel d'Aubigny, tenant of honors and lordships in Normandy and England and viceroy of the North as local justice of Yorkshire and Northumberland *c*.1107–*c*.1118.[134] Robert's more frequent colleagues at the *curia regis* from the Norman administration were John bishop of Lisieux, Henry's chief justice for Normandy,[135] William de Tancarville, chamberlain,[136] and Geoffrey archbishop of Rouen.[137]

---

[128] *OV* vi. 174–5; *Regesta* ii. nos. 1019, esp. 1015a, 1204; Bates, "Prosopographical Study of Anglo-Norman Royal Charters," 94–5 100–1; see Chapt. 2, 29–30.

[129] For Hollister's ranking of these individuals as *curiales*, see "Rise of Administrative Kingship," 888.

[130] For Ranulf, see *Regesta* ii. ix, nos. 1015a, 1062, 1091, 1128, 1183, 1204, 1243, 1245, 1247–9, 1289; *GOE*, 28, 159–60 & n., 172, 175, 179n., 235; Bishop. *Scriptores Regis*, 30; Hollister, *Henry I*, 361, 363.

[131] For Roger, see *Regesta* ii., nos. 1062, 1091, 1128, 1243, 1245, 1247–9, 1280, 1283, 1289.

[132] *Regesta* ii., nos. 1062, 1091, 1128, 1243, 1245, 1247–9, 1280, 1283, 1289. *GP*, 474–5. Henry of Huntingdon (1996), 586–9, against which, see Hollister, *Henry I*, 332–3. See also *GOE*, 39, 48, 135, 162, 190n.

[133] Hollister, "Rise of Administrative Kingship," 878, 884, 886, 888; *GOE*, 39–40, 46, 48, 75, 101, 108–9, 115, 128n., 139, 145, 166, 169, 171, 178, 182, 231–2, 270; Reedy, "First Two Bassets of Weldon," 241–5, 295–8; Reedy, *Basset Charters*, v, viii–x; Reedy, "Origins of the General Eyre," 694, 697, 699, 702–3, 706, 708–9, 714–16. William Giffard, as bishop of Winchester (1107–29), perhaps should be counted as a bureaucratic associate if he functioned as a baron of the Exchequer; see *Regesta* ii. nos. 1243, 1248–9, esp. 1283, 1289; *EEA* viii. xxxiv–xxxv.

[134] *GOE*, 26, 35, 37, 39, 123, 147, 181n., 246, 281; *Charters of the Honour of Mowbray*, xviii–xxv; White, "Household of the Norman Kings," 149–51.

[135] *Regesta* ii. nos. 1091, 1183, 1204.

[136] *Regesta* ii., nos. 1015a, 1062, 1183, 1204, 1243, 1245, 1247–8, 1280, 1289.

[137] For Archbishop Geoffrey, *Regesta* ii. nos. 1019, 1091, 1183, 1204, 1247–8, 1289; for the archbishops' roles in Norman administration, see Chapt. 2, 32.

The court also provided relationships with England's two metropolitans, Archbishop Ralph d'Escures (transl. 1114–22) of Canterbury, former abbot of Sées (Orne), then (1108–14) bishop of Rochester (Kent), and the king's former chaplain, secretary, and *familiaris* Thurstan, archbishop elect of York (1114; consecr. 1119).[138] They might be at court regarding some aspect of their ongoing dispute over Canterbury's claim of primacy over York: Thurstan, to obtain consecration without making a profession of obedience to Ralph, and Ralph opposing Thurstan's consecration unless he did so.[139] Another example might have occurred at or close to the Norman council Henry I summoned for October 7, 1118, when Archbishop Ralph consulted with Henry on his way to plead his case to the pope.[140] There were probably also a few behind-the-scenes meetings in the royal household between Robert and his later curial colleague Brian fitz Count, Stephen of Blois count of Mortain, and the Beaumont twin brothers Waleran count of Meulan and Robert earl of Leicester.[141] There may have even been some opportunities for the king's son to observe the twins' father, the king's premier adviser, Robert de Beaumont count of Meulan and earl of Leicester, at work. So respected was his counsel that he was deemed to speak with the voice of an oracle. Professor Sally Vaughn has shown that the count's advice on a variety of issues between 1100 and 1115 made him the architect of a politics based on winning agreements by amiable concessions which could be repudiated later. As the king's son was fulfilling the aims of his first career, the count of Meulan's was coming to a close; and in 1118 he died.[142]

Presence in his father's household and court also led before 1120 to Robert's participation, along with his brothers Richard and William Aetheling, in at least one of his father's military campaigns. Robert and his siblings served with an adjunct unit of the royal household's mercenary force known as the *familia regis*. Lay and ecclesiastical magnates also maintained such groups within their households. Later on, Robert had one himself. The core of the royal *familia*, under the high command of the constables and master marshal, consisted of mercenary knights led by their captains. It also could be supplemented by family members and landless aristocratic *iuvenes*, household officials, curial *familiares*, and tenants-in-chief. Members served as domestic guards, mobile field forces, and castle garrisons.[143]

---

[138] For Ralph, see *Regesta* ii., nos. 1091, 1182, 1204, 1243, 1245, 1247–9; for Thurstan, see nos. 1062, 1091, 1204.

[139] *Regesta* ii. no. 1091; Eadmer, 237–8; Hugh the Chanter, 62–3; *C & S* i. 709–16. For another example, but without evidence of Robert's presence, see *JW* iii. 140–1. For further discussion of the primacy dispute, see also Chapt. 2, 37.

[140] *Regesta* ii. no. 1183; *OV* vi. 202 & n., 203; Eadmer 248–9; *GP*, 208–9.

[141] *Regesta* ii. nos. 1182, 1243, 1245; *OV* vi. 42–3: for Stephen's early years, see King, *King Stephen*, esp. 9–11; for Waleran and Robert, see *Regesta* ii. no. 843; *GR* i. 734–7; King, "Brian fitz Count," 538.

[142] *GR* i. 736–7; Henry of Huntingdon (1996), 596–601; *ASC a*.1118; *Regesta* ii. nos. 1019, 1091; only one of Robert of Meulan's attestations of Henry I's *acta* is datable to 1100 × 18: no. 1200; others show that 1116 was the last year in which he was active; Vaughn, "Robert of Meulan and Raison d'Etat in the Anglo-Norman State," 361–9, 372; Vaughn, *Anselm of Bec and Robert of Meulan*, 164–8, 217–18, 230–4, 284–5, 347, 351, 353, 356–9.

[143] Chibnall, "Mercenaries and the *Familia Regis* under Henry I," 15–23; Prestwich, "War and Finance in the Anglo-Norman State," 24–34; Hollister, *Military Organization of Anglo-Norman England*, 65, 118, 124, 167–8, 171–6; Morillo, *Warfare under the Anglo-Norman Kings*, 60–6.

The known pre-1120 example is the famous battle of Brémule (Eure) on August 20, 1119 between Henry's forces and those of King Louis VI of France (1108–37) and several Norman baronial allies during the second of Henry's defensive Norman wars (1117–19). Brémule for Clito was to be the opportunity to gain his ducal inheritance and his father's freedom.[144]

Each conflict initially pitted against Henry the already mentioned alliance of external princes, the king of France, the counts of Anjou and of Flanders. The first attracted Norman baronial sympathizers and the second, those especially in active rebellion in the duchy. In each conflict death and diplomacy reduced Henry's main external foes to one, King Louis VI of France. For successive counts of Flanders, Robert II and Baldwin VII, it was death. Two months before Brémule, Baldwin died from a wound incurred in his attack on Eu (Seine-Maritime), complicated by overindulgence—food and fornication were both blamed; and his successor Charles "the Good" did not renew hostilities with Henry and in fact renewed the Anglo-Flemish alliance in 1119.[145] And Henry I detached Fulk V by a peace treaty, as he had earlier in 1113. Betrothal of William Aetheling to Fulk's daughter Matilda sealed the first agreement; marriage to her anchored the second. Also in each case Anglo-Norman overlordship of Maine was recognized: in the first, by Fulk's swearing fealty to Henry for Maine; in the second, with the county as Matilda's dower.[146]

Brémule ended a campaign King Louis had been waging in eastern Normandy as part of the full-scale war he had resumed with King Henry in 1117. Intermittent hostilities characterized by cross-border raiding and seizures of castles had continued even after peace had been made supposedly ending the earlier fighting (1111–13). The seriousness of events brought Henry I to Normandy soon after Easter 1116. His sons Robert, Richard, and William Aetheling joined him over the next three years.[147] Orderic Vitalis seems to imply that by Brémule Robert and Richard already had achieved distinction as knights (*milites egregii*), although the chronicler's *Historia Ecclesiastica* does more to make the latter fit the mold, on the basis of his martial exploits both before and after the battle.[148]

The best example concerns Richard's command of the fortified village of Le Grand Andely (Eure) in the Norman Vexin in 1118. His garrison was overwhelmed through treachery, then forced to surrender to King Louis after having taken refuge in a church. The king released Richard, who then went back to warring for his father with the *familia regis* and narrowly escaped capture on another occasion during a foray into the French Vexin. Robert's arrival at his father's court around October 1118 may mean that he also fought for his father, particularly in December

---

[144] *OV* vi. 236–7.
[145] *Warenne Chronicle*, 70–3; *OV* vi. 190–1 & nn.; Suger, *Vie de Louis VI*, 196–9; *GR* i. 730–1; Hollister, *Henry I*, 251 & n.
[146] *OV* vi. 180–1; *ASC a*.1110; Hollister, *Henry I*, 231 & n. 115; Green, *Henry I*, 149; Aird, *Robert Curthose*, 255–6.
[147] *ASC a*.1116; *Regesta* ii. no. 1183 (Robert), nos. 1204 (William, Robert, and Richard); Hollister, *Henry I*, 244.
[148] *OV* vi. 216–19, 228–9, 246–9.

at the battle of Alençon, where Count Fulk of Anjou inflicted on Henry I the greatest defeat of his reign.[149]

In any case, Robert was with Richard and William Aetheling in the army of 500 King Henry led from his forward position at Noyon-sur-Andelle (Eure) to confront Louis's force of 400 on the nearby field of Brémule. Louis's army included Normans who took part in the battle, notably the "Pretender" William Clito and William Crispin, and several others like Stephen of Aumâle and lord of the great English honor of Holderness, who did not, out of fear of losing their English lands if they were captured. Orderic Vitalis portrays the battle as a kind of chivalrous tournament between knights, in the course of which only three were killed: "They were all clad in mail and spared each other on both sides out of fear of God and fellowship in arms; they were more concerned to capture than to kill the fugitives."[150]

The reality, given the reported battle scenes, probably was a good deal different, particularly regarding casualties. Henry won in large part because of the strategic advantage he gained by having succeeded in deploying his army on the battlefield before being attacked; and Louis commenced the fighting in a disorganized manner and without a plan of battle. The formation crucial to Henry's victory was his army's wedge-shaped dense mass of dismounted knights supposedly divided into two lines and protected some distance to the front by two lines of mounted knights. The wedge's first line was reinforced with foot soldiers and archers, and among its dismounted knights were Robert, William Aetheling, and apparently the *familia regis* (*fidentiores milites*). Successive charges of Louis's forces were unable to break the wedge, although Henry himself in its second line was almost killed by William Crispin when he managed to fight his way to the king through or around the first line. The French army's losses from attacking the Anglo-Norman lines finally saw its numbers so reduced that retreat became necessary to save what was left. However, Henry of Huntingdon credited the infantry unit in which Robert and his brothers fought with turning the tide of battle. Then Louis's withdrawal became a rout when it came under attack from Anglo-Norman cavalry. King Louis, William Clito, and other escapees made their way back to Le Grand Andely (Eure).[151]

During the year following Brémule, King Henry continued to triumph over Louis. At the instigation of Amaury of Évreux, the French king soon returned to the duchy with an army of priests and their parishioners levied by their bishops. Louis's goal was to restore Breteuil to Eustace de Pacy as well as other lordships to other of William Clito's dispossessed supporters. However, on September 17 Henry I's replacement for Eustace, Ralph de Gael, aided by an advance force of the *familia regis* Henry sent with his son Richard, forced Louis to abandon his attack

---

[149] *ASC a.*1118; Symeon of Durham, 252; *OV* vi. 206–9, 216–21; 228–9, 246–9; John of Marmoutier, "Additamenta ix," 155–61; *Regesta* ii. no. 1183; Hollister, "War and Diplomacy in the Anglo-Norman World," 74 & n.

[150] "Ex Brevi Chronico Gemmeticensi," 775; "Ex Brevi Chronico Ducum Normanniae," 787; *OV* vi. 234–7, 240 & n., 241; *Warenne Chronicle*, 76–7; Crouch, *The Image of Aristocracy in Britain*, 126–7.

[151] *Warenne Chronicle*, xxv–xxviii, 72–9; see also Suger, *Vie de Louis VI*, 196–9; *ASC a.*1119; Henry of Huntingdon (1996), 462–5; Van Houts, "The Warenne View of the Past 1066–1203," 103, 110–13; esp. Morillo, *Warfare under the Anglo-Norman Kings*, 171–3; Bradbury, "Battles in England and Normandy," 6 & n. 29, 7–9.

on Breteuil and to withdraw from Normandy. Norman rebels were either crushed or made peace with the victorious Henry.[152]

In October, at the Council of Rheims and before Pope Calixtus II, the French king accused Henry of unjustly invading Normandy, imprisoning Robert Curthose and Robert de Bellême, dispossessing William Clito of his inheritance, and inciting his vassal, Count Theobald of Blois, to rebel against him. Calixtus demanded that Henry and his nephew rectify these injustices during a private meeting with the king in November in or near the border castle of Gisors (Eure). But Henry not only was able to avoid condemnation and sanctions from both council and pope, but he succeeded in gaining a declaration from Calixtus that, in effect, the issue of his tenure of Normandy was closed.[153]

Henry's crowning achievement came in the next year. Louis VI, given his lack of Angevin and Flemish allies or significant Norman supporters, plus the refusal of papal intervention on his behalf, agreed to a proposal from the victorious Henry he had rejected in 1115. It saved both of their political faces, but not William Clito's. Louis accepted the homage of William Aetheling for Normandy, thereby emphasizing his overlordship, while sparing Henry as a king from the role of his vassal, but also legally abandoning William Clito's claim to the duchy.[154]

On November 25, 1120 Henry embarked from Barfleur (Manche) for a triumphant return to England, leaving behind his sons William Aetheling and Richard, daughter Matilda, and other relatives and nobles to follow on other ships. Before the day ended, it produced the greatest political and dynastic crisis of Henry's reign. His son Robert's whereabouts at this time are unknown, but they increasingly would be recorded because of the dramatic change in his status set in motion by his brother William's unexpected death.

The Aetheling, his half-brother Richard, and half-sister Matilda, and all other fellow passengers and crew, except for one survivor, perished when their vessel, the "White Ship," sailing after the king at night, was wrecked after hitting a rock off Barfleur. Richard's recent heroics had built up so much capital with his father that he, not Robert, had taken the lead in obtaining mitigated punishment due his sister Juliana and brother-in-law Eustace de Pacy for their rebellion in 1119.[155] Abbot Suger of Saint-Denis reflecting particularly on the Aetheling's fate saw fulfillment of Geoffrey of Monmouth's prophecies of Merlin about the lion's "cubs being turned into fish." Thinking more of the calamity's political impact, William of Malmesbury put it very simply: "it changed everything."[156]

---

[152] *OV* vi. 242–9; Suger, *Vie de Louis VI*, 198–9, is a face-saving effort for Louis; Hollister, *Henry I*, 265–6.

[153] *OV* vi. 256–65, 282–91; Hugh the Chanter, 76–7; *GR* i. 734–7; Eadmer, 258–9; Suger, *Vie de Louis VI*, 112 & n., 113; Thomson, *GR* ii. 368; Hollister, *Henry I*. 266–9.

[154] *GR* i. 734–7; *ASC a*.1119, 1120; *JW* iii. 144–5; *Warenne Chronicle*, 80–3 & n., 84–5; Green, *Henry I*, 161–4.

[155] *OV* vi. 278–9, 296–307; *ASC* a.1120; *GR* i. 758–63; Eadmer, 288–9; Symeon of Durham, 259; Henry of Huntingdon (1996), 466–7, 594–5; *JW* iii. 146–9; Hugh the Chanter, 99.

[156] *GR* i. 762–3: *res mirum in modum mutatae*, freely translated; Suger, *Vie de Louis VI*, 98–101; *HRB* 146–7, ll. 84–5. For Orderic Vitalis's use of the prophecies of Merlin see *OV* vi. xviii & nn., and 380 & n. 5, 381–9, esp. 384–5; Suger, *The Deeds of Louis the Fat*, 185, n. 2, contains useful bibliography.

Henry I, a widower since Matilda's death in 1118, suddenly found himself without a legitimate male heir in the direct line. Their only other child, Matilda, was married to the Salian Emperor Henry V. The dynastic and political implications of this situation were obvious to all, as Henry of Huntingdon reported: Henry's nephew William Clito was undeniably now his sole legitimate heir.[157] This endangered Henry's suppression of Norman rebellion, destroyed the basis for the Angevin alliance and attendant Continental territorial settlement, and in England fueled the quiet development of support for Clito's eventual succession.[158] So, in an effort to repair the root cause of this damage, Henry I sought a new marriage which would lead in 1121 to his union at 53 with Adeliza of Louvain in hopes of replacing William with a new male heir.[159] But in the short term the king also sought to strengthen his family's position at court by increasing his illegitimate son Robert's presence and status.[160]

Henry's intentions are evident from the obvious difference between the number of Robert's recorded appearances at court between 1113 and 1120 and those in the portion of 1121 when he was still "Robert the king's son." As already seen, his pre-1121 annual rate was extremely low.[161] After the Aetheling's death and before his elevation to comital rank, in the year 1121 Robert attested a total of nine of his father's charters on at least four different occasions between January and the end of May:[162] Henry had begun to elevate Robert's status as a *familiaris*; and to institutionalize his eminence in that regard he made him an earl before the end of the next year. Gloucester probably was selected for Robert's comital title because the shire held the greatest amount of his demesne estates, including one in Gloucester, his most valuable and strategic castle-borough Bristol, and at Tewkesbury the *Eigenkloster* of his English honor. A second career was under way, perhaps celebrated by the first Anglo-Norman earl of Gloucester's participating in Tewkesbury Abbey's grand dedication on October 24, 1121 by Theulf bishop of Worcester and the bishops of Llandaff, Hereford, and Dublin.[163]

---

[157] Henry of Huntingdon (1996), 594–5.
[158] Hollister, "War and Diplomacy in the Anglo-Norman World," 84; Hollister, "The Anglo-Norman Succession Debate of 1126," 25.
[159] *GR* i. 762–3; Henry of Huntingdon (1996), 466–9; *JW* iii. 148–9; *ASC a.*1121; *OV* vi. 308–9; "Ann. Winchester," 46.
[160] Round saw the connection between the White Ship disaster and Robert's promotion to earl: *Geoffrey de Mandeville*, 434.
[161] See 22; also Chapt. 2, 29–30.
[162] See n. 125; *Regesta* ii. nos. 1241, 1243, 1245, 1247–9, 1280, 1283, 1289.
[163] *JW* iii. 150–1; see Chapt. 4, 99 & n. 109.

# 2
# A Second Career: Royal Counselor and Official
## c.1121–1135

The first—baronial—career Henry I created for his son Robert was supplemented by a second one in response to the death of Robert's half-brother William Aetheling in November 1120.[1] The new career, like the first, was the king's doing and was formally announced, as it were, by his creating Robert, the earl of Gloucester. But unlike the baronial career which gave the king's son limited political importance beyond his lordships, in time this second one made Robert a major figure at his father's court. As one of Henry's most trusted counselors, Earl Robert became associated with the most pressing political issue of the king's reign after the early 1120s, the royal succession. This involvement led to Robert's third and most famous career, championing his half-sister Matilda's claim to their father's throne. Furthermore, the sense of having lost elements of the second one helped the earl of Gloucester to justify changing his allegiance from their cousin King Stephen of Blois to her.[2]

On January 29, 1121, according to John of Worcester, Henry I, following the advice of Ralph archbishop of Canterbury and his magnates in council, married the conventionally described beautiful and modest Adeliza, daughter of Godfrey VII count of Lorraine. If there was some truth in the concern John attributed to Ralph and the council that Henry's libido be again channeled by a *coniunx legalis*, the more likely aim was to regain a legitimate male heir against a possible claim to the throne from his nephew William Clito; and there is every reason to believe that the marital plan was primarily Henry's.[3]

More than likely the king's son was among those his father had consulted in council about his Lotharingian marriage plan. Royal scribes recorded Robert's presence at court on several occasions in January both before and after the nuptials.[4] Increased attendance at this time and for the remainder of the reign is a sign that the king had a new career in mind for Robert. He would now be a means of strengthening the family's influence at court among his close associates and counselors,

---

[1] See Chapt. 1, 28.   [2] See Chapt. 6, 189–90.
[3] Eadmer, 290; *JW* iii. 148–9; Henry of Huntingdon (1996), 466–9; *GR* i. 758–9; *OV* vi. 307–8; Hollister, *Henry I*, 280–1.
[4] Robert was at court on multiple occasions in January: *Regesta* ii. nos. 1241, 1243, 1247–9. Newman, *Anglo-Norman Nobility*, 182–96, examines individuals' attestations of royal *acta* on a yearly basis, but its methodology is not without limitations.

his *familiares*. So frequently did Robert attest his father's *acta* that even with his infrequent attestations (0.87 per year) between 1113 and 1121, his overall annual rate during the reign still ranks first among non-household lay members.[5] Among those whose periods of royal service were at all comparable with his between January 1121 and the date of his father's death in late 1135, Robert's rate (5.5 per year) was only exceeded by officials whose services were regularly needed by King Henry and his central administration. These were the king's chief of staff, Bishop Roger of Salisbury (1102–39), the chancellor Geoffrey Rufus (1123–33), and his assistant, the master of the royal scriptorium and keeper of the seal, Robert *de Sigillo* (1121–35).[6]

The transition between careers was almost seamless. The earl's first career had been a virtual apprenticeship for the second. Robert's education prepared him for a variety of possible roles in his father's increasingly document-based governmental machine, which demanded at least rudimentary knowledge of Latin.[7] He already knew the chief officials of his father's English and Norman administrations, Roger bishop of Salisbury and the justicier John bishop of Lisieux (1107–41), the chancellor Ranulf (1107–22), the chaplain and keeper of the seal Richard de Capella (*c*.1107–1121), William d'Aubigny, *pincerna*, and Geoffrey Brito archbishop of Rouen (1111–28). The earl's association with Ranulf was cut short in 1121 by the chancellor's accidental death—falling from his horse and being trampled by some nag ridden by a monk—but continued with his successor Geoffrey Rufus.[8] Socially Robert fit right in with many of his lay colleagues. Like them, he was one of his father's "new men," nobodies metaphorically raised, as Orderic Vitalis wrote, from dust, and transformed by the king like many of them such as Brian fitz Count, William d'Aubigny *pincerna*, and William de Pont-de-l'Arche by marriage to a rich heiress.[9] Robert's holdings in Normandy and South Wales gave him several likely common interests with other trans-Channel and Marcher types among the *curiales*. Fellow fee-holders in Normandy included William d'Aubigny *pincerna* (Saint-Martin, d'Aubigny); Robert de la Haye (La Haye-du-Puits); Humphrey de Bohun (Saint-Georges de Bohon, Manche); and Hugh Bigod (Corbon, Calvados). Henry de Pomeroy (La Pommeraye) and Hugh Bigod (Savenay, Les Loges, Calvados) also were Robert's fellow tenants of

---

[5] Hollister, "Rise of Administrative Kingship," 888. For criticism and defense of calculating individuals' rates of attendance at court based on the number of the attestations of royal *acta* divided by their years of service, see Bates, "Prosopographical Study of Anglo-Norman Royal Charters," esp. 89–102; Hollister, *Henry I*, 499–506; Keefe, "Counting those who Count," 135–45. The pioneering work in this methodology in Anglo-Norman Studies is Crosby, "The Organization of the English Episcopate under Henry I," 3–88.

[6] Seventy-seven attestations in 14 years; I recalculated Roger of Salisbury's attestations for 1121–35 and came to an annual rate of 10.9 based upon 152 attestations for the fourteen-year period. Calculating the annual rate for Hollister's Henry of Blois as abbot of Glastonbury and bishop of Winchester based on his service to the king from 1126 to 1135 instead of Hollister's 1129–33 would give him a 2.4. For Robert *de Sigillo*, see Christelow, "Chancellors and Curial Bishops," 63.

[7] Clanchy, *From Memory to Written Record*, 58–9; Hollister, *Henry I*, 493–4; Hollister. "Anglo-Norman Political Culture," 10–14.

[8] Henry of Huntingdon (1996), 468–71; *Regesta* ii. xii; *GOE*, 229; Green, *Henry I*, 107; Chapt. 1, 23.

[9] *OV* vi. 16–17; Southern, "The Place of Henry I in English History," 206–33; for excellent critiques, see Mooers, "Patronage in the Pipe Roll of 1130," 284–5; *GOE*, 139–57.

the bishop of Bayeux. Brian fitz Count (Abergavenny), Bishop Roger of Salisbury (Kidwelly), and Miles of Gloucester (Brecon) were neighboring Marchers. Trans-Channel holdings predisposed their lords to favor England and Normandy being under a single rule, while Marchers looked for a king who respected their special jurisdictions and could protect them from the Welsh.[10]

The new earl's colleagues included representatives of virtually every echelon of Henry I's administration in England and Normandy, from Roger bishop of Salisbury and John bishop of Lisieux to local justices, sheriffs, and *vicomtes*. If one narrows the list of men who served with Robert to the ten most frequent, his closest associates were mostly members of the realm's central administration, with his closest associates the chiefs of staff and chancery personnel, the chancellor, and Robert *de Sigillo*. One unofficial member was the earl's curial partner and fellow super-insider Brian fitz Count, who among his other already noted attributes was a possible royal household constable. Fitz Count also may have had a claim on the constableship of Oxford castle after he purchased the office and part of the land of the former castellan Nigel d'Oilli; a second was the curial magnate, William II de Warenne earl of Surrey, whose storied career featured transformation from dispossessed rebel of 1101 into favored royal *familiaris* and marriage to Robert of Meulan's widow Isabel.[11]

Henry I's Norman administration had some of its own personnel, utilized some royal household members, and developed an Exchequer at Caen modeled on England's.[12] Henry I's chief justiciar Bishop John of Lisieux and fellow justices and stewards Robert de la Haye and Robert de Courcy represent the Norman-based type.[13] The constable William fitz Odo, his subaltern Henry de Pomeroy, and William of Glastonbury, a possible constable, seem to have been seconded from the royal household in some way for service in the duchy. Aside from other evidence, William and Henry are mentioned by name in the description of the royal household of *c*.1136.[14]

Earl Robert's main associations within the Norman administration were with the bishop of Lisieux, Robert de la Haye, and Robert de Courcy, and three other

---

[10] I have omitted William II of Mauduit, court chamberlain or receiver, of Saint-Martin-du-Bosc (Eure) because he had little political importance as a *curialis* and very few associations with Gloucester at the royal court: *PR 31 Henry I* (Green), 30, 106; *Regesta* ii. nos. 1689–90; note the absence of his name from Hollister's list of important *curiales*: "Rise of Administrative Kingship," 888; see also *GOE*, 261–2. See Appendix 2.1 for royal *acta* attested by *curiales* and Earl Robert.

[11] *OV* vi. 174–5; see also *Regesta* ii. nos. 1091?, 1183?, 1204, for John of Lisieux; no. 1364, for John as archdeacon of Sées; *PR 31 Henry I* (Green), 110; *GOE*, 247 & n; Keats-Rohan, "Devolution of the Honour of Wallingford," 315; King, "Brian fitz Count," 538; Hollister, "The Taming of a Turbulent Rebel: Henry I and William de Warenne," 137–44; Crouch, *The Beaumont Twins*, esp. 41; see Chapt. 5, 126–7.

[12] *Regesta* ii. no. 1584 & n.; Round, "Bernard, the King's Scribe," 424–6; Haskins, *Norman Institutions*, 88–122; Le Patourel, "Normandy and England," 10–21; Hollister, "Rise of Administrative Kingship," 874–5; *GOE*, 258; Bates, "Origin of the Justiciarship," 9; Chapt. 3, n. 131

[13] Respectively, the two Roberts rank 29th and 35th in Hollister's list: "Rise of Administrative Kingship," 874, 888; Round, "Bernard, the King's Scribe," 425–6; *GOE*, 242–3, 258.

[14] Church, "Constitutio Domus Regis," xxxviii, 208–11; for William of Glastonbury, see *PR 31 Henry I* (Green), 11; *Regesta* ii. nos. 1581, 1764; *GOE*, 253, 256, 266–7; Hollister, "Rise of Administrative Kingship," 871–2.

bishops, Hugh archbishop of Rouen, and his suffragans, John of Sées and Audoin of Évreux.[15] Meetings of the Norman Exchequer court and of enlarged versions of the *curia regis* provided for most of Earl Robert's known encounters with them.[16] Archbishop Hugh of Amiens was the chief of King Henry's Norman lieges. Charters show Hugh holding court, appearing as the responsible chief legal officer, and as a royal judge.[17] In spite of Earl Robert's many associations with the archbishop, these failed to influence Hugh to consecrate Gloucester's illegitimate son Richard bishop of Bayeux in 1133.[18] Audoin and Archbishop Hugh were with Henry when he died and, with an act nicely illustrating how the secular and ecclesiastical might be intertwined, bound the lay barons in attendance, including Earl Robert, under oath not to abandon the body except by mutual agreement, and to conduct it with an honor guard to the coast (for transport to England for burial).[19]

The bishop of Salisbury with whom Robert met more often from 1121 was not politically the same Roger the king's son had encountered earlier. During the 1120s, the bishop emerged as the king's most influential adviser, especially following the death of Robert de Beaumont in 1118. Roger realized the full potential of his position as King Henry's chief of staff and periodic viceroy with effective control of the household, the Winchester Treasury, including meetings there of the *curia regis* related to the business of the Exchequer, and the judicature: as William of Malmesbury put it, "the very kingdom."[20] In one of his most illustrative gestures, in the mid-1120s the bishop centralized control of finance by creating the new office of court treasurer and putting in his nephew Nigel as incumbent.[21] However, Queen Matilda and then William Aetheling took precedence over him at viceregency courts until their deaths, respectively, in 1118 and 1120.[22]

Initially there was no special mark to distinguish Robert's new curial position. I suspect that for a time he was more valuable to his father as a force among

---

[15] Haskins, *Norman Institutions*, 87–105; Green, "Le Gouvernement d'Henri I<sup>er</sup> en Normandie," 71–2. For the ranking of Norman *curiales*, see Hollister, "Rise of Administrative Kingship," 888.

[16] *Regesta* ii. no. 1356.

[17] *Regesta* ii., e.g., nos. 1721, 1736, 1830 (England), 1696–7, esp. 1699 (judicial), 1554, 1688, 1742, esp. 1764 & 1918, 1910 (chief of Norman lieges); *RBE* ii. 644?; see also Bates, "The Earliest Norman Writs," 266–84; Green, *Henry I*, 105–6.

[18] *OV* vi. 442–3.

[19] *OV* vi. 448–9; the words in parentheses were not in the text, but the destination was clearly understood by those present: see Chapt. 5, 127.

[20] "Constitutio Domus Regis," 195–215; *OV* vi. 530–1; *HN* (1998), 64–5; *GR* i. 736–9; *GS* (2004), 72–3: second to the king in all of the government's business; *ASC a.*1118, 1123, 1125; *GP*, 210–1; *Dialogus de Scaccario*, 64–5; note Roger's ranking as a *curialis*: Hollister, "Rise of Administrative Kingship," 888.

[21] Hollister, "Origins of the English Treasury," 269–73. *Regesta* ii. no. 963, significantly attested by Roger and the chancellor; Kealey, *Roger of Salisbury*, 48–50; *GOE*, 51; Green, *Henry I*, 182–3, 237, 303–4; Hollister, *Military Organization of Norman England*, 123–4, 133, 188–9.

[22] For Roger's roles, see *Regesta* ii. nos. 946, 959, 963, 1000, 1211 (baron of the exchequer); nos. 1614, 1989; Kealey, *Roger of Salisbury, Appendix 1*, nos. 11–18, 23–5 (viceregal); see also nos. 8–10 & nn., 22 & n. (partly episcopal); "Ann. Winchester," 47; Bates, "The Origins of the Justiciarship," 11 & n. 87; *GOE*, 34, Chapt. 3, *passim*; *GP*, 210–11; *Regesta* ii. nos. 1472, 1488, 1614, 1814 & n.?, 1977, 1989 & n.; nos. 1000–1, 1190 (in Queen Matilda's name); nos. 1189, 1191–2, 1201–2 (in William Aetheling's name); Hollister, "The Origins of the English Treasury," 269–73; Hollister, "Rise of Administrative Kingship," 876.

potential supporters and warrantors of his *acta* than as a close adviser. He would have functioned much as he had in the very earliest event in his life reported by Orderic Vitalis in which he is listed as one of those who validated a confirmation charter in favor of Saint-Évroul Abbey in 1113 with their *signa*, but was not the one who advised Henry to issue it.[23] However, sometime between April to May 1121 and November 1122, Henry I, more than increasing Robert's presence at court, reinforced this informal boost in stature and virtually proclaimed it by creating Robert earl of Gloucester. An earldom also could lead to increased authority in one's titular shire; and King Henry accomplished this in Robert's case by making the constable of Gloucester castle his son's vassal. As a mark of the title's potential importance, the king had created only two earls, Robert de Meulan (Leicester) and his brother-in-law David (Huntingdon), before Robert; and Gloucester would be his last one.[24]

Comital rank was the highest title for a lay member of the aristocracy in Norman England.[25] In the diplomatic protocol of the royal court, earls as a group enjoyed the highest ranking among the king's lay magnates. As witness-lists of Henry I's *acta* show, earls, when listed together, were only outranked at great meetings of the *curia regis* by members of the immediate royal family, sometimes including members of the royal household, and by members of the higher clergy.

The term used for earls most often in post-Conquest England was borrowed from the Norman one for count, *comes*, just as Norman *vicecomes* for *vicomte* was used for post-1066 English sheriffs. But the inspiration for the Anglo-Norman earl did not derive from Norman counts who originated in the tenth century as close relatives of the ducal house and were charged with defense of border districts like the counts of Mortain, Évreux, and Eu. Anglo-Norman earls' ancestors were Anglo-Saxon. They had exercised jurisdiction within their earldoms as royal viceroys, in connection with which they presided over the shire court along with the bishop and commanded the fyrd. They also shared with the king through a payment called the third-penny a third of the proceeds of justice of their shires. Several of their privileges are mentioned in legal treatises written in Henry I's and Stephen's reigns. The widely circulated "Instituta Cnuti," translated between 1066 and 1123/4, states that earls shared certain revenues with the king and enjoyed equal legal standing with bishops in some matters because of the excellence of their order.[26] The "Leges Edwardi Confessoris," a new collection without known Anglo-Saxon

---

[23] *OV* vi. 174–5; Robert count of Meulan was the adviser; text calendared in *Regesta* ii. no. 1019 (suspect).

[24] *HN* (1998), 62–3; *Regesta* ii. nos. 1347, 1372–3; see also no. 1301; Round, "Creation of the Earldom of Gloucester," in *Geoffrey de Mandeville*, 422–34. Round's dating has yet to be narrowed successfully. See Appendix 2.1 for Earl Robert's status in Gloucestershire. See also *OV* vi. 20, *Regesta* ii. nos. 1015a, 1032n.; Green, *Aristocracy of Norman England*, 268.

[25] Green, *Aristocracy of Norman England*, 11, 268, 342.

[26] "Instituta Cnuti," III. 55, 57: *Die Gesetze* i. 614–15; Liebermann, "On the Instituta Cnuti Aliorumque Regum Anglorum," 98–9; O'Brien, "Legal Treatises as Perceptions of Law in Stephen's Reign," 191 & n. 40; O'Brien, "The *Instituta Cnuti* and the Translation of English Law," 177, 185–91, 196; for Anglo-Saxon earls, see Stenton, *Anglo-Saxon England*, 539–40; Lewis, "The Early Earls of Norman England," 208–10; Sharpe, "Address and Delivery in Anglo-Norman Royal Charters," 33–4; *PR 31 Henry I* (Green), 60; See *Dialogus de Scaccario*, 98–9, written in the late 1170s by Richard fitz

origins, believed to date from 1135–54, awarded to earls an amercement second in amount only to the king's from violators of the King's Peace.[27]

Robert adopted *consul*, from its ancient Roman basis a virtual self-proclamation of judicial and military supremacy, as his most favored new comital title. He used it in the superscriptions of his *acta* in combination with *Henrici regis filius* in the address clauses and in the legend on his seal. The earl's steward Geoffrey de Waterville proudly sported his consular title on his own. Robert's education may have inspired him to use the term; the widely influential Isidore of Seville's *Etymologies*' ranking of *consul* in titles of dignity is an even more likely immediate influence. Nevertheless, perhaps from his exposure to royal governmental usages— even because both terms somehow figured in his father's grant of the earldom— Robert occasionally used *comes* in superscriptions and in the legend of his own pennies minted in the 1140s. Furthermore, there is reason to believe that the earl wrote *comes* in personally subscribing a vassal's *actum*.[28]

One of the earliest signs of the enhanced responsibilities his new status brought Robert was not curial but military. In 1123 after having held a council at Woodstock, the king placed Robert and Ranulf earl of Chester in command of a great military force to thwart a challenge to his rule in Normandy. Robert was assigned charge of the Cotentin, within easy range of his headquarters at Torigny-sur-Vire, and Ranulf, custody of the royal citadel at Évreux.

Henry had learned of another planned uprising by a group of Norman barons sympathetic to William Clito's claim to the duchy. Their leader was Amaury IV de Montfort count of Évreux. Chief among his confederates was Waleran of Meulan; and Waleran by marriage drew into the plot his new brothers-in-law, Hugh de Montfort of Montfort-sur-Risle (Eure), William Lovel lord of the nearby French lordship of Bréval, and Hugh lord of Chateauneuf-en-Thimerais (Eure-et-Loir) in the county of Chartres. Amaury gained the support of Count Fulk V of Anjou, who had his own grievances against Henry, but invaded the duchy from the south with William Clito in support of his dynastic claim.[29] Henry chose to strike at Montfort-sur-Risle from Rouen and summoned Robert earl of Gloucester and Nigel d'Aubigny from the Cotentin in the west and other areas to assist in his siege of the castle. Details of their forces' participation are lacking, but after a month of enduring the effects of it Amaury's garrison surrendered.[30]

---

Nigel, Bishop Nigel of Ely's son, for the third-penny's definition; for commentary, see Round, *Geoffrey de Mandeville*, Appendix H, 287–96.

[27] "Leges Edwardi Confessoris," 27.2: *Die Gesetze* i. 651; O'Brien, "Legal Treatises as Perceptions of Law in King Stephen's Reign," 185–9.

[28] BL, MS Sloane 1301, fol. 227v (*consul*); Patterson, *EGC*, nos. 6, 42, 68, 82–4, 119, 157, 162, 283 (*consul*) no. 110, 156, *Cart. Langley*, no. 41 (*comes*); Warner & Ellis, no. 36; *HN* (1998), 2; for the tradition that Henry I created Robert *consul* and *comes*, see *Mon. Angl*. ii. 61; the earl's half-brother Reginald of Cornwall and son-in-law Ranulf of Chester occasionally used *consul*: King, "Introduction," 28; Hudson, "Diplomatic and Legal Aspects of the Charters," 155 & n.; Crouch, *The Image of Aristocracy*, 43–4, 92, 97; Chapt. 1, 10, Figure 1.1.

[29] Symeon of Durham, 267–8; Hollister, *Henry I*, 292–4; Crouch, *Beaumont Twins*, 14–17.

[30] *OV* vi. 334–5; Hollister, *Henry I*, 294–5.

Knights of the *familia regis* and other forces also fought at the decisive battle of Bourgthéroulde on March 26, 1124, which was a complete rebel rout and led to the war's speedy end. Orderic Vitalis, whose *Historia Ecclesiastica* noted Robert's presence at Montfort-sur-Risle and also named the royal commanders at Bourgthéroulde, Ranulf of Chester, Henry de La Pommeraye, Odo Borleng, and William de Harcourt, did not mention him.[31] I suspect that, at the time, Robert was with his father at Caen. In spite of the paucity of recorded details about the new earl of Gloucester's military activities, he gained the praise of William of Malmesbury in his *Gesta Regum Anglorum*, written by *c*.1125. William singled out the earl's knightly expertise and valor and recalled how King Henry relied upon him to defeat disloyal barons in Normandy.[32] Orderic does mention the fates of various rebels, among them that of Waleran of Meulan, to which should be added the political fortunes of his younger twin, Robert of Leicester, who did not join the rebellion. Waleran suffered five years of captivity (1124–9). During the rebellion and then Waleran's imprisonment Robert of Leicester carefully observed the etiquette of outward loyalty by making occasional visits to court and as a result suffered no punishment for his brother's behavior. But, at the same time, Henry did nothing to promote him as a *curialis*. Finally in 1129 the king freed Waleran, restored his lands, minus his castles, and welcomed the two brothers to the inner circle of his courtiers. As David Crouch has argued, the death of William Clito in 1128 made a Norman rebellion less likely and Waleran less dangerous; furthermore, the Beaumont brothers could be valuable allies. The two, along with Earl Robert, were among those who attended Henry as he lay dying in late 1135.[33]

Court protocol began to express the earl of Gloucester's increased curial stature by according his name first place in the witness-lists of the king's various *acta* after any bishops mentioned, in groupings of earls,[34] as the only layman (other than the king, queen, and David king of Scots),[35] among tenants-in-chief and other witnesses.[36] The exceptions were rare occasions when both Robert and his first cousin Stephen count of Mortain attested royal *acta*. Up to 1130 Stephen outranked Robert. But, from that year until King Henry's death, court protocol, evidently recognizing the rank Robert had achieved, began to award him primacy of place in

---

[31] *OV* vi. 348–50 & n., 351–2; *GND* ii. 234–7; *ASC a*.1123, 1124; *RHG* xii. 784; see also *JW* iii. 156; *GR*, i. 798–9, suggests that King Henry called on Robert more than once; Hollister, *Henry I*, 298–301 & nn.; Morillo, *Warfare under the Anglo-Norman Kings*, 173–4.

[32] *GR* i. 734–5, 798–9; Thomson in *GR* ii. 6, 397–8.

[33] *Regesta* ii., nos. 1607?, 1688–90, 1693, 1699, 1702, 1711, 1918 (for Waleran), 1391, 1428, 1451, 1547, 1559, 1569, 1587, 1688, 1693, 1710, 1715, 1719, 1736, 1740, 1764–5,1902, 1908, 1910 (for Robert); *OV* vi. 448–9; Hollister, "Rise of Administrative Kingship," 888 & n., in which list of *curiales* the brothers rank last; Crouch, *The Beaumont Twins*, 24–8; Chapt. 5, 126–7.

[34] *Regesta* ii. nos. 1372, 1391, 1426–7, 1474, 1559, 1575, 1587, 1702, 1680, 1656, 1934, 1687, 1719, 1715, 1711, 1688–90, 1693, 1736, 1740, 1742, 1764–5, 1757, 1911, 1896, 1908, 1912; exceptions: nos. 1590, 1588, 1932, 1668, 1691–2.

[35] *Regesta* ii. nos. 1373, 1620, 1841, 1973, 1546.

[36] *Regesta* ii, nos. 1875, 1347, 1600–1, 1459, 1463, 1483, 1562, 1586, 1581, 1643–4, 1721, 1713, 1724, 1700, 1726, 1717–18, 1737, 1777, 1892, 1917, 1915, 1919, 1916.

the lists. As will be seen below, his father's change in attitude toward Stephen may have manifested itself in a reduction in his fiscal patronage.[37]

From his presence at courts and councils his father held as he traveled with elements of his household staff about his trans-Channel Anglo-Norman realm, Earl Robert of Gloucester became involved with some of the weightiest issues in Anglo-Norman politics between c.1121 and his father's death. His curial contacts occurred over half the time in England, often at the king's great retreat at Woodstock (Oxon.), where Henry maintained a menagerie of exotic animals, and at the kingdom's administrative centers, Winchester and Westminster; those in Normandy, mostly at the ducal capital of Rouen.[38] Because of Anglo-Norman magnates' trans-Channel attributes, regional *curiales*' frequent additional roles as the king's *familiares*, and the interconnections between the royal court and other jurisdictions, the earl and his associates formed an "imperial" bureaucracy.[39]

The earl participated in a number of ways.[40] His most common activity was warranting as a witness his father's recorded acts. Some were pleas heard in the king's presence (*coram rege*)—the abbot of Fécamp recovering forest tithes withheld by the king's own huntsman—and *conventiones* resolving disputes between contending parties, such as one between the abbot of Peterborough and the bishop of Lincoln about the parish church of Peterborough.[41] Others were various types of grants and policies for which the king sought conciliar approval, such as his grant of revenues to Fontevrault Abbey.[42] There also were more occasions when the new earl was called upon with other important *curiales* to validate his father's *acta* with his *signum*; one of these put Earl Robert in the company of the king, John bishop of Lisieux, and Robert de la Haye, respectively Henry's justiciar and steward for Normandy, and two administratively important Norman bishops, Audoin of Évreux and John of Sées.[43] Sometimes, the king validated his transactions with his own *signum*.[44] In less formal settings Earl Robert, when traveling with the king in England or Normandy, like other *curiales* sometimes was utilized to warrant his

---

[37] Before elevation to earl of Gloucester: in *Regesta* ii.: Stephen, nos. 1183, 1243; Robert, no. 1245; as earl of Gloucester to 1130: Stephen, nos. 1588 & n. (1129?), poss. 1932 (1129 x 35); Robert: none; 1130–5: Stephen, poss. no. 1932 (1129 x 35); Robert, nos. 1934, 1740, 1757, 1908; note King, *King Stephen*, 19. It would be interesting to see how Robert and Stephen were ranked in the register of earls and barons King Henry supposedly maintained: *De Nugis Curialium*, 438, 470–1. Stephen attested Henry I's *acta* over a period of about 23 years (from c.1112): Theobald, in roughly 28 years (1107–35): For these chronologies, see LoPrete, *Adela of Blois*, 152–3, 309–11, 335 (Theobald's sole comital authority, 1120–35).

[38] *GR* (1998) i. 740–1; Henry of Huntingdon (1996), 470–1; Patterson, *EGC*, no. 70 & n.; Hollister, "Rise of Administrative Kingship," 888n.

[39] Church, "Constitutio Domus Regis," li; Le Patourel, *The Norman Empire*, 179, 190–221; Bates, *The Normans and Empire*, 98–115. For reservations concerning non-magnate members of the aristocracy, see Green, "Unity and Disunity in the Anglo-Norman State," 128–34; Crouch, "Normans and Anglo-Normans: A Divided Aristocracy?," 51–67. See Appendix 2.2 for charter evidence of Earl Robert's most frequent curial associates.

[40] See Hudson, "Henry I and Counsel," 109–26.

[41] *Regesta* ii., e.g., nos. 1689, CCXLIX; see also nos. 1700, CCLI, 1911.

[42] *HN* (1998), 8–9; e.g., *Regesta* ii. nos. 1687, CCXLVIII.

[43] *Regesta* ii., e.g., no. 1442; I have omitted several other names; see also, e.g., nos. 1441, 1691.

[44] e.g., *Regesta* ii. nos. 1441, 1575, 1581.

father's writs alone or with one or only a very few colleagues.[45] Then, when the royal entourage lacked chancery personnel, the earl "partnered" with fellow *curiales* like William of Glastonbury and Robert de la Haye as messengers to carry drafts or the king's authorization to secretarial facilities and to have the writs or other *acta* executed under their authority.[46]

The earl's joint participations with colleagues involved him with several legatine councils of Archbishop William of Corbeil (1123–36). The first, May 13–16, 1127 at Westminster, banned simoniacal practices and marriage for subdeacons and those in higher orders.[47] The second council after Easter 1132 at London was Archbishop William's last of the reign and ended the diocesan boundary conflict between St. David's and Llandaff.[48]

The earl also witnessed efforts of his father and a papal legate to resolve the longstanding quarrel between the archbishops of Canterbury and York over the former's claim of primacy over the latter. Two Norman courts the earl attended, possibly at Rouen in March and definitely at the ducal capital in October 1125, were associated with meetings between legate Cardinal John of Crema and the king to craft a formula the two strong-minded opponents and Henry would accept.

William of Corbeil of Canterbury (1123–36) had rekindled the quarrel by insisting that Archbishop Thurstan of York (1114–40; consecr. 1119) acknowledge his primacy as a condition for consecrating him. After Thurstan refused, the two resumed their jurisdictional battle at Rome before Pope Calixtus II (1119–24) and the curia. Instead of issuing a definitive judgment, the pope commanded that a council be held in England to settle the dispute under the presidency of a papal legate. This led to the first of the above-mentioned courts, during which the legate John of Crema and the two archbishops met with King Henry in a futile attempt to reach an agreement prior to the council.[49] The second court after Michaelmas 1125 followed John of Crema's visitation of English dioceses and monasteries earlier in September. John hammered out a compromise, but it failed to hold up. Back in Rome, the two archbishops found themselves with a jurisdictional resolution imposed on them which effectively ended the dispute.[50]

---

[45] e.g., *Regesta* ii., nos. 1653, 1682, 1684, 1718, 1898, 1919, 1925, 1938, 1941, 1952.

[46] *Regesta* ii., e.g., nos. 1949 *per* William of Glastonbury; no. 1951 *per* Robert de la Haye; see also no. 1722, a notification from Woodstock *per* Miles of Gloucester: Haskins, *Norman Institutions*, nos, 8, 11, pp. 101–2. For the attestation of writs and explanation of the *per* protocol, see *Regesta* ii. xxvii & nn.; Van Caenegem, *Royal Writs in England*, 150 & nn., 158–9, 163; *Facsimiles of English Royal Writs*, xiv–xv.

[47] *Regesta* ii., e.g., no. 1483 & n.; Henry of Huntingdon (1996), 476–7; *JW* iii. 168–73; *C & S* ii. 743 & n., 744–9; Brett, *The English Church under Henry I*, 47, 81, 121.

[48] *Regesta* ii. nos. 1736–7?; Henry of Huntingdon (1996), 488–9; *C & S* ii. 757–61; Nicholl, *Thurstan, Archbishop of York*, 109–10; Brett, *The English Church under Henry I*, 82; Hollister, *Henry I*, 379; Cowley, "The Church in Medieval Glamorgan," 91–3; Davies, *Conquest, Coexistence, and Change: Wales 1063–1415*, 182–3.

[49] *Cart. Reading* i. no.1 & n., for Dr. Kemp's exhaustive analysis; *Regesta* ii. no. 1427. See also Symeon of Durham, 278 (read 1125 for 1126), 281; *JW* iii. 160–5; for the controversy, see esp. Nicholl, *Thurstan, Archbishop of York*, 36–100; also Brett, Brooke, and Winterbottom, in Hugh the Chanter, xxx–xlv; *C & S* ii. 730–1 & n., 732; Hicks, "The Legatine Mission of John of Crema," esp. 301; Bethell, "William of Corbeil and the Canterbury York Dispute," 156; Barlow, *The English Church*, 143.

[50] *Regesta* ii. no. 1426, establishes the October meeting because of the presence in the charter's witness-list of Alexander bishop of Lincoln and of the abbot of St. Alban's, who accompanied the

Two courts associated with King Henry's recognition of Gregory of St. Angelo as the legitimate pope involved Robert of Gloucester in actions with broad western European religious and political implications and meetings with European notables. A papal schism broke out after the death of Honorius II in 1130, when Roman factions chose two different popes, the Cardinal Deacon Gregory of St. Angelo as Innocent II and Cardinal Peter Pierleone as Anacletus II. Innocent won the support of Abbot Peter the Venerable of Cluny (Saône-et Loire) and Bernard abbot of Cistercian Clairvaux (Aube) and, soon, of the French and German churches. Henry I probably decided to recognize Innocent due to Cluniac influence.[51] Family members were or had been associated with Cluny. Henry's sister Countess Adela of Blois had been a retiree at Cluniac Marcigny (Saône-et-Loire) since 1120; his nephew Henry had been a member of the Cluny community. The king himself had founded Reading Abbey in 1121 as a Cluniac house and contributed to the building costs of the mother house's great church, Cluny III. He had welcomed Abbot Peter to visit English Cluniac houses and Henry of Winchester in 1130.[52]

In 1131 the king took advantage of the good offices of his nephew Count Theobald of Blois to recognize Innocent on politically friendly territory at Chartres. On January 13 the formal process witnessed by Theobald, Earl Robert of Gloucester, a delegation of Norman bishops led by Henry's Cluniac protégé Archbishop Hugh of Amiens, and several of the king's *curiales* and earls involved Henry kneeling before Innocent and paying him reverence.[53] Later, on a Sunday in May, Innocent returned Henry's political favor by visiting him at Rouen; and Earl Robert was again among the participants in the court which marked the grand occasion. Among the Anglo-Normans present with Robert was his half-sister Matilda. Innocent's party included several well-known celebrities, Abbot Bernard of Clairvaux, and King Louis VI's chief minister and ultimate biographer, Suger abbot of Saint-Denis, an admirer of Henry.[54] Had Gloucester's interactions with the two been personally beneficial? Within four years Innocent ordered the consecration of Earl Robert's bastard son Richard as bishop of Bayeux; and when Earl Robert chose to found a Cistercian monastery as the *Eigenkloster* of his lordship of Glamorgan in 1147, Bernard sent his brother Nivard to the ceremony as his representative.[55]

---

legate and archbishops on their return to Rome: *ASC a.*1125; and Hugh the Chanter, 204–7, indirectly supports this by describing the compromise after naming the travelers; *C & S* ii. 732, attributes the compromise to the post-Michaelmas meeting with the king; Bethell, "William of Corbeil and the Canterbury York Dispute," 156; esp. Barlow, *The English Church*, 143. For John of Crema's council, see *C & S*, ii. 733–41.

[51] *OV* vi. 392–3, 418–21; Henry of Huntingdon (1996), 486–7; *HN* (1998), 12–19; Bloch, "The Schism of Anaclitus II and the Glanfeuil Forgeries," 159–82; Nicholl, *Thurstan, Archbishop of York*, 103–5; Hollister, *Henry I*, 460–1; Barlow, *The English Church*, 273. For another view, see Green, *Henry I*, 209.

[52] *Letters* of Peter the Venerable i. no. 49, p. 150; ii. 131, Kemp, *Cart. Reading*, i. 13–19; Hollister, *Henry I*, 282–7, 413–18; LoPrete, *Adela of Blois*, 408. At the time of Abbot Suger's visit to Rouen, Henry and Louis VI were at peace: Symeon of Durham, 283.

[53] *Regesta* ii. no. 1687 [no. CCXLVIII]; Henry of Huntingdon (1996), 486–7; *OV* vi. 420 & n., 421; Hollister, *Henry I*, 447, 460–1; Bloch, "The Schism of Anaclitus II and the Glanfeuil Forgeries," 168, n. 34.

[54] *Regesta* ii. no. 1691; Hollister, *Henry I*, 461–2.     [55] *OV* vi. 428–9; see Chapt. 4, 93.

In 1135 Earl Robert and colleagues ratified Henry's only surviving Norman legislation, the Truce of God ordinance of 1135, by their "common counsel and approval."[56] The ordinance increased ducal authority over this originally ecclesiastical movement. On the basis of canons of the Council of Lillebonne in 1080, which Henry I confirmed with his seal, the duchy's *vicomtes* were to remain the last resort for failed efforts by bishops to enforce provisions of the Church's peace. The ordinance made it even more the king's peace. Trials by battle for those accused of killing during truces were to take place in the king's court, terms governing related contingencies were set by the king, and collection and division of amercements between bishops and the king were under his control.[57]

Barons like Earl Robert also could on occasion serve with justices on judicial panels. A Norman example from 1111 reveals among several, Robert Count of Meulan, William II de Warenne earl of Surrey, along with Geoffrey archbishop of Rouen and Henry I's Norman chief justiciar John bishop of Lisieux. On at least one occasion during the late 1120s, Robert and his colleague Ranulf earl of Chester acted similarly on a panel very likely associated with the Norman viceregency court at Caen. The two earls' names appear, sandwiched between those of the two major officers of the ducal Exchequer and courts there, Bishop John of Lisieux, and the steward Robert de la Haye, regarded as the institutions' second in command, as fellow addressees in a royal writ. They and unnamed relevant local *vicomtes* were mandated to uphold (as justices) traditional proprietary rights enjoyed by the canons of Bayeux.[58]

In 1131 the earl of Gloucester acted individually like a royal justice, a *missus dominicus*, when he officially took in hand William Ghot's fee of Laleu (Orne), which the king had purchased from his heirs and had earmarked as a gift to the bishop of Sées.[59] Robert served his father in a similar capacity two years later when he conducted the famous inquest of the bishopric of Bayeux's landed possessions immediately after the death of Bishop Richard II. He himself testified because of his tenurial relationship with the bishop and proudly proclaimed that he was one of Sainte-Marie's barons and his Lady's standard-bearer by hereditary right.[60]

Robert's most famous policy involvement had to be the one in January 1127 dealing with his father's choice of his legitimately born daughter Matilda as his heir.[61] Roles the king assigned Robert, I suspect in the mid-1120s, in connection

---

[56] *Très Ancien Coutumier de Normandie*, c. lxxi; *Regesta* ii, no. 1908; Haskins, *Norman Institutions*, 120; Green, *Henry I*, 219, 241.

[57] *OV* iii. 26–7; Haskins, *Norman Institutions*, 104 & n.

[58] Haskins, *Norman Institutions*, 91–2, cal. in *Regesta* ii. no. 1002; *Cart. Bayeux*, i. no. 34; *Regesta* ii. no. 1589; the writ was noticed, but only exploited to show John of Lisieux's status, by Round, "Bernard, the King's Scribe," 427; another example may be *Regesta* ii. no. 1907, but its text is incompletely calendared and not found as listed in Deville, *Analyse d'un ancien cartulaire de S. Étienne de Caen*, no. 34. For the personnel and institutions mentioned, see Haskins, *Norman Institutions*, 88–103, esp. 99 & 100; Hollister, "Rise of Administrative Kingship," 874–5; Green, "Henry I and the Aristocracy of Normandy," 168–9.

[59] *Regesta* ii. nos. 1688, 1698: Haskins, *Norman Institutions*, nos. 10–11, pp. 299–300.

[60] *RHG* xxiii. 699; Navel, "L'Enquête de 1133 sur les fiefs de l'évêché de Bayeux," 13–14; *Regesta* ii. no. 1893; for the term *missus dominicus*, see *Regesta* ii. xix.

[61] See the most useful discussion of this subject in Hudson, "Henry I and Counsel," 109–26. For evidence of the court's composition about this time, see Green, *Henry I*, 193 & nn.

with promoting the empress for dynastic and political puposes may be the first evidence of the earl's rise in status as an adviser.

By this time Henry I's effort to replace his drowned heir with another legitimate son from his marriage to Adeliza of Louvain had clearly failed. Henry's most direct heirs, theoretically at least, were his brother Duke Robert of Normandy, a captive since the battle of Tinchebrai in 1106, Curthose's son William Clito, and his daughter the Empress Matilda. The Clito had the best claim based on the 1101 treaty of Alton between his father and uncle.[62] But he was anathema to Henry as the perennial pretender to the duchy of Normandy backed periodically by combinations of Count Fulk V of Anjou, the count of Flanders, King Louis VI of France, and disaffected Norman barons. Just two years before Henry V's death, the military threat from the alliance resurfaced with the added menace of William's marriage to Fulk's daughter Sibyl, engineered by the Norman revolt's ringleader, Amaury count of Évreux. It took a great victory by Henry's forces at Bourgthéroulde in March 1124 and success in moving his cousin Pope Callixtus II to annul Clito's nuptials in August on the basis of consanguinity for the challenge to be squelched.[63] Probably more remote, but still possible candidates were the sons of Henry's sister Adela countess of Blois, Theobald IV count of Blois, and Stephen, whose royal uncle's patronage had turned him into a super-magnate. Henry had given him the county of Mortain and the English honors of Boulogne, Eye, and Lancaster and then in 1125 marriage to Matilda, heiress to the rich Continental county of Boulogne.[64]

The Empress Matilda's stock as her father's successor had begun to rise within two years of her brother William's death. Circumstantial evidence collected by Karl Leyser indicates that the empress, as early as May 1122, was planning to visit England, arguably to discuss the succession with her father at his invitation. At this time Henry V's health was seriously in decline from cancer, which may have given a sense of urgency to the intended meeting. However, Charles the Good, Louis VI of France's ally against Henry I, prevented Matilda's passage across his lands to a port for her crossing to England. There were later opportunities, but missed; consequently, the meeting of the king and the empress never took place before her husband's death on May 23, 1125.[65] Nevertheless, as soon as the king learned of the event, he dispatched messengers to recall Matilda and she, after giving her situation some consideration, joined him in Normandy.[66] Henry V's death also gave his

---

[62] Chapt. 1, 7–8.
[63] For the marriage of Clito and its annulment, see *GR* i. 762–3; *HN* (1998) 4–5 & n.; *OV* vi. 164–5, 332–3; Suger, *Vie de Louis VI*, 250–1; Aird, *Robert Curthose*, 254–73.
[64] *HN* (1998), 4–7; Hollister, *Henry I*, 308–13. On the candidates' eligibility and plans for Henry and Matilda to meet before 1125 about her succession, see Leyser, "The Anglo-Norman Succession 1120–1125," 226–9, 234–41; Chibnall, *Empress Matilda*, 37–42; King, "Stephen, Count of Mortain and Boulogne," 271; on Stephen's early life, see Lewis, "The King and Eye: A Study in Anglo-Norman Politics," 569, 571, 579–80; King, "Stephen of Blois, Count of Mortain and Boulogne," 274–5, 280; King, *King Stephen*, 9–13, 20–8; LoPrete, *Adela of Blois*, 335.
[65] Leyser, "The Anglo-Norman Succession 1120–1125," 234–41; Chibnall, *The Empress Matilda*, 38–9.
[66] *HN* (1998), 4–5; *Regesta* ii. no. 1448, as Brian Kemp noted, corrupt or a forgery: *Cart. Reading* i. no. 5n., no. 1459; Robert of Torigny, "Chronica," 111; Hollister, "The Anglo-Norman Succession Debate of 1126," 27; Chibnall, *Empress Matilda*, 40–4.

former father-in-law a valuable opportunity to repair the diplomatic damage to his 1119 peace treaty with Fulk V count of Anjou caused by William Aetheling's death. Apparently, by the end of Henry's Christmas court of 1126, a remarried Matilda was widely expected. Unbeknownst to the court, Henry planned to replace an Angevin daughter-in-law with an Angevin son-in-law. Enter his son Robert, elite insider.

To accomplish this dynastic goal, by early 1127 but possibly some months before, we have either the first indication of Earl Robert's standing as one of the king's elite advisers or the act which made him one. Henry I chose Robert and two other trusted *familiares*, Brian fitz Count and John bishop of Lisieux, to work out the details of his marital scheme in secret, without even the knowledge of Roger of Salisbury, as the bishop later complained.[67] C. Warren Hollister provided a logical reason for the king's decision: Bishop Roger was the leader of a court faction which favored the imprisoned Robert's Curthose's son William Clito rather than Matilda as the king's eventual successor.[68]

All three curial insiders were Henry's creatures: Earl Robert, obviously most of all, closely followed by Brian, who had been sent to Henry's household for promotion. There the king educated and knighted him. Sometime between 1114 and 1119, when the king made Brian lord of Abergavenny in Upper Gwent (Monm.), he granted the young man marriage to the heiress of the valuable and strategic lordship of Wallingford.[69] Brian was one of the most rewarded with the king's fiscal patronage, but his total benefits amounted to less than half of what Earl Robert received.[70] The three were predictably unquestioning supporters and in two of the cases, Robert and especially John, men with strong Continental connections.

Evidently, as step one in his Angevin marriage plan, Henry, having started the process of obtaining the baronage's oaths of fealty to Matilda's succession as his heir at his Christmas court of 1126 held at Windsor, accomplished it at London on January 1, 1127, the feast of the Circumcision. Ecclesiastical and lay barons swore fealty to the empress's future status if the king died without a legitimate male heir. Members of the hierarchy were first, then the lay magnates, David king of Scots, followed by Stephen of Blois count of Mortain and Boulogne, then Robert earl of Gloucester.

According to William of Malmesbury, the event's chief source, Stephen's precedence over Robert came after the two had contended for the position, with the

---

[67] *HN* (1998), 10–11: "Eius matrimonii nullum auctorem, nullum fuisse conscium, nisi Rotbertum comitem Gloecestriae, et Brianum filium comitis, et episcopum Luxouiensem." For arguments in favor of Henry I's marital negotiations in 1127, see Chibnall, *The Empress Matilda*, 54–5 & n.; see also Hollister, "The Anglo-Norman Succession Debate of 1126," 27–8; but, as Dr. Chibnall has noted, William of Malmesbury's *HN* supports the Angevin marriage being Henry I's plan following Henry V's death.

[68] Hollister, "The Anglo-Norman Succession Debate of 1126," 25, 27–8.

[69] *LCGF* no. 26, p. 61; Davis, "Henry of Blois and Brian Fitz Count," 302–3; *Regesta* ii. no. 1062; Keats-Rohan, "The Devolution of the Honour of Wallingford," 311–15, esp. 315; *GOE*, 247–8; King, "Brian fitz Count," 538; Green, *Henry I*, 133.

[70] Mooers, "Patronage in the Pipe Roll of 1130," 285, 293. Brian fitz Count's total pardons were about £161.

count pleading the rights of a nephew and Robert that of a son. Taken at face value, royal son should trump royal nephew. But with the issue of legitimate heir before the council, it is arguable that Robert's illegitimacy put him behind his cousin in the oath-taking line; Malmesbury even refers obliquely to Robert's birth status by noting Henry's recognition of him as his son in the account of the council.[71] Yet the earl's legitimacy may not have been an issue at all. As we have seen, it was certainly not an issue in shifting the ranking court protocol assigned Earl Robert and Stephen between 1121/2 and 1135.

The baronage's 1127 conditional acceptance of Matilda's succession opened the way for active negotiations with Count Fulk for her marriage to Geoffrey; but political developments over the winter of 1126–7 made Henry I the suitor. At his Christmas court Louis VI proclaimed his renewed commitment to William Clito's claim to Normandy and urged his barons to help him. In January Louis gave him marriage to Queen Adelaide's half-sister Jeanne de Montferrat and a territorial base for attacking Henry by granting him a fee in the French Vexin. Norman baronial support for Clito was fanned when he appeared soon after with an armed force before Gisors. Then, on March 2, 1127, the count of Flanders, Charles the Good, was murdered by some of his own men in the church of Saint Donatian, Bruges (Belgium), and before the end of the month Louis used his influence as the count's overlord to secure the succession for Clito. In spite of measures Henry took to weaken Clito within Flanders, his nephew had secured two bases from which to attack and the active allegiance of many Norman barons. And to top off his problems, Henry faced the possibility of a resurrected triple alliance of France, Anjou, and Flanders.[72]

It is not known what the marriage plan in final form by May 1127 provided for Geoffrey le Bel's status; terms of the agreement between the two fathers were not recorded. The boy's future enjoyment of a condominium with Matilda, such as his father Fulk V gained by marrying King Baldwin II of Jerusalem's heiress daughter Melisende, would seem a possibility.[73] We do know that Matilda was dowered with castles; and it is likely that they included at least Domfront, Argentan, Exmes (Orne) in southern Normandy, and possibly Ambrières, Gorron, and Châtillon-sur-Colmont (Mayenne) in northern Maine.[74] And besides making peace with Anjou, the marital agreement detached Count Fulk from his alliance with Louis VI of France against King Henry's interests in Flanders.[75] Initially the empress may

---

[71] *HN* (1998), 6–9; *ASC* a.1127; *JW* iii. 166–7; Symeon of Durham, 281; another swearing supposedly occurred at Westminster on April 29, 1128: *JW* iii. xxxv, 176–83; but this probably should be regarded as a misdated other version of the 1127 event; the speeches smack of Thucydidean invention; see also *JW* iii. 182 n. 7; the text (pp. 178–9) alleges that Robert yielded to Stephen on the basis of his seniority; see also *GND* ii. 240–1; Henry of Huntingdon (1996), 700–1; Hugh the Chanter, 218–19; Chibnall, *The Empress Matilda*, 51–2.

[72] *OV* vi. 370–1; Hollister, *Henry I*, 318–22; Green, *Henry I*, 195–9.

[73] Chibnall, *The Empress Matilda*, 56–7; Green, *Henry I*, 201–3; Mayer, *The Crusades*, 82–3.

[74] Robert of Torigny, "Chronica," 128; *GND* ii. 274–5; *OV* vi. 454–5; Henry of Huntingdon (1996), 476–7; for various views, see Chibnall, *The Empress Matilda*, 56–7, 66; Crouch, *Reign of King Stephen*, 33; Hollister, *Henry I*, 290–1, 324–5.

[75] See Chapt. 1, 25.

not have been charmed by the idea of marrying Geoffrey. She was the crowned dowager empress who had participated in the governmental affairs of the western Empire; Geoffrey was a mere stripling eldest son of a count. In time, however, she accepted her father's scheme.[76]

Because of Robert's and Brian's advisory role regarding the Angevin marriage, King Henry chose them to escort Matilda to her betrothal on May 22, 1127 before Archbishop Geoffrey at Rouen.[77] The next year on June 17 the two were married at Le Mans (Sarthe). A week before, Henry I knighted his 15-year-old prospective son-in-law in an elaborate ceremony at Rouen.[78]

Still another council dealt with Matilda's interconnected succession and marriage issues. The assembled baronage at Northampton on September 8, 1131 had to consider what to do with this reluctant bride who had left her teenaged husband and returned to Normandy. The council supported Matilda's return to Count Geoffrey. Oaths of fealty to her succession were demanded from those who had not sworn previously and renewals from those who already had. Earl Robert was in attendance, but there is no record of the actual oath-takings to cast light on his ranking as a *familiaris*.[79] The same evidential problem pertains to another possible council supposedly held for such oath-takings before Henry I's death.[80]

Another status-boosting event for Earl Robert occurred in late 1126 which suggests, if not a second shift in King Henry's confidence from Bishop Roger to the earl, given the chief-of-staff's exclusion from planning for Matilda's succession, at least a second assignment of a role for Robert related to the royal succession at Roger's expense. About September 11, when Henry and Matilda landed in England from Normandy, her maternal uncle David, king of Scotland since 1124 and earl of Huntingdon, met them and quickly joined Earl Robert's elite circle of insiders.[81] Before the end of the year at his and Matilda's urging, King Henry transferred custody of his brother Robert Curthose from the bishop of Salisbury at his Devizes castle (Wilts.) to Earl Robert. About this time Brian fitz Count also was given charge of the less important prisoner, Waleran count of Meulan, whom the king brought from Normandy.[82]

---

[76] Symeon of Durham, 282; *HN* (1998), 4–5; *GND* ii. 240–1; Chibnall, *The Empress Matilda*, 55 & n., 56.

[77] *HN* (1998), 8–9 & n.; *ASC a.*1127; Henry of Huntingdon (1996), 476–7; Robert of Torigny, "Chronica," 112; *GND* ii. 240–1; *OV* vi. 390n.; Chartrou, *L'Anjou*, 21–2; Hollister, *Henry I*, 323 n. 168. After witnessing the marriage with Henry I, Fulk left for the Latin Kingdom of Jerusalem to marry King Baldwin II's heiress daughter Melisende: Mayer, *The Crusades*, 82, 299 n. 43.

[78] John of Marmoutier, 179–81.

[79] Henry of Huntingdon (1996), 486–9; Symeon of Durham, 281–2; *HN* (1996), 18–21; *Regesta* ii. nos. 1712–16, of which nos. 1713, and esp. 1715, reflect his premier standing in court protocol; Chibnall, *The Empress Matilda*, 57, 59–60.

[80] Howden, *Chronicon* i. 187 (oaths of fealty to Matilda and her son Henry); see Round, *Geoffrey de Mandeville*, 31n.; but note Chibnall, *Empress Matilda*, 61.

[81] *Regesta* ii. nos. 1448, 1451; *ASC a.*1126; Symeon of Durham, 281; Henry of Huntingdon (1996), 476–7; Hollister, "The Anglo-Norman Succession Debate of 1125," 25; Chibnall, *The Empress Matilda*, 43–4.

[82] *Peterborough Chronicle, a.*1126; *OV* vi. 356–7, 380–1; *ASC, a.*1126; *JW* iii. 212 & n., 213; *Cart. Gloucester* i. 15; Hollister, "The Anglo-Norman Succession Debate of 1126," 25–6; Crouch, *Beaumont*

As a compliment to his sister, about 1129 Robert founded a priory at Bristol in honor of St. James the Greater, whose relic hand the empress had brought from Germany. And he emphasized his personal commitment to Matilda by attending one of her courts in England sometime during 1126 × 31.[83]

Likely by around 1127 to 1129 Henry I provided Robert with a major power base in eastern England, in Kent and several adjacent counties. The king assigned him command of castles at Dover and Canterbury and provided a complementary landed presence by allowing him to inherit in right of his wife the lion's share of the tenancy-in-chief of Countess Mabel's uncle, Haimo II *dapifer* and sheriff of Kent.[84] The grant of the two castles may have been connected with one or both events in 1126–7 involving Robert with royal policy, the transfer of his uncle Robert Curthose from Roger of Salisbury's to his custody and especially the baronage's oath to support the succession of his sister Matilda. The two castles which controlled the great entry road to London from the Continent put Robert in place to thwart any future claimant to the throne other than Matilda gaining access to the heart of the kingdom, the most obvious being Stephen of Blois.[85]

Robert's share of his late uncle-in-law's barony yielded him lands with a major portion of Haimo II's former demesne income arguably well over £64 and fifteen undertenants owing the services of almost twenty-three knights. Authority over the two castles, I suspect especially Canterbury, gave Robert some influence over the office of Kent's sheriff. The cumulative effect of these windfalls made Robert the dominant figure in Kent by 1135, mirroring to some extent his position in Gloucestershire as earl.[86]

In a mark of special trust, the king chose Robert and Brian fitz Count to conduct an audit of the Treasury at Winchester during 1128–9. From one perspective their assignment reflects the royal household's functional flexibility;[87] but politically it looks like another slap at Roger of Salisbury. Investigation of any kind supposedly should have been his ultimate responsibility and any irregularity ultimately his fault. The Winchester bureau was the seat of his power as chief of Henry's administration and his nephew Nigel as court Treasurer had oversight of it.[88] It was there since at least late Anglo-Saxon times that sheriffs deposited revenues due the king annually from their counties. Members of the *curia regis* utilized a checkerboard accounting device mimicking an abacus to audit the sheriffs' payments at Easter

---

*Twins*, 25; Aird, *Robert Curthose*, 277 & n. Curthose died at Cardiff castle in 1134 and was buried at St. Peter's Abbey Gloucester.

[83] *Regesta* iii. no. 898; on the basis of the dating, the earl of Chester could be either Ranulf I or II; Hollister, "The Anglo-Norman Succession Debate," 37 n. 37. For the priory of St. James, see Chapt. 4, 119.

[84] *GND*, 248–9; *OV* vi. 516–18; *PR 31 Henry I* (Green), 51, shows Robert de Crèvecoeur owing £166 13*s*. 4*d*. for part of Haimo *dapifer*'s land; the two Roberts were both pardoned danegeld: *PR 31 Henry I* (Green), 53; Douglas, *Domesday Monachorum*, 55 & nn., illustrates the division, relies on later evidence; *GOE*, 124n.; Hollister, "Magnates and 'Curiales' in Anglo-Norman England," 76 & n., 79; for discussion of their possible political connections and dates, see Chapt. 3, 69.

[85] See 41–2.     [86] Chapt. 3, 57, 68 & n. 89.

[87] Church, "Constitutio Domus Regis," li.

[88] Hollister, "The Origins of the English Treasury," 264–73; Round, *Commune of London*, 76–8; *GOE*, 34, 47.

and Michaelmas. The two *curiales* apparently checked the moneys on hand and inventoried items stored there such as treasure, regalia, and records such as the Domesday Book.[89] They may have uncovered some irregularities. It is perhaps no coincidence that the Exchequer roll for 1129–30, which followed the audit, records replacements of sheriffs and remedies for shortfalls in the renderings of their annual farms.[90]

There have been plausible theories about the arrest and trial of the Treasury chamberlain Geoffrey I de Clinton on a charge of treason in 1130. Might the events have resulted from Robert's and Brian's audit? Had Roger earl of Warwick, on whom Geoffrey had been foisted as an honorial tenant of seventeen knights' fees, instigated the process? Geoffrey, falsely charged according to Henry of Huntingdon, was found innocent at his trial presided over by King David of Scotland during the Easter court Henry I held at Woodstock.[91] De Clinton was an honorial tenant of Earl Robert for a fee of five knights. If his indictment was politically motivated and at Roger of Salisbury's instigation, perhaps it was the bishop's cautious and indirect attack on the king's daughter Matilda, her uncle David, and her brother Robert of Gloucester for his political position being challenged in 1126.[92] If so, the verdict quashed it.

There are other indications of a decline in fortunes for the bishop late in the reign. Roger mysteriously lost his Marcher lordship of Kidwelly, which King Henry had given him in 1106. In a move reminiscent of the transfer of Robert Curthose to Robert, the king installed as new lord Maurice de Londres, one of the earl of Gloucester's vassals in England and Glamorgan, separated from Kidwelly by the Beaumont lordship of Gower.[93] Interestingly, the same year that Roger lost custody of Curthose, a *conventio* attested by Maurice de Londres settled a jurisdictional dispute in Glamorgan between Earl Robert and Urban bishop of Llandaff before the *curia regis* meeting at King Henry's great manor of Woodstock. Perhaps, if this was not the occasion for the transfer of Kidwelly, it had something to do with it.[94]

One has to wonder, from the sum of these events between 1126 and 1130 involving Robert of Gloucester and, in various ways, Roger of Salisbury, if the bishop had not become the loser in a pro-Angevin party power struggle. If this was the case, then the arrest and trial of Earl Robert of Gloucester's vassal and Treasury chamberlain Geoffrey I de Clinton might have been Bishop Roger's counterattack.

---

[89] *Regesta* ii. no. 963; *PR 31 Henry I* (Green), 101–3; Campbell, "Significance of the Anglo-Norman State in the Administrative History of Western Europe," 179 & n.; Poole, *The Exchequer in the Twelfth Century*, 35–41, 70–2; 174–9; Hollister, "Rise of Administrative Kingship," 877–9; *GOE*, 40–3; Biddle and Keane, "Winchester in the Eleventh and Twelfth Centuries," 304–5.
[90] Note Professor Judith Green's conclusions in *PR 31 Henry I* (Green), xxx–xxxi, and *GOE*, 61–2, 65.
[91] Henry of Huntingdon (1996), 486–7; *OV* iv. 276–7; *Cart. Warwick*, 4–5; *GOE*, 93; Crouch, "Geoffrey de Clinton and Roger Earl of Warwick," 119–20; Green, *Henry I*, 203, esp. 207–8.
[92] *RBE* ii. 289. For the candidacy of Roger earl of Warwick as instigator of Geoffrey's arrest, see Crouch, "Geoffrey de Clinton and Roger Earl of Warwick," 119–20; but see also Green, *Henry I*, 207.
[93] Kealey, *Roger of Salisbury*, 21, 106–7; Davies, *Conquest, Coexistence, and Change: Wales 1063–1415*, 41, 469; Davies, "Henry I and Wales," 140; Lloyd, *A History of Wales* ii. 430.
[94] *Regesta* ii. no. 1466; Patterson, *EGC*, no. 109 & n.

Edward Kealey suggested that his grudging support for Matilda's succession may have won him from Henry a charter in 1131 reconfirming his possession of Malmesbury Abbey.[95] Perhaps it also was as much a peace offering as a consolation prize.

Robert's auditing was associated with a larger fiscal role he enjoyed as a trusted *familiaris*. Royal charters suggest that within about two years of their special audit he and Brian fitz Count were functioning with other *curiales* as "barons" of the Exchequer. At this time "exchequer" signified the checkered accounting cloth used by semi-annual meetings of the king's court at the Winchester treasury to audit the required annual renderings of sheriffs. Such courts could deal with general legal as well as fiscal business. Witness-lists in two of such *acta* include Robert's and Brian's names along with others of the *curia regis* associated with fiscal meetings, the justiciar Roger bishop of Salisbury, the chancellor Geoffrey Rufus, and very possibly, Henry of Blois as bishop of Winchester.[96]

By 1130, Robert had become his father's most favored *curialis* and *familiaris* if the apportionment of the king's fiscal patronage is any indication.[97] Even though this assessment is based on the lone surviving pipe roll for Henry I's reign, an extant fragment from the roll for 25 Henry I suggests that the beneficiaries recorded in the roll of 1129–30 like the earl had enjoyed their fiscal perks over a number of years.[98] The fiscal patronage largely consisted of King Henry's pardons by royal writ to Robert, certain fellow *curiales*, and others through their influence (*de amore*) from various types of taxes. For great landlords like Earl Robert the most burdensome was danegeld, the non-feudal land tax periodically levied on lords' demesnes by the Anglo-Norman kings; in the role of 1129–30 at a rate of 2*s*. per hide (typically 120 acres). City aids (the *auxilium civitatis*) were the urban counterpart to danegeld. Murder fines (the *murdrum*) were charged to lords on whose lands murders had been committed. Pleas producing owed amercements fell under royal jurisdiction for reasons including breach of the king's peace, contempt of royal writs and commands, and failure of justice.[99] Exactly when Robert first received these exemptions, whether together or singly, and for how long, cannot be determined.

---

[95] *Regesta* ii. no. 1715; *HN* (1998), 18–21; Kealey, *Roger of Salisbury*, 152.

[96] *Historia Monasterii S. Augustini Cantuariensis*, nos. 7, 14; *Regesta* ii. nos. 1643–4 (*dei gratia rex* in the *intitulatio* is suspicious); see also nos. 1391, 1764–5; *Dialogus de Scaccario*, xx–xxvii, 22–5; Poole, *The Exchequer in the Twelfth Century*, 103–8; Hollister, "The Origins of the English Treasury," 273; *GOE*, 40–4. On the emerging position of the chancellor, see Hollister, "Rise of Administrative Kingship," 879 & n. 34; for the bishop of Winchester, see possibly *Regesta* ii. no. 1641; *Dialogus de Scaccario*, xxi, 24–7; (formal membership under Bishop Richard of Ilchester); for Henry of Blois, see Appendix 2.2, 187; for complementary evidence about Earl Robert and barons of the exchequer, see Christelow, "The Fiscal Management of England under Henry I," 166–71.

[97] Mooers, "Patronage in the Pipe Roll of 1130," 292–3, 305, 307. My calculations for the total financial benefits received by Earl Robert and others are based on their pardons in Exchequer years 1128–9 and 1129–30 in PR 31 Henry I for danegeld, city aids, amercements and fines, pardons to others through Robert's and other royal favorites' influence, and awarded gifts; these tabulations differ from some of those for Earl Robert and several others in Mooers, "Patronage in the Pipe Roll of 1130," esp. 305.

[98] Hagger, "A Pipe Roll for 25 Henry I," 133–4 & n. 5.

[99] *Leges Henrici Primi*, c.10. For *auxilium civitatis*, see Stephenson, "Aids of the English Boroughs," 457, 459, 467, 470. Hudson, *The Formation of the English Common Law*, 29–30, 62–3.

But the evidence of 1129–30 at least allows us to view this aspect of the earl late in his father's reign and in comparison to other politically significant individuals at the same time.

It reveals a quantifiable feature of Robert's prime standing among his father's *curiales* and *familiares*. Although Earl Robert was the second-highest beneficiary of his father's current danegeld pardons in 1130, considering all elements of royal fiscal patronage the pipe roll reveals, Gloucester was the most favored. His total past and current monetary benefits, including adjusted danegeld figures for Somerset and Worcestershire, exceeded the next-highest recipient of these favors, the bishop of Salisbury, by about £98.[100] The only other *familiares* and *curiales* whose rates of attestation exceeded Robert's, the chancellor Geoffrey Rufus, Henry of Blois bishop of Winchester, and Robert *de Sigillo* the *magister scriptorii*, enjoyed lesser total benefits of, respectively, £80, £123, and a paltry 5s. 6d. Even Stephen of Blois, who had been one of the most favored by his royal uncle, received about £113 less than Earl Robert according to the composite schedule of the count's exemptions from danegeld and other benefits in the pipe roll of 1129–30.[101] In fact, the pipe roll for that Exchequer year may tell a more important story about the king's nephew. Stephen's exemption level declined significantly—mostly for danegeld, but also for city aids. His largest losses occurred in Essex, Hertfordshire, and Lincolnshire. In Essex alone Stephen lost a past exemption of £22 16s. 4d.[102] It may be that this reduction of fiscal patronage was part of the king's measures to clip the count of Mortain's political wings in England. Protocol still accorded Stephen a place of honor at court as a member of the royal family, but from about 1130 his name tended to be listed after his cousin Robert of Gloucester's in witness-lists of royal *acta*; and the control of Dover and Canterbury castles Henry gave to the earl seems, a least in part, aimed at deterring any ambition Stephen might have to seize the throne after his death.[103]

Seventy-two percent of Robert's £339 came from pardons from payments of danegeld. Exemptions from this levy were King Henry's most common form of fiscal favoritism, and Robert was the greatest beneficiary. With one of the largest known English honors, by 1130 including the land of Countess Mabel's uncle Haimo II *dapifer*, Robert's potential liability would have been enormous.[104]

---

[100] Current danegeld pardons: Roger of Salisbury, £148; Earl Robert, £123; counting all past and current pardons: Earl Robert, danegeld: £244, with estimates for Somerset and Worcestershire, £263; *auxilium civitatis*: £39; *murdrum*: £23; pleas: £12; *pro amore*: £1, for a rounded-out total of about £339; Bishop Roger, about £241. For the best example of my methodology, see Professor Edward Kealey's *Roger of Salisbury, Appendix 4*; see also Chapt. 3, Appendix 3.1.

[101] Davis, *King Stephen*, 3rd edn., 8; Hollister, "Rise of Administrative Kingship," 888. Robert *de Sigillo* predictably was in line for ecclesiastical preferment: *PR 31 Henry I* (Green), 63. Stephen of Blois's pardons totaled about £227.

[102] *PR 31 Henry I* (Green), 45, 47; danegeld pardons overall fell from £132 to £68.

[103] See 35–6. I agree with Professor King that the reductions in exemptions follow no general pattern, but there is a case for placing them within the broader context I have hypothesized: see King, "Stephen of Blois, Count of Mortain and Boulogne," 285; King, *King Stephen*, 27–8.

[104] See Chapt. 3, 57.

The remaining 28 percent mostly came from exemptions from payments of *auxilium civitatis*, murder fines, and amercements from various pleas.[105]

A very few of Henry I's favorites also parlayed the high favor they enjoyed into awards of fiscal exemptions to members of their followings and clients; and the amounts forgiven are another dimension of the patronage the *familiares* themselves enjoyed. Robert of Gloucester was one of only eleven recipients of this benefit for two men forgiven danegeld in Buckinghamshire.[106]

As a final gesture of trust in his *familiaris* son, before his death on December 1, 1135, Henry I placed Falaise castle (Calvados) with its treasury under Gloucester's command. While he lay dying at his hunting lodge at Lyons-la-Fôret (Eure) near Rouen, the king ordered Robert to take funds from the Falaise treasury to pay the household's knights and to distribute as alms to the poor. Later, with the castle under his control, after he learned of his cousin Stephen's accession as king, the earl surrendered it.[107]

Robert earl of Gloucester's interactions with his curial colleagues were not limited to the *curia regis*. Robert and Miles of Gloucester crossed paths at the Gloucestershire county court and the court of the honor of Gloucester, possibly at Gloucester castle during the earl's visitations.[108] Suit of court also may have brought Geoffrey I de Clinton before the earl. The same obligation accounts for the earl's presence at the bishop of Bayeux's honorial court and theoretically would have required his attendance at the archbishop of Canterbury's as well for his share of Haimo II *dapifer*'s fee.[109]

The earl himself was visited in 1128 by Archbishop Thurstan of York to witness the finalizing of a *conventio* between Robert and Roger abbot of ducal Fécamp (1107–39) regarding Robert's rights over its priory of Saint-Gabriel (Calvados) as *patronus*. The archbishop's name appears first in the list of the *actum*'s witnesses. Since Fécamp was a ducal abbey and the very foundation of Saint-Gabriel had been approved by the first Anglo-Norman king William I, Robert's colleague, arguably, was present as King Henry's representative. Thurstan's Bessin roots as the son of a priest of Condé-sur-Seulles near Bayeux and Creully (Calvados) may have contributed to his availability for the task.[110]

Court life was not all business. It also provided a special ambience of the royal court available for savoring by the titled and privileged, especially during the multi-day festal celebrations of Christmas, Easter, and Pentecost. They could be

---

[105] See n. 100.
[106] *PR 31 Henry I* (Green), 81; Mooers, "Patronage in the Pipe Roll of 1130," 297–8.
[107] *OV* vi. 448–9; Robert of Torigny, "Chronica," 129; *Regesta* ii. no. 1919; Haskins, *Norman Institutions*, 308.
[108] *Regesta* ii. no. 1657; Patterson, *EGC*, nos. 80, 110, 283.
[109] *Cart. Bayeux* i. no. cii; see also no. xlii; see Chapt. 3, 57.
[110] Patterson, *EGC*, no. 70; *CDF*, no. 1410, p. 521; witnesses include Richard II fitz Samson bishop of Bayeux (1107–33) and several representing Abbot Roger and Earl Robert, including his son William and *dapifer* Geoffrey de Waterville; Abbot Roger's far outnumber those any of the other party's, so the abbot's court is the more likely location; several of his lay witnesses also are found in the witness-list of an *actum* of Henry I in favor of Fécamp (*Regesta* ii. no. 1562); see also *Regesta* 1 (1998), no. 357 & n.

*A Second Career* 49

occasions for demonstrating and relishing one's rank amidst the pomp and pageantry of court ceremonial. Bishops Alexander and Nigel made grand entrances at court with great escorts of knights.[111] Earls enjoyed special status, Robert even more so as he became more noticeably his father's *familiaris* in the 1120s. If, as Walter Map claimed, the king maintained a register of his earls and barons, the earl of Gloucester's name would have led the list.

There was sumptuous banqueting on vast arrays of food and wine to be enjoyed and opportunities, presumably as observer or participant, for engaging in various sports and games ranging from jousting, cheered on by admiring ladies, to chess and dice. The ladies themselves presented opportunities for flirting and possible sexual liaisons. Given Robert's reputation for being a devoted follower of Venus, it would be rash to exclude the earl from being a participant.[112]

Geoffrey of Monmouth in the process of seeking Earl Robert's patronage seems to have sent him a copy his *Historia Regum Britanniae*, which was intended to conjure up for him and others of his class the glories of Britain's past through tales of King Arthur and his court. In Geoffrey's prime example, Arthur celebrated defeating and killing the Roman tribune of Gaul Frollo with a great feast on Pentecost at his capital Caerleon in Glamorgan. Mass was celebrated, followed by processions for the king and queen amidst music and singing, crown-wearing, awarding bishoprics, baronies, and castles, and banquets served by opulently liveried staff. Elegantly dressed ladies were on hand to be tempted by the valorous in post-prandial games.[113]

A mutual appetite for Romance history produced the most far-reaching of Earl Robert of Gloucester's relationships with his colleagues. Several of them were *litterati*, particularly Alexander bishop of Lincoln, who supposedly, after learning about Merlin, urged Geoffrey of Monmouth to publish the wizard's prophecies, commissioned Henry of Huntingdon's *Historia Anglorum*, and may have compiled a dictionary of Anglo-Saxon legal terms.[114] Henry bishop of Winchester and Brian fitz Count are known for their letter-writing—the latter also for his composition of a tract in favor of the Empress Matilda's succession.[115] Nigel bishop of Ely, Alexander's brother, may have written the *Constitutio domus Regis*, the description of the royal household of *c*.1136.[116] One might have expected one or more of these closest associates to be his literary confrères. Instead, it was a colleague Gloucester hardly ever saw who evidently wanted to borrow a book.

---

[111] *GS* (2004), 72–3; the monks of Ely saw Nigel's accession somewhat differently: *LE*, 283–4; Hollister, "The Origins of the English Treasury," 270–3.

[112] *De Nugis Curialium*, 426–7, 438–9, 470–3; Geffrei Gaimar, ll. 6501–3, 6511–16.

[113] *HRB*, 208, 210, 212, 214; Short, "Gaimar's Epilogue and Geoffrey of Monmouth's *Liber Vetustissimus*," 338. For references of likely interest to Earl Robert in the *HRB*, see Tatlock, *The Legendary History of Britain*, 68–9, 90, 104–5, 120–1, 170.

[114] Reeve in *HRB*, viii, 142–3; Greenway, Henry of Huntingdon (1996), lxvi–lxvii; see also pp. 4–9; Smith, "Alexander," 647; Gransden, *Historical Writing* i. 194; Kealey, *Roger of Salisbury*, 24; Bartlett, *England under the Norman and Angevin Kings*, 503.

[115] *LCGF*, no. 26, p. 61; King, "The Memory of Brian fitz Count," 76–7, 89–91.

[116] Kealey, *Roger of Salisbury*, 24; however, note Church, "Constitutio Domus Regis," xliv.

Simple details of Earl Robert's literary curial relationship come from a story the vernacular historian Geoffrey Gaimar recounted about one of the sources for his *Estoire des Engleis*. Gloucester's fellow *curialis* was Walter Espec, a major baronial figure and royal official in the north of England. He was lord of Helmsley and Wark, sheriff and local justice in Yorkshire, founder of Cistercian Rievaulx, Kirkham Priory (Yorks.), and Wardon Abbey (Beds.), and friend of Rievaulx's famous historian-monk and abbot Ailred.[117] The two barons saw very little of each other at the royal court, but Walter, who reputedly had an impressive command of Norman history, by some means asked Robert to send him a book about the early history of Britain the earl had commissioned to be adapted from Welsh texts. Scholars generally agree that the book probably was an early version of Geoffrey of Monmouth's *Historia Regum Britanniae* (now *De gestis Britonum*). Robert sent Walter the book, which passed as gift or loan via a network of several aristocratic households until it was presented to Geoffrey Gaimar.[118]

Espec's curial association with Earl Robert may not have been the only factor involved in his request for the book.[119] Walter and Robert also had a personal connection based on land a close relative held of the earl. One of Walter's nephews, sons of his sister Albreda and Geoffrey I de Trailli (also Trelly), Geoffrey II was one of the earl's medium-ranking honorial tenants with a fee of four knights based on Yelden and Chellington in Bedfordshire. The manors had in the Domesday era belonged to Geoffrey bishop of Coutances but had been confiscated from his heir Robert de Mowbray for rebellion by King William Rufus and then granted to Robert fitz Hamon or his posthumous son-in-law Robert.[120] Rebellion also ended any further curial or literary relations between the two bookmen when they went separate political ways—in 1138 Robert declaring for the Empress Matilda's cause and Walter one of the royalist army's leaders at the battle of the Standard for King Stephen's.[121]

Henry I's death on December 1, 1135 brought to an end Robert of Gloucester's second career. It had given Robert, along with the loftiest aristocratic title available to a layman, an earldom with heightened authority in the center of his demesne stronghold and a life at the center of royal power in the Anglo-Norman realm. That brought Robert association with the men who were the principal cogs in the royal administrative machinery, most frequent participation in his father's curial

---

[117] Damian-Grint, *The New Historians of the Twelfth-Century Renaissance*, 49–53; Dalton, "Espec, Walter," 602–3; Green, *Henry I*, 176, 317; *GOE*, 245–6; Gransden, *Historical Writing* i. 187–8, 212–13.

[118] *Regesta* ii. no. 1463; Geffrei Gaimar, ll. 6436–7, 6447–55, & p. 349; Ailred of Rievaulx, 186; Baker, "Ailred of Rievaulx and Walter Espec," 94–5. Professor Ian Short's chronology for the composition of the *Estoire* would place Walter Espec's request of the earl at the end of Henry I's reign: "Gaimar's Epilogue and Geoffrey of Monmouth's *Liber Vetustissimus*," 337–8; Chapt. 6, 178–9.

[119] Short, "Gaimar's Epilogue and Geoffrey of Monmouth's *Liber Vetustissimus*," 338.

[120] *DB Bedfordshire (Phillimore)*, 3.4, 10 & n.; *RBE* i. 289; *CIPM* i. no. 530: Sanders, *English Baronies*, 133–4. Geoffrey II, not Geoffrey I, is the Gloucester tenant and nephew of Walter Espec: see him and his other brothers, nephews of Walter Espec, attesting King Stephen's confirmation of Walter's foundation of Wardon Priory: *Regesta* iii. no. 919.

[121] King, *King Stephen*, 90–4; Baker, "Ailred of Rievaulx and Walter Espec," 93–4; see Chapt. 5, 140.

actions, ultimately membership in his father's innermost circle of advisers, and, along with a trusted few, the power to wield royal authority in the king's name as his legate. Direct access to royal patronage made Robert its greatest fiscal beneficiary.

Robert of Gloucester, Professor Ian Short has argued, may have had a copy of Geoffrey of Monmouth's work in hand when he crossed the Channel to join King Stephen in Normandy in 1137.[122] If the earl read any of its references to his father's court, they likely would have sharpened his sense of the lost curial status he was suffering under King Stephen. More reminders were soon to come.

---

[122] Short, "Gaimar's Epilogue and Geoffrey of Monmouth's *Liber Vetustissimus*," 336–9.

## APPENDIX 2.1 THE EARL OF GLOUCESTER IN GLOUCESTERSHIRE

The great question which has puzzled scholars in recent years is not Anglo-Norman earls' curial prominence or possible enjoyment of the third-penny. Rather, the issue has been the degree to which a comital title translated into the exercise of tangible authority at the shire level. On the one hand, study of Anglo-Norman royal *acta* has shown that operational control had become the responsibility of the sheriff, theoretically as the earl's deputy, setting the courts in motion and executing their judgments, to borrow Van Caenegem's phrase.[123] Otherwise, in general, earls might preside over the shire court along with the bishops and sheriffs and receive the third-penny.[124] They enjoyed a precedence of honor among the suitors of their shire courts, second only to the local bishop, given the responsibility "to pronounce upon the laws of God and secular matters with just deliberation."[125] Nevertheless, Graeme White explained royal *acta* addressed to earls as just efforts to give the documents greater weight.[126]

However, Professor Ralph Davis provided evidence suggesting that earls, along with bishops and sheriffs, were the primary officials responsible for overseeing certain actions in their shire courts.[127] For example, in one of these writs King Henry, addressing Henry earl of Warwick and William sheriff of Warwickshire, held them alone responsible for seeing that a potential plaintiff against the abbot of Abingdon appear in the abbot's court for justice and nowhere else.[128] Davis showed that at least seven different earls, including Worcester, Warwick, and Leicester, issued writs implying their authority over their sheriffs.[129] In three writs, Waleran count of Meulan, acting as earl of Worcester, commanded (*praecipere*) his bailiffs and ministers of Worcestershire that certain monasteries were to enjoy various benefits from his manor at Droitwich (Worcs.).[130] Even more to the point, the count, again acting as earl of Worcester, commanded William de Beauchamp (de facto hereditary sheriff of Worcestershire and constable of Worcester castle) to quitclaim the prior and monks of St. Mary's Worcester of forest fees and all pleas of the forest at Taddington (Glos.).[131] David

---

[123] Stenton, *Anglo-Saxon England*, 539–40; Lewis, "The Early Earls of Norman England," 209–10, 222–3; Chibnall, *Anglo-Norman England*, 19; Sharpe, "Address and Delivery in Anglo-Norman Royal Charters," 34, 42; White, "Earls and Earldoms during King Stephen's Reign," 78–9.

[124] Round, *Geoffrey de Mandeville*, 273; Stenton, *English Feudalism*, 229–34; *GOE*, 118–19; Green, "Financing Stephen's War," 92. See also Richardson and Sayles, *Governance*, 19–20, 25–6.

[125] *Leges Henrici Primi*, 7, 2; 31, 3, p. 135; Hudson, *The Formation of the English Common Law*, 34–7. For later twelfth-century evidence, see *Cart. Gloucs.*, nos. 374–5.

[126] White, "Continuity in Government," 125.

[127] See, e.g., *Regesta* ii. nos. 732, 1044, 1151, 1445–6, 1845. Davis, *King Stephen*, 3rd edn., 125–41.

[128] *Regesta* ii. no. 654 (1103?). See also a writ (?1138–41) of King Stephen addressed to Waleran of Meulan as earl of Worcester making his responsibility more emphatic: *Cart. Worcester*, no. 84.

[129] Davis, *King Stephen*, 3rd edn., 127–8.

[130] BL, MS Cotton Faustina A.iii., fols. 279v–280r: *Westminster Abbey Charters*, no. 489; *Cart. Gloucester* ii. no. 542; White, "King Stephen's Earldoms," 69; White, "The Career of Waleran, Count of Meulan and Earl of Worcester," 29 & n.; see also a similar writ of Waleran in favor of Reading Abbey: *Mon. Angl.* iv. 56, and White, "The Career of Waleran, Count of Meulan and Earl of Worcester," 29 & n.

[131] Davis, "Some Documents of the Anarchy: The Sheriffdom of Worcester," 170–1; Crouch, *Beaumont Twins*, 39 & n. shows that by confirming a grant made by William to Bordesley Priory (Worcs.), Waleran acted as the sheriff's overlord. For the Beauchamp sheriffs, see also Mason, *Cart. Beauchamp*, xlviii–lii.

Crouch also has argued that several of Warwickshire's sheriffs were subject to the first earls of Warwick, Henry de Beaumont (1088–1119) and his son Roger (*c*.1119–53), by being either comital vassals or appointees.[132] Paul Latimer approached the subject of comital power at the shire level from another perspective by describing how certain individuals gained de facto comital power by acquiring the *comitatus*, the king's lands and courts in a shire.[133]

The kind of earldom Henry I originally conferred upon Robert, aside from extra dignity at court, involved at the shire level joint presidency with the bishop of the shire court and primacy among suitors in deciding matters at its meetings. This seems apparent from the two extant writs Henry I addressed to him. In the earlier of the two, which has been attributed to June 3–10, 1123, the king notified Theulf bishop of Worcester (1115–23) and Earl Robert of his grant of the land of Eadric son of Chetel to Walter of Gloucester.[134] In 1130, Henry addressed the then bishop Simon (1125–50), Robert earl of Gloucester, Miles (of Gloucester) the constable (and the sheriff), and all his barons and *fideles*, both French and English, of Gloucestershire. The king gave notice to them that he was confirming to St. Peter's Gloucester Scott's Quarry (in Harescombe, Glos.) given to the abbey by Roger of Berkeley; and that the abbey was to hold the manor as freely as the manor of Standish (Glos.) to which it belonged.[135] Perhaps reflecting an occasion when the earl's presence was not deemed necessary, another writ of Henry's addressed the bishop and Miles and all his barons of Gloucestershire without any mention of Robert.[136]

Robert's earldom also brought him the third-penny, which added £20 to his annual income.[137] In addition, perhaps through a separate action by 1130, the king ensured the earl's dominant position in his titular city by making the county sheriff Miles de facto hereditary constable of the royal castle at Gloucester the earl's vassal.[138] Such dual tenure of the shrievalty and local constableship was a privilege several other sheriffs enjoyed.[139] William of Malmesbury's *Historia Novella* contains the vassalic relationship's only description: "She [the Empress Matilda] was thereafter received at Gloucester by Miles, its castellan under the earl, who in the time of King Henry had done homage and sworn fealty to him. For that is the chief place of his earldom."[140] This concession to the earl conformed to a pattern David Crouch has shown Henry I followed in Warwickshire, Leicestershire,

---

[132] Crouch, "Geoffrey de Clinton and Roger Earl of Warwick: New Men and Magnates in the Reign of Henry I," 113–16.
[133] Latimer, "Grants of 'Totus Comitatus' in Twelfth-Century England," 137; *GOE*, 118–23; Green, *English Sheriffs*, 12–13, 16, esp. 14, for Earl Robert of Gloucester's strategy to gain influence over the sheriff of Kent; Green, "Financing Stephen's War," esp. 92.
[134] *Ancient Charters*, no. 10; *Regesta* ii. no. 1395; Green, *English Sheriffs*, 42; see also Walker, "Miles of Gloucester, Earl of Hereford," 68.
[135] *Cart. Gloucs.* ii. no. DCXVi; *Regesta* ii. no. 1657.
[136] *Regesta* ii. ii. nos. 1384, 1496, 1407, 1565.
[137] *PR 31 Henry I* (Green), 60; Round, *Geoffrey de Mandeville*, 287–8, 290–6, esp. 292.
[138] *HN* (1998), 62–3; Walker, "Miles of Gloucester, Earl of Hereford," 66–8; Green, *English Sheriffs*, 42; *GOE*, 256–7 & nn.; for royal *acta* addressed to, or attested by, Miles the constable (as castellan), see, e.g., *Regesta* ii. nos. 1646?, 1657–8; (as household officer) 1717–18, 1810.
[139] Green, *English Sheriffs*, 11, 16; Morris, *The Medieval English Sheriff*, 117, 151; Hollister, "Rise of Administrative Kingship," 888.
[140] "Recepit illam postea in Gloecestram Milo, qui castellum eiusdem urbis sub comite habebat, tempore regis Henrici dato ei homagio et fidelitatis sacramento. Nam eadem ciuitas caput est sui comitatus." *HN* (1998), 62–3; *JW* iii. 270–1, referred to Earl Robert as Miles's lord.

and Northamptonshire by granting or continuing for their earls degrees of influence over their sheriffs.[141]

In recognition of his vassalage, Miles came at least twice to the earl's court at Gloucester to gain proprietary favors. On one occasion, Miles obtained Robert's confirmation of his grandmother Adeliza's grant of fourteen burgesses of the family's fee in the town to St. Peter's Abbey. On the other one, at his request, the earl granted to his recently founded priory Lanthony (Secunda) freedom from tolls on comital land in England and Wales.[142] Miles may have provided Earl Robert as his lord with *hospitalitas* at Gloucester castle on such occasions.

In other respects, Miles appears to have been quite independent from Robert's feudal overlordship. Gloucestershire's traditional shrieval duties remained Miles's responsibility. He had held the two offices since succeeding his father Walter a year or so before 1130. Miles's family had been sheriffs of Gloucestershire from the time of his grandfather Roger de Pîtres, first post-Conquest sheriff. Furthermore, the new sheriff also held the offices of royal justice as well as the newly established regular office of shire justice in Gloucestershire and several other counties.[143]

Another relevant source of Miles's political independence was the fact that the sheriff and local constable was, like his father, a royal *curialis* and *familiaris*. He acquired the basis for these by receiving from the king shortly after his father's death confirmation of the court constableship Walter had held; and a close relationship developed between the king and his constable.[144] Gerald of Wales remembered Miles as a special royal counselor; both Miles and Payn fitz John influenced the king's appointment of Robert de Béthune to the bishopric of Hereford in 1131.[145]

---

[141] Crouch, "Geoffrey de Clinton and Roger, Earl of Warwick," 115; see also Crouch, "Oddities in the Early History of the Marcher Lordship of Gower," 134.

[142] Patterson, *EGC*, nos. 83 & n., 110; *Cart. Gloucs.* i. 81 states that Adeliza's grant was made in 1125 and involved fourteen lands; her son Walter had fifteen burgesses as tenants according to the "Evesham K" survey of Gloucester of *c*.1096 × 1101: Ellis, *A General Introduction to Domesday Book* i. 446n.; *DB Gloucestershire* (Phillimore), EvK, 1, G 1.

[143] Walker, "Miles of Gloucester, Earl of Hereford," 66–7 & n., 68; *GOE*, 256–7; Hollister, "Rise of Administrative Kingship," 886; Reedy, "The Origins of the General Eye in the Reign of Henry I," 688–724.

[144] *Regesta* ii. no. 1552; Hollister, "Rise of Administrative Kingship," 888.

[145] Gerald of Wales, *Itinerarium*, 34; Walker, "Miles of Gloucester, Earl of Hereford," 70.

## APPENDIX 2.2

### Robert of Gloucester's chief associates, c.1121–47

| Rank | Name | *Acta* jointly attested |
|---|---|---|
| 1. | Robert *de Sigillo* (31) | 1459, 1466, 1546, 1581, 1586, 1590, 1601, 1687–8, 1690–1, 1693, 1700, 1702, 1711, 1713, 1715, 1719, 1724, 1736, 1740, 1742, 1764–5, 1777, 1892, 1908, 1911–12, 1915, 1917. |
| 2. | William de Warenne earl of Surrey (27) | 1391, 1426–8, 1442, 1474, 1559, 1587, 1656, 1668, 1680, 1687–91, 1693, 1715, 1719, 1736, 1740, 1742, 1757, 1764–5, 1896, 1911. |
|  | —Brian fitz Count (27) | 1427, 1459, 1463, 1483, 1535?, 1562, 1581, 1643–4?, 1656, 1668, 1687–90, 1692–3, 1713, 1715, 1719, 1721, 1724, 1736, 1757, 1777, 1908, 1911, 1934, 1973. |
| 3. | Roger bishop of Salisbury (26) | 1335, 1347, 1391, 1428, 1459, 1466, 1483, 1562, 1575, 1641, 1643–4, 1656, 1668, 1711, 1713, 1719, 1721, 1724, 1736–7, 1740, 1742, 1757, 1764, 1777. |
| 4. | John bishop of Lisieux (23) | 1427–8?, 1442, 1466, 1559, 1575, 1581, 1587–8, 1680, 1687–93, 1702, 1908, 1912, 1915–17, 1932. |
|  | —Hugh Bigod (23) | 1391, 1427, 1601, 1680, 1687–90, 1693, 1711, 1713, 1715, 1719, 1724, 1736–7, 1742, 1757, 1764, 1777, 1892, 1908, 1915. |
|  | —Nigel nephew of Roger bishop of Salisbury and bishop of Ely (23/10) | 1454, 1459, 1477, 1554, 1562, 1586, 1623, 1641, 1688–91, 1693, 1700, 1707, 1709–10, 1715, 1736, 1740, 1746, 1827, 1852, 1757, 1759, 1776–7, 1782, 1784, 1787, 1902, 1908–9. |
| 5. | Alexander bishop of Lincoln (20) | 1391, 1426, 1459, 1463, 1568, 1668, 1711, 1713, 1715, 1719, 1721, 1724, 1726, 1736–7, 1740, 1742, 1764–5, 1811?, 1911. |
| 6. | Geoffrey fitz Payn (19) | 1581, 1600–1, 1668, 1693, 1700, 1711, 1719, 1724, 1726, 1737, 1740, 1742, 1764, 1892, 1915–17, 1973. |
| 7. | Henry bishop of Winchester (18) | 1372, 1391, 1427, 1443–4, 1466, 1711, 1713, 1715, 1721, 1724, 1736, 1740, 1742, 1757, 1764–5, 1990. |
| 8. | Thurstan archbishop of York (16) | 1391, 1427–8?, 1459, 1463, 1474, 1546, 1563, 1581, 1587, 1692, 1711, 1713, 1715, 1719, 1721, 1736. |
|  | —William of Corbeil archbishop of Canterbury (16) | 1391, 1426–8, 1474, 1483, 1711, 1713, 1715, 1719, 1724, 1737, 1740, 1765, 1896, 1990. |
|  | —Geoffrey Rufus chancellor (16) | 1391, 1459, 1562, 1643–4, 1656, 1668, 1711, 1713, 1715, 1719, 1721, 1724, 1736, 1742, 1764. |
|  | —Audoin bishop of Évreux (16) | 1427–8?, 1441–2, 1466, 1466, 1546, 1581, 1656, 1687, 1690, 1693, 1892, 1908, 1932. |
| 9. | John bishop of Sées (15) | 1428?, 1441–2, 1581, 1588, 1687–91, 1693, 1700, 1702?, 1740, 1764, 1908. |
|  | —Hugh archbishop of Rouen (15) | 1427–8?, 1466, 1474, 1575, 1687–91, 1693, 1700, 1736, 1892, 1908, 1932. |

(*continued*)

Continued

| Rank | Name | *Acta* jointly attested |
|---|---|---|
| 10. | Robert de Vere (13) | 1668, 1680, 1719, 1736–7, 1764, 1757, 1777, 1892, 1915–17, 1919. |
|  | —Miles of Gloucester (13) | 1656, 1711, 1713, 1715, 1117–18, 1724, 1736–7, 1740, 1742, 1764–5. |
| 11. | Robert de Courcy steward (12) | 1719, 1726, 1742, 1742, 1757, 1764–5, 1892, 1908, 1915–17 |
| 12. | Humphrey II de Bohun (11) | 1693, 1711, 1715, 1719, 1736, 1740, 1742, 1757, 1764, 1777, 1892. |
| 13. | Aubrey de Vere (10) | 1668, 1715, 1736, 1740, 1742, 1757, 1764–5, 1915, 1934. |
|  | —Robert de la Haye (10) | 1427, 1442, 1575, 1581, 1680, 1689–91, 1698, 1702? |
|  | —Payn fitz John (10) | 1466, 1668, 1711, 1713, 1715, 1724, 1736, 1740, 1742, 1764. |
| 14. | William fitz Odo (9) | 1391, 1427, 1441, 1586, 1680, 1700, 1719, 1908, 1912. |
| 15. | Richard II bishop of Bayeux (8) | 1546, 1575, 1588, 1600–1, 1687–8, 1702. |
|  | —Richard Basset (8) | 1711, 1715, 1736, 1742, 1757, 1764–5, 1777. |
|  | —William d'Aubigny, *pincerna* (8) | 1391, 1581, 1588?, 1600–1, 1620, 1656, 1692, 1702, 1990? |
| 16. | Ranulf II earl of Chester (7) | 1391, 1428, 1575, 1715, 1719, 1736, 1740. |
|  | —Geoffrey de Clinton (7) | 1426, 1428, 1483, 1588?, 1687–8, 1715. |
| 17. | William de Pont de l'Arche (6) | 1483, 1562, 1586, 1656, 1715, 1777. |
|  | —Rabel de Tancarville (6) | 1587, 1687–8, 1691, 1693, 1719. |
| 18. | Eustace fitz John (5) | 1459, 1575, 1668, 1711, 1740. |
|  | —Stephen count of Mortain (5) | 1588?, 1932, 1934, 1740, 1757, 1908. |
| 19. | Humphrey I de Bohun (4) | 1347, 1391, 1427, 1600?–1. |
|  | —William of Glastonbury (4) | 1581, 1764, 1915, 1949. |

# 3
# The Making of a Super-Magnate

In describing his patron Robert earl of Gloucester for posterity, William of Malmesbury cited as his preeminent attributes regal birth, Norman martial prowess, Flemish handsomeness, and French nobility. Whatever one may think of the list, with its device of ethnic portraiture, it omitted the eminent status Henry I created for Robert, super-magnate, with its endemic landed mentality.[1]

This proprietary stature mostly was due to the territorial proceeds from the marriage Henry engineered for him to Mabel fitz Hamon. As we already have seen, *ipso facto* Robert became lord of a trans-Channel barony. In Normandy it consisted of the house of Haimo's patrimonial lands in Lower Normandy plus a key office in Caen and two tenancies-in-chief; in England, the honor of Gloucester; and in South Wales, the Marcher county of Glamorgan with its dependency, the lordship of Gwynllŵg. On the basis of the English and Welsh lordships alone Robert became transformed *iure uxoris* into a class A baronial tenant-in-chief of the king with an income in the range of £500.[2]

After Mabel's uncle Haimo II sheriff of Kent died childless by the late 1120s, the king allowed Robert to inherit over half of his English barony. This raised Robert's demesne income to over £564 from the two insular sources alone. His father's total additional grants may have made him the largest demesne lay landlord in England and catapulted the earl of Gloucester into the most select category of the Anglo-Norman landed aristocracy, AA class super-magnates.[3]

In Lower Normandy, *iure uxoris*, the king's son became the most important honorial tenant of the bishop of Bayeux for the service of ten knights. Wace described Mabel's father as lord of Torigni-sur-Vire (Manche) and Creully (Calvados) and of many lands about Creully. His barony evidently consisted of demesne at Évrecy and Torigni and subinfeudated estates.[4] To provide this *servitium debitum* Robert had the service of knights of whom some were almost certainly enfeoffed, while others may have belonged to his household.[5] He utilized Torigni as

---

[1] *GR* i. 798–9.    [2] *GOE*, 57; see Chapt. 1, n. 91 and Chapt. 4, 82.
[3] See Chapt. 1, 16. Haimo II, *dapifer* under King William Rufus, lost his shrievalty of Kent *c*.1115 (*Regesta* i. no. 451; *Regesta* ii. nos. 1093, 1669n.), but attested an *actum* of Henry I as *dapifer* datable to 1119 × 23 (no. 1404); see also *PR 31 Henry I* (Green), 50–3; Douglas, *Domesday Monachorum*, 55; *GOE*, 201; for details, see 68–9; see Map 1, 239; see Chapt. 1, n. 91.
[4] Wace, *Le Roman de Rou* ii., ll. 11073–6, p. 296; Navel, "Recherches sur les institutions féodales en Normandie," 128; see also Chapt. 1, 16 & n.; Chapt. 2, 44.
[5] *RHG* xxiii. 698–9; *RBE* ii. 645; Gleason, *An Ecclesiastical Barony*, 45 & n.; Navel, "Recherches sur les institutions féodales en Normandie," 127. Henry II later confirmed a grant to the abbey of Saint-Martin Troarn by Robert and his men from his fee: Delisle-Berger, i. no. 28, p. 126.

his honorial administrative center (*caput*).[6] When Robert's son Earl William of Gloucester (1147–83) held the honor both Évrecy and Torigni were utilized in this way.[7] Fitz Hamon also had some interest at Ecajeul near Mézidon (Calvados) and in Langrune-sur-Mer (Calvados) from which he made a gift to Saint-Martin's Troarn.[8] The Register of Tewkesbury Abbey (Glos.), founded by Robert, states that he was lord of Esterville (Calvados);[9] and Ducy-Sainte-Margarite and Chouain (Calvados) may have been held of him as well.[10]

Proprietary actions taken by Fitz Hamon's twelfth-century heirs may reveal some other of his barony's pre-1107 details. Mabel's husband Earl Robert consented to the gift of land at Bazenville (Calvados) to Savigny Abbey by Robert fitz Ernesius.[11] Robert did the same regarding the gift of two mills at Montaigu (Calvados) by William de Magny-le-Freûle (Calvados) to the abbey of Saint-Étienne Caen.[12] The earl granted Asnières (Calvados), acquired from the bishop of Bayeux, to a local figure of increasing importance by the 1120s, William Crassus II.[13] Robert's son and successor Earl William granted the church of Écrammeville (Calvados) to the priory of St. James Bristol.[14] William's brother Richard, who held Creully (*c.*1138?–75), granted Bayeux Cathedral his mills at Mesnilbuye (Calvados?).[15] Earl Robert's grandson Philip de Creully (1175–98 × 1202) gave Notre Dame du Voeu of Cherbourg (Manche) his fee and demesne at Arreville (Manche, arr. Valognes, cant. Quettehou), the abbey of Saint-Lô at Coutances a messuage at *Monfai* (Manche), and the abbey of Sainte-Marie de Longues, Le Manoir (Calvados, cant. Ryes, arr. Bayeux).[16] Another grandson Roger of Creully, Philip's brother, granted land at Maupertuis (Manche) and Clermont to Longues.[17] Three virgates at Mathieu (Calvados) were given Sainte-Trinité Caen by another grandson, Richard, in 1221.[18]

The connections of several later Gloucester fees to Fitz Hamon are obscure. Creully was a likely dependency of his lordship; and his posthumous son-in-law

---

[6] *GND* (1995) ii. 248–9; Wace, *Le Roman de Rou* ii., ll. 11199–201, p. 300. See also the less reliable "Extrait de la chronique de Normandie," in *RHG* xiii. 253.

[7] AD du Calvados, H. 6510, no. 90, fol. 22b (mod. fol.), transcr. in B.N., MS latin nouvelle acquisition 1020, fol. 399r; Patterson, *EGC*, no. 186.

[8] *Regesta* i. (1998), no. 281 (II), p. 848; PRO 31, 8/140B, pt. 3, p. 340; *CDF*, no. 480; transcr. of Avranches, Bibliothèque Municipale, MS 20, fol. 80r (for which I am indebted to Professor David Bates); Deville, *Analyse d'un ancien cartulaire de l'abbaye de Saint-Étienne de Caen*, 20.

[9] BL, Additional MS 36985, fol. 10v.

[10] *Les Actes de Guillaume le Conquérant et de la reine Mathilde pour les abbayes caennaises*, no. 8, p. 88.

[11] *CDF*, no. 824, p. 299.

[12] *Neustria Pia*, 631; *CDF*, no. 453, p. 158; Delisle-Berger, i. no. cliv, p. 274.

[13] *Regesta* ii. no. 1601; iii. no. 63; Delisle-Berger, i. no. 73; Vincent, "The Borough of Chipping Sodbury and the Fat Men of France (1130–1270)," 144 & n., Fig. 1, 145; this William or his namesake then made a gift to the priory of Ardenne near Caen for his father's soul in 1138: AD du Calvados, H.1; printed in *Neustria Pia*, 702–3; *Gallia Christiana* xi, "Instrumenta IX," 78. See also n. 22.

[14] Patterson, *EGC*, no. 38.

[15] *Cart. Bayeux* i. no. cclxxiii, pp. 321–2. See also *RHG* xxiii, 501.

[16] PRO, 31, 8/140B, pt. 1, no. 14, pp. 106–7; *CDF*, no. 951. Delisle-Berger, ii. nos. DCCVII, 366, DCCXXXV. For another grant from Le Manoir by Philip's brother Roger, see *Chartes de l'abbaye de Jumièges* ii. no. CLXXVI, pp. 132–3.

[17] PRO, 31, 8/140B, pt. 2, pp. 90–1 (original in AD du Calvados); poss. *CDF*, no. 1454.

[18] *Charters and Customals of the Abbey of Holy Trinity Caen*. ii: *The French Estates*, no. 26; Patterson, *EGC*, no. 6 & n.

Robert certainly acted as lord in the 1120s. In 1128 the earl made a *conventio* with the abbot of Fécamp regarding the priory of Saint-Gabriel in this capacity. However, Richard son of Turstin Goz, lord of Creully, and his son Turstin had founded Saint-Gabriel in 1058 as a dependency of Fécamp Abbey. I believe they were honorial tenants of Fitz Hamon's family.[19] Perhaps the reason that Gloucester rather than a member of the Goz family was acting in 1128 as lord of Creully in dealing with the priory is that the Creully fee had escheated to its Gloucester mesne lord. Creully continued after Earl Robert in his family, first in the hands of his son Richard (d. 1175) and then of Richard's heirs. Earl Robert also held a fee at Saint-Clair-sur-l'Elle (Manche), likely appurtenant to his Creully lordship.[20]

Fitz Hamon also may have been lord of Sainte-Scolasse-sur-Sarthe (Sarthe), a castellany straddling the southern Norman boundary with the county of Maine. He could have acquired it by 1098 in connection with his alliance with Roger de Montgomery and his redoubtable wife Mabel de Bellême, possibly through his marriage to their daughter Sibyl.[21] The lordship more than likely belonged to the earldom of Gloucester at least from the time of Fitz Hamon's posthumous son-in-law Robert. William Crassus III (d. -1219), the likely son of the previously named recipient of Asnières from the earl, owed the service of one knight at Sainte-Scolasse-sur Sarthe.[22]

There are no contemporary figures to indicate what Earl Robert's Norman holdings yielded to him in demesne and feudal income. The earliest extant Norman Exchequer rolls from 1180 and 1184 give little detailed information.[23] However, the inquest of the bishop of Bayeux's barony that Robert held for his father in 1133 reveals other indications of his feudal and political strength. The proceedings survive, as John Horace Round demonstrated, in two versions made from two different groups of data from a seventeenth-century transcription of the original text of the

---

[19] Wace, *Le Roman de Rou* ii. ll. 4025–8; Patterson, *EGC*, no. 70 & n.; *Regesta* i (1998). no. 257; Musset, "Naissance de la Normandie," 95–8, esp. 96 (for Richard as lord). Turstin de Creully, apparently Richard's son, along with other landholders, gave all he possessed at Tailleville (Calvados) *c.*1069? to Saint-Martin's Troarn: *CDF*, no. 463. Turstin's brother Vital was a monk at Fécamp and rose to be abbot of Bernay and, subsequently, of Westminster: Musset, "La Contribution de Fécamp à la reconquête monastique de la Basse-Normandie," 65; Knowles, *HRH*, 76. A Richard de Creully, perhaps Turstin's father and Fitz Hamon's vassal, was present at the *Ordinatio* of Robert's foundation, Tewkesbury Abbey, in 1105: *Mon. Angl.* ii. 81.

[20] Patterson, *EGC*, no. 6 & n.; *Cart. Bayeux* i. no. 156, p. 195; *RHG* xxiii. 633, 694; Navel, "Recherches sur les institutions féodales en Normandie," 140. Richard, known as Richard fitz Count and Richard of Creully, married the sister of Robert de Montfort (Robert of Torigny, "Chronica," 269).

[21] Fitz Hamon belonged to the following of the house of Montgomery during the second half of the eleventh century in the Alençonnais and pays de Sées. See his attestations of Montgomery *acta*: e.g., PRO 31, 8/140B iii. 186; *Mon. Angl.* vi, pt. 2, p. 1109; *CDF*, no. 656; Fitz Hamon also donated to the Montgomery-favored Saint-Martin's Troarn (PRO, 31, 8/140B iii. 327; *CDF*, no. 473; Du Motey, *Origines de la Normandie*, 233, 306.

[22] *Regesta* iii. no. 63; *RHG* xxiii. 611; Powicke, *The Loss of Normandy*, 340; Vincent, "The Borough of Chipping Sodbury and the Fat Men of France (1130–1270)," 144–7. Concerning the lack of charter evidence of Gloucester overlordship, see Power, "Guérin de Glapion," 157.

[23] In 1180 and 1184, with the *vicomté* of Bayeux held at farm, the farmer was acquitted £15 from the earl's land, only the equivalent of slightly over £3 15*s*. in English pounds sterling; exactly what income source this sum represents is uncertain: *Pipe Rolls of the Exchequer of Normandy for the Reign of Henry II 1180 and 1184*, 29, 97; Keefe, *Feudal Assessments*, 122.

inquest: one pertaining to the bishopric's tenants around the beginning of the twelfth century and the other contemporary with the inquest.[24]

The earlier version shows what Robert's status in the Bessin would have been had he simply been content with his wife's inheritance. The bishop's own military needs and his obligations to the duke of Normandy and king of France were provided by 38 honorial barons providing a total of 119.5 knights' fees. Forming the uppermost group along with Robert fitz Hamon were Roger Suhard (8 knights), the *vicomte* of the Bessin Ranulf (7.5), Roger Malfilastre (7), and Roger of Saint-Sauveur (*vicomte* of the Cotentin) (7); below, in the next echelon, were fees of 5 knights: Richard (*vicomte* of Avranches) earl of Chester, Engeram de Spineto, Hugh de Crèvecoeur, and (Walchelin) Maminot; following them were two fees of 3 knights, nine fees of 2 knights, ten fees of single knights, and four of half-knights. Of the thirty-eight episcopal tenants, Robert fitz Hamon's mesne lordship of 10 knights was the largest. As can be seen, about a third (12) were lordships of 5–8 knights; an "upper crust" of six of these held between 7–8 knights' fees. Twenty-five fees supported fewer than 4 knights; and the majority, fourteen of them, were valued at either one-half or a single knight.[25] In this feudal milieu, Robert, merely as Fitz Hamon's successor, would have enjoyed no more prominence than among the uppermost echelon of the bishopric's second- or third-tier vassals.

Furthermore, the real sociopolitical strength of some of his honorial colleagues in the Anglo-Norman realm was far stronger than the size of their Bayeux holdings. For example, in addition to his ducal office and fee as *vicomte* of Avranches (Manche), Richard of Chester (5) was a major English tenant-in-chief whose honor of Chester alone stretched over 20 counties with a Domesday value of over £794.[26] Roger I Bigod (0.5) not only held the offices of sheriff of Norfolk and steward in the royal household, but belonged to the inner circle of Henry I's earliest advisers. His honor of Framlingham (Suff.) with a Domesday value of c.£450 had 125 enfeoffed knights by 1135.[27] Hugh II de Montfort (8), Henry de Port (3), (Hugh) Maminot (5), and Hugh de Crèvecoeur (5) held English baronies owing castle-guard at Dover castle (Kent) over which King Henry gave authority

---

[24] (1) *RBE* ii. 645–7; (2) *RHG* xxiii. 699–702; D'Anisy, *Extrait des chartes* ii. 425–31; Haskins, *Norman Institutions*, 15n.; Stenton, *English Feudalism*, 13n.; Navel, "L'Enquête sur les fiefs de l'évêché de Bayeux," 13–38; Round, "The Bayeux Inquest of 1133," 201–16.

[25] *RBE* ii. 645–6; as Haskins, *Norman Institutions*, 16n., pointed out, the actual number reported in the inquest of 1133 was 117.75; the better version of the inquest printed in *RBE* ii. 645–7 reported 119.5; on the two versions of the inquest, see Round, "The Bayeux Inquest of 1133," 201–16. The inquest did not state that the bishop had a fee of 100 knights; it only showed how 100 knights supplied its military quotas owed to the king of France and the duke of Normandy. In the Norman inquest of knights' fees of 1172, 120 knights were reported for the bishopric: *RBE* ii. 625.

[26] Loyd, *Anglo-Norman Families*, 28; Lewis, "Formation of the Honour of Chester," 41–3; Hollister, "Anglo-Norman Civil War: 1101," 319; Hollister, "Henry I and the Anglo-Norman Magnates," in *MMI*, 183; for the lands around Saint-Sever (Calvados) belonging to Richard of Chester as *vicomte* of Avranches, see Musset, "Naissance de la Normandie," 123; Bates, *Normandy before 1066*, 115.

[27] Sanders, *English Baronies*, 46–7: Roger died in 1107; Hollister, "Henry I and the Anglo-Norman Magnates," in *MMI*, 185.

to his son Robert.[28] Hugh Maminot and later his son Walchelin also were tenants of Robert's honor of Gloucester.[29]

Earl Robert's political nemesis-to-be in King Stephen's reign, Waleran count of Meulan, was another fellow Bayeux episcopal tenant. As elder coheir from 1118 of the great premier *familiaris* of the earl's father, Robert de Meulan earl of Leicester, Waleran held the county of Meulan in the French Vexin and all of his father's Norman lands except for the great lordship of Breteuil, which was his twin brother Robert earl of Leicester's share in the duchy. The center of Waleran's extensive Norman holdings lay in the Risle Valley, but two of his knights' fees at Epaignes (Eure), Selles, and the forest of Brotonne were held of the bishop of Bayeux.[30]

In 1133, Waleran's personal political stature in the Bayeux barony may not have concerned Earl Robert, but Waleran was stronger than at first glance. In addition to the count's two knights' fees, his first cousin Robert de Neubourg held another two and his brother-in-law Hugh IV de Montfort-sur-Risle, eight.[31] However, Hugh and his eight fees were unavailable for any Beaumont family supporting role. Both Waleran and Hugh and other Norman allies had risen in 1123 against Henry I partly to support the dynastic claim of William Clito. It was to be the last mustering of the coalition of Norman baronial dissidents aided and abetted by the count of Anjou and Louis VI of France that King Henry I would have to face on Norman soil. At the rout of the Norman forces which made this so on March 26, 1124, the battle of Bourgthéroulde east of the Risle near the abbey of Bec, both Waleran and Hugh were among those captured, and their lands, presumably including their Bayeux fees, were taken into the king's hands.[32] Henry released Waleran and restored him to favor after five years, but kept Hugh in custody, not only at the time of the Bayeux inquest, but for the remainder of his reign because he had refused an offer of freedom in exchange for a pledge of peace.

Henry's successor King Stephen would keep Hugh de Montfort a captive, but in one of his first acts in early 1136 he granted de Montfort's Norman honor, likely including the eight fees held of the bishop of Bayeux, to Count Waleran.[33] Considering the argument Earl Robert later used to justify his transfer of fealty from King Stephen to his half-sister Matilda, Gloucester might well have viewed

---

[28] Round, "The Bayeux Inquest of 1133," 212; Navel, "Recherches sur les institutions féodales en Normandie," 127; Hollister, *Henry I*, 175.

[29] For Hugh Maminot (d. -1131), son of Gilbert Maminot bishop of Lisieux (d. 1101), see *Regesta* ii. nos. 497, 515; Sanders, *English Baronies*, 97; the fees of the Maminot barony owing castle-guard at Dover were at Hartwell (Northants) and at Bretinghurst, part of Camberwell (Surrey), held of the honor of Gloucester: *DB Surrey* (Phillimore), 30.2; Round, "Castle Guard," 147, 155–6; *VCH Northants*. i. 295, 374b; *VCH Surrey* iv. 31. For Hugh's son Walchelin, see Chapt. 5, 140–2.

[30] *Regesta* ii. no. 843; *RBE* ii. 646; *RHG* xxiii. 700; Navel, "Recherches sur les institutions féodales en Normandie," 127; Navel, "L'Enquête de 1133 sur les fiefs de l'évêché de Bayeux," 31, nn. 72–3. For the Beaumont brothers, see Crouch, *The Beaumont Twins*, 3–10 & *passim*; White, "Career of Waleran, Count of Meulan and Earl of Worcester," 24 & n.

[31] For the de Montfort family and Hugh IV, see Robert of Torigny, "Interpolations," 260–1: *GND* ii. 176–7; Loyd, *Anglo-Norman Families*, 68; Douglas, *Domesday Monachorum*, 67–70; White, "The Career of Waleran Count of Meulan," 24 n. 3; Hollister, *Henry I*, 294–5.

[32] *OV* vi. 330–7; 346–357; Robert of Torigny, "Chronica," 107; Robert of Torigny, "Interpolations," 296: Crouch, *The Beaumont Twins*, 14–24; Hollister, *Henry I*, 292–301.

[33] *OV* vi. 356 & n., 357; Crouch, *The Beaumont Twins*, 29–30.

this build-up of Waleran's personal territorial standing in the heartland of his Norman power as one of the king's earliest affronts.[34]

But perhaps Stephen was thinking of counterbalancing Robert's accumulation of strength in the Bayeux episcopal barony during the pontificate of Richard II fitz Samson of Bayeux (1107–33). The king's son had not been content to be just his posthumous father-in-law's territorial successor there. In the Bayeux inquest's contemporary second version of 1133, while proclaiming himself to be Sainte-Marie's hereditary standard-bearer, the earl testified that he had in effect increased his knights' fees from Fitz Hamon's ten to at least 25.[35]

In spite of the fact that the earl claimed that some fees had been granted to him by the bishop, and at least one of them, the Malfilastre fee, with the agreement (*concessu*) of the cathedral chapter and the king, Robert was the moving force behind his acquisitions. A later bishop of Bayeux, Philip de Harcourt (1142–63), and Pope Eugenius III (1145–53) blamed him for taking the fees and the earl never denied it—indeed made a *conventio* with Philip by which he abandoned claim to some fees in return for holding others temporarily. Since we know that Robert had the most personal of ties to Bishop Richard's family through his sister Isabelle, that relationship may well have influenced the transfer of fees to Robert: his bastard son by her may have been named for his "uncle."[36] However, King Henry's influence would have come into play, not only because of his status as overlord, but also because he seems to have intended to make Robert the major political force in the Bessin. Sometime, perhaps after *c*.1129 but before his death, Henry I made the hereditary *vicomte* of Bayeux and new earl of Chester, Ranulf II, Robert's son-in-law by engineering his marriage to Robert's daughter Mabel. This gave Robert a putative ally holding of the bishop a total of 12.5 fees backed up by the force of his ducal offices of *vicomte* in the Bessin and Avranchin and especially some 52 knights from his Briquessart (Calvados) and Saint-Sauveur (Manche) fees.[37] And in 1133, after Bishop Richard's death, the king made Robert's son by Isabelle, Richard, lord of the Bayeux fee by giving him the bishopric.[38] In effect, Henry I was creating a zone of political strength for Robert like those he arranged for him in England in the southwest and Kent.[39]

[34] See Chapt. 5, 138.

[35] *RHG* xxiii. 700; Navel, "Recherches sur les institutions féodales en Normandie," 127; the text of *c*.1100 makes no mention of Robert fitz Hamon as the bishop's standard-bearer: *RBE* ii. 645.

[36] Patterson, *EGC*, no. 6; in the inquest of 1133 Robert declared that the fees were held of the bishop: *RHG* xxiii. 700–1; Round, *Family Origins*, 214–16; Gleason, *An Ecclesiastical Barony*, 47 & n. Robert's tenure of the Suhard fee and of several others was later challenged by Bishop Philip de Harcourt; see Chapt. 4, 123–4.

[37] Ranulf II became earl of Chester *c*.1129; *HN* (1998), 80–1, suggests that he was the earl when he married the earl of Gloucester's daughter, but that is not certain; Ranulf was heir to 7.5 fees (or as recorded later, 9.5) as *vicomte* of the Bessin and to 5 as earl of Chester: *RBE* ii. 645; *RHG* xxiii. 700, 702; *Regesta* iii. no. 180; for his ducal fees, see *RBE* ii. 626; White, "King Stephen, Duke Henry, and Ranulf de Gernons," 561; Navel, "Recherches sur les institutions féodales en Normandie," 127; Navel, "L'Enquête de 1133 sur les fiefs de l'évêché de Bayeux," 28 n. 26, 29 n. 36; *CP* iii. 164–7; Cronne, "Ranulf de Gernons, Earl of Chester," 105, 109; see Genealogical Chart, xxi.

[38] *OV* v. 210 & n., 211n., vi. 428 & n., 429n.; Pezet, "Les Barons de Creully," 312–13; Beziers, *Histoire sommaire de la ville de Bayeux*, 220; Navel, "L'Enquête de 1133 sur les fiefs de l'évêché de Bayeux," 23 n. 2. See also Haskins, *Norman Institutions*, 120; Gleason, *An Ecclesiastical Barony*, 23–5.

[39] See Chapt. 1, 16; Chapt. 2, 44; Chapt. 3, 57, 68–9.

## The Making of a Super-Magnate 63

The earl of Gloucester's strength in the Bessin also seems to have been bolstered by holding the office of *bailli* or *prévôt* of Caen—perhaps like the *vicomte*'s situation at Bayeux.[40] Robert before 1138 certainly controlled (if not held) the office. A pancarte of that year issued by his son Richard bishop of Bayeux mentions the earl's gift of a prebend belonging to the office (*prefectura*) of the priory of Sainte-Marie Ardenne, near Caen.[41] The earl also appears to have, at the very least, functioned as castellan of Caen in 1138, when he, with a complement of 100 knights, kept the castle from falling to King Stephen's partisans.[42] Consequently, it appears that Robert's office, titled or de facto, like the later administration of Caen under Earl Robert's nephew Henry II, combined military with domainal functions.[43] Such authority in the ducal town may have been more valuable to the earl than the income from his wife's patrimonial estates.[44]

Caen was emerging as the second ducal capital. The then duke, William, had begun *c*.1060 to enclose the town with a wall and had a palace built, the walled enclave of which included a two-storied rectangular hall measuring 8 m × 16 m, residential chambers, and the chapel of Saint-George. He and Duchess Matilda further enhanced the site by founding in new suburbs between 1059 and 1066 the two great abbeys Sainte-Trinité and Saint-Étienne, dedicated on, respectively, June 18, 1066 and September 13, 1077. Henry I added the keep *c*.1120, which became the meeting-place for his justices, and another hall called the Hall of the Exchequer, measuring inside 30.70 m × 11.2 m.[45] The end result, as Professor David Bates has noted, was a prime example of calculated urban development to enhance ducal rule.[46]

Exactly how Caen's bailliage came to Robert through his Fitz Hamon marriage is uncertain. The most detailed account is that of the canon of Bayeux, Wace, of about 1155. According to the poet-historian's *Roman de Rou*, while campaigning for the king in the Bessin against Duke Robert Curthose in 1105, Fitz Hamon purchased four prominent burgesses of Caen from their captor, one Robert de

---

[40] Yver, "Les Châteaux forts en Normandie," 45.
[41] AD du Calvados, H.1; *Gallia Christiana* xi. Instr. IX, 77–8; *Neustria Pia*, 703; it is possible that, since the grant was made for his father's soul, it occurred *c*. Dec. 1135. A house in Caen confirmed to the priory in 1154 by Henry fitz Empress may have been related to Earl Robert's grant: *Regesta* iii. no. 22. The priory began as a chapel founded by Aiulphus a Foro and his wife Asselina in 1121. The great church was dedicated by the bishop of Bayeux in 1138 and was the occasion for producing the pancarte: *Neustria Pia*, 702. For the *prévôté* (*prepositura*) of Caen, see Musset, *Les Actes de Guillaume le Conquérant et de la reine Mathilde pour les abbayes caennaises*, nos. 11–12; *RADN*, nos. 171–2; correct "district" in Patterson, *EGC*, no. 192.
[42] *OV* vi. 516–17.
[43] See Stapleton, *Magni Rotuli Scaccarii Normanniae Sub Regibus Angliae* i. xxxi–xxxii & n., xxxv; *Pipe Rolls of the Exchequer of Normandy for the Reign of Henry II 1180 and 1184*, 41; Powicke, *Loss of Normandy*, 50–8, 72; Böuard, *Le Château de Caen*, 12; Boussard, *Le Gouvernement d'Henri II Plantegenêt*, 332–3.
[44] In 1180 Henry II's seneschal for Normandy was allowed £1,000, the equivalent of some £250 in English pounds sterling, from the farm of this office and similarly £300 (£75) for custody of the castle: *Pipe Rolls of the Exchequer of Normandy for the Reign of Henry II 1180 and 1184*, 40–1.
[45] Böuard, *Le Château de Caen*, 10, 12, 63, 66–70; Yver, "Les Châteaux-forts en Normandie," 54, estimates the walls' date as *c*.1058. See also Bates, *Normandy before 1066*, 115. For the foundation and dedication dates of the two abbeys, see Musset, *Les Actes de Guillaume le Conquérant et de la reine Mathilde pour les abbayes caennaises*, 13–15; see also n. 46.
[46] Bates, *Normandy before 1066*, 178; Chibnall, *OV* iii. 8 n. 5, 12 n. 1.

Saint-Remi-des-Landes. The lord of Torigni and Creully then gave the men to Henry I in return for the *garde* (bailliage) of Caen. The king in turn persuaded the men by promises of rewards to arrange the town's surrender to him; and upon the plot's success fulfilled his bargain with Fitz Hamon and made the bailliage a heritable fief.[47]

Aside from the improbability of Fitz Hamon's gaining any position at Caen from Henry by haggling with him, other elements of Wace's story also may be the product of artistic license. Orderic, the most attentive of contemporary chroniclers to details of Henry I's capture of Caen, mentions nothing of Fitz Hamon's bargaining, of the king's promises to the captive burgesses, or of the measures the conspiratorial burgesses took to achieve Caen's surrender. In fact, Orderic attributes the town's surrender to the residents' fear of suffering the destruction which befell Bayeux for failing to surrender to Henry.[48] Henry of Huntingdon only supports the bribery element of Wace's tale in his fleeting comment that Henry won Caen by money.[49] Finally, if Fitz Hamon did gain something at Caen from the king, he only enjoyed it briefly. According to William of Malmesbury, Fitz Hamon, soon after Henry's seizure of Caen in 1105, was wounded in the head fighting for the king at the siege of Falaise and survived incapacitated mentally until 1107.[50]

The largest number of estates, and the most valuable in feudal terms, which came to Robert with Mabel's marriage were in England and Wales. They belonged to, respectively, the later earldom's honors of Gloucester and Glamorgan and the latter's dependency, the lordship of Gwynllŵg. Fortunately, both for the purpose of revealing Robert's baronial physique and for accounting for his ability to support his later military leadership in the Angevin war against Stephen, these are the best known.

The original "endowment" of Robert's English honor of Gloucester was estates his father-in-law had acquired from William II and Henry I. A major group confiscated after the Norman Conquest from the great Saxon thegn Beorhtric fitz Algar gave the honor a Severn Valley and southwestern topographical orientation. It included large estates like Tewkesbury, Thornbury, and Fairford in Gloucestershire,[51] Hanley Castle, with Malvern and Bushley in Worcestershire,[52] Iddisleigh, Littleham,

---

[47] Wace, *Roman de Rou* ii. pp. 299–301, ll. 11163–11238, esp. ll. 11233–11236; *CP* v. 683. David, *Robert Curthose*, 166n., gives a summary of Wace's story including King Henry's grant of Caen as a fief to Fitz Hamon and his heirs. See also Gleason, *An Ecclesiastical Barony*, 23; Aird, *Robert Curthose*, 233.

[48] *OV* vi. 78–9 & n. [49] Henry of Huntingdon (1996), 452–3.

[50] *GR* i. 722–3. See Hollister's commentary on this passage: *Henry I*, 189n.

[51] *DB Gloucestershire* (Phillimore), 1.24–39, 47, 50; *PR 1 John*, 35; Patterson, *EGC*, nos. 46, 179. For Beorhtric's estates, see Williams, "A West-Country Magnate of the Eleventh Century: The Family, Estates and Patronage of Beorhtric Son of Algar," 41–67, esp. 63–7. For an estate which seems to have been granted first to Sainte-Trinité of Caen: *Regesta* i (1998), no. 65; *DB Devon* (Phillimore), 1.13.1; see Map 2, 240.

[52] *DB Gloucestershire* (Phillimore), 1.34; WoC4; *DB Worcestershire* (Phillimore), 2.30–1; E4; EG1; *EEA* xxxiii. nos. 85, 131; *Regesta* ii. no. 1413.

and Winkleigh in Devon,[53] Ashmore, Cranborne, and Frome St. Quintin in Dorset,[54] and Binnerton and Crowan, Connerton in Gwithian, and Trevalga (Meledam) in Cornwall.[55] These estates had been reserved as an appanage for Queen Matilda, but after her death in 1083 were kept in the royal demesne. Although they had been earmarked for Henry, his brother King William Rufus gave them instead to his favorite, Robert fitz Hamon. One reason was to reward Robert for his and his family's loyalty during the baronial revolt of 1088 against the king's succession.[56] Other estates of the honor of Gloucester formerly held by the queen, such as Mapledurham in Hampshire and Marlow in Buckinghamshire, also may initially have come to Fitz Hamon.[57] The total Domesday value of all of Queen Matilda's demesne estates that Mabel fitz Hamon brought to the king's son has been estimated to be about £500.[58]

Other components of the English honor the king's son came to enjoy were estates confiscated from Domesday-era Anglo-Norman super-magnates. In Cornwall, Breage, Phillack, and possibly Sancreed came from William count of Mortain.[59] However, far more important were "contributions" from Geoffrey bishop of Coutances and the Conqueror's half-brother, Odo bishop of Bayeux. Either after Geoffrey's death in 1093 or most likely after William Rufus's confiscations c.1095 from Geoffrey's heir, Robert de Mowbray, came the honor's most strategically and economically important holding, the castle-borough of Bristol, the finest port in the southwest, with its Gloucestershire suburban Barton[60] and many other former Coutances manors like the 112 acres of meadow and woodland at Bedminster (Som.) across the river Frome from Bristol.[61] Adjoining the Barton were the hamlets of Mangotsfield, Stapleton, and Easton (later, St. George).[62]

---

[53] *DB Devon* (Phillimore), i.1. 61, 63–4; *CPR Henry VII* ii. 94; *Mon. Angl.* v. 259.

[54] *DB Dorset* (Phillimore), 1.15–17; PRO, E.132/2/13, m.1; *CPR Henry VII* ii. 94; Patterson, *EGC*, no. 179.

[55] *Mon. Angl.* ii. 69; iv. 335; *DB Cornwall* (Phillimore), 1.5, 14, 16–17; *EEA* xi. no. 139n.; *VCH Hampshire*, iii. 86; Picken, "The Feudality of Pendrim Manor," 126, 133. Matilda's other Cornish estates were at Carworgie and Codford Farleigh (alias Coswarth): *DB Cornwall* (Phillimore), 1.15, 18; tenure of these last two by Fitz Hamon or Earl Robert has not been established. Earl Robert also held Sancreed and Germoe; Picken, "The Descent of the Devonshire Family of Willington from Robert Earl of Gloucester," Appendix, no. 1 & n., 102, 104.

[56] *GR* i. 510–13; *OV* iv. 128–9, 220–1; see also Le Patourel, *The Norman Empire*, 345 & n.

[57] *DB Hampshire* (Phillimore), 1.8; Marlow may have included estates at Great (Bishop of Bayeux) and Little (Queen Matilda) Marlow: *DB Buckinghamshire* (Phillimore), 4.18; 52.1; Patterson, *EGC*, nos. 66, 166; *Chron. Abingdon* ii. 96.

[58] *GOE*, 57; Chapt. 1, n. 91.

[59] *DB Cornwall* (Phillimore), 5.4.17; 5.12,3. Sancreed was located in the hundred of Penwith and would have belonged to Alverton (*DB* (Phillimore), 5.1,11 & n. See also Picken, "Descent of the Devonshire Family of Willington from Robert Earl of Gloucester," Appendix no. 1.

[60] BA, 5139 (487): *EEA* xxxiii. no. 85; *Mon. Angl.* ii, no. 87, p. 81; Cronne, *Bristol Charters*, 24–6; Walker, *Bristol in the Early Middle Ages*, 9; Walker, "Bristol under the Normans," 102, claiming Queen Matilda as Bishop Geoffrey's predecessor; against this, see Sharp, *Bristol Castle*, "Appendix I," 68–9 & nn. Fitz Hamon's chaplain Robert held Bristol's church of St. Peter and granted it to Tewkesbury Abbey: BAO, 5139 (238).

[61] *DB Somerset* (Phillimore), 1.7; *Regesta* iii. no. 1000; *BF* i. 42.

[62] BA, 5139 (487); *EEA* xxxiii. no. 85; *CPR Henry VII* ii. 94; Cronne, *Bristol Charters*, 20–4, 43; Walker, *Bristol in the Early Middle Ages*, 8–9; Sharp, *Accounts of the Constables of Bristol Castle*, xvii–xviii, xxxvi–xxxvii, xlvii–xlix.

Other Gloucester manors from the Coutances–Mowbray source stretched from the southwest to the Midlands; for example, Sowton (alias Clyst Fomison) in Devon,[63] Barrow Gurney in Somerset,[64] Wingfield in Wiltshire,[65] Winterborne in Dorset,[66] Finmere and Shelswell in Oxfordshire,[67] and in Northamptonshire, manors such as Addington Parva, Barton Seagrave, Cranford, and Raunds.[68]

Contributions to the honor of Gloucester also came from estates confiscated from Bishop Odo of Bayeux. In Oxfordshire, Finmere and Burford are of particular interest. Burford became a valuable demesne manor through early development. The vill was located at a convenient eastern approach to the Cotswolds, prime sheep-raising country, and connected by major roads with Oxford to the east and Gloucester and Malmesbury to the west and southwest, respectively. Fitz Hamon realized its potential for manorial income from commerce and promoted it, as did his immediate Gloucester family successors.[69]

Finmere provides a case of manorial consolidation. After the Conquest, the vill had been partitioned unequally between Geoffrey of Coutances and Odo of Bayeux. But the first two Norman kings' policy of utilizing the two bishops' former estates to endow new barons resulted in the vill's institutional "reunification" as a single manor either under Robert fitz Hamon or Henry I's son Robert.[70]

Henry I added at least one manor to the honor by summarily imposing Robert fitz Hamon as lord upon an incumbent tenant-in-chief. The king used this tactic to reward Fitz Hamon at the expense of William Mauduit I at Fyfield in Hampshire. As a result, Fitz Hamon's successor, the king's son Robert, could command William de Eynesford and his wife to perform service for the manor to William Mauduit II as mesne lord.[71] Aisthorp in Lincolnshire, held by Robert before he became earl of Gloucester, was another of Henry's feudal rearrangements. The king's son appears in the Lindsey Survey of *c*.1115 as tenant of a mesne lord, William Turniant, one of the two sons and heirs of the sheriff of Lincolnshire and Yorkshire, Osbert the priest, who died about the same time. Aisthorp may have come to Robert as his

---

[63] *DB Devon* (Phillimore) i. 3.93; ii. 3.93.   [64] *DB Somerset* (Phillimore), 5.32.
[65] *DB Wiltshire* 5.3; *VCH Wiltshire* vii. 70–1; Professor Richard Sharpe's study makes less likely the claim of Hollister, "Magnates and 'Curiales' in Early Norman England," 70, that Rufus kept Mowbray's inherited Coutances English honor in his hand until his death.
[66] *DB Dorset* (Phillimore), 5.1–2; *BF*, 750.   [67] *VCH Oxfordshire* i. 427; vi. 286.
[68] *DB* i. 220b; *VCH Northamptonshire* i. 309; "Northamptonshire Survey," 377, 388–9.
[69] *DB Oxfordshire* (Phillimore), 7.36; PRO, C47/45/388a, no. 1.; Stenton, "The Road System of Medieval England," 241; see also Chapt. 4, 101.
[70] *DB* i. 155b, 221 (listed under Geoffrey's lands in Northants.); *VCH Oxfordshire* vi. 117; *VCH Northamptonshire* i. 312.
[71] Patterson, *EGC*, no. 152 & n.; *Regesta* ii. nos. 1719, 1255 & n.; but note Mason, *Cart. Beauchamp*, xxvii, nos. 161–3 & n. Henry I acted similarly with Nigel d'Aubigny: *Charters of the Honour of Mowbray*, xxv & nn. For Mauduit, see *DB Hampshire* (Phillimore), 5.9; *VCH Hampshire*. iii. 158; iv. 366; White, "Financial Administration under Henry I," 60–2; Richardson & Sayles, *Governance*, Appendix iii, 429–36; *Winchester*, 9n., 17, 41–3, 370, 390; Hollister, "Origins of the English Treasury," 213, 215–16, 221; Hollister, "Rise of Administrative Kingship," 235; Barlow, *William Rufus*, 148 & n.; *GOE*, 261–2, 247 & n.

posthumous father-in-law's successor, as certainly was the case at nearby Marston.[72] However, another possible scenario is that after Turniant succeeded Osbert, Henry I seized Turniant's lands for failing to fulfill an agreement with him to pay for inheriting a priest's lands; then, while Aisthorpe was in his hands, the king gave the estate to Robert.[73]

Elements of the future earl of Gloucester's honor such as Bickmarsh in Warwickshire,[74] Chaddesley Corbet and Eldersfield in Worcestershire,[75] Kemerton, Marshfield, and Oxenton in Gloucestershire,[76] Keynsham in Somerset,[77] Luton in Bedfordshire,[78] Great Gransden in Huntingonshire,[79] and Kilkhampton[80] in Cornwall were former *terrae regis*. Two manors in Suffolk belonging to the mother of the Saxon Earl Morcar which became *terra regis* probably were granted by William Rufus to Fitz Hamon. Cornard was given by Robert fitz Hamon with one of his daughters to St. Mary's Malling; and burghal Sudbury belonged to Fitz Hamon's Gloucester heirs.[81] So did Kingston-Buci with Southwick (Sussex), which Fitz Hamon and his wife Sibyl utilized for a residence.[82]

Another substantial proprietary windfall came Robert's way after his wife Mabel's uncle, Haimo II *dapifer* and sheriff of Kent, died without direct heirs by the late 1120s. Henry I then divided Haimo's English honor between Robert, *iure uxoris*, and the *dapifer's* nephew, Robert de Crèvecoeur (Calvados) lord of Chatham (Kent) and heir of a former tenant of Bishop Odo of Bayeux. Gloucester owed his father nothing, so far as is known, for his wife's portion; however, de Crèvecoeur had to pay the king 250 marks to enjoy his share.[83]

---

[72] In the Domesday Survey the estate was held by Gilbert de Gant: *Lincolnshire Domesday*, 24/1, p. 105. Fitz Hamon's brother Haimo II *dapifer* also held an estate in Bradley Wapentake. *Lincolnshire Domesday*, L9/1, p. 248; *Regesta* ii. no. 1930; *CRR* i. 263; *BF* ii. 1064; Patterson *EGC*, no. 236. Aisthorpe, along with Marston, passed to Herbert, chamberlain of David king of Scots, *iure uxoris* William Turniant's niece Milicent, whom Henry I had given in marriage to Herbert: Clay, *Early Yorkshire Families*, 13. See Chapt. 1, 19.
[73] *Chron. Meaux* i. 86–7: Turniant had failed to pay what he had pledged to the king for inheriting the lands of a priest.
[74] *DB Warwickshire* (Phillimore), 43.2; *EEA* xxxiii. no. 85.
[75] *DB Worcestershire* (Phillimore), E6; 28.1; *CPR Henry VII* ii. 94; *BF* i. 139.
[76] *DB Gloucestershire* (Phillimore), 1.20, 25, 41; *CPR Henry VII* ii. 94; *EEA* xxxiii, no. 85.
[77] *DB Somerset* (Phillimore), 1.28; Winchester Cathedral Library, MS XXB, pp. 64–5: Vincent, "The Early Years of Keynsham Abbey," Appendix 1, p. 106; *PR 33 Henry II*, 163.
[78] *DB Bedfordshire* (Phillimore), 1.2a–b, 3; 40.1; 57.4; *Gesta Abbatum Monasterii Sancti Albani* i. 113; *VCH Bedfordshire* ii. 350.
[79] *DB Huntingdonshire* (Phillimore), 1.5; Patterson, *EGC*, no. 71; *VCH Huntingdonshire* ii. 297, 301.
[80] *DB Cornwall* (Phillimore) 1.5; *CPR Henry VII* ii. 94; Patterson, *EGC*, no. 179.
[81] *Regesta* ii. no. 791. See *DB Suffolk* (Phillimore), 1. 97–8. A daughter Fitz Hamon gave to St. Mary's Malling was either one of the two Henry I made abbesses, Cecilia of Shaftsbury and Hawisia of Romsey, or a fourth unnamed one: Green, "Robert fitz Haimon," 119; Knowles, *HRH*, 219, 222. The estate at Cornard which had belonged to Earl Morcar's mother was the one which came into Fitz Hamon's hands; for other manorial segments there, see *DB Suffolk* (Phillimore), i. 14.29; ii. 25.43; 43.4; and 76.4.
[82] BL, Add. MS 36985, fol. 5; Patterson, *EGC*, no. 177 & n.
[83] *GND* ii. 248–9. *PR 31 Henry I* (Green), 51–2; Douglas, *Domesday Monachorum*, 55 & n., 56. For Robert, Mabel fitz Hamon's first cousin, see *Calendar of Charter Rolls* ii. no. 2, 300; *Regesta* ii. nos. 1222, 1255–6, 1283; Sanders, *English Baronies*, 31; Loyd, *Anglo-Norman Families*, 35–6; Colvin,

From Haimo II *dapifer* the king's son gained estates with a Domesday value of about £128. Their locations extended his English honor into Kent, Essex, and Surrey, and added to its presence in Lincolnshire by reason of manors held in chief of the king and of mesne lords.[84] Along with these acquisitions came the services and feudal dues of fifteen honorial tenants with quotas totaling almost twenty-three knights.

Robert's share of Haimo's barony in Kent consisted at least of tenancies held in chief and of the archbishop of Canterbury. Land in Canterbury for which he was pardoned 10s. for *auxilium civitatis* and valuable Mereworth with a Domesday income of £19 passed to Robert's honor of Gloucester probably before 1135 as a tenancy-in-chief.[85] Furthermore, in Canterbury, Earl Robert held both the castle and perhaps appurtenant land in the bailey just inside Worthgate seemingly as Haimo's successor as royal castellan.[86] Eltham, a former mesne tenure held of Odo bishop of Bayeux, had a Haimo origin.[87] Brasted and Milton were held of the archbishop; both belonged to a group of five estates Earl Robert's heir William held for the service of three knights.[88]

Robert's accumulated demesne, enfeoffed vassals, and particularly control of the strategic royal castles of Dover and Canterbury must have made him the dominant political figure in Kent by his father's death. There were times in the late 1120s and early 1130s when William I de Eynesford and his son were sheriffs there that Robert enjoyed some claim to their loyalty. Both were the earl's honorial tenants; and although they were minor ones, Robert is known to have had a long-standing jurisdictional relationship with them. Furthermore, one of the two Williams was indebted to Robert for having assumed financial responsibility for his proffer for the county, likely the shrievalty or enjoyment of other royal rights.[89] By 1138, if not earlier, Earl Robert also gained at least three important allies among the Kentish lay baronage who supported his rising against King Stephen: William Peverel of Dover, successor to three Domesday tenants of Bishop Odo, William's nephew and the

---

"A List of the Archbishop's Tenants by Knight-Service in the Reign of Henry II," 11–12; Eales, "Local Loyalties in Stephen's Reign: Kent," 91, 96–7; Navel, "L'Enquête de 1133 sur les fiefs de l'évêché de Bayeux," 29 n. 45.

[84] Hollister, "Magnates and 'Curiales' in Early Norman England," 76. Haimo sheriff held Tooting (Surrey) of the abbot of Chertsey: *DB Surrey* (Phillimore), 8.25.

[85] *DB Kent* (Phillimore), C1; 1.1–3; 2.16; 12.1–4; *RBE* i. 190. In 1129–30, Haimo also had held the city apparently at farm for the king: *VCH Kent* iii. 206a–b; see also Urry, *Canterbury under the Angevin Kings*, 41. In 1130 Rualon the sheriff owed the farm: *PR 31 Henry I* (Green), 50; later in the pipe roll appears the account of the *auxilium* owed but pardoned: the archbishop of Canterbury, £11 12s.; Earl Robert, a mere 10s.: *PR 31 Henry I* (Green), 53.

[86] *OV* vi. 516–17. Haimo gave Leeds Priory land in the castle area just inside Worthgate: Urry, *Canterbury under the Angevin Kings*, 214–15.

[87] *DB Kent* (Phillimore), 5.30, 96; *Mon. Angl.* vi. pt. 1, 452–3.

[88] Colvin, "A List of the Archbishop of Canterbury's Tenants by Knight-Service," 6, 11; *VCH Kent* iii. 212b; *Domesday Monachorum of Christ Church Canterbury*, 36, 81–2, 103, fol. 7r.

[89] *PR 31 Henry I* (Green), 51; *RBE* i. 289; Patterson, *EGC*, no. 152 & n,; *GOE*, 212, 247; for the important Eynesford genealogy, see Douglas, *Domesday Monachorum*, 44–7. Sheriffs as a rule did not have custody of royal castles; *GOE*, 122–3. Paul Latimer provides an excellent example of the income from royal rights, the county [*comitatus*], of Shropshire being given by Henry I to Queen Adeliza in 1126: "Grants of 'Totus Comitatus' in Twelfth-Century England," 140; the evidence for Kent is problematic; see also Davis, *King Stephen*, 3rd edn., 140.

earl's undertenant, Walchelin Maminot, and Robert de Crèvecoeur, Gloucester's first cousin by marriage and co-beneficiary of the Haimo *dapifer* inheritance. All had lands elsewhere and reasons for abandoning their allegiance to Stephen, but shared a potential common association with Earl Robert in Kent, which might explain why they followed his political lead in supporting Matilda. All three owed ward-service to Dover castle, which was under the earl's authority. Thus, Dover castle under Maminot's immediate command rose against Stephen in 1138, just as it had refused admission to him as an uncrowned claimant in 1135. And Leeds castle, which belonged to Robert de Crèvecoeur's lordship of Chatham, yet reportedly Earl Robert's in 1138, was his probably because Crèvecoeur supported him.[90]

King Henry's division also brought his son some of Haimo II's extensive holdings in Essex as a tenant-in-chief. In the Pipe Roll of 1129–30 Robert appears forgiven for a past aid (*auxilium civitatis*) due from his demesne in Colchester. In the *dapifer*'s day the estate's Domesday contents included a house, courtyard, fifteen burgess tenants, and an appurtenant hide's-worth of land. Elsewhere, among the most valuable of Haimo's other manors which became tenancies of Robert's honor, were Greensted, Little Wigborough, and Stambourne, together with Toppesfield.[91]

Several of the honor of Gloucester's subinfeudations in Surrey show Robert's and Mabel's succession to her uncle's estates there as well. Haimo's manor at Camberwell (Surrey) was used by Earl Robert to enfeoff Robert of Rouen;[92] Rotherhithe, which in 1086 belonged to Camberwell, made Osbert Eightpence of London one of the earl's military tenants.[93]

Robert's English honor is notable for its urban holdings. Most of these locations are revealed in the Pipe Roll of the Exchequer year 1129–30 from the aid called *auxilium civitatis* forgiven him from these places. There are no entries for Bristol, Tewkesbury (Glos.), or Burford (Oxon.). Even so, the total sum for which he was pardoned was the highest among his fellow super-magnates, at least partial evidence of his standing as England's premier lay baronial urban landlord.[94] Bristol, a late Anglo-Saxon *burh* which had been part of the Domesday royal manor of Barton Regis, had been entirely "mediatized" by King William Rufus to Robert's

---

[90] *OV* vi. 518–19 & n. (but mentioning Peverel's Shropshire castles); *The Chronicle of Battle Abbey*, 140–1; Henry of Huntingdon (1996), 712–13, 718–19; Robert of Torigny, "Chronica," 134–5. For the ward-duty owed to Dover castle, see *RBE* ii. 615, 617; key discussions of castle-guard are in Round, "Castle Guard," 144–59; Painter, "Castle-Guard," 450–9; Hollister, *The Military Organization of Norman England*, 136–66. Colvin, "A List of the Archbishop of Canterbury's Tenants by Knight-Service in the Reign of Henry II," 12; Hugh de Crèvecoeur, who was a fellow honorial baron with Earl Robert of the bishop of Bayeux, held one knight's fee of Gloucester deriving from former Haimo *dapifer*'s fee in Kent: *RBE* i. 190; ii. 645; *RHG* xxiii. 699–700.

[91] For the *auxilium civitatis*, see Chapt. 2 n. 99; *DB Essex* (Phillimore), 28.9, 11, 13, B3b; for examples of Gloucester subinfeudations, see Patterson, *EGC*, nos. 71, 115, 174; *Rotuli de Dominabus et Pueris et Puellis*, 80n.; *CRR* iv. 261; *VCH Essex* iv. 59. Colchester, the city, fortifications, tower, and castle had been given to Eudo *Dapifer* (d. 1120) by Henry I in 1101: *Regesta* ii. no. 552.

[92] *DB Surrey* (Phillimore), 30.2; *Mon. Angl.* iv. 393–4; *VCH Surrey* iv. 28.

[93] *DB Surrey* (Phillimore), 30.2; *Mon. Angl.* v, 87; *RBE* i. 189; *VCH Surrey* iv. 87.

[94] For the *auxilium*, see *Dialogus de Scaccario*, 108–9; Mitchell, *Taxation in Medieval England*, 244, 259–60, 264–5; Hoyt, *The Royal Demesne in English Constitutional History*, 112–15; *GOE*, 76. Whether the *auxilium* was based on size of population or of land, alternatives pointed out by Green, does not affect the status of those indebted for it, or forgiven it, as landlords. See Appendix 3.1, also Map 2, 240.

father-in-law as its landlord. Tewkesbury and Burford were both developing burghal manors which had been confiscated by the king from their former tenants before being granted to Robert fitz Hamon.[95] North of Bristol, Earl Robert had burghal holdings at his titular capital and county town Gloucester[96] and close by at Winchcombe (Glos.), where its only pardoned aid was Earl Robert's.[97] In Wiltshire at Salisbury he had a presence at the headquarters and episcopal seat of the administrative head of his father's government, Bishop Roger.[98] Robert's status was quite different at nearby Winchester (Hants.), the Anglo-Norman realm's administrative capital. There, among royal *curiales* and local landlords the amount for which the earl was pardoned was only surpassed, in ascending order, by the chancellor Geoffrey Rufus, the sheriff of Hampshire and chamberlain of the treasury William de Pont de l'Arche, the chief justiciar Roger of Salisbury, and the king's nephew Henry bishop of Winchester.[99] South of London at Guildford in Surrey the earl's pardoned city aid of a mere 2s. suggests a very small tenurial presence.[100] Within London Robert held one of the town's sokes; it must have been sizeable property and only slightly less than Roger bishop of Salisbury's.[101] Further east in Canterbury (Kent), the primatial seat, the aid forgiven Earl Robert suggests holdings assessable at less than one-twentieth the amount of the archbishop's.[102] North in Essex at Colchester, as just seen, Robert's landed interests perhaps were about double what they were in Gloucester.[103]

Another distinctive feature of Robert's honor was its concentration in six Severn Valley and southwestern shires where just about 60 percent of its geldable demesne lay in 1130. The earl had a proprietary presence by 1129–30 in every one of the twenty-four southern and southwestern English shires, including and fully south of Lincolnshire, Norfolk, Cambridgeshire, Huntingdonshire, Northamptonshire, Warwickshire, and Worcestershire. However, its major concentration was in Gloucestershire (22 percent), Somerset (6 percent), Wiltshire

---

[95] *DB Gloucestershire* (Phillimore) 1.21, 24–6, 34–5, 37–9; *DB Oxfordshire* (Phillimore), 7.36; Cronne, *Bristol Charters*, 20–4; Patterson, "Bristol: An Angevin Baronial Capital under Royal Siege," 171–2. See also Chapt. 4, 94, 101–2.
[96] *DB Gloucestershire* (Phillimore), G1, G4; Evk1; Ellis, *A General Introduction to Domesday Book* ii. 447n.; *PR 31 Henry I* (Green), 62–3; in s.xiii, the estate was considered a soke: *PR 5 John*, 40.
[97] *DB* i. 162c; Ellis, *A General Introduction to Domesday Book* ii. 446n. –7n.; *PR 31 Henry I* (Green), 62–3.
[98] *PR 31 Henry I* (Green), 16, 18; Kealey, *Roger of Salisbury*, Chapt. 2, 82–6; *GOE*, esp. 5, 38–50, 273–4.
[99] *PR 31 Henry I* (Green), 32; *Winchester*, Survey I, no. 96; Survey II, nos. 139 & n., 475; Patterson, *EGC*, nos. 102–3; for Pont de l'Arche, see *GOE*, 267–8; esp. Hollister, "The Origins of the English Treasury," 215; Hollister, "Rise of Administrative Kingship," 881. Note that Fitz Hamon's and later the earldom of Gloucester's holdings were in different parts of Winchester.
[100] *PR 31 Henry I* (Green), 40: paid into the treasury, 84s.; the earl of Gloucester forgiven 2s. and owed 14s.
[101] *PR 31 Henry I* (Green), 116, 118, *auxilium civitatis* for 1129 pardoned for Roger, £8 10s.; for Earl Robert, £7 5s.; *DB* i. 2; *OV* vi. 516–18; *CPR Henry VII* ii. 94; Patterson, *EGC*, no. 179; listed, *EEA* xv. no. 229; *PR 3–4 Richard I*, 306.
[102] *PR 31 Henry I* (Green), 53.
[103] *DB Essex* (Phillimore), B3b; *PR 31 Henry I* (Green), 62, 109; for Gloucester, see n. 96 and Appendix 3.1.

(8 percent+), Dorset (15 percent), Devon (7 percent+), and Cornwall (2 percent). As will be seen, in this proprietary heartland were located some of the honor's most valuable demesne manors.[104]

Most of the residential and administrative centers the earl utilized lay in Gloucestershire. Bristol, together with Barton Regis, Robert developed as his baronial capital.[105] He gave increased substance to Gloucester as his titular city some 35 miles to the north, when more than being landlord of his posthumous father-in-law's former burgesses, he could hold feudal courts to which the de facto hereditary royal constable of the castle felt compelled to pay suit, and he acted as *patronus* of its great Benedictine abbey St. Peter's.[106] Robert kept Tewkesbury, a further 11 miles on, more as a major retreat. Although he sponsored both an emerging borough and *Eigenkloster*, Benedictine St. Mary's Abbey, he never built a castle to complete the ideal baronial triad. Instead, within easy reach of the hunting around Hanley Castle and Malvern Chase, he maintained a great hall where his sergeanty tenant Richer of Eldersfield (Worcs.) likely served at table clad in red stockings on Christmas Day.[107] All three centers were connected via the river Severn and by the Roman Bristol–Gloucester–Tewkesbury–Worcester–Chester road.[108] The great Domesday manor of Cranborne (Dors.), where Robert occasionally resided with Countess Mabel and his household, held court, and enjoyed the benefits of Tewkesbury's priory and hunting, was accessible by main and secondary roads connected to the nearby ports of Southampton (Hants.) and Wareham (Dors.), and to regional hubs like Dorchester (Dors.), Ringwood (Hants.), Marlborough (Wilts.), Salisbury, and Winchester.[109]

Rich demesne resources from Bristol's Barton also were readily available to the east of the castle past the market and beyond the Lawfords Gate; and farther south beyond Brislington lay Keynsham on the Avon toward Bath.[110] Thornbury was just off the Roman road about 13 miles north of Bristol, and huge 21-hide Fairford (Glos.), about 7 miles east of Cirencester (Glos.) and about 9 miles south of the demesne's eastern salient at Burford (Oxon.).[111] Fairford was close to the

---

[104] Davis, *King Stephen*, 3rd edn., 13n., cited a hidage total for the honor of Gloucester I have revised since writing Patterson, "William of Malmesbury's Robert of Gloucester." See Appendix 3.1 and also Chapt. 2, 33 & n.

[105] Patterson, *EGC*, no. 119; BL MS Sloane 1301, fol. 227v; *OASPG*, xxi–xxxii, 12; Patterson, *EGC*, nos. 82–4; Barton Regis apparently could yield over £22.5 at the beginning of the thirteenth century: *PR 3 John*, 53; £40 19s. 5 ½ d. in 1261–2: PRO, C.132, file 27–5, m.41. For Bristol's development, see Chapt. 4, 95–9, 101–2.

[106] Patterson, *EGC*, nos. 83, 110; Moore, "The Evesham MSS and 'Evesham K'," G1–4; see also Chapt. 4, 116–17.

[107] *JW* iii. 282–3, for the "magnificam domum": Patterson, *EGC*, no. 216; Jones, "The Borough of Tewkesbury," 110; Le Patourel, *The Norman Empire*, 317–18. See also Chapt. 4, 99, 102–3.

[108] Unless otherwise noted, references to roads are based on Stenton, "The Road System of Medieval England," Hindle, *Medieval Roads*, and Ordnance Survey Maps.

[109] Patterson, *EGC*, no. 157, 283; see also Chapt 4, 93–4.

[110] *DB Gloucestershire* (Phillimore), 1.21; Sharp, "The Barton," in *Bristol Castle*, xxxvi–lxiii; *DB Somerset* (Phillimore), 87 a, a.

[111] For Thornbury and Fairford, see *DB Gloucestershire* (Phillimore), 1.47, 50. For the earl's management of his demesne, see Chapt. 4, esp. 94–105.

Bristol–London road, which went toward Oxford through Malmesbury and Faringdon and then on to London via Oxford, Tetsworth, High Wycombe, and Uxbridge. From Tewkesbury (Glos.), Bushley with Pull (Worcs.) west of the Severn would have been within easy reach. Hanley and Malvern (Worcs.) were a few miles farther north.

Regional subinfeudations for vassals made from the Gloucester honor prior to 1136 added bulk to the demesne's heartland. There are good reasons to believe that lands in Bristol belonging to the baronies of Odo Sor (15 knights' fees), Richard of St. Quintin (10), Gilbert of Umfraville (9), and Richard Foliot (4) had been enfeoffed to them by then.[112] Odo's father Robert, Richard's predecessor Herbert, and, I believe, Gilbert all had been enfeoffed under Robert fitz Hamon, albeit elsewhere.[113] Richard Foliot died before the end of 1135 and had been succeeded in his Gloucester fee by his son Robert.[114] Elsewhere in Gloucestershire were Sor, de la Mare (10), Maisi (9), Oriescuilz (10), and Foliot estates.[115] William fitz John of Harptree (10), Roger Witeng (7), and Robert de Gurnay (9), and possibly Odo Sor were established in Somerset; the large sub-honors of William fitz Odo of Torrington (10) and of Walter Clavill (10) in Devon; Guuiz (5) and Waspail (5) estates in Dorset; and Roger Waspail (5) in Wiltshire.[116] And it was not uncommon for such honorial tenants to be landlords in multiple shires of the heartland.

Nevertheless, the "heartland" was no homogeneous domain. Interspersed with both Robert's and his honorial tenants' estates were important holdings of other landlords: in Gloucestershire Walter fitz Richard de Clare of Striguil (Chepstow) held demesne valued at 49 hides; and Miles of Gloucester the hereditary sheriff, 105.5 hides. In Dorset, Roger bishop of Salisbury's lands were almost double those of Robert; and Walter of Salisbury, William Martel, and Waleran count of Meulan held demesne estates in the 80-hide range. In Wiltshire, Roger of Salisbury's demesne dwarfed Robert's; the bishop of Winchester's was more than double in size; and both Robert earl of Leicester and Walter of Salisbury's were about half the size of Gloucester's.

The accumulated assets of the honor of Gloucester alone made the once landless royal bastard Robert a super-magnate, to borrow Warren Hollister's felicitous label.

---

[112] All held Gloucester honorial baronies by the end of 1135: *RBE* i. 288–92: also *Liber Niger Scaccarii* i. 53–4, 161–4; *Cart. Bristol*, no. 72, a charter of Robert fitz Harding (d. 1171), granted his son Maurice Bristol properties held of the baronies of Richard Foliot, Richard of St. Quintin, and Gilbert of Umfraville; for Odo Sor, see Patterson, *EGC*, no. 121; Patterson, "Robert Fitz Harding of Bristol," 110; Patterson, "Bristol: An Angevin Baronial Capital under Royal Siege," 173 & n.; see also Chapt. 4, 100.

[113] *Cart. Abingdon* i. L 122, p. 75, L 123, p. 76; *Regesta* ii. no. 813. For Robert Sor, see *Mon. Angl.* ii. no. xxxix, p. 71.

[114] *RBE* i. 291; *Liber Niger Scaccarii* i. 164; note a charter of Foliot's widow Beatrice: *Cart. Bristol*, no. 586; see Chapt. 4, 100, 105.

[115] e.g., *EEA* xxxiii. no. 84 (Sor); *PR 5 Richard I*, 118 (Oriescuilz); *Ancient Charters*, no. 45 (de la Mare); *PR 31 Henry I* (Green), 62 (Maisi); BCM, Select Charter no. 15: Jeayes, *Descriptive Catalogue of the Charters and Muniments*, no. 15; Cheney, *Roger, Bishop of Worcester*, Appendix I, no. 33 (Foliot). See also: *RBE* ii., e.g., 429, 485.

[116] *RBE* ii. 558–9 (Torrington; Clavill); 485 (Waspail); *Rotuli Normanniae* i. 8–9 (Fitz John); *CIPM* iii. 249 (Gournay); *PR 9 John*, 220 (Witeng); *Cart. Forde*, nos. 619–20, 625 (Sor).

## The Making of a Super-Magnate 

In W. J. Corbett's classification of Conquest-era feudal lords according to their worth, the earl was one of only three class AA barons; the other two were Bishop Roger of Salisbury and Stephen of Blois count of Mortain.[117] Robert ranked second of the three. According to the Exchequer roll surviving from Henry I's reign for the year 1129–30, Robert's English geldable demesne, on the basis of past and current pardons for the dues, contained a total of about 2,443 hides, with exemptions of about £244; in 1130 alone, approximately 1,229 hides, with £123 forgiven. However, the accounts of Worcestershire and Somerset, where the earl held demesne, are missing from the roll; so the earl's hidage and geld exemption totals for both past and current danegelds probably should be higher by about 192 hides and £19. Furthermore, if barons' geld exemptions for the *auxilium civitatis* are considered, Robert's would grow by a combined 782*s*. 8*d*. for the two assessment periods or by 351*s*. 4*d*. for the one for 1130. Robert of Gloucester's adjusted grand total for that year would be 1,501 hides, below Roger of Salisbury's 1,585 and well above Stephen of Blois's possible 1339.[118] Among English tenants-in-chief whose lands were exempted from danegeld and the *auxilium civitatis* in 1130, only Gloucester's £140 and Roger bishop of Salisbury's forgiven £158 featured such enormous amounts.[119] Translating hidage into acreage produces demesnes for Roger, Robert, and Stephen, respectively, of 190,200, 180,120, and 160,680. In other indications of wealth suggested by the number of their enfeoffed knights in England, Earl Robert's roughly 282 were only surpassed by Stephen's possible 291.[120] While there is no way to accurately calculate the ranking of the three relative to each other, Robert and Stephen were about equal and probably both outranked Bishop Roger.[121] In any case, Robert stood well above class A potential allies and rivals like the earls

---

[117] Hollister, "Henry I and the Anglo-Norman Magnates," in *MMI*, 178; William John Corbett, Chapt. XV, *The Cambridge Medieval History*, reprn. edn. (Cambridge, 1957), 510–11. For Robert's pardons, see Appendix 3.1; for Stephen's and Roger's, see Chapt. 2, nn. 100–1.

[118] For Worcestershire, see Bushley with Malvern forest, Eldersfield, Hanley Castle, and Queen Hill with total Domesday hidage of 11 hides and mentioned in a confirmation charter of Earl Robert's son William: *DB Worcestershire* (Phillimore), 2.30, 36; E4.44; E5.45; E6.46; Patterson, *EGC*, no. 281. For Somerset, the earl of Gloucester's son Robert in 1154–5 was forgiven danegeld equivalent to 85 hides: *PR 2 Henry II*, 31; Keynsham, alone, had a possible Domesday value of some 50 hides (*DB Somerset* (Phillimore), 1.28). I have included sums forgiven for *auxilium civitatis* in calculating Robert's and Stephen's hidage. See also my former estimate in Patterson, "William of Malmesbury's Robert of Gloucester," 994 n. 41. Professor Davis's list of Stephen's geldable demesne, uses both past and current danegeld exemptions: *King Stephen*, 3rd edn., 8; see *PR 31 Henry I* (Green), 10 & n.

[119] Davis, *King Stephen* (1967), 8–9; 3rd edn., 13n. Stephen was pardoned £69; Kealey, *Roger of Salisbury*, 96, *Appendix 4*; Hollister, "Henry I and the Anglo-Norman Magnates," in *MMI*, 178 & nn.; Keefe, *Feudal Assessments*, 97, 173, 190, 243 n. 70.

[120] To calculate Earl Robert's fees owing service in England c.1135, I have counted those created before Henry I's death ("old fees") and those constituting the earl's share of his wife's late uncle Haimo II dapifer's barony (259.50 plus 22.83 "Kent fees"): *RBE* i. 189–90, 288–91; *Liber Niger Scaccarii* i. 161–5; Douglas, *Domesday Monachorum*, 55 n. 16. However, Earl Robert may not have enjoyed the service of all 282 knights in England. Later evidence shows that at least 39 (which could be 41) fees were held in Robert's two Welsh lordships and the service of 5 fees was due in Normandy: *PR 33 Henry II*, 142; *PR 2 John*, 57; but see also *RHG* xxiii. 715; Bishop Roger had 40.5 fees: I disagree slightly with Professor Thomas Keefe's total for the earl of Gloucester as of 1166; however, I have relied upon his evidence for Roger and for Stephen's English honors of Boulogne, Eye, and Lancaster: Keefe, *Feudal Assessments*, 158, 97, 173; 164 & n., 169 & n., 176 & n.

[121] See Davis, *King Stephen*, 3rd edn., 8, 13 n.

of Chester and Warwick, Richard of Clare, Stephen of Richmond, Baldwin de Redvers, and Brian fitz Count.[122] The age of the class of immediate post-Conquest super-barons like Odo of Bayeux, Robert of Mortain, Roger de Montgomery, and Hugh earl of Chester had long passed. Ranulf II earl of Chester, whose post-Conquest predecessor Earl Hugh had enjoyed English holdings in 1086 rated at 8,901 hides with a value of £890, was now in the second rank.[123]

There are no records contemporary with Robert to indicate what his vast honor de Gloucester yielded in annual income. However, its manorial income alone could range as high as £784 during the Exchequer year 1183–4, when Earl Robert's granddaughter and the earldom's heiress Isabel was in King Henry II's wardship. When we consider that the same source which passed to Robert *iure uxoris* yielded a total Domesday income of probably at least £564, it is difficult not to see the earl's estate management policies, which will soon be discussed, behind some of the increased income.[124] Bristol undoubtedly was Robert's greatest source of income, and its ready cash yields must have been a major asset for the administrative center (*caput honoris*) he was developing there. Robert certainly recognized the burghal manor's financial potential and promoted it. During Isabel of Gloucester's wardship Bristol produced between 17 percent and 23 percent of the honor of Gloucester's total income.[125]

Robert's final territorial dividends gained from his Fitz Hamon marriage were two adjacent lordships in South Wales, Glamorgan and Gwynllŵg, roughly across the Bristol Channel from Bristol. The political, military, and economic value of the two to the king's son probably would have been considerable by 1135 even if late twelfth-century reports for their military and financial yields, 47 knights and almost £226, are divided by half, seemingly extreme adjustments.[126] Both lordships also would be fertile grounds for recruiting native mercenaries. Their two fortified *capita* ports, Cardiff and Newport (Monm.), must have solidified, if not completed, Robert's domination of the Bristol Channel and lower Severn Valley, and reinforced his position in the southwest of England.

The two lordships had not been built up in the ways Robert's English honor had, but had been carved out from territory which Robert fitz Hamon and his men had conquered from native Welsh princes in Gwent and the former kingdom of Morgannwg with King William Rufus's blessing. Military conflicts with the Welsh,

---

[122] Hollister, "The Aristocracy," 46–8; Hollister, "Henry I and the Anglo-Norman Magnates," in *MMI*, 178–87.
[123] Lewis, "The Formation of the Honor of Chester," 42. See also Barraclough, "Earldom and County Palatine of Chester," 12; Hollister, "The Aristocracy," 47–8.
[124] *PR 34 Henry II*, 109–10; Latimer, "Estate Management and Inflation: The Honor of Gloucester," 191 & n. 18. The honor's gross income from all sources could reach £845: *PR 33 Henry II*, 14–16, 135, 163; Professor Painter, *English Feudal Barony*, 70 & n., underestimated the honor's income; for demesne income derived from Robert fitz Hamon and Haimo II *dapifer*, see *GOE*, 57; Chapt. 1 and in this chapter, 57. For Isabel of Gloucester, see Patterson, "Isabella Countess of Gloucester," 416.
[125] Painter, *Feudal Barony*, 166. See Chapt. 4, 95, 100, 102.
[126] For the Exchequer year 1184–5 during the wardship of the earldom of Gloucester's heiress Isabel, £121 13s. 7d. from Glamorgan, £100 3s. 5d. from Gwynllŵg: *PR 31 Henry II*, 5–6; scutage exempted for 47.25 knights' fees in the two lordships in 1202: *PR 4 John*, 283; see Map 2, 240.

as well as the Scots, were part of the Anglo-Saxon inheritance of Anglo-Norman kings; and King Edward the Confessor instituted a system to defend part of the frontier with Wales which prefigured William the Conqueror's later Marcher lordships. In 1051 he installed his French nephew Ralph of Mantes as earl of Hereford to defend the province; and Ralph in turn settled vassals, Richard fitz Scrob, Osbern Pentecost, and one Hugh, as regional castellans served by corps of mounted knights at Richard's Castle, Ewias Harold, and apparently Hereford. Edward's measures, however, were both temporary and more defensive than colonial. The Conqueror's were just the opposite.[127] His three Marcher lordships, the earldoms of Chester, Shewsbury, and Hereford, all became expansionist and colonizing in nature.

In the lower Severn Valley William I's first earl of Hereford, William fitz Osbern, already had pushed across the lower Wye and established himself on the southwestern side with Chepstow castle before his death in 1071. The king himself made an armed expedition to St. David's in 1081 and established a vill (*villa*) at Cardiff, some kind of fortified settlement likely by the remains of a Roman fortress on the east bank of the river Taff. The fledgling site was stable enough for a mint to be established there which issued William I's pennies and then Henry I's up to *c*.1135.[128]

William apparently had no ambition for conquest of the region. He was satisfied with obtaining acceptance of his Cardiff base from southwest Wales's hegemonic prince Rhys ap Tewdwr; in return, Rhys won the king's recognition of his personal status for an annual payment of £40. However, King William Rufus encouraged more aggressive action against the Welsh. The policy change may have emerged from consultations with his *familiares* at Gloucester in early 1093. Then, the death of Rhys ap Tewdwr at the hands of Bernard of Neufmarché, conquistador of Brecon, toward the end of April likely unleashed a new wave of Norman conquistadores on South Wales. In the words of the *Brut y Tywysogyon*, "Rhys ap Tewdwr, king of the South, was slain by Frenchmen who were inhabiting Brycheiniog—with whom fell the kingdom of the Britons."[129] Robert fitz Hamon would have been a natural choice to lead a campaign of conquest beyond the Usk along the south coast. He was a favorite of Rufus and, with Bristol and his other demesne "heartland" territories, particularly those in Gloucestershire, he possessed the perfect base and available resources for such a mission.[130]

While Bernard de Neufmarché was establishing his lordship of Brecon from the conquered kingdom of Brycheiniog, Fitz Hamon seized lands along coastal plains in lower Gwent from the son of Caradog ap Gruffydd, Owain Wan, and in the

[127] See Lloyd, *History of Wales* ii. 357–78, 392–459; Barlow, *William Rufus*, 320–1; see also the useful study of Walker, "The Norman Settlement in Wales," 131–43.
[128] "Ann. Margam," *a*.1081; Crouch, "Slow Death of Kingship in Glamorgan," 27–8; Hague, "The Castles of Glamorgan and Gower," 426–7; Blackburn, "Coinage and Currency under Henry I," 70–2.
[129] *Brut y Tywysogyon*, *a*.1093 (as corrected), p. 19; Smith, "Kingdom of Morgannwg," 8–11; Crouch, "Slow Death of Kingship in Glamorgan," 27–9; see also Babcock, "Rhys ap Tewdwr, King of Dehebarth," 21.
[130] Barlow, *William Rufus*, 73, 77, 85, 321; for the king's encouragement of Fitz Hamon, see also Crouch, "The Transformation of Medieval Gwent," 17–18.

adjacent kingdom of Morgannwg at the expense of its prince, Iestyn ap Gwrgant. Territory between the Usk and Rhymney rivers he enfeoffed to a Robert de la Haye and it became known as the lordship of Gwynllŵg; between the Rhymney and Ogmore rivers Fitz Hamon established his own domain, called the Shire Fee.[131]

Exactly how he accomplished this feat is not known; an amphibious attack from Bristol or elsewhere in Gloucestershire is one possibility; an expedition by land through Gwent with a crossing at the ford of the Severn at Gloucester, another.[132] While little credence can be given to the tradition preserved by the Welsh antiquarian Rhys Merrick that Fitz Hamon achieved his conquest with the help of twelve knights, William de Londres, Richard de Grainville, Pain de Turberville, Robert de St. Quintin, Richard Seward, Gilbert de Umframville, Raymond de Sully, Roger Berkeroles, Peter Sor, John Fleming, Oliver St. John, and William Esterling, some members of these families do appear to have been involved.[133] Gilbert de Umfraville, Herbert de St. Quintin, and Robert Sor attested Fitz Hamon's charters as his vassals, and their families, along with the de Londres of Ogmore, were among the earliest established lords in the lordship of Glamorgan during the twelfth century: the de Londres of Ogmore, Sors of St. Fagan, and Umfravilles of Penmark, as tenants of the Shire Fee, Fitz Hamon's domain; and the Grainvilles of Neath, St. Quintins of Talyfan, Turbervilles of Coety, by reason of seizing land in the Upland dominated mostly by the Welsh, in time as semi-independent Member lords in Glamorgan's own March.[134]

In the Shire Fee Robert fitz Hamon may have transformed an earlier fortification of William the Conqueror at Cardiff into a motte-and-bailey castle to serve as his headquarters or *caput*. The motte, with base and top diameters of, respectively, 250 and 90 feet, rose to a height of some 20 feet and utilized the remains of the Roman fortress for curtain walls. Demesne estates at Llantwit, Roath, and Leckwith provided immediate support. One of Fitz Hamon's charters granting a branch of the river Taff to Tewkesbury Abbey (Glos.) mentions a borough which would have developed under his aegis; and another grant in favor of the abbey involving St. Mary's church and tithe of Cardiff's revenues suggests probable rents and taxed commercial activities there before his death in 1107.[135]

With no prior Saxon or Anglo-Norman royal demesne, sheriff, or shire court in Morgannwg, Fitz Hamon was able to establish his new lordship as a private shire,

---

[131] Smith, "Kingdom of Morgannwg," 6–8; possibly not the Norman *curialis*; d.s.p. based on marital and tenurial evidence: Clark, *Cartae et alia* i. no. 35; Patterson, *EGC*, nos. 156–7; *Cart. Gloucester* ii. nos. dix–dxi; Crouch, "Slow Death of Kingship in Glamorgan," 21–30, 33.

[132] Nelson, *Normans in South Wales*, 106–7; Smith, "Kingdom of Morgannwg," 10. On the obscurity of the process, see Crouch, "Slow Death of Kingship in Glamorgan," 29.

[133] Merrick, *A Booke of Glamorgan Antiquities*, 29–30.

[134] *Mon. Angl.* ii. no. lxxxvii, 81; *CPR Henry VII* ii. 94; *Chron. Abingdon* ii. 96; *RBE* i. 288–9; Smith, "Kingdom of Morgannwg," 17–22–3, 27–8; Richard de Grainville held land of Maurice (de Londres of Ogmore) and a mill with multure at Pendoylan (Glam.) of Richard de St. Quintin as lord of Llanblethian by 1130: Birch, *Neath Abbey*, Appendix II, p. 309.

[135] *CPR Henry VII* ii. 94; Clark, *Cartae et alia* i. no. XXXIV; Walker, "Cardiff," 111; Griffiths, "Medieval Boroughs of Glamorgan and Medieval Swansea," 335; Hague, "The Castles of Glamorgan and Gower," 427; Pounds, *The Medieval Castle in England and Wales*, 7, 158; Grant, *Cardiff Castle, its History and Architecture*, 25–8, 51.

likely resembling that of Earl Hugh of Avranches and his immediate successors, who had *totus comitatus* in their county of Chester. That involved receiving all royal demesne, except for rights over the bishopric of Chester, gaining control of the shrieval office, and utilizing the shire court also as an honorial one.[136] In neo-colonial Glamorgan all land was held either by Fitz Hamon as demesne or of him as dependent fees; and his newly created court, called the county court or court of Cardiff, enjoyed jurisdiction over his vassals' feudal issues;[137] its chief officer, the sheriff, was under his authority.[138] Several of Earl Robert of Gloucester's charters addressed to the current bishop of Llandaff and sheriff of Glamorgan indicate that there were occasions when the two presided over the court together just as in Anglo-Saxon and post-Conquest England.[139]

After Robert became Glamorgan's lord, his vigorous effort to subject all freemen within the Shire Fee to the jurisdiction of his court caused a major conflict with the bishop of Llandaff, Urban (1107–33). One of the bishop's ambitions was to be lord of an independent episcopal barony with jurisdiction over his own tenants. Such a goal would have been abhorrent to Robert, given his lordship's seigniorial tenurial model; but, as will soon be seen, he and the bishop would work out a compromise under the king's auspices with the bishop a vassal, but also a quasi-Member lord.[140]

Earl Robert succeeded in expanding his predecessor's conquests west of the river Ogmore, at least along the coastal lowland, the *Bro Morgannwg*, to the east bank of the stream Afon Cynffig; near its mouth he established Kenfig, a fortified demesne settlement.[141] Robert certainly claimed as demesne the area farther on between the Afon Cynffig and the river Avan known as Margan or Morgan, much of which he used as foundation endowment for his *Eigenkloster* Margam Abbey, even though one possible reason for the foundation may have been the tenuousness of his control.[142] His Shire Fee also may have reached the east bank of the river Neath, possibly at Briton Ferry (West Glam.) and slightly upriver, where the earl more likely built a castle and installed his Devon tenant Richard de Grainville as constable. A demesne castle and borough were there when Robert's son William was earl.[143] Richard founded Neath Abbey in 1130 from lands across the Neath he had seized from the Welsh for his own Member lordship, which included a castle-borough

---

[136] Barraclough, "Earldom and County Palatine of Chester," 9–11; Lewis, "Formation of the Honor of Chester," 37–8, 43, 45; Crouch, "Administration of the Norman Earldom," 70; Latimer, "Grants of 'Totus Comitatus' in Twelfth-Century England," 137.

[137] Clark, *Cartae et alia* i. no. XXXV; *Cart. Gloucester* ii. no. DIX; see also *Regesta* ii. nos. 1307 & n., CXLIV.

[138] For the view that acquisition of regalian rights came from the Anglo-Normans' conquests of Welsh kingdoms, see, e.g., Edwards, "The Normans of the Welsh March," 169–75; against this view, see Davies, "Kings, Lords and Liberties in the March of Wales," 44–7, 53–61; Davies, "The Law of the March," 13–14; Crouch, "Slow Death of Kingship in Glamorgan," 20–2. See also Birch, *Neath Abbey*, no. IIA*e*, 324–6; Patterson, *EGC*, no. 246: a charter of Earl William of Gloucester conferring regalian rights on Neath Abbey (West Glam.) is a forgery: Birch, *Neath Abbey*, 50.

[139] Patterson, *EGC*, nos. 68, 84; 119 (sheriff alone).

[140] Patterson, *The Scriptorium of Margam Abbey*, 8–9. See Chapt. 4, 122–3.

[141] Patterson, *EGC*, no. 68.    [142] Patterson, *The Scriptorium of Margam Abbey*, 11.

[143] Patterson, *EGC*, nos. 159 & n., 242, 246: identification of *ponte* in no. 246 is uncertain; Birch, *Neath Abbey*, 48, identified the site as Llandeilo-Talypont or 58n., Llandeilo-Talybont; Hague, "Castles of Glamorgan and Gower," 432; *PR 31 Henry II*, 5–8, 155; Birch, *Neath Abbey*, 227–32.

called, like the earl's, Neath.[144] Service as the earl's constable would have given de Grainville the logical opportunity for his ultra-riparian conquests.

Even if Earl Robert was successful in this Neath demesne venture, it is likely that his Shire Fee's military and administrative control of the Vale, considering the buffer-zone purpose of Margam Abbey's foundation, ended around the river Afan, where he had fisheries.[145] The foundation charter's designation that his grant to the monks started at the lip of the mountains in effect recognized his Shire Fee's northern limits. In former Morgannwg's upland, the *Blaenu Morgannwg*, the native princes not only successfully resisted further Anglo-Norman conquests, but their potential threat must have led both de Grainville and Earl Robert to make agreements with them at some point in hopes of warding off raids or, even worse, major counter-attacks. David Crouch has suggested that fighting among the native princes in 1127 occurred at least partly in reaction to Anglo-Norman pressure and that further Anglo-Norman conquests in 1127 × 30 fueled major Welsh attacks on the colonists after Henry I's death in 1135.[146]

Robert's diplomacy must have led to the establishment of one or more native prince's lands as a Member lordship. Between the Afan and Neath rivers Caradog (*c*.1078–1148?), eldest son of Iestyn ap Gwrgant and married to a daughter of Gruffudd ap Rhys ap Tewdwr, ruled the Welsh lordship of Afan, or Afan Wallia. In addition to Afan, Caradog was overlord of three other lordships in the *Blaenau Morgannwg*, blocking Norman advance from west to east: Glynrhondda, Miskin, and Rhuthun. Farthest east, the lordship of Senghennydd was held by a member of the family of its mid-twelfth-century lord, Ifor ap Meurig, married to a daughter of Gruffudd ap Rhys ap Tewdwr.[147]

In the mountains of Gwynllŵg, Earl Robert as lord of Newport faced the formidable sons of the first successor-prince Owain Wan, Morgan and Iorwerth. By the end of 1136 the two had rolled up most of the lordship except for Earl Robert's *caput*, Newport. But instead of attempting total conquest they were amenable to an agreement which would legitimize their position. Robert, predictably anxious over conditions in Normandy and England associated with King Stephen's accession, needed hostilities to cease. So, possibly with Morgan taking the lead, the parties agreed to a *conventio* by which Robert was recognized as lord in return for his recognition of the brothers' conquests and an award of additional land at Rumney.[148]

The death of Henry I on December 1, 1135 changed the status of Earl Robert's far-flung lands. What had been accumulated for him and kept free from challenge

---

[144] Birch, *Neath Abbey*, 21–2, 36–7, 58, 323–4 (Appendix 2A.a, 2A.b).

[145] Patterson, *EGC*, no. 119.

[146] "Ann. Margam," 12; information about the agreements comes reportedly from the lost cartulary of Neath Abbey: Davis, *Medieval Cartularies of Great Britain*, 77–8; Merrick, *A Booke of Glamorganshires Antiquities*, 38–40, 49, 53; Smith, "Kingdom of Morgannwg," 30; Crouch, "Slow Death of Kingship in Glamorgan," 32–3.

[147] Lands granted by de Grainville were west of the river Neath to the Tawe; evidence for Earl Robert's agreement contains no territorial details, but Caradog's Member lordship extended from the Neath to the river Afan; Evens, "The Lords of Afan," 18–20; Smith, "Kingdom of Morgannwg," 24–7.

[148] Crouch, "Slow Death of Kingship in Glamorgan," 33–4; Crouch, *Reign of King Stephen*, 59; Crouch, "The Transformation of Medieval Gwent," 11.

under his father's benign eyes now became subject to his successor's confirmation and continued recognition. While security of tenure was becoming widely accepted in post-Conquest England, tenants-in-chief like Earl Robert might well feel that their holdings were at risk. As George Garnett put it, "the tenures...held of the last king might be deemed, strictly speaking, to have lapsed because the lord of whom they had held was dead."[149] Understandably, then, Robert, like most of the baronage in England, performed homage and fealty to Stephen in return for his recognition of, and expected continued support for, their lordships' tenure. As will be seen, the earl obtained the first element from King Stephen in early 1136, even though the two distrusted one another, but within less than three years, not the second, so the earl claimed. This in part justified his renunciation of his fealty to Stephen and championing of his half-sister Matilda's claim to their father's throne. Then, what had served as appanage for a curial baron now, particularly the southwestern and Severn Valley heartland of the honor of Gloucester, became the strategic backbone of support for the empress's cause in England.

---

[149] Garnett, *Conquered England*, 187; Stenton, *English Feudalism*, 161; Hudson, *Land, Law, and Lordship in Anglo-Norman England*, 107; Davis, *King Stephen*, 3rd edn., 151; however, regarding expected warranty by mesne lords, see *Hudson, Land, Law, and Lordship*, 54, 67–8, 71, 107; and 54 n. 181 for tenants-in-chiefs' jeopardy and, earlier, Holt, "Politics and Property in Early Medieval England," 57.

## APPENDIX 3.1

Pardons for Danegeld and Urban Aids in the Pipe Roll of Exchequer Year 1129–30

|  | | *Previous* | | *Current* |
|---|---|---|---|---|
| A. *Auxilium Civitatis* | | | | |
| | Cambridge | 7s. | p. 46 (36) | — |
| | Canterbury | — | | 10s. p. 68 (53) |
| | Colchester | 75s. | p. 138 (109) | 60s. p. 138 (109) |
| | Gloucester | 34s. | p. 79 (62) | 33/4 p. 80 (63) |
| | Guildford | — | | 2s. p. 52 (40) |
| | London | 145s. | p. 147 (116) | 104s. p. 149 (118) |
| | Salisbury | 25s. | p. 21 (16) | 12s. p. 23 (18) |
| | Winchester | 118/8 | p. 41 (32) | 116/8 p. 41 (32) |
| | Winchcombe | 26/8 | p. 79 (62) | 13/4 p. 80 (63) |
| | Totals | 431/4 | | 351/4 |

B. Danegeld

| | | | |
|---|---|---|---|
| Bedfordshire | 56s. | p. 103 (82) | 56s. p. 104 (83) |
| Berkshire | — | | 12s. p. 126 (99) |
| Buckinghamshire | 144s. | p. 101 (81) | 144s. p. 102 (81) |
| Cambridgeshire | 48s. | p. 46 (36) | 48s. p. 47(36) |
| Cornwall | 72/10 | p. 159 (126) | 72/10 p. 161(127) |
| Devon | 217s. | p. 156 (123) | 200s* p. 158 (124) |
| Dorset | 450s | p. 14 (11) | 450s. p. 16 (12) |
| Essex | 116/6 | p. 57 (45) | 116/6 p. 60 (47) |
| Gloucestershire | 613s. | p. 79 (62) | 613s. p. 80 (63) |
| Hampshire/Honor of Arundel | 32s. | p. 43 (34) | Membrane lost |
| Hertfordshire | 30/6 | p. 62 (48) | 30/6 p. 62 (49) |
| Huntingdonshire | 32s. | p. 48 (37) | 32s. p. 49 (38) |
| Kent | 41s. | p. 66 (52) | 41s. pp. 67–8 (53) |
| Lincolnshire | 16s. | p. 114 (90) | 16s. p. 121 (96) |
| Norfolk | — | | 22/2 p. 95 (75) |
| Northamptonshire | 20/9 | p. 84 (66) | 20/9 p. 86 (68) |
| Oxfordshire | 62s. | p. 4 (4) | 20s*. p. 5 (4) 68s. p. 6 (5) |
| Suffolk | 100/14 | p. 98 (78) | 102s. p. 99 (79) |
| Surrey | 128s. | p. 50 (39) | 128s. p. 51 (40) |

| | | | |
|---|---|---|---|
| Sussex | — | | 8s. p. 72 (56) |
| Warwickshire | — | | 10s. p. 108(86) |
| Wiltshire | 247/6 | p. 21 (16) | 247/6 p. 23 (18) |
| Totals | 2,428/3 | | 2,458/3 |

| | | |
|---|---|---|
| *Auxilium civitatis* | +431/4 | +351/4 |
| | 2,860 = 1,430 hides | 2,810 = 1,405 hides |
| Somerset DB demesne | +170/0 = 85 | 170/0 = 85 |
| Worcestershire demesne | 22/0 = 11 | 22/0 = 11 |
| Totals | 3,052 = 1,526 hides | 3,002 = 1,501 hides |

An asterisk indicates a missing or questionable portion; dashes, the absence of an entry for the earl of Gloucester. Subtotals with fractions have been rounded to the nearest whole numbers. Page numbers refer both to *PR 31 Henry I* and, in parentheses, to the new edition of Professor Judith A. Green.

# 4
# Feudal Baron

King Henry I's promotion of his firstborn son Robert produced one of the greatest of all Anglo-Norman feudal lords. Along with tenure of high office, lineage and land had been the major components of the nobility's successful rise in early eleventh-century Normandy. To its members, a lord's welfare meant not merely his family's perpetuation through male heirs, but successful provision for his sons and daughters, as well as use of them, particularly through marriage, to increase the family's social, economic, and political standing. Land was the aristocracy's great provider—of sites for castles and halls, manorial and feudal income, dowers, marriage portions, appanages, and services from tenants, particularly military ones, knights; development by shrewd landlords could increase its potential.[1] For viewing the baronial side of Robert of Gloucester family and land are the keys.

Robert prided himself on his royal lineage and broadcast the fact in his charters. The title he adopted in their address clauses stated that he was the king's son and his appended seals made symbolic reference to royal birth.[2] Mabel's family ties were alluded to in comital subinfeudations by referring to the lands as hers, as given with her permission or advice, or by Robert's confirming an action of her father.[3] Robert's rearing prepared him for the exercise of lordship which came with marriage to the Fitz Hamon heiress.

While there is nothing comparable known about Mabel's background, there is a hint of some involvement in the affairs of her father's honor which antedated her marriage. In 1105, months after a severe head wound received in attacking Falaise deprived Fitz Hamon of his senses, establishment of Tewkesbury Abbey's obedientiary system supposedly was accomplished in his presence and with his consent as founder, together with his wife Sibyl and daughter Mabel. Whatever may have been the real state of Fitz Hamon's health and whereabouts, Tewkesbury's record of the *Ordinatio* portrays mother and daughter attesting it as warranters, presumably as lady and heiress.[4] In any case, after marrying Robert she filled the subordinate role feudal custom dictated for married ladies. In the conventional phraseology in

---

[1] Painter, "Family and the Feudal System," 195–219; for the precariousness of baronial families and their holdings, see Holt, "Feudal Society and the Family in Early Medieval England: I. The Revolution of 1066," 193–212; Green, *Aristocracy of Norman England*, "Aristocratic Society," 327–60.

[2] Patterson, *EGC*, 24, e.g., nos. 166, 283; Archibald, "The Lion Coinage of Robert Earl of Gloucester," 72–3.

[3] Patterson, *EGC*, no. 119; Patterson, *The Scriptorium of Margam Abbey*, Appendix III, no. 271; *Mon. Angl.* ii, no. xxvii, p. 70: ref. *EEA* xxxiii, no. 85n. (as B text).

[4] BL, MS Cotton Cleopatra A.vii, fols. 96v–97r (mod. fol.): *Mon. Angl.* ii. no. lxxxvii, 81 (September 27, 1105); Knowles, *MOE*, 431–9, esp. 437; Cownie, *Religious Patronage in Anglo-Norman England*, 48–9; Hollister, *Henry I*, 189. For Robert, see Chapt. 1, 16–17.

which she was remembered by her family, Mabel was "a lovely and noble woman, a lady who was both obedient to her husband and blessed in being the mother of numerous and very fair children."[5] And what the historical record has preserved of her ambience supports this for a time. She visited various *capita* of their honors with Robert and could approve a transaction with him, attest his *acta*, and possibly issue them jointly with him. Also, some of her own inheritance was set aside for her by Robert, apparently as demesne; had she made grants of it during his life, she would have done so with his permission. On the other hand, evidence to be considered shortly shows that, in time under certain circumstances, she exercised seigniorial authority.[6] During her husband's captivity after the Rout of Winchester, she acted as regent; and in the *conventio* Robert made with Miles of Gloucester prior to departing for Normandy in 1142, he had Mabel not only warranting it by oath, but pledging to hold him to the agreement, as much as she could. If she failed it seems that she would take Robert's non-compliance to their honorial court for, presumably, tenants' withdrawal of service.[7]

With Robert and Mabel, there was no repetition of her family's dynastic catastrophe. Between c.1113 and 1134 the couple produced six children, the eldest William, four other sons, and one daughter, according to Robert of Torigny, writing within four years of Henry I's death.[8] The boys' names, William, Robert,[9] Richard,[10] Haimo,[11] and Roger, believed to be their youngest son,[12] and the girl's, Mabel,[13] honored ancestors from Robert's and Mabel's families. Robert also

---

[5] *HN* (1998), 8 & n., 9.

[6] Patterson, *EGC*, nos. 84, 156–7, 283; Glanville, VI.3; Patterson, *EGC*, nos. 31, 86, 167, 171; *EEA* xxxiii. no. 85n.

[7] Chapt. 5, 164.

[8] *GND* ii. 248–9, where the chronicler calls Mabel fitz Hamon "Sibyl"; but later changes the name to Matilda: Van Houts, *GND* i. lxxx. Robert's genealogical accuracy has been questioned: White, "The Sisters and Nieces of Gunnor Duchess of Normandy," 132; Van Houts, "Robert of Torigni as Genealogist," 215–33, effectively makes the case for his accurate genealogies; see also Van Houts, in *GND* i. lxxxiv, lxxxix. For the Gloucester progeny, but needing revision, see *CP* v. 686n.; see also Genealogical Chart, xxi.

[9] *EGC*, no. 171; Robert's tenure of family land in England, albeit acquired, argues for his legitimacy; see 85.

[10] *Chart. Chester*, nos. 121, 141, 148, 163–4, 176–7n., 180; *CP* v. 686n. Richard's legitimate birth is established by the fact that he became lord of Creully, his mother's patrimonial land. See 88.

[11] Haimo's being named for his mother's grandfather (or uncle) and designation as Earl Robert's son leaves little doubt: Caen, AD du Calvados, H.1 (*Neustria Pia*, 703); Patterson, *EGC*, no. 71 & n. Unlike his brothers, Robert and Richard fitz Count, Haimo, so far as is known, did not receive any family land; although he attested a *conventio* in Normandy involving the priory of Sainte-Marie d'Ardennes in 1138, he, like his brother Roger, was maintained in his father's household as late as 1147 and in his brother Earl William's before seeking the patronage of his cousin, King Henry II: Patterson, *EGC*, nos. 34–5, 71, 119, 280. See also 87.

[12] Illegitimacy would have been an impediment to Roger's later elevation to the episcopate; in a tradition incorporated into a late medieval text of William fitz Stephen's *vita* of Thomas Becket, Roger asserts that his mother was Mabel: *MTB* iii. 104; vii. no. 649, p. 258; Cheney, *Roger, Bishop of Worcester*, 6–7; see also *EGC*, nos. 34–5 & n., 119, 280; *The Letters of John of Salisbury* ii. no. 196. Roger seems to have been named for his maternal grandfather, Roger de Montgomery.

[13] *Chart. Chester* no. 122. Her chosen name in Chester charters is Matilda. John Horace Round, followed by Lewis Loyd, mistakenly believed that Earl Robert had another daughter Mabira (Mabel/Matilda?) who was the mother of Jordan de Chambernowne: *CDF*, no. 547; Loyd, *Anglo-Norman Families*, 26. The mother in question was the daughter of Earl Robert's son Robert and Hawisia de Redvers: AD du Calvados, 2.H.2, no. 767, fol. 137r; transcr. in PRO, 31, 8/140B, iii. no. 23, p. 23;

fathered two other sons, the already mentioned bastard Richard who became bishop of Bayeux,[14] and Philip, whose legitimate birth is suspect for reasons to be discussed later. Robert's family, like so many aristocratic ones, was an extended one. Legitimate and illegitimate children alike bore the patronymic "fitz Count" or "fitz Earl," often with the added qualifier "of Gloucester"; and even more distant relatives were identified this way.

The initial stage of the children's nurturing is completely veiled from us, although Roger seems never to have forgotten the influence of his mother. In time, Robert provided his sons with at least some elements of his own upbringing. The author of the *Gesta Stephani* reported that their martial skills had been honed through regular practice with arms, training which predictably would have been initiated by their father.[15] Exposure to the arts probably would have occurred at the appropriate age for each of the boys, possibly tutored by the household clerk, Master Picard. For Roger, the experience came at about age 10 in 1142. As his first cousin, the then King Henry II, reminded him years after he had become bishop of Worcester (1164–79), his uncle Robert, "the good earl," had the two of them educated at Bristol castle. They were tutored there between 1142 and 1144 by a certain Master Matthew in letters and good behavior.[16]

The Gloucester domestic household (*domus*) can be expected to have provided livery and maintenance for Robert's and Mabel's children when in residence.[17] The future earl William and his budding bachelor brothers Robert, Haimo, and Roger were recipients at various times, and the last three even after William succeeded their father (1147–83). Demesne estates, particularly honorial *capita* like Bristol, Cranborne, and Tewkesbury, plus possibly Fairford, appear to have been favored sites. Bristol served as a refuge for Earl Robert's supporters and one of his sons even in his absence.[18]

Appanages as mesne tenures also supported the family.[19] At the same time, as will be seen, there were limitations in Earl Robert's ability or willingness to "appanage" them. And the reactions of several sons, disappointed for either reason, reveal how violence could result. Countess Mabel received some of her own land at Rumney in Gwynllŵg. Robert gave their eldest, William, land at an unidentified

---

Bearman, *Redvers Charters*, no. 114n.; Picken, "The Descent of the Devonshire Family of Willington from Robert Earl of Gloucester," no. 6. G. H. White also believed that a Mabel, daughter of Earl Robert, married Aubrey de Vere: *CP* xi. 106n. Another Mabel supposedly married Gruffudd ap Ivor lord of Senghenydd: Clark, *Cartae et alia* i. 149n.

[14] See Chapt. 1, 12.

[15] *GS* (2004), 168; William fitz Stephen, "Vita S. Thomae," 104–5. For Picard, see Chapt. 4, 108.

[16] Details of this conversation survive in only one manuscript of William fitz Stephen's Life of Thomas Becket, BL, MS Lansdowne 398, fol. 30v: *MHTB* iii. 104; Gervase of Canterbury i. 125; Knowles, *Episcopal Colleagues of Thomas Becket*, 22 & n., 23; Cheney, *Roger, Bishop of Worcester*, 7–8 & n., 9; Cheney, "William fitz Stephen and his Life of Archbishop Thomas," 147–8; Barlow, *Thomas Becket*, 85.

[17] "Inventio S. Nectani Martyris," 411.

[18] *GS* (2004), 56–7; Fairford was a dower manor of Earl Robert's posthumous daughter-in-law, Countess Hawisia of Gloucester: Patterson, *EGC*, no. 2 & n. Earl Robert's domestic household (*domus*) and hall (*aula*) are mentioned in the "Inventio S. Nectani Martyris," 414.

[19] Holt, "Politics and Property in Early Medieval England," 11 & n. 49, 57.

Ashley in Gloucestershire, which the recipient later gave to St. James's Priory Bristol. However, there is reason to believe that this holding was but a small part of the Gloucester heir's larger assets. William as earl used language denoting previous possession in granting the priory, the Pentecost fair, prisage of wine, and customs from anything brought to Bristol by water.[20]

The earl also created an appanage for his namesake son. It consisted of estates from the honor of Gloucester in Somerset granted before the earl's death, but more likely at least after his espousal of the Empress Matilda's cause in 1138. Doubt expressed by Robert about his ability to warrant his grant of £20-worth of lands at Pawlett and £5-worth at Rowberrow (Som.) to Robert fitz Harding of Bristol suggests that the war was under way between his father's Angevin party and King Stephen's royalists. Robert's Somerset demesne contained some 85 hides, as it apparently was rated for danegeld at the start of Henry II's reign.[21] The earl's son also acquired land in Cornwall before his death prior to 1166, but the evidence of this acquisition, wording of his subinfeudation of Connerton to Richard Butler, shows that at the time Robert's brother Earl William of Gloucester was his mesne lord.[22]

Earl Robert provided his likely youngest son Roger (b. c.1134) with some landed maintenance after having supported him in his household. Archbishop Thomas Becket later described him as the somewhat precocious child of his father's old age, his favorite son, and dedicated from the first to the service of God. Following completion of his already mentioned instruction in the arts, Roger was aimed toward a future ecclesiastical career by being sent for further study in the schools of Paris. There in the 1150s he came under the influence of the distinguished theologian Robert de Melun.[23] Earl Robert and possibly later Roger's brother, Earl William, appear to have partly supported his advanced education by granting him the church and possibly the entire rich manor of Keynsham as a benefice.[24] Both master and

---

[20] Patterson, *EGC*, nos. 31, 35–7, 167; *Mon. Angl.* iv, 335, no. 1; *Cartae Antiquae Rolls 1–10*, no. 313; I am indebted to Prof. Nicholas Vincent for transcriptions of these materials. Ashley Down, just a mile or two north of the priory, may be the property in question: see *The Place-Names of Gloucestershire* iii. 94; see also i. 85; ii. 96; Walker, "The 'Honours' of the Earls of Hereford in the Twelfth Century," 176; *PR 2 Henry II*, 30, perhaps more provision for Countess Mabel.

[21] *Redvers Charters*, no. 111n.: *CPR Henry IV* iii. 15; Patterson, "Robert Fitz Harding of Bristol," 111; *PR 2 Henry II*, 31; *VCH Somerset* vi. 268; for Earl Robert's adoption of Matilda's claim to the throne, see Chapt. 5, 137–8; Chapt. 6, 178, 184–5.

[22] Bowles, *A Short Account of the Hundred of Pentwith in the County of Cornwall*, Appendix, no. 2, attested by his wife Hawisia de Redvers; contrary to Vincent, "Early Years of Keynsham Abbey," 95, n. 1., the donor was not Earl William of Gloucester's son Robert (d. 1166), whose wife was named Agnes: e.g., *PR 6 Richard I*, 96. The beneficiary of the charter, Richard Butler, Stephen de Beauchamp, mentioned in the text, and the witness Hugh de Loges all appear in another charter of Robert's son Robert along with his *sponsa* Hawisia de Redvers: *Redvers Charters*, no. 111. Contrary to Crouch, "Earl William of Gloucester and the End of the Anarchy," 69–70, 73, I believe that Earl Robert's son Robert, not Earl William's, was the more likely beneficiary of a charter of Henry II granting Eudo *Dapifer*'s fees in England and Normandy to his cousin Robert, son of the earl of Gloucester: Antony House, MS PG/B2/6, no. 3763: see also 89 & n. 47.

[23] Bodl., Tanner MS 3, fol. 3; *MHTB* vii. no. 649, p. 258; Patterson, *EGC*, no. 119; Cheney, *Roger, Bishop of Worcester*, 6–7 & n., 8–10; *EEA* xxxiii. xlviii–ix.

[24] Patterson *EGC*, nos. 34–5, 280; Cheney, *Roger, Bishop of Worcester*, 13. See also the foundation charter of Keynsham Abbey (Som.) published by Nicholas Vincent in which Earl William of

pupil were given English bishoprics by King Henry II in March 1163, Hereford to Robert and Worcester to Roger—his first cousin completing the patronage of his family and remembering its support for his mother and him.[25]

For contrast, there is Richard, also a bishop, not the last born but the first of Robert's sons. Unlike Roger, he could not in due course be supported by family land as an appanage because he was illegitimate.[26] His story ends up being as much about Henry I helping his son as providing an important benefice for his grandson. Assuming that Richard had satisfied the 30-year canonical age requirement for bishops in 1133, when his grandfather gave him the bishopric of Bayeux, then he was born by c.1104;[27] and the name of Richard's mother, Isabelle de Douvres, plus the likely whereabouts of Robert about this time, place his son's birth and infancy in the Bayeux–Caen area. Richard was no mere bastard product of one of Robert's bachelor escapades. Isabelle belonged to an old-time Bayeux ecclesiastical family which was as distinguished for its career successes as for its non-observance of clerical celibacy. She and her brother Bishop Richard II of Bayeux (1107–33) were the offspring of a priest's son, Samson de Douvres, bishop of Worcester (1096–1112), former ducal chaplain, archdeacon, and treasurer of the Bayeux Cathedral chapter and local large landowner. Samson's brother Thomas, who also served as the chapter's treasurer, became archbishop of York (1070–1100); Samson's son Thomas II held the see in 1109–14 after the pontificate of Gerard.[28]

Richard's childhood is a complete blank, but at some point King Henry provided him with a promising future by taking him into his service as a royal chaplain. The royal chapel was a virtual episcopal nursery.[29] Henry chose for his next opportunity to help his grandson and son Robert the death of Bishop Richard II in Easter week 1133. He immediately sent Robert to conduct an inquest of the bishopric's feudal holdings, but, I believe, also to influence the cathedral chapter to elect Richard. Robert and his father are known to have previously swayed Bishop Richard and the

---

Gloucester represents himself and his brother, then Bishop Roger, as equal (*pariter*) founders of the abbey: Vincent, "Early Years of Keynsham Abbey," Appendix I, 106.

[25] Roger had been in Henry's entourage in at least one of his Channel crossings in 1156: *Mon. Angl.* iv. no ix, pp. 538–9; Holt, *Acta of Henry II and Richard I*, 430H; Cheney, *Roger, Bishop of Worcester*, 9; Barlow, *Thomas Becket*, 85; Knowles, *Episcopal Colleagues of Archbishop Thomas Becket*, 22 & n., 23.

[26] As the earl's son: AD du Calvados, H.1: facsm. in D'Anisy, *Extraits* ii. Plate XXVII, fig. 1. See also *Cart. Bayeux* i. no. cii; *Gallia Christiana* xi. Instr. LXXVIII; for Richard's illegitimacy, see *OV* vi. 442–3; *Concilia Rotomagensis Provinciae* ii. 234.

[27] See Chapt. 1, 12.

[28] A necrology of Bayeux Cathedral mentioned the death of Isabelle, mother of Bishop Richard, son of the earl of Gloucester, on April 24: Beziers, *Histoire sommaire de la ville de Bayeux* (Caen, 1773), 220; *Journal de Verdun* (Oct., 1760), 276. *Neustria Pia*, 743: Du Monstier called Bishops Richard II and III, respectively, uncle and nephew; Navel, "L'Enquête de 1133 sur les fiefs de l'évêché de Bayeux," 23; Pezet, *Les Barons de Creully*, 312–13, claimed that Isabelle died at Bayeux in 1166; Gleason, *An Episcopal Barony*, 23–5; Barlow, *The English Church*, 58; Bates, *Normandy before 1066*, 97, 130, 261; *EEA* xxxiii. xxxvii–xxxix; Burton, *EEA* v. xxi–xxvi.

[29] *CDF*, no. 590; *Regesta* ii. no. 1909 (witness-list incompletely calendared); *OV* vi. 428 & n., 429 & nn., 442–3; Haskins, *Norman Institutions*, 120.

chapter to grant Robert custody of certain fees. The chapter probably nominated the earl's son and the king confirmed it.[30]

However, Henry had to intervene again. The archbishop of Rouen, Hugh of Amiens, refused to consecrate Richard because of his bastardy. Henry then put pressure on Pope Innocent II to dispense Richard from this impediment and command Hugh to perform the consecration. Hugh's maneuverings and the royal–papal exchanges played out for two years, but Richard got his position and Robert a compliant overlord in 1135.[31] However, a day of reckoning for the earl of Gloucester lay ahead under Richard III's successor, Philip de Harcourt (1142–63).[32]

Haimo first enters Gloucester family history in 1138 when he appears in Normandy with his half-brother Richard bishop of Bayeux and very likely his father at the bishop's dedication of the Premonstratensian priory of Sainte-Marie Ardenne (Calvados). On the same occasion Haimo attested a *conventio* made between the canons and a local priest about some property and his father also made a gift to the priory.[33] Haimo was likely a landless bachelor knight at the time and was maintained in the Gloucester household. Apparently Haimo continued to be supported in this way for the remainder of his father's life and even after his brother William's accession as earl.[34] Eventually, though, he must have felt the need to seek patronage elsewhere and joined his cousin King Henry's service, but he failed to live long enough to receive any; he was killed on the king's Toulouse campaign of 1159 waged to gain the county of Toulouse claimed as part of Queen Eleanor's inheritance.[35]

Lack of his father's patronage is the dominant theme of Philip's life. He may well not have been a *filius a legali coniuge*. His personal disability is suggested first by the fact that if Robert of Torigny's attribution of five sons to Robert and Mabel is correct, five legitimate ones can be accounted for without Philip.[36] Another reason for questioning his legitimacy is that although he campaigned vigorously for the Angevins during much of the war against King Stephen, his father Earl Robert never created any appanage for him; and he only acquired military command of Cricklade (Wilts.) and possibly of Cirencester (Glos.).[37] Philip evidently banked

---

[30] *Gallia Christiana* xi. 360–1; Chapt. 2, 39; there were, however, justices and custodians of the bishopric about this time addressed in a writ of King Henry witnessed solely by Earl Robert: *Regesta* ii. no. 1898.
[31] *OV* vi. 428–9, 442–3; Robert of Torigny, "Chronica," 124; *Concilia Rotomagensis Provinciae*, 234; Hollister, *Henry I*, 448–9.
[32] See esp. 123–4.
[33] AD du Calvados, H.1: *Neustria Pia*, 702–4; *Gallia Christiana* ix, Instrumenta XI, 78.
[34] Patterson, *EGC*, nos. 71, 119.
[35] Roger of Howden i. 217; Warren, *Henry II*, 83–8.    [36] *GND* ii. 248–9.
[37] *GS* (2004), 180–1; Crouch, *Reign of King Stephen*, 216–17 & n., believed that the Empress Matilda made Philip an earl to give him some status. Proof was the dating clause of a s.xiii^med calendared text of a letter sent by a Gloucester vassal to John bishop of Worcester (1151–7) in Tewkesbury Abbey's inventory of *acta*, BL MS Cotton Cleopatra A.vii; the clause as transcribed reads: *m'lto t'p're ant'q'm phillipp' Com(es)* [Philip Earl] *h'uit castellm de Chichelade et de Cirencestre'*: fol. 78v; *Mon. Angl.* ii. no. xxxix, 71. However, the *phillipp' Com'*, absent any confirming evidence from diplomatic or narrative sources, is best explained as an haplographic error of the calendaring scribe, whose eye skipped over the *fil'* before *Com(itis)* [son of the Earl] or even "fil" *Com(itis)* [*Glouc(estrie)*] [son of the earl of Gloucester] in the original. For examples of haplography see, e.g., Picken, "The Descent of the

so much on victory to gain landed wealth from among its spoils that when his father's military leadership and fortunes seemed to fail, he abandoned his father's party for the king's. Even then he may have had to rely on his own efforts to obtain a socially advantageous marriage; and the best he could do was an obscure unnamed niece of Roger III of Berkeley, a modest tenant-in-chief and minor vassal of his father.[38] A sudden and protracted illness ended Philip's notoriously violent career. When he recovered, the contrite earl of Gloucester's son joined the Second Crusade, probably became a Hospitaller, and died soon after.[39]

Another Richard, known during his lifetime as Richard fitz Count, was most likely legitimately born. He acquired a sub-tenure of his family's Norman honor, the lordship of Creully, which his father had ruled in 1128; he died in 1175, lord of Creully, a barony owing the duke of Normandy the service of three knights,[40] to which his firstborn son Philip and his other heirs would succeed, with Creully, not Gloucester, as their toponym.[41] How all of this came about began with another Gloucester family opportunistic rebel.

Sometime after Earl Robert repudiated his fealty to King Stephen in 1138 the earl or Countess Mabel most likely installed Richard at Torigni-sur-Vire—although Creully is another possibility—to wage war on Stephen and seize his Norman lands. Richard's brothers were utilized at Bristol and Wareham in similar roles. As a result Stephen's lands at Saint-Clair and Mathieu fell into the earl of Gloucester's hands and Stephen's tenant at Thaon and Villiers, William de Saint-Clair, had to recognize both Gloucester and Angevin overlordship.[42] Richard probably was involved because he later admitted harm he had done to the church of Bayeux during the Anarchy.[43]

---

Manor of Willington from Robert Earl of Gloucester," 110–12. For further discussion of Philip, see Chapt. 5, 174; see also Crouch and Trafford, "The Forgotten Family in Twelfth-Century England," 39, for possible proprietary remedy.

[38] *GS* (2004), 190–1; *RBE* i. 289; Sanders, *English Baronies*, 114 & n.; see Chapt. 5, 174–5.

[39] *GS* (2004), 190–1; Philip seems to have joined the contingent led by Hugh archbishop of Rouen in 1147: *CDF*, no. 98; Philip is the likely brother to whom Roger, then bishop of Worcester, referred as a Hospitaller during an argument with Henry II: William fitz Stephen, "Vita S. Thomae," *MTB* iii. 105.

[40] Robert fitz Hamon was lord of Creully: Wace *Le Roman de Rou* ii. ll. 11073–6, p. 286; Robert of Torigny, "Chronica," 269; two knights' fees held in 1133 of the bishop of Bayeux by the post-Conquest *curialis* Eudo *Dapifer* at Mathieu (Calvados) and Saint-Clair-sur-l'Elle (Manche) became part of the Creully barony of 3 knights belonging to Earl Robert's son Richard fitz Count: *RHG* xxiii. 694, 700; *RBE* ii. 644, 646; Navel, "Recherches sur les institutions féodales en Normandie," 140–1; Navel, "L'Enquête de 1133 sur les fiefs de l'évêché de Bayeux," 32 n. 76, 40; Powicke, *The Loss of Normandy*, 337–8; after Eudo died in 1120 Henry I gave his Norman fees, which included episcopal estates at Thaon (Calvados) and Villiers (Manche), to the future king, Stephen of Blois; their undertenants in sequence were the brothers William and Haimo de Saint-Clair, who during the Anarchy recognized Gloucester and Angevin overlordship: BN, MS latin nouvelle acquisition 1022, nos. 211–14, 216, fols. 191–2; *Cart. Colchester* ii. 153–7; Farrer, *Honors and Knights' Fees* ii. 287–8; Loyd, *Anglo-Norman Families*, 88–9; see also Map 1, 239; these holdings might have formed at least part of the lord of Creully's third fee, but one Earl Robert also held there could have been a component: *RHG* xxiii. 633, 694; Patterson, *EGC*, no. 6 & n.

[41] *Cart. Bayeux* i. nos. cclxxiii–cclxxiv; e.g., Delisle-Berger ii. no. 757; NA, PRO 31, 8/140B, i. no. 14, pp. 106–7; ii. no. 4, pp. 90–1; *CDF*, no. 1454, p. 535; *CP* v. 686n: See also n. 40.

[42] Patterson, *EGC*, no. 6; BL, MS latin nouvelle acquisition 1022, no. 211, fol. 191; no. 213, fol. 192; no. 216, fol. 191; no. 214, fol. 192; no. 216, fol. 192; BL, MS latin nouvelle acquisition 1023, no. 216, fol. 30.

[43] *Cart. Bayeux* i. nos. cclxxiii–cclxxiv.

But more was going on in the Bessin and Cotentin than Angevin civil war. Richard commanded the Gloucester *caput* fortress of Torigni-sur-Vire from 1151 until October 1154, if not earlier. Under his castellanship Torigni underwent two sieges conducted by Duke Henry, whose cause the Gloucester family championed, but for a notable exception. The garrison survived one siege in 1151 because the new duke had to withdraw to face an invasion of the duchy by King Louis VII; but in the second one during the month of October 1154, Richard was forced to capitulate after fifteen days.[44] In the absence of source-based explanations for his resistance to Henry, modern scholars have cast the earl's son variously as a rebel either against the new duke of Normandy or, like Philip, against his family; and Henry, as restorer of ducal rights.[45]

However, only the family rebel theory makes sense. Certainly ducal recovery of Torigni was not Henry's goal. After Richard's surrender, Gloucester comital authority was restored there, obviously with Henry's agreement. Fitz Count's brother Earl William made use of Évrecy and held a great meeting of his court at Torigni c.1155–60 at which a concord was reached between two rival claimants to properties; and his mother Countess Mabel, who acted as *domina* in the honor for William, probably held sway there as well.[46]

Perhaps Richard, having been established at Torigni during the civil war, after Robert's death refused to leave because of dissatisfaction with his prospects of a possible appanage (likely Creully) or the lack of one. In response, I believe either the apparent Gloucester family council of Countess Mabel, Earl William, and his brother Robert, Countess Mabel herself, or William himself finally called in Henry as overlord and family ally to dislodge Richard. After failing to do so in 1151, Henry in an 1154 charter discovered by Professor David Crouch in effect deprived Richard of any *Dapifer* fees; he awarded them to Richard's brother Robert or his namesake nephew, and the name of Richard's brother Earl William appears first in the list of witnesses.[47]

After both possible beneficiaries died by 1166, an opportunity presented itself for Henry to whittle down William of Gloucester's power by awarding Creully to Richard. Perhaps this was behind the earl's brother Roger accusing his royal cousin of vast disseisins of William when the king and then bishop of Worcester met near Falaise in July 1170 and William's failure to respond to the king's inquest of Norman knights' fees in 1172.[48] Henry II (1154–89) bore Richard no ill will for

---

[44] Robert of Torigny, "Chronica," 161, 180–1; *Regesta* iii. no. 66; *CDF*, no. 1441.

[45] e.g., Yver, "Les Châteaux-forts en Normandie," 109 & n.; Warren, *Henry II*, 53; Boussard, *Le Gouvernement d'Henri II Plantagenêt*, 401; Crouch, *Reign of King Stephen*, 284–5; King, *King Stephen*, 266.

[46] Patterson, *EGC*, nos. 172, 186; AD du Calvados, H.6510, fol. 22b (mod. fol.): transcr. in BN, MS latin nouvelle acquisition 1020, fol. 299r.

[47] Patterson, *EGC*, no. 171; Antony House, MS PG/B2/6, no. 3763, p. 509: Crouch, "Earl William of Gloucester and the End of the Anarchy," 69–70. I am grateful to the staff of the Cornwall Record Office for obtaining the Antony House manuscript for my study. I believe an even better case may be made for Earl Robert's namesake son as the beneficiary, rather than the earl's grandson. Henry called the former his *cognatus* in NA, C.56/98, m.12: *A Medieval Cornish Miscellany*, no. 4, pp. 107–8; and the extreme youth of Earl William's son Robert militates against his being the beneficiary.

[48] BL, MS Lansdowne 398, fol. 31: William fitz Stephen, "Vita S. Thomae," 105; *RBE* ii. 644; Warren, *Henry II*, 216 (with loose translation).

his earlier armed resistance. Fitz Count was welcome at his courts and died in seisin of his *Dapifer* tenancy-in-chief.[49] Reconciliation with Bishop Philip de Harcourt's successor Henry eased the way for Richard's possession of the episcopal *Dapifer* fee, and possibly Creully as well.[50] However, Richard's behavior created lasting bad blood between him and his elder brother: Richard's name never appears in the witness-lists of *acta* generated at William's courts. On visits to England, Fitz Count sought the hospitality of his sister, Countess Matilda (Mabel) of Chester, and nephew Earl Hugh (1153–81).[51]

Robert's marriage to Mabel fitz Hamon epitomizes the social, political, and economic advantages the institution offered to the Anglo-Norman aristocracy, albeit increasingly under the jurisdiction of the Church. But Henry I's prerogative controlling the marriages of tenants-in-chiefs' various family members had to have been the moving force.[52] All of these aspects were repeated most clearly in the marriage, celebrated before the king's death, of Robert's and Mabel's daughter Mabel (aka Matilda) to Ranulf II de Gernons earl of Chester (1129–53) and hereditary *vicomte* of Bayeux.[53] As we already have seen, the king's various forms of patronage gave Robert a long and varied relationship with the comital family. Ranulf may not have felt complimented by the *maritagium* of Chipping Campden (Glos.) Robert provided for his daughter. Unless the manor either was the kind of village Reginald Lennard showed could have had more than one lord or had somehow come undivided into Earl Robert's hands, from the age of the Domesday Survey the estate had belonged to the earldom of Chester. Robert and Ranulf both potentially benefited politically in the central Midlands and in the Bessin.[54] Dynastically, the marriage favored the earl of Gloucester. Earl Ranulf could entertain little hope of gaining the earldom of Gloucester in the event of Robert's death because of his father-in-law's supply of putative legitimate male heirs; Earl Robert, on the other hand, could envision a future grandson as earl of Chester and *vicomte* of Bayeux. He had that prospect in mind in 1146 when he won from Bishop Philip de Harcourt agreement to retain control of the Chester episcopal fee until the heir should appear.[55]

What had been accomplished politically by the Chester match probably was somewhat replicated by a marriage alliance between Earl Robert and the powerful

---

[49] *CDF*, nos. 456, 530, 550; Delisle-Berger, *Recueil: Introduction*, 427; i. nos. cccv, ccccxxxviii–ccccxxxix; ii. no. cccclxvii; *Gesta Henrici Secundi* i. 51; Eyton, *Court, Household, and Itinerary of King Henry II*, 118, 127–8, 176 & n., 177.

[50] *Cart. Bayeux* i. no. cxliv; Delisle-Berger, i. 539n.; Navel, "L'Enquête de 1133 sur les fiefs de l'évêché de Bayeux," 40.

[51] *Chart. Chester*, nos. 121, 141, 148, 163–4, 176–7, 180. Richard never appears as a witness in Earl William's many *acta*.

[52] *Select Charters*, "Charter of Liberties," c. 3: transl. *EHD* ii. no. 19; Green, "A Lasting Memorial: The Charter of Liberties of Henry I," 61.

[53] The marriage took place during Henry I's reign: *HN* (1998), 81 & n.; Farrer, *Honors and Knights' Fees* ii. 53–4; *Chart. Chester*, nos. 41n., 59 & nn.; Crouch, *Reign of King Stephen*, 137. Countess Matilda was reported to be more than 50 years old in 1185: *Rotuli de Dominabus et Pueris et Puellis*, 15.

[54] Lewis, "Formation of the Honor of Chester," 45, 56, 63. The gift of an estate at Chipping Campden to Bordesley Abbey by the Gloucester vassal Hugh de Gundeville was confirmed by Earl William of Gloucester: Queen's College MS 88, fol. 217r.

[55] Patterson, *EGC*, no. 6.

earl of Devon, Baldwin de Redvers, created by the likely 1140s marriage between Robert's namesake son and Hawisia (d. 1213 × 19), Baldwin's daughter. If Robert's and Baldwin's putative sovereign, the Empress Matilda, sanctioned the nuptials, I have found no evidence of it. The young Robert granted Hawisia's *maritagium*, the manor of Puddleton (Dors.), to Quarr Abbey (Devon) with the consent of his *sponsa*.[56] The union further strengthened Earl Robert's leadership in the baronial coalition which had formed against King Stephen in the southwest. Its major figures were, besides Gloucester, his half-brothers Earl Reginald of Cornwall and Robert fitz Roy, lord of Okehampton (Devon), and the father of his daughter in law, Earl Baldwin of Devon.[57]

Philip's marriage to a niece of the Gloucestershire magnate Roger III of Berkeley, lord of Berkeley and Dursley (Glos.), was even more devoid of royal influence and, more to the point, his family's. Even though Earl Robert was Roger's overlord for two knights' fees, the nuptials seem more like the fruit of an agreement between Roger and Philip than between Earl Robert and Roger.[58] According to the marriage's place in the *Gesta Stephani*'s chronology the event occurred after Philip's change of loyalty from the Angevins to King Stephen in 1146 and was associated with a sworn pact by which Philip assumed responsibility for Roger's protection.[59]

The prime marriage example of Earl Robert's family involved his heir William and Hawisia, daughter of Robert II earl of Leicester. The wedding occurred within a couple of years after Gloucester's death (prob. 1148 × 9) when William would have been in his thirties.[60] Such a long bachelordom, including most of the years of the Anarchy, suggests that Robert consciously had held William back for just the right

---

[56] Robert's marriage to Hawisia de Redvers is clearly established by a charter of his granting Connerton (in Gwithian), Cornwall, to Richard Pincerna and attested by his *sponsa* Hawisia de Redvers: Bowles, *A Short History of the Hundred of Penwith*, Appendix, no. 2; Picken, "The Descent of the Devonshire Family of Willington from Robert Earl of Gloucester," no. 3, pp. 105–6, no. 4, pp. 107–8, forthcoming as no. 2194 in *The Acta of Henry II*, for which I am indebted to Professor Nicholas Vincent. See also *Redvers Family Charters*, 11, nos. 7n., 42n., 67n., 111 & n. Hawisia was not the wife of Earl Robert's grandson Robert; that Robert, who died in 1166, left a widow named Agnes, as shown by entries in the Pipe Rolls of Richard I: e.g., *PR 3 Richard I*, 18; "Ann. Margam," 16.

[57] See the meticulous study of Judith Green, including her cautionary remarks, "Family Matters," 161–3.

[58] *RBE* i. 289. The marriage of Richard fitz Count to an unnamed sister of Robert de Montfort, Waleran of Meulan's nephew, poses even greater challenges to determine the responsible parties and their motives, because the event is undated: Robert of Torigny, "Chronica," 269; see Crouch, *Beaumont Twins*, 29–30 & n. 5.

[59] "Philippus autem...iniurias Rogerio irrogatas aegre ferens, hinc quia eum sub defensionis suas iure tutandum susceperat, inde quia neptem suam uxorandi copula iuratam habebat..." *GS* (2004), 190. The English translation, ignoring the crucial meaning of *inde*, makes it seem that Philip was motivated by two parallel reasons, a sworn defense pact and marriage to Roger's niece, instead of the second's following from the first one.

[60] My estimate is based on the best evidence for the latest date of Robert's and Mabel's marriage from the Northamptonshire Survey, 1115 × 18, instead of *c.*1113: William was Robert's and Mabel's firstborn: *GND* ii. 248–9. William was listed among witnesses for his father in a *conventio* with the abbot of Fécamp in 1128: Patterson, *EGC*, no. 70. According to the author of the *Gesta Stephani*, William by 1147 was *senior aetate*: *GS* (2004), 139–40, which in contemporary thought would put a person at 40 years or more. Gilbert Foliot's letter to Earl William of Gloucester in which he refers to William as a *homo licet etate iuuenis* appears to be flattery or a put-down: *LCGF*, no. 88; see also Genealogical Chart, xxi.

match. If the earl had the Beaumont comital house of Leicester in his marital plans, as I suspect he did, perhaps it was Earl Robert of Leicester's failure to openly break with the royalist faction which delayed Gloucester's marital overtures. Robert of Leicester's brother Waleran had declared for the Angevins in 1141, but Robert during the decade only went as far toward changing sides as making himself scarce at Stephen's court. In the end, it seems that the force of baronial treaty-making among magnates with landed interests in the Midlands and southern Welsh March, likely dating from *c.*1148, led to Earl William of Gloucester's becoming Earl Robert II of Leicester's son-in-law around this time. One of these *conventiones*, probably of the same vintage as the one between Earl William of Gloucester and Earl Roger of Hereford, mentions another treaty between Roger and Earl Robert of Leicester with Earl William, already associated with Leicester as the latter treaty's guarantor. This more personal marriage agreement would seem more likely to have followed a bit later, especially after William had complete authority over his earldom, possibly as early as January 1148.[61] Before that point, his mother may have promoted the Beaumont tie. She was conducting the earldom's business either by herself, jointly with William, or through an apparent family regency council consisting of herself, William, and his brother Robert.[62] Besides making peace between the two families, with the Leicester marriage William now had potential allies of the Midlands' two dominant lords. And whether offered by Robert of Leicester as legitimizing bait or as a face-saving surrender, Hawisia's *maritagium* consisted of Wareham and some other Dorset estates seized by the earl's father during the war.[63]

To great Anglo-Norman landed families like Earl Robert's, demesne not only was their most immediate support, but its uses can also help to define their personalities.[64] Some gaps between his recorded appearances at the royal court must represent periodic visits to the demesne manors of his great trans-Channel barony. A few glimpses of them may be gleaned from charter evidence. These mostly show occasions when Countess Mabel or their sons William, Haimo, and Roger attested the earl's *acta* while attending him along with the servants of his household as he perambulated his English and Welsh demesne manors and held courts at Bristol, Cardiff, and Cranborne (Dors.), or visited some location in Normandy.[65] Mabel and William also could preside over courts with the earl; the foundation of Neath Abbey by Richard de Grainville and his wife Constance in 1130 may have been one of them.[66] A tradition preserved at Robert's *Eigenkloster* Tewkesbury Abbey

---

[61] Patterson, *EGC*, no. 96 & n.; *Regesta* iii. no. 612 may be Robert's only attestation of a royal charter; Crouch, *Beaumont Twins*, 85; Crouch "A Norman *Conventio* and Bonds of Lordship," 308–9; see Chapt. 6, 205.

[62] Patterson, *EGC*, nos. 86, 167 (yet admitting William's authority), 171. William started issuing his own *acta* in January 1148: Patterson, *EGC*, nos. 178–9. Crouch, *Reign of King Stephen*, 236–7, makes a case for William's initiative.

[63] e.g., BL, MS Cotton Otho B.xiv, fol. 34v; Crouch, *Beaumont Twins*, 85 & nn., 197n. See also Chapt. 6, 205.

[64] Painter, *Feudal Barony*, 152; Miller and Hatcher, *Medieval England*, 179–80.

[65] BL, MS Sloane 1301, fol. 227v; Patterson, *EGC*, nos. 70, 84, 119, 156–7, 283.

[66] "et hoc concesseru(n)t...an(te) comite(m) et comitissam. et ante Will(el)mu(m) filiu(m) suu(m). Hec om(n)ia dam(us)...et Rotb(er)ti consul(is) gloecestrensis. et mabilie uxoris sue comitisse.

held that he might be accompanied by the abbot and twelve monks. Another occasion would have been at Tewkesbury at Christmas, when one Richer from nearby Eldersfield (Worcs.) waited on tables outfitted in red hose according to the terms of his serjeanty tenure.[67]

The most complete record of such a gathering at Bristol appears in the earl's foundation charter for Margam Abbey issued shortly before his death in late 1147, when he was served by Hubert steward (*dapifer*), Hugh de Gundeville constable, his clerks, Adam de Ely, Henry Tusard, and Elias, and his physician Picot.[68] On another of these occasions the priest Philip granted his share of Holy Trinity Church Bristol and himself to Tewkesbury Abbey by a script placed in the hands of the abbot in the presence of the earl and his barons.[69] Robert might enfeoff Fulk fitz Warin, decide inheritance, or confirm proprietary actions by a vassal or his father-in-law. Manors' residential resources should not be overlooked, and some had the added delights of hunting for example, in the forest east of Bristol, Cranborne Chase, Malvern Chase, Hanley north of Tewkesbury, and Kibur forest by Cardiff. Perhaps in Gloucestershire one might have caught sight of the great earl in pursuit of game in company with his falconer Benefrei (or Renefrey) and archer Hinganus.[70]

The identities of Earl Robert's demesne estates reveal themselves in various ways. For example, Bristol, Gloucester, Burford, Cardiff, Newport, and Tewkesbury emerge from the contents of charters.[71] Chronicle and inquest evidence reveals Torigni-sur-Vire and Évrecy.[72] Sudbury's status can be deduced because it was available to be given by his son Earl William to his granddaughter Amicia as her *maritagium*.[73] A comparison of estates in the Domesday Survey known to have passed to Earl Robert from Countess Mabel's father and uncle and the king with demesne mentioned in the Exchequer accounts of the honor of Gloucester during the wardships of Robert's granddaughter Isabel in the 1180s or under King John yields the identities of the likes of Fairford, Thornbury (Glos.), and Burford (Oxon.).

Cranborne, as described by the Exon Domesday, reveals in spite of its anachronistic features the range of assets a great rural manor containing a demesne farm and tenanted lands might offer Robert as sole landlord.[74] Each of the two parts occupied about 3.5 hides (*c.*420 acres). Multure from four mills and pannage from its woodlands must have been valuable sources of income. Cereal and livestock were Cranborne's main products. Among the latter were 10 cows, 51 pigs, and 40 goats; but the manor's flock of 1,037 sheep was the principal asset. In 1086 the manor yielded £30.[75]

---

et Will(el)mi filii sui comsid(er)acionis [*sic*] et uolu(n)tate": WGAS, GBO216 A/N 1: Clark, *Cartae et alia*, i. no. 67.

[67] Bodl., MS Top. Glouc.d.2, fol. 15r; *Mon. Angl.* ii. 61?; Patterson, *EGC*, no. 216.
[68] Patterson, *EGC*, no. 119.
[69] *Mon. Angl.* ii. 70–1, no. xxxiv; Patterson, *EGC*, no. 269.
[70] *Cart. Langley*, no. 41; *Catatalogue of Ancient Deeds* iii. 448.
[71] Patterson, *EGC*, nos. 10, 42, 46, 156. For demesne lands, see Maps 1 & 2, 239–40.
[72] *GND* ii. 248–9; Wace, *Le Roman de Rou* ii., ll. 4025–8, 11073–6; *RHG* xxiii. 608, 634.
[73] *DB Suffolk* (Phillimore), i. 1.97; *Regesta* ii. no. 1178; *Westminster Abbey Charters*, no. 72 & no. 130n; *CRR* i. 186; BL, MS Cotton Appendix xxi, fol. 29b–30; Patterson, *EGC*, no. 169 & n.
[74] Lennard, *Rural England*, 237.    [75] *DB* iv: *Exon Domesday*, fol. 29; *DB* i. 75b.

Evidence from the manor more contemporary with Robert provides a virtual catalogue of products which would have been available to him for consumption or sale, as well as other seigniorial sources of revenue.[76] His choices included cheese, chickens, lambs, piglets, deer calves, wool, flax, bees (honey), and hay. Dues were collected from tenants for rights of forage for their pigs and of pasturage for their cattle, for use of his mill, for gathering timber for housing and hedging, and for tithes; and there were amercements for hunting, and proceeds from the view of the earl's forester.[77] The small St. Mary's Priory Fitz Hamon left behind in 1102 when he transferred the community's abbatial status to St. Mary's Tewkesbury would have been a potential source of spiritual and clerical services.[78]

Local manorial bailiffs, the *prepositi* or *ministri* of comital charters' address clauses, would have been responsible for collecting the various revenues. A charter Earl Robert issued at Newport shows how such sums might then be sent to honorial *capita*. He advised the monks of Montacute Priory (Som.) that they could claim 36s. of Gwynllŵg's revenues at his castle there.[79]

Robert's manorial retentions reveal a basic policy, common to baronial landlords, to which he adhered from the time he first acquired demesne: retain the most valuable and geographically concentrated estates, including burghal holdings regardless of their income yields or location. It is just one rather exceptional snippet, but the 20s. Ralph burgess owed to the earl from his Winchester land illustrates such tenures' attractive ready cash.[80] The curialist in Robert also was reluctant to part with urban locations such as Winchester and London which might provide him with hospitality and other resources while attending the *curia regis*.[81]

The result was the demesne heartland revealed by the Pipe Roll of 1129–30, with 60 percent located in a contiguous block of six Severn Valley and southwestern shires, Gloucestershire, Somerset, Wiltshire, Dorset, Devon, and Cornwall. And within four of them were ten of the honor's roughly fifteen probably most valuable demesne manors: Ashmore and Cranborne (Dors.), Keynsham, possibly Brislington (Som.), Bristol with Barton, Fairford, Thornbury, and Tewkesbury (Glos.) with nearby *membrum* Hanley Castle, and Eldersfield, and Malvern (Chase) (Worcs.).[82] In Gloucestershire alone there were burgesses at Winchcomb, Tewkesbury, Gloucester, and Bristol.[83]

---

[76] Patterson, *EGC*, nos. 157, 283.   [77] PRO, E.132/2/13, m.1; Patterson, *EGC*, no. 51.
[78] Calthrop, "Priory of Cranborne," 70.   [79] Patterson, *EGC*, no. 156.
[80] Patterson, *EGC*, no. 103; see also Davis, "London Lands and Liberties of St. Paul's," 48, 57; Green, *Aristocracy of Norman England*, 148.
[81] The earl's son William still enjoyed hospitality from land at Winchester: Patterson, *EGC*, no. 103.
[82] *DB* (Phillimore): *Dorset*: Ashmore, Cranborne, 1. 16–17; *Somerset*: Brislington, not mentioned; Keynsham, 1.28; *Gloucestershire*: Bristol with Barton, 1.21; 5.20; Fairford, 1.50; Tewkesbury, 1.24–6, 37–9; Thornbury, 1.47; *Worcestershire*: Malvern, 2.31 (1086 in forest; bishop of Worcester); Bushley (aka Bisley, Worcs.) belonged to Malvern forest: *PR 6 Richard I*, 4; the earl of Gloucester disputed its service with the bishop: *Red Book of Worcester* iv. xxiv; Malvern Chase (or forest) included Great Malvern and Little Malvern: *VCH Worcester* ii. 317; iii. 450; Pull (*DB Worcestershire* (Phillimore), E4.44) also belonged to Malvern forest: *PR 6 Richard I*, 4; the earl also disputed service due from it with the bishop: *Red Book of Worcester* iv. xxiv.
[83] Darby & Terrett, *Domesday Geography of Midland England*, 43–8. The 60% includes danegeld and relevant *auxilium civitatis* sums pardoned and an estimated danegeld pardon for Somerset.

The image of Robert as an unexceptional landlord suggested by the obvious logic of his demesne retention is radically upgraded to "energetic and forward-thinking landlord" when improvements he made are added to the proprietary equation. If the ideal in baronial headquarters was for them to include castle, monastery, and borough, Robert aggressively pursued it in various ways. In Normandy, as Robert of Torigny put it, in perhaps his earliest efforts, once Henry I had put the *caput* of Mabel's patrimony under his son's authority, Robert fortified Torigni with very high towers, the strongest of walls, and steep ditches.[84] At Cardiff in Glamorgan he may have rebuilt the motte-and-bailey castle protecting the vill and mint which he inherited from his posthumous father-in-law, ultimately from his grandfather William I; the mound alone had a circumference of 90 feet at the top and 250 at the base.[85] In the late 1120s he resumed Fitz Hamon's conquest of Morgannwg and expanded the Shire Fee westward beyond the river Ogmore, possibly to please Countess Mabel, but even more to preempt his own vassals' territorial ambitions. Geographically, Robert's first effort was the territory of Kenfig, where he is rightly credited with founding a fortified settlement close to the sea on the Afon Cynffig. Next came the area between the waters of the Afon Cynffig and the Avan called Morgan or Margan, which he used as the endowment of his great Cistercian *Eigenkloster* Margam Abbey in 1147. Finally, beyond a developing native Member lordship he recognized, Afan, Robert may well have established the castle-borough of Neath on the east side of the river Neath.[86] What constructive measures he took, if any, in his dependent lordship of Gwynllŵg are unknown. But he did use Newport as the lordship's administrative *caput* by the early 1130s and referred at that time to the borough and castle as his own.[87]

No such obscurity pertains to Bristol, which Robert transformed into a virtual baronial capital. In no other of the earldom of Gloucester's *capita* do we see in such detail the contributions the earl made to achieve the ideal baronial demesne triad of castle, borough, and monastery, the first and third, cultural agents respectively of "hard" and "soft" power.[88] He completely changed the previous motte-and-bailey castle, attributed to Bishop Geoffrey of Coutances, which had guarded the neck of the peninsula on which the former Anglo-Saxon *burh* was located and which

---

[84] Robert of Torigny, *Chronica*, ed. Delisle, ii. 88; Wace, ll. 11199–201; *GND* ii. 248–9. Note the uncertainty of Prof. Jean Yver about the dating of Robert's work: "Les Châteaux-forts en Normandie," 100–1.

[85] Tradition attributes the castle to Robert: *Chroniques anglo-normandes*, 105; Walker, "Cardiff," 107, 111; Griffiths, "Medieval Boroughs of Glamorgan and Medieval Swansea," 335; Hague, "Castles of Glamorgan and Gower," 427–8; Grant, *Cardiff Castle*, 27–8, 51; Blackburn, "Coinage and Currency under Henry I: A Review," 57.

[86] Patterson, *EGC*, no. 68, for evidence of Kenfig; Beresford, *New Towns of the Middle Ages*, 555–6; Crouch, "Slow Death of Kingship in Glamorgan," 30, 32–4. According to a tradition preserved by Rice Merrick, Robert's son William rebuilt Kenfig: *A Booke of Glamorganshires Antiquities*, 51, also 42, 49; Birch, *Neath Abbey*, 21–2; Smith, "Kingdom of Morgannwg and the Norman Conquest of Glamorgan," 30–2; Griffiths, "Medieval Boroughs of Glamorgan and Medieval Swansea," 338; Evans, "The Lords of Afan," 18–19.

[87] Patterson, *EGC*, nos. 156, 162, 280.

[88] Le Patourel, *The Norman Empire*, 317–18; Bates, *The Normans and Empire*, 4, 18–19, 50, 76, 97–8, 123, 158.

accorded the only direct access by land. Work under Robert's direction was under way perhaps as early as the late 1120s and involved leveling of the motte and raising with Caen stone a great square keep, irregularly aligned, with four corner towers of about 84 feet × 84 feet, not counting a forebuilding at the northeast corner. While its proportions were surpassed by his grandfather's White Tower of London at 118 feet × 97 feet and paled in comparison to Colchester (Essex) at 110 feet × 151 feet given by Henry I in 1101 to Eudo *Dapifer*, it was more grand than several lay baronial counterparts, such as William d'Aubigny's Castle Rising keep (Norf.) of 78.5 feet × 68.5 feet and Aubrey de Vere's Castle Hedingham (Essex) of 54 feet × 58 feet. Robert also is credited with construction of an adjacent aisled hall 54 feet × 108 feet.[89] He surrounded the bailey with a curtain wall with rectangular mural towers and at least one gate, and probably had a new moat dug.[90] The author of the *Gesta Stephani* was in awe of the earl's completed efforts. Among the events of 1138, he observed, "Bristol...is the most strongly fortified of all its [England's] cities...; where it is considered more exposed to a siege and more accessible, a castle rising on a vast mound, strengthened by wall and battlements, towers and divers engines, prevents an enemy's approach." The keep, which the young Henry fitz Empress knew well, may have been the inspiration for the later king's at Dover.[91]

These features were not the basic reason for the castle's effective defenses. The location of the borough it protected was surrounded, except for the castle-guarded land approach by the rivers which intersected at its west end; on the south, the Avon and on the north, its tributary the Frome. Bristol's value as a demesne manor also was enhanced by its location. The intersecting rivers and junction of roads made it the natural market for its Cotswolds and Mendips hinterland. Its inland protected harbor, the finest in western England, made it a hub for regional and overseas trade which, as William of Malmesbury marveled, extended to Ireland, Norway, and elsewhere. Its wealth was legendary. As an indication of its long economic importance, Bristol had belonged to the system of royal burghal mints since Saxon times. Seven moneyers struck issues of Henry I's silver pennies.[92] Three of them, Farthegn, Iordan, and Rodbert, were active at the same time and are known to

---

[89] BL, Additional MS 36985, fol 15; PRO, E.164/1 *a*.1147; Symeon of Durham 215; *Little Red Book of Bristol* i. 207; Cronne, *Bristol Charters*, 24; Carus-Wilson, "The Norman Town," 4; Walker, *Bristol in the Early Middle Ages*, 8–9; adding the forebuilding lengthens the keep's north wall to 108 feet: Ponsford, "Bristol Castle," i. 19, 27–9, 31, 43–6, 83, 103, 145–9; Fifteenth-century William Worcestre left Latin and English descriptions of Bristol castle; the Latin one is the more reliable, based on William's personal measurements; *The Topography of Medieval Bristol*, nos. 396, 422; Harvey, *William Worcestre: Itineraries*, 399–400; *Regesta* ii. no. 552; Brown, *English Castles*, 66, 69; Fernie, *The Architecture of Norman England*, 55, 61. For the distinction between royal and baronial castles, see Painter, "English Castles in the Early Middle Ages: Their Number, Location, and Legal Position," in *Feudalism and Liberty*, 135.
[90] *William Worcestre Itineraries*, 399–400; Patterson, *EGC*, nos. 199–200; Ponsford, "Bristol Castle" i. 88, 99, 107, 103, 115, 119, 127, 137, 140, 143–4; ii. 316–17, 333; Cronne, *Bristol Charters*, 23; Marshall, "Excavations in the City of Bristol," 11.
[91] *GS* (2004), 56–7; Ponsford, "Bristol Castle," 146–9.
[92] *GP*, 446–7; *GS* (2004), 56–7; *Vita Wulfstani*, 42–3; Cronne, *Bristol Charters 1378–1499*, 15–16; Carus-Wilson, "Origins," 2–3; Stenton, "The Road System of Medieval England," 4–5 & n.; Blackburn, "Coinage and Currency under Henry I: A Review," 49–76, esp. 69.

have minted Earl Robert's "Lion" pennies.[93] A burgeoning burgess population, fed by immigration, was in the process of doubling by *c*.1150 from an estimated Domesday-era 2310. It spilled over into suburbs: east of the castle, the market; across the Frome river to the north and northwest, respectively, "new town" and Bilswick; and across the Avon bridge to the south, Bedminster fees. Burgesses' ranks included potters, soap makers, weavers and mercers, furriers, cobblers, butchers, wine and corn merchants, moneylenders, and landlords; at the social peak were families like the De la Warres and Cordwainers and especially the urban patrician Robert fitz Harding, whose fortune came from wine, land, and moneylending.[94]

Together with the Barton, Bristol's goods and revenues were the immediate support for Robert and his family, his castle garrison, and probably part of his local administration. I suspect that the volume may account for *magistri* like Picard and the notary Richard of Ilchester he utilized, and may have influenced the development from the hall, where Richard served, of an exchequer for Robert's entire barony by his death.[95]

As landlord Robert would have enjoyed burgage rents or landgable, possibly with entry fees and reliefs, tolls, stall fees at the Michaelmas fair, purchase and sales taxes, custom from chalk for tanning, prisage of wine, possible multure, brewing and baking charges, and the proceeds of justice.[96] Also at his disposal was the town's burghal militia Professor Warren Hollister viewed as still fighting under the Saxon obligation of fyrd service during the Anarchy. I suspect that this force supplemented the castle's household knights in an attack on Bath in 1138.[97]

Earl Robert's second major building project produced the monastic component for his capital, the just-mentioned priory of St. James, which he founded as a cell of his English honorial *Eigenkloster*, Tewkesbury Abbey.[98] Robert and the current abbot of Tewkesbury, Benedict (1124–37), saw to it that all of the proprieties required by the competing seigniorial and canonical systems were observed. On the side of the lay founder and patron, *iure uxoris*, of the abbey, the assent of Earl Robert witnessed by the very *uxor* herself, Countess Mabel; and for the Church, at the request of Abbot Benedict, the confirmation of the arrangement by the diocesan, Simon bishop of Worcester (1125–50).[99] There is reason to believe that the earl initiated the process in the very late 1120s. The choice of the house's patron saint suggests that he was selected as a compliment to the earl's half-sister, the Empress Matilda. She returned to England in 1126 from Germany with the

---

[93] Archibald, "The Lion Coinage of Robert Earl of Gloucester," 75.
[94] Walker, *Bristol in the Early Middle Ages*, 9, 19–21; Russell, *English Medieval Population*, 286; Patterson, "Robert Fitz Harding of Bristol," 109–21; on urban class structure, see Reynolds, *English Medieval Towns*, 74–7; Archibald, "The Lion Coinage of Robert Earl of Gloucester," 76; see Chapt. 5, 171–2.
[95] Patterson, *EGC*, 10, 13, no. 188, where the exchequer is first mentioned in a charter of Earl William. For the hall as Richard's place of work, see Chapt. 1, 21.
[96] Patterson, *EGC*, no. 283 (rents for storage places at the fair; renders for chalk for leather), 84 (tolls), 110 (tolls), 151 (relief), 180 (earl's market at Michaelmas), 185 (comital bakery, brewery, mill).
[97] *GS* (2004), 58–9; Hollister, *Military Organization of Norman England*, 231.
[98] Fernie, *The Architecture of Norman England*, 228.
[99] *Mon. Angl.* ii. 70; *EEA* xxxiii, no. 85n.

relic hand of St. James the Greater and ultimately presented it to Reading Abbey. Robert was closely associated with Matilda in 1127–8, so naming his priory after the saint out of respect for her is quite plausible.[100] In addition to the standard benefits which attracted monastic founders, Robert may have been thinking like other Anglo-Norman barons of the priory as his mortuary church.[101] His endowment consisted of lands and tenements almost certainly in Bristol and the immediate vicinity. A confirmation charter in favor of the priory from Robert's son Earl William may identify some of their whereabouts: twenty houses in St. Peter's parish, thirty-one houses in the market east of the castle, and twelve by the priory's cemetery north of the river Frome.[102]

The site the earl picked was just across Bristol's northern Frome river bridge in a suburban area of Stapleton soon known as "new vill." Only the Romanesque church's original nave and fragments of the west cloister have survived. The nave and east end with choir once measured 37.5 yards. The nave is a simple single-storied arcaded hall with five bays and clerestory. Round pillars with scalloped capitals support the arcading. A no longer extant Lady chapel extended southward from the choir. The most interesting architectural feature is the façade of its gabled west front, structurally divided into four tiers. The second is decorated with elongated overlapping arcading enclosing three windows; the third contains a wheel-window made up of a central circle surrounded by eight smaller ones; under the gable in the fourth is a small lancet. Robert continued supporting the priory at least to about 1138 by helping to build the small Lady chapel measuring 7 by 21 yards. He provided stone, quarried from his base at Caen, by tithing the supply being used at this time for the construction work on his castle.[103]

The earl also is credited with other improvements, but more tenuously attributed, within the borough and its emerging suburbs. His hand is thought to have been behind building or rebuilding several parish churches. In the town center at the intersection of Corn and Broad Streets, St. Ewen's, which the earl gave to a local priest Thurstan, is thought by some to be one of them. The earl or his son William may have built St. Michael's parish church northwest of the Frome bridge. Robert possibly walled in the lowland marsh at the town's western headland.[104]

---

[100] Patterson, *EGC*, no. 199; *Regesta* iii. no. 898; *ASC a*. 1126: Matthew Paris, *Chronica Majora* ii. 159, for the arrival of the relic at Reading Abbey in 1133; *EEA* xxxii. no. 85 & n.; Leedom, "William of Malmesbury and Robert of Gloucester Reconsidered," 251–2; Leyser, "Frederick Barbarossa," 489, 491–2, 494; Walker, *Bristol in the Early Middle Ages*, 19–20; Jackson, *Excavations at St. James's Priory, Bristol*, 6, 8; Fernie, *The Architecture of Norman England*, 228. For the comparable development of neighboring St. Augustine's founded by Robert fitz Harding, see Dickinson, "The Origins of St. Augustine's, Bristol," 111–20.

[101] BL, Cotton Cleopatra A.vii, fol. 75; Jackson, *Excavations at St. James's Priory, Bristol*, 16, 18, 32–3; Knowles, *MOE*, 562–8; Le Patourel, *Norman Empire*, 317–18; for a general treatment, see Chibnall, *The World of Orderic Vitalis*, 47; Green, *Aristocracy of Norman England*, 391–428; Golding, "Anglo-Norman Knightly Burials," 36–7.

[102] Patterson, *EGC*, no. 207; see also BA, 5139 (488): *Mon. Angl.* iv. 335, for a transcript of which I am grateful to Nicholas Vincent; Jackson, *Excavations at St. James's Priory, Bristol*, 9.

[103] Patterson, *EGC*, no. 200 [corrected, *c*.1138, on the basis of the estimated duration of the castle construction: see 96]; *EEA* xxxiii. no. 85 & n.; Jackson, *Excavations at St. James's Priory Bristol*, 6, 8, 16, 18–19, 20, fig. 8, 21, figs. 9–10, 13; Pevsner, *North Somerset and Bristol*, 390.

[104] Carus-Wilson, "The Norman Town," 4–5.

However, Robert's subinfeudations and policies indirectly did promote the development of the suburban "new borough of the meadow" across the river Frome to the north, Bilswick to its west, the Old Market just east of the castle, and Bedminster, south of the river Avon. The earl's foundation of St. James's provided a magnet for settlement and this potential was increased even more when his son William designated the priory as the area's parish church.[105] His subinfeudations of Bilswick and part of Bedminster to Robert fitz Harding and the rest of Bedminster to the Templars indirectly contributed to the suburbs' development. The Temple fee quickly became a mini-town of rent-paying craftsmen and merchants complete with a conventual church built, as recent excavations have established, in the typical Templar round-church style.[106]

Earl Robert regarded Tewkesbury as the most important of his northern group of demesne estates, which included Hanley (Castle), Eldersfield, and Malvern (of lesser value) in southern Worcestershire, west across the Severn. After Waleran of Meulan retaliated for the Angevins' burning and sacking of Worcester in 1140 by wasting Tewkesbury and Earl Robert's great house, it is likely that Robert was the one who rebuilt the hall on a new site on Holm Hill.[107] However, the most extensive evidence about improvements he made at the 100-hide Domesday manor is the liberties he granted to his tenants, creating a chartered borough.[108] Otherwise, his known contributions to the manor's fabric, aside from maintenance of his great hall, involved his honorial abbey. Robert is credited with showering St. Mary's with gifts. Some were certainly monetary and must have helped to further the abbey church's rebuilding and enabled its consecration by the bishops of Worcester, Hereford, Llandaff, and Dublin on Monday October 24, 1121.[109] But there is at least one example of a structural addition the earl made to the magnificent Romanesque church, featuring in the choir a three-storey elevation of arcade, gallery, and tribune with walkway. The sixteenth-century traveler John Leland recorded an epitaph from Robert fitz Hamon's chantry chapel which attributed a spire on the church's magnificent tower to the earl.[110] However, the architectural development of the church after completion of the choir and transepts by c.1100 leaves the possibility of his contribution to construction of the great nave, famous for its massive 28-foot pillars.[111]

---

[105] Patterson, *EGC*, no. 205.
[106] Lees, *Records of the Templars in England in the Twelfth Century*, 58; Brown, "Excavations at Temple Church, Bristol," 115–16, 119–20; Carus-Wilson, "The Norman Town," 5–8.
[107] Jones, "The Borough of Tewkesbury," 110; see Chapt. 5, 153.   [108] See 102–3.
[109] *GR* i. 800–1; ii. 361; BL, Additional MS 36985, fols. 4–4b, 14b; *EEA* xxxiii, no. 85; Patterson, *EGC*, nos. 180, 260, 268, 283; *JW* iii. 150–1 (*a*.1121), 154–5; "Ann. Tewkesbury," *a*.1123; Zarnecki, *Romanesque Art*, 53; Boase, *English Art*, 92–4; *English Romanesque Art*, no. 538. Thurlby, "The Norman Church," 89, presents the persuasive case for 1121.
[110] Leland, *Itinerary* vi. 92: "Robertus Consul ejus gener aedificauit pyramidam turrim." Thurlby, "The Norman Church," 89, believes that the upper parts of the central tower were not completed by his chosen consecration date of 1121. See also Kidson, "The Abbey Church of St. Mary at Tewkesbury in the Eleventh and Twelfth Centuries," 6, and Hulsey, "Tewkesbury Abbey: Some Recent Observations," 23, 28, 31.
[111] Thurlby, "The Elevations of the Romanesque Abbey Churches of St. Mary at Tewkesbury and St. Peter at Gloucester," 36, estimates completion of the church except for the tower possibly by the abbey's consecration; see Fernie, *The Architecture of Norman England*, 160, 162.

Perhaps outranking major manorial building improvements as demesne policy was Robert of Gloucester's patronage of burgesses, evident on several levels. It began with his status as perhaps Anglo-Norman England's preeminent lay baronial urban landlord. He was one of a select group of sole lords of important English towns; and his, Bristol, was almost the realm's richest in the eyes of the *Gesta Stephani*'s author and certainly was developing into the second- or third-ranking one by the late twelfth century. Also suggestive is that, measured by the aid Henry I levied in 1129–30 on the urban holdings of landlords in thirty-two towns, the *auxilium civitatis*, and from the *familiares* who received pardons, Robert's total was the highest among individual laymen; and his position in Bristol was not even taken into account because of the town's "mediatized" status, to use Sir Frank Stenton's useful term.[112]

The earl, by 1135, partly through marriage, possibly by his own initiative, also had become lord of tenants by knight-service who can be considered burgesses such as William fitz Otto of London, goldsmith, and Osbert Eightpence.[113] Furthermore, I suspect that under Earl Robert some of his major honorial barons like Richard de St. Quintin (10), Gilbert de Umfraville (9), and Richard Foliot (4) had mixed socio-economic "personalities." Their Gloucester honorial baronies included subinfeudated properties in Bristol which made them urban landlords and possible tenants themselves.[114]

Robert's basic policy was to enhance the attractiveness for merchants and tradesmen of residence in his boroughs through the social and economic advantages of being tenants. There was no particular high-minded principle behind Robert's support of men who in some places like Tewkesbury prior to his time technically were no more than villeins. The earl had no qualms about exacting forced labor from peasants in Normandy and England when it suited him.[115] Good business and shrewd political sense made Robert an ally of the rising "class" of freemen. His boroughs could be honeypots of readily available cash from basic rents for the urban plots or burgages and from a variety of other charges. The result only becomes visible later especially at Bristol under Robert's son and successor William when he could realize between 19 percent and 26 percent of his income. The earl of Leicester came to realize 30 percent to 35 percent of his annual income from his titular town.[116] William's annual income from Bristol is not broken down by category, but we know some of the sources such as burgage rents or landgable, reliefs, proceeds of justice, fairs, stall rents, multure from mills, and import and export duties.[117]

---

[112] *GS* (2004), 56–7; Mooers "Patronage and the Pipe Roll of 1130," 295–6 & Table 4; Stenton, *English Feudalism*, 234 & n.; see Chapt. 3, 69–70.
[113] For William fitz Otto, see Green, *Henry* I, 250; for Osbert, see n. 134; Chapt. 5, 158–9, 164.
[114] Richard Foliot was dead by 1135 and succeeded by a son Robert: *RBE* i. 291; see also *Cart. Bristol*, nos. 72, 586; a second Richard Foliot was active during the tenure of Earl Robert's successor William: BCM, Select Charter no. 15: *Descriptive Catalogue*, ed. Jeayes, no. 15.
[115] *CDF*, no. 734, p. 268; *GS* (2004), 150–1; Patterson, *EGC*, no. 46.
[116] Painter, *Feudal Barony*, 166; Postan, *The Medieval Economy and Society*, 167.
[117] BL, Harley Charter 75.A.31 (landgable); Patterson, Bristol: An Angevin Baronial Capital under Royal Siege,' 173–4 & n. 18.

One accomplished this goal by granting or confirming various liberties to burghal communities and, in Robert's age of increasing reliance upon records, by charter; and Robert joined a post-Conquest trend by doing so himself.[118] His royal grandfather and especially barons of the March in South Wales had promoted burghal development; and his father and some fellow barons such as Archbishop Thurstan of York and Robert de Meulan continued the trend, particularly by grants of burghal liberties. But for immediate inspiration his own posthumous father-in-law's charter of liberties for Burford is a logical candidate. It is the earliest such text to survive.[119]

Robert confirmed Robert fitz Hamon's charter. While the charter only can be dated to the period of his earldom, what the posthumous son-in-law confirmed reveals the proprietary privileges he favored and that he was guided by his predecessor's values. Besides listing burgesses' rights over their houses, property, and inheritance, the charter limited the right to purchase wool and hides in the vill's market to its burgesses and granted them the liberties and customs enjoyed by Oxford's gild-merchant.[120] These recognized burgesses' enjoyment of a gild-merchant, restricted non-members' rights to trade, and granted burgesses immunity from tolls in England and Normandy and the privilege of not pleading in a court outside of the borough.[121]

Robert and William also recognized or granted some liberties for Bristol. However, their only known details appear in John Lackland's charter of liberties granting the burgesses as earl of Gloucester "reasonable gilds" (*gildas rationabiles*) "such as they had during the time of Earls Robert and William."[122] The Conqueror's Domesday Survey recognized Bristol's burgesses as distinct from the population of Barton Regis to which they belonged; and the burgesses gave testimony to the commissioners as if from their own hundred. James Tait made a compelling case for the enjoyment of post-Conquest burgage rights by their Anglo-Saxon burghal predecessors. Thus, Bristol's burgesses, in return for payments of landgable, already were free from serfdom's appurtenances and likely able to dispose of their messuages by means such as sale, rent, and mortgage by the time Robert fitz Hamon became the borough's landlord, let alone his successor.[123]

---

[118] Reynolds, *English Medieval* Towns, 53.

[119] *EHD* ii. nos, 270, 283, 298; 282, 292; Reynolds, *English Medieval Towns*, 102, 104–5. Beresford, *New Towns of the Middle Ages*, 535–6, 539–41, 558–62, 553–7, 569. For Henry I's charter for London, see Green, *Henry I*, 249 & n., 250.

[120] PRO, C.47/45/388a, no. 1: transl. in *EHD* ii. no. 286 (with misprint *wood* for *wool*; Patterson, *EGC*, nos. 42–3 & n.

[121] *Select Charters*, 167–8: transl. in *EHD* ii. no. 300; Patterson, "Bristol: An Angevin Baronial Capital under Royal Siege," 177–8. See Postan, *Medieval Economy and Society*, 214–18, regarding gild-merchants.

[122] Cronne, *Bristol Charters*, 25, believed that the reference was to possible craft gilds, but at the same time considered that either Robert fitz Hamon or Earl Robert might have granted the burgesses a gild-merchant; but see also Cronne's remarks in *Bristol Charters*, 64. See Patterson, *EGC*, 5, no. 10; transl, in *EHD* ii. no. 285; John married Isabel, Earl William of Gloucester's heiress, on August 29, 1189; she died on October 14, 1217: Patterson, "Isabella Countess of Gloucester," 417; Fleming, "Christchurch's Sisters and Brothers: Canterbury Obituary Lists," 142.

[123] *DB Gloucestershire* (Phillimore), 1.21; Tait, *The Medieval English Borough*, Chapt. IV; Reynolds, *English Medieval Towns*, 36, 93.

Robert's and William's awards of gilds presumably would have conferred enjoyment of self-governance and monopoly in trading to members of certain crafts, as Professor H. A. Cronne suggested; but with the mode of Burford's charter in mind, a gild-merchant seems the more "reasonable" benefit enjoyed under the first two earls. In that case much the same appurtenant liberties would have been involved and exercised by traders such as vintners, corn-merchants, and cordwainers. Burghal jurisdiction was not awarded to any group. It was still being exercised under Earl William.[124] Regardless of the Bristol gild's nature, I suspect that its terms would have enumerated, or at least made reference to, past liberties and included the right to trade free from tolls throughout the earl of Gloucester's lands and the important tenurial immunity from pleading beyond Bristol's walls. The latter would become a bone of contention between the borough and royal officials during Henry II's reign.[125]

How much all of Earl Robert's attention to Bristol affected his income is empirically beyond reach. But what evidence is available gives the impression of significant impact. Bristol's revenues, at farm (*firma*, a predetermined fixed amount), gave its Domesday lord Bishop Geoffrey of Coutances 42 marks or £28; in 1185, when Bristol and the rest of the earldom of Gloucester were in King Henry II's wardship and with its revenues owed in the same way, the borough yielded £119. In addition, as already noted, this sum, together with the other of Bristol's annually farmed revenues to the end of the twelfth century, constituted from between 19 percent and 26 percent of the honor of Gloucester's income.[126] The accuracy of what Geoffrey's 42 marks represent certainly can be questioned, but it is hard not to see in a comparison of the two farmed yields a dramatic upward trend in Bristol's revenues and Earl Robert's responsibility for it at some level.

The earl also improved the status of his tenants at Tewkesbury and Cardiff, where burghal settlements antedated him, by granting them liberties. Determining exactly what they were is difficult because the source is an undated thirteenth-century text which attributes them to Robert and his son William without further clarification.[127] Professor Ralph Griffiths has suggested about 1125 × 28 for Cardiff's, when the earl began minting his father's coins there.[128] But even the conservative handling of the evidence this situation requires leaves little doubt about the effect of his most likely actions.

---

[124] Cronne, *Bristol Charters*, 24–5; Gross, *Gild Merchant* ii. 24–8; Reynolds, *English Medieval Towns*, 102. For comital jurisdiction, see *Cart. Bristol*, no. 30; Patterson, *EGC*, nos. 77, 151, 184–5.
[125] Patterson, "Bristol: An Angevin Baronial Capital under Siege," 177–8.
[126] Cronne, *Bristol Charters*, 21–2, 43–4, criticized by Walker, *Bristol in the Early Middle Ages*, 15–17; *DB Gloucestershire* (Phillimore) 1.21; *PR 31 Henry II*, 154; Patterson, "Bristol: An Angevin Baronial Capital under Royal Siege," 173. The best reason for interpreting the economic impact on Robert conservatively is the stability in the number of moneyers active at Bristol during the reigns of Henry I and Stephen: Archibald, "The Lion Coinage of Robert Earl of Gloucester," 75; Blackburn, "Coinage and Currency under Henry I: A Review," Table 5, p. 69; see 96.
[127] Patterson, *EGC*, no. 46 & n.
[128] See, e.g., 83, 92, for the possibilities of joint grants; Griffiths, "The Borough of Cardiff," 335–6, believed that the list of liberties derived from a confirmation charter of Earl William of Gloucester, a most plausible theory, but not provable; e.g., Walker, "Cardiff," 120.

Tewkesbury enjoyed a location like Bristol's, at the confluence of two rivers, the Severn and Warwickshire Avon, and at a Severn crossing, but two other lesser rivers, the Carron and the Swilgate, fed the Avon at opposite ends of the village. The result was a natural trading hub potential which Robert's paternal grandmother Queen Matilda had appreciated and enhanced by establishing a market. Not surprisingly, by 1086 its tenant population included thirteen whose identified status as burgesses and annual rent suggest that their personal and tenurial condition probably was similar to that of Bristol's Domesday burgesses.[129] Cardiff, as already seen, had begun as an Anglo-Norman colonial plantation on the east bank of the river Taff, utilizing the ruined site of a Roman fortress. By the early years of the twelfth century the vill had a motte-and-bailey-castle, priory, parish church indicative of a resident population, and a mint like an English borough. Already by Robert fitz Hamon's time the borough was yielding rents and market customs which enabled him to grant a portion to Tewkesbury Abbey.[130]

Terms to retain and attract rent- and toll-paying tenants in Robert's two boroughs were his liberties' main thrust. Burgesses merely had to pay a painless 12*d*. in quit rent. In return they commuted a wide range of disabilities and fiscal obligations to which villeins were commonly bound: there was to be no payment of heriots or reliefs to inherit a burgage; no license had to be obtained from the lord for sons and daughters to marry; burgesses were free to devise in any way burgages they had purchased, saving the earl's service; hereditary succession to burgages without seigniorial oversight was recognized; burgesses could brew and bake without seigniorial license or payment of a fee; nor was there any obligation for them to use the lord's mill or facilities for fulling and dyeing cloth unless they wished; burgesses were free to sell their cow, horse, or any goods without the lord's license and free of tolls; others were not, including monks, unless they had charters exempting them; burgesses also were exempt from pleading in a hundred court other than the borough's.

Some liberties from this amalgam seem originally to have been applied only to one or the other borough. Exemption from tolls at Gloucester, if not a copyist's error for Bristol, and in Gloucestershire seems more appropriate for Tewkesbury's burgesses; the toll-free status of goods bought or sold in the market for the bishop's own use but not his men's, more for Cardiff's.[131] Furthermore, whatever Cardiff's liberties were, as opposed to Tewkesbury's, Robert just may have granted them to the settlers at Neath before his death. His successor William did this by charter, in which he addressed his tenants as burgesses and in taking the action he used diplomatic language which could be used for confirmations.[132]

---

[129] *DB Gloucestershire* (Phillimore), 1.24–6; *VCH Gloucestershire* viii. 175, 199; Finberg, *Gloucestershire Studies*, 63.
[130] *CPR Henry VII* ii. 94; Cowley, "The Church in Medieval Glamorgan," 95–6; Cowley, *The Monastic Order in South Wales*, 270.
[131] See Patterson, *EGC*, no. 159; other convenient summaries of liberties attributed to both earls may be found in Jones, "The Borough of Tewkesbury," 147; Walker, "Cardiff," 120–1.
[132] Patterson, *EGC*, no. 159 & n. For the use of *dare et concedere* in confirmations, see Hudson, *Land, Law, and Lordship in Anglo-Norman England*, 72–7.

A still higher level of social patronage became a virtual alliance through Earl Robert's special relationships with the upper echelon of burgess society. Key burgesses not only were honorial tenants, but were treated as *familiares*. Robert enlisted a Bristol burgess Lewin fitz Ailric to be chamberlain of his household with possible responsibilities in an inchoate central fiscal bureau at Bristol.[133] Gloucester inherited Osbert Eightpence from his uncle-in-law Haimo as an honorial tenant of a knight's fee, but Osbert was no simple knight. He was a rich and powerful London burgess. His wealth apparently derived from successful dealings in the local money market; and his standing in the borough's burgess community must have led to his gaining the offices of royal justice and sheriff of London and Middlesex in the period *c*.1136 × 43 from both King Stephen and the Empress Matilda. His clerk as sheriff was the later illustrious Thomas, son of Osbert's kinsman and fellow burgess Gilbert Becket.[134] By the early 1140s Earl Robert included Osbert among his most trusted honorial barons. Eightpence was one of eight such men held responsible on the earl's side for making public the terms of his treaty with Miles of Gloucester should it become necessary; and in 1146 Osbert was again one of eight to warrant the earl's treaty with Philip bishop of Bayeux regarding Robert's surrendering claim to Norman fees he had held in the Bessin.[135]

Robert fitz Harding of Bristol provides an even better example because of Fitz Harding's preeminent socio-economic status in Earl Robert's *caput* and because the earl's assimilation of him into the honorial baronage can be traced in almost ascending tenurial order. Fitz Harding ranked at the summit of Bristol's burgess class, a true urban patrician. Although barely visible, the sources of the wealth which enabled him to buy knights' fees, loan money, amass a considerable fortune, and found an *Eigenkloster* which came to overshadow his overlord's priory were at least the land and money markets. I suspect that his Bristol messuages, on which his tenurial status as a burgess was based, provided the fuel for his financial dealings; without doubt they created the tenurial tie with Earl Robert. If Marion Archibald's interesting speculation is correct that Robert fitz Harding was the moneyer *Rodbertus* active at Bristol under the Empress Matilda and the earl during the Anarchy, profits from that enterprise would be a likely Fitz Harding financial pillar.

Fitz Harding was the scion of a regional Saxon thanage family whose lands were subsumed into the post-Conquest Norman tenurial system, and possibly the son of the post-Conquest Bristol moneyer under Henry I.[136] Fitz Harding's share of patrimony there likely became burgage tenures of the developing urban manor of the honor of Gloucester. Some of these may well have made him a demesne tenant of Earl Robert after the king's son acquired Bristol *iure uxoris*. But Fitz Harding

---

[133] See 110–11.
[134] *Regesta* iii. nos. 527–9, 531; Reynolds, "Rulers of London," 354; Brooke & Keir, *London*, 212 & n., 214, 372; Green, *English Sheriffs*, 38; Barlow, *Thomas Becket*, 26–7, 282.
[135] Patterson, *EGC*, nos. 6, 95.
[136] Patterson, "Robert Fitz Harding," 109–10; Williams, *The English and the Norman Conquest*, 120, 122. See also Lewis, "Formation of the Honor of Chester," Appendix 2, 67–8; Archibald, "The Lion Coinage of Robert Earl of Gloucester and William Earl of Gloucester," 76 & n.; the grant was made to Robert and pertained to the manor of Berkeley, not Bristol: *Regesta* iii. no. 310; Patterson, "The Ducal and Royal *Acta* of Henry Fitz Empress in Berkeley Castle," 120 & n., Appendix no. 2.

certainly was a mesne tenant of the earl from messuages he held of Gloucester honorial barons Gilbert de Umfraville, Richard of St. Quintin, and Richard Foliot. Such tenures were the basis for Fitz Harding's status as a Bristol burgess. However, at some point Earl Robert granted him a knight's fee in Bedminster, just south of the borough across the river Avon in Somerset, which accomplished his burgess's metamorphosis to honorial knight.[137] It could be that the Bedminster fee was another of Fitz Harding's purchases for which the evidence has not survived, sold by Earl Robert to help pay the costs of his military needs during the war against Stephen. Regardless of his tenurial status, by the end of Earl Robert's life, if not earlier, Fitz Harding was sitting at his court, attesting as an honorial baron his lord's foundation of Margam Abbey.[138] To mark his elevated status, in the early 1140s he began the process of founding a community of Augustinian canons, ultimately St. Augustine's abbey, in his Bilswick fee. Even then, Fitz Harding's aristocratic rise was not yet complete. Soon after Earl Robert's death Henry fitz Empress made Fitz Harding a tenant-in-chief with additional lands and a castle at Berkeley at Roger of Berkeley's expense. Also in 1153 Fitz Harding's family was further assimilated into the aristocracy by a marriage, arranged by a formal treaty, between his heir Roger and the heiress daughter Alice of the Gloucestershire tenant-in-chief Roger of Berkeley.[139] And within a year or so the former Bristol burgess tenant of Earl Robert raised up in the very Bedminster fee that he held of the earl of Gloucester a chartered borough with the then King Henry's help to rival his overlord's *caput*.[140]

If the *acta* of Robert of Gloucester's heir William are any indication, his father contributed to an honorial culture of burgess participation in comital proceedings.[141] With the metamorphoses of knights and select burgesses and their joint participation in the exercise of honorial business in the honor of Gloucester, distinctions at least between burghal and feudal elites were becoming blurred in the course of the twelfth century.

Robert fitz Harding, Earl Robert's tenant both of demesne and of a knight's fee, is a perfect topical transition to the much larger part of the Gloucester trans-Channel barony which consisted of lands variously granted in fee—subinfeudated—to vassal-tenants before 1136. One example possibly from 1136 × 66 shows that Robert could support knights from his demesne before making grants to them in fee. He apparently did so sometime after 1135 with £20-worth of land at unidentified *Badewenstemendas* for Fulk fitz Warin.[142] It was the wealth, castles, and vassals particularly in England that Orderic Vitalis thought explained the earl's ability to sponsor the Empress Matilda's claim to the Anglo-Norman throne against King Stephen.[143]

---

[137] BA, AC/D.13/1; Patterson, *EGC*, no. 219; *Cart. Bristol*, no. 72 & n.
[138] Patterson, *EGC*, no. 119.    [139] Patterson, "Robert Fitz Harding," 111–14.
[140] Cronne, *Bristol Charters*, 32–6.
[141] Patterson, *EGC*, nos. 36–7, 48, 69, 71, 85, 98, 124, 155, 168.
[142] BL, MS Sloane 1301, fol. 227v.; also in a more abbreviated transcript in Bodl., MS Dodsworth 97, fol. 73r; *RBE* i. 292; *Liber Niger Scaccarii* i. 165. For the distinction between *de vetere* and *de novo* fees, and the meaning of *super dominium*, see Keefe, *Feudal Assessments*, 7–8.
[143] *OV* vi. 516–19.

Most of the subinfeudated portion of the earldom of Gloucester consisted of fees owing the services of knights. Such enfeoffments were one of the ways, in addition to household knights and mercenaries, military tenants-in-chief of the king like Robert raised the quotas of knights (*servitia debita*) they owed the king as well as such forces for themselves. Knights' fees also were potential sources of revenue for their overlords; for example, when granted with military service commuted to annual fixed payments; were in wardship; or were subject to feudal taxes such as relief or scutage.[144]

Robert's 282.3 knights fees belonged to 93 tenants. Just under half of them were obligated to provide the services of multiple knights. Twenty-one held from 5 to 15 knights' fees; and those few with the highest number of fees formed Earl Robert's honorial baronage: Odo, Robert Sor (15), William de la Mare (10), Robert de Clavill (10), Richard de St. Quintin (10), William Fitz John (10), Elias Oriescuilz (10), Robert de Meisi (9), Robert de Gurnay (9), Gilbert de Umfraville (9), and the unnamed son of William fitz Baldwin (9).[145]

Earl Robert's pre-1136 tenants unsurprisingly represent all three of his Anglo-Norman and Welsh lordships. Most held fees of the honor of Gloucester, but at least seventeen of the 93 held some 39 fees of the earl's two Welsh lordships.[146] Among these, the Walenses (Llandough), Nerbers (St. Athan), Wintons (Llandow), Butlers (St. Donats), Cogans (Cogan), and Penarths (Penarth) were tenants of the Shire Fee in Glamorgan.[147] Families like those of Roger of Berkerole (Wentloog), William fitz Robert, Azo brother of Leomerus, Roger fitz Mauger, Herbert son of Herbert chamberlain, and Roger of Bergvalle held fees in Gwynllŵg.[148] Others, like the Sors (also le Sore; St. Fagan), the de Cardiffs (Llantrithyd), the Umfravilles (Penmark), the de Londres (Ogmore), the St. Quintins (Llanbelthian, Pendoylan [Shire Fee], Talyfan), and the Grainvilles (Neath), were the earldom's tenants in both England and Glamorgan;[149] the Guuiz, in England, but with service in Normandy.[150]

The paucity of relevant evidence, especially Robert's charters and references to his grants, makes it very difficult to say how many of the ninety-three honorial tenants by knight-service Earl Robert had enfeoffed or how many of their pre-1136

---

[144] Hollister, *Military Organization of Norman England*, Chapts. 4, 6–7.
[145] *RBE* i. 288–9; *Liber Niger Scaccarii* i. 161. The surnames are either from attestations of Robert's *acta* or from Earl William of Gloucester's list of pre-1136 tenants. On honorial barons, see Stenton, *English Feudalism*, esp. 86–98; Green, *Aristocracy of Norman England*, 198–9, 207. Admittedly the demarcation line between the elite groups and slightly lower fee-holders is somewhat arbitrary; Stenton, *English Feudalism*, 86–98.
[146] Barons of the honor of Gloucester in 1186-7 were pardoned scutage for 41 fees in Wales, probably meaning in both Glamorgan and Gwynllŵg: *PR 33 Henry II*, 142.
[147] *RBE* i. 289, 291; *GCH* iii. 17, 22–7; Nicholl, *Normans in Glamorgan*, 52, 58–63, 65, 75–7, 92–3; for members of families who held Glamorgan fees and attested *acta* of Robert fitz Hamon, see Patterson, *The Scriptorium of Margam Abbey*, 2 n. 6.
[148] *RBE* i. 290–1; *CIPM* iii. 248; Nicholl, *Normans in Glamorgan*, 45n.
[149] *RBE* i. 288; *GCH* iii. 17, 22–5, 27, 32, 97, 337; Nicholl, *Normans in Glamorgan*, 13–14, 17, 21–2, 24–6, 34, 53–8, 61, 68–72, 77–86, 90, 101, 107, 110, 113, 116–17, 143, 152; see in this volume 45, 65, 72 & n., 76, 106, 119, 134.
[150] *RBE* i. 289; *RHG* xiii. 715; *PR 3 John*, 57 (Norman service).

*servitia debita* he had established. In fact, the quota of knights Robert owed to the king (*servitium debitum*) is unknown. As a result, the extent to which the enfeoffment attributable to Robert's tenure satisfied, exceeded, or fell short of this military obligation of a tenant-in-chief cannot be determined.[151] To cite an example of the documentary problem, there is only one surviving text of an original enfeoffment of a knight by the earl with a knight's fee, but, because it is an incomplete transcript, we cannot be sure if the grant was in fee farm or knight-service.[152] And it is true of all types of enfeoffments attributed to Robert that even when such evidence exists, it sometimes is not possible to determine when in Robert's tenure of his various lordships he made the grants or whether these grants were original or mere confirmations.

Even the lists of tenants by knight-service which come from his son Earl William's reply to Henry II's Inquest of 1166 are incomplete. Robert granted Bedminster, just south across the Avon from Bristol, to the patrician Robert fitz Harding for the likely service of one knight.[153] He enfeoffed William of Berkeley, cousin of the earldom's tenant Roger III of Berkeley and founder of Kingswood Abbey, with a knight's fee at Eldersfield, near Tewkesbury.[154] Nigel fitz Arthur, Robert fitz Harding's son-in-law, received a half-knight's fee at Combe (in Wotton-under-Edge, Glos.).[155] Halberton (Devon) was divided into two manors, Halberton Boys and Halberton Abbot, for, respectively, William de Bosco and Gregory de Turri, each with a service obligation of one half-knight.[156]

These Halberton fractional fees and others like them may have been disguised serjeanty tenures, for some form of non-military service, or fee farms, fixed annual rents. Robert certainly employed them. By grants in serjeanty, he could hunt accompanied by at least one of his bowmen, Hinganus, and Benefrei, whom he had apparently provided with, respectively, an estate at Hawkesbury and market rights at Fairford (Glos.);[157] a dog from William de Cardiff per year in return for a half-knight's fee at Queen Hill (Worcs.) could flush out game.[158] And, as already noted, Robert could feast on Christmas, likely at Tewkesbury, waited on by one Richer, attired in red hose, for an estate at Elderfield in return for his service.[159] The grant of Oxenton (Glos.) to Robert *parvus* gave Gloucester a mounted escort

---

[151] The earldom's *servitium debitum* was not among those of 77 secular fiefs Round included in his list: *Feudal England*, 253–6; or in Sidney Painter's in his reduced group of 65: *Feudal Barony*, 24–30, esp. 25 & nn. See Sanders, *English Baronies*, 6 & n.

[152] Bodl., MS Dodsworth 97, fol. 73.

[153] Henry fitz Empress confirmed the grant without indicating the service due: *Regesta* iii. no. 1000; but, contrary to Walker, *Cart. Bristol*, xii, see John count of Mortain (as lord of the honor) confirming the manor, as Fitz Harding held it for the service of one knight, first to Maurice and then to Maurice's son Robert: BA, AC/D.13/1; see also a confirmation to Maurice by Earl Robert's granddaughter Countess Isabel: BA, MS 36074/32 (c).

[154] *BF* i. 139; *RBE* i. 289; *PR 31 Henry I*, 133; Patterson, *EGC*, no. 194; Barkly, "Earlier House of Berkeley," 193, 198–203, 222; *LCGF*, 510–13.

[155] GRO, D.471/T.1/1–2; *Regesta* iii. no. 306. Nigel was married to Robert fitz Harding's daughter Aldeva.

[156] Summerson, *Crown Pleas of the Devon Eyre of 1238*, no. 168n.

[157] *Catalogue of Ancient Deeds* iii. 448 (Robert only recognized as lord); *Cart. Langley*, no. 41.

[158] Patterson, *EGC*, no. 211.    [159] Patterson, *EGC*, no. 216.

at his own expense; if Robert *parvus* was sent alone on the earl's business, he was allowed 2*d.* per day and was assured that if his horse died, he would receive a replacement or its value.[160] I suspect at Bristol castle, a gatekeeper Thomas received estates at Redland and at Ashley (Glos.) for his service.[161] Cash to support a small manorial presence Robert retained at Camberwell south of London near Lambeth in Surrey was made available to him by annual rents of half a gold mark—in effect possible commutations of military service or fee farms—for at least lands he granted from the manor to Reginald Poinz and Robert of Rouen.[162]

Ecclesiastical benefices granted by Robert supported several of his administrative clerks. Master Picard, described as the earl's clerk and *nutritus*, may also have been his household tutor if the Latin term is a mistake for *nutricius*. Robert gave him chapels at Binnerton (in Crowan) and at Germoe, along with the churches of Breage, Gwithian, Phillack, Sancreed, Crowan, and Trevalga in Cornwall.[163] A grant specifically made in free alms involved St. Owen's (Norman, *Euen*) church, Bristol, given by Robert to a priest named Thurstan who may have served as a household chaplain.[164] The earl's clerk Adam of Ely was supported at least in part by four burgages in the suburban market just east of Bristol castle, but his service obligations for them are unknown.[165]

Robert of Gloucester, like other magnates, functioned as landlord of his barony's demesne and as overlord of its tenants through an administrative structure which mirrored the king's, although less developed. Its center was the earl's household staff, with comparable major officers, stewards, butlers, chamberlains, constables, clerks, and chaplains who could address his domestic as well as bureaucratic needs.[166] The earl excelled in recruiting men with reputations for learning, especially *magistri*, to perform clerical tasks, as well as in including urban and business types in his household among his trusted *curiales*.[167]

Stewards (*dapiferi*) usually were magnates' most important officials. They traditionally supervised their lords' halls, and custom recognized that they could serve as their lords' legal alter egos. In this capacity they could represent their lords

---

[160] BL, Additional MS 28206, no. 167, fol. 122v.    [161] Patterson, *EGC*, no. 273.
[162] Patterson, *EGC*, nos. 250–2; Stenton, *English Feudalism*, 172–4, 179; Lennard, *Rural England*, 111–12; Pollock and Maitland, *History of English Law*, i. 293. Robert of Rouen gave his land to the nuns of Augustinian Haliwell, London, which gift Earl William of Gloucester may have confirmed: Patterson, *EGC*, 113 & n.; *VCH Surrey* iv. 28. The Poinz fee was at Camberwell and descended in the family: Bodl., MS Dodsworth 102, fol. 90b; Antony House, PG/B2/6, no. 3511, p. 420, no. 3797, p. 512; *VCH Surrey* iv. 30.
[163] BL, MS Cotton Cleopatra A.vii, fol. 76 (mod. fol.): Picken, "Descent of the Devonshire Family of Willington from Robert Earl of Gloucester," p. 94 & Appendix nos. 1 & n., 2 & n., correcting Patterson, *EGC*, 10, no. 202; but to date I have found no tenurial association of the earl's son Robert with Ilchester: see *VCH Somerset* iii. 183 for royal tenure in the twelfth century. Picard also held the church of Écrammeville (Calvados), but his tenure of it only can be dated to the time of Earl William of Gloucester: Patterson, *EGC*, no. 38; Barlow, *William Rufus*, 15n; Chibnall, in *OV* i. s.v. *nutricius*, and Chibnall *The World of Orderic Vitalis*, 132, for military tutor; *nutriti* also stood for those who had been raised in a monastery; Latham, *Revised Medieval Latin Word-List*, 317.
[164] Patterson, *EGC*, 13, nos. 275–6; *EEA* xxxiii. no. 86.
[165] *EEA* xxxiii. 12, no. 77; BA, 5139 (139), 5139 (448).
[166] Mason, "Barons and their Officials in the Later Eleventh Century," 243–62.
[167] See 31, 104–5.

in hundred or shire courts or act as their lords' legates *a latere*.[168] Earl Robert employed stewards for his Norman and English honors. Two served him in Normandy, an undertenant of William de Mohun, Hubert de Pierrepont, and William Crassus, who presided over a *conventio* in 1138 between the canons of Ardenne and the priest of Saint-Germain-la-Blanche-Herbe (Calvados), apparently at Robert's honorial court.[169] Three members of the Oxfordshire D'Almary family, Gilbert, Herbert, and Robert, held stewardships during Earl Robert's tenure of the honor of Gloucester.[170] Another steward of Gloucester's English honor also came from a service family like the D'Almarys. Geoffrey de Walterville or Waterville was a possible Cambridgeshire Gloucester tenant.[171] His father Ascelin, the Domesday tenant of Marholm (Northants.) held of Peterborough Abbey, seems, as Edmund King has argued, to have served as the abbot's *dapifer*. From Ascelin's attestations of Robert fitz Hamon's *acta*, he seems to have served Earl Robert's predecessor in some capacity. Geoffrey's elder brother Hugh followed in their father's footsteps at Peterborough Abbey.[172]

Geoffrey, through his performance of his duties, is the best known of all Earl Robert's household officials. In one comital charter Geoffrey, addressed as *dapifer* and clearly as such chief officer of the earl's court, had responsibility for ensuring the tenure of certain lands which had been given to St. Peter's Abbey Gloucester.[173] In another from 1135 × 38, Earl Robert used Geoffrey to cause an Earl Gilbert (probably lord of Clare, lord of Chepstow, and later earl of Pembroke) to be seized of the Bedfordshire manor of Luton. But as an illustration that a Gloucester

---

[168] *Leges Henrici Primi*, 42, 2; Stenton, *English Feudalism*, 74–9. A William butler (*pincerna*) attested Richard de Grainville's foundation charter for Neath Abbey along with some Gloucester personnel, but I have been unable to determine if he was one of Earl Robert's household officials: see Nicholl, *The Normans in Glamorgan*, 68.

[169] For Hubert de Pierrepont, see AD du Calvados, H.7824, for a transcript of which I am indebted to Professor Daniel J. Power; Hubert seems to have had a landed interest at Clayhanger (Som.) before 1185: *Records of the Templars in England*, 59; for William Crassus, see AD du Calvados, H.1: *Gallia Christiana*, Instrumenta IX, p. 78; Vincent, "The Borough of Chipping Sodbury and the 'Fat Men' of France," 144–5 & n. 20, for which I am endebted to Professor Vincent. See also Patterson, *EGC*, nos. 6, 38, 186; *RHG* xxiii. 620.

[170] Hubert *dapifer* and Robert D'Amary appear in a charter written at Earl William of Gloucester's court by an unidentified scribe, BCM, no. 15; Patterson, *EGC*, nos. 84, 95, 119, 283; *CPR Henry IV* iii. 15; for the D'Amary family of Bletchingdon (Oxon.), see *VCH Oxfordshire* vi. 58. For tenures held as an undertenant of Keynsham Abbey (Som.) through Earl William of Gloucester's grants, see *CRR* xi. 563; xii. 225, 237, 315, 380; *Mon. Angl.* vi. pt. 2, 452–3; for Stockwood by Keynsham, see *CPR Edward II* ii. 114. For Hambledon (Bucks.), see *CRR* xi. 563; xii. 237, 380. For Winkfield (Wilts.), see *CRR* x. 11. See Green, *Aristocracy of Norman England*, 208–9: The Gilbert *dapifer* referred to in a charter of Robert fitz Hamon may not be Gilbert D'Almary, as Green suggested, but rather Gilbert de Umfraville: in one of Henry I's charters to Tewkesbury Abbey granting rights to assart, the king addressed Walter sheriff of Gloucestershire first, followed by Gilbert de Umfraville, arguably responsible for the Gloucestershire sites of Fitz Hamon's honor (*Regesta* ii. no. 853). Even more persuasive is another of the king's charters confirming to Tewkesbury Abbey land a serjeant of Fitz Hamon had sold to the abbey and forbidding de Umfreville to require the abbey to answer for service from the land (*Regesta* ii. no. 1979).

[171] Patterson, *EGC*, no. 83; also nos. 6, 70, 95, 110; Warner & Ellis, no. 36 & n., Plate XXIII; Sanders, *English Baronies*, 97n.

[172] For service to Peterborough, see *PR 31 Henry I*, 83; *Regesta ii*. no. 1733; King, "The Knights of Peterborough Abbey," 42, 44, 46; King, *Peterborough Abbey*, 32–3.

[173] Patterson, *EGC*, no. 83; see also nos. 70, 95.

steward's authority might extend to honorial tenants, the steward in turn dispatched Walter de Chesney (*de Querceto*), who held a fee of five knights of the honor, to perform the actual installation.[174] Geoffrey adopted a fine equestrian seal proudly bearing his comital office's title in its legend: +SIGILLV(M) GAVFRIDI DE WATERVILLA DAPIFER[I CSVLIS?].[175] He married Asceline, an heiress to the barony of Bourn (Cambs.).[176]

At least three sheriffs are known to have headed Robert's administration for the honor of Glamorgan and its dependent lordship of Gwynllŵg. A William sheriff of Cardiff belonged to a group of Anglo-Normans Pope Calixtus admonished for harming the church of Llandaff in 1119.[177] A shadowy Ralph's only documentary appearance is a testimonial to the importance of his shrieval office. Earl Robert had him dispatched to Woodstock with a select group of his honorial tenants to witness his 1126 treaty with Bishop Urban of Llandaff in 1126 before the king and his court.[178] Robert Norreys, the next known office holder, was active during the 1140s and into the early years of Earl William's administration. He held the Member lordship of Penllyn for the service of 2 knights, but he may not have gained it until William of Gloucester became lord of Glamorgan.[179] Norreys's authority in Glamorgan surpassed that of ordinary honorial *dapiferi* in England because the court of Cardiff over which he presided served as both honorial and private shire's court. Perhaps his most revelatory manifestation is an occasion at Earl Robert's Bristol court when he witnessed a writ-charter addressed to himself which would have been presented to him later at Cardiff by the beneficiary.[180]

For maintenance of his chamber and household's finances, Robert chose a Bristol burgess and budding landlord in Somerset as undertenant of at least three different lords. Lewin chamberlain, also known as Lewin son of Ailric of Bristol or Lewin of Brislington, also continued in this role under the earl's son. Lewin was

---

[174] BL, MS Cotton Otho D.iii, fol. 41; *Gesta Abbatum Monasterii Sancti Albani* i. 116–17; *RBE* i. 289; Williams, "William the Chamberlain and Luton Church," 726; but corrected by Douglas, "Frankalmoin and Jurisdictional Immunity," 29 & n., 30; *English Lawsuits*, i. 249–50; *EEA* i. Appendix. I, no. 15; see also Saltman, *Theobald, Archbishop of Canterbury*, "Charters," no. 229; Crouch, *Reign of King Stephen*, 306; *VCH Bedfordshire* i. 314–15; Richardson and Sayles, *Governance*, 286–7 & nn.; for doubt about the identity of Earl Gilbert, see *VCH Bedfordshire* ii. 350 & n.; however, I support recent scholars' identification of the Cotton document's "Earl Gilbert" with Gilbert earl of Pembroke.

[175] Warner & Ellis, no. 36 & n.

[176] For conflicting views, see King, *Peterborough Abbey*, 39; Sanders, *English Baronies*, 19.

[177] Clark, *Cartae et alia*, i. no. LVII; William may or may not have been the William sheriff of Cardiff who represented Robert fitz Hamon when Robert de la Haye made a gift of Gwynllŵg land to Montacute Priory: *Cartae* i. no. XXXV; a William de Cardiff seems to have been the same individual Earl Robert enfeoffed with Queen Hill (Worcs.) and held a likely pre-1136 fee of one knight in England and of half a knight's service in Wales: *BF* i. 139; *RBE* i. 289; *Liber Niger Scaccarii* i. 163; Patterson, *EGC*, no. 109; the family held the Glamorgan lordship of Llantrithyd: *GCH*, 17–18; Nicholl, *The Normans in Glamorgan*, 69; Dowdeswell, "Some Ancient Deeds," 165.

[178] Patterson, *EGC*, no. 109.

[179] Rice Merrick preserved a tradition that Norreys was enfeoffed by Earl William: *A Booke of Glamorganshires Antiquities*, 53–4, 82–3; Patterson, *EGC*, nos. 68, 84, 119; Patterson, *The Scriptorium of Margam Abbey*, 3, 6–7. *RBE* i. 291, and *Liber Niger Scaccarii* i. 164, indicating that the fee of Robert Norreys is vacant by the end of 1135, is in error, unless the sheriff of the 1140s and later was a Robert II.

[180] Patterson, *EGC*, no. 182. For the jurisdictional scope of the Cardiff court, see Chapt. 3, 76–7.

active in estate-building as early as 1130, when he acquired Houndstreet in Marksbury (Som.) from the abbot of Glastonbury, Henry of Blois.[181]

Whether Lewin's responsibilities extended beyond the *camera curie* to a central fiscal body which I believe Earl Robert maintained in the early years of his tenure is an unanswerable question. So too is whether this "bureau," at least under Earl Robert, was the chamber. Great landed magnates needed some kind of organization for the financial administration of their estates; and several such facilities have been established, for example, for his son-in-law Ranulf II of Chester and contemporaries Robert I and II of Leicester.[182] Earl Robert's successor William certainly had one at Bristol called an exchequer (*scaccarium*) to which his harper William paid a dish of beans once a year.[183] The fact that military tenants from all three of the earldom's principal honors were included in the list of the honor of Gloucester's pre-1136 military tenants submitted to King Henry II for his inquest of 1166 suggests that the Norman and Welsh lordships' revenues also went to the honor of Gloucester's *caput*.[184] Presumably these would have included the aids Robert levied on his tenants by knight-service, although the only one any contemporary source specifically mentions is the scutage he demanded in lieu of tenants' sending their knights.[185] Reliefs, the inheritance tax paid for lords' recognitions of heirs' succession to their fees, was probably another. Income from the estates of minor heirs and unmarried heiresses in wardship probably was rendered there as well.[186]

Staff for the Gloucester facility would have come from Robert's household clerical personnel, his notably numerous masters, as well as clerks, and chaplains. *magistri*, by definition, were products of higher learning gained from cathedral or monastic schools. Clerks and chaplains presumably also were reasonably literate. Theoretically, then, they were capable of receiving revenue, managing accounts, and creating records, including charters.[187] Their retention by Robert's son and

---

[181] Bodl., MS Wood empt. 1, fol. 208v: *Cart. Glastonbury* ii. no. 1028 & p. 562; *EEA* viii. no. 62 & n.; *Cart. Cirencester* i. xxiv, no. 187; ii. no. 630; Patterson, *EGC*, nos. 7, 36–7, 182; Stenton, *English Feudalism*, 71–3. For another chamberlain of Earl William of Gloucester, Helie, see BCM, Select Charter no. 15.

[182] Stenton, *English Feudalism*, 69–70; Crouch, *Beaumont Twins*, 163; Crouch, "Administration of the Norman Earldom," 82, shows that this facility was the chamber; see also 83–6; and, e.g., English, *The Lords of Holderness*, 93; Greenway, *Charters of the Honour of Mowbray*, lxvi–lxix.

[183] Patterson, *EGC*, no. 188.  [184] *RBE* i. 288–92; *Liber Niger Scaccarii* i. 161–5.

[185] *GS* (2004), 150–1.

[186] Earl Robert showed knowledge of relief in his charter of liberties for Cardiff and Tewkesbury: Patterson, *EGC*, no. 46; and in a *conventio* he made with the abbot of Fécamp, he agreed about how the abbot and prior of Saint-Gabriel should divide reliefs and revenues: *EGC*, no. 70. For circumstantial evidence of wardship, see, e.g., mention of the fees held of the earl by the son of William fitz Baldwin and by, e.g., the Gournay, Greinville, and de Clinton families: *RBE* i. 288–9; *Liber Niger Scaccarii* i. 161–2.

[187] Patterson, *EGC*, 9–10, 12–14, 26–7. In general, see Clanchy, *From Memory to Written Record*, 53, 56, 65, 227–8; *GOE*, esp, 43, 135, 157–9; note the functional distinction Crouch sees between chaplains and clerks: "Administration of the Norman Earldom," 83–6; Webber's commentary on the force of clerks' and chaplains' attestations of Chester *acta* is persuasive; contrary to her minimalist views of the evidence for a writing office under Earl William of Gloucester ("The Scribes and Handwriting of the Original Charters," 138), it shows that he maintained one: Patterson, *The Scriptorium of Margam Abbey*, 26–7; for another charter written for the Gloucester vassal Richard Foliot by an unidentified scribe at Earl William's court, see BCM, no. 15; *Descriptive Catalogue*, ed Jeayes, no. 15.

their professional mobility—Adam of Ely's, Richard of Ilchester's, and Master Elias's departures from Earl William's service for Henry II's and Queen Eleanor's—testify to their "saleable" skills.[188] Robert's chaplain Herbert even followed the traditional promotional route of chaplain-clerks to a bishopric, Avranches.[189]

Such staff members' administrative roles, except for the famous notary Richard of Ilchester and, I believe, Adam de Ely, are mainly indicated in extant evidence by their work names. Some individuals labeled masters like Picard and Henry Tusard also were identified as clerks.[190] Herveus, the self-described *scriptor* of one of Earl William's original charters, identified himself as both *magister* and clerk.[191] Several household chaplains, who might, but not necessarily, be in priestly orders and administer the sacraments, apparently also functioned as clerks on the basis of such occasional designations.[192] This was true of the royal scriptorium and the contemporary administrations of the earls of Chester and Leicester, although in both administrations *capellani* were never referred to as *clerici*.[193] Given the vagary in the administrative status of Robert's clerical personnel, they are best considered members of a household "secretarial pool," available for a variety of tasks, the clerical department, for lack of a better term. Earl Robert may have given Adam of Ely, former clerk of Robert of Leicester and dean of the collegiate church of Wareham (Dors.), who grandly proclaimed in his charters that he was the earl of Gloucester's clerk, a leadership position in the group;[194] and as a result, as David Crouch suggested, he may have influenced the comital fiscal body's development into an exchequer.[195]

Master Herveus, the clerk in Earl William's household who wrote charters as a member of his writing office, illustrates how staff from Robert's generic household clerical department could be assigned secretarial functions. Four *magistri* and clerks, Adam of Ely, Picot, Henry Tusard, and Elias, were available for the drafting and execution of the charter recording Earl Robert's foundation of Margam Abbey at his Bristol court in 1147.[196] Furthermore, a charter Herveus wrote as his colleague Adam de Ely's scribe suggests that by William's tenure, if not earlier, the group of assigned scribal clerks to what we call the writing office had developed a fledgling structure under the leadership of Adam as chief clerk.[197]

Because only copies of Earl Robert's charters survive, no master or clerk can be shown paleographically to have written his *acta*. And none of Gloucester's *acta* even bears a revealing *qui conscripsit hanc cartam* clause attached to the name of an

---

[188] Patterson, *EGC*, 12–14; Amt, *The Accession of Henry II in England*, 41.
[189] Patterson, *EGC*, 13.
[190] Patterson, *EGC*, 10, 13, no. 38; Picken, "The Descent of the Family of Willington from Robert, Earl of Gloucester," Appendix nos. 1–2, pp. 102, 104.
[191] Patterson, *EGC*, 10, 17, no. 75; also nos. 97, 188.   [192] Patterson, *EGC*, nos. 157, 283.
[193] Crouch, *Beaumont Twins*, 148, 151; Crouch, "Administration of the Norman Earldom," 83: see also Webber, "The Scribes and Handwriting of the Original Charters," 139 & n. 12.
[194] BA, 5139 (139), 5139 (448); see also Patterson, *EGC*, 12; Crouch, *Beaumont Twins*, 46 & n., 166.
[195] Crouch, *Beaumont Twins*, 46 & n., 166.   [196] Patterson, *EGC*, no. 119.
[197] BA, 5139 (448); Patterson, *EGC*, 25–7; see n. 198; see also Crouch, *Beaumont Twins*, 153–4, 166; Webber, "The Scribes and Handwriting of the Original Charters," 139 & n. 12, 140–1; Crouch, "Administration of the Norman Earldom," 85.

Figure 4.1. Seal of Robert earl of Gloucester altered and used by his son and successor William (1147–83). NLW, Penrice and Margam Estate Record, no. 20.
© by permission of Llyfrgell Genedlaethol Cymru/The National Library of Wales.

attesting clerk to at least associate its production with the individual. However, there is evidence that a writing office was functioning during Robert's tenure. To begin with, the earl authenticated his *acta* with appended seals, regardless of their internal or external provenance; in fact Countess Mabel may have had her own.[198] The seal (Figure 4.1), as the numismatist Marion Archibald has confirmed, was essentially the same as Earl William's extant ones: thus, wax, round, on the obverse, a lion passant to the dexter, with a lily or conventional flowering plant behind it, bearing the legend +SIGILLVM RODBERTI (possibly abbreviated) (or ROBERTI) GLOENCESTRIE CONSVLIS; and possibly on the reverse, an intaglio gem, the image of a helmeted bust to the dexter between two figures of Nike, below which is an eagle rising regardant between two standards with the legend +AQVILA SV' ET CVSTOS COMITIS. Crude lettering of VV I[LLEL]MI as opposed to that of the rest of the legend shows that the legend on its metal matrix was changed by excising RODBERTI (or ROBERTI) and in its place recutting VV ILLELMI. Furthermore, as Archibald has noted, the flowering plant is a likely allusion to Isaiah 11:1, with the rod arising from the stem of Jesse, which would nicely stress Robert's royal lineage.[199]

*Acta* issued in Earl Robert's name mainly fall into two groups identifiable by the distinctive formulas of their address clauses. Those with wording especially typical of monastic and episcopal *acta* such as *Sciant presentes et futuri quod...*, *Notum sit omnibus tam presentibus et futuris...*, and *Karitatis uestre... notifico...* strongly suggest that they were the work of beneficiaries' scribes rather than bureau staff the earl maintained.[200] On the other hand, *acta* with notification clauses reading

---

[198] Patterson, *EGC*, no. 283; Clark, *Cartae et alia* v. no. 720, p. 1683; see n. 223.
[199] NLW, Penrice & Margam Deed, no. 20 obverse; legend partly damaged, but with personal examination aided by a 1970s photo: +SIGILLVM WI[LLEL]MI GLOENCESTRIE CONSVLIS; see Figure 4.1; Patterson, *EGC*, 24; and Archibald, "The Lion Coinage of Robert Earl of Gloucester," 73–4; Harvey and McGuinness, *A Guide to British Medieval Seals*, 43.
[200] Patterson, *EGC*, 21 & nos. 156, 283; *OASPG*, xlix–l; Chaplais, "The Original Charters of Herbert and Gervase Abbots of Westminster (1121–1157)," nos. 1–3, 5–6, 8; see also Davis,

*Sciatis me*...or *Sciatis quod*..., which were increasingly popular with lay lords, were arguably the office's products.[201] Ironically, the only known original *actum* apparently produced at one of Earl Robert's honorial courts, Richard de Grainville's foundation charter for Savignac Neath Abbey, was written not for the earl but for a vassal and, to judge by the wording of the address clause, by an "alien" non-comital ecclesiastical scribe.[202]

Finally, Earl Robert maintained or perhaps utilized an archive of some sort to complement his writing office. The very agreement the earl made in 1126 with Bishop Henry of Llandaff records that Robert had a copy of it (*contrascriptum*).[203] Also, if Robert failed to keep the agreement of the *confederatio amoris* he made around July 1142 with Miles of Gloucester, Countess Mabel pledged to make legal record of it known, which presupposes a retained half of the chirograph for her reference.[204]

Earl Robert's *acta* reveal his household's key military official, the constable. Baronial constables could be commanders of the household's corps of knights as well as of castle garrisons. Sir Frank Stenton stated long ago that early records favor the latter function.[205] But the early honor of Gloucester may provide an exception. It seems that Earl Robert used constables in both capacities, like the royal constableships of Walter of Gloucester and his son Miles. Richard constable may be found attached to Robert's household at both Cranborne and London, where there were no castles; and if, as I suspect, he was Richard de Grainville, the self-proclaimed constable of the earl of Gloucester, then he was also the garrison commander of Robert's castle at Neath.[206]

Richard's likely successor was Hugh de Gundeville. He appears in only one of Robert's *acta* issued at Bristol, and because he also was supported on the Gloucester demesne until well after the earl's death, Hugh's constableship was only domestic.[207] Like Fulk fitz Warin, Hugh was actually, and not just notionally, enfeoffed with

---

*The Kalendar of Abbot Samson of Bury St. Edmunds*, e.g., nos. 7–9; Patterson, *The Scriptorium of Margam Abbey*, 59; for episcopal *acta*, see Cheney, *English Bishops' Chanceries*, 69–74. For the address clause formula *omnibus / uniuersis Christi fidelibus* which appears in the late 1170s, see Vincent, "Early Years of Keynsham Abbey," 97.

[201] *Sciatis me*: Patterson, *EGC*, 21 & nos. 6, 42, 68, 83–4, 119, 152; *Sciatis quod*: *EGC*, nos. 82, 157. For an example of an ecclesiastical beneficiary's drafting, see *EGC*, nos. 156, 283.

[202] WGAS, GB0216 A/N 1: Clark, *Cartae et alia* i. no. lxvii; Birch, *Neath Abbey*, Appendix II, both with errors in the address clause; Wilcox, "The Foundation Charter of Neath Abbey," 18. Butler, "The Foundation Charter of Neath Abbey," 214–16; Patterson, *The Scriptorium of Margam Abbey*, 15n., 30 & n., Appendix III, no. 271. The text begins, "Notum sit omnibus tam futuris quam presentibus quod ego..." For the additional criteria I have applied in this description and for an example of a charter issued by a comital scribe for a vassal at an honorial court under Earl William of Gloucester, see Patterson, "Vassals and the Norman Earldom of Gloucester's Scriptorium," 342–3. Note Earl Robert's first-person subscription: Figure 1.1, 10.

[203] Patterson, *EGC*, no. 109.  [204] Patterson, *EGC*, no. 95.

[205] Stenton, *English Feudalism*, 79–81.

[206] Patterson, *EGC*, nos. 152, 157, 283; Birch, *Neath Abbey*, 36, 56, "Appendix," nos. VII, XI, IIA.b. Richard also had his own castle in his Member lordship west of the river Neath.

[207] Patterson, *EGC*, no. 119; *RBE* i. 291; *Liber Niger Scaccarii* i. 164. A castellan Robert might install at Sherborne (Wilts.), which he captured during the Anarchy, is called a constable: *EGC*, no. 171; Stenton, *English Feudalism*, 80.

two Gloucester fees before 1166. These were centered on Pimperne and Tarrant Gunville in Dorset. To these were added several other Gloucester estates. One was called *Estentona* or *Eastenest*, which might be Exton in Hampshire or, I believe more likely, Easton, part of the earl's manor of Barton and administratively associated with the constable of Bristol, albeit in later evidence; the other, at Chipping Campden in Gloucestershire, where he established a borough.[208] Like Hubert de Pierrepont and the chaplain Warin, Hugh joined Robert of Gloucester apparently after earlier service to William de Mohun lord of Dunster. And just as several of Gloucester's clerks did, Hugh remained for a time in Gloucester service before finally "jumping" to King Henry's.[209] The king's temporary seizure of Bristol castle around 1173–4 may have had something to do with the constable's change of loyalty.[210] In any case, Hugh became one of Henry's lesser *familiares*, won further estates from him, and before his death *c*.1181 among his roles served the king as general factotum, ambassador, sheriff, royal justice, baron of the exchequer, and guardian and one of the councilors of the young King Henry.[211]

In feudal terms, the most central institutions of the earl of Gloucester's administrative system were his three honorial courts. On the one hand, his enfeoffed tenants were bound to attend them and, on the other, he as lord was obliged to seek the counsel of these men in court concerning the business of the Gloucester barony.[212] The notification clauses of Robert's charters addressed to his *barones*, *amici*, and *fideles* in effect are recognitions of their curial role.[213] In one such *actum* Robert notified this group in his Norman barony of the terms of his proprietary agreement with the bishop of Bayeux.[214] One of the honor of Gloucester's seven Ditton fees was awarded to a certain Gregory after his claim had been considered in Earl Robert's presence.[215] His *concordia* with Bishop Urban of Llandaff in 1126 in effect recognized that the lordship of Glamorgan's court meeting in Cardiff castle would be where suits involving judicial duel by the bishop of Llandaff's men against Robert's direct or mesne tenants would be settled.[216] Robert's 1128 *conventio* with the abbot of Fécamp recognized his Norman court's potential role in choosing a prior for Saint-Gabriel's near Caen and in approving any sale, mortgage, or grant of its lands.[217]

---

[208] *Cart. Cirencester* iii. nos. 808–9; Vincent, "Hugh de Gundeville," 127–8 & nn., 129; Appendix, nos. 1–2, 7–8.; Sharp, *Accounts of the Constables of Bristol Castle*, xxxvi–xxxvii, liii–lv. On Chipping Campden, see Patterson, *EGC*, no. 226, and 90. Both my and Nicholas Vincent's identification of *Estentona* and *Eastenest* are conjectural.

[209] PRO, 31, 8/140B, iii. no. 41 (but dated 1142 × 63); Patterson, *EGC*, 13–14, nos. 85?, 96, 111; *EEA* vi. no. 136; *Documents and Extracts Illustrative of the Honour of Dunster*, 4; see n. 208; royal favor was being extended to Hugh as early as 1155–6: *PR 2 Henry II*, 30, 49–50, 61; *Cartae Antiquae Rolls 11–20*, no. 620; Vincent, "Hugh de Gundeville," 125–6, 131.

[210] Patterson, "Bristol: An Angevin Baronial Capital under Royal Siege," 178–9.

[211] BL, Sloan Roll xxxi. 4, no. 34: *Basset Charters* no. 34; West, *The Justiciarship in England*, 48 & n.; Vincent, "Hugh de Gundeville," 131–4.

[212] *Leges Henrici Primi*, 55, 1–3; Stenton, *English Feudalism*, 42.

[213] On honorial barons, see Green, *Aristocracy of Norman England*, 198.

[214] Patterson, *EGC*, no. 6; for Glamorgan, no. 68; for England, no. 82; for a more general address, see nos. 157, 283; *Cart. Langley*, no. 41.

[215] *RBE* i. 288–9; *Liber Niger Scaccarii* i. 161.    [216] Patterson, *EGC*, no. 109.

[217] Patterson, *EGC*, no. 70, in which the Gloucester court interestingly is called a chapter.

Except for the Ditton case we never see Earl Robert dispensing justice to an honorial tenant, but at least his scope of jurisdiction is known. In England he enjoyed the usual baronial franchises of *soc, sac, toll, team,* and *infangentheof.* These gave him the right to hold manorial and honorial courts for his men, to receive profits of justice, to collect tolls and have jurisdiction over transactions on his land, and to hang thieves caught on his land with stolen goods in their hands.[218] Robert's situation in his Norman honor of Évrecy probably was similar. The appearance of an apparent tenant before Robert's *dapifer*, William Crassus, to donate land to Saint-Gabriel's Priory provides a glimpse of his feudal jurisdiction, which custom and the duchy's earliest, albeit end-of-century, law code, the *Très Ancien Coutumier*, recognized. The code's general principle about franchises was that unless claimed as ducal, all others belonged to the baronage.[219] However, those pleas which were claimed put most of what would be classified in England as pleas of the sword solely under ducal jurisdiction or enjoyed by ducal grant. These included murder, rape, robbery, various types of homicide, arson, and assaults.[220] Even though the *Très Ancien Coutumier* often narrowly defines these reserved pleas in terms of peculiar circumstances and indicates some division of jurisdiction with lords, it would be unwise to conclude that anything outside these perimeters was baronial. As the century-earlier *Consuetudines et Iusticie* put it, there was more regarding ducal-royal and baronial jurisdictions than was recorded.[221] Furthermore, since it is doubtful that Robert's lord for Évrecy, the bishop of Bayeux, held franchises for pleas of the sword, in the absence of direct evidence it might be argued that Earl Robert also did not.[222]

In Glamorgan, the situation was quite different. There, as already noted, Robert inherited from Mabel's father both a private shire with jurisdiction in theory comprehending both civil and criminal pleas and also some regalian rights enjoyed by Gwynllŵg's previous native princes. In a donation to Montacute's priory at Malpas in his lordship of Gwynllŵg Robert granted its court the same immunity his own enjoyed. Right of wreck, to judge from Earl William of Gloucester's confirmation of his father's grants to Neath Abbey, may have been one of them.[223]

Glimpses of Robert exercising authority indirectly over his honors come from certain writs and charter notifications he addressed to their chief officers. These *acta* all had beneficiaries who had first obtained them from the earl and then presented them to one of his Norman or English stewards or to his Welsh sheriff for reference and execution.[224] In a text copied in the cartulary of St. Peter's Abbey

---

[218] *Leges Henrici Primi* 9, 4–4a; 9, 11; 20, 20, 1a–2; 24, 1–4; 59.19; Hurnard, "The Anglo-Norman Franchises," 450; Stenton, *English Feudalism*, 100–11; Roffe, "From Thegnage to Barony," 157–76; Hudson, *The Formation of the English Common Law*, 43–5.

[219] *Très Ancien Coutumier*, c.lix.1; see also c.liii.

[220] *Très Ancien Coutumier*, cc.xv–xvi, xxxv, liii, lix, lxvii, lxix–lxx; "Consuetudines et Iusticie," in Haskins, *Norman Institutions*, 27–30, 278; Appendix D, 281–4; Bates, *Normandy before 1066*, 122.

[221] *Très Ancien Coutumier*, c.lix, and, e.g., c.lxvii.2; "Consuetudiunes et Iusticie," c.xiii, p. 284.

[222] Gleason, *An Ecclesiastical Barony*, 89–91.

[223] Patterson, *EGC*, nos. 156, 246; *Mon. Angl.* v. 259 (confirmation by King John); Appendix XI, II A.e, 325 (Clark, *Cartae et alia* v. no. 720, p. 1683); Birch, *Neath Abbey*, 50, 58; the text of Earl William's charter is clearly spurious, as Birch saw.

[224] Patterson, *EGC*, e.g., nos. 6 (Normandy), 83 (England), 68 (Glamorgan), 109 (*uicecomiti uel preposito de Kardi*), no. 162 (sheriff [of Glamorgan] and *prévôt* of Newport).

Gloucester against possible loss, Robert advised Geoffrey de Waterville of grants by Miles of Gloucester's grandmother Adelisa to St. Peter's Abbey Gloucester and wished that the steward see that the abbey suffer no damage or controversy because of them.[225] Individual honorial tenants also could be managed. A writ preserved by the Mauduit family for possible legal use, informing possibly William I of Eynsford and his wife that he had granted land formerly held by Robert de Mauduit to his brother William, commanded them to render the same service to William as they had to Robert.[226] No direct communications survive from Robert to local manorial fiscal and judicial officers referred to generically as *ministri* or more individually as *prévôts* (*praepositi*) and bailiffs (*bailivi*). Earl William certainly communicated with such personnel and there is reason to believe that Robert did as well.[227] Even so, Michael Clanchy believes that most business directions in this period were communicated verbally through messengers.[228]

Many of Robert's extant grants reflect the contemporary proprietary piety which sought spiritual benefits in return for grants of revenues and lands, especially from monks and on a grander scale, from monastic foundations. Ironically, the Anarchy is notable for the latter.[229]

Various organizational developments within western monasticism which took root in the Anglo-Norman realm attracted the earl's patronage, just as they did his father and, in general, the Anglo-Norman baronage.[230] Robert personally supported the Benedictine Order by grants to St. Peter's Gloucester and its Glamorgan priory, Ewenny,[231] his inherited *Eigenkloster* St. Mary's Tewkesbury[232] and his foundation St. James's Priory, Bristol,[233] and Cluniac Montacute's priory of Malpas (Monm.).[234] He also favored even more reformed communities deriving from Tiron,[235] Savigny,[236] and especially Cîteaux,[237] and the more socially involved Augustinian and Norbertine or Premonstratensian canons.[238] Finally, at least one

---

[225] Patterson, *EGC*, no. 83.
[226] Patterson, *EGC*, no. 152; regarding its preservation, see Mason, *Cart. Beauchamp*, xii, no. 161 & n.; *GOE*, 247.
[227] Patterson, *EGC*, e.g., charters as patents nos. 68, 283; mention of bailiffs and *prévôts*: 156 (Newport), 162 (Gwynllêg) 271 (Kenfig); *ministri*: nos. 82, 110; for Earl William, see *EGC*, no. 69; Chaplais, *English Royal Documents*, 4–7, 19.
[228] Clanchy, *From Memory to Written Record*, 89–90; see a documentary defense of the use of written *acta* in Crouch, "The Acts of Waleran II," 77–81.
[229] *Mon. Angl.* ii. 71, 73, 75–6; Patterson, *EGC*, nos. 68, 83, 156–7, 169 & n., 242–3; Clark, *Cartae et alia* i. no. 67; Postles, "Religious Houses and the Laity in Eleventh to Thirteenth-Century England," 11–12.
[230] Ward, "Fashions in Monastic Endowment," 436; in general, see Green, *The Aristocracy of Norman England*, Chapt. 12, *passim*; Thomas, "Lay Piety in England," 179–92; Holdsworth, "The Church," 216–28.
[231] Patterson, *EGC*, nos. 68, 82, 84.  [232] Patterson, *EGC*, nos. 180, 283.
[233] Patterson, *EGC*, nos. 199–200, 260–1.  [234] Patterson, *EGC*, nos. 156–7.
[235] Patterson, *EGC*, no. 193; Thompson, "The First Hundred Years of the Abbey of Tiron," 104–17.
[236] Patterson, *EGC*, nos. 242?–243.  [237] Patterson, *EGC*, no. 119.
[238] Patterson, *EGC*, no. 110; *Gallia Christiana* xi. Instrumenta IX, 78; Knowles, *MOE*, 205; the Premonstratensian example involved Saint-Gabriel (Calvados), dedicated in 1138 by Earl Robert's son Richard bishop of Bayeux.

of the two major western military orders generated by the Crusading Movement, the Templars, benefited from Robert's grants.[239]

His offerings included lands, churches, revenues, quittances from tolls, and at least for Montacute's priory at Malpas, jurisdictional immunity for its court. Not surprisingly, the major beneficiaries probably were Margam and Tewkesbury, with the addition of St. James's. At the same time, Robert was watchful of the possible effect of his patronage on his "bottom line" as a landlord. For purchases and sales at least at Cardiff and Tewkesbury Robert's and William's Customs decreed that only those monks, Templars, and Hospitallers who had charters exempting them were to be free from tolls.[240]

In return, Robert sought personal salvation for himself and family gained through the prayers and works of monastic grantees. One of his charters for Tewkesbury Abbey was for the salvation of his and his wife's parents; another for Ewenny Priory added their ancestors' and successors' salvation. He supported a tenant's pursuit of salvation for himself and his wife by confirming his grant to St. Peter's Gloucester.[241] But a vassal could return the favor. Richard de Grainville and his wife Constance put the salvation of Earl Robert, Countess Mabel, and their son William before their own in founding Neath Abbey.[242]

Broader purposes lay behind some of these overtly religious acts. The just-cited foundation of Neath Abbey by Richard de Grainville and his wife, which occurred in Earl Robert's and Countess Mabel's presence, was as much a political act as a religious one. In response, as it were, the personal subscription Robert evidently wrote on the foot of Richard's and Constance's charter—that he had taken the abbey into his protection—is a virtual proclamation of his feudal overlordship. Several of Robert's own grants have political overtones. The freedom from tolls he gave to the canons of Lanthony Priory, if made *c.*1136, could well have been an effort to court the support of its *patronus*, Miles of Gloucester; but it is equally possible that it was a reward for an ally who had reaffirmed his vassalage.[243] Tiron (Eure-et-Loire), founded in 1109 by the reform-minded monk Bernard, attracted patronage of some sort from Earl Robert, supposedly in 1140.[244] If this date is correct, after Robert joined the Angevin side against King Stephen, the earl's motivation may have been to compliment Matilda or particularly Robert fitz Martin, notable patron of the order and fellow adherent from the early 1140s of the empress.[245]

---

[239] Pattersom, *EGC*, no. 258. The evidence for a donation to the Hospitallers only cites an earl of Gloucester prior to King John: *Rotuli Chartarum*, 16.
[240] Patterson, *EGC*, no. 46.   [241] Patterson, *EGC*, nos. 283, 68, 82.
[242] See 114; Postles, "Religious Houses and the Laity in Eleventh to Thirteenth-Century England," 43–4.
[243] Patterson, *EGC*, no. 110, no. 94n.
[244] "Vita B. Bernardi Abbatis de Tironio," 174; *ASS* ii (April), 246a; Patterson, *EGC*, no. 193. Robert is listed among those who made gifts, gave lands, or built cells.
[245] *Regesta* iii. nos. 274, 394, 498, 581, 632, 651, 898–9; Cowley, *The Monastic Order in South Wales*, 19–20, 63, 198–9; less likely would be to favor Miles of Gloucester: Chibnall, *Empress Matilda*, 100 & n.

The earl's grant of a prebend in Caen to the abbey of Sainte-Marie Ardenne in 1138, which his son Richard bishop of Bayeux dedicated in that year, was aside from other considerations a gesture of paternal support.[246]

The earl's own well-being may have been on his mind. While his foundation and endowment of St. James's Priory was an important, perhaps most important gift to Tewkesbury Abbey, the result added a key demesne improvement to the baronial capital Robert was creating. St. James's was a component of Robert's planned development of Bristol as *caput* of his barony; and the choice of St. James as patron saint had to be a compliment offered to his half-sister the empress.[247] Robert's grant of a fee in Bedminster to the Templars while promoting an increasingly popular Crusading order may have been a disguised sale.[248] Margam's foundation, aside from offering the prospect of secretarial services, could have served any or all of the following ends: to win the support of the Cistercians Bernard of Clairvaux and his protégé Pope Eugenius III for the Angevin cause; to ward off Eugenius III's commanded excommunication and interdict for continued retention of episcopal fees in the Bessin; to create a spiritual cordon sanitaire against Welsh aggression on the western border of the Shire Fee; even to counterbalance the attraction of Richard de Gainville's Neath Abbey for Robert's vassals' patronage with its attendant political implications.[249] Robert's donation of land to Savigny at Briton Ferry by the mouth of the Neath river in the lower part of his demesne outpost may have been calculated to serve a similar purpose.[250]

Confirmations of tenants' acts of proprietary piety also made them his own. Examples include Saint-Étienne Caen, Savigny, St. James's Bristol, St. Peter's and Lanthony Priory Gloucester, Tewkesbury, Montacute, Ewenny Priory, and Neath.[251] A charter the earl granted to Ewenny between 1140 and 1147 in effect put donations made by its founder Maurice de Londres and Gilbert de Turberville and the earl's additions on equal footing.[252] A monastic beneficiary also could view the earl's confirmation of a tenant's donation as ultimately Robert's gift. In 1126 Richard fitz Nigel granted St. Peter's Abbey Gloucester a mill and some land at Paygrove and Wooton St. Mary's by Gloucester as an entry gift for his two sons joining the community; and in a separate action Earl Robert confirmed the gift.[253] However, when the abbey recorded the donation in its *Historia*, which was a list of benefactors for whom the community was to pray, the earl appears without mention of Richard as the donor. The monks were right. Ultimately Robert was the

---

[246] Patterson, *EGC*, no. 192.    [247] See 117.
[248] Harper Bill, "The Piety of the Anglo-Norman Knightly Class," 67; see 117–18.
[249] Patterson, *The Scriptorium of Margam Abbey*, 35–6; see also 117.
[250] The grant was at *Ponte*, which has been identified with Briton Ferry, Bridgend, and Llandeilo-Talyfont: *Rotuli Chartarum* i. 174; Patterson, *EGC*, no. 242; Birch, *Neath Abbey*, 58 & n.; Birch, *Margam Abbey*, 327; Chibnall, *The World of Orderic Vitalis*, 48, 50.
[251] In the case of Savigny, Robert fitz Ernesius gave land at Bazenville (Calvados) with Earl Robert's consent: *CDF*, no. 824, p. 299; imperfect copy in *Rotuli Chartarum*, 63.
[252] Patterson, *EGC*, no. 68.
[253] Patterson, *EGC*, nos. 82 & n. ("concedo et confirmo"); see also no. 262; *Cart. Gloucester* i. no. ccxcii; ii. nos. mlxxi, mlxxii (the charter mentions only one son, William); "Historia," *Cart. Gloucester* i. 107 (Robert as donor), 118 (Richard and his wife donating, Earl Robert confirming); *OASPG*, xxxi.

donor: as he stated in his confirmation, the gifts had come from his fee; furthermore, his confirmation had been solicited as extra security for the gifts' survival.[254]

Another side of the earl of Gloucester's seigniorial relations with the Church reveals further shades of his proprietary attitudes and how, in three illustrative cases, his actions had to take into consideration the potential punitive force of the Church. For contrast, there is the quarrel Robert resolved in 1146 between Abbot Roger of Tewkesbury (1137–61) and Bishop Uthred of Llandaff (1140–8). At issue were conflicting proprietary claims to moor land between the Taff and Ely rivers and tithes at Merthyr Mawr and those belonging to the chapel of St. John, claimed by the abbot as appurtenant to St. Leonard's Newcastle. Robert fitz Hamon's conquest of Morgannwg led, as previously mentioned, to the bishop's becoming the lord of Glamorgan's vassal and the abbot's resulting added vassalage for assets held in Glamorgan. Over a decade earlier Robert had implicitly recognized the bishopric of Llandaff as a virtual Member lordship, but in the process of settling this dispute neither any seigniorial interest of his was at stake nor ecclesiastical influence exerted because the bishop had accepted the lord of Glamorgan's jurisdiction.[255]

On the basis of Robert's intervention and consent, as the charter Bishop Uthred gave to Roger and his community stated, the bishop confirmed to them all tithes, alms, and benefices they currently held or would be given canonically in his diocese. The bishop also conceded that anyone wishing to be buried at Tewkesbury might be, regardless of the bishopric's rights in this matter. In return, the abbot and community would surrender claim to all tithe they had from the earl's demesne plowlands between the Taff and Ely, two parts of the tithe of Merthyr Mawr, and the tithe pertaining to St. John's chapel appurtenant to St. Leonard's Newcastle.[256] Evidently Abbot Roger had on his side the vaguely worded grant of Robert fitz Hamon of the tithes of all revenues from his demesne lands in Wales of the church of St. Leonard Newcastle, and possibly equally vaguely worded confirmations of the earl and King Henry I.[257]

A first example of the earl's protection of his seigniorial status in dealings with ecclesiastics comes from a *conventio* he made with Roger abbot of Fécamp in 1128 without any hint of external pressure. Their pact boiled down to a simple uncontentious updating of a prior agreement between their predecessors. In 1058 the father-and-son tenants of Creully, one of the lord of Évrecy's fees, gave the small church of Saint-Gabriel and a market with some unspecified appurtenances by the river Seulles (Calvados) as a monastic cell to the great ducal abbey of Fécamp (Seine-Inférieure). The two founders, Richard and Turstin, probably were moved by the advice of Turstin's brother Vitalis, who was a member of the community. In 1080 their donation was confirmed by King William I in a great Norman

---

[254] Milsom, *The Legal Framework of English Feudalism*, 120–1; Hudson, *Land, Law, and Lordship in Anglo-Norman England*, 211–29, esp. 212; Hudson, *The Formation of the English Common Law*, 94–117, esp, 100–3.
[255] *LEA*, no. 3; Cowley, *The Monastic Order in South Wales*, 166.   [256] *LEA*, no. 3.
[257] PRO, C.66/580, m.1; *CPR Henry VII* ii. 94; Patterson, *EGC*, no. 283; *Regesta* ii. 1535, 1978; no. 497 in its present state is spurious. See 123–4, for Earl Robert's dispute with the bishop of Bayeux.

assembly. Out of respect for the various tenurial relationships which Saint-Gabriel's foundation involved, a key provision required that should the community increase to such an extent that an abbot and monks be placed there, the abbot would be chosen by the abbot of Fécamp with the advice of the ruler of Normandy (as lord of Fécamp) and the lord (*senior*) of Creully (apparently referring to a Goz heir or successor). No mention was made of a member of the house of Haimo as the fee's lord, but we do know that Robert fitz Hamon's grandfather was; and Robert's role in the 1128 agreement is proof that he was Creully's *senior* as well.[258]

In 1128 Robert, acting as lord (*senior*), and Roger abbot of Fécamp made the already mentioned illustrative *conventio* because the Saint-Gabriel community had further developed. Apparently, over time it had grown, become ruled by a prior, and functioned as a feudal landlord. There were now three parties, abbot, prior, and earl, with immediate interests to protect. The result was a compromise between the three authorities, with the two superior ones, abbot and earl, spelling out its terms. Particularly relevant ones provided that for a prior to remain permanently that situation needed the election and counsel of the abbot and earl, the aforesaid lord of Creully, along with unanimous agreement from the chapters of the two houses. Should the prior be elevated to a higher grade, be deposed, or die, a successor from Fécamp found worthy by the abbot, the earl the lord of Creully, and each chapter, was to be installed. The prior was to be elected in the chapter of Fécamp by the abbot, each chapter, and with the earl's consent. Evidently, since Saint-Gabriel was a fee held of the lord of Creully, its feudal dealings with tenants were not Earl Robert's direct concern. Consequently, the abbot and prior divided performances of homage, oaths of fealty, reliefs, and revenues between them. However, Robert's proprietary interests were protected in the event that an alienation of land to another magnate was planned. That needed the lord of Creully's, the abbot of Fécamp's, and both chapters' advice and consent.[259]

A second case of the earl's proprietary relations with the Church involving Robert and Bishop Urban of Llandaff (1107–34) posed for the first time a serious challenge to Gloucester's seigniorial status and the threat of ecclesiastical weapons being used against him. It emerged within a decade or so of Robert's acquisition of the lordship of Glamorgan. The core issue was the degree of Urban's tenurial and jurisdictional independence and its corollary, the degree of the bishop's jurisdiction over his own tenants. It was the product of Robert fitz Hamon's conquest of Morgannwg accompanied by the seizure of the native *clas* churches and of lands, tenants, and revenues belonging to them as well as to previous bishops of Glamorgan. Fitz Hamon had died in 1107 without the tenurial and jurisdictional relationship between the Marcher lord of Glamorgan and the bishop being defined, particularly for the lands remaining in the bishop's possession in the Shire Fee.

Urban was an imposing opponent, a member of a distinguished native ecclesiastical family, and elected apparently without interference from the then lord of Glamorgan. His profession of obedience to Archbishop Anselm of 1107 indicates

---

[258] Patterson, *EGC*, no. 70; *Regesta* i (1998). no. 257; Bates, *Normandy before 1066*, 208.
[259] Patterson, *EGC*, no. 70 & n.

his acceptance of his see's subordination to Canterbury's primacy. However, Urban was not prepared to accept the Anglo-Norman colonial status quo of 1107, as well as encroachments by the bordering dioceses of Hereford and St. Davids, in large measure because of his ambitions to complete the transformation of his bishopric into a territorial diocese with its seat at Llandaff.[260] To judge from the settlement of issues he later made with Earl Robert, he also aimed to win for his estates the status of an ecclesiastical Marcher barony. The means he used to accomplish his diocesan restoration were several weapons employed in Latin ecclesiastical culture, documentary and hagiographical collections which included forgery, and appeals to papal authority and sanctions.[261] The last along with his own "spiritual sword" were apt weapons against lay barons.

The campaign which ultimately affected Earl Robert began in 1119 with Urban's appeal to Pope Calixtus II (1119–24), King Henry I's distant cousin, against the lay lords by letter and in person at the Council of Rheims. Calixtus responded with a command addressed to thirteen named baronial perpetrators in South Wales to return their purloined items without delay or face confirmation of Urban's judgment.[262] Among those named by Calixtus was William sheriff of Cardiff, but not the king's son Robert. Because of this relationship and the fact that the pope was Henry's cousin, it may have been diplomatically preferable for Robert's chief administrator in Glamorgan to be threatened. In any case, we hear no more of this campaign from extant evidence until 1126, when Earl Robert and Bishop Urban settled their differences in an agreement made at Woodstock before King Henry I, the *curia regis*, and a delegation of Robert's Glamorgan court led by Ralph sheriff of Cardiff. It was clearly the result of very hard bargaining and likely brought to fruition by the good offices of Robert's father.

The text of the *concordia* was carefully preserved in the great hagiographical and documentary compilation called the *Book of Llandaff*.[263] Without explicitly stating so, the agreement recognized Urban's bishopric as a virtual ecclesiastical Member lordship within Glamorgan and, as the earl's later *acta* addressed to Urban's successor Uthred show, as presiding official in the *curia comitatus* along with the sheriff.[264] Such tenurial integration was a clear victory for Robert. At the same time divisions of jurisdiction between Robert and Urban favored the bishop; any of the earl's men regardless of health could become the bishop's tenants; and the bishop had full rights of justice over his own men. Only when pleas requiring trial by battle arose between tenants of the two or between the bishop's men and undertenants of the earl's vassals were the ordeals to take place in the earl's castle. Even so, the bishop received some compensation, since securities were to be given in the

---

[260] Walker, "The Medieval Bishops of Llandaff," 14–15; Crouch, "Urban: First Bishop of Llandaff," 1, 3–9; *GCH* iii. 28, 87; BL, Harley Roll A.3; *Canterbury Professions*, 36; *LEA*, Appendix, no. 1.

[261] Crouch, "Urban: First Bishop of Llandaff," esp. 9–13 (except for dates on p. 9); Cowley, "The Church in Medieval Glamorgan," 464–7; Huws, "The Making of *Liber Landavensis*," 133–60.

[262] *Liber Landavensis*, 87–8, 93–4: Clark, *Cartae et alia* i. xx; Crouch, "Urban: First Bishop of Llandaff," 11, 13; Cowley, "The Church in Medieval Glamorgan," 91–4.

[263] *Liber Landavensis*, 27–9 with partial facsm.; Clark, *Cartae et alia* i. no. L; Patterson, *EGC*, no. 109; cal. in *Regesta* ii. no. 1466; Crouch, *LEA*, Appendix, no. 3.

[264] Patterson, *EGC*, nos. 68, 84; Patterson, *The Scriptorium of Margam Abbey*, 8–9.

bishop's court and he was to have their proceeds as if the trial took place in his court. However, territorial restorations to Urban were few: William de Cardiff's mill and its land, along with a fishery on the Ely and 100 acres between the Taff and Ely rivers. On balance, if the agreement was a compromise, the outcome favored the earl on the tenurial issue which would have most concerned him.[265] Another indication of Robert's success may be that when Urban resumed his campaign in 1128 against Glamorgan's lay lords with a threatened excommunication, neither the earl nor his sheriff was among the eleven individuals threatened by the then Pope Honorius II with confirmation of an excommunication by Urban if they were recalcitrant.[266] Furthermore, in spite of his *conventio* with Urban, there is reason to believe that the conditions of the Anarchy permitted Gloucester to control the bishopric of Llandaff's temporalities following the death of Bishop Urban in 1133 and to influence the election of his successor Uthred in 1140.[267]

A third example reveals Robert's fighting a rearguard defense of his interests in Lower Normandy against combined episcopal and papal pressure. As already noted, Robert not only was the vassal of 10 knights' fees held from the bishop of Bayeux for his honor of Évrecy, but also added perhaps 17.5 more sometime during the pontificate of his overlord Bishop Richard II (1107–33). If not without the protest of Robert's son Bishop Richard III (1135–42), at least by exploiting conditions of the Angevin war of succession, Earl Robert seized an additional possible 14.5 fees: the 2 fees of Ilbert and Gilbert de Lacy, the earl of Chester's 12.5 (5 as the earl of Chester; 7.5 as *vicomte* of Bayeux), and estates of the Eudo *Dapifer* fee of 2 knights held by Stephen of Blois before his accession as king. By the mid-1140s Robert's Norman fee grand total had climbed to as many as 53 or slightly less.[268]

In 1142 Robert's comfortable relationship with his episcopal overlord changed when his son Richard died. The new bishop Philip de Harcourt (1142–63) was not only a partisan of Robert's enemy King Stephen but was an aggressive reformer determined to recover his bishopric's lands and rights. Philip quickly won the support of Bernard of Clairvaux's pupil Pope Eugenius III (1145–53), but had to take into account his new overlord the duke of Normandy Geoffrey of Anjou. Robert may have succeeded in ignoring Philip's demands for several years, but in March 1145 the earl faced the threat of at least excommunication from the bishops of Worcester and Bath at the pope's command. He only paid heed to the issue about eighteen months later in a *compositio* he issued at Devizes before the Empress Matilda in September 1146.[269]

---

[265] David Crouch awarded "a little victory" to Urban: "Urban: First Bishop of Llandaff," 13; see Cowley "The Church in Medieval Glamorgan," 93–4.
[266] *Liber Landavensis*, 37–8; Clark, *Cartae et alia* i. no. LVII.
[267] Patterson, *The Scriptorium of Margam Abbey*, 8–9 & nn.
[268] Patterson, *EGC*, no. 6; *RHG* xxiii, 698, §435, 700–1, §439 (fees held by Robert fitz Hamon and Earl Robert); for the other fees, see *RHG* xxiii, §439, §441–3, pp. 700–1; Navel, "L'Enquête de 1133 sur les fiefs de l'évêché de Bayeux," 15–19 & nn. There are problems with the number of Eudo *Dapifer*'s Norman fees, see n. 40; the grand total includes the honor of Évrecy's fees.
[269] *Cart, Bayeux* i. nos. cxc (18 March 1145), cxcviii (10 March 1146/7 [corrupt]: addressed to Thomas archbishop of Canterbury, instead of Theobald, and the bishops of Worcester and Bath) with an interdict as an added penalty), xlii; Patterson, *EGC*, no. 6 & n.

On the surface Philip scored a smashing victory. Robert had agreed to putting at his tenurial risk, excluding Évrecy, perhaps as high as 77 percent of his fees. However, on closer examination, Robert only surrendered about 4.5 fees to the bishop; and he was able to postpone the possible surrender of 27.5 more for undetermined dates in the future, 15 to be held until the bishop's death; 12.5 when an heir to the Chester land would be recognized by the duke of Normandy. So, on the face of it, the *compositio* was a limited success for the earl.[270] However, he may have triumphed. There is no evidence that Robert ever returned any land to the bishop of Bayeux. In May 1147 a frustrated Eugenius III commanded the two English bishops to excommunicate the earl and place his lands under interdict if he violated the *compositio* and, after being warned, was unwilling to correct his action within forty days of their receipt of his letter. I suspect that Gloucester simply ignored the pope's fulminations and opted instead to mollify his mentor Bernard of Clairvaux by founding Margam Abbey. The great abbot was pleased enough to send his brother Nivard to the event at Bristol to receive the endowment.[271]

Finally, an episode from *c*.1145–6 shows that the same baronial power which had to be controlled or corrected by *conventiones* could be solicited to aid the Church. No less a figure than the abbot of St. Peter's Gloucester, Gilbert Foliot (1139–48), recommended use of the earl's secular arm to resolve an ecclesiastical dispute. In two letters to Archbishop Theobald of Canterbury he urged the primate to excommunicate a former deposed abbot of Cerne in Dorset, William Scotus, who contumaciously had returned to the abbey, and to command the earl of Gloucester to accomplish his removal. Gilbert felt confident that Earl Robert would not fail to obey.

Foliot had become involved in the Cerne case out of loyalty to his prior Bernard, who had been elected by the Cerne community to succeed Scotus, deposed for lax practices. But Bernard had never received abbatial blessing from the local diocesan Jocelin of Salisbury (1142–84) because of his scruples about making a gift to the bishop in return for the blessing. This had given William Scotus an opening to return with the support of a sympathetic faction within Cerne.

Earl Robert was a logical choice to resolve the dispute because he was a patron of St. Peter's Abbey, earl of the shire where Cerne was located, leader of the Empress Matilda's cause, which Abbot Gilbert supported, and to 1145 held sway supreme between the Channel and the river Severn after his victory in 1143 over King Stephen at Wilton. Furthermore, Gilbert felt that the earl could move Jocelin to act. Archbishop Theobald took Foliot's suggestion and dispatched a letter to Robert; but Scotus and his party were no pushovers. Foliot learned that Scotus's supporters attacked the messenger bearing Theobald's letter, pulled him from his horse, and seriously wounded him. With the letter undelivered and messenger imprisoned at Cerne, Abbot Gilbert again wrote Archbishop Theobald with

---

[270] *Cart. Bayeux* i. no. xli; *Regesta* iii. no. 58; Patterson, *EGC*, no. 6 & n.
[271] *Cart. Bayeux* ii. no. cxci, 364 (date corrected to 24 May 1147); *EGC* no. 119 & n.; Cowley, *The Monastic Order in South Wales*, 23 & n.; Patterson, *The Scriptorium of Margam Abbey*, 34; see also in this volume, 119.

various suggested actions to get Earl Robert, his son William, and the bishop of Salisbury to act. It is unknown whether Robert ever was galvanized into action against the rebellious Abbot Scotus and his confrères; but it is known that Scotus successfully retained his office, which suggests that if Robert ever received a command from Theobald, nothing came of it. Nevertheless, Foliot's depiction of Robert reflects how he might be perceived in one place as a potential *miles Christi* while embroiled with the Church as its enemy in another.[272]

---

[272] *LCGF*, esp. nos. 51–2; Appendix III, ibid., 507–9; *GS* (2004), 148, 150; Morey & Brooke, "The Cerne Letters of Gilbert Foliot and the Legation of Imar of Tusculum," 523–5; Saltman, *Theobald*, 86–7; *GFAL*, 80–1.

# 5

# The Empress's Champion

Robert earl of Gloucester's third and final career began on December 1, 1135, when his father, "the Lion of Justice," died at his castle at Lyons-la-Forêt near Rouen after a short illness. The event created another example of a pan-European twelfth-century phenomenon, political upheaval arising from the basic instability of dynastic power and problems posed by interregna.[1] Once again, a family death changed Robert's life, but instead of the results being molded by his father, this final career was the earl's own doing, though not without help from an array of supporting characters.

King Henry I left England forever for Normandy sometime after August 2, 1133. Terrifying celestial and terrestrial phenomena, as if portents of dire events to come, were recorded by chroniclers. Earl Robert of Gloucester, who may well have made the crossing with his father, seems to have remained in the duchy over the next roughly two years and three months. The earl periodically frequented courts his father held at Rouen and Falaise castle, site of one of the king's treasuries. On one occasion at Caen in 1135 his son Richard represented him.[2]

On a Monday evening in late November 1135 while hunting at Lyons-la-Forêt near Rouen, King Henry I unexpectedly fell ill and his condition soon worsened. Neither of the two first cousins who had vied for precedence in swearing to Matilda's succession in 1127 was in attendance upon the king at the time. Stephen of Blois was in his county of Boulogne. Earl Robert's whereabouts are unknown, but upon hearing of his father's illness, he made what might be considered his first move indicative of his view of the Anglo-Norman royal succession. Consistent with Robert's acceptance of his ineligibility to succeed his father and obvious filial piety, the earl, instead of maneuvering to seize power, rushed along with other magnates to the king's side.[3]

At Lyons-la-Forêt Robert joined the royal entourage, which included some of the elite of the Anglo-Norman aristocracy, Hugh archbishop of Rouen and former abbot of Reading, Audoin bishop of Évreux, four other earls and counts, Robert's brother-in-law Rotrou II count of Mortagne, the two Beaumont twins Waleran count of Meulan and Robert earl of Leicester, and their stepfather William II de

---

[1] Bisson, *The Crisis of the Twelfth Century*, 182–6, 269–78; Garnett, *Conquered England*, Chapt. 3.
[2] *Regesta* ii. nos. 1757, 1764–5, 1777. See also nos. 1892, 1896, 1898, 1908, 1911–12, 1915–17, 1919; *OV* iii. 344–5; vi. 434–7; *ASC a*.1135 (for 1133); *JW* iii, 208–11. For Richard fitz Count, see *Regesta* ii. no. 1909; *CDF*, no. 590; Haskins, *Norman Institutions*, 106–7.
[3] Robert of Torigny, "Chronica," 127; *HN* (1998), 24–5; *GS* (2004), 18–21; Hollister, *Henry I*, 473–4.

Warenne earl of Surrey, as well as other magnates, members of the royal household, castellans, and probably some of the household's complement of stipendiary knights.

Henry I prepared for death by confessing his sins and receiving the Eucharist, arranging for other pious acts, and chose his great foundation Reading Abbey (Berks.) for his burial. He also directed Earl Robert as his executor to withdraw £60,000 from the treasury at Falaise to pay salaries and "mercies" to members of his household and mercenaries.[4] Some attendees later claimed that Henry designated a successor, but if so, the name they heard was not the same.[5]

Whether the dying Henry did so did not matter. The Norman barons attending the king, Robert included, responded by setting up a regency government—calmly ignoring their oaths of 1127. The germ of this body evidently was a *coniuratio*, a pact Archbishop Hugh and Bishop Audoin of Évreux pressured all those present at King Henry's death to form under oaths sworn to one another not to leave the body, unless by common consent, until it was brought to the coast for transport to England for burial.[6] Most often the ad hoc administration appears functioning through the apparatuses of councils; but it always was a nebulous group in which any ebb and flow of personal influence on its decisions is mostly invisible to us.

From Lyons-la-Forêt Robert, the other *coniurati*, and an enormous following conveyed his father's body to Rouen. From there, on the basis of the terms of the *coniuratio*, and reports of Robert conducting his father's body for burial, it seems likely that the earl and his sworn colleagues continued with the royal remains via Pont-Audemer and Bonneville to Caen to await a favorable wind for the crossing to England. Until the weather cooperated, Henry's body lay in the abbey of Saint-Étienne, where his father was entombed.[7]

While the cortege was still at Rouen, William de Warenne was assigned responsibility for the defense of Rouen and the region of the Caux; and William de Roumare, half-brother of Ranulf earl of Chester *vicomte* of the Bessin, and Hugh de Gournay were dispatched to defend the duchy's frontiers. The responsibility for these measures, according to Orderic Vitalis, came from from the counsel of wise men (*consultu sapientium*), certainly members of the ad hoc ruling group. Unfortunately Orderic did not record their identities, but after the group sent word to Theobald IV count of Blois to come and assume rule of the duchy, Robert of Gloucester is the only person any source mentions in connection with the process.

---

[4] *OV* vi. 448–9; *HN* (1998), 24–7; White, "King Stephen's Earldoms," 51.

[5] *HN* (1998), 24–5; *LE*, 285. See Chapt. 6, 184, 192.

[6] *OV* vi. 448–9; Chartrou, *L'Anjou de 1109 à 1151*, 39; LePatourel, *Norman Empire*, 143. The *coniuratio* was an association of oath-takers with pre-medieval origins. Impetus for formation could come from some authority or be popularly driven; the element of oaths led to potential ecclesiastical, ultimately papal judicial involvement: Du Cange, *Glossarium* ii. 507; *OV* i. s.v. coniuratio, 274; Patterson, "Anarchy in England," 198–9. The burgesses of London formed their commune by a comparable device: *HN* (1998), lviii–lix, 94–5. The Lisbon-bound mariners of the Second Crusade, who departed from Dartmouth (Devon), formed a shipboard *coniuratio*: *De Expugnatione Lyxbonensi: The Conquest of Lisbon*, 56–7 & n. 5, 104–5, 176–7; Patterson, "Anarchy in England," 198–9; see also nn. 35, 39.

[7] *OV* vi. 448–51; Henry of Huntingdon, 702–3; Robert of Torigny, "Chronica," 127; *Letters of Peter the Venerable* i. no. 15; ii. 104; *ASC* a.1135.

Theobald had several recorded meetings with the barons, at Rouen, Le Neubourg (Eure), and at Lisieux (Calvados); but there may only have been two councils, with Lisieux being an error for Le Neubourg. Apparently the multiple meetings were to ensure the maximum acceptance of Theobald's rule. Robert of Torigny reported that at the Lisieux meeting Earl Robert spoke with Count Theobald, presumably about some aspect of his governance.[8]

The empress herself was the cause of the regents' decision. She was a female, and custom definitely favored legitimate male inheritance. Her marriage to Count Geoffrey V of Anjou, with obvious future dynastic implications, had been accomplished probably without promised baronial approval; and in the past the count of Anjou had been the Normans' enemy.[9] However, most importantly, Matilda and Geoffrey had fomented a civil war in Normandy during the last months of King Henry's life and continued it even more aggressively against the baronial regency regime.

The conflict had started over Geoffrey's failure to gain from Henry at Matilda's urging key castles in the southern duchy, Domfront, Argentan, and Exmes, claimed as part of her *maritagium*.[10] Matilda and Geoffrey also supposedly demanded that her father swear fealty to them for all castles in England and Normandy as his heirs.[11] Rebuffed, Geoffrey turned to raiding Normandy through Maine, in which he had besieged Henry's son-in-law Roscelin *vicomte* of Maine and incinerated his castle at Beaumont-le-Vicomte (Sarthe).[12]

Henry I's death unleashed an even more aggressive campaign for Matilda to become her father's successor—according to some, jointly with her husband.[13] Geoffrey immediately sent her to Normandy, where Guigan Algason, who commanded Argentan, Exmes, and Domfront, recognized her lordship within the first week of December. The count himself, accompanied by William Talvas, disinherited heir of Robert de Bellême, invaded with a joint Angevin–Manceux army. The count's campaigning in the duchy was stopped, but not before gaining for him and Matilda a virtual Marcher lordship and territorial springboard in the Passais and lower Hiémois for future conquests. Hostilities formally ceased through a six-month truce Count Theobald succeeded in winning from Geoffrey in order to obtain a respite from Angevin attacks until the political situation in England allowed the new king to assume personal leadership of Normandy's defense. For his part, the count of Anjou needed to address baronial rebellions in Anjou.[14]

---

[8] Robert of Torigny, "Chronica," 128–9.; *OV* vi. 42–3, 454 & n. 2, 455.
[9] See, e.g., Douglas, *William the Conqueror*, 54–76; Chartrou, *L'Anjou de 1109 à 1151*, Chapt. 1; Hollister, "Anglo-Norman War and Diplomacy," *MMI*, 275, 281, 286.
[10] *OV* vi. 444–5; Chartrou, *L'Anjou de 1109 à 1151*, 37.
[11] Robert of Torigny, "Chronica," 128.
[12] *OV* vi. 444 & n., 445; Norgate, *England under the Angevin Kings* i. 269–70; Loyd, *Anglo-Norman Families*, 16.
[13] Henry of Huntingdon (1996), 708–11; Robert of Torigny, "Chronica," 128.
[14] Orderic Vitalis claims that Geoffrey offered the truce, which Theobald accepted; John of Marmoutier, that Stephen sought it: *OV* vi. 454–7; John of Marmoutier, 225; Robert of Torigny; 128–9; see Map 1, 239.

Matilda's and Geoffrey's rebellion also revived the old pro-Angevin Norman baronial faction of Henry I's earlier wars. Other barons simply acted independently in their own interests and after Stephen's accession remained aloof from succession politics. One such was Rabel de Tancarville (Seine-Maritime), a major Norman lord and the late king's chief chamberlain for Normandy, who fortified his own castles, seized the great ducal castle at Lillebonne (Seine-Maritime), and held out for a good year or more.[15]

Private feuds added another dimension to Normandy's turmoil. One of the best known shows how they could be intertwined with the war of Anglo-Norman royal succession. A war over succession to the great Norman honor of Breteuil involving Robert of Leicester as incumbent with William de Pacy as claimant pitted soon-to-be Blesian protagonists Robert and his brother Waleran and their ally Richer II, lord of nearby Laigle (Orne), against Angevin supporters, William Talvas and Roger de Tosny.[16]

With William Clito dead, it was logical for Earl Robert of Gloucester and the Anglo-Norman regency group to turn to one of Henry I's four nephews of the house of Blois, sons of Henry's sister the dowager Countess Adela and the late Count Stephen-Henry of Blois, Chartres, and Meaux, as the king's eligible male successor. Neither William, the eldest, the family's own mysterious outcast, nor the youngest, Henry, was a realistic possibility. But the latter, pluralist abbot of Glastonbury and bishop of Winchester, would be a valuable ally to any Blesian claimant to the throne.[17]

Realistically, the choice was between Bishop Henry's two older brothers, the elder and current count of Blois and count palatine of Champagne, Theobald IV/II (1107–52), and Stephen lord of the county of Mortain and of the county of Boulogne, and of several English honors.[18] By good fortune Stephen had disembarked from the ill-fated White Ship in 1120 just before it sailed and so had not perished with William Aetheling and his distinguished companions.[19]

Theobald had a long record of involvement in Norman affairs. He fought for his uncle Henry against King Louis VI of France and Count Fulk V of Anjou in the frontier wars of 1111–13 and 1117–19. The count also had maintained personal ties to Henry and to Anglo-Norman curial circles by periodic visits to the royal court. On one occasion, after crossing from Normandy with his uncle in November 1120, Theobald and and the court received the horrific news of William Aetheling's drowning in the wreck of the White Ship. No *curialis* dared

---

[15] *OV* vi. 482 & n., 483; *GOE*, 141–2;, 151, 275, 283, 285, 287; Hollister, "The Aristocracy," 43; Chibnall, "Normandy," 96 & n.; Crouch, *Reign of King Stephen*, 60.
[16] *OV* vi. 444–7, 456–9, 466–7; Robert of Torigny, "Chronica," 125, 128; Chartrou, *L'Anjou de 1109 à 1151*, 38; Chibnall, *Empress Matilda*, 64–5; Thompson, "William Talvas," 171–6; Thompson, "Family and Influence," 215–26, Thompson, "The Lords of Laigle," 183–4, 186, 188–9; Thompson, *Power and Border Lordship in Medieval France*, 64–5, 79, 82.
[17] King, "Henry of Winchester," 7; see also Chapt. 2, 46, and Chapt. 5, 130; Genealogical Chart, xxi.
[18] For the family, see Davis, *King Stephen*, 3rd edn., 4–11; Knowles, *MOE*, 702; Brett, *English Church under Henry I*, 103n.; Keefe, *Feudal Assessments*, 158–9; for Stephen's English holdings, see Chapt. 3, 73.
[19] *OV* vi. 296–7.

to approach the king with the news, but at the count's suggestion a small boy was sent weeping with the details to Henry.[20]

Even so, the author of the *Gesta Stephani* called Stephen perhaps quite accurately Henry I's favorite nephew. The king's patronage had made him one of three Anglo-Norman super-magnates. His total holdings may have yielded wealth exceeding Earl Robert of Gloucester's.[21] But for all of Stephen's trans-Channel super-magnate tenurial status, he never became a curial regular, even though, when he did attend court, protocol usually assigned him first or second place in lists of witnesses to the king's *acta*.[22]

It is unknown if the regency government even considered Stephen as King Henry's successor. If it had, there were possible reasons for disregarding him. One could have been Stephen's tarnished political reputation for his incompetent and corrupt administration of Alençon in 1119. That had driven its burgesses to revolt and led to Fulk of Anjou's intervention and to King Henry's greatest defeat in the ensuing battle. A second possible negative was Stephen's attempt in 1127, at Henry's instigation, to drive William Clito from Flanders, where he had been installed as count by Louis VI. Not only was the effort unsuccessful, but Clito's counterattack forced Stephen to accept a truce for three years.[23]

Nevertheless, Stephen's resourcefulness trumped all considerations against him or positives in favor of Theobald. Having learned of his uncle's death, Stephen immediately sailed from Wissant on the river Somme to England, bypassed Earl Robert's opposing garrisons at Dover and Canterbury, and won the support of London and, aided by his brother the bishop, of Winchester and the royal administration headed by Bishop Roger of Salisbury.[24] Then, after William of Corbeil, archbishop of Canterbury, had been persuaded by the sworn testimony of Hugh Bigod that Henry had changed his mind on his deathbed and designated Stephen as his heir, Stephen was anointed king in Westminster Abbey on December 22, 1135. Within a few months he could announce Pope Innocent II's recognition of his right.[25]

While Robert and Theobald were engaged in their governmental discussion, an emissary from the count's younger brother Stephen brought news of Stephen's

---

[20] *Regesta* ii. nos. 1019n., 1244, 1247 & n. (Windsor), 1249 (Windsor), 1590, 1607, 1687 (Chartres), 1692; *OV* vi. 300–1; Round, *Geoffrey de Mandeville*, 429.

[21] *GS* (2004), 4–5; *OV* vi. 42–3; Davis, *King Stephen*, 3rd edn., 6–7 & n., 8–11; King, "Stephen of Blois, Count of Mortain and Boulogne," 280; Crouch, *Reign of King Stephen*, 11–24; Hollister, "The Anglo-Norman Succession Debate of 1126," 148 & n., 149; Hollister, "Henry I and the Anglo-Norman Magnates," in *MMI*, 178–7, 186–7; Chartrou, *L'Anjou de 1109 à 1151*, 42; King, *King Stephen*, 9–12, 20–8.

[22] For Stephen's curial service in Normandy, see *Regesta* ii. nos. 1337 (*OV* vi. 324–5), 1356; also nos. 1019n. (*OV* vi. 174–5), 1102, 1183*, 1243, 1245+, 1547, 1588 & n.* (not a chancery product), 1740+, 1757+, 1761, 1795, 1830, 1932*, 1934+, 1941, 1973: *acta* with ranking favoring Stephen ahead of Robert are marked with asterisks; those placing the earl ahead of Stephen, with plus signs; Hollister, "Rise of Administrative Kingship," 888.

[23] *OV* vi. 204–9, 370–3, 378–9; *GS* (2004), 4–5; Suger, *Vie de Louis VI*, 248–51; Hollister, *Henry I*, 252 & n., 319–22. For consideration of Stephen's popularity, see King, "Stephen of Blois, Count of Mortain and Boulogne," 271.

[24] I must disagree with Bradbury, "The Early Years of the Reign of Stephen," 20, about a prearranged plan for Stephen's coup.

[25] Richard of Hexham, 147–8; *Regesta* iii. no. 271.

coronation. Consequently, the regency council, which would have included Robert, changed its allegiance to Stephen; and Theobald begrudgingly accepted the fait accompli of an ordained king. Orderic Vitalis reported that the barons wanted to avoid holding their fees from two different lords. Earl Robert, as a fellow major trans-Channel baron, concurred. In keeping with the conciliar action the earl surrendered Falaise castle with its treasure, apparently to the new king's messenger. By so doing, Gloucester either directly or indirectly also thwarted a move on Falaise by his sister and her Angevin husband.[26] He also refused to be drawn away from his recognition of Stephen by early attacks in support of his sister's claim to the throne by his half-brother Reginald in the Cotentin near his own *caput* Torigni-sur Vire. Reginald was allied with the then exiled Devon tenant-in-chief Baldwin de Redvers and his close ally and honorial tenant Stephen de Mandeville, lord of Erlestoke (Wilts.) and Magneville (Manche). Baldwin, as will be seen, had rebelled against Stephen for personal reasons, and was defeated, disinherited, and exiled. He then had fled, first to Geoffrey of Anjou's court, and then with Geoffrey's and Matilda's encouragement gone to the Cotentin to take his revenge on the king, possibly utilizing the Redvers Norman *caput*, Néhou (Manche), as his base for preditory raids.[27]

Robert's half-uncle King David of Scotland became his niece's first explicit advocate in England. On learning of Stephen's seizure of the Anglo-Norman throne, mindful of the 1127 oath he had sworn to her succession, David invaded northern England and captured castles in Cumberland and Northumberland. In areas which fell under his control, he took oaths and hostages from the more important nobles to honor their earlier oaths regarding the royal succession. Matilda's uncle supported her cause; yet while serving it, he also strove to recover territories in northern England to which his kingdom had a claim. Then King Stephen responded by leading a large force which stopped David's advance short of Durham on 5 February 1136. Faced with the prospect of an uncertain outcome of a likely pitched battle with the king's army, during February 1136 David made peace with him by a *conventio*, the first Treaty of Durham, which awarded him control of Carlisle and Cumberland. These conquests were added to his honor of Huntingdon and were to be held by his son Henry in return for his homage. Matilda's claim to the throne was completely ignored.[28]

In spite of the previous evidence of the earl of Gloucester's acceptance of Stephen's succession, William of Malmesbury and the anonymous author of the

---

[26] Robert of Torigny, "Chronica," 128–9; *OV* vi. 454–5; *HN* (1998), 30–1; Strickland, "Against the Lord's Anointed," 57. I must disagree with Marjorie Chibnall's hypothesis of contacts between Earl Robert and Matilda in December 1135 as inconsistent with this chronicle evidence; the sole charter of the empress (*Regesta* iii. no. 805: 1135 × 39) she cites in support depends on her dating, which she admits is only a possibility; Chibnall, "The Empress Matilda as a Subject for Biography," 190–1; Chibnall, "Introduction," in *King Stephen's Reign*, 2.

[27] See 138.

[28] John of Hexham, 287–8; Richard of Hexham, 145–6, 150–1; *GS* (2004), 52–3; Henry of Huntingdon (1996), 706–7; Barrow, "The Scots and the North of England," 244–6; Green, "Aristocratic Loyalties on the Northern Frontier," 94–7; Stringer, *The Reign of Stephen*, 28; Dalton, *Conquest, Anarchy and Lordship*, 204. Contrary to King, *King Stephen*, 53, I believe the chroniclers have David's motivation about right.

*Gesta Stephani*, both imply, for different partisan reasons, that Robert's delaying to perform homage to King Stephen was a sign of his disloyalty.[29] And the witness-lists of Stephen's *acta* do show that Robert did not arrive at court in England until sometime after March 22, 1136, the feast of Easter, as Malmesbury claimed.[30] Earl Robert apparently had not met Stephen at Reading Abbey (Berks.) for Henry I's funeral on January 5. On the contrary, Orderic Vitalis reported that, after a month of waiting, weather had finally permitted the body escorted by several monks from Saint-Étienne Caen to be transported across the Channel.[31] And according to a continuatuion of John of Worcester, Stephen carried the king's bier on his own shoulders to the abbey with the help of accompanying nobles.[32]

The most obvious reason for Robert's delayed arrival at court is that he had been detained in Normandy until around Easter 1136, likely attending to the defenses of his lordships in and around the Bessin. As already seen, the duchy was in turmoil from private baronial wars and pro-Angevin attacks in the Cotentin, so that some of the earl's extensive fortification of Torigni-sur-Vire may well have required his supervision at this time.[33]

In any case, Robert's attestation of Stephen's famous Charter of Liberties for the Church issued at his Oxford court at the end of March or very early April 1136 shows that at most the earl only missed the festal curial meeting by about ten days or so; and it is even possible that he met the king earlier between the two courts at either Westminster or Wallingford.[34] Whenever that was, the king received his cousin "with favor and distinction" and then the two agreed to the terms of the most famous *conventio* of the king's entire reign. Court protocol still accorded him first place among baronial witnesses to royal *acta*.[35]

Precedents for their agreement were grants and confirmations of lands, especially through treaties or *conventiones* the king made with individual lay barons such as at least two he made with Miles of Gloucester c. January 4, 1136. Stephen made it clear in them that their terms constituted a *conventio* between him as lord and Miles as vassal; no mention was made of Miles's vassalage to the earl of Gloucester.[36] In one, among other things, he granted as Miles's patrimony custody of Gloucester castle in fee and heredity; in another, probably hereditary tenure of Gloucestershire's shrieval office as well.[37]

---

[29] *HN* (1998), 32–3; *GS* (2004), 12–15.　　[30] *Regesta* iii. nos. 945–8 & n., 271.
[31] *OV* vi. 450–1; Patterson, "Stephen's Shaftesbury Charter," 491 n. 51.
[32] *JW* iii. 214–17.
[33] *OV* vi. 456–7; Robert of Torigny, "Interpolations," 306–7: *GND* ii. 248–9; as Jean Yver has noted, this is one of the two most likely times for Earl Robert's work at Torigni: "Les Châteaux-forts en Normandie," 100–1.
[34] *Regesta* iii. nos. 945–8 & n.; Galbraith, "Royal Charters to Winchester," 384; Patterson, "Stephen's Shaftesbury Charter," 487; King, "Introduction," 12.
[35] *GS* (2004), 14–15: Robert was received at court *gratiose et excellenter*; *Regesta* iii. nos. 271, 284?, 337, 340, 616, 818?, 945–8, 952; Round saw the *conventio* (sealed by oaths like the *coniuratio*) as one of the defining characteristics of Stephen's reign: Round, *Geoffrey de Mandeville*, 176; King, "Dispute Settlement in Anglo-Norman England," esp. 118–19; Crouch, "A Norman *Conventio* and the Bonds of Lordship in the Middle Ages," esp. 306–16; see in this chapter nn. 6 and 39.
[36] *Regesta* iii. nos. 386–7; no. 388 cannot be classified in this regard because of its extensive damage.
[37] Respectively, *Regesta* iii. nos. 387 and 388.

Some scholars, due to the charters' references to the hereditary tenure of castle and shrievalty being held from Stephen as king and Miles as baron-tenant, eliminated the mesne lordship over Miles as constable that Henry I had granted Earl Robert and which, as such, would have been offensive to Earl Robert. However, the grants merely recognized the de facto status of the tenures his family already had enjoyed. More importantly, would Robert have felt wronged, given that Miles recognized his vassalage to him after his arrival in England in 1139? To be sure, soon after, Matilda at Gloucester in effect confirmed Stephen's grants of the constableship and shrievalty to reward Miles for his loyalty—even to keep it—without any evidence of Robert's displeasure; and two years later, when Matilda boxed up all her previous diplomatic dealing with, and grants to, Miles, including those regarding the castle and shrievalty, in a huge pancarte, Robert did not renege from attesting it.[38]

The *conventio* between Stephen and Robert provided for the earl's performance of homage and pledge of loyalty in return for the king's continued maintenance of his *dignitas*, presumably comprehending Gloucester's personal and proprietary status, respectively the *vita et honor* of similar lord–vassal quid pro quos. Such agreements were by nature conditional; Robert's with Stephen represents no political deviation from his initial acts recognizing Stephen in Normandy.[39] Stephen even showed Robert some personal favor by issuing in 1135 × 38 a charter for Tewkesbury Abbey of which the earl was *patronus*.[40]

Earl Robert soon demonstrated his commitment to the king by participating in Stephen's three-month siege of Baldwin de Redvers at Exeter between roughly June and August. As Robert Bearman has shown, the shrievalty of Devon which had been a key element of the Redvers power had been lost to the local rival Meulles family of Okehampton; and Baldwin sought to exploit the disputed royal succession by withholding his homage until he received the shrievalty from the new king. When this was not forthcoming by around May 1136, Baldwin seized and fortified the castle and borough of Exeter. That prompted Stephen first to send an advance force, which took the borough by surprise, and then to follow with the main body of his army, which settled down to a prolonged siege of the castle. The earl of Gloucester seems to have been part of the advancing royal army, participated in the siege, and apparently celebrated its surrender with his cousin.[41]

The author of the *Gesta Stephani* believed that a traitorous baronial faction which had influenced Baldwin to rebel against Stephen existed in the king's besieging army; and Professor Ralph Davis associated Earl Robert with the group.[42]

---

[38] Davis, *King Stephen*, 3rd edn., 19; King, *King Stephen*, 60–1; see 147 & n., 123.
[39] *HN* (1998), 32–3; *GS* (2004), 14–15; Patterson, "William of Malmesbury's Robert of Gloucester," 988 & n.; Patterson, "Anarchy in England," 197; Bloch, *La Société féodale*, 350–3; King, "Dispute Settlement in Anglo-Norman England," 115–30, esp. 125; King in *HN*, xliv–xlvi; see also nn. 6, 35.
[40] *Regesta* iii. no. 868, more likely issued 1136 × 38, rather than Davis's 1136 × 39.
[41] *Regesta* ii. nos. 825–6; Loyd, *Anglo-Norman Families*, 85; Sanders, *English Baronies*, 137; Bearman, "Baldwin de Redvers," 19–20; Hollister, *Henry I*, 344, 503, 505. *Regesta* iii. nos. 340 (Hittisleigh, Devon), 337 (during the siege of Exeter), 284?, 952 (post siege?); *GS* (2004), 30–7; King, *King Stephen*, 63–4 & n., prefers Hurstbourne (Hants.) rather than Hittisleigh.
[42] *GS* (2004), 40 & n., 41; Davis, *King Stephen*, 3rd edn., 24; notice the influence in Bradbury, "The Early Years of the Reign of Stephen," 28; Finberg, in his *Lucerna*, 216, advanced an attractive theory that Robert of Bampton was an ally of Baldwin.

However, Baldwin was motivated not by fifth columnists or devotion to the empress's cause, but by hope of regaining control of the Devon shrievalty. And as for Robert's being a party to any anti-Stephen faction at this time, except for charter evidence, no major source mentions his presence at the siege. Furthermore, the conspiracy-membership theory is countered by Robert's abandonment of Matilda and loyalty to Stephen from December 1135 and to some degree by the record of Robert's attendance at Stephen's court during 1136.[43]

In between 1136–7 visits to court, Gloucester attended to his own affairs. Bristol, which Earl Robert had been developing as his principal *caput*, especially the castle, to as late as *c*.1138 certainly would have received some of his attention. As a result of all of the structural improvements to the town and castle, when King Stephen attacked Bristol in 1138, he gave up because of its impregnability.[44]

This also is a likely time for Robert to have dealt with attacks led by the scions of the native princely houses on his lordships in South Wales.[45] The threat to Anglo-Norman settlements posed by native uprisings supposedly led to three attempts by King Henry to return to England; and his death gave further impetus to the Welsh attacks.[46] Glamorgan may have been affected.[47] There is reason to believe that in *c*.1135 × 7 Earl Robert obtained peace by entering into a *conventio* with native lords in which each side accepted the hereditary tenure of land currently held by the other, thus at least diplomatically recognizing Iustin ap Gwrgant's family's right to the Blaenau Morgannwg and the house of Gloucester's to the Bro Morgannwg.[48] Furthermore, Robert's constable Richard de Grainville for his Member lordship made territorial concessions to pacify native princes as well.[49]

The safety of Earl Robert's lordship of Gwynllŵg in lower Gwent was another matter. A Welsh uprising occurred in Upper Gwent led by its joint rulers, Morgan ap Owain and his brother Iorwerth, and moved down the Usk river valley towards Newport, Gwynllŵg's *caput*. As a result, as David Crouch long ago pointed out, the earl made a *conventio* with Morgan and Iorwerth at his Bristol court, very likely between 1136 and his departure for Normandy in early 1137. By its terms, the two brothers accepted the status of vassals in return for a grant of a paltry 300 acres from the earl's demesne moor of Rumney (Monm.) in Gwynllŵg.[50]

---

[43] Esp. *GS* (2004), 40–1, and Henry of Huntingdon (2006), 706–9; Crouch, *Reign of King Stephen*, 58n. See also *Regesta* iii. nos. 271 (Oxford), 337 (Exeter), 340 (Hillsleigh), 616 (Oxford), 945–8 (Westminster), 952 (Exeter); nos. 284 (Exeter?) and 818 (Gillingham, Dors.) are suspect. For *Regesta* iii. nos. 945–6 and 947–8 being issued on two different occasions, see Chapt. 6, 195.

[44] *GS* (2004), 64–7; see also Chapt. 4, 96.

[45] e.g., Crouch, "Robert of Gloucester and the Daughter of Zelophehad," 230; Crouch, "Slow Death of Kingship in Glamorgan," 30–3.

[46] *OV* vi. 444–5; "Ann. Dore," *a*.1135; "Ann.Winchcombe," *a*.1136.

[47] Smith, "The Kingdom of Morgannwg and the Norman Conquest of Glamorgan," 30. See also, for contrast, "Ann. Margam," 13–14; Davies, "Henry I and Wales," 134; Crouch, "Slow Death of Kingship in Glamorgan," 32–3.

[48] Rice Merrick, *A Booke of Glamorganshires Antiquities*, 39–40; *Medieval Cartularies of Great Britain*, 77–8; see Beverly Smith's comments in "The Kingdom of Morgannwg and the Norman Conquest of Glamorgan," 7–8, 29–30; Crouch, "Slow Death of Kingship in Glamorgan," 32.

[49] Rice Merrick, *A Booke of Glamorganshires Antiquities*, 39–40, 49; Crouch, "Slow Death of Kingship in Glamorgan," 33–4, 41; *HN* (1998), 38–9, for the date of Earl Robert's crossing to Normandy.

[50] *Cart. Bristol*, no. 49 & n.; Crouch, "The March and the Welsh Kings," 267, 272–3; Lloyd, *A History of Wales* ii. 475.

Continued military and political threats to Stephen's rule in Normandy finally brought the king there in the third week of March. Neither the former regency government nor Stephen's fledgling Norman administration had succeeded in suppressing baronial factionalism over the royal succession and the private wars to which it gave openings. A large delegation of *curiales* and barons which did not include Robert of Gloucester saw the king off at Portsmouth. Gloucester crossed over himself from England before Easter, April 11. But if it is true that before leaving England for the duchy he tested the political waters for loyalty to Matilda and put his affairs in order, we may have the first positive evidence of his doubts about Stephen's adherence to their *conventio*.[51]

Gloucester joined them on at least two occasions during the spring, at Bayeux with his son Bishop Richard, at Évreux (Eure), and then possibly later at Pont-Audemer (Eure).[52] At the Évreux court Gloucester probably witnessed several political measures Stephen took to mollify opposition and gain key adherents in the duchy: formally making peace with Ralph de Tancarville whose castles he had just captured; releasing the imprisoned Roger de Tosny; and entering into *conventiones* with Rotrou of Mortagne and Richer de Laigle. It also was the occasion at which the king dispensed patronage to Waleran of Meulan and awarded his brother Count Theobald an annuity of 2,000 marks of silver as compensation for losing out in the Anglo-Norman succession. Winning Theobald's acceptance of the new political order complemented the agreement Stephen won from Normandy's overlord Louis VI in May at some unknown location whereby his son Eustace would hold the duchy of Louis in return for his homage.[53]

Gloucester's possibly most loyal act came within a few weeks. Count Geoffrey invaded Normandy in May via the Hiémois and made Caen, the duchy's virtual second capital and one of Earl Robert's strongholds, a major strategic target. In attacking Caen Geoffrey may have been aiming to jostle his brother-in-law to change sides and gain the center of royal administration in Lower Normandy. Some believed that the earl of Gloucester already had joined the Angevins; but in spite of the count's possible hopes and these suspicions, as Orderic Vitalis reports, the castle and garrison, which would have been under Robert's control, remained loyal to the king.[54]

Stephen aimed to drive Count Geoffrey from the duchy by mustering an army at Lisieux. An important component was going to be a force of Flemish mercenaries under the command of William d'Ypres, illegitimate grandson of Count Robert the Frisian of Flanders, unsuccessful claimant of the County of Flanders in 1127. William had entered Stephen's service in 1136, during which his rapid rise among

---

[51] *HN* (1998), 36–9; *Regesta* iii. no. 827, misdated: see the definitive assessment by King, *King Stephen*, 70 & n.

[52] *Regesta* iii. nos. 594 & n., 69 & n., 749; the dating of nos. 594 & 69 is based upon March 25: see *Handbook of Dates*, 4–5.

[53] *OV* vi. 454–5; Henry of Huntingdon (1996), 708–9; Robert of Torigny, "Chronica," 132; Chartrou, *L'Anjou de 1109 à 1151*, 53; Crouch, *Reign of King Stephen*, 64–5.

[54] *OV* vi. 482–3; Robert of Torigny, "Chronica," 132; Chartrou, *L'Anjou de 1109 à 1151*, 53; Patterson, "William of Malmesbury's Robert of Gloucester," 990; Helmerichs, "King Stephen's Norman Itinerary," 94–5. See also Crouch, *Reign of King Stephen*, 63 & n.

the king's *familiares* was marked by receiving the honor of Eye. The mercenary captain and force had been indepensable to Stephen from the beginning of his 1137 Norman expedition.[55]

However, at Livarot (Calvados) there was serious quarreling between the Norman and Flemish forces and much blood was shed on both sides. John of Marmoutier reported that the quarrel was between William d'Ypres and Reginald of Saint-Valéry over rank. Robert of Torigny believed that the animosity between the groups originated at Livarot due to a Fleming's theft of a small amount of wine from Hugh de Gournay. In any case, the upshot was that Stephen's army broke up. Some of its commanders and their dependents simply deserted without notice. Outraged, Stephen pursued them to Pont-Audemer, where he tried without success to restore them to a reliable fighting force. Failing in this, the king abandoned his plan for a campaign against Count Geoffrey and accepted a truce with him for three years in return for 2,000 marks payable each year and the first year paid immediately.[56]

The Livarot episode seems to have been the most likely setting for an incident reported exclusively by William of Malmesbury which scholars agree was related to bad blood between the Normans and Flemings in Stephen's army.[57] Not long after Earl Robert's arrival in Normandy, Stephen, at the urging of William d'Ypres, devised a plan to take Robert prisoner because of his suspected Angevin sympathies. Forewarned, Robert avoided capture and remained away from court in spite of frequent invitations. The king then decided on a more subtle tactic to deal with the earl. Stephen publicly admitted responsibility and according to a formula agreeable to Robert swore never to do such a thing again; and to give his oath greater weight the king made the archbishop of Rouen surety for their *conventio* by placing Hugh's hand into Robert's.[58] All told, a wonderful story that will be presented as a piece of Gloucester propaganda in Chapter 6.

Stephen abandoned the challenges of eliminating armed opposition in the southern March, especially the bridgehead Matilda and Geoffrey held at Argentan and the area of her dowry and in the Cotentin. Instead, he very mistakenly decided, as Ralph Davis succinctly described, to return to England and leave full restoration of order to William de Roumare, Roger *vicomte* of the Cotentin, and other justiciars, who did not include the earl of Gloucester.[59] Stephen departed for England during Advent, sometime after November 28, 1137, taking with him the Beaumont brothers and many other magnates.[60] Robert of Gloucester remained in Normandy and, as probably correctly described at this time by William of Malmesbury, "Like a man positioned in a watchtower, Robert was considering the

[55] *OV* vi. 370 n. 4; 482–3; Crouch, *Reign of King Stephen*, 18n., 26–7.
[56] *OV* vi. 484–7; Henry of Huntingdon (1996), 708–9; John of Marmoutier, 225; Robert of Torigny, "Chronica," 132–3; Chartrou, *L'Anjou de 1109 á 1151*, 53–4; Chibnall, *Empress Matilda*, 73; Bradbury, *Stephen and Matilda*, 41–2.
[57] Chibnall, *Empress Matilda*, 73 & n. 41; King in *HN*, 39 & n. 99. The E text of *ASC* written *c.*1155 only mentions the plot to kidnap Earl Robert, without details. The Winchester Annals paraphrase the account (King in *HN*, ci & nn., cii) but are even later: Gransden, *Historical Writing*, 252 & n.
[58] *HN* (1998), 38–9.
[59] *OV* vi. 491–5—Orderic exaggerating numbers; Chartrou, *L'Anjou de 1109 à 1151*, 54–5; Davis, *King Stephen*, 3rd edn., 24–6; Chibnall, *Empress Matilda*, 73.
[60] *OV* vi. 494–5; Henry of Huntingdon, 708–11; Robert of Torigny, "Chronica," 133.

future turn of events and pondering how he could avoid being considered unfaithful toward God and man because of the oath he had sworn to his sister."[61] If a late November dating of a royal charter by Professor Davis is correct, Richard bishop of Bayeux may have brought Stephen his father Earl Robert's last loyal greeting.[62]

Immediately after Pentecost, May 22, 1138, Robert sent legates bearing a formal denial of his fealty (*diffidatio*) to the king.[63] William of Malmesbury claimed that Robert's act followed a traditional practice. It did to a degree, and the earl's act and the verb the chronicler used to express it, *diffidiare/diffidare*, are no longer thought to be so innovative.[64] Earl Robert's rationale for changing to the Angevin side, as reported by his apologist William of Malmesbury, was that King Stephen had illegally become king, broken their agreement, and violated his oath to Matilda's succession. Furthermore, both the advice of learned churchmen he had sought on the matter and direction from a papal letter (*decretum*) mandated his obedience to the oath he had taken to honor his oath in favor of Matilda's succession.[65]

Leaving for later discussion the earl's lay and ecclesiastical authorities concerning oaths, Stephen's most demonstrable offence would have been depriving Robert of his former curial status. Stephen replaced Robert as favored royal confidant and insider with the Beaumont Waleran of Meulan. As early as Easter 1136 the king forged a familial bond with the count by betrothing to him his 2-year old daughter Matilda (d. 1137).[66] By early 1137 the count of Meulan could supersede Gloucester in a royal charter's witness-list.[67] To compound Robert's sense of loss, by then yet another royal favorite had the king's ear instead of Gloucester, the already mentioned Flemish mercenary captain, William d'Ypres. Almost as a corollary to this situation went the absence of curial or military assignments such as he had held under his father; Waleran and his brother Robert were appointed *legati* to pacify Normandy soon after Easter 1136.[68] Gloucester could rightly consider that he was losing out in the battle for places of influence with the new king to a Beaumont family phalanx.[69] His political future under Stephen would revert to the more baronial life his father had mapped for him before William Aetheling's death.

---

[61] *HN* (1998), 40; translation mine.   [62] *Regesta* iii. xl, no. 681.
[63] For the date of Earl Robert's *diffidatio* immediately after Pentecost (22 May), see *HN* (1998), 40–1. Henry of Huntington (1996), 712–13, followed by Robert of Torigny, claimed Robert was in rebellion after Easter, which fell on 3 April 1138: "Chronica," 136; *OV* vi. 514–17 would place the event in June. A much later source, *Chronicon Thomas Wykes*, 22, claims English castles were promised Robert, but there are problems with those identified.
[64] *HN* (1998), 40–1, 38–9; Gillingham, "1066 and the Introduction of Chivalry into England," 224 & n.; Du Cange, ii. s.v., 112–14; King, in *HN*, xlviii; Crouch, *Reign of King Stephen*, 77 & n.; Dalton, "In Neutro Latere: The Armed Neutrality of Ranulf II earl of Chester," 48, nn. 39, 41, p. 49.
[65] *HN* (1998), 38–43, esp. 42–3 (*decretum*), 120–1 (*mandatum*).
[66] *OV* vi. 456–7 & n.; Henry of Huntingdon (1996), 754–5; *Cartulary of Holy Trinity, Aldate*, 232; *Chronicon Valassense*, 8, states that Stephen granted Waleran the earldom of Worcester on the occasion of the marriage: see also Houth, "Galeran II comte de Meulan," 634; Crouch, *Reign of King Stephen*, 44 & n.
[67] *Regesta* iii. no. 594; Patterson, "William of Malmesbury's Robert of Gloucester," 990–1; Crouch, "Robert of Gloucester and the Daughter of Zelophehad," 231.
[68] *GS* (2004), 46–7; *OV* vi. 456–9, 462 & n., 463; Davis, *King Stephen*, 3rd edn., 66, 142; Crouch, *Beaumont Twins*, 31.
[69] Patterson, "William of Malmesbury's Robert of Gloucester," 990–1; Crouch, "Robert of Gloucester and the Daughter of Zelophehad," 231.

Compounding Earl Robert's grievance over Waleran's promotion may well have been Stephen's granting his new favorite estates of the royal demesne in Worcestershire and Warwickshire, beginning with the borough of Worcester probably in early 1136 and others by *c*.1138, when Stephen created his favorite earl of Worcester. As a result Robert had to countenance his rival's acquisition of a territorial center of influence near his own concentration of demesne and subinfeudated estates in and around Tewkesbury in northern Gloucestershire.[70]

There is reason to believe that in Robert's mind Stephen had also violated his *dignitas* by either disseising him of land or attempting to do so. Even though there is no solid proof for such actions before the earl's repudiation of fealty in 1138, there are possible cases. Earl Robert's demesne manor at Burford (Oxon.) is potentially the best one. Several of the king's *acta* place him at the borough before 1139 and at least once in 1136 × 7, but in no case do any of the king's *acta* reveal his exercise of lordship of the manor. So we are left wondering whether these instances were mere royal stopovers imposing on Gloucester's hospitality or an occupation which was cut short by the earl's later return in force from Normandy.[71]

Knowing what we know about William d'Ypres's pre-1137 entry into Stephen's service makes Dartford in Kent one of several other possible examples from Earl Robert's holdings. Moreover, William's tenure of the manor by 1137 would partly explain the animus Gloucester had for d'Ypres beginning by the end of this year.[72]

It also is possible that the already mentioned pro-Angevin fighting in the Cotentin in which his half-brother Reginald de Dunstanville and Baldwin de Redvers were notable leaders exerted some influence on Robert's *diffidatio*.[73] Some Angevin arm-twisting certainly played a role. Before Geoffrey invaded Normandy in June 1138, he had won the earl to his side with "pleas and promises" and made a pact (*concordia*) with him at Easter (April 3). Exactly what the agreement included can only be guessed; but it is reasonable to assume that it involved Robert's support for Matilda in return for restoration of his *dignitas*.

Robert's *diffidatio* was more than his declared denial of fealty to King Stephen; it was a declaration of war on his cousin on behalf of his sister's claim to the Anglo-Norman throne. England would be the major battleground. As the seat of royal government, it was the key to Matilda's prospects as it had been for Stephen's; and for Robert personally, England was the area of his greatest landed wealth, which he would have to defend against Stephen's predictable retaliatory disseisins.

---

[70] Patterson, "William of Malmesbury's Robert of Gloucester," 991; Crouch, *Beaumont Twins*, 30–1. Waleran's foundation charter for Bordesley Abbey (f. November 22, 1138), which mentions some of the estates, presupposes his prior tenure of them: printed, King, "Waleran, count of Meulan, earl of Worcester," 178–9; for the charter's use of *dedisse* and *confirmasse*, see Hudson, *Land, Law, and Lordship*, 76. For the date of the earldom, see Crouch, *Reign of King Stephen*, 86 & n. 6; King, *King Stephen*, 106.

[71] *Regesta* iii. nos. 349–51, 398; nos. 349 (possibly) and 398 (definitely) were issued 1136 × 7. *OASPG*, no. 41; Bishop, *Scriptores Regis*, no. 583. Earl Robert did not attest any of the *acta*.

[72] *VCH Kent* iii. 208a (*terra Regis* in hands of Haimo sheriff); *Regesta* iii. no. 98; *PR 2 Henry II*, 65. For the dating of William d'Ypres's entry into King Stephen's service, see 135; for views about him attributable to Gloucester by 1137, see King, *HN* (1998), xlvii, 38–9.

[73] *OV* vi. 490–5, 510–17.

Whether or not Robert saw himself by this declaration as assuming leadership of his sister's party, we cannot know for sure; but a segment of the English baronage certainly recognized his leadership to some degree, for in response to news of the earl's *diffidatio* many barons rebelled as well. He believed that the dynastic fate of his nephews depended on what actions he took.[74]

Stephen responded to Robert's act of defiance by attempting to seize all of his English holdings. William of Malmesbury claimed that only Bristol survived in Robert's hands. Whatever his actual losses were, Robert had anticipated the king's reaction. Looking first to his own survival, as well as to any military advocacy role in England he might assume, he had taken steps to prepare a secure redoubt for himself at his English *caput* and to have his men initiate hostilities in anticipation of his arrival. The same messengers he had sent to announce his withdrawal of homage to Stephen proceeded on to Bristol with instructions for the castle to be provisioned, for it to receive all who sought refuge there, and for its garrison to start harrying his enemies.[75]

Across the great Severn estuary the earl could count on the additional security of his two Welsh lordships and, before long, the support in one way or another of other neighboring Marcher lords, Brian fitz Count of Abergavenny and Miles of Gloucester of Brecon. Gilbert fitz Gilbert de Clare, who succeeded his uncle Walter as lord of Striguil (Chepstow, Monm.), a supporter of Stephen elsewhere, did nothing to disrupt the political solidarity of the southeastern March for the Empress Matilda: perhaps the fruit of a grant Earl Robert made to him of Luton church and land (Beds.).[76]

In England the just-mentioned uprisings gave Robert a varied group of military and political allies which reveals unusually detailed information about an inchoate early twelfth-century affinity.[77] By definition, such a group provided a great lord certain regional support or control for a particular purpose through the loyalty and service of men who were not feudal tenants. Such a following contradicts the long-held view of post-Conquest honorial societies and their feudal armies being made up of military tenants.[78]

Nevertheless, the composition of the earl of Gloucester's initial followers shows that in 1138 his "favorers" (*faventes*) as Orderic Vitalis called them, as a group, were far from blindly committed Angevins. A nominally major member, David king of Scots, reveals very mixed loyalties; another, the great Yorkshire baron

---

[74] *HN* (1998), 42–3; *OV* vi. 516–19; *GS* (2004), 56–7; Gervase of Canterbury i. 104.

[75] *HN* (1998), 42–3; *GS* (2004), 56–7.

[76] Crouch, "The March and the Welsh Kings," 280–1; Crouch, *Reign of King Stephen*, 130; *CP* x. 348 & n., 349 & nn., 350 & nn. For Earl Robert's estate at Luton, see Chapt. 3, 67; Chapt. 4, 173.

[77] *OV* vi. 516–19; Henry of Huntingdon (1996), 712–13, and Robert of Torigny, "Chronica," 134–5, record very similar lists. I have added William fitz Odo of Torrington, who is not on any of the lists, because he rose against the king at the same time.

[78] The construct was an element of fourteenth- and fifteenth-century society; antecedents were present in the twelfth century: Crouch, *Reign of King Stephen*, 166–7; McFarlane, *England in the Fifteenth Century*, 30–1, 34–5; Payling, *Political Society in Lancastrian England*, 111, 189; King, "The Anarchy of King Stephen's Reign," 133–4; Hicks, *Bastard Feudalism*, 104–8, 119; see also Coss, "Bastard Feudalism Revised," esp. 29–30, 32–4, 44, 55–6; Crouch, "Debate: Bastard Feudalism Revised," esp. 167–8, 170–3; Green, *The Aristocracy of Norman England*, 213–18.

Eustace fitz John, only indirect initial attachment and ultimately hardly any at all. David may have been in contact with Earl Robert prior to his revolt.[79] David renewed hostilities with Stephen in January 1138 after being implored by Matilda, and then launched a full-scale invasion of England in April. Yet, after suffering a crushing defeat in the battle of the Standard at Northallerton (Yorks.) on 22 August, he made a *conventio* with Stephen which, like the one of 1136, ignored Matilda's succession, gained English territory, and the earldom of Northumberland for his son Henry. Eustace, on the other hand, had switched from royalist to Angevin because King Stephen had deprived him of Bamburgh in 1137 for being a suspected Angevin sympathizer. He had gravitated politically away from Stephen to David as the more likely protector of his landed rights and then fought for the Scots' king at the famous August battle; but he kept himself aloof from both Matilda and Earl Robert.[80]

The west, southwest, and Welsh March, the region of Earl Robert's greatest strength, were where most of his known followers were located, which suggests the general influences of Robert's power and of common interests. The former may account for the presence among the *faventes* of Robert son of Alfred of Lincoln, castellan of Wareham, the port of which provided direct Channel entry from Normandy to the earl of Gloucester's domanial heartland.[81] Either William de Mohun lord of nearby Dunster or members of his administration felt some attraction to the lord of Bristol. Robert was able to attract into his service from William's Hugh de Gundeville, Hubert de Pierreponte, and possibly Warin chaplain.[82]

The security of the March after King Stephen failed to stop Welsh attacks through surrogates Baldwin fitz Gilbert de Clare and Robert fitz Harold of Ewyas in 1136 and effectively left the region to its fate was a reason for a number of the rebels to join the empress and Earl Robert.[83] The earl's nephew-in-law William fitz Alan was sheriff of Shropshire and castellan of Shrewsbury.[84] William Peveral of Dover and Walchelin Maminot, uncle and nephew, both had proprietary interests at Ellesmere (Salop).[85] Ralph Paynell of Dudley castle (Worcs.) was close to the Shropshire border.[86]

---

[79] Green, "Family Matters," 160; Dalton, "Eustace Fitz John," 359–64; *GOE*, 250–2; for King David, see also Chapt. 2, 45.

[80] *GS* (2004), 52–3; John of Hexham, 287, 293, 300; Richard of Hexham, 146, 177–8; Dalton, "Eustace Fitz John," 368–71; Green, "Aristocratic Loyalties on the Northern Frontier," 96–7; King, *King Stephen*, 53–4, 90–4.

[81] Green, "Family Matters," 147–64; Sanders, *English Baronies*, 99. The social connection between Robert of Lincoln's wife Bence and a countess of Gloucester was likely to have been Hawisia, Earl Robert's posthumous daughter-in-law, not his wife Mabel (Green, "Family Matters," 161): *Wulfric of Haselbury*, 157. For Wareham, see *HN* (1998), 124–5; *GS* (2004), 84–5.

[82] Loyd, *Anglo-Norman Families*, 66; *CP* xii. 37–9; Bearman, "Mohun, William de, Earl of Somerset," 515–16; see Chapt. 4, 115.

[83] *GS* (20043), 18–23; Crouch, "The March and the Welsh Kings," 256–8.

[84] *OV* vi. 520–1 & nn.; *JW* iii. 250–1; *GOE*, 250–2, 284–7.

[85] *Mon. Angl.* iii. 522; *Cart. Shrewsbury* i. nos, 15 & n., 19 & n., 28, 40, 43b; Eyton, *Antiquities of Shropshire* x. 233; Walchelin also was the son-in-law of Robert de Ferrers, who remained loyal to Stephen: *OV* vi. 520–1.

[86] *JW* iii. 250–1.

The personnel of this quasi-affinity contained some very feudal types, military tenants of Robert's honor of Gloucester. William fitz John of Harptree and William fitz Odo of Torrington represented the elite of Robert's honorial baronage, owing the service of ten knights;[87] Walchelin Maminot, Robert's castellan at Dover in 1138, was a mesne tenant or a rear-vassal of the honor as heir of the Domesday tenant-in-chief Gilbert Maminot. His fees at Bretinghurst in Surrey and Hertwell in Northamptonshire provided the services of three knights of the total of twenty-four owed for the castle-guard of Dover by the Maminot honor of West Greenwich.[88]

Two others lack traditional vassalic profiles in some way and were really allies bound by some feudal paraphernalia. Ralph Lovel of Castle Cary (Som.) had sworn fealty and performed homage to Robert, but his fee was not a Gloucester tenure.[89] Morgan ab Owain, the native lord of Usk (Monm.), had sworn fealty to the earl at his Bristol court and received a subinfeudated token 300 acres in Rumney marsh in the lordship of Gwynllŵg.[90]

Of the freebooter Geoffrey Talbot II, rebel castellan at Hereford, *cognatus* of Gilbert de Lacy of Weobly, it could be said that Stephen drove him into Earl Robert's service. After Stephen drove Geoffrey from both Hereford and Weobly, his renegade castellan fled to the hospitality of Bristol castle, the garrison of which Robert had ordered to provide for such refugees, and both Geoffrey and Gilbert joined the earl's corps of household knights. Talbot fought in attempts in 1138 and 1140 to capture Bath (Som.) and died of wounds in the second one commanded by the earl himself and was honorably buried in St. Peter's Abbey Gloucester, arguably predictably under Robert's aegis.[91]

By the 1140s Robert's regional support had long since been augmented by Baldwin de Redvers, whom Matilda created earl of Devon in 1141, and the great Breton lord of Totnes (Devon) Alfred fitz Judhael, whom de Redvers had drawn in as a sworn ally. Stephen de Mandeville as honorial tenant of Baldwin and Earl Robert was a link between the two earls; Gloucester's two tenants Fitz John and Fitz Odo were similar assets.[92] And Robert tightened the bond between the networks still further by marrying his son Robert to Baldwin's daughter Hawisia.

---

[87] *RBE* i. 255–6; ii. 288; "Constitutio Domus Regis," 208–9; Sanders, *English Baronies*, 48 & n. 5.; *GOE*, 19n., 253, 283, 285; Loyd, *Anglo-Norman Families*, 103–4; William was the brother of Eustace and Pain fitz John: Davis, in *GS* (2004), xxix; for another view, see Keats-Rowan, *Domesday Descendants*, 920.

[88] *OV* vi. 518–19; Henry of Huntingdon (1996), 712–13; *Domesday Book: Kent*, 5.36–7; *RBE* i.195; ii. 617, 646; *The White Book of Peterborough*, no. 245L; Round, "Northamptonshire Survey," 374; Sanders, *English Baronies*, 97 & nn.; Navel, "Recherches sur les institutions féodales en Normandie," 127; Loyd, *Anglo-Norman Families*, 57; *VCH Surrey* iv. 31; Round, "Castle Guard," 146–7, 155–6; Painter, "Castle-Guard," 146–7, 150–1; Hollister, *Military Organization of Norman England*, 150–1, 157–61 (rebuttal of Painter in support of Round).

[89] *GS* (2004), 66–7; Clark, *Cartae et alia* i. no. clxxx, p. 185; Sanders, *English Baronies*, 27: the theory that Ralph was the heir of Walter of Douai by a first wife has been countered by Davis in *GS* (2004), xxviii & n., xxix.

[90] Crouch, "Slow Death of Kingship in Glamorgan," 32–3 & n., 41.

[91] *GS* (2004), 58–9 & n., 60–5; *JW* iii. 248–9, 276–7, 290–1; *GS* (2004), 108–11.

[92] Sanders, *English Baronies*, 64; Bearman, "Baldwin de Redvers," 42 & n., 44 & n.; Green, "Family Matters," 154.

We finally see likely fragmentary evidence of a southwestern affinity after his victory over Stephen at Wilton in 1143, when Earl Robert and his following could be said to rule half of England from sea to sea; and mints on the lands of four great lords who were not Robert's vassals or tenants were producing silver pennies in the earl's name with dies sent from Bristol.[93]

In retrospect, the rebellions of 1138 in England were failures. For one thing, the empress and the earl of Gloucester were abroad and would remain absent for roughly eighteen months more. For his part, the king acted decisively. Even before he learned of his cousin's *diffidatio*, Stephen dealt with Geoffrey Talbot and then led a campaign against other western rebels. Only at the absent earl of Gloucester's *caput* Bristol was the king foiled by the fortress's natural defenses.[94] However, undismayed by this reverse, he attacked and took in order Castle Cary, Harptree, Dudley, Shrewsbury, and very likely Wareham.[95]

Individual rebels and whatever forces they could muster remained isolated, with insufficient numbers to challenge King Stephen in the field.[96] He could mete out ruthless punishment to those besieged garrisons which responded to honorable terms of surrender with mockery. For such behavior, at least some of Shrewsbury's garrison and commander Ernulf de Hesding, William fitz Alan's uncle, were hanged.[97]

Stephen also employed effective surrogates against other rebels. In the southwest, William fitz Odo of Torrington and William de Mohun of Dunster were left to be dealt with by Stephen's formidable Henry de Tracy.[98] In the east, Queen Matilda shut off Walchelin Maminot in Dover castle by land and used ships from her county of Boulogne to complete the siege by sea. On the advice of his father-in-law Robert of Ferrers, recently made earl of Derby, and with the example of the Shrewsbury garrison's fate, Walchelin Maminot surrendered and made his way to the empress. William d'Ypres took Canterbury and Earl Gilbert fitz Gilbert, Leeds, with the result that from 1138 William d'Ypres became politically unchallengeable in Kent.[99]

Meanwhile, there was plenty to keep Robert of Gloucester and his sister and brother-in-law occupied in Normandy. Robert and Count Geoffrey were involved in discussions which would lead to their Easter pact.[100] In early October, in his first recorded appearance as his sister's military champion, he assisted in the count's siege of Falaise. During the year Robert's overall campaigning for Geoffrey helped bring much of the Bessin, including Caen and Bayeux, and perhaps some of the Oximin under his authority at least for a time.[101]

Once Earl Robert had joined the Angevins and a successful attack on Stephen in England became a credible possibility, planning for it probably took up much of

---

[93] See 171.   [94] *GS* (2004), 64–7: *HN* (1998), 42–3.   [95] See 167.
[96] See *GS* (2004), 66–9, for the sentiments and condition of Castle Cary's garrison.
[97] *JW* iii. 250–1; *GS* (2004), 66–9; *OV*, vi. 520–1 & nn., 522–3.   [98] *GS* (2004), 82–3.
[99] *OV* vi. 520–1; Henry of Huntingdon (1996), 712–13; Robert of Torigny, "Chronica," 136; *Regesta* iii. nos 821?, 68, 274.
[100] See 138.
[101] Robert of Torigny, "Chronica," 136; *OV* vi. 514–17, 526–7; Norgate, *England under the Angevin Kings* i. 306–8; Chartrou, *L' Anjou de 1109 à 1151*, 56; Crouch, *Beaumont Twins*, 38.

1138–9.[102] Matilda evidently intended to launch a two-pronged campaign against Stephen: a diplomatic one involving an appeal to Pope Innocent II to reverse his initial endorsement of the king back in 1136; and a military assault to dethrone Stephen in England. Her diplomatic success would legitimize her claim to the Anglo-Norman throne and consequently her invasion—all very reminiscent of the *ex post facto* Norman propaganda justifying the attack on King Harold Godwinson by Matilda's grandfather. Innocent heard the appeal at the Second Lateran Council, which began on April 8, 1139, and the negative result left only a military option.[103]

As her plan developed, Matilda included her stepmother Queen Adeliza and her husband William d'Aubigny, *iure uxoris* lord of Arundel, uncle King David, and brother Earl Robert most of all. Aided by hindsight, we can see that Matilda staked her hopes for success on an invasion at two different sites along the south coast, by herself with Robert in command and by a second body led by Baldwin de Redvers with possibly her brother Reginald in tow. In its fully developed form, Baldwin's force was to land first at Wareham in hopes of drawing King Stephen's attention and allowing Robert and Matilda in her main force to disembark unopposed in Sussex near Arundel.[104]

The roots of Robert of Gloucester's role as champion of Matilda's succession and leader of her party appear in the post-invasion strategic role envisioned for him as well as in his participation in his sister's pre-invasion diplomatic effort aimed at achieving it. The earl's Gloucestershire demesne heartland was planned to provide an initial safe haven for her. Robert's impregnable Bristol would be their ultimate redoubt. For Matilda Gloucester would provide her the site of former festal royal crown-wearings with potential assets of castle, borough, abbey, and the adjacent suburban palace at Kingsholm supported by the demesne manor of King's Barton.[105] To reinforce their position in the county and Gloucester Robert and his sister set about ensuring the support of the sheriff and constable of Gloucester castle, Miles. Details of their diplomatic efforts are contained in one of the Anarchy's most important historiographical additions, the missing portion of a clumsily drafted *pancarte* in favor of Miles of Gloucester issued in its final form by the empress at Gloucester around the end of June 1141 and discovered by Professor Nicholas Vincent.[106]

Part of this text contains an excerpted *conventio* Matilda had made with Miles of Gloucester from her headquarters at Domfront by means of exchanged wordings

---

[102] *Regesta* iii. no. 567, the dating of which has been established by Marjorie Chibnall: *Empress Matilda*, 74; *OV* vi. 534–5.
[103] *LCGF*, no. 26, p. 61, ll. 15–16, 22–3; p. 65, ll. 132–54; John of Salisbury, *Historia Pontificalis*, 83–5; *GFAL*, 105, 112 & n.; Chibnall, *Empress Matilda*, 75. For an earlier hearing in 1136 before the pope, see Constable, "Peter the Venerable, the Lateran Council of 1139," 254–5; King, *King Stephen*, 104.
[104] See 131.
[105] *ASC a*. 1087 (1086); *Regesta* ii. no. 490; *GR* (1998) i. 508–9; Biddle, "Seasonal Festivals and Residence: Winchester, Westminster and Gloucester in the Tenth to Twelfth Centuries," 53, 55, 59 & n.; Herbert, *Medieval Gloucester*, 18–19; see Map 2, 240.
[106] BL, MS Sloane 1301, fol. 422r–422v *c.s.*xvii[in], completing *Regesta* iii. no. 391 (misdated) after *forestam de Dena*. For dating, see King, *King Stephen*, 163n. I am indebted to Nicholas Vincent for providing me with a transcript of the text.

carried by two named messengers sometime between her brother's *diffidatio* of late May 1138 and starting for England at the end of September 1139. In the final product, made with the advice and command of Count Geoffrey, Matilda granted in fee and heredity a list of Gloucestershire properties her father had held in return for Miles's homage. Geoffrey swore to Miles that he would maintain the agreement, as did Matilda. The empress also placed her brother Robert earl of Gloucester as surety by oath (*obsidem per fiduciam*) to Miles. Were she to renege from their agreement, Robert with Miles would withhold service to her until she satisfied Miles only by his leave. And finally, Earl Robert attested first among the agreement's witnesses.[107]

The document's political implications are as significant as its strategic ones. First of all, it is the earliest expression of a partnership between Matilda and Earl Robert, with him taking the lead in the formation of a putative West Country-based party. The politically cautious earl would not have agreed to his possible involvement with the Gloucestershire sheriff and constable without having come to some agreement himself either directly or indirectly with Miles. One of John of Worcester's Gloucester continuators reported under events of 1138 in an only partly inaccurate account that the two, having denied their fealty to King Stephen, bound themselves in a *coniuratio* and urged the ex-empress through messengers to come to England.[108] Miles still remained openly loyal to Stephen in January 1139 and possibly later, so at the time of Matilda's *conventio* with him the constable of Gloucester was playing a double game.[109]

Although no word about Miles's obligation to Matilda appears in the digested text of their *conventio*, the constable of Gloucester reacted accordingly by going on the warpath in advance of the empress's arrival. Like Earl Robert, he became a magnet for some of Stephen's enemies, attacked the king's friends, and pillaged their lands in the Gloucestershire region. At Miles's urging, his son-in-law Humphrey de Bohun, lord of Trowbridge (Wilts.), fortified his castle and joined the rebellion.[110]

The empress involved the dowager queen Adeliza and her husband William d'Aubigny in her invasion plans through a flurry of letters in order for their great castle at Arundel (Sussex) to provide initial security and their nearby Sussex coast a protected site for the disembarkation of an expeditionary force. Arundel offered easy connections with the earl's Bristol by both main roads and secondary tracks.[111] Kent was undesirable as a landing site after Earl Robert's *diffidatio*.

Arrangements likely were reached between Matilda and her stepmother with the passive agreement of her new husband. While Robert of Torigny stated that the

---

[107] BL, MS Sloane 1301, fol. 422r. The messengers were Elias Giffard and Humphrey fitz Odo ("per Elia(m) Giffard et Humfr(idum) filium Odonis qui verba inde inter nos portauerunt." For their affiliation, see King, *King Stephen*, 118.
[108] *JW* iii. 252–3; see also 270–1; see McGurk in *JW* iii. xliv–xlv & n.
[109] *Regesta* iii, nos. 366, 473, 667: court appearances datable to January 1139 in varying degrees of certainty; for a range of views, see Round, *Geoffrey de Mandeville*, 284; Crouch, *Reign of King Stephen*, 78–9, 107 n. 3; McGurk, *JW* iii. xlv; King, *King Stephen*, 119n.
[110] *GS* (2004), 90–1; *JW* iii. 270–1.   [111] *HN* (1998), 60–1.

invitation to Arundel came from William d'Aubigny, both William of Malmesbury and a continuator of John of Worcester make flimsy excuses for Queen Adeliza allowing this situation to happen; and Malmesbury blamed her, not d'Aubigny, for the empress's later forced departure from Arundel castle. Furthermore, Arundel was Adeliza's dower.[112]

Matilda's plans were put into execution during summer 1139 by Baldwin's landing with a sizeable force at Wareham harbor, formerly held by Angevin-friendly Robert son of Alfred of Lincoln, but at this time under Stephen's control. Given the situation, Baldwin moved immediately to, and seized control of, nearby royal Corfe castle (Dors.). All of this occurred around the time a tempestuous council at Winchester began on August 29, presided over by recently appointed papal legate Henry bishop of Winchester. Its aim was to apply sanctions against the king for his recent arrest of Bishop Roger of Salisbury and his nephew Alexander bishop of Lincoln and seizure of Roger's and his nephew's castles. Roger and his relatives had been the victims of a plot engineered by Waleran of Meulan, who capitalized on fears about the bishops' loyalty with the empress's invasion looming and on envy of their wealth and power. Before a meeting of the king's court at Oxford in June 1139, with the assistance of his twin brother Robert and ally Alan count of Brittany, Alan's men lured Roger's into a brawl. Roger, his son the chancellor Roger le Poer, and Alexander were arrested, but Nigel of Ely avoided capture. Stephen charged the bishops with breaking the king's peace, and judged their attempt to avoid surrendering their castles as signs of good faith to be proof of their treasonous designs and justification for condemnation and seizure of the castles. Waleran thus replaced at a stroke the core of the old guard of Henry I's central administration and gained for the king Roger's Sherborne, Salisbury, Devizes, and Malmesbury; Alexander's Newark (Notts.) and Sleaford (Lincs.); and Nigel's Ely, and Aldreth (Cambs.). Among the replacements of Roger's family in Stephen's central administration was the new chancellor, a protégé of Waleran, Philip of Harcourt, who later bedeviled Robert of Gloucester as bishop of Bayeux.[113]

As the Winchester council was adjourning on September 30, the other and main element of Matilda's invasion plan was implemented with her landing with Robert and their force near Arundel. As an omen of what was to come, an annalist at Plympton Priory recorded that the sky had turned blood red; his was not the sole sighting.[114] Both armies' landings had occurred in spite of Stephen's efforts to prevent them.

The empress's forces, William of Malmesbury reports, probably on good authority, numbered 140 knights consisting of both Matilda's and Earl Robert's men, if not

---

[112] Robert of Torigny, "Chronica," 137; *JW* iii. 268–9; *HN* (1998), 60–1.

[113] *HN* (1998), 50–9, 64–9; *GS* (2004), 72–80 & n., 81, 84–5; *OV* vi. 530–5; *LE*, 314–15; *JW* iii. 280–1; Henry of Huntingdon (1996), 718–23; *Councils* i. 768–79; Kealey, *Roger of Salisbury*, 178–89; Davis, *King Stephen*, 3rd edn., 29–30; Yoshitake, "The Arrest of the Bishops in 1139 and its Consequences," 101–2, see also Chapt. 2, 62 and Chapt. 4, 123–4.

[114] *HN* (1998), 60–1; *JW* iii. 268–9, and Robert of Torigny, "Chronica," 137, give respectively October and August for the landing; Orderic Vitalis says autumn: *OV* vi. 534–5; Round, *Geoffrey de Mandeville*, 278–83. For omens, see "Ann. Plympton," 28.

others. How they were mustered and the fleet collected which transported them or even their Continental port of embarkation is unknown. Barfleur, much used in the past for *transfretationes* to and from the south coast, is a likely choice.[115] One thing is for certain: Earl Robert of Gloucester arrived in England as his sister's chief commander and sponsor; and if Robert of Torigny is correct, Countess Mabel either accompanied him or met him at Arundel.[116]

The king did not fall for the de Redvers' bait, but immediately upon hearing of the landing broke off other campaigns and headed for Arundel with Bishop Henry. As the royalist army began to deploy for a siege, Robert, leaving Mabel and the empress behind, left for Bristol in the dark of night via back roads with a small escort of barely a dozen knights before Stephen was able seal off all means of escape. Gloucester succeeded in spite of efforts by the king and his brother to capture him: Stephen, by giving hot pursuit, and Henry, by mistakenly guarding only the main routes. The bishop's failure apparently led some second-guessers to believe that he had made a pact of friendship with the earl. Probably by common agreement, the empress, with her sister-in-law, remained in Arundel castle. The dowager queen was left to deny to Stephen her responsibility for the presence of the Angevin army by claiming that she only had intended to offer Matilda and Robert hospitality.[117]

Robert and Matilda, in choosing for him to travel "light and fast," probably had chosen the best option, regardless of the outcome. Remaining in Arundel together would have risked all on successfully breaking out or on hoping to win unpredictably favorable terms of surrender. On the other hand, a free Robert could secure their power and bring forces to rescue Matilda and Mabel or, if he were not in time before they had to surrender, he would at least have an army as a bargaining chip for favorable terms. In the latter scenario, there was even the possibility that chivalrous norms about treatment of women might move Stephen to let Matilda and Mabel go.[118] In any case, it is safe to assume that the earl was attending to his primary obligation to preserve the war by seeing to the security of Bristol and organizing Angevin supporters.

Surprisingly, Stephen not only allowed his dynastic rival and his chief military opponent's wife to leave their hosts, but provided them with an escort of his brother Henry and Waleran of Meulan. Was it chivalry, misplaced generosity, or tactical stupidity?

Some chroniclers heap criticism on the king for bad judgment on the basis of one or more character flaws. The most shrewd observer, the anonymous author of the *Gesta Stephani*, plausibly claimed that the king had accepted the pragmatic advice of his episcopal brother: rather than fight the empress in one place and have her

---

[115] "Ann. Reading," 11, says that Matilda came from Anjou.
[116] Robert of Torigny, "Chronica," 137.
[117] "Ann. Winchester," 51; "Ann. Worcester," 378; *GS* (2004), 86–9; *HN* (1998), 60–1, for the escort of 12; Robert of Torigny, "Chronica," 137.
[118] On this point, see Gillingham, "1066 and the Introduction of Chivalry into England," 31. William of Malmesbury referred to "the custom of honorable knights" in discussing one aspect of Stephen's treatment of the empress at this time: *HN* (1998), 62–3.

brother wage war against him in another, send the empress to her brother at Bristol and defeat them both in one place.[119] Even though he apparently took that advice, Stephen still imposed terms which included a truce probably covering the duration of her travel, an escort, and a limitation on how far east forces of her brother could advance to meet her party. Apparently Calne in Wiltshire was at least one of the points. There they were met by Robert, who had mobilized a military escort to conduct his sister safely to Bristol. At that point Waleran turned back, while Bishop Henry continued onward.[120]

By the time Earl Robert met his sister, he already had been acting on her behalf by rallying two major figures to their side. While traveling to Bristol from Arundel, the earl met first with his old curial colleague Brian fitz Count at Wallingford. Brian is not in Orderic Vitalis's or other chroniclers' lists of the 1138 rebel castellans. Like Miles of Gloucester, he only publicly joined the Angevin party in 1139.[121] However, there is reason to believe that Fitz Count had privately favored Matilda's succession, but waited for her arrival before formally changing sides. Once Brian had the news, he fortified Wallingford and vigorously warred on the king.[122]

Earl Robert also made contact with his vassal and pre-invasion ally surely to plan for future cooperation, possibly secured by oath.[123] Miles probably had made it possible for Fitz Count to meet the earl. King Stephen's response to Brian's rebellion was to make for Wallingford with a large army. He was unable to take the castle by direct assault and so fell back on the strategy of a tight siege by building and garrisoning two siege castles. He then turned to deal with Humphrey de Bohun at Trowbridge (Wilts.) and along the way captured Miles's castle at South Cerney (Glos.). But back at Wallingford, Miles suddenly arrived at night with his own impressive force. He completely overwhelmed Stephen's garrisons and easily took back South Cerney.[124] Thus saved, Wallingford became the eastern Angevin salient in the Thames Valley. The constable of Gloucester's help was not forgotten. Around 1141 × 2, Brian and his wife Matilda gave Miles the Marcher lordship of Abergavenny, contiguous with his honor of Brecon, to be held for the nominal service of three knights.[125]

After Robert escorted his sister to Bristol from their rendezvous location, she stayed with him for at least a month, during which the two utilized their secure headquarters to broadcast her arrival, to meet with supporters, and for Matilda to receive oaths of fealty. One of those who came was Miles, who afterwards conducted

---

[119] *GS* (2004), 88–91; see also *OV* vi. 534–5; *JW* iii. 268–9; Henry of Huntingdon (1996), 722–3, the least critical.

[120] *GS* (2004), 88–91; *HN* (1998), 62–3.

[121] Brian remained loyal to King Stephen into 1138: *Regesta* iii. nos. 383–5; King, "Brian fitz Count," 538.

[122] *HN*, 60–1; Robert of Torigny, "Chronica," 137; *GS* (2004), 90–1.

[123] Robert of Torigny, "Chronica," 137; *GS* (2004), 90–1; possibly *JW* iii. 270–1; Robert of Torigny only reports that Robert announced the empress's arrival to Brian and Miles. See Round, in *Geoffrey de Mandeville*, 284–5.

[124] *GS* (2004), 90–5; Robert of Torigny, "Chronica," 137; Davis, *King Stephen*, 3rd edn., 40–1.

[125] *Ancient Charters*, no. 26 & n.; *Regesta* iii. no. 394; iv, Plate XIII & n.; Walker, "The 'Honours' of the Earls of Hereford," 191.

her to her Gloucestershire royal stronghold for another round of similar activities. The highlight of the Bristol events must have been Miles's recognition of Matilda as his lady and the kingdom's heir; at Gloucester, Miles's formal performance of homage to her, evidently in return for her confirmation of, among other things, his hereditary tenure of Gloucester castle and county shrievalty.[126]

As the Angevin party developed, Earl Robert of Gloucester manifested various aspects of his leadership, the office of commander-in-chief (*offitium ducis*), as William of Malmesbury called it.[127] Its obvious basis was his military function, but diplomatic efforts to increase or retain his supporters were important features of it as well, whether through personal approaches, likely letter-bearing legates, or simply involving himself in the affairs of allies and vassals. There survive examples of the earl's approaches to vassals, Miles of Gloucester and Geoffrey II de Clinton, and allies such as Henry, son Robert d'Oilli, constable of Oxford castle, and Brian fitz Count and, possibly later in his absence, his wife Matilda of Wallingford. By the likely 1140s marriage of his son Robert to Baldwin de Redvers's daughter Hawisia, the earl solidified a geopolitically important alliance and indirectly expanded his own network of supporters with Baldwin's vassals and allies.[128]

As in his situation as his father's *familiaris*, Earl Robert, along with Brian and Miles, became a force within the empress's inner circle of advisers. However, asfar as Matilda was concerned, the earl was her chief *familiaris*. He exercised viceregal powers during 1140 in creating their brother Reginald earl of Cornwall, either at her direction or with her tacit approval after the fact; he would be her choice to lead a delegation of her advisers to a peace conference with royalists and he and Matilda would approve a peace proposal from Henry bishop of Winchester, the papal legate.[129] Also, over the next few years Robert's name would be accorded first-place listing before Miles and Brian when the three acted as sureties for the empress, and in the witness-lists of her *acta* according to usual court protocol.[130]

However, Miles's stock would rise with Matilda, so much so that she would grant him the earldom of Hereford on July 25, 1141, and then possibly having taken his advice attack Bishop Henry at Winchester without Earl Robert's knowledge.[131] By 1142 the new earl of Hereford could even challenge his vassalage to Robert. When Robert made a *conventio* with Miles to guarantee his continued prosecution of the war against Stephen during his absence in Normandy, the two appear in the

---

[126] *Regesta* iii. no. 391 and adding in part from BL, MS Sloan 1301, fol. 422r: "con(cessi) in feod(o) et hered(itate) et heredibus suis custodiam turris Glocestr(ie) cum toto castello et viceco(m) itatu(m) Glocestr(ie) comitat(us) in feodo et hereditate..."; *JW* iii. 270–3, but erring on the length of her stay at Bristol.
[127] *HN* (1998), 72–3.
[128] *HN* (1998), 60–1, 86–9, 96–7; *GS* (2004), 56–7; *JW* iii. 270–1 *Chart. Hereford*, no. 2; *Cart. Oseney* iv, no. 39a; *Eynsham Cartulary*, no. 71; *Select Documents of the English Lands of the Abbey of Bec*, no. xlvii (dated 1122 x 47); see Chapt. 4, 90–1.
[129] *HN* (1998), 72–5, 78–9, also 96–7.
[130] *Regesta* iii. nos. 275, 634; 43, 68, 111, 115, 274–5, 277, 296, 316, 316a, 328, 343, 369–71, 393, 400, 518, 581, 587, 629, 634, 645–6, 697, 699–700, 702, 911.
[131] *Regesta* iii. no. 393; *JW* iii. 298–9; see 154–5, 160 & n., 191.

agreement as allies, not as lord and vassal. Only the earl of Hereford's death in a hunting accident on Christmas Eve 1143 prevents us from seeing the outcome of this rivalry.[132]

Another who joined what William of Malmesbury called Earl Robert's party about this time was John fitz Harold lord of Sudeley, just south of Winchcombe (Glos.). Also, by the end of the year or early in 1140, Nigel bishop of Ely, first deprived of his castles and then driven from his bishopric by Stephen, took refuge at Bristol under Earl Robert's protection and became an Angevin ally.[133] By early 1140 the pro-Angevin party gained one of its most valuable allies, John fitz Gilbert, the Marshal, Stephen's master marshal, royal constable of Marlborough, and lord of Ludgershall (Wilts.). Like the majority of the baronage and previous royal servants, John recognized Stephen and remained loyal through 1138, possibly into 1139.[134] However, his loyalty was suspect enough for Stephen to attack him in Marlborough perhaps a month or more before Matilda's and Robert's landing. John was described by a pro-Angevin and a pro-royalist writer as "devious, a man of great cunning." His capacity for double-dealing continued into 1140.[135] However, from 1141 he became one of the Angevin party's staunchest members and his Wiltshire castles protected the "right flank" of the Angevins' eastern salient.[136]

The political sympathy at this time of Gilbert Foliot, abbot of royal St. Peter's Gloucester, is unknown, but he may have been a crypto-Angevin. He had been nominated for the abbacy by his cousin Miles of Gloucestr at a time when the sheriff and royal constable was overtly loyal to Stephen, but secretly moving toward involvement with the Empress Matilda's cause.[137] Gilbert even may have had connections to Earl Robert of Gloucester through one or two relatives, possibly a Robert fitz Richard Foliot who was one of the honor of Gloucester's medium-ranking honorial tenants and Richard of Ilchester (Som.), the earl's notary.[138] In any case, soon after appointing Gilbert abbot, King Stephen must have sensed that he had an Angevin sympathizer on his hands, because his heretofore patronage of the abbey completely or almost totally ceased after 1139 until a new abbot Hamelin had succeeded Gilbert in 1148.[139] Even if Gilbert had not been predisposed to the Angevin side, there would have been enormous pressures on him to join it after Matilda's move from Bristol to Gloucester in the fall of 1139 added to the already present strengths enjoyed there by Miles of Gloucester and his overlord Earl Robert and turned the town into a major Angevin power base. In spite of these factors

---

[132] Patterson, *EGC*, no. 95 & n.; *GS* (2004), 148–9, 160–1.

[133] *JW* iii. 274–5, 280–1; Henry of Huntingdon (1996), 722, dates Nigel's expulsion as "post Natale [1139]"; *HN* (1998), 62–3; *GS* (2004), 90–1, 100–1.

[134] "Constitutio Domus Regis," 134; *Regesta* iii. nos. 288, 342, 384–5, 418, 435, 579, 712, 749, 868, 963.

[135] *HN* (1998), 76–7; *GS* (2004), 106–7; *JW* iii. 268–9.

[136] *Regesta* iii. nos. 68, 275, 277, 316a, 393, 581, 634, 699, 700, 702, 791; Crouch, "Marshal, John," 811–12.

[137] *JW* iii. 262–7; Brooke, "Foliot, Gilbert," 218; see 143–4.

[138] *RBE* i. 291; Patterson, *EGC*, 13; for the prolific Foliot family, see *GFAL*, 32–51, esp. 38 & n. Richard fitz Robert's place in the family remains a mystery.

[139] *Regesta* iii. nos. 346–50, 356; then nos. 357–61; Knowles, *HRH*, 53. Gilbert became bishop of Hereford: Barrow, *EEA* vii. xl.

Gilbert maintained a low political profile until after Earl Robert's victory at Lincoln in February 1141 and the earl had brought his royal captive to Matilda at Gloucester on his way to Bristol.[140] By 1143–4 Gilbert was able to write the major Angevin Brian fitz Count that he had met often with Earl Robert and heard him quote a passage from the *Book of Numbers* justifying a daughter's right to be her father's heir in a letter which expressed the most extensive justification for rebelling against King Stephen any apologist for Matilda wrote.[141]

Noticeably absent from Gloucester's own followers and indeed from Matilda's party were the earl's son-in-law, Ranulf earl of Chester, and William de Roumare. Like so many other barons, the brothers had accepted Stephen as king, but in 1138–9 had not yet taken Robert's *diffidatio* as a cue to rebel or joined the Angevin cause for any other reason.[142] Their political loyalties were heavily influenced, like David of Scotland's, by territorial ambitions. For them, it was preservation and expansion of their holdings in the Midlands, especially those they regarded as inheritance from Ranulf's namesake father and from their thrice-married mother Countess Lucy of Bolingbroke. One of Ranulf's sought-after prizes was the lordship of Carlisle and Cumberland, which his father Ranulf "le Meschin" had surrendered to Henry I as the price for succeeding to the earldom of Chester.[143] But, as Paul Dalton has argued, Ranulf's and William's main proprietary target was Lincolnshire and estates Lucy had held, including rights in Lincoln castle.[144]

In 1136 King Stephen provoked Earl Ranulf by granting Carlisle to Henry son of King David of Scotland as part of the first Treaty of Durham and then by seating Henry in a place of honor at his right at the Easter court of 1136. In 1139 William de Roumare would have been aggrieved by Stephen's conferral of the earldom of Lincoln upon Henry, and disappointed by the compensation offered him in the form of the earldom of Cambridge, as Marjorie Chibnall has argued.[145] In spite of such insults, Ranulf and William remained loyal to Stephen and the king managed not to jostle the half-brothers into Angevin ranks.[146] Even their bold seizure of Lincoln castle in 1140 by the ruse of sending their wives on a social call to the castle, calling for them unarmed, then seizing weapons and overpowering the guards, failed to break relations with Stephen formally. For after a brief siege the king made a peace

---

[140] *JW* iii, 270–3; *HN* (1998), 62–3, 86–7; *Regesta* iii. nos. 111, 343; *GS* (2004), 102–3, 114–15; see also 156 in this volume. Earl Robert also was becoming personally involved with St. Peter's: *EGC*, nos. 84?, 68, poss. 83; *OASPG*, no. 12.

[141] *Numbers* 36; *LCGF*, no. 26, pp. 61–2. About this time Brian fitz Count omitted Gilbert's name from a list of Angevin supporters in a letter he wrote to Henry bishop of Winchester: King, "The Memory of Brian fitz Count," 75–98, esp. 90.

[142] *OV* vi. 296–7; *Regesta* iii. nos. 67, 271, 598, 679, 818–19, 944–8.

[143] Davis, "King Stephen and the Earl of Chester Revised," 659; Davis, *King Stephen*, 3rd edn., 161–5.

[144] Dalton, "*In Neutro Latere*: The Armed Neutrality of Ranulf II Earl of Chester," 41–3; esp. Dalton, "Aiming at the Impossible: Ranulf II Earl of Chester and Lincolnshire in the Reign of King Stephen," 109–34.

[145] Chibnall, *Empress Matilda*, 93–4.

[146] Richard of Hexham, 146; John of Hexham, 287; *Regesta* iii. no. 271, also nos. 67, 598; *OV* vi. 494–5; Davis, "King Stephen and the Earl of Chester Revised," 658–9; Sharpe, "Norman Rule in Cumbria," 63.

with the two brothers which left them in control of the castle.[147] It was Stephen's doing, as will be seen, that relations between the three changed dramatically at Christmas 1140. Even after joining up with his father-in-law for the battle of Lincoln and welcoming him to his court, Ranulf only gave the Angevin cause lukewarm support well into the 1140s. He had his own priorities and mistrusted both sides.[148]

Before the end of 1139 Robert of Gloucester set about earning the military reputation which led William of Malmesbury in an encomiastic outburst to rank him above Julius Caesar.[149] In response to his 1138 message from Normandy to begin hostilities, his *Bristoenses* had attempted, albeit unsuccessfully, to capture royalist Bath.[150] The earl himself initially profited from a military partnership he formed with his vassal Miles of Gloucester to employ their own and joint forces against royalist centers in the Angevin western regional power base. Their various operations supported the basic strategy the empress had promoted from Normandy regarding the tactical role of the earl's power base as well as their own proprietary self-interests.[151] Allegedly, these military actions in 1139–40 were for Robert at least calculated campaigns measured in terms of the likelihood of success and of minimal loss of his men's lives.[152] He succeeded in recapturing William fitz John's Harptree castle. His mere presence in the general neighborhood of Humphrey de Bohun's Trowbridge castle around October of this year was enough to cause Stephen to suspend his siege operations and thus eliminate at least this threat to an important Wiltshire ally.[153] In early 1140, the earl recovered John fitz Harold's Sudeley, which Miles of Gloucester had been unable to do.

However, not all of the earl's military engagements were successes even in his demesne heartland. He himself led an attack on Bath (Som.) only some 13 miles from Bristol before August 15, 1140, but his force was detected by royalist scouts and may have faced at least one or more of their ambushes before meeting the king's main body. When the earl's men did face it, they were no match for Stephen's men. With heavy casualties, including Geoffrey Talbot, Robert and his men were forced to beat a hasty retreat to Bristol.[154] Earlier in 1140 Gloucester was unable to capitalize on an opportunity to seize Devizes castle for the empress. It had been reputedly the greatest of Bishop Roger of Salisbury's castles, but had come into Stephen's hands in 1139 after the bishop's arrest, forfeiture of his castles, and threatened hanging of his son Roger le Poer before its gates.[155]

---

[147] Crouch, *Reign of King Stephen*, 138 & Appendix I, 143–4; Dalton, "*In Neutro Latere*: The Armed Neutrality of Ranulf II Earl of Chester," 45–7.

[148] Notice the absence of Ranulf's attestations of the empress's *acta* and the comment by William of Malmesbury about Ranulf's appearance at the Rout of Winchester in 1141: *HN* (1998), 102–3; Dalton, "*In Neutro Latere*: The Armed Neutrality of Ranulf II Earl of Chester," 43–8.

[149] *HN* (1998), 60–1.   [150] *GS* (2004), 58–63.

[151] See 144.   [152] *HN* (1998), 72–3.

[153] *GS* (2004), 96–7; Patterson, "William of Malmesbury's Robert of Gloucester," 994 & n.; see Chapt. 3, 72.

[154] *JW* iii. 290–1.

[155] Henry of Huntingdon (1996), 720 & n., 721–3; *OV* vi. 530–2 & n., 533 & n., 534–5; *GS* (2004), 72–81; *HN* (1998), 44–9; Kealey, *Roger of Salisbury*, Chapt. 6, pp. 173–89; Davis, *King Stephen*, 3rd edn., 28–30; Yoshitake, "The Arrest of the Bishops in 1139 and its Consequences," 98; on Waleran's role, see Crouch, *Beaumont Twins*, 43–5; for Roger le Poer, see *Regesta* iii. x.

Unexpectedly, a Flemish stipendiary knight of Robert's gone rogue, Robert fitz Hubert, and his men captured the castle in a surprise attack. They had previously been in King Stephen's service, had occupied Malmesbury castle, and had been forced to surrender it to William d'Ypres, whereupon they joined the earl. Thinking that Fitz Hubert had acted on his behalf at Devizes, Earl Robert dispatched a son, William, Robert, or Philip, with a large force to garrison the castle. However, Fitz Hubert, emboldened by his success, thought of establishing a lordship for himself and refused admission to Robert's men and renounced his allegiance to him.

Earl Robert did not fail to gain Devizes for lack of trying. His ex-mercenary imagined that he also might gain admission to nearby Marlborough castle and then seize it. However, its wily castellan John fitz Gilbert, a political fence-sitter still, instead imprisoned him and his escort. The earl then negotiated with John for custody of Fitz Hubert to take him before Devizes and threaten him with hanging if his men did not yield the castle. However, after a repeat performance and the garrison again refused, the earl got the satisfaction of hanging his wayward mercenary high. When the garrison did surrender later, it was to Stephen, who turned it over to Hervey Brito, his earl of Wiltshire. The Angevins only got possession of Devizes when a group of rustics bound by *coniuratio* intimidated Brito's men to yield.[156]

Several episodes involving the earl reveal aspects of his political standing with his half-sister. In an effort to stop the violence, Bishop Henry of Winchester, as papal legate, organized during the summer of 1140 a meeting of representatives from the two warring factions at Bath to hash out a compromise peace agreement. King Stephen's queen Matilda, Archbishop Theobald, and the legate represented the royalists. The empress sent Robert as chief of her delegation of advisers. Although the effort failed, the legate traveled to the Continent in September to seek the advice of his brother Count Theobald of Blois and King Louis VII of France about terms for another agreement. In this case, Earl Robert approved the draft Henry brought back together with Matilda, but Stephen killed its chances by procrastinating with his decision.[157]

In September 1140 a raid by Earl Robert against William Peverel's town of Nottingham (Notts.) indicates the earl's willingness to expand the theater of war beyond his immediate power base. The few known details provide no clues to his particular motivation, but the fact that he staged the operation at the urging of one ally, Ralph Paynel, and utilized some troops of at least one other, Roger earl of Warwick, gives us a glimpse of Robert's tactical interaction with his allies. Conquest was not the object in this case. An undefended Nottingham simply was turned over to the attackers to plunder. Some unfortunate residents who had taken refuge in churches perished when the town was put to the torch; others were led away into captivity to Gloucester.[158]

---

[156] *GS* (2004), 104–9, 116–17; *HN* (1998), 62–3, 74–7, attributes the hanging to John fitz Gilbert; see also *JW* iii. 284–91.
[157] *HN* (1998), 76–9.  [158] *JW* iii. 290–3; Bradbury, *Stephen and Matilda*, 81–2.

Some of Gloucester's actions during 1139–40 were cooperative undertakings with Miles of Gloucester or in some way complementary to the constable's own campaigns. Early in 1140, together the two took their forces to Cornwall to help Robert's brother Reginald against King Stephen, who had brought a force to roll back the latter's territorial advances in the county. Allegedly they thought that their expedition was an opportunity to catch King Stephen cut off from reinforcements and to defeat him.[159] The foray also may have served Robert's own interests, since the county contained a cluster of Robert's estates.[160] Reportedly, both the earl and Miles also went together with a large force to bargain with John fitz Gilbert for the use of Robert fitz Hubert to obtain Devizes.[161]

Miles on his own in 1139 had come to the rescue of Brian fitz Count at Wallingford. In November troops from Gloucester, presumably under the constable's authority, fell upon and burned royalist Worcester, possibly as Ralph Davis surmised, to distract Stephen from returning to Wallingford. In 1140 Miles went on to take Winchcombe just north of Tewkesbury on January 20 and South Cerney (Glos.) and, as already noted, attempted to regain Sudeley. Waleran, with the Angevin devastation of Worcester in mind, took revenge on the Angevins by wasting Earl Robert's Tewkesbury manor and burning his great hall.[162] Perhaps several months into the new year, with the help of Geoffrey Talbot Miles also besieged and captured royalist Hereford.[163]

An issue which potentially complicated relations between Robert and Miles was the fact that from as early as 1138 the constable had been waging a private war with Gilbert de Lacy over a share of the honor of Weobly (Herefs.). Following Earl Robert of Gloucester's *diffidatio*, in the hope of gaining royal confirmation of his proprietary claim, Gilbert sided with the empress because King Stephen had confirmed Miles's tenure of the disputed estates. Geoffrey Talbot's seizure of Weobly castle as his cousin Gilbert's ally, if not the immediate *casus belli*, was part of it.[164]

Whatever its purpose, the Nottingham raid was the harbinger of the single external campaign upon which so much of Gloucester's historical reputation rests; among medieval chroniclers and annalists, if they noted any feat of his, it is more

---

[159] *GS* (2004), 100–3; *HN* (1998), 74–5.
[160] *GS* (2004), 102–5; *HN* (1998), 62–3, 72–5; Walker, "The 'Honours' of the Earls of Hereford in the Twelfth Century," 176, 178, 198. For Earl Robert's elevation of Reginald to the earldom of Cornwall, see 148.
[161] *JW* iii. 288–9; however, I am not confident that some of the details of this account are plausible; see also McGurk, in *JW* iii. xl.
[162] *GS* (2004), 94–5; *JW* iii. 274–5, 282–3; Crouch, *Reign of King Stephen*, 113; Davis, *King Stephen*, 3rd edn., 40–1; King, *King Stephen*, 120–1, for a range of opinions about the authority for the Worcester attack.
[163] *GS* (2004), 92–7; *HN* (1998), 64 & n., 65; *JW* iii. 272–7, 282–3. *GS* (2004), 94–5 seems to link together Miles's attacks on South Cerney and Hereford. On the Peace movement in England at this time, see Patterson, "Anarchy in England," 194–6; see also Dalton, "Churchmen and the Promotion of Peace in King Stephen's Reign," 84–94.
[164] Patterson, *EGC*, no. 94 & n; Davis, *King Stephen*, 3rd edn., 39; also Davis, "Treaty between William Earl of Gloucester and Roger Earl of Hereford," 139–46; Wightman, *The Lacy Family in England and Normandy*, 167–77, 181–7; see 141.

often than not his capture of King Stephen at the battle of Lincoln on February 2, 1141.[165] However, with beautiful irony, promotion of his sister's cause was not involved.

The earl of Gloucester's initial interest was the rescue of his daughter Matilda countess of Chester from capture by King Stephen. Late in 1140, as already noted, Robert's son-in-law Ranulf II earl of Chester and William de Roumare seized the royal keep at Lincoln through trickery. Stephen, to retain even his nominal loyalty, at first recognized the earl of Chester's seizure.[166]

However, the townsmen of Lincoln chafed under Ranulf's rule and around Christmas 1140 petitioned Stephen to come to their aid. He did, and with such speed that Ranulf barely escaped with a few knights from one of the town's gates as the king was being welcomed at another. The earl made for Chester but left behind Countess Matilda and William's wife Matilda, daughter of Richard de Redvers, under siege in the castle. Ranulf immediately begged his father-in-law, the Empress Matilda, and, among others, Miles of Gloucester for help in rescuing the two Matildas and pledged fealty to the empress and future loyalty to her cause.[167]

In spite of Ranulf's previous political indifference to him, Earl Robert could not ignore his daughter's plight. He mustered a force which included a large component of Welsh troops from Iorwerth of Gwent and, joined at some point by Miles of Gloucester, Baldwin de Redvers, and Brian fitz Count, marched to meet Earl Ranulf and his men. Robert kept the purpose of the campaign a secret from his army either to insure the element of surprise or possibly because of the personal nature of the mission.[168] It is estimated that Robert's force junctioned with Ranulf's at Claybrook (Leics.), where the Fosse Way intersects with Watling Street, and then advanced forward along the Fosse Way. Earl Robert was in overall command of the composite army and ultimately designed its order of battle; evidently he saw it as an opportunity to settle the succession quarrel.[169] Stephen gave him the opportunity.

From the direction they had advanced, at Lincoln the combined army would have found its way forward toward the walls obstructed by the river Witham and a canal known as the Fossdyke linking the Witham with the Trent farther to the east. Most scholars agree that the Angevin army attacked from the southwest, but which water barrier, the Witham or the Fossdyke, it forded and by what means remain disputed points. Whichever one was crossed, it was forded, not by swimming the river Trent as William of Malmesbury claimed. Stephen facilitated the army's crossing

---

[165] e.g., *ASC* a.1140 (recte 1141); "Annales Anglosaxonici breves...cum continuatione Latina," 6; "Annales monasterii de Bello," 53; "Annales Wintonienses cum contin. S. Augustini Cantuar." 80; John of Hexham, 308.

[166] *OV* vi. 538–9; *HN* (1998), 82: *GS* (2004), 110–11; Cronne, "Ranulf de Gernons," 109; Round, "Stephen and the Earl of Chester," 87, 90–1; Davis, "King Stephen and the Earl of Chester Revised," 654–60. See 150–1.

[167] *OV* vi, 538–41; *HN* (1998), 80–3; *GS* (2004), 110–11; John of Hexham, 307; Henry of Huntingdon (1996), 724–5.

[168] *HN* (1998), 82–5; *LE*, 321; *LE*, 321.

[169] *Regesta* iii. no. 393; *HN* (1998), 82–5; *GS* (2004), 110–11; Henry of Huntingdon (1996), 724–5; 726: "dux magnus"; 726–7; John of Hexham, 307: "Rodbertus dux et dispositor praelii"; Beeler, *Warfare in England*, 109. See also *HRB*, 5: "dux Claudiocestriae."

## The Empress's Champion

to the plain sloping upward to the city's walls by stationing a small guard along the south bank instead of the north at the most likely fording location; that group was easily overwhelmed, which left no opposition to crossing and the allies' easy disposition for battle.[170]

That was not the king's only mistake. Stephen, on receiving news of the Angevins' approach, had called a council of war to seek advice about the best strategy to follow. Probably the best one was to flee in order to raise an adequate force with which to return and fight the Angevins, but also to leave behind household troops to withstand Robert's and Ranulf's siege along with the burgesses. Instead, he chose the option of a pitched battle against a superior force.[171]

The opposing armies' disposition on the plain followed the accepted Anglo-Norman practice of men-at-arms supported by dismounted knights in the center, with mounted knights to the rear of men-at-arms on the wings. As has been plausibly suggested, Robert commanded the Angevin center, Ranulf the right, and possibly Miles of Gloucester the left. In the same tripartite formation and combination of knights and men-at-arms, Stephen was opposite Robert, William d'Ypres and William of Aumale earl of York opposite Ranulf and five earls, Hugh Bigod of Norfolk, William III de Warenne of Surrey, Simon of Northampton, Waleran of Worcester, and Alan of Richmond.[172] It is doubtful that there was much oratory on either side or that ceremonial combat occurred. Orderic Vitalis states that when the opposing lines were formed, fighting commenced.[173]

Nevertheless, Henry of Huntingdon records Thucydidean-like motivating speeches prior to the commencement of hostilities. Part of one delivered by Baldwin fitz Gilbert de Clare bears mentioning. He compared Robert's bravery to a hare's and reduced his leadership to the few accomplishments of an idle boaster.[174]

The earl of Gloucester's behavior on that day February 2, 1141, was a total rebuttal of such charges. The initial impact of the opposing forces was indecisive and costly to both sides. Then Stephen's right gave way and its leaders, William's d'Ypres and Alan of Richmond, fled. Panic set in. Waleran and his fellow earls followed suit, dooming the left. The royal center still held on, but ultimately was overwhelmed; and as this happened, Lincoln's burgesses took flight. Defenseless in this posture against charging Angevin knights, they were simply cut down. All but abandoned except for a few members of his household, Stephen valiantly fought on with a Norse double-headed axe until he too was captured by Robert or by a knight William de Cahagnes. As befitted a chivalrous victor, Robert received Stephen with kindness. It was the Feast of the Purification of the Virgin Mary,

---

[170] *HN* (1998), 84–5; *GS* (2004), 112–13; Henry of Huntingdon (1996), 724–5; e.g., Ramsay, *The Foundations of England* ii. 397–9; Norgate, *England under the Angevin Kings* i. 316–17; Beeler, *Warfare in England*, 109–13; Bradbury, *Stephen and Matilda*, 90–2.

[171] *GS* (2004), 112–13; *OV* vi. 540–3.

[172] The main sources conflict with one another in some details. I have arbitrarily made adjustments like the placement of Earl Robert: Henry of Huntingdon (1996): 724–39; Robert of Torigny, "Chronica," 139–40; and *OV* vi. 542–3; and of the commentaries on them I have found Bradbury, *Stephen and Matilda*, 94–6, the most useful; see also Beeler, *Warfare in England 1066–1188*, 113.

[173] *OV* vi. 542–3; *HN* (1998), 84–5; Henry of Huntingdon (1996), 726–37.

[174] Henry of Huntingdon (1996), 726–31, 734–5.

under whose patronage William of Malmesbury later was to write that his patron had fought. To some the judgment of God in the Angevin–royalist dispute had been rendered.[175]

Earl Robert's victory and capture of the king won him the first explicit expression of Matilda's favor since their arrival in England. The earl brought his royal captive to her at Gloucester and there, in a gesture reminiscent of his becoming his uncle Duke Robert's jailor roughly fifteen years earlier, the empress awarded Robert the captive king to be held for the rest of his life. The earl then led Stephen to Bristol, where he was first held, as William of Malmesbury claimed, benignly confined merely to his quarters until he was found beyond these limits on several nights. That supposedly resulted in his being put in irons.[176]

Gloucester's capture of Stephen soon had Norman repercussions. After hearing of it, Count Geoffrey re-entered the duchy with demands that nobles surrender their castles to him by right. In response, about mid-March, a council presided over by Archbishop Hugh of Rouen met at Mortagne (Orne) to decide their response to Geoffrey. However, instead of surrendering, the barons appealed to Count Theobald of Blois to accept rulership of both Normandy and England. Theobald refused and offered to recognize the count on condition that the city of Tours be restored to him and that Stephen be released and regain his former lordships.[177]

The Count of Blois's offer, whether Geoffrey considered it or not, must have shown that King Stephen's cause in Normandy was doomed. Opposition to Angevin rule began to collapse. Rotrou count of Mortagne went over to Geoffrey and Robert earl of Leicester followed suit, but apparently with a plan designed to protect both his and his brother Waleran's trans-Channel landed interests: Leicester would remain outwardly loyal to Stephen and look after their affairs in England; Waleran would join the Angevins in England and protect their interests in Normandy. In pursuit of this, Robert of Leicester obtained from Count Geoffrey a truce for himself and for Waleran pending his arrival from England. Waleran did indeed submit to Matilda in England. He then traveled to the duchy and came to terms with Geoffrey. More strategic desertions of Stephen continued. All of central and eastern Normandy, including the Roumois, except for Rouen, was now in Geoffrey's hands. In Lower Normandy only a few areas still held out against him in the southwest.[178]

In England, Matilda and her party set to winning the realization of the oaths that had been sworn to her succession at London in 1127. At Gloucester she had received counsel from her followers. On February 17, 1141 she left for Cirencester,

---

[175] *OV* vi. 542–5; *HN* (1998), 84–7; *GS* (2004), 112–13; Henry of Huntingdon (1996), 724–7, 732–3, 736–9; *JW* iii. 292–3; *ASC a*.1140 (*recte* 1141); Robert of Torigny, "Chronica," 139–42; John of Hexham, 307–9; "Ann. Winchester," 52; "Ann. Waverly," 223; Bradbury, *Stephen and Matilda*, 96–8.

[176] *HN* (1998), 86–7; *GS* (2004), 114–15; *JW* iii. 292–3; *OV* vi. 544–5; Henry of Huntingdon (1996), 738–9; *ASC a*.1126, 1140 (*recte* 1141).

[177] *OV* vi. 546–9.

[178] *OV* v. 546–51; Robert of Torigny, "Chronica," 142; *OV* vi. 546–51; White, "The Career of Waleran Count of Meulan and Earl of Worcester," 35–6; Crouch, *Beaumont Twins*, 50–2; Chibnall, *Empress Matilda*, 106–7, 112–13.

where she received the town's submission.[179] About the same time, Matilda and her brother Earl Robert sought the support of the Church for the legitimacy of the new order. Both made diplomatic approaches to the papal legate Bishop Henry of Winchester to recognize her as her father's heir and rightful queen.

Henry agreed to meet the Angevins on an open plain outside of Winchester; the site was at Wherwell about nine miles to the north. The meeting occurred on Sunday March 2 and resulted in a *conventio* between Matilda and Henry. In return for the legate's acceptance of her as *domina* and continued fealty, Henry would have authority over all the chief affairs of the realm, especially grants of abbacies and bishoprics. Earl Robert first of all, Miles of Gloucester, and Brian fitz Count were the concord's guarantors, which supports the likelihood that Robert, if not all three, was somehow involved in the *conventio*'s formulation.[180]

As a result of the agreement, on the next day Winchester submitted to Matilda, and Henry received her at Winchester Cathedral with a grand ceremonial procession. Bernard bishop of St. David's marched on her left, Henry on the right, amidst the chanting of the nuns of St. Mary's Abbey (Nunnaminster). Matilda received the royal crown and Bishop Henry anathematized all who refused to accept their new monarch. Other attendees included major clergy such as Alexander bishop of Lincoln, Nigel bishop of Ely, Seffrid bishop of Chichester, Gilbert Foliot abbot of St. Peter's Gloucester, Roger abbot of Tewkesbury, along with Earl Robert, Reginald earl of Cornwall, Brian fitz Count, Miles of Gloucester, and several other important laymen.[181]

Very shortly after this, at the legate's suggestion, Archbishop Theobald of Canterbury met with Matilda at Wilton. The primate had hesitated to recognize Matilda without Stephen's permission. So the archbishop and a group of bishops and laymen sought and received her agreement for them to visit the imprisoned king for that purpose. Stephen agreed for them to become the empress's subjects.[182]

Following a stopover at Reading, where she received the submission of Robert d'Oilli castellan of Oxford castle and discussed with him its surrender, Matilda moved to celebrate Easter on March 30, 1141 at Oxford. D'Oilli was the stepfather of Earl Robert's namesake half-brother, the son of Edith of Greystoke, a supporter and locally important tenant-in-chief; and it is likely, as Round suggested, that this relationship influenced the castellan's change of loyalties as well. Earl Robert may have attended the Oxford court and been in his sister's retinue since Bristol.[183]

This was a logical time for Matilda to have begun long-term measures for her security at Oxford. She chose Earl Robert, whose great work at Bristol she had seen personally, to improve the town's defenses by adding earthworks. To protect approaches to Oxford as well as possible retreat routes toward Earl Robert's Bristol and the Severn Valley, she had a string of fortifications built at Woodstock,

---

[179] *JW* iii. 292–5.   [180] *HN* (1998), 86–9.
[181] *Regesta* iii. no. 343; *GS* (2004), 118–19; *JW* iii. 294–5; *HN* (1998), 86–9; Chibnall, *Empress Matilda*, 97–8.
[182] *JW* iii. 294–5; *HN* (1998), 88–91.
[183] *GS* (2004), 116–17; *JW* iii. 294–5; *Regesta* iii. no. 645; Round, *Geoffrey de Mandeville*, 65–6; *CP* xi, Appendix D, 108–9.

Bampton, Radcot (Oxon.), and Cirencester (Glos.), and may well have chosen her brother for these efforts as well. Mottes seem to have been raised at Woodstock by Henry I's famous hall, at Radcot (to guard the Thames crossing), and by the nuns' church at Cirencester, and Bampton's church tower fortified.[184]

Another council held the Monday after Easter week, April 7, at Winchester by Archbishop Theobald and the higher clergy, with the papal legate Henry presiding, formally proclaimed Matilda *domina* of England. The Benedictine historian William of Malmesbury was present and is a major source for the proceedings. Stephen's brother made the case for transferring allegiance from the king to the empress. Stephen had been allowed to succeed in order to preserve peace in the realm since Matilda had failed to come to England to claim the throne. However, Stephen had violated the peace by his many injustices; the judgment of God (the battle of Lincoln) had delivered him into Matilda's hands; and peace needed to be preserved. Before the council adjourned, many of Stephen's party were excommunicated, most notably the former king's *dapifer* William Martel.[185]

Enormously significant for the future course of events was the appearance at this council of a delegation of London's burgesses and of a clerk bearing a letter from Queen Matilda. The Londoners and the queen both asked for Stephen's release and restoration to the throne. Both appeals were rejected; and in response the burgesses only stated that they would do what they could to persuade the rest of their fellow Londoners to accept the council's decision.[186]

However, the danger this uncertain acquiescence represented was not immediately apparent. Resistance to the new regime seemed mainly confined to Kent, where Stephen's queen Matilda held out with the support of Stephen's mercenary captain William d'Ypres. Yet at the same time seeds of decline in Angevin fortunes were being sowed by the very claimant to the throne.

The Empress Matilda was beginning to demonstrate the imperious arrogance for which she became notorious. Not only did she ignore advice from her uncle, her brother, and the legate, but she would not show them the courtesy of rising to greet them when they came before her on bended knee with a request. Obedience to her will was all that mattered. The first dramatic price she and her party would pay for that occurred after her entry into London.

This had been made possible by the empress making key diplomatic moves as she advanced on the city from her new headquarters at Oxford towards Midsummer. At St. Albans (Herts.) she and a prominent delegation of Londoners came to terms for the city's surrender. At Westminster she won over the support of Geoffrey de Mandeville, castellan of the Tower, by a charter recovering his family's fortunes and creating him earl of Essex. This nicely supplemented the loyalty of London's royal justice and sheriff Osbert Eightpence that Matilda seems already to have gained, as

---

[184] See n. 184; *Regesta* iii. xliv, nos. 400 (suspect), 571 & n., 628 & n., 854 & n.; *HN* (1998), 90–1, 126–9; *GS* (2004), 138–41; *ASC* a.1140, p. 202; *JW* iii. 294–5 & n.; Beeler, *Warfare in England*, 132; Renn, *Norman Castles in Britain*, 100, 144, 289, 349 (except for construction dates); Round, *Geoffrey de Mandeville*, 65–6; Crouch, *Reign of King Stephen*, 201n.
[185] *HN* (1998), 90–7.     [186] *HN* (1998), 94–7.

a writ the empress addressed to him strongly suggests. Osbert was an honorial tenant of Earl Robert for one knight's fee consisting of estates in Surrey and in the Gloucester honor's London soke, but had not joined the earl in his change of loyalty in 1138. But from this time forward Osbert not only remained loyal to Matilda, but was relied upon by the earl as a valued Gloucester honorial tenant.

Giving credibility to Matilda's agreements as guarantors both earlier and later were the very leaders of her entourage she had begun offending by her imperious behavior, especially Earl Robert, according to William of Malmesbury, along with Miles of Gloucester and Brian fitz Count. Not even David king of Scots and Bishop Henry of Winchester were accorded due respect.[187] Nevertheless, they all remained faithful. Not so the Londoners. Instead of dealing with her new subjects cautiously, given the advance warning she had been given about the uncertainty of their acceptance of her as *domina*, the empress demanded a *donum* from the wealthiest burgesses. She also declined the Londoners' petition to be governed by the laws of King Edward instead of those of her father and again refused to free Stephen, even as a monk or pilgrim. Some who attended her court she treated disrespectfully and drove from her presence.

Outraged by their overall treatment and encouraged by the approach of an army of Queen Matilda, the empress's "loyal" Londoners rose up against her before she could enjoy her coronation or crown-wearing in Westminster Abbey on June 24; and she, Earl Robert, and her entourage were forced to flee to avoid capture. In their absence rioting burgesses looted their quarters.[188]

The loyalty of London was not the only casualty of Matilda's political rigidity. Either before or soon after her flight, Bishop Henry asked her that his nephew Eustace be granted seisin of his father's Continental baronies, the counties of Boulogne and Mortain. Matilda declined the appeal. In response, he began to retreat from his support for her. He stayed away from her court in spite of being summoned and instead met with Queen Matilda regarding their family claims. Henry all but repudiated his fealty to the empress by widely broadcasting his complaints against her, particularly her violation of the oath she had sworn to him and the baronage at the previous Council of Winchester, and annulling his former excommunications of Stephen's followers.[189]

Matilda retreated to Oxford, where she had previously set up her court, and began mustering supporters. Earl Robert of Gloucester, almost certainly with the empress's blessing, accompanied by a small retinue, hurried to Winchester in an attempt to somehow pacify the bishop, but in vain. Given Matilda's recalcitrance about the issues affecting the house of Blois, Gloucester's mission was a fool's errand.

---

[187] *HN* (1998), 96–7; *JW* iii. 294–7 & n.; *GS* (2004), 120–1; *Regesta* iii. nos. 274, 392, 497, 529, also no. 275; Crouch, *Reign of King Stephen*, 174. For Osbert, see Patterson, *EGC*, nos. 6, 95, 210; *RBE* i. 189; Round, *Geoffrey de Mandeville*, 374–5; Round, *The Commune of London*, 109, 114, 116; Brooke & Keir, *London 800–1216*, 212 & nn., 332, 372; Reynolds, "The Rulers of London in the Twelfth Century," 342; Crouch, *Reign of King Stephen*, 173 & n.; King, "The Memory of Brian Fitz Count," 90.

[188] *Regesta* iii. no. 275, 634; *HN* (1998), 88–9, 96–9; *GS* (2004), 120–7; *JW* iii. 296–7; Henry of Huntingdon (1996), 738–9; Robert of Torigny, "Chronica," 141; King, *King Stephen*, 163 & n.

[189] *GS* (2004), 122–5, challenges Malmesbury's and John of Worcester continuation's versions of Bishop Henry's political change of sides: *HN* (1998), 100–1; *JW* iii. 296–9; see also Chibnall, *The Empress Matilda*, 105–7; esp. Crouch, *Reign of King Stephen*, 180–1.

If Gloucester realized this, his effort may have been a manifestation of his stoical sense of duty. However, William of Malmesbury states that Robert and others had told his sister that the bishop of Winchester had always been disloyal to her, and charter and other chronicle evidence shows Matilda being supported by an inner circle of *familiares* around this time, particularly her uncle the Scots' king, brother Gloucester, Brian fitz Count, and Miles of Gloucester.[190] In any case, the result was that Matilda abandoned diplomacy and opted for pressuring Henry by occupying Winchester castle with a military force.[191]

Matilda appeared without warning at Winchester with a considerable force on July 31, 1141. There is conflicting evidence about the town's loyalty to the empress, but she was received in the royal castle located in the southwest corner of the town by West Gate and summoned the politically relapsed Bishop Henry to her presence. Taken completely by surprise, Henry temporized. Instead of responding as directed, he prepared his castle-palace Wolvesey at the town's southeastern corner for defense, sent word to Stephen's supporters for help, and then fled from the town to the safety of his other castles. Perhaps at this point, the empress besieged the bishop's castle.[192]

William of Malmesbury, perhaps thinking in hindsight to belittle the royalist victory which he would have to report, claimed that few came with the Empress Matilda other than King David, Earl Robert, Earl Miles of Hereford, Ranulf earl of Chester, and a few barons, but he elsewhere mentions by name two more magnates and many other victorious royalists with captives. Echoing his patron's pique with his son-in-law, Malmesbury made it a point to mention Ranulf of Chester's tardiness in coming to Winchester. At the same time, to enhance his patron's military reputation, the chronicler also reported that Earl Robert came with few baronial colleagues.[193] In reality, just on the basis of chronicle evidence, the empress's force contained a roster of major Angevin leaders. In addition to those Malmesbury listed, among others also present were Robert's brothers Reginald of Cornwall, Robert fitz Edith, and Henry fitz Nest, and also Baldwin de Redvers earl of Devon, Roger earl of Warwick, the marshal, John fitz Gilbert of Marlborough, William fitz Alan, Brian fitz Count, Robert d'Oilli constable of Oxford castle, Roger de Nonant of Totnes, and William de Mohun of Dunster, whom Matilda elevated to the earldom of Somerset.[194]

---

[190] *Regesta* iii. no. 393; for the recorded presence of *familiares* and others, see esp. nos, 68, 275, 328, 377, 393, 629, 634, 645–6, 648, 791, 899; *HN* (1998), 98–101; *GS* (2004), 124–7; Chibnall, *Empress Matilda*, 101, 106–7, 174–5.

[191] *JW* iii. 298–9; *GS* (2004), 126–7; *HN* (1998), 100–1, 107n. A John of Worcester continuator claimed that Matilda acted without her brother Robert's knowledge and apparently on Miles of Gloucester's advice. In virtue of Miles's service, the empress created him earl of Hereford: *JW* iii. 298–9; *Regesta* iii. no. 393.

[192] *GS* (2004), 126–7; *HN* (1998), 100–3; *JW* iii. 298–9; John of Hexham, 310; *Winchester* i. 302–5, 323–8, esp. 326. Henry had built his palace in 1138: "Ann. Winchester," 51; Round, *Geoffrey de Mandeville*, 123–35; Painter, "The Rout of Winchester," 70–5; Hill, "The Battle of Stockbridge, 1141," 173–7; Bradbury, *Stephen and Matilda*, 108–11.

[193] *HN* (1998), 100–1.

[194] *HN* (1998), 102–3 (William of Salisbury and Humphrey de Bohun), 116–17; *GS* (2004), 128–9; John of Hexham, 310; Davis, *King Stephen*, 3rd edn., 138.

Henry of Winchester's call for help brought Stephen's Queen Matilda with William d'Ypres and a large force of well-equipped Londoners. Still another force consisted of likely mounted knights and archers. Henry's own recruiting efforts provided old baronial loyalists, to whom he added hired mercenaries. And within Winchester, the garrison of the bishop's fortified palace, instead of capitulating, on the bishop's orders beat off the Angevin attackers by hurling firebands from the parapets and firing large parts of the city. Apparently the Angevins may have torched buildings themselves, because Earl Robert won praise for refraining from burning churches.[195]

The Angevin besiegers soon found themselves doubly under siege, sandwiched between Bishop Henry's garrison within Winchester and Queen Matilda's and the bishop's forces without. Furthermore, the combined royalist army was fast closing Winchester's access roads and the possibilities for provisioning the trapped Angevins. In an effort to counter this, perhaps as many as 200 of them, among whom were John the Marshal and the empress's and Earl Robert's brothers, Robert fitz Edith, and Henry, were sent out to Wherwell Abbey (Hants.), close to 9 miles northwest of Winchester. The aim was to fortify it with a castle to protect the nearby ford of the river Test, a key link in a supply route to Winchester from the Thames Valley. But royalist forces under William d'Ypres attacked the expeditionary force before the construction was completed, drove the garrison to take refuge in the abbey church, and then forced the survivors to surrender after burning the abbey church.[196]

Starvation now was added to the woes facing Matilda's besieged force. Faced with an untenable position, Earl Robert and the other leaders of the Angevin force decided to stake all on a breakout at the Westgate, and Robert was in command of this effort. The plan called for Matilda in the vanguard of the escaping column to make for John the Marshal's castle at Ludgershall via the Stockbridge road and causeway across the river Test, and thence via Devizes to Gloucester. Robert and the rearguard of some 200 knights were to prevent royalist forces from following.

On Sunday September 14, the Feast of the Exaltation of the Cross, the plan was put into action. But royalist pressure finally proved too much for the column to maintain order; men scattered and the retreat became what has become known to all students of the period as the Rout of Winchester.[197]

Matilda did indeed make it to Gloucester, accompanied by Brian fitz Count, her brother Reginald, and a few men by way of the designated friendly castles, but terrified, riding a horse astride like a man, and on the final leg of her journey tied

---

[195] *HN* (1998), 102–5; *GS* (2004), 128–31; Henry of Huntingdon (1996), 740–1; John of Hexham, 310; *JW* iii. 298–301; "Annales Plymptonienses," 28; "Annales Anglosaxonici breves," 6.

[196] *GS* (2004), 130–3; *HN* (1998), 102–5; John of Hexham, 310; *JW* iii. 298–301; see also a very different account of these events in the thirteenth-century *Histoire de Guillaume le maréchal* (i. 8–11, ll. 183–224); also *History of William Marshal*, ll. 245–78, for the Marshal tradition about these events and John's loss of an eye; Hill, "The Battle of Stockbridge, 1141," 174–6. See also Round, "The Rout of Winchester," 130–1; Painter, "The Rout of Winchester," 158–9; Chibnall, *Empress Matilda*, 114; Crouch, *Reign of King Stephen*, 185; Bradbury, *Stephen and Matilda*, esp. 110–11; King, *King Stephen*, 170.

[197] *GS* (2004), 130–3; *HN* (1998), 104–5; for John the Marshal's alleged role and a different chronology, see *History of William Marshal*, ll. 195–212; Hill, "The Battle of Stockbridge," 174–6.

to a litter like a corpse on a bier. According to the *Gesta Stephani*, the shock of the rout had brought on a condition in her resembling a nervous breakdown. Perhaps the friendship and service of Brian fitz Count rendered to the empress which she and her son Henry later memorialized in their charters for Reading Abbey were partly based on the comfort Brian gave to Matilda at this time. King David was captured three times, but each time purchased his freedom; after the third experience he fled quickly to Scotland. Matilda's adviser Miles managed to escape, but only by shedding his armor and insignia of rank; he reached Gloucester utterly exhausted and half-naked.[198]

With the breakup of the Angevin column, Earl Robert and his men were finally cornered at Stockbridge before they could make it across the Test. They made a brave fight of it, but were overwhelmed and Earl Robert was taken prisoner by William de Warenne and a group of Flemings. Gloucester had refused to flee almost certainly to ensure his sister's escape. However, as William of Malmesbury reported, Robert also viewed self-serving flight as beneath his dignity.[199]

The earl was brought before Queen Matilda, as her husband had been led before the empress after the battle of Lincoln, then handed over to William d'Ypres, and imprisoned at Rochester castle.[200] William of Malmesbury reported his patron's stoical acceptance of his fate.[201] Robert seems to have endured his imprisonment in relative comfort and with few restrictions. At Rochester castle, as long as the queen was present, Robert was allowed to visit churches below the castle and to speak with anyone. And he was able to purchase horses with revenue he received from his estates in Kent. Only after her departure was he restricted to the keep.[202] However mild the effect of capture was on Robert, it brought progress of the empress's cause to a standstill and a virtual stalemate in the civil war.

Ironically, the earl's valiant sacrifice of himself to save Matilda produced the clearest expression of the position he had come to enjoy in the Angevin party. It is apparent from negotiations for his and Stephen's release that Earl Robert was as important to Angevin fortunes as Stephen to the royalists'. Implicit in this equation was that Matilda, the free uncrowned *domina Anglorum*, was incapable of advancing her cause without Robert. Worse still, some believed that the Angevins faced defeat without him.

Countess Mabel managed the diplomatic exchanges for Earl Robert and Queen Matilda for the king. Initially, a group of earls proposed simply an even exchange, Robert for Stephen; but Earl Robert rejected the plan on the grounds of the inequality of earl and king. He would only agree if all his followers who had been

---

[198] *Regesta* iii. nos. 703–4; *HN* (1998), 106–7; *JW* iii. 300–3; *GS* (2004), 134–5; John of Hexham, 310–11; see also *History of William Marshal*, ll. 213–36.

[199] *HN* (1998), 104–7, but see also 114–15; John of Hexham, 310–11; see also *GS* (2004), 132–7; *JW* iii. 302–3; Henry of Huntingdon (1996), 740–1; "Ann. Winchcombe," *a*.1141.

[200] John of Hexham, 311; *GS* (2004), 134–5; Henry of Huntingdon (1996), 740–1; *Regesta* iii. nos. 703–4; *JW* iii. 202–3; Hill, "The Battle of Stockbridge, 1141," 174–7. See also Chibnall, *Empress Matilda*, 199, for commentary on the *amor* Brian fitz Count rendered to Matilda and her son according to their Reading charters.

[201] *HN* (1998), 106–7, 114–15.

[202] *HN* (1998), 114–17; Gervase of Canterbury i. 120–1.

taken prisoner were freed as well. However, Stephen's partisans among the baronage refused this condition because of the ransoms they would lose. Next, Robert was offered a status in Stephen's subsequent administration second only to the king, with authority over all matters, if he would change sides. Robert jokingly replied to what he must have viewed as a preposterous offer, given Stephen's penchant for other favorites, that he could only consider this proposal when he was free. The royalist response was to threaten him with perpetual imprisonment in Boulogne. Robert countered by saying that in that event Countess Mabel would simply send the king to Ireland. Negotiation dragged on over the next several months, with messengers conveying various plans from the countess and queen.[203]

Robert finally was persuaded by his own followers to accept a compromise. They convinced him that if a settlement was not made, they would be overwhelmed one by one. Consequently, he accepted the idea of mutual exchange but, in the face of solid royalist opposition, had to give up freedom for his men. Instead, all territory the empress's followers captured during Stephen's imprisonment was to be retained by them. Stephen, as befitting his dignity, would be released first, but a mechanism to ensure that each side kept its promise to release its prime captive also became part of the final agreement. On the day Stephen was released at Bristol he would leave Queen Matilda and his son Eustace as sureties for Robert's release. He would then travel within three days to Winchester, where Earl Robert, having been brought from Rochester, would be freed upon Stephen's arrival. Then the earl would leave his son William there as a hostage for the queen's release. Robert would then return to Bristol and free Queen Matilda and Eustace. Furthermore, William of Malmesbury alleged that Bishop Henry and Archbishop Theobald swore to make themselves the earl's prisoners if the king broke his word. Both ecclesiastics also were to write sealed letters, which Robert was to retain, describing this condition to the pope and requesting him to rescue them and the earl from imprisonment should this happen. On November 1, 1141, the peace agreement was implemented. Stephen was released at Bristol and two days later at Winchester, Earl Robert.[204] Gained? Merely a temporary truce.

A period of relative military quiet ensued until the beginning of Lent 1142, when the penitential season imposed a truce between the royalist and Angevin sides. Once free, Earl Robert returned to Matilda's court at Oxford, where he found himself reunited with, among others, Brian fitz Count and John fitz Gilbert.

Councils were held by each party in efforts to rally followers. The royalist one on December 7 was called by the legate Henry and mainly concerned itself with his efforts to justify his changes of loyalty and to excommunicate Matilda and her followers. Matilda summoned her supporters to a secret meeting at Devizes toward the end of Lent 1142. There she would be advised about the post-Rout of Winchester status of her political fortunes, by the likes of Earl Robert, accompanied by his steward Geoffrey de Waterville, Miles earl of Hereford, and most significantly both the earl of Worcester, Waleran of Meulan, and his sheriff William de

---

[203] *HN* (1998), 116–19; *JW* iii. 302–5 (an incomplete account, because the text ends); *ASC a*.1140 [*sic*].
[204] *HN* (1998), 106–9, 118–21; *JW* iii. 304–5; *GS* (2004), 136–7; "Ann. Winchcombe," *a*.1141.

Beauchamp, in keeping with the peace Waleran made with Count Geoffrey in Normandy the previous year. The magnates' deliberations would lead to Robert of Gloucester's second major contribution to Count Geoffrey of Anjou's conquest of Normandy and an impressive affirmation of his leadership status in the Angevin party in England.[205]

The earl of Gloucester's primacy among Matilda's barons was reaffirmed as an unintended result of the Devizes conference. The assembly concluded that Matilda's cause in England needed a dramatic boost to break the atmosphere of stalemate resulting from Robert's and Stephen's releases. Consequently, envoys of rank were dispatched abroad to bring over Count Geoffrey from the Continent to defend his wife's and sons' inheritance. However, on the delegates' return on June 14, the reassembled meeting was told that Geoffrey would only discuss the prospect of his coming to England with the earl of Gloucester. Robert was the only one he knew; no one else would do.[206]

Robert was implored to go, but he refused at first, fearing the fickleness of Angevin supporters' loyalty and their uncertain ability to defend Matilda in his absence. However, in the end, with no real alternative, Robert agreed, but he demanded hostages from those of the highest rank to accompany him to Normandy in order to assure their continued service to the empress and their presence at Oxford to defend her.[207] I suspect that in some cases the earl made *conventiones* with individuals which were duly recorded to avoid later disputes over fulfillment of their terms. One such survives between Earl Robert and Miles of Hereford, which also reflects upon their mutual status of lord and vassal.

First of all, it was drafted in the form of a bipartite chirograph, thereby providing each party with a copy for possible later use. As a *conventio* adapted to the current political circumstances, observance of it was sworn to by Robert, but secured by Miles by placing his son Mahel in Robert's custody as a hostage. Furthermore, notable vassals were named as guarantors of each man. They would be responsible for withdrawing service from their lord if he failed to observe the terms within forty days of a violation; but in the case of Earl Miles, his men also would give their services to Earl Robert. Countess Mabel, in an amazing revelation of her domestic authority, also swore that she would keep Robert to the agreement insofar as she was able, and that if he reneged on it, she would do what she could to restore it; if she could not accomplish this, if necessary, she would make legal record of it known. And as pledges to accomplish that were listed a representative roster of Robert's honorial *curiales*: Geoffrey de Waterville (steward), Hubert steward, Richard de Grainville (constable), Osbert Eightpence, Odo Sor, Gilbert de Umfraville, Richard de St. Quintin (honorial tenants), and Reginald de Cahagnes (possible tenant). On behalf of Earl Miles his son and heir Roger swore that if his father strayed from observance, he would withdraw from service until Miles returned to it. And three honorial tenants of Miles were to make a record of the agreement known in court if that became necessary.

---

[205] *HN* (1998), 108–11, 124–7; *Regesta* iii. no. 116 & n.; but, for dating, see *BS*, no. 514.
[206] *HN* (1998), 122–5.   [207] *HN* (1998), 122–5; Robert of Torigny, "Chronica," 143.

## The Empress's Champion

What the two men pledged reflects on their own individual concerns. Robert wanted assurance that for the duration of the war against Stephen Miles would continue to fight for the empress. Miles wanted to know that Robert would maintain his personal well-being and his lands, that if anyone wished to harm him, Robert would help him, and that Robert in turn would hold himself to the war between the empress and Stephen and not to other ones.

About their lord–vassal relationship nothing was said. It was only pledged that after the war was over, prudent men as hostages and securities would be taken for preserving concord between the two men. As Ralph Davis observed, the *conventio* was one-sided in favor of Miles, illustrating the difficulties Earl Robert faced to guarantee loyalty to Matilda in his absence and the frailty of the bond of vassalage his father had created for him.[208]

Sometime after June 24 Robert set sail for Normandy from Wareham, where he had put his son William in command of both the town and the castle. With the earl went a group of knights likely to have included at least his household corps and the baronial hostages. Halfway across the Channel a storm scattered all but two of his ships. Fortunately for his mission Robert and his most faithful retainers were on one of them which made a safe landing and proceeded to Caen.

From there, the earl sent word of his arrival to Count Geoffrey, who came for the planned strategy meeting. In response to the request Robert brought, Geoffrey procrastinated, citing many impediments to his coming to England; but the one stressed was that a number of castles in the duchy were in rebellion against him. Robert felt the only hope for bringing Geoffrey to England was to remove this objection. So the earl assisted Geoffrey in capturing at least ten castles. However, when this was accomplished, the count only raised new objections. One may well have been his worry over a possible rebellion in Anjou.

Nevertheless, while Robert's mission failed in its purpose, his participation in Geoffrey's campaign contributed to Angevin objectives in Normandy. The ten castles, including Mortain, which a Gloucester family copy of the *Historia Novella* attributed to Robert, and two other castles mentioned in other sources, show that King Stephen's honor of Mortain was the main prize, with Briquessart, *caput* of the Norman barony of Earl Ranulf of Chester, and several castles in the Bessin and Cotentin additional dividends. Robert of Torigny viewed these conquests as establishing the count's rule over the men of the Cotentin and Avranchin, in effect completing Geoffrey's conquest of western Lower Normandy.[209]

No later than the beginning of November 1142, Robert returned to England without his brother-in-law. According to William of Malmesbury, Robert had

---

[208] *BS*, no. 212 & facsm. facing p. 152; Patterson, *EGC*, no. 95 & n.; among commentaries, see Round, *Geoffrey de Mandeville*, 379–83; Davis, "The Treaty between William Earl of Gloucester and Roger Earl of Hereford," 142; Crouch, *Reign of King Stephen*, 235; King, "Dispute Settlement in Anglo-Norman England," esp. 121, 124.

[209] *HN* (1998), 124–6 & n., 127; Robert of Torigny, "Chronica," 143; Chartrou, *L'Anjou de 1109 à 1151*, 62–3; King, *King Stephen*, 184–5; the copy based upon a Gloucester text is Ce¹, BL, MS Royal 13.D.ii, fol. 123r: *HN* (1998), 126n., 127: Tinchebrai (Orne), Saint-Hilaire (Manche), Briquessart, Aunay, Bastebourg, Trévières, Vire, Plessis-Grimoult, Villers-Bocage (Calvados), and Mortain (Manche).

assembled quite a flotilla, 52 ships, with a force of between 300 and 400 knights, the size of which, as Marjorie Chibnall has pointed out, is problematic to say the least. In any case, the earl's *transfretatio* was successful and he landed his force at Wareham.[210]

Gloucester did not return to England empty-handed. As a concession to the Devizes council's request and, not improbably, to the earl for his military contributions, the count sent his and Matilda's eldest son Henry with his uncle as guardian in hopes that by seeing him the English barons might better be motivated to fight, supposedly, "for the cause of the lawful heir." As Edmund King has noted, this translated quotation from William of Malmesbury's *Historia Novella* reflects the Angevin party's emerging focus on Henry fitz Empress as legal heir to the throne. It is an idea also attributed anachronistically to Henry's uncle, Robert earl of Gloucester, by the author of the *Gesta Stephani*, but in fact applied by Robert and Miles of Gloucester in their *concordia amoris* not long before Robert's visit to Geoffrey as well as in Matilda's charters.[211]

In conjunction with his role as Henry's guardian, Earl Robert in time established the 9-year-old in his household at Bristol castle. There the earl arranged for the boy to be tutored in letters and knightly manners with his own son Roger by Master Matthew, possibly from St. Augustine's Abbey, recently founded (1140) by his patrician vassal Robert fitz Harding. The great scholar and translator Adelard of Bath may have had some association with Henry, since he dedicated his treatise on the astrolabe to him. Years later, then duke of Normandy and count of Anjou, Henry recalled the experience at St. Augustine's with fondness; and apparently Roger even later, as bishop of Worcester, did as well.[212]

The England Robert found on his return with the young Henry was far from the condition in which it had been when he had left for Normandy. In fact, it was news of this state of affairs that had caused the earl to terminate his Norman stay. Before the end of September 1142, King Stephen had taken advantage of the earl's absence to burn Wareham and capture the castle which the earl had entrusted to his son William. With this accomplished, he moved against Matilda at Oxford. First he overwhelmed the forts she had established in the vicinity guarding approaches to the town. Then, on September 26, he broke through Oxford's fortifications, which Earl Robert had improved, and laid siege to the castle with the empress trapped inside. Her own forces regrouped at Wallingford, but hesitated to attack the king.[213]

---

[210] *HN* (1998), 128 & n., 129; Poole, "Henry Plantagenet's Early Visits to England," 449; Chibnall, *Empress Matilda*, 117.

[211] *HN* (1998), lxvii & n., 126–7; *GS* (2004), 12–15; Robert of Torigny, "Chronica," 143; Patterson, *EGC*, no. 95; *Regesta* iii. xlvi, nos. 634–5; Chibnall, *Empress Matilda*, 102, 109, 115, 117; Poole, "Henry Plantagenet's Early Visits to England," 450.

[212] William fitz Stephen, "Vita S. Thomae," 104; Gervase of Canterbury i. 125; BA, DC/E/45: Patterson, "Ducal and Royal *Acta* of Henry fitz Empress," 118, facsm. 130; *Regesta* iii. xlvi, no. 996; Poole, "Henry Plantagenet's Early Visits to England," 449–50; Brooke and Brooke, "Henry II Duke of Normandy and Aquitaine," 81; Cheney, *Roger, Bishop of Worcester*, 7–8; Haskins, "Henry II as a Patron of Literature," 72–4; Dickinson, "The Origins of St. Augustine's Bristol," 112–20, esp. 115.

[213] *GS* (2004), 138–43; *HN* (1998), 126–9; *ASC, a.*1140 [*sic*]; Gervase of Canterbury i. 124.

Earl Robert's initial movements after landing show that he came with a strategic plan in mind which took precedence over rushing to help his sister at Oxford. He also felt that his amphibious force was insufficient to confront Stephen immediately. The first phase involved retaking Wareham because of its geopolitical importance to himself and the Angevin party in the southwest. He and his men quickly took control of the harbor and borough, apparently with little difficulty. But the castle was well fortified and stoutly defended by its garrison commanded by Herbert de Lucy, so the earl relied upon siege tactics, over about a three-week period, to force the royalists into submission. The king's handpicked troops negotiated their honorable departure. The earl was asked for the customary truce, which he chivalrously granted, for time to request the king to come to their relief; if he did not do so by the agreed-upon date, the garrison would surrender. When Stephen declined the request, Robert reclaimed the castle and oversaw improvements to its defenses.

Robert next moved to strengthen the Angevin hold on the lower Dorset region as a protection to Wareham by seizing Lulworth castle from its turncoat constable, William of Glastonbury, and capturing and fortifying the isle of Portland, which belonged to the bishop of Winchester.[214] The earl's entire Dorset campaign likely postponed his advance on Oxford for about a month. He had banked on besieged Matilda looking after herself until his arrival, a calculated gamble. However, the earl still had the Angevin heir to the throne in reserve.[215] As it happened, she had looked to her own safety, although not as her brother probably had expected.

Just before the castle's food supplies were completely exhausted, Matilda escaped in the dark of night—one account says by being let down from the tower by ropes—escorted by three trusty knights, across the moat, past the besiegers and their pickets over six miles to safety at Wallingford. Her escape so astonished the author of the *Gesta Stephani* that he claimed that the empress had crossed miraculously dry-footed over the castle's moat without getting her clothes wet. To William of Malmesbury, writing what would be the last episode of his *Historia Novella*, there were four knights, a walk on foot to Abingdon, and then a horseback ride to Wallingford. Her escape also was miraculous.[216]

For his part, sometime after the beginning of Advent 1142, on November 29, Robert of Gloucester began organizing his relief effort for Matilda by commanding predictably through messengers and letters all supporters of the empress to muster at Cirencester, which was located in the heart of his and his allies' dominated territory. The likely combination of a castle at the Augustinian abbey and a town would have served him well as his headquarters and gathering point for his campaign. A network of roads leading from Angevin strongholds near and far converged on the town; and at least one, via Malmesbury and Faringdon, would put the gathering force within easy striking range of Oxford. Robert's summonses and their politically

---

[214] *HN* (1998), 128–30 & n., 131; *GS* (2004), 144–5; Gervase of Canterbury i. 124; Ce¹, fol. 123v: *HN* (1998), 130n.
[215] *HN* (1998), 128–31; Gervase of Canterbury i. 124.
[216] *GS* (2004), 142–5; *ASC a.*1140; *HN* (1998), 132–3; Henry of Huntingdon (1996), 742–3; John of Hexham, 310.

undifferentiated recipients indicate that he was marshaling a broadly based Angevin army and that his authority to do so was recognized.

The opportunity for the earl to turn the military tables on Stephen at Oxford never came about. It took until about mid-December or slightly later for his muster to be completed. Then, shortly before Christmas, when Robert had begun moving his army on Oxford, he learned of Matilda's escape. He might have deployed his troops to recover the town and castle, whose garrison had surrendered after Matilda escaped. However, he chose to join his sister, possibly to reunite mother and son, and an opportunity to recover Oxford was lost. This left Wallingford as the Angevins' eastern bastion in the upper Thames Valley.[217]

Nevertheless, Earl Robert of Gloucester significantly improved the Angevins' fortunes in 1143. Stephen apparently resumed hostilities against the Angevins early in the year with the earl's recovered Wareham as his major target. With Normandy all but lost the king needed more than ever to contain Robert and the southern Angevins; and one way to do that would be to cut off reinforcements for them from the duchy by recapturing Wareham. The king's well-equipped forces inflicted considerable damage upon the town and its environs, but failed to take the castle due to the earl's improvements to its defenses. The king withdrew northeast to Wilton (Wilts.), where he planned to fortify a castle at the Benedictine nunnery in which the empress's mother had resided before her marriage to King Henry and worn the veil to ward off ambitious suitors. Stephen also was reinforced there by his brother Henry with a large force and by many other barons with their men.

The author of the *Gesta Stephani* believed that Stephen intended for the fortress to inhibit the earl of Gloucester's raids in the region. Wilton, like Cirencester, was a great hub of roads. It was only 6 miles from Salisbury, which was held by its Angevin castellan, William. And Wilton as a forward military base would provide the king with a southwestern salient into Robert's and the Angevins' southwestern power base comparable to Wallingford's function for the Angevins in the Thames Valley, as Jim Bradbury has aptly observed. Stephen's plans were not realized. They triggered a full-scale counterattack by Robert on July 1 and a pitched battle, in which the king narrowly escaped capture a second time.[218]

Gloucester had not been taken unawares by Stephen's move on Wilton. The earl had kept himself well informed about the king's movements by an effective intelligence network of scouts, as John Prestwich pointed out. Advance warning of Stephen's change of plans allowed Robert time to muster his principal *coadiutores*, according to the *Gesta Stephani*, to oppose the king: representing the earl's family, apparently his son Philip; from allies, Miles of Gloucester and William of Salisbury; and from mercenaries, the villanous captain Robert fitz Hildebrand.

---

[217] *HN* (1998), 130–3; *GS* (2004), 138; Gervase of Canterbury i. 125; Coulson, "The Castles of the Anarchy," 70–1 & n.; Davis, *King Stephen*, 3rd edn., 70; Stenton, "The Road System of Medieval England," 241. Earl Robert's construction of the castle at Cirencester may have led to Philip of Gloucester's appointment as castellan, which another source attributes to the empress: see Chapt. 4, 87, n. 37.

[218] *GS* (2004), 144–7; Beeler, *Warfare in England*, 135; Renn, *Norman Castles in Britain*, 347; Bradbury, *Stephen and Matilda*, 125.

The earl deployed his men in three squadrons, supposedly about equal in number to Stephen's.[219]

Robert immediately gained the tactical advantage by striking first at sunset on July 1, with the royalist army at ease and the king taking his rest in Wilton Abbey. The earl deployed his men in three wedge-shaped squadrons, possibly arranged to form a single striking force aimed at the king's center. In his haste to face Robert's surprise attack, either Stephen staked the outcome of the battle on disposing the three divisions of his army with the greatest strength on the flanks or a chaotic rush to battle determined this array. Either way, when Robert sent his combined forces against the center of the royalist army, they shattered it, driving all before them.

Much of the royal army scattered into the countryside. Some took refuge in Wilton's houses and churches, only to be burned to death when the earl of Gloucester and his men fired the town in an orgy of sanctioned plunder and destruction in the mopping-up phase of the battle. Especially notable was their violation of the abbatial church from which those who had hoped for sanctuary were dragged out bound. Stephen almost was taken prisoner again and Bishop Henry barely escaped as well. Many were led back to Bristol in chains. Among them was William Martel, Stephen's steward, who had bravely fought on longer than most of the royalists. Stephen chivalrously ransomed him by turning over to Robert mighty Sherborne castle (Dors.), which Martel had commanded. Earl Robert returned to his baronial headquarters laden down with booty. His fine piece of generalship counterbalanced the Angevin defeat at Winchester with the royalist Rout of Wilton.[220]

To the theologically minded author of the *Gesta Stephani* Robert and some of his allies in time faced divine retribution for their Wilton violence. The earl lost a son, likely Philip; Miles of Gloucester was killed in a hunting accident; the mercenary Fitz Hildebrand's innards were slowly consumed by worms; and William of Salisbury suffered from frightening nightmares and a slow and painful death.[221]

Actually, in several ways the Angevin civil war benefited Earl Robert, first of all by seizure of his enemies' lands. Perhaps by 1144, in Normandy Robert won part of the late Eudo *Dapifer*'s fee Henry I had given to Stephen of Blois near Creully and with it overlordship of William de Saint-Clair.[222] Two knight's fees of the Lacy

---

[219] *GS* (2004), 146–9; the agents are called *nuntii*; Prestwich, "Military Intelligence under the Norman and Angevin Kings," 16.

[220] *GS* (2004), 146–9; Henry of Huntingdon (1996), 740–3; Gervase of Canterbury i. 125–6; "Ann. Waverly," 229; "Ann. Tewkesbury," 46.

[221] GS (2004), 148–9; for Robert's son, likely Philip, see Chapt. 4, 87–8, 91; Cronne, *Reign of King Stephen*, 203.

[222] Transcriptions of charters in BN, MS latin nouvelle acquisition 1022, establish that churches at Thaon and Villiers belonging to a fee held by William de Saint-Clair as undertenant of Eudo *Dapifer* of the bishop of Bayeux passed to the mesne lordship of Stephen count of Mortain, the Empress Matilda (presumably 1138 × 44), and Mabel countess of Gloucester (presumably after 1138): nos. 211, 213, 214, 216, fols. 191–2; for Mabel, see also BN, MS latin nouvelle acquisition 1023, fol. 30; *CDF*, nos. 798–9; Patterson, *EGC*, no. 6 & n.; Loyd, *Anglo-Norman Families*, 88–9. I have found no evidence that Geoffrey de Mandeville actually recovered this land by means of a charter from the Empress Matilda in 1141: *Regesta* iii. no. 275; Hollister, "Misfortunes of the Mandevilles," 123; Chibnall, *Empress Matilda*, 109; see also Chapt. 4, n. 42.

family may have been fruits of Earl Robert's 1142 *compositio* with Miles of Gloucester. Gloucester's seizure of his son-in-law Ranulf's estates held of the bishop of Bayeux very likely occurred when he and Count Geoffrey captured the earl of Chester's castles during that year. In England, Robert's taste for episcopal lands yielded him Bishop Henry of Winchester's manor at Damerham (Wilts.) close by his own demesne manor of Cranborne (Dors.) and Sherborne castle and hundred (Dors.) from Stephen.[223] Probably between 1139 and 1141 Robert seized Robert earl of Leicester's holdings in Wareham and nearby.[224]

The *Gesta*'s mention of Earl Robert's acquisition of mighty Sherborne castle in Dorset as ransom for his captive William Martel and a joint charter issued by Earl Robert's widow and heir not only show how Gloucester gained such power in the county, but suggest how it might be exercised in other areas under his control. As a result, Robert gained the hundreds of Sherborne and Axminster, the market of Sherborne, the toll and all tithings from the manor of Sherborne, judicial pleas involving trial by ordeal of battle and water, saving only the rights of the Crown. Lands and their men, from knights to rustics, were swept into the earl's control. With it, he probably could impose works and other obligations upon manorial tenants.[225] Robert's local influence in 1145/6 also is indirectly indicated by Gilbert Foliot's advice to Archbishop Theobald of Canterbury about binding the earl to expel the miscreant ex-abbot William.[226]

Reflection on the battle of Wilton also was an occasion for the *Gesta Stephani*'s author to view Robert's territorial profit from the war in broader terms. The earl and his allies had achieved a kind of dominion in the southwest: "the earl and his supporters…made the kingdom subject to them far and wide, demolished with spirit and valour castles belonging to the king's men, in unchecked triumph built others for their more effectual subjugation, and without any resistance from anyone put almost half of England, from sea to sea, under their own laws and ordinances. This lordship of his the earl very greatly adorned by restoring peace and quietness everywhere, except that in building his castles he exacted forced labour from all and, whenever he had to fight the enemy, demanded everyone's help either by sending knights or by paying scutage. And there was indeed in those regions a shadow of peace but not yet peace complete."[227]

The so-called seas between which Robert and his allies prevailed at this time were the river Severn and the Channel.[228] Empirical evidence of the extent of Gloucester's centralized governmental reach and the relationship he had with his allies in this region survives in the coinage his mints and those maintained by allies

---

[223] Patterson *EGC*, no. 6 & n. See 148–9, 164–6; Chapt. 2, 53; Dalton, "*In Neutro Latere*: The Armed Neutrality of Ranulf II Earl of Chester in King Stephen's Reign," 50–1; I agree with Crouch, *Reign of King Stephen*, 200n.
[224] BL, MS Cotton Otho B.xiv, fols. 32, 33–33v, 34, 37, 39–39v. Crouch, *Reign of King Stephen*, 156.
[225] *GS* (2004), 148–9; Patterson, *EGC*, no. 171 & n.
[226] *LCGF*, no. 52, p. 90; see also Chapt. 4, 124–5.
[227] *GS* (2004), 148–51; *ASC a*.1140 [*sic*], attributed the division to an effect of King Stephen's imprisonment; see also John of Hexham, 309, and Robert de Torigny, "Chronica," 141. An excellent survey of this subject is in Crouch, *Reign of King Stephen*, Chapt. 9, esp. 151–67.
[228] Davis, "Authorship," xxv.

produced. The earl's mints at Cardiff and Bristol functioned during his father's reign and Stephen's. In the latter's, initially the royal system continued with its centralized control over silver content, the production of dies, and minting carried out by royally appointed local moneyers. Bristol's mint produced Stephen's first issue, the "Watford" type. As the Angevin revolt progressed, local moneyers fell under the influence of local lords, so that, in areas under Angevin dominion, coins might be irregular issues in Stephen's and Matilda's names—in some cases, even in those of local lords like Eustace fitz John or Robert earl of Leicester.[229] Robert of Gloucester is exceptional first of all because to date only his mints in his castle-boroughs, Bristol, Wareham, and Cardiff, are known to have produced the empress's pennies in the whole of the southwest, lower Severn Valley, and South Wales, and perhaps the majority of them minted anywhere.

However, secondly and with greatest relevance to the subject of Gloucester's regional dominion, at least from about 1143 until his death Earl Robert began minting silver pennies in his own name. The spectacular hoard of them found at Box (Wilts.) between 1993 and 1994 containing 36 whole ones and 8 cut-halfpennies is a treasure trove of information. Obverse sides bear variations of an image of a lion passant to dexter, plausibly inspired by the obverse of Robert's seal, within an inner circle. A legend between the inner and an outer circle reads: "+Rob'.Com'.Gloc'." for *Rob(ertus) Com(es) Gloc(estrie)*; reverse sides, versions of a cross pommée superimposed on a fleur-de-lys above a saltire pommée. In place of a legend within concentric rings are the moneyers' names and the locations of their mints (Figure 5.1).

In discussing the Box hoard, the numismatist Marion Archibald has been able to show that the pennies represent three different issues, minted from dies probably cut at Robert's Bristol mint, the *domus monete* on Castle Street, for moneyers such as Farthegn, Iordan, and Robert to use there and by others at local mints. One of these was Wareham's, a Gloucester demesne holding since 1139 × 41; but others, at Castle Combe, Marlborough, Trowbridge, and Salisbury (Wilts.), belonged to Robert's Angevin allies, a likely Dunstanville, John fitz Gilbert, Humphrey de Bohun, and William of Salisbury (d.1143) and his brother Patrick, respectively. Besides the prima facie evidence of Robert's regalian pretension, use of the same dies and maintenance of very similar weight by all of the network's mints presumably under allies' control indicates both a system of centralized oversight exercised by Robert from Bristol and a high degree of political deference to him as the Angevins' leader from barons who were not his vassals: as already noted, the best evidence of a Gloucester affinity. Marion Archibald went so far as to characterize Earl Robert's southwestern zone of such scope as "a fully operational separate state" functioning "along similar lines to the royal government in London."[230]

---

[229] For Henry I's reign, see Blackburn, "Coinage and Currency under Henry I: A Review," 49–81, Tables 5 & 6; for Stephen's in general, see Mack, "Stephen and the Anarchy 1135–1154," 85–112; Blackburn, "Coinage and Currency," 145–205; for a summary, see Crouch, *Reign of King Stephen*, 330.
[230] Patterson, *EGC*, no. 185; "*CIPM*, no. 729; *Regesta* ii. no. CCLXXXIX; *BF* no. 181; Cronne, *The Reign of King Stephen*, 237–9; Blackburn, "Coinage and Currency under Henry I: A Review," 64–5, 71–4; Mack, "Stephen and the Anarchy 1135–1154," 38–41, 59–60, 85–88; Archibald, "The Lion Coinage of Robert Earl of Gloucester and William Earl of Gloucester," 71–2 & fig. 1, 73 & fig. 2, 74,

**Figure 5.1.** a–d: Obverse and reverse of silver pennies issued in the name of Robert earl of Gloucester at Bristol by local moneyers *c.*1143–*c.*1147: a–b, by Farthegn; c–d, by Iordan. BM, CMB 394387; CMB 394388.

© The Trustees of the British Museum.

The author of the *Gesta Stephani* was correct in assessing the effect of the earl's dominion as, "a shadow of peace but not yet peace complete." To begin with, even in the earl's demesne heartland, there were royalist pockets like Malmesbury (Wilts.) and Bath (Som.).[231] Furthermore, Gloucester's treaty with Miles of Gloucester shows how tenuous political loyalty might be.[232] And Angevin loyalty

76–7, 82–4, Plate 1, esp. nos. 1, 3, 11, 17, 22; see nos 1, 3 at Figure 5.1 above, issued, respectively, by the moneyers Farthegn (Faretein) and Iordan at Bristol. My own readings, courtesy of the British Museum's Department of Coins and Medals, differ only slightly from Dr. Archibald's: Figure 5.1a–b: +RO[ ]LO (obverse); [+ ]ARETEIN [ ] (reverse); c–d: +ROB CO [ ]OC (obverse); [ ]IOR [ ]RI. For the obverse of Earl William of Gloucester's seal, his father's in modified form, see Figure 4.1, 113.

[231] *GS* (2004), 150–1; Davis, *King Stephen*, 3rd edn., 70, 72; Green, "Financing Stephen's War," 95–9.
[232] Davis, "Henry of Blois and Brian Fitz-Count," 300; Davis, *King Stephen*, 3rd edn., 90–1, 131, 138; but regarding William de Mohun's political status, note Edmund King's caution in accepting

did not guarantee benign governance. Brian fitz Count in his embattled Angevin outpost at Wallingford defended his and his men's practice of brigandage in order to survive.[233] Plundering, wasting of estates, violations of churches, and assaults on non-combatants were commonly practiced by Angevins and royalists alike. And what could be more illustrative of the unpredictable chaotic fruits of war than the case of the former royal treasurer and constable of Portchester castle (Hants.), William de Pont de l'Arche.

William, an Angevin since 1141, came under attack by the troops of Bishop Henry of Winchester, likely at Porchester in 1143. Feeling in danger of being overwhelmed, he appealed for help to the Empress Matilda, who sent the Flemish mercenary Robert fitz Hildebrand to the rescue. But instead of aiding William, Robert seduced his wife, imprisoned the hapless constable in his own castle, and then declared for King Stephen and Bishop Henry.[234]

Following Wilton, in 1144 the earl of Gloucester decided to eliminate the royalist threat of Malmesbury. He tightened the noose on the royalist garrison commanded by Walter de Pinkney by building three castles nearby and by dispatching his ally William Peveral of Dover with a company of mercenaries to build a castle at the village of Cricklade (Wilts.). Located between Malmesbury and Oxford and protected on all sides by water and marsh, it enabled William to stage attacks on the two royalist centers and block any royalist relief efforts for Malmesbury. Stephen responded by rushing to Malmesbury with a reportedly large force and, with the garrison amply supplied, went on the offensive by besieging Robert's castle at Tetbury (Glos.) about three miles northwest of Malmesbury. Having likely learned through his intelligence network of this threat, Robert countered by raising an even greater force to lead against his cousin. Under the earl's command was a truly Angevin army composed of his own men, knights and footmen from Bristol and other towns, Welsh mercenaries, and allies, notably the new earl of Hereford, Miles's son Roger.

Faced with a pitched battle against a superior force, Stephen followed his counselors' advice to break off the Tetbury siege temporarily and to draw Gloucester away from the area by attacking Winchcombe and a castle built there by Earl Roger. Robert did not take the bait; but it cost the Angevins Winchcombe and led to various motte-and-baileys being thrown up by the king elsewhere in Gloucestershire. Evidently this multiplication of castles with likely undermanned garrisons made easy pickings for two marauding renegade Flemish mercenary brothers, Henry and Ralph Caldy and their men.

---

Ralph Davis's assessment: "The Memory of Brian Fitz Count," 83; Dalton, "*In Neutro Latere*: The Armed Neutrality of Ranulf II Earl of Chester in King Stephen's Reign," 49–50; White, "Were the Midlands Wasted during Stephen's Reign?," 37.

[233] *HN* (1998), 70–3; *GS* (2004), 152–3; *ASC a.*1137; Davis, "Henry of Blois and Brian Fitz Count," 299, and 300–2 (transl. in King, "The Memory of Brian fitz Count," 90–1); Davis, *King Stephen*, 3rd edn., 82–6; Thomas, "Violent Disorder in Stephen's England: A Maximum Argument," 139–70. The bibliography of this controversial subject is too extensive to cite.

[234] *GS* (2004), 150–3; Chibnall, *Empress Matilda*, 100.

Robert's efforts against Malmesbury failed, but along with the standard horrors of siege warfare, they produced drama on both sides. Walter de Pinkney was captured, but neither reason, torture, nor the rigors of imprisonment succeeded in persuading him to order his garrison to surrender. The earl of Gloucester's Cricklade gambit lost him the services of William Peverel. According to the author of the *Gesta Stephani*, Peverel became guilt-ridden over sins he had committed during his Cricklade-based compaigns and in expiation for them joined the Second Crusade and bravely died in battle. His successor was Philip of Gloucester, who convinced his father to build a motte-and-bailey castle to thwart attacks of the royalist garrison at Oxford against Angevins in the region; and Earl Robert selected a site farther east in Berkshire by the village of Faringdon in the summer of 1145. However, that strategy more than just backfired. It turned into a Gloucester family civil war.

Stephen responded to Faringdon's challenge by raising a reportedly massive army of Londoners; and he quickly staged a full-scale and incessant assault on the fortress. Although Philip pleaded with his father to come to its rescue, perhaps because Robert saw that his opponents outnumbered his force and prospects were low for raising additional men quickly, he refused. Faringdon's men then were forced to surrender and in despair, I believe, at the Angevin party's prospects and his own, Philip turned his talents for brutal warfare against his father and his allies. He was stopped by a lengthy illness during which he came to feel remorse for his behavior; then, rather than rejoining the Angevins, he followed William Peverel's penitential path. To Henry of Huntingdon and the author of the *Gesta Stephani*, Faringdon was a bad omen for the Angevin cause.[235]

The Faringdon debacle and Robert's failure to take Malmesbury were points in a gradually developing downward trend in his military and political fortunes. Other potentially threatening royalist pockets were not eliminated in the region in which the earl was supposedly strongest. Just north of Gloucester, Winchcombe castle remained in royalist hands. Bath was still under the control of its royalist bishop Robert. Other royalist castle holdouts included Barnstable and Torrington in Devon, and possibly Dunster by the Somerset coast near Bristol.

Robert also was losing members of his following. Earl William de Mohun of Somerset's service was held up to ridicule by Brian fitz Count probably by the end of 1142–3 at the latest—and he lost his comital title. Henry de Tracy, Stephen's surrogate in Devon and Somerset, had so crushed William militarily that the lord of Dunster would no longer fight against him.[236] Roger earl of Warwick may have stopped attending the empress's court as early as 1142 and appeared at the king's by around 1146, if not earlier.[237] The alliance Roger of Berkeley made with Earl Robert's turncoat son Philip may have led in 1146 to Berkeley's lord being taken prisoner by Robert's Angevin ally Walter of Hereford to keep the castle from falling

---

[235] *GS* (2004), 170–81, 188–9, 212; *LCGF*, no. 27, p. 66n.; for Ralph Caldy's brush with proprietary piety, see *Cart. Gloucs.* i. no. 146. *GS* (2004), 182–5; Henry of Huntingdon (1996), 746–7, quoted by Robert of Torigni, "Chronica," 149–50, and "Ann. Waverly," 231; see also Chapt. 4, 87–8.
[236] *GS* (2004), 82–3; King, "The Memory of Brian fitz Count," 77–8; Davis, *King Stephen*, 3rd edn., 138; Bearman, "Mohun, William de," 516; see 142.
[237] *JW* iii. 290–1; *Regesta* iii. nos. 494, 597; Davis, *King Stephen*, 3rd edn., 131, 142.

into royalist hands; but even such extreme measures as a charade hanging outside his castle's walls failed to gain the garrison's surrender.[238] Robert's son-in-law Ranulf of Chester even formally abandoned his loose Angevin ties in the same year and made an agreement with King Stephen which among its benefits effectively granted to the earl the town and castle of Lincoln for the foreseeable future; and as if to emphasize that Ranulf's change of loyalty meant abandoning his father-in-law, the king gave him land at the port of Grimsby on the Humber mouth (Lincs.) Earl Robert had inherited through his wife from Haimo II *dapifer*. The earl of Chester helped Stephen capture Bedford castle (Beds.) and went so far as to to join the king in an attack on Brian fitz Count's Wallingford. Robert also fared no better from Ranulf after Stephen arrested him, demanded surrender of Lincoln in exchange for his freedom, and the earl went to war with the king. But of all these losses in personnel, Philip of Gloucester's treason, with its personal, political, and military implications, must have hit his father hardest. If the embattled earl had any reaction to his son's remorse and expiation by joining the Second Crusade, it is unknown.[239]

The Second Crusade also depleted Angevin ranks.[240] The shock of the Muslim conquest of Edessa and much of the county in 1144 had moved Pope Eugenius III to organize a new crusade to come to the aid of the first colonial state created by the First Crusade. The pope's reissued bull *Quantum praedecessores* of 1146 offered participants a range of spiritual and material benefits. Enthusiasm for participation was fanned by popular preachers, especially Cistercian Abbot Bernard of Clairvaux in France and Bishop Arnulf of Lisieux in Normandy, and was strongly supported by King Louis VII of France.

The Anglo-Norman aristocracy had strong associations with the Crusading movement. Gloucester's uncle, Duke Robert, and Stephen's namesake father were among its heroes, the latter even with a somewhat tainted reputation. Queen Matilda's father Eustace and her uncles Godfrey and Baldwin I had joined the First Crusade and the last two had been the Latin Kingdom of Jerusalem's first two monarchs. She, the king, and the empress all were patrons. Royalist barons, notably William III de Warenne earl of Surrey, as well as Angevins, were caught up in Crusading fervor. Earl Robert of Gloucester had become a landlord and possibly patron of the Templars. Around 1146 the earl lost his major ally in his Cotswolds campaigns when William Peverel left his strategic command post and joined the crusade. Two of the earl's important supporters in the southwest, Baldwin earl of Devon and his boon companion and militarily valuable vassal Stephen de Mandeville lord of Erlestoke (Wilts.), both took the Cross.[241]

---

[238] *GS* (2004), 190–1.
[239] *GS* (2004), 184–5, 190–1; Henry of Huntingdon (1996), 748–9; *ASC* a.1140 (for 1146), p. 201; Robert of Torigny, "Chronica," 151–2; *Regesta* iii. no. 178; *The Lincolnshire Domesday and the Lindsey Survey*, L9/1, 5, p. 248; see also Patterson, *EGC*, no. 6 & n.; Dalton, "The Armed Neutrality of Ranulf II Earl of Chester," 52–3; Davis, *King Stephen*, 3rd edn., 88–94; White, "Were the Midlands Wasted during Stephen's Reign?," 37–8; King, *King Stephen*, 223–5, 227–9, 239–40; see also Chapt. 4, 88.
[240] *GS* (2004), 192–3.
[241] *Regesta* iii. esp. nos. 843–4, 850–1, 853–5, 858, 861–2; *Historia Pontificalis of John of Salisbury*, 54 & n. Davis, *King Stephen*, 3rd edn., 87–8; Berry, "The Second Crusade," 463–81, 487; Constable,

Even Gloucester's sister lost confidence in him and possibly the prospects of her own cause. In 1146 Matilda approached Stephen to see if a peaceful resolution to the conflict could be reached. Her chief negotiator, however, was not her champion Robert, but her brother Reginald. To add to Robert's embarrassment, as already noted, his renegade son Philip had captured his own uncle while Earl Reginald was traveling under a truce to the parley. Probably in response to the pressures he was facing, in September 1146 before the empress and her court at Devizes, Robert of Gloucester made an agreement with his Norman mesne overlord Philip bishop of Bayeux about his tenure of lands in the Bessin which probably eliminated the threats of excommunication and interdict upon his lands from the bishops of Worcester and Bath formally commanded by Pope Eugenius III.[242]

In 1147 the 14-year-old Henry fitz Empress returned to England with a small retinue of mercenaries, intending to come to the aid of his embattled supporters. Expectation of the young man's success ran high among them until realization spread that Henry's force was not a large army and was underfunded. Few joined him when he announced an attack on Cricklade (Wilts.) and not surprisingly the venture failed, as did another action against nearby Purton (Wilts.). He could neither pay his mercenaries nor even fund their retreat to Normandy. But when he applied first to his mother and then to his uncle Earl Robert, each pleaded the lack of cash to spare. As Ralph Davis probably rightly surmised, Henry's escapade was a distraction to Matilda and Robert and the best way to get the Angevin heir back in Normandy was to deny him money. The boy's cousin King Stephen supported their goal, albeit understandably from a different perspective, and when asked, gave Henry return fare to the Continent.[243]

Shortly afterwards, what was to be Earl Robert's last field action met with defeat and complete embarrassment. One of Brian fitz Count's men seized the bishop of Winchester's castle at some unknown site called *Lidelea* and set about harrying the countryside. Bishop Henry brought up an army, built two siege castles, and settled down to a siege. Earl Robert then came to the garrison's rescue with a very large force which included three earls. He attacked the siege castles, but in the process allowed himself to be taken by surprise by King Stephen and a relieving army. Capitalizing on his advantage, Stephen drove Robert and his men into a panicked flight back to Bristol. That was embarrassment enough, but more followed. Robert tried to muster a new army to send against the king; but neither promised rewards nor threats could produce one.[244]

Robert earl of Gloucester died on October 31, 1147, at Bristol after suddenly falling ill with a fever and was laid to rest in St. James's Priory, according to sixteenth-century Tewkesbury Abbey sources, in a tomb of green jasper located in

"The Second Crusade as Seen by Contemporaries," 213, 226, 261, 263; Chibnall, *Empress Matilda*, 149n.; Tyerman, *England and the Crusades*, 24–32, esp. 32; Crouch, *Reign of King Stephen*, 208n. For the earl of Gloucester, see Chapt. 4, 17–18.

[242] Patterson, *EGC*, no. 6; *Cart. Bayeux* i. no. cxc, pp. 237–8; see Chapt. 4, 123–4.

[243] *GS* (2004), 204–5 & n., 206–7; Robert of Torigny, "Chronica," 154; Davis, *King Stephen*, 3rd edn., 94; Crouch, *Reign of King Stephen*, 220. For a different interpretation, see Chibnall, *Empress Matilda*, 146.

[244] *GS* (2004), 208 & n., 209–11; possibly located in Crondall (Hants.).

the middle of the choir.[245] Several monastic annalists, including Tewkesbury Abbey's, recorded that his death was marked by an eclipse. The pro-royalist author of the *Gesta* could not resist reporting a rumor that the earl died unconfessed. But at St. Swithun's Winchester the earl was memorialized as "a good man and the most faithful of all of England's magnates." Robert's last known act was not military at all, but pertained to the welfare of his soul and of his lordship of Glamorgan: the foundation of Margam Abbey for a community of Cistercian monks.[246]

Gervase of Canterbury recalled that the Empress Matilda was so demoralized by the state of things that before Lent 1148 she left England for Normandy and her husband's protection.[247] She did not enjoy the hindsight which would have revealed that her brother had kept alive the prospects for an Angevin succession and, as we are about to see, had arranged for that cause and his partly self-engineered reputation as its champion to enjoy an even more lasting life.

---

[245] "Ann. Margam," 14; *Cartae Antiquae Rolls 1–10*, no. 317; Bodl., MS Top. Glouc. d.2, fol. 15r: *Mon. Angl.* iv. 335; BL, Additional MS 36985, fols. 15–16; note also PRO, E.164/1, *a.*1147. The east end of the priory has long since disappeared; the sixteenth-century antiquarian John Leland described the tomb as gray marble and supported by six pillars: Dugdale believed that Robert's remains were moved to Tewkesbury Abbey sometime later; *The Itinerary of John Leland*, 91; Jackson, *Excavations at St. James's Priory, Bristol*, 8–9, 12.

[246] "Ann. Tewkesbury," 47; "Annales Plymptonienses," *a.*1147; "Ann. Winchester," *a.*1146 [*sic*]; *GS* (2004), 210–11; Patterson, *EGC*, no, 119 & n.; Patterson, *The Scriptorium of Margam Abbey*, 34–7.

[247] *ASC a.*1140 (for 1148), 202n.; Gervase of Canterbury, i. 133.

# 6

# The Earl and the Chronicler

Soon after bringing Matilda's war of succession to England in 1139, Robert earl of Gloucester took a step to justify the cause for which he was fighting and more than likely to enhance his own future reputation. He commissioned William, preceptor of Benedictine Malmesbury Abbey, about 28 miles from Bristol, to write a history of their times and of occurrences according to the will of God. While its future author and his patron knew of each other, their means of contact are unknown.[1]

Earl Robert of Gloucester's solicitation of a distinguished literary figure to explain Matilda's and his war against Stephen of Blois should come as no surprise. He belonged to the literate elite of early twelfth-century society and is the preeminent example of a secular baronial literary patron. Aside from what has been surmised about his literacy and education, the earl by 1139 already knew of William of Malmesbury's *Gesta Regum Anglorum* and according to later evidence probably had been approached by William via a presentation copy for patronage. On the same grounds, Geoffrey of Monmouth, who would become the age's most widely circulated historian, used the same tactic after dedicating his *Historia Regum Britanniae* first to the earl. Robert certainly impressed the poet Serlo of Wilton and very likely the transmitter of Arabic science Adelard of Bath.[2] To sustain his reading habits, as already noted, Robert also maintained a personal library. Among its holdings at one time or another would have been the *Gesta Regum Anglorum* and *Historia Novella* and *Historia Regum Britanniae*. Their dedications imply that they were sent to the earl and the rubricated incipit of the famous Margam Abbey library copy of the *Historia Novella* (Ce[1]) supports this claim (Figure 6.1).[3]

The earl also was no stranger to literary commissioning. Well before approaching William of Malmesbury, he added to his book collection by having a vernacular history (*geste*) of Britain's kings adapted from Welsh sources. At some point the earl sent the book to his occasional curial colleague Walter Espec at his request. It later became by means of another transfer to Constance, wife of a Lincolnshire tenant of the Gant family, Ralph fitz Gilbert, a source for Geoffrey Gaimar's *Estorie des*

---

[1] "Abbreviatio Amalarii," 128–9; see Norgate, *England under the Angevin Kings* i. 94 & n., for the "friend Robert" William addressed in the preface, possibly Robert of Gloucester; but note Thompson, *Literacy of the Laity in the Middle Ages*, 172–5; Pfaff, "The 'Abbreviatio Amalarii' of William of Malmesbury," 79–80.

[2] Thomson, *GR* ii. xxxiii, n. 26, 6, 10–11; for the revisions of the *GR* and their dates, see Thomson, *GR* i. xiii–xxvi; ii. xvii–xxxv. Adelard dedicated his *Quaestiones Naturales* to the bishop of Bayeux, Robert's son Richard: Burnett, "Bath, Adelard of," 340; see also Chapt. 1, 10–11; for the evidence of Earl Robert's receipt of these presentation copies, see n. 3.

[3] See Figure 6.1, 179, and 182–3.

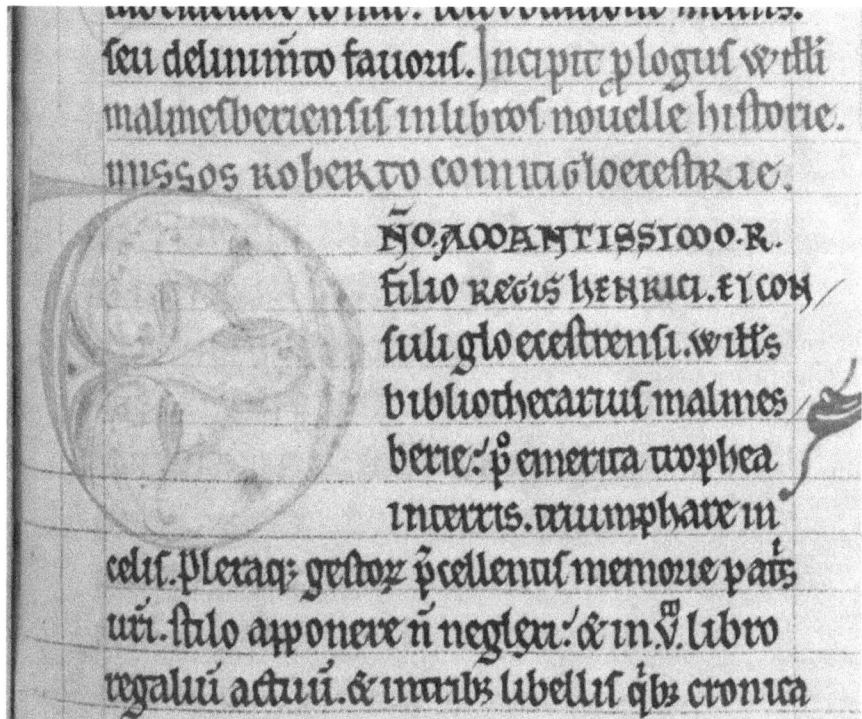

**Figure 6.1.** The rubricated Prologue of Margam Abbey's copy in an unidentified hand of William of Malmesbury's *Historia Novella* sent to Robert earl of Gloucester. BL, MS Royal 13 D.ii, fol. 110r, col. a, ll. 30–2; partial text of dedication to the earl, ll. 30–41.
© British Library/Granger.

*Engles*, the earliest surviving historiographical work written in French, possibly between March 1136 and April 1137.[4] Although the circumstances surrounding the earl's commission are unknown, this effort establishes him as a participant in the Anglo-Norman realm's insular multicultural environment and, with the added details of the book's travels, as an agent in the lay baronage's assimilation of Celtic culture through "hard and soft power."[5] Furthermore, scholars have accepted that

---

[4] *Geffrei Gaimar Estoire des Engleis*, ll. 6447–58 & pp. xxv, 349, esp. 455 re. l. 4636; Short, "Gaimar's Epilogue and Geoffrey of Monmouth's *Liber Vetustissimus*," 337–9; Gillingham, "The Context and Purposes of Geoffrey of Monmouth's *History of the Kings of Britain*," 105 & n. 33; for other meanings and uses of "translate," see Damian-Grint, *The New Historians of the Twelfth-Century Renaissance*, 20–32, esp. 24–5; see also Brooke, "Geoffrey of Monmouth as a Historian," 97. Ian Short's dating of 1136 × 7 for an existing text of the *HRB* is not affected by the date of Henry of Huntingdon's exposure to the work at Bec: Henry of Huntingdon (1996), lxi, 558–9, 582–3; Robert of Torigny, "Chronica," 65; Dumville, "An Early Text of Geoffrey of Monmouth's *Historia regum Britanniae* and the Circulation of Some Latin Manuscripts in Twelfth-Century Normandy," 17–23; Bates, "Robert of Torigni and the *Historia Anglorum*," 176–8; Pohl, "When Did Robert of Torigni First Receive Henry of Huntingdon's *Historia Anglorum* and Why Does it Matter?," 164.

[5] Bartlett, *England under the Norman and Angevin Kings*, 482–506; Bates, *The Normans and Empire*, 4, 19, 50, 82–3, 87, 97–8.

the earl's book was an early version of Geoffrey of Monmouth's *Historia Regum Britanniae*; and that, plus Robert's patronage of Geoffrey himself, makes the earl a contributor to the dissemination of the Arthurian legend.[6] Still more interesting: if John Gillingham is correct, the spark which led ultimately to Earl Robert's acquisition of the *Historia Regum Britanniae* from Geoffrey was the Welsh attacks on Anglo-Norman colonial settlements in South Wales in 1135–6 which Robert had helped to quell by a treaty with the invading Welsh princes.[7] Not for nothing did the earl, his family, and his Bristol and Cardiff *capita* gain various places in later medieval romance verse chronicles; and his death was cause for him to be mourned as a lost Cicero and Virgil in Serlo of Wilton's funeral eulogy.[8] Gloucester's exercise of lordship in his Welsh lands envisioned more than seigniorial exploitation, administrative and demesne development, even political compromises, and sought to maximize what he had acquired by marriage or conquest by learning of its past.

Earl Robert's first two careers primed him to solicit a self-serving history of his time. He had been raised by his father to be a *miles litteratus* and became one of those clerical and lay officials upon whom the king's administration relied by reason of their varying literate skills.[9] The literary atmosphere of his father's court would have been an inspiration. Robert's curial colleague Alexander bishop of Lincoln, as already noted, was Henry of Huntingdon's patron and reputedly urged Geoffrey of Monmouth to publish more about the prophecies of Merlin. Robert's two stepmothers, Queens Matilda and Adeliza of Louvain, were patrons of historians. Matilda already had commissioned William of Malmesbury to write the *Gesta Regum Anglorum* and Adeliza, an unknown David for a now lost history of Henry I.[10] And Anglo-Norman poets Benedeit, author *The Voyage of St. Brendan*, and Philippe de Thaon, through his *Bestiaire*, wrote for, respectively, Matilda and Adeliza. Matilda's lavish generosity, known far and wide, is said to have attracted flocks of scholars, especially foreigners.[11]

The earl of Gloucester's commission gained the expertise of the English historian, who saw himself as the successor of Bede and whom modern scholars consider England's greatest since the monk of Jarrow. William was about the same age as

---

[6] Short, "Gaimar's Epilogue and Geoffrey of Monmouth's *Liber vetustissimus*," 338; but see Damian-Grint, *The New Historians of the Twelfth-Century Renaissance*, 106; Leckie, *The Passage of Dominion: Geoffrey of Monmouth and the Periodization of Insular History in the Twelfth Century*, 78–86; Gransden, *Historical Writing* i. 203; see also Chapt. 1, 11.

[7] e.g., Bell, *L'Estoire des Engleis*, li; Short, "Gaimar's Epilogue and Geoffrey of Monmouth's *Liber vetustissimus*," 340; Gillingham, "The Context and Purposes of Geoffrey of Monmouth's *History of the Kings of Britain*," esp. 110–16; see also Chapt. 2, 78.

[8] *Serlon de Wilton Poèmes latins*, no, 15, ll. 11, 13: "Plangite Robertum...Marcum...Maronem"; Solan, "A Study of the Life and Works of Serlo of Wilton," 50, 144. "Cont. Wace," 103–5; *The Metrical Chronicle of Robert of Gloucester* ii. 633–6.

[9] *GR* i. Letter III, 10–13, §447 (798–9); *GOE*, 157–63; Hollister, *MMI*, 311–12; Hollister, *Henry I*, 495; Chapt. 1, 10–11; Chapt. 2, 30.

[10] *GR* i. xiii–xv, Letters I–II, 2–9; Thomson, *GR* ii. 6–7: the Tt recension; Thomson, *William of Malmesbury*, rev. edn., 7, 18, 36–7. Legge, "L'Influence littéraire de la cour d'Henri Beauclerc," 682–6. David's work is lost; Henry I also had several works from Fleury dedicated to him: Brett, "John of Worcester and his Contemporaries," 114, 118; see also Chapt. 2, 49.

[11] *GR* i. 756–7; Letters I–II, 2–9; Legge, *Anglo-Norman Literature*, 8–26; Bartlett, *England under the Norman and Angevin Kings*, 497; note also Clanchy, *From Memory to Written Record*, 215–16.

his patron, born possibly as early as 1085 × 90 of Saxon and Norman parents. He had been placed in Malmesbury at a very early age, became a professed monk, was educated in the liberal arts, and ultimately served as the abbey's precentor and librarian.[12]

Malmesbury Abbey in William's day under the leadership of Abbot Godfrey of Jumièges (1084 × 91–before 1106) was becoming re-established as a center of Benedictine culture; William not only contributed to the process as supervisor of scribes, copyist, and collector of books for the library, but became himself the abbey's most illustrious embodiment as an author and man of letters.[13] Currently nineteen original works and thirteen edited collections have been attributed to him, a surprising number of which survive in his own hand. These included biblical commentary, hagiography, the liturgy, florilegia of stories from western literature and of precepts for a religious life, and history. His edited collections represent great categories of early western pagan and Christian writing: biblical commentary, grammar, philosophy, theology, canon law, and history.

The works and authors William of Malmesbury cited in his various writings reveal the breadth of his learning; leading modern scholars to consider him a true polymath. Of such resources Professor Rodney Thomson has identified some 400 works by 200 pagan and Christian authors of which William had reading knowledge.[14] Malmesbury shared St. Jerome's love for the pagan classics and also his pangs of conscience about it. Virgil and Cicero were William's favorite authors and classical topoi often chosen modes for expressing himself. Among patristic authors, he relied heavily upon Jerome and St. Augustine. Carolingian resources for William included Paul the deacon, Rabanus Maurus, Paschasius Radbertus, and John Scotus Erigena; among the more proximate and contemporary, Ivo of Chartres, Lanfranc, and St. Anselm.[15]

William's training in the arts, a process he somewhat emotionally describes in the Prologue of the *Gesta Regum Anglorum's* second book, led him to become the kind of literary specialist Robert of Gloucester was looking for.[16] By the time Earl Robert commissioned Malmesbury, he had produced the *Historia Pontificalis*, the *Gesta Pontificum Anglorum*, *De Antiquitate Glastonie Ecclesie*, and the final draft of his *Gesta Regum Anglorum*. In them he had applied critical skills which

---

[12] *GR* i. "Prologue," 1–8; 796–7; Galbraith, *Historical Research in Medieval England*, 15, 17, 23; Farmer, "William of Malmesbury's Life and Works," 39; Southern, "Aspects of the European Tradition of Historical Writing IV: The Sense of the Past," 253; Southern, *Medieval Humanism*, 160–1; Gransden, *Historical Writing* i. Chapt. 9; King, *Anarchy of King Stephen's Reign*, 2; Thomson, *William of Malmesbury*, rev. edn., 4–6; Thomson, "Malmesbury, William of," 348; Bartlett, *England under the Norman and Angevin Kings*, 624; Chibnall, *Anglo-Norman England*, 215.

[13] Knowles, *HRH*, 55; Thomson, *William of Malmesbury*, rev. edn., 4–5; Thomson, "Malmesbury, William of," 348.

[14] Farmer, "William of Malmesbury's Life and Works," 39; Thomson, *GR* ii. xlvi–xlvii; Thomson, *William of Malmesbury*, rev. edn., 10, 202–14, Chapt. 3; Sharpe, *A Handlist of Latin Writers*, no. 2114; Sharpe, *Additions and Corrections*, no. 147; Gransden, *Historical Writing* i. 166.

[15] Thomson, *William of Malmesbury*, rev. edn., 41–4, 46–9; Gransden, "Prologues in the Historiography of Twelfth-Century England," 55–66, 69–78.

[16] *GR* i. 150–3; Gransden, "Prologues in the Historiography of Twelfth-Century England," 150–3; Thomson, *William of Malmesbury*, rev. edn., 14–15.

have been another major reason for modern scholars' admiration for him as a historian: aggressive imaginative pursuit and use of a wide range of source materials from the written and oral to the visual, architectural, and artifactual; determining the reliability of collected data by the application of rational criteria; and the ability to revise his work on the basis of new evidence or reconsideration of prior judgments. The first of these involved consultation of such items as chronicles, annals, biographical and hagiographical works, charters, visitation of local archives to consult sources, even correspondence with another historian, John of Worcester; the second, such criteria as sources' reliability, authority, style, age, and content and relationship to their historical context.[17]

Nonetheless, William also had failings which have not gone unnoticed: he could be inconsistent in applying his criteria, credulous, mythologize when dealing with recent events, deferential to propaganda, biased, and capable of embroidering on a single shred of evidence—even of using forged documents.[18] Not surprisingly, some of these scholarly pluses and minuses, as we shall see, are present in Malmesbury's *Historia Novella*, particularly in treatments of his patron.[19]

Robert had good reason to expect favorable treatment from Malmesbury. Rodney Thomson has suggested that Robert's knowledge of William's *Gesta Regum Anglorum* may have stretched back even to about 1126. The earl almost certainly received a presentation copy of the work's version of *c.*1135 from William to solicit his patronage.[20] Presentation copies such as these were implicit solicitations for patronage in the pre-printing Middle Ages.[21] Geoffrey of Monmouth's *Historia Regum Britanniae* even included in its dedication a request for Robert's possible corrections.[22] Malmesbury's *Gesta Regum Anglorum* was tailored especially for the earl, with a very personal dedication and an epilogue of three chapters brimming with complimentary remarks about him which included praise for his support for the arts and writers and generosity toward Tewkesbury Abbey.[23] Furthermore,

---

[17] Southern, "Aspects of the European Tradition of Historical Writing IV: The Sense of the Past," 255; Gransden, *Historical Writing* i. Chapt. 9, esp. 169–70, 174–7, 181–2; Gransden, "Prologues in the Historiography of Twelfth-Century England," 58–9, 70–6; Thomson, *William of Malmesbury*, rev. edn., Chapt. 2, esp. 16–24; Scott, *The Early History of Glastonbury*, 10, believes in a probable meeting with John of Worcester.

[18] Malmesbury, *GP*, 104–5; Southern, *St. Anselm and his Biographer*, 247 & n.; Gransden, *Historical Writing* i. esp. 176–7; Thomson, *William of Malmesbury*, rev. edn., 24–5; Bradbury, *Stephen and Matilda*, 125; Scott, *The Early History of Glastonbury*, 32: Malmesbury could reject oral testimony, but deferred to it from reliable men.

[19] See 187–97.

[20] Thomson, *GR* ii. xxxiii, n. 26, 6; the **A** and **C** versions, respectively. For the revisions of the *GR* and their dates, see *GR* i., xiii–xxvi, esp. xxii–xxiv; ii. xvii–xxxv, esp. xxxii–xxxv, 6; Thomson, *William of Malmesbury*, rev. edn., 37.

[21] Crick and Walsham, *The Uses of Script and Print*, 30; Gransden, "Prologues in the Historiography of Twelfth-Century England," 61–3.

[22] BL, MS Royal 13 D.ii, fol. 124r. col. a, but an empty topos; see also *HRB*, ll. 17–23, p. 5; Wright, *The Historia Regum Britanniae of Geoffrey of Monmouth*, 5: xii–xv; Gransden, "Prologues in the Historiography of Twelfth-Century England," 73.

[23] *GR* i. Letter III, 10–13, 798–801. Thomson, *William of Malmesbury*, rev. edn., 6–8. Thomson and Winterbottom have revised Stubbs's designation of manuscripts deriving from three editions of the *GR* designated as **A**, **B**, and **C**: Stubbs, William of Malmesbury, *GR* i. xliii–xliv & ff. They have introduced a new **T** as the version (or a transcript) made for the Empress Matilda, and established that

included in the later *Gesta Regum Anglorum* were two letters written around 1126, respectively, to Matilda's uncle King David of Scotland and to the empress herself from the community of Malmesbury and very possibly from William himself; and they show what direction their loyalties were in advance of the succession crisis of 1135. Both letters sought to free the community from the rule of their titular abbot, Bishop Roger of Salisbury, holder of the abbacy in plurality since 1118, and to obtain Matilda's influence for a free election. The first letter sought David's help in this enterprise. The second one recognized Matilda to be her father's legitimate heir. Both are thought to be William of Malmesbury's work.[24]

Malmesbury began work by late 1140 on Earl Robert's commission. The work was dedicated to the earl and called appropriately the *Historia Novella* ("The History of Recent Events"). As will be seen, to William, this era's most defining thread had been the struggle to procure the Anglo-Norman throne for Matilda as Henry I's heir, in which his patron had always been her unflinchingly loyal advocate. Since Earl Robert had initially accepted Stephen of Blois's succession instead of Matilda's, that awkward fact had to be explained. For these reasons, William's history would be largely an apologia, but, as Reginald Darlington once put it, with a partisanship that makes it all the more interesting. Malmesbury's text records events only as far as December 1142, quite possibly because he died the next year;[25] and the earl's copy gave him or a family member later opportunities to polish his image further.[26]

To fulfill his commission William of Malmesbury recounted the defining story of the current Anglo-Norman realm. What the establishment of Christianity and of a monastic culture in Britain was to Bede's *Ecclesiastical History*, the dynastic struggle over succession to King Henry I was to Malmesbury's *Historia Novella*. William told his story with an overall bias in favor of Matilda's cause and interwove with it an apologia for his patron's pro-Angevin politics and a panegyric of him. More than any other of his fellow historians William shows how the principals in his story and the course of the succession struggle were affected by factors such as emerging customs of inheritance, feudal relations, and the roles of the papacy and members of the English Church; and if the function of a single institution were to be singled out as pivotal in the story's issues, use, observance, or violation of oaths would rank first.[27]

---

Stubbs's A manuscripts derive from the second major revision and his C & B manuscripts from the third: *GR* i. xiii–xxvi; ii. xvi–xxxiv.

[24] *GR* i. Letters I–II, 2–9; Thomson, *GR* ii. esp. xxii–xxiii, 6–10; Thomson, *William of Malmesbury*, rev. edn., 36–7; Weiler, "William of Malmesbury, King Henry I, and the *Gesta Regum Anglorum*," 169; see also Chibnall, *Empress Matilda*, 47.

[25] *HN* (1998), 2–3; Malmesbury's mention of being commissioned to write the *HN* by Robert is the first of many classical topoi the author employed in the work: Gransden, "Prologues in the Historiography of Twelfth-Century England," 55–60, 62–3, 65–6, 70–6; Stubbs, in William of Malmesbury, *GR* i. xxxvii; Darlington, *Anglo-Norman Historians*, 9; Bradbury, "The Early Years of the Reign of Stephen," 17, 24; Smalley, *Historians in the Middle Ages*, 92; King, "Anarchy of King Stephen's Reign," 6–7. For the *HN*'s dates of composition, see King, xxx–xxxiii; and of interest, Gullick, "How Fast Did Scribes Write? Evidence from Romanesque Manuscripts," 39–58. For the illness which may have caused William's death, see 197–8.

[26] King, *HN* (1998), esp. xci–xciv; see also 183, Figure 6.1, 179; 198–9 in this volume.

[27] Patterson, "Anarchy in England 1135–54," 189–200.

Key elements of Malmesbury's Matilda theme are laid out with lawyerly logic. The empress was Henry I's legitimate daughter whose royal lineage was traceable back centuries in the house of Wessex through her mother Edith/Matilda. Due to the death of her brother William Aetheling, her father made her his *heres legitima* and later confirmed this on his deathbed. Fealty to her succession, failing a legitimate male heir to Henry, had been sworn by the Anglo-Norman baronage on several occasions at great councils.[28] Furthermore, Matilda's Angevin marriage was an integral part of her father's succession plan. Readers could see that the groundwork for it had been laid prior to the 1127 conciliar fealty to Matilda's succession and that the nuptials took place relatively soon afterwards. The union's purpose was to make peace with the county of Anjou and to restrain its power. Matilda's and Geoffrey's sons, particularly Henry (the future Henry II), thus were the heirs to the Anglo-Norman throne.[29]

To Malmesbury, Matilda's right made Stephen of Blois effectively a *rex illicitus*, an illegal ruler, because he had broken his oath to Matilda's succession; and Matilda had to vindicate her claim by force of arms. This was the old Norman case against Harold Godwinson all over again, of which Malmesbury was well aware from his knowledge of William of Poitiers and William of Jumièges.[30] William also made it clear that Archbishop William of Canterbury and Stephen's supporters were oathbreakers as well. But at the same time, Malmesbury recognized that Stephen was a duly anointed king and labeled his supporters *peruersi*—perverters—not as the Gloucester comital copy of the *Historia Novella* called them perjurers.[31]

Malmesbury also took extra care to ensure that readers of his *historia* would not miss his patron's role in supporting his sister and especially his justification for doing so. Elaboration of this Gloucester theme occupies much of Book 1 and appears briefly again in a detailed résumé of Earl Robert's role in Book 3.[32] There, as Malmesbury's translated words put it, "It has occurred to me...to make into a parcel, as it were, the main points scattered through my text bearing on the conduct of Robert, earl of Gloucester, King Henry's son, and to present them in a recapitulation for the reader to evaluate."[33]

In a nutshell, William's position was that his patron was true-blue in loyalty to his sister's succession from the first.[34] At the very beginning of the succession issue, the baronage's sworn fealty to Matilda in 1127, Earl Robert had vied with Stephen for precedence in swearing.[35] Then are noted Robert's association with his father's Angevin marriage plan for Matilda and his presence at Henry's deathbed confirmation of her right of succession.[36] After his father's death and Stephen's coronation, Earl Robert in Normandy anguished over the course he should take regarding the royal succession. Submitting to Stephen would mean violating his oath to Matilda; but given the extent of support for Stephen, backing his sister or his nephews

---

[28] *HN* (1998), 6–9, 18–21, 24–5.  [29] *HN* (1998), 124–7.
[30] Thomson, *William of Malmesbury*, rev. edn., 69, 124, 207.
[31] BL, MS Royal 13 D.ii, fol. 110b: *erga p(er)iuros*; *HN* (1998), 2 & n. *e*.
[32] *HN* (1998), 4–43, 112–15.  [33] *HN* (1998), 112–13, esp. 112–33.
[34] Smalley, *Historians in the Middle Ages*, 91.  [35] *HN* (1998), 8–9.
[36] *HN* (1998), 10–11, 24–5.

would be a futile gesture and likely be damaging to his own welfare: better to dissimulate and attempt to persuade the baronage to honor their oaths to the empress. Thus, Robert came to Stephen's court after Easter 1136, where his formal submission occurred. This involved swearing fealty, but, knowing that Stephen would be unable to keep his word, only on condition that the king would maintain his dignity and would keep the agreement.[37] Thus Robert's first political volte-face was explained away and the fiction of unflinching loyalty to Matilda preserved.

In expectation, as it were, of Stephen's violation of their pact, in 1137 Earl Robert canvassed the level of barons' support for their oaths to Matilda and put his own affairs in order before joining the king in Normandy. After the earl arrived, the king began to fulfill Robert's expectation of perfidy. First Stephen, egged on by William d'Ypres, attempted to take the earl prisoner in an ambush. Peace was restored between the king and earl by the openly repentant king swearing a new oath to the earl never to attempt such treachery again, and reinforcing this pact by pledging the archbishop of Rouen as security. Yet, at the same time, Stephen cheated Robert of what possessions he could. Gloucester remained in Normandy outwardly loyal for the rest of the year while inwardly committed to his original duplicitous plan.[38]

Finally, in 1138 immediately after Pentecost (May 22), Earl Robert formally renounced his fealty and homage and joined the Angevins.[39] He was justified in doing so because Stephen had unlawfully seized the throne in violation of his oath to Matilda and had broken their pact. Furthermore, many ecclesiastics whom Robert had consulted had warned him of the shame and danger to his salvation failure to honor his oath to the empress would bring him. In addition the tenor of an *apostolicum decretum*, a papal pronouncement of some sort, but less likely a papal letter, which Malmesbury promised to include later in his *Historia*, directed the earl to obey his oath.[40] As a result, the earl was compelled by the opinions of respected ecclesiastics and the papal text to get on with supporting the empress.

The next step was for Earl Robert to undertake political and military actions on his sister's behalf against King Stephen.[41] To Malmesbury, Robert's leading role in the royal succession drama was so evident that in many passages referring to Gloucester's activities he is simply referred to as "the earl."[42] No other Angevin supporters the *Historia Novella* mentions, such as King David of Scotland, Brian fitz Count, or Miles of Gloucester, are given such a starring role. Especially noteworthy are the low-key activities Malmesbury reported for Matilda's royal uncle. He had been a member of Matilda's inner circle in the late 1120s, was perceived then as such by William and the Malmesbury community, and swore fealty to her succession first among the lay baronage in 1127.[43]

---

[37] *HN* (1998), 26–7, 30–3.    [38] *HN* (1998), 36–41.
[39] *HN* (1998), 40–1.
[40] *HN* (1998), 40–2 & n., 43; Malmesbury used *epistolae* and *scripta* for "letters": *GP*, 182–3; *HN* (1998), 14–15, 24–5; *sigillatim breuia* for sealed writs: 120–1; later Malmesbury referred to the papal *mandatum* the earl had remembered to obey the oath he had sworn to his sister in his father's presence: *HN* (1998), 120–1.
[41] *HN* (1998), 60.    [42] *HN* (1998), e.g., 32, 36, 38, 72.
[43] *ASC a.*1126; *GR* i. "Letter I," 2–5; *HN* (1998), 8, 30, 98, 102, 112.

By contrast, the *Historia Novella* portrays Robert of Gloucester as the chief leader of the empress's party.[44] He alone is mentioned canvassing the Anglo-Norman baronage's level of loyalty to her in 1135–7 and 1140 and, in the latter case, urging the magnates of England to respect their former oaths.[45] Matilda's 1139 arrival in England was under his auspices.[46] The *Historia* cites only Robert from the delegation of Matilda's advisers whom she sent in 1140 to parley with Stephen about a possible peace; and it is the earl who with Matilda agreed to peace terms later proposed by Bishop Henry of Winchester.[47] After his victory at Lincoln, Robert and the empress each sent messengers to Bishop Henry urging her recognition as King Henry's successor.[48] As far as Count Geoffrey of Anjou was concerned, Robert was the only baron of Matilda's party who was acceptable to represent the baronage in negotiations to gain his participation in the English theater of war in 1142.[49] Finally, the *Historia* shows that even Stephen's party recognized Earl Robert's primacy in the Angevin party. During his captivity following the Rout of Winchester he was plied with the offer of a place tantamount to that of chief of staff and premier counselor in Stephen's administration; and he was treated as the king's equal in the mutual exchange treaty which resulted in their release.[50]

Although his name alone might not suffice on occasion to warrant certain promises Matilda made, Robert also is portrayed as Matilda's virtual viceroy. He created his half-brother Reginald earl of Cornwall in 1140.[51] Then, during the following summer, the earl won barons' adherence to her cause by promises and threats delivered by his legates and imposed peace through the rule of law in areas loyal to Matilda.[52]

Without explicitly saying so, the *Historia* also presents Angevin campaigns against Stephen as mainly the earl's. His force of 140 knights escorted Matilda to England in 1139. Although Ranulf earl of Chester won mention in connection with the battle of Lincoln, Earl Robert receives most of the *Historia*'s attention and credit for the victory. Malmesbury reports the earl afterwards leading his royal captive before the empress and then being awarded custody of Stephen as his prize.[53] Although the earl was one of four barons Malmesbury listed as joining in the attack on Winchester later in 1141, Robert's army is given exclusive attention in the chronicler's account and the earl is depicted as making the command decision to retreat, placing Matilda in the vanguard, and heroically making possible her escape from the rout.[54] In 1142 Robert's assistance to Geoffrey of Anjou in Normandy is credited with the capture of ten castles.[55]

No autograph or "Malmesbury Authorized Version" of William's *Historia Novella* has survived for assessing the value of Earl Robert's patronage. The work exists only as copies in ten surviving medieval manuscripts. By collating their *Historia* texts modern scholars first classified them in three (A, B, and C) and

---

[44] *HN* (1998), 112–13.   [45] *HN* (1998), 36–9, 72–3.   [46] *HN* (1998), 60–1.
[47] *HN* (1998), 76–9.   [48] *HN* (1998), 86–9.   [49] *HN* (1998), 122–5.
[50] *HN* (1998), 116–21.   [51] *HN* (1998), 73–5.   [52] *HN* (1998), 96–7.
[53] *HN* (1998), 82–7.   [54] *HN* (1998), 104–7.   [55] *HN* (1998), 126–7.

then two (AB and Ce) labeled groups.[56] Building on their findings, Edmund King established Malmesbury's text from readings from one of them (AB) and a second post-obit edition aimed at enhancing Earl Robert's image from the other (Ce), thus doubling the potential for appreciating the earl's patronage.[57] The earlier and most important representative of this promotional text (Ce[1]) is in a codex from the library of the earl's foundation Margam Abbey, identified by the manuscript's early thirteenth-century *ex libris* inscription (Figure 6.2).[58]

The history which William of Malmesbury wrote on Earl Robert's commission (AB) is the obvious basis for evaluating the two as, respectively, a historian and apologist.[59] The chronicler himself with classical topoi invited readers to do this at

Figure 6.2. *Ex libris* inscription in an unidentified hand of Margam Abbey's codex containing copies of William of Malmesbury's *Gesta Regum Anglorum* and *Historia Novella* and Geoffrey of Monmouth's *Historia Regum Britanniae (De Gestis Britonum)*. BL, MS Royal 13 D.ii, fol. 173v, col. b.
© British Library/Granger.

---

[56] A Group: Bodl., MS Laud Misc. 548; Oxford, All Souls College, MS 35; Cambridge, Trinity College, Wren Library, MS R.7.10; B Group: BL, MS Royal 13 B.xix; Bodl., MS Bodley 712; Cambridge, Trinity College Wren Library, MS R.7.1; C Group: BL, MS Royal 13 D.ii (Ce[1]); BL, Additional MS 38129 (Ce[2], a descendant of a duplicate of Ce[1]; Ce is their ancestor); BL, MS Royal 13 D.v (Cd). For their classifications, see Hardy, William of Malmesbury, *GR* ii. xxiii–xxv; Stubbs, William of Malmesbury, *GR* i. lxv–lxix, lxxxii–lxxxiii; Mynors, William of Malmesbury, *HN*, xli–xliii. King, *HN* (1998), lxvii–lxxix; BL MS Arundel 161 (Cm) is a copy of MS Royal D.v. I have collated nine passages relating to Earl Robert in the ten medieval manuscripts.

[57] See the definitive case presented by Professor King in the new text of the *Historia* he edited, *HN* (1998), lxxvi–lxxxix, xciii–xciv & n. The Margam library's *ex libris* inscription reads: *Liber monachor(um) s(an)c(t)e marie de margan*, on fol. 173v, col. b, below the last line of the text; for paleographical dating, see n. 58 & n. 155; see above Figure 6.2.

[58] BL, MS. Royal 13 D.ii (the main text of William of Malmesbury, *HN*); Additional MS 38129. MS Arundel 161 contains copies of several sections BL, MS Royal 13 D.5; Hardy, William of Malmesbury, GR ii. xxii; Mynors, William of Malmesbury, *HN*, xl–xliii; King, *HN* (1998), lxxiv–lxxx; Birch, *Margam Abbey*, 278; see Patterson, *The Scriptorium of Margam Abbey*: see p. 102 for Margam Clerk 11's treatment of minims' feet in his endorsement on NLW, P & M Charter no. 73, Plate XXVIIIi; Jennifer Sheppard argues that *ex libris* marks are not proof of books' production at a library's house: "The Twelfth-Century Library and Scriptorium at Buildwas," esp. 196–7; see n. 155.

[59] Note the general comment of Stubbs in William of Malmesbury, *GR* ii. cxli; Round, *Geoffrey de Mandeville*, 115; Davis, *King Stephen*, 3rd edn., 144; Gransden, *Historical Writing* i. 180, 183; Thomson, *William of Malmesbury*, 35 & n.; Bradbury, "The Early Years of the Reign of Stephen," 17; Bradbury, *Stephen and Matilda*, 24, 43; King, *Anarchy*, 6; King, *HN* (1998), esp. lxxix.

least for the first role, writing that his *historia* was based only on the truth as he knew it "without any concession to dislike or favor" and that he "always dreaded putting in writing, for transmission to posterity, anything that [he] did not know to be factual."[60] Robert of Gloucester's *gesta* were not included in a previous year's events, William informs us, because at the time he was ignorant of them and because he always sought to put into writing only what he knew to be "established fact."[61] In reporting Bishop Roger of Salisbury's excuse for repudiating his oath of support for the empress's succession, William tellingly adds, "In saying this I would not wish it to be thought that I accepted the word of a man who knew how to adapt himself to any occasion according as the wheel of fortune turned."[62] And he defended his reporting by adding, "Yet at the same time, I merely, like a faithful historian, add to my narrative what was thought by people in my part of the country."[63] At least once, Malmesbury even admits that the motives he attributed to the earl for attacking Stephen at Lincoln in 1141 were his own surmises.[64]

Foremost among the *Historia Novella*'s assets are details for which the work is the sole source, especially those involving Malmesbury's patron. A good number have added value as important elements of Earl Robert's three careers. Early on, the *Historia* presents the essential element of Robert's social metamorphosis, his father's recognition of him as his son, several signature features of Robert's curial career, the new earl of Gloucester's additional award of the royal constable of Gloucester's vassalage, and his membership in his father's elite group of advisers.[65] For the third career, there are examples of Robert's exercise of viceregal power, mustering and strategic authority, political initiatives in recruiting and diplomatic dealings, and allusions to the curial status he enjoyed as the empress's *familiaris*.[66]

Particularly valuable are the images of his patron the chronicler left scattered throughout his *Historia*.[67] There is the king's son, proud of his royal lineage, well educated in the arts, and possessed of a prudence and wisdom admired by both friend and foe.[68] He practiced the virtues expected of an ideal knight, prowess, bravery, chivalric courtesy, but loyalty above all else, "for which he deserved to be praised for all ages."[69] His politics and military tactics were well considered, calculated, prudent, and diplomatic.[70] Yet he fought the most famous battle of the

---

[60] *HN* (1998), 2–3, 112–13, also 122–3; Gransden, "Prologues in the Historiography of Twelfth-Century England," 56, 71–2.
[61] *HN* (1998), 122–3. [62] *HN* (1998), 10–11. [63] *HN* (1998), 10–11.
[64] *HN* (1998), 80. [65] *HN* (1998), 8–9, 10–11, 62–3.
[66] *HN* (1998), 130–1 (mustering), 72–3, 78–9, 86–7, 96–7, 100–1 (diplomatic), 104–5, 130–1 (strategy), 72–5 (viceregal), 88–9, 96–7(curial status).
[67] Gransden, *Historical Writing* i. 171 & nn., 173, 205; Thomson, *GR* ii., xliii. Malmesbury did not use the Suetonian topical format, however: Schütt, "The Literary Forms of William of Malmesbury's 'Gesta Regum'," 255–6, 260; Galbraith, *Historical Research in Medieval England*, 17. See also William's assessment of Earl Robert in *GR* i., esp. 798–801.
[68] *HN* (1998), 8–9, 30–3, 42–3, 112–13, 122–3; see also Henry of Huntingdon (1996), 726–9; *GS* (1996), 168–9.
[69] *HN* (1998), 24–5, 60–1, 84–7, 104–7, 114–15; see also *HN* (1998), 106–9, 112–13, 120–1.
[70] *HN* (1998), 30–1, 40–3, 72–3, 96–7, 118–21; see also *GS* (2004), esp. 104–5, 144–7, 172–3; Prestwich, "Military Intelligence under the Norman and Angevin Kings," 16. The *GS* (2004), 206–7, reported the earl of Gloucester's stinginess toward his nephew, Henry fitz Empress; on the author's supposed royalist bias, see King, "The *Gesta Stephani*," 203–5.

Anarchy, Lincoln, in large part for personal reasons, in order to avenge the wrong King Stephen had done to his son-in-law and to save his daughter Countess Mabel of Chester from capture by King Stephen, and kept the reason secret from his men.[71]

Some of Earl Robert's biographical details enjoy the added strength of complete or at least partial confirmation by independent sources: his diplomatically alluded-to bastardy;[72] the earl's presence at his father's death;[73] Robert's oath after Stephen's with other magnates to accept Matilda's succession;[74] Stephen's unlawful succession and violation of his oath to Matilda;[75] Robert's defiance of the king;[76] the earl's landing in England with Matilda in 1139;[77] diplomatic involvement with allies;[78] his 1141 participation in the battle of Lincoln, capture of Stephen, followed by his own capture as a result of the Rout of Winchester; and exchange for Stephen.[79]

King Stephen's failure to sustain the earl of Gloucester's *dignitas*, shorthand for his personal status and lands and the *sine qua non* condition for Robert's homage, is one of William of Malmesbury's most important Gloucester revelations. In my view, the *Historia*'s allegation of its violation was the driving force behind Earl Robert's exculpatory renunciation of homage:[80] his cited legal arguments and ecclesiastical imperatives were just window dressing. Robert could accept not being king; he could not stomach loss of the benefits of his first two careers, particularly the second. That had occurred between 1135 and 1138 by being replaced among the royal *familiares* by Waleran of Meulan and William d'Ypres and passed over for curial assignments.[81] Geoffrey of Monmouth's dedications of his *Historia Regum Britanniae* seem to record the shifts in political prominence from Robert to the new king and his power broker.[82]

Stephen's other alleged violation of Robert's *dignitas*, disseisins or attempted ones, is often not viewed in this context, but rather as the king's retaliatory sanctions for the earl's *diffidatio*. However, the chronicler may have been chronologically correct. What Malmesbury wrote was that Stephen robbed or cheated Robert of his possessions as much as he could, "quibus poterat possessionibus uellicabat."[83]

---

[71] *HN* (1998), 82–5.   [72] *HN* (1998), 8–9; *GS* (2004), 12–13.
[73] *HN* (1998), 24–5; *OV* vi. 448–9.
[74] *HN* (1998), 24–5; Henry of Huntingdon (1996), 706–7; *JW* iii. 176–81 (not entirely reliable). Sources which merely mention the event have been omitted.
[75] *HN* (1998), 40–3; Henry of Huntingdon (1996), 700–1; "Annales Wintonienses cum contin. S. Augustini Cantuar.," 82; Robert of Torigny, "*Chronica*," 127 (from Henry of Huntingdon).
[76] *HN* (1998), 40–3; *OV* vi. 516–19; *GS* (2004), 56–7; Henry of Huntingdon (1996), 712–13; *JW* iii. 248–9.
[77] *HN* (1998), 60–1; *OV* vi. 534–5; *GS* (2004), 86–7; *JW* iii. 268–9.
[78] *HN* (1998), 72–5, 96–7; Chapt. 5, 148.
[79] *HN* (1998), 82–7, 100–7, 114–21; *GS* (2004), 128–33, 136–7; *JW* iii. 292–3, 302–3; Henry of Huntingdon (1996), 724–33, 740–1; John of Hexham, 308, 310–11; *ASC a*.1140 (*recte* 1141).
[80] *HN* (1998), 40–3; Gillingham, "1066 and the Introduction of Chivalry into England," 48–9; esp. Garnett, *Conquered England*, 217.
[81] HN (1998), 32–3; Patterson, "William of Malmesbury's Robert of Gloucester," 990–1; Crouch, "Robert of Gloucester and the Daughter of Zelophehad," 231.
[82] Crick, *Summary Catalogue*, nos. 39, 48–9, 107, 128, 133, 136, 170, 199.
[83] *HN* (1998), 38–9; see Patterson, "William of Malmesbury's Robert of Gloucester," 988–9; King in *HN* (1998), xlviii–xlix; Davis, *King Stephen*, 3rd edn., 35; Chibnall, *Empress Matilda*, 78; King, *King Stephen*, 86–90; Bradbury, *Stephen and Matilda*, 68; however, the post-*diffidatio* disseisins are not at issue.

And as we have seen, Dartford (Kent) and especially Burford (Oxon.) may be examples. There are obvious limitations as evidence, but, especially in the case of Burford, the king's visits to Earl Robert's demesne manor prior to his *diffidatio* could have had the earl at least feeling that the king was about to reclaim the manor as royal demesne.[84] Henry of Huntingdon apparently believed in at least the general truth of Earl Robert's deprivation by giving him a motivating speech to the dispossessed before the battle of Lincoln in 1141.[85]

Utilization of sources is one of Malmesbury's most praised attributes as a historian; and it is one of his *historia*'s ornaments. Literary works Malmesbury employed in the *Historia* were biblical, classical, and patristic, predictably for the edification and enjoyment of ecclesiastical readers, but possibly to appeal to a widely read patron. They are small in number by comparison to some of Malmesbury's other historical works, undoubtedly due to the *Historia*'s polemical focus and incomplete text. Most classical citations are from the *Aeneid* of Virgil, one of William's two most favorite pagan authors.[86] However, only three of these allusions were used to explain or embellish Earl Robert's *gesta*. One was a general reference to his bravery; another, to the difficulty in obtaining his release from captivity following the Rout of Winchester; and the third, to his steadfast resistance during that time to offers of future personal benefits if he changed sides.[87]

Malmesbury included transcriptions of letters of Hugh abbot of Reading and archbishop of Rouen to Pope Innocent II regarding Henry I's death and of the papal legate Peter of Porto, and a version of King Stephen's entire 1136 Charter of Liberties to the Church minus its witness-list.[88] William also referred to the contents of several other such sources. In a very famous example, he promised to publish the "apostolic decretal" mandating Earl Robert to obey his oath to Matilda in a later book of the *Historia*.[89]

William's own participation in events and his own assessments of them led to his reports of the two legatine Councils of Winchester in, respectively, 1139 and 1141.[90] He also exploited various types of oral testimony. He attributed his information most often to what he called rumors, widely held beliefs or reported details, and well-established data. The melodramatic oath-swearing contest of 1127 came from a report.[91] Malmesbury learned about the earl's landing in England from Normandy with 140 knights in 1139 from "trustworthy informants."[92]

---

[84] See Chapt. 5, 138.    [85] Henry of Huntingdon (2004), 726, 728.
[86] See King, *HN* (1998), Index of Quotations and Allusions (134); Thomson, *GR* ii. 457–66; Thomson, *William of Malmesbury*, rev. edn., 10, 16, 48 & n., 49, 214, also 51.
[87] *HN* (1998), 2–3, 118–19, 120–1.
[88] *HN* (1998), 14–19, 24–7, 34–7.
[89] *HN* (1998), 42: "Adde quod etiam apostolici decreti pre se tenorem ferebat, precipientis ut sacramento, quod presente patre fecerat, obediens esset. Cuius decreti paginam posteriori libello indicere curabo." See also *HN* (1998), 120–1. William possessed a Canon Law collection, the *Quesnelliana*, in which his own copy has been identified, Oxford, Oriel College MS 42: Thomson, *William of Malmesbury*, rev. edn., 11n., 20, 34, 46, 64–6, 96 & n., 124, 132; he also knew the "Collectio Lanfranci," 46, 66, 131–3, and apparently the "Decretum" of Ivo of Chartres, 43, 46, 144.
[90] *HN* (1998), 46–7, 90–1.
[91] *HN* (1998), 8–9: *ut fertur*. For other examples, see *HN* (1998), 106–9.
[92] *HN* (1998), 60–1.

The just-noted story of Bishop Roger of Salisbury's excuse for repudiating his oath to the empress was based both upon the chronicler's memory of conversations with Roger and on a supposedly common belief in the chronicler's part of the country.[93] William also overheard the bishop's well-founded misgivings about attending the Council of Oxford in 1139.[94]

An unnamed personal source for Malmesbury may well have been King Stephen's brother, Henry of Blois bishop of Winchester and papal legate, as evidence collected by Edmund King suggests. Henry, like Roger, would have been a logical pipeline for information about the royal court.[95] He or Earl Robert also would have been likely sources for the episode in the *Historia Novella* about the bishop's and Waleran of Meulan's escort of the empress partway to Bristol from the siege of Arundel in 1139.[96] Both men for William were the trustworthy types on whose testimony he could rely, as he explained elsewhere.[97]

Roger is the only personal source the *Historia Novella* specifically identifies, but there is a far more important one to which its author made no reference. The Gloucester story William of Malmesbury did not tell, and a major story indeed, is the contribution of information his patron Earl Robert of Gloucester made to his own commissioned work.[98] This identification depends on circumstantial evidence to be sure, but yields some reasonable examples.

Certain episodes Malmesbury included in the Matilda and Gloucester leitmotifs of his work point to William's patron as their anonymous source, whether transmitted directly by him or via a Gloucester official or even a family member. In a case for likely comital origin Edmund King put so well, the *Historia Novella's* rubric listing of Norman castles Earl Robert helped his brother-in-law Count Geoffrey capture in 1142 "seems almost like an extract from a letter home."[99] An interpolated reference in the *Historia Novella* to Countess Mabel as "having been given him (Earl Robert) in marriage...a true beauty and excellent woman, a lady who was both obedient to her husband and blessed in being the mother of numerous and very fair offspring" might have come from Earl Robert. The remark strikes all the husbandly aristocratic chords. Almost the same list of attributes gave Robert's paternal grandfather William I greater reason to love Queen Matilda I and, as will be seen, Robert may have read it. A likely Tewkesbury Abbey scribe has the earl "speak" at least once of Mabel as his spouse.[100]

Henry I's deathbed confirmation of the royal succession to Matilda appears to be another instance of Robertian origin. The earl was present and the reported

---

[93] *HN* (1998), 10–1.  [94] *HN* (1998), 46–7.
[95] King, *HN* (1998), xxiii–xxiv & nn.  [96] *HN* (1998), 62–3.
[97] *HN* (1998), xxxiii–xxxiv, 60–1; *GR* i. 16–17.
[98] King, *HN* (1998), xxxiii–xxxiv, 10–11; see also *GR* i. 16–17.
[99] BL, MS Royal D.ii, fol. 123; *HN* (1998), 126n.; King, *King Stephen*, 184.
[100] *HN* (1998), 8 & n. *e*; "Tulit ex Mathilde liberos multos, quae, et marito morigera et prole fecunda, nobilis uiri animum in sui amoris incitabat aculeum": *GR* i. 500–1; Patterson, *EGC*, no. 283; Truax, "From Bede to Orderic Vitalis: Changing Perspectives on the Role of Women in Anglo-Saxon and Anglo-Norman Churches," 48; Newman, *The Anglo-Norman Nobility in the Reign of Henry I*, 41–4; Fenton, *Gender, Nation and Conquest in the Works of William of Malmesbury*, 63–4, singles out this passage as an example of aristocratic bias.

episode was a nice piece of supportive propaganda for the *Historia*'s earl of Gloucester story as well as for the Matilda theme. The account had a royalist concocted counterpart according to which, predictably, Henry I designated Stephen of Blois as his successor.[101] Regarding Malmesbury's version, first of all one has to wonder why the king would make such a last-minute gesture in favor of Matilda when she and her husband were rebelling against him. Three recorders of the scene, Orderic Vitalis, Archbishop Hugh of Rouen, who was present at Henry's death, and Peter abbot of Cluny, who may have learned details from a messenger bearing Hugh's letter to the pope, are silent about any succession arrangements the king may have had in mind. Furthermore, the anonymous *Gesta Stephani* reported that Stephen's supporters claimed that the dying king repented of having forced his barons to swear to support Matilda's succession and intended for them to decide the issue.[102] One may conclude, then, that Henry I either made no definitive pronouncement about the succession or left the issue to be settled by the baronage.

The *Historia Novella*'s rationale for Earl Robert's performance of homage to Stephen in early 1136, to be examined, could have been another self-serving Gloucester transmission or simply be Malmesbury's exculpatory interpretation of his patron's act.[103] There seems little doubt about the status of the tale about King Stephen's treacherous attempt to kidnap Earl Robert at Livarot (Calvados) in 1137; their mode of reconciliation not only is traceable to Robert or a member of his traveling staff, but reflects badly on his reputation as a likely fabrication. The E text of the *Anglo-Saxon Chronicle* supports only the barest version: Stephen's attempt to capture Robert, foiled by the earl's discovery. However, even these few details may derive from the same source as the *Historia Novella*'s story and were written *c.*1155+, well after the alleged event. Orderic Vitalis states that Earl Robert's loyalty to Stephen was suspect, but mentions no attempt to capture Gloucester with or without the counsel of William d'Ypres. Orderic does mention quarreling in Stephen's army caused by animosity between the Norman magnates and Flemings, but the only plotting was by Normans against the Flemings. Robert of Torigny reports dissension between the two groups caused by the theft of a small cask of wine by a Fleming named Hugh de Gournay. John of Marmoutier only recognized a rivalry over leadership between William d'Ypres and Reginald of Saint-Valéry as the cause of the dissension. Furthermore, no contemporary source makes reference to Stephen's oath-swearing involving the archbishop of Rouen, Stephen, and Gloucester; but given the importance of the event and of the principals involved, one would expect such news to be recorded.[104]

[101] *LE*, 285; *The Historia Pontificalis of John of Salisbury*, 84–5; note George Garnett's wry comment about Hugh Bigod's later seizure of Norwich castle: *Conquered England*, 232, esp. 189; see also Crouch, *Reign of King Stephen*, 30–1; King, *King Stephen*, 48–9, 301–2.
[102] *OV* vi. 448–9; *HN* (1998), 24–7, 38–9; *The Letters of Peter the Venerable*, i. no. 15; ii, 104; *GS* (2004), 12–13; *GFAL*, 119; Crouch, *Reign of King Stephen*, 67; for more opposing views, see Bradbury, *Stephen and Matilda*, 24–5; King, *King Stephen*, 74–5.
[103] See Gransden, "Prologues in the Historiography of Twelfth-Century England," 74–6, for other examples.
[104] See also *OV* vi. 484–5 & n., 486–7; John of Marmoutier, 225; Robert of Torigny, "Chronica," 132; *ASC a.*1140 & nn.; Whitelock in *ASC* xvi–xvii & n.; *The Peterborough Chronicle*, xv–xxviii, esp. xxv, lxxxvi–lxxxvii; King, *HN*, xcv–xcvi.

Because of the complete diversity of the reported circumstances of the military fiasco at Livarot one is inclined to dismiss them all. However, the accounts do not carry equal weight as evidence. The Angevin historian John of Marmoutier personally may not have been as close to events or as contemporary with them as Orderic Vitalis, but his information about the Angevins came from a known informant, Engelran de Bohun, who served the Angevins during the Anarchy, and thus should be given the greater credence.[105] One detail Malmesbury shares broadly with John of Marmoutier's *Historia Gaufridi Ducis* is the person of William d'Ypres. So the story probably has value as evidence of Earl Robert's enmity for d'Ypres and by then the tenuousness of the earl's loyalty to the king.[106]

The *Historia* explicitly attributed to the earl of Gloucester opinions that Robert had solicited from many ecclesiastics about the obligation to honor his oath to Matilda. Their answers in distilled form were that observance was the only way to avoid disgrace in this life and to win salvation in the next. As Edmund King has noted, some confirmation of this claim comes from a letter Abbot Gilbert Foliot of St. Peter's Gloucester wrote to Brian fitz Count sometime in 1143 × 4.[107] Among the points Foliot made: he had heard the earl of Gloucester frequently cite a passage from the *Book of Numbers* in support of the Empress Matilda's right to be her father's heir; inheritance by daughters is supported by divine, natural, and human law; he had frequently solicited opinions from important individuals, including ecclesiastics, regarding the charge that Matilda was illegitimate because of her parents' invalid marriage; however, St. Anselm had ruled that Matilda's parents were free to marry. All together, not proof of the *Historia*'s report, but enough, absent contradictory evidence, to dismiss a charge of prevarication.[108]

In addition to the surveyed ecclesiastical opinions, the meaning (*tenor*) of an apostolic (papal) *decretum* also had informed the earl of Gloucester's conscience.[109] Malmesbury omitted the text of the papal *decretum* from the *Historia*, although he promised to include the document (*pagina*) in a later book. He never did so, even though his recapitulation of Gloucester's reasons for his abandonment of loyalty to King Stephen in Book 3 provided a logical opportunity.[110] The nature of the document is unknown. There is general scholarly belief that the *decretum* would have come, were it a papal letter, from Innocent II (1130–43) during the early years of Stephen's reign.[111] However, there is solid evidence that Innocent accepted Stephen as king throughout his entire pontificate. The pope refused to accept Matilda's argument in favor of her claim to the throne at the Lateran Council of 1139; and there are four of the pope's letters to Stephen and one to Peter the Venerable abbot

---

[105] John of Marmoutier, 174, 225.   [106] See Chapt. 5, 136.
[107] King in *HN* (1998), 42n.
[108] *LCGF*, no. 26; see *GFAL*, 108, 116–22; Crouch, "Robert of Gloucester, and the Daughter of Zelophehad," 232–3; Garnett, *Conquered England*, 233; see also Chapt. 5, 150.
[109] *HN* (1998), 42–3; Patterson, "William of Malmesbury's Robert of Gloucester," 992–3.
[110] *HN* (1998), 42–3, 112–13; Patterson, "William of Malmesbury's Robert of Gloucester," 992–3.
[111] For Innocent II's letters, see Richard of Hexham, 147–8; *Regesta Pontificum Romanorum*, ed. Jaffé, esp. i. nos. 7765, 7804, 8026, 8123; Appleby, *The Troubled Reign of King Stephen*, 48; Holdsworth, "The Church," 210 & n.; Frost, in Hollister, *Henry I*, 482n.; Bradbury, *Stephen and Matilda*, 25. For another view, see also Crouch, "Robert of Gloucester and the Daughter of Zelophehad," 231 & n. 8; see 185 & n. 40.

of Cluny indicating de facto recognition of Stephen over the 1135–43 period.[112] It also seems unlikely that the *decretum* was some Canon Law papal decretal. William of Malmesbury not only was familiar with canonical literature, but he had his own personal collection; and he also possessed some archival materials from Canterbury, including papal letters to Anselm. The only clue Malmesbury provides is that it pertained to the oath he had taken to his sister's succession in 1127. But whatever the text was, William clearly believed in its existence. The best explanation for its absence from the *Historia Novella*, unless we wish to accuse William of lying or having gullibly accepted a falsehood, is that the document had been promised to Malmesbury by Robert or a member of his household, but not been delivered before William was forced to cease writing.[113]

Examples such as the preceding may not even exhaust the possible unattributed Gloucester sources of William of Malmesbury's material about Earl Robert gleaned from "trustworthy sources, wide reports, or well-established information." Other possibilities include the exact size of the force the earl brought to England with the empress in 1139 and the number of his household knights who shortly afterwards accompanied him to Bristol.[114]

In the reported negotiations in late 1141 between royalists and Angevins for the release of King Stephen and Earl Robert, we have an actual example of how Gloucester details could have been transmitted to Malmesbury. Robert, Countess Mabel, pro-Angevin and royalist barons were the protagonists. Legates bore drafts of the terms for release of the two between royalists and Countess Mabel. Security for Robert's release after Stephen's was provided by sealed letters to the pope containing the final agreement, given to Robert for safe-keeping. He provided for that, according to Malmesbury, by putting them in a safe place. That, if another known case of documentary retention for Robert is any guide, would be in Countess Mabel's hands. Only the means by which Malmesbury acquired all this information in 1142 is missing from his account, but a good case may be made for its being the countess.[115]

In spite of his *Historia*'s positive features, Malmesbury may be taxed for lapses from complete objectivity. For his part William of Malmesbury produced in his *Historia Novella* a persuasive polemic and apologia slanted in favor of Matilda's succession and Earl Robert of Gloucester's chief leadership. His patron did not need to wink at him to convey the kind of contemporary history guided by divine providence he wanted.

Devices Malmesbury used to achieve the desired effect in the *Historia Novella* include omission of damaging details, use of false data and argument perhaps out of deference to, or trustingly accepted from, his patron, and distortion in

---

[112] Patterson, "William of Malmesbury's Robert of Gloucester," 992–3; Bradbury, *Stephen and Matilda*, 25; but see also Holdsworth, "The Church," 210 & nn.; Crouch, "Robert of Gloucester and the Daughter of Zelophehad," 242n.; King, *HN* (1998), li–lii.
[113] *HN* (1998), 40–3; Patterson, "William of Malmesbury's Robert of Gloucester," 993 (revised); Crouch, *Reign of King Stephen*, 123–4.
[114] *HN* (1998), 60–1 (respectively, "Testimonio ueridicorum relatorum" and "ut audiui").
[115] *HN* (1998), 116–21.

several forms. Malmesbury was not being innovative by such practices, just for the most part adding to the list already known from the corpus of his other historical works.[116] While some are marks against the norms of historical objectivity and of the author's own stated claims of adherence to them—even to soliciting criticism for any departures noticed by readers—these gestures are literary topoi. Consequently, from this perspective, the *Historia* as a polemical work deserves to be judged partly as such. If so, many of the *Historia*'s historical deficiencies are its assets and Malmesbury's "faults," ironically elements of his art![117] The interesting thing is that instead of diminishing the importance of the work, they reveal a side of scholarly William as a writer and observer of current events who could produce the most extensive expression of partisan writing of the Anarchy.

Details which would undermine his theses of Matilda's right of succession and of his patron's complete and unfailing loyalty to her are just not mentioned. For example, the chronicler knew enough about the care of Henry I's body at Rouen and Caen prior to its being transported to England, yet reported nothing of the embarrassing baronial *coniuratio*, overtures to Theobald, or Robert's participation in these proceedings. Furthermore in continuing his account of Norman events following Henry's death, Malmesbury states that while Stephen hastened to England (to claim the throne), the Empress Matilda and her brother Robert remained in Normandy, creating the false impression of their political association at this time.[118] Early signs of Gloucester's loyalty to Stephen following his fealty also are passed over. The *Historia* ignores Robert's presence in the king's army which besieged Baldwin de Redvers at Exeter castle later in 1136.[119] It does report Robert's crossing to Normandy in 1137, but without mentioning that the earl did so in part to join the king's court. Instead, Malmesbury, after implying that Earl Robert had to remain loyal to Stephen because of the continued support Stephen enjoyed from the baronage, made his text focus on an alleged plot of Stephen to capture Robert, their insincere reconciliation, and the earl's attention to his own affairs during the rest of the year.[120]

Another clear example comes from the story William tells about the hanging of the renegade Flemish mercenary, the "cruel and savage" Robert fitz Hubert. Malmesbury intended it to be a morality tableau in the *Historia Novella* about the just fate mercenaries might expect from their deviant careers. It appealed nicely to the widespread loathing this group, particularly Flemings, enjoyed in Earl Robert's day: they fought for money and used crossbows. The problem for Malmesbury was that his patron had been Fitz Hubert's employer. Not surprisingly, then, that fact is not mentioned.[121]

Malmesbury also included in his history details which in historical value range from the dubious to the downright fallacious. Many seem to perform important

---

[116] Gransden, *Historical Writing* i. 176–8; Scott, *The Early History of Glastonbury*, 1.
[117] *HN* (1998), 2–3, esp. 112–13, 122–3; Stubbs, William of Malmesbury, *GR* ii. cxli.
[118] *HN* (1998), 26–7.
[119] *GS* (2004), 30–42; *Regesta* iii, nos. 284, 952; Davis, *King Stephen*, 3rd edn., 22–4.
[120] *Regesta* iii. nos. 69, 594; *HN* (1998), 36–41.
[121] *HN* (1998), 62–3, 74–7; *GS* (2004), 92, 104–9; *JW* iii. 284–9; Crouch, *Reign of King Stephen*, 162.

supporting roles for his history-turned-apologia. Their source arguably was Earl Robert, a family member, or one of his administrative officials.

First of all, there is the already mentioned episode of Henry I's deathbed confirmation of both England and Normandy to the Empress Matilda which was witnessed by Robert of Gloucester. The section in the *Historia* where this passage is located has the flavor of an *ex post facto* promotion of Earl Robert's loyalty to his sister's succession. Immediately before the confirmation passage and like an introduction to it, Malmesbury states that also coming to the deathly ill Henry was "his son... [the] earl of Gloucester... who for his steadfast loyalty and distinguished merit, has pre-eminently deserved that the recollection of him shall live for all time."[122]

Malmesbury progresses very little in his narrative before providing an example of deference to a patron who was understandably sensitive about his birth status by only mentioning that his father had acknowledged him as his son before becoming king.[123] Later on, to foster the aura of Earl Robert's consistent loyalty to Matilda and to separate him from the *peruersi* referred to in his *Historia*'s Prologue, William used a fallacious *post quod, ergo propter quod* argument to justify Robert's performance of homage to King Stephen. It was based on the earl's pragmatic submission to realpolitik until a more propitious opportunity emerged for backing Matilda, his concern for not endangering the future prospects of his two infant nephews as heirs to the throne, and the belief that the king would violate his homage's conditions in any event. At the time William was writing, he knew well how the *conventio* had fared.[124]

The tale's characterization of Robert's homage exemplifies how William of Malmesbury could use exaggeration to score polemical points. Having taken the decision to submit, "Therefore he (the earl) did homage to the king conditionally, namely for as long as the king maintained his rank (*dignitatem*) unimpaired and kept the agreements (*pacta*)."[125] What Malmesbury's text did not add was any indication that such acts were by nature conditional, imposing on lord and vassal reciprocal obligations to respect each other's *vitam et honorem*. Furthermore, Stephen made similar arrangements like this with other barons at the start of his reign.[126] And it is now known that William of Malmesbury was not original in his use of forms of the verb *diffidiare/diffidare* to describe Earl Robert of Gloucester's

---

[122] *HN* (1998), 24–5; Ralph de Diceto i. 248; Crouch, *Reign of King Stephen*, 30–1.
[123] *HN* (1998), 8–9.
[124] *HN* (1998), 30–3; Patterson, "William of Malmesbury's Robert of Gloucester," 987–8; Crouch, "Robert of Gloucester and the Daughter of Zelophehad," 228–9; Bradbury, *Stephen and Matilda*, 21; Gransden, "Prologues in the Historiography of Twelfth-Century England," 74–5.
[125] *HN* (1998), 32–3, 40–3; see also *GS* (2004), 22–5. On homage, fealty, and investiture, see Brown, *Origins of English Feudalism*, 29; Le Goff, *Time, Work, and Culture in the Middle Ages*, 239–44.
[126] *Leges Henrici Primi*, 43.8–9; Patterson, "Anarchy in England," 197 & n.; Patterson, "William of Gloucester's Robert of Gloucester," 987–8 & nn.; King, *HN*, xliv & n., xlv–xlvi. See Brown, *Origins of English Feudalism*, 29; Strickland, *War and Chivalry*, 233; Le Goff, *Time, Work, and Culture in the Middle Ages*, 255; King, "Dispute Settlement in Anglo-Norman England," 125.

repudiation of his fealty to King Stephen in 1138. The chronicler also was correct in claiming that there was precedent for the practice.[127]

Hyperbole was certainly at work in Malmesbury's claiming unqualified steadfastness of Robert's support for Matilda and of his unselfishness and self-sacrifice involved with his efforts on her behalf.[128] Another fertile area for distortion involved the chronicler's portrayal of his patron's personality. Keeping to the stylistic logic of an apologia, William provides readers only with a composite Earl Robert of complimentary attributes.[129] Uncomplimentary details are ignored. We read nothing of the man of strong passions who served Venus as a most willing volunteer, nothing of inducements to change sides from the Angevins, nothing of appetite for territorial gain or political animosity for its loss, nor jealousy for loss of stature at court.[130] There is no opportunity for us to sift the charges of fecklessness, timidity, and laziness from a supposed detractor for grains of truth.[131] In other examples, Marjorie Chibnall has shown how Malmesbury turned the Angevins' precipitous flight from London and massive defeat at Winchester in 1141 into an orderly retreat and defeat of its small military force.[132]

William of Malmesbury's inclination to publish material favorable to Gloucester may not just have sprung from his instincts to please his patron; an organizational peculiarity of his *Historia* may be indicative of the reason. He inserted a summary of Earl Robert's motives and actions in support of Matilda's succession into the text of Book 3, strangely in the midst of his running account of the events of 1142. The abruptness of this placement suggests that the chronicler may have sensed that he might not be able to finish his *Historia*; and posterity needed to be reminded of his apologia's key points in favor of Earl Robert and the Angevin succession.[133]

The reason, I believe, was Malmesbury's declining health due to an illness he reported around 1140. This might explain a series of careless dating mistakes in his *Historia Novella*. In Book 3 the date of Matilda's arrival at Winchester in the summer of 1141 to confront Bishop Henry was weeks too late.[134] In the recapitulation of Robert of Gloucester's career the date of Robert's *diffidatio* is a year off and *gesta* of 1142 are attributed to 1143.[135] In theory, had the author been in reasonably good health, he could have corrected such anomalies, but he also may not

---

[127] Gillingham, "The Introduction of Chivalry into England," 224 n. 69; see also Chapt. 5, 137 & n.
[128] Patterson, "William of Malmesbury's Robert of Gloucester," 986, 991–2 & n. (but Brill is incorrect).
[129] *HN* (1998), 2–3, 24–5; e.g. 72–3, 96–7, 104–7.
[130] *De Nugis Curialium*, 426–9; *OV* vi. 514–17; Robert of Torigny, "Chronica," 136, reports that Robert made a concord with Count Geoffrey; Patterson, "William of Malmesbury's Robert of Gloucester," 991–2.
[131] Henry of Huntingdon (1996), 734–5.
[132] *HN* (1998), 98–105; Chibnall, *The Empress Matilda*, 105, 113.
[133] *HN* (1998), 8–9, 112–15; *JW* iii. 178, 180, for confirmation. Stubbs, William of Malmesbury *GR* ii. cxxxviii–cxxxix, believed that William had given up the study of history and was distracted from properly investigating key details by reading and transcribing work; the activities are hardly mutually exclusive. But see Farmer on this point: "William of Malmesbury's Commentary on Lamentations," 289.
[134] *HN* (1998), 106–7 & n. 254.   [135] *HN* (1998), 112 & n., 113.

have been inclined to do so because his mind by then had turned to topics pertaining to things eternal rather than temporal before he died, possibly in 1143.[136]

William of Malmesbury's *Historia Novella* soon acquired a double posthumous existence. As copies were made and circulated, among them appeared over time texts of a distinctly second edition which was even more focused on William's patron and, because of this and other features, has revealed a Gloucester family provenance. This altered *Historia* is best represented among its ten extant medieval manuscripts by the copy in the already noted grand codex from Margam Abbey.[137] Joining the new *Historia Novella* are two other copies of works dedicated to Robert, William's *Gesta Regum Anglorum* and Geoffrey of Monmouth's *Historia Regum Britanniae (De Gestis Britonum)*, which makes the codex a memorial volume to the founder. Like its two companions, this *Historia Novella* is written in the same slightly left-leaning, stylistically transitional, compact, and often angular proto-Gothic book hand of *c.*1180 (s.xii$^{ex}$). Indicative signs are certainly later than the s.xii$^{med}$ Stubbs believed, but not 1190s or s.xiii$^{in}$: stubby trailing-headed *a*s; finishing minims with upward ticks; stems of majuscules with both upward ticks and inchoate finished feet; disappearance of tailed-*e* for *ae*; saucer-shaped, angular bracket and horizontal stroke suspension signs; and ampersands for *et*.[138] Like the codex itself, this *Historia Novella* has a new story to tell, about how possibly Earl Robert, but certainly his family, used the work to further polish especially the earl's image. Their efforts suggest more expanded roles for Robert as Malmesbury's patron.

The *Historia*'s consistency of focus especially on Earl Robert has led to theories that it was a house of Gloucester product, that a copy was annotated in various ways by a single editor, Earl Robert's son Roger, or possibly the earl himself, and that a clerk in the service of Roger after he had become bishop of Worcester (1164–79) might have "written up" the annotated *Historia* at Worcester. Whether such an event ever happened may never be known; it is more likely that the edited *Historia* was copied one or more times to create the text in the Margam codex.[139] On the basis of access to the *Historia*, during its formative period of *c.*1143 × *c.*1180, Earl Robert, Countess Mabel, William, and Roger, or clerks under their direction seem the most likely potential editors. As for single editorship, as will be seen, more than one family member may have been responsible for the same annotation.

The commissioned work dedicated to Earl Robert presumably would have been sent to Robert after Malmesbury's death, and the Margam copy, based on its edited ancestor, states in its rubricated incipit that its three books were sent to Earl Robert: "Incipit p(ro)logus Will(elm)i malmesberiensis in libros nouelle historie.missos RobeRto comiti GloecestRie." Bristol, the earl's baronial capital, would have been

---

[136] Farmer, "William of Malmesbury's Life and Works," 53, noted that William had commented on his illness in his Miracles of the Virgin written *c.*1140; Farmer, "William of Malmesbury's Commentary on Lamentations," 289; Thomson, *William of Malmesbury*, rev. edn., 6.

[137] See 187 & n.

[138] Stubbs, William of Malmesbury, *GR* i. lxxxi (s.xii$^{med}$). I may differ slightly from King, *HN* (1998), lxxiv, and Crick, *Summary Catalogue*, nos. 112, 183–5. For the criteria for my dating of Ce¹: Ker, *English Manuscripts*, 34–9; see also Hardy, William of Malmesbury, *GR* ii. xxii; Mynors, Thomson, and Winterbottom, *GR* i. xiii n., xxix; ii. xvi (s.xii²).

[139] King, *HN* (1998), xci–xciv.

the text's most likely destination.[140] Roger had potential access to the work during the period of his membership in the Gloucester household for some years after William succeeded their father. Furthermore, after Roger became bishop of Worcester (1164–79), there is evidence that he visited Bristol.[141] And there is a story about him reported by William fitz Stephen, Thomas Becket's biographer, which, without much mental extrapolation, might suggest an interest in promoting his father's reputation with an improved *Historia Novella*.[142] But his brother William had even more potential access to the volume. As earl of Gloucester from 1147, he was most frequently in residence at Bristol until his arrest by Henry II and death in 1183—even criticized for his domestic traits.[143] Earl William and his mother Countess Mabel also had a more documented relationship to comital affairs than Roger. They were issuing joint charters for about a year following Earl Robert's death; and before Mabel's death in 1156 she was making a grant with William's permission and exercising administrative responsibility in the earldom's Norman holdings.[144]

Of the second edition's elements most revelatory of Gloucester influence, rubrications and interpolations, rubrications as a group are so focused on Earl Robert that it is easy to see him as their annotator and for some the source of the information as well.[145] Seventeen rubrics introducing chapters especially call attention to his activities, guiding readers to the major phases of the earl's role in the war of succession. Not to be missed are his first appearance in England after Stephen's accession and performance of homage to him; Robert's visit to Normandy and Stephen's plots against him; how and why the earl withdrew his homage; his arrival in England with the empress; and the earl's battle (of Lincoln) and capture of the king. In one, pointing to his effort to arrange a *foedus pacis* between Stephen and the empress at Bath in 1140, Robert shared "billing" with Bishop Henry of Winchester, Archbishop Theobald, and Stephen's Queen Matilda.[146] Several rubrics deal with his rescue or recapture of Angevin garrisons and of the empress; several also covered his retreat from Winchester, his capture, his temptation during captivity, his trip to Count Geoffrey of Anjou, and assistance in capturing ten Norman castles. Lest anyone miss Malmesbury's promotional points, a rubric also alerted readers to a recapitulation of the earl's deeds. In addition, the subsequent Margam text includes several interpolations of "Robert" to identify the "earl" who was being discussed to

---

[140] Ce¹, BL, Royal MS 13 D ii., fol. 110r, col a, ll. 30–2; *HN* (1998), lxxv n. 312, also lxx, n. 292; see Figure 6.1, 179.

[141] Cheney, *Roger, Bishop of Worcester*, no. 67 & n.: *EEA* xxxiii, no. 223 & n. I suspect that *EEA* xxxiii, no. 158, Plate II was written by a Bristol scribe.

[142] BL, MS Lansdowne 398, fols. 30v–31r: William fitz Stephen, "Vita S. Thomae," 104–5; Cheney, "William Fitz Stephen and his Life of Archbishop Thomas," 139–56; Cheney, *Roger, Bishop of Worcester*, 47–8.

[143] BL, Additional MS 28206, fol. 122v; Patterson, *EGC*, nos. 36–7, 48, 69, 71, 85, 98. 124, 155, 168, 182, 282; *GS* (2004), 120–1; Patterson, "William, Second Earl of Gloucester," 39–40.

[144] Patterson, *EGC*, nos. 86, 167, 171–7. For Roger's and Henry II's famous altercation, see n. 142.

[145] See 199–200.

[146] *HN* (1998), 76n. The rubrications especially focused on Earl Robert's activities are in Ce¹, fols. 112v, 113v, 115v, 117v, 118r–118v, cols. a–b, 120r–v, 121v–122r, 123r–123v, cols. a–b: William of Malmesbury, *HN*, 17, 21, 44, 47, 50, 58, 60, 64, 67, 72–3, 74–6.

ensure unmistaken attribution or reference to the earl of Gloucester.[147] One of them describes Countess Mabel's conjugal qualities and another one upgrades her husband to "beloved."[148] There is a chance that Robert interpolated the phrase praising Countess Mabel from what he had read in his presentation copy of Malmesbury's *Gesta Regum Anglorum*.[149] The earl, who had been one of the hostages by oath for the Empress Matilda's treaty of July 1141 to further reward and foster Geoffrey de Mandeville's pro-Angevin change of loyalty after King Stephen's defeat and capture at the battle of Lincoln, might well have had the *conventio* in mind as the interpolator of the earl of Essex's oath of fealty to his sister.[150] The fact that the altered *Historia* does not substitute Robert's favored title of *consul* for *comes* should not disqualify the earl from having been an editorial contributor. He employed both terms in the address clauses of his *acta* and although *consul* appeared on his seal, *comes* did so on his coinage.[151]

Single editorship of some interpolations is open to challenge. The just-cited phrase concerning Countess Mabel could have originated from an offspring such as Roger or William. Countess Mabel's hand might be favored for adding *dilecti* besides *viri*, but again, William's or Roger's cannot be ruled out. Anyone from the Gloucester family could have inserted appropriately declined forms of "Robert" to enhance references to "the earl."[152]

Production of the Margam codex was another of the house of Gloucester's promotional efforts for Earl Robert. Countess Mabel's death in 1156 rules out her involvement.[153] With Roger and his eldest brother William the likeliest sponsors on the basis of the manuscript's dating and this text's arguable provenance, Bishop Roger's candidacy would be stronger if it could be proved that he possessed a copy of the *Historia Novella*. As bishop of Worcester, he readily had available the well-known resources for documentary and literary production of the bishopric and priory.[154] Earl William had greater potential access to the presumed location of the books ultimately copied to form the Margam codex and the availability of a more fully documented functioning writing office and staff than is presently known for Roger.[155] Furthermore, affiliation with Margam makes William a more likely donor of the abbey's codex than Roger. The earl was a very active patron of his

---

[147] As noted by King, *HN* (1998), lxxxiii & n.
[148] BL, MS Royal 13 D.ii, fol. 110v, col. b, ll. 18–21: *data ei in matrimonium...beata*.; *HN* (1998), 8–9, 116–17; William of Malmesbury, *HN*, 4–5, 66–7.
[149] See 178.
[150] *HN* (1998), 102 & n. *g*; *Regesta* iii. no. 275; Round, *Geoffrey de Mandeville*, 384–7; King, *King Stephen*, 164 & n. 105.
[151] See King, *HN* (1998), lxxxii–lxxxiv & n., lxxvi–lxxxvii, 2–3: For Earl Robert's use of *comes*, see Patterson, *EGC*, 22–4 (needing revision), no. 110, BL MS Sloane 1301, fol. 227v and the subscription on WGAS, GB0216 A/N 1 (Clark, *Cartae et alia* i. no. LXVII); and Archibald, "The Lion Coinage of Robert Earl of Gloucester and William Earl of Gloucester," 73–80.
[152] King, *HN* (1998), lxxxiii & nn., 116–17; 118 & n. *b*. 119; see n. 147.
[153] "Ann. Margam," 48.
[154] *Cart. Worcester*; King, *HN* (1998), xxvi; Cheney, *English Bishops' Chanceries*, 9–10, 16, 33n., 51, 94–5, 116; *EEA* xxxiii, l, lxii; Cheney, *Roger, Bishop of Worcester, 1164–1179*, 99–100, 102–5, 108–9; Hoskin, *EEA* xxxiii, lxiv; Thomson, *A Descriptive Catalogue of the Medieval Manuscripts in Worcester Cathedral Library*, xx & n., xxiii; Gameson, *The Manuscripts of Early Norman England*, 15.
[155] For the writing office of Earl William, see Patterson, *EGC*, 9–21; *GS* (2004), 210–11; Patterson, *The Scriptorium of Margam Abbey*, 26–7, 31; Hoskin, *EEA* xxxiii, no. 86n.; see also n. 58.

father's foundation, whereas there is absolutely no known example of the bishop of Worcester's playing such a role. Also, William, not his father or brother Roger, became a patron of William of Malmesbury's abbey.[156]

Accordingly, I believe a scribe in Earl William's service probably copied the *Historia Novella* from his father's annotated copy, along with Malmesbury's *Gesta Regum Anglorum* and Monmouth's *Historia Regum Britanniae* to form the codex Ce[1] during approximately the eighth to ninth decade of the twelfth century. Much later, an as yet unidentified Margam scribe entered the *ex libris* inscription, "Liber monachor(um) s(an)c(t)e marie de margan," on the end folio.[157] No effort had been made to correct this *Historia's* various deficiencies. That, I suspect, represents Earl William of Gloucester's implicit ratification of the contents.[158]

Both *Historia Novella*s suffered a centuries-long form of literary entombment in their respective manuscript groups. The various copies survived in codices which included copies of his *Gesta Regum Anglorum*, but remained mostly unmined by subsequent historians until the nineteenth century. Although the *Gesta Regum Anglorum* was used by historians over the next few centuries, the *Historia* versions were seldom quoted or otherwise influenced their accounts.[159] The main reason was the popularity among medieval English historians of Henry of Huntingdon's *Historia Anglorum*, the Worcester chronicle written by John of Worcester with its continuations, and Robert of Torigny's *Chronica*.[160] Roger of Howden's *Chronica* provides an extreme example of Henry of Huntingdon's influence. The episodes featuring Robert are solely those chosen by the archdeacon of Huntingdon and the relevant passages are either quoted verbatim or virtually so from Huntingdon's *Historia Anglorum*.[161] In the case of Ralph de Diceto's *Abbreviationes Chronicorum*, its source was Robert of Torigny for events between 1123 and 1147. In only one passage, a very digested version of the 1127 oath to Matilda, it is just possible that Ralph's source might have been the *Historia Novella*.[162] Ralph also is indicative of

---

[156] Patterson, *EGC*, nos. 116, 120–35, 241?
[157] BL, MS Royal 13 D.ii, fol. 173v, col. b, s.xiii[1]. The hand does not belong to any Margam scribe I have identified up to c.1225: Patterson, *The Scriptorium of Margam Abbey*. Stubbs, William of Malmesbury, *GR* i. lxxxi, believed Earl Robert was the donor.
[158] BL, MS Royal 13 D.ii, fol.113v: "Q(u)om(od)o et quibus de causis. rob(ertus) comes homagiu(m) regis abdicauit"; *HN* (1998), 40 n.c.
[159] Stubbs, William of Malmesbury, *GR* i. xci–xciii; Mynors, William of Malmesbury, *HN*, xxxviii–xl; Thomson & Winterbottom, *GR* i. xiii–xxi; King, *HN* (1998), xciv–cvii, esp. xcvi & n., revising King in *Anarchy of King Stephen's Reign*, 1–2, on the *HN*'s influence on *ASC*. Ralph Niger's *Chronicon I* brief treatment of Stephen's reign stresses the rise of the Angevin dynasty and ignores Earl Robert of Gloucester; see *Chronicon*, 92. John of Hexham's few mentions of Earl Robert ("Historia," 307–8, 310–11) do not rely on the *HN*; see Gransden, *Historical Writing* i. 261; Gransden, *Historical Writing* ii.
[160] King, *HN* (1998), xcv–xcvii & n. Richard of Hexham only notes Earl Robert's attestation of Stephen's charter of liberties for the Church: "De Gestis Regis Stephani et de Bello Standardii," 149. For Ralph de Diceto's reliance upon Robert of Torigny, see his accounts of Earl Robert's participation in the Rout of Winchester in his "Abbreviationes Chronicorum," i. 23, 254nn.
[161] *Chronica Magistri Rogeri De Houedene* i. 193, 196–7, 199–205, 208; Henry of Huntingdon (1996), 712, 722, 724–40, 746.
[162] Ralph de Diceto i. 23, 245 & n.; *HN* (1998), 8–9. There is no support in the *HN* for the oath Ralph reports and Stubbs cites: Ralph de Diceto i. 246–7 & n.: see King, *HN* (1998), xcvii & n.–xcviii.

another historiographical trend; he was more interested in recording benchmarks in the rise of the new Angevin dynasty than tracing the history of the Anarchy. Thus, when he and other historians recorded an event relating to the Angevin succession, particularly like the baronage's oath of 1127 to Matilda's succession, Robert's participation might be noted, but not within Malmesbury's context.[163] Gervase of Canterbury's *Chronica* and *Gesta Regum*, which provide the most complete summary at the end of the twelfth century of Earl Robert's military role in the Anarchy, exemplify both trends.[164]

The great exception is Matthew Paris. Even at the center of historical writing which developed at St. Albans (Herts.) by the early thirteenth century, bypassing the *Historia Novella* as a source for Earl Robert's *gesta* was initially standard practice. Roger of Wendover knew of the *Historia*—even had a copy of it, the *Gesta Regum Anglorum*, and Geoffrey of Monmouth's *Historia Regum Britanniae*—and recorded the death of the *Historia Novella*'s author in his *Flores Historiarum*; but he relied on the same basic sources for Stephen's reign as his predecessors.

Matthew Paris, however, made use of the *Historia Novella*. His *Chronica Majora*'s treatment of Stephen's reign incorporates Roger of Wendover's *Flores Historiarum* and its sources, such as Robert of Torigny. As Richard Vaughan has argued, the folios of a first recension of Roger's *Flores* became in effect a first draft of the *Chronica* through Matthew's using its folios to place his quoted or rewritten passages from Roger's *Historia Novella* as marginalia. The text thus revised and continued when copied became the *Chronica Majora*. Many of these Malmesbury borrowings pertained to Earl Robert's activities. Gloucester's arrival in England after Easter 1136 and the initial wording of his performance of homage are almost quotations. Then, in a wonderful piece of creative writing, Matthew transformed Robert of Gloucester's conditional oath to Stephen into "As long as you maintain me as a senator, I will do the same for you as emperor."[165] Some versions of the marginalia also appear in Paris's own *Flores Historiarum*.[166]

The *Chronica Majora*'s entries relating to Earl Robert represent the single most comprehensive medieval historical presentation of Earl Robert of Gloucester's role in the Anarchy. In addition to those just mentioned, the work includes Robert's withdrawal of his father's treasure from, and surrender of, Falaise following news of Stephen's accession; the castles the earl held against Stephen in 1138; his arrival with Matilda in England in 1139; his participation in the battle of Lincoln; his capture at the Rout of Winchester and exchange for Stephen in 1141; Robert's participation with Geoffrey of Anjou in capturing Norman castles in 1142; and

---

[163] Ralph de Diceto i. 255.
[164] Gervase of Canterbury i. 105, 109–15, 120–6, 130, 140; ii. 73–4; *JW* iii. 252, 268, 290, 298, 302; Henry of Huntingdon (1996), 724, 726, 728, 730, 732.
[165] Roger of Wendover, *Chronica, Sive Flores Historiarum* ii. 234–5; Matthew Paris, *Chronica Majora* ii. 164. Roger's copy was BL, MS Royal D.v; Vaughan, *Matthew Paris*, 21–2, esp. 24–31, 129 & n.; King, *HN* (1998), lxxiii & n., lxxiv, xcviii–c; Gransden, *Historical Writing* i. 367–8 & n.
[166] Matthew Paris, *Flores Historiarum* ii. 58: compare "Robertus…conservaret." with Matthew Paris, *Chronica Majora*, 164: "R(obertus) sibi homagium…suam sibi servaret"; and *HN* (1998), 32: "homagium regi fecit…sibi pacta seruaret."

the earl's loss of Faringdon.[167] But even though Matthew Paris brought the *Historia Novella* back to life, it was mostly without its author's points of view.

Anglo-Norman annals as a class ignored William of Malmesbury's always loyal champion of Matilda's succession. Almost by their very nature, even when their entries record events involving Earl Robert in some way, they appear like scribes' random selections. Ironically, Scribe 24, the author of the annals of Margam Abbey, Earl Robert's own foundation, made use of his house's copy of the *Historia Novella* or another source utilizing it, but only records dramatic *gesta* of his in 1141 and his founding role and death in the account of 1147. Tewkesbury's only noticed the earl's capture and exchange for Stephen, his victory at Wilton, and death.[168] Even the E text of the *Anglo-Saxon Chronicle*, which could editorialize—even interpret—and took note of important happenings involving Robert between 1126 and 1137, from a Gloucester source or even the *Historia Novella*, reports them almost entirely apolitically.[169]

The *Winchester Annals* covering the years 1066–1202, written in the late twelfth century to *c.*1202, is the major exception in this genre.[170] It not only quotes widely from Malmesbury's *Gesta Regum Anglorum*, *Gesta Pontificum*, and *Historia Novella* for entries in the 1066–1142 segment, but often mines the *Historia* verbatim or summarizes passages dealing with the years 1126–42, especially some thirteen dealing with Earl Robert's pro-Angevin activities and alienation from Stephen. However, showing his own partisanship, the annalist, instead of incorporating Malmesbury's apologia for Earl Robert's joining the Angevins, included the earl among those whom he denounced for doing so against their consciences and for personal gain.[171]

Critical evaluation of the *Historia* happened only after history became established as an academic discipline in the nineteenth century and higher criticism, comparable to that applied to study of the Bible, began to be applied to Western Europe's ever-increasing published accumulation of historical texts and documents. This led to modern scholarly editions of the *Historia* by Sir Thomas Duffus Hardy (1840), Bishop William Stubbs (1889), Roger Mynors and H. A. Potter (1955), and most recently Edmund King (1998) and of Malmesbury's contemporaries,

---

[167] Matthew Paris, *Chronica Majora*, 165 (but surrendered to Theobald of Blois), 165, 167, 170, 172–4, 177.

[168] "Ann. Margam" i. 14; "Ann. Tewkesbury" i. 46–7; Gransden, *Historical Writing* i. 29–30. Compare *HN* (1998), 20: "Plene porcorum...destituebantur....Tunc...usupauerat..." with "Ann Margam," 13; the closely related chronicle, Trinity College Dublin MS 507, only records Stephen's capture at Lincoln and release by Earl Robert and his foundation and death under the year 1151: TCD, MS 507, *a.*1141, *a.*1151; Patterson, "The Author of the 'Margam Annals,'" 198–202.

[169] *ASC a.*1126, 1127, 1135, 1140; compare with *a.*1100; King, *HN* (1998), xcv–xcvi; King, "Dispute Settlement in Anglo-Norman England," 115.

[170] Luard, *Ann. Mon.* ii. x–xii; "Ann. Winchester," 48; Appleby, "Richard of Devizes and the Annals of Winchester," 70–1; Gransden, *Historical Writing* i. 252 & n. 47, against the attribution of authorship to Richard of Devizes.

[171] "Ann. Winchester," 27 (1067), 28 (1069), 30 (1072), 31 (1075), 39–40 (1098), 41 (1100), 48 (1126), 49 (1129, 1130?, 1131, 1132?), 50 (1134, 1136?), 50–3 (1137–42), esp. 50, for *de purchacio*, which is the basis of my rendering of "personal gain." See in general Luard, "Ann. Winchester," xvi; King, *HN* (1998), ci–cii.

particularly Orderic Vitalis, Henry of Huntingdon, and the anonymous author of the *Gesta Stephani*, and the *acta* of the Anglo-Norman kings, of the Empress Matilda and her husband and son, Geoffrey V count of Anjou and Henry fitz Empress. Appreciation of William of Malmesbury has been enhanced by new editions of his works and commentaries on his scholarship.[172]

Bishop Stubbs, as commentator and editor of the *Historia Novella*'s Ce[1] text, effectively began modern critical analysis of the work and its author. For study of the Anarchy, John Horace Round's document-based *Geoffrey de Mandeville* (1892) became the catalyst. Several of the great study's many contributions related to Robert of Gloucester and the *Historia Novella*. Round separated Robert's marriage chronologically from his elevation to comital rank, thereby correcting the impression that they happened in tandem created by William of Malmesbury's *Historia Novella* and perpetuated by Tewkesbury Abbey tradition. In addition, Round's book established the dating parameters within which Robert's reception of the earldom occurred, which to date have remained unchanged, and contributed to an understanding of the office itself. However, Round, like his teacher Stubbs, recognized only the chronicler's bias. Only from the 1960s did scholars aggressively begin questioning the quality of Malmesbury's and the *Historia*'s reporting, particularly its portrayal of Robert of Gloucester.[173] This approach may have the potential for revealing Malmesbury's scholarly pluses and minuses as a historian on the basis of this work, but also is problematic because of the nature of the evidence and the differing interpretations it can generate.[174]

Robert fitz Roy earl of Gloucester died suddenly of a fever on October 31, 1147 at Bristol shortly after founding Margam Abbey and was buried at his earlier monastic foundation, St. James's Priory.[175] Earl Robert's reputation survived independently of the *historia* he commissioned partly to perpetuate a historical persona for himself. Shortly after his death, the poet Serlo of Wilton eulogized him in effusive terms which rivaled those Malmesbury had applied to the earl in his *Gesta Regum Anglorum* and *Historia Novella*.[176] Even the anonymous author of the *Gesta Stephani*, an ardent royalist who wanted to throw a little dirt Robert's way and recalled his bastardy and reported a rumor that he had died unshriven, in the same breath called him "a man of proved talent and admirable wisdom."[177] Walter Map praised the late earl's prudence and learning, but could not resist passing on a gossipy tidbit about his sexual appetite.[178]

---

[172] *GR* i & ii; *GP*; William of Malmesbury, *HN*; Scott, *The Early History of Glastonbury*; and e.g., Thomson, *William of Malmesbury*, rev. edn.; Gransden, *Historical Writing* i; the bibliography of this and related literature is too extensive to include here.
[173] e.g. Patterson, "William of Malmesbury's Robert of Gloucester," 983–97; Crouch, "Robert of Gloucester and the Daughter of Zelophehad," 227–43; Gransden, "Prologues in the Historiography of Twelfth-Century England," 70–6; Davis, *King Stephen*, 3rd edn., Appendix III, 144–6; King, *HN* (1998), "The Historical Value of the *Historia Novella*," xxxiii–lxviii.
[174] See, e.g., Chibnall, "The Empress Matilda as a Subject for Biography," 191.
[175] See Chapt. 5, 176 & n. 245.   [176] *Serlon de Wilton: Poèmes latins*, no. 15, p. 94.
[177] *GS* (2004): 12–13.
[178] *De Nugis Curialium*, 426–9; *GS* (2004), 12; Henry of Huntingdon (1996), 734.

At the time of his death Robert could not have foreseen the outcome of the struggle for the throne he had led in England or the place in history he would enjoy as the result of his efforts. His ignominious flight from the field of battle at *Lidelea* must have been fresh in his mind. His sister Matilda left England for Norman retirement by early 1148 and her cause in England to the fortunes of baronial sponsorship and the future success of her son Henry, self-proclaimed rightful heir and the Angevin party's since 1141–2. Her brother Robert's death must have been a blow to her imperious self-confidence after having lost the services of Miles of Gloucester through death and Brian fitz Count to some form of retirement, possibly monastic. And since 1146 she had been under the threat of excommunication to abandon Devizes castle, a headquarters since 1141, and restore it to Bishop Jocelin of Salisbury, Bishop Roger's successor, in a scenario much like that which Earl Robert had faced with Bishop Philip de Harcourt in the Bessin.[179]

Death deprived Robert of Gloucester of taking his battle for his sister's cause any further. In the end, the convergence of baronial, dynastic, and ecclesiastical developments coupled with Henry fitz Empress's determination not to give up the fight led to the Angevin dynastic victory for which Robert of Gloucester had fought. The politically divided baronage, as Professor Ralph Davis illustrated long ago, tired of the military stalemate by the end of the 1140s and had begun to make peace within itself through key interconnecting alliances.[180] The nuptials of Earl Robert's heir and successor William and Hawisia, daughter of Robert II earl of Leicester and niece of Gloucester's old nemesis Waleran of Meulan, was a key element of that process and led to the alliance of the earls of Gloucester, Leicester, Chester, and Hereford. And how appropriate it was for Hawisia's *maritagium* to include the Leicester estates her posthumous father-in-law Robert of Gloucester had seized during the civil war.[181]

The Church already had dealt a crippling blow to Stephen's dynastic hopes when Archbishop Theobald of Canterbury at the direction of Cistercian Pope Eugenius III, prodded by his former abbot Bernard of Clairvaux, declined to anoint Eustace in 1152. The deaths of Stephen's queen Matilda (1152) and effective heir Eustace (1153) effectively sealed the king's dynastic doom.[182]

The outcome was the so-called Treaty of Winchester in November 1153, which in Sir James Holt's words, "breathes the atmosphere of the Anarchy." Of its many terms, two particularly could be considered post-obit victories for Earl Robert. Stephen remained the realm's *rex coronatus* and Henry became the fictional son and heir; and familial and baronial rights to hereditary possession were recognized and guaranteed by feudal oaths and threats of ecclesiastical sanctions. As if putting paid

---

[179] *Regesta* iii. no. 634–5; King, *HN* (1998), lxii–lxiii, lxvii, 126–7. Chibnall, *Empress Matilda*, 112, 148–51; King, "Brian fitz Count," 540; see also Chapt. 4, 123–4.
[180] Patterson, *EGC*, 5 & n.; Stenton, *English Feudalism*, 250–7; Davis, *King Stephen*, 3rd edn., 75–95, 108–24; Crouch, *Reign of King Stephen*, 233–9, 245–7, 270–7; King, *King Stephen*, 258–300; Amt, *The Accession of Henry II in England*, 7–18; Patterson, "Anarchy in England," 194–7; Dalton, "Churchmen and the Promotion of Peace in King Stephen's Reign," 93–4.
[181] See Chapt. 4, 91–2; Chapt. 6, 205.
[182] Davis, *King Stephen*, 3rd edn., Chapt. 9 & 113–15, 117–18.

to his father's military and political sponsorship of his aunt, Earl William of Gloucester joined other barons in attesting the charter containing many of the treaty's terms. Almost anticlimactically, Stephen died in October 1154 and Henry fitz Empress ascended the Anglo-Norman throne, crowned on December 19, 1154.[183]

William of Malmesbury's death well before his patron's probably spared him from making the earl's fall in fortune in 1146–7, like his capture and imprisonment in 1141, into another example of his not letting adversity humble him.[184] As "the great earl," to use John of Salisbury's expression, lay dying, racked with fever, about October 31, it is hard not to think that in lucid moments his emotions did not oscillate between anger and despair. High on Robert's list of disappointments must have been his military fiasco at *Lidelea* and Philip's betrayal. The earl lacked the benefit of our hindsight that he had kept alive the potential for the Angevin succession, even that he had helped prepare the way for the "empire" of Henry II and Eleanor of Aquitaine, or, more to the point of this chapter, that some nine centuries later he would still be offering battle in self-defense and for the empress through not one apologia he and his family had helped to create, but two.[185]

As the discussion of this chapter shows, the collective persona of Robert earl of Gloucester was very much a product of his three careers. The patron of the *Historia Novella* originated in one way or another from all of them. The earl may have been capable of occasional dishonesty and of actions based on impulse. However, his most defining qualities often seem reducible to the learning and prudence Walter Map noted. Pragmatic shrewdness influenced the earl's recognition of Stephen, burghal patronage, and *conventiones* with ecclesiastics and Welsh princes. Robert was immensely proud of his royal lineage. He was a man of honor who, I believe, would not have rebelled against Stephen had he not perceived that the king had broken their *conventio*; he certainly refused to betray Matilda out of self-interest when given the chance during his captivity. Surely there would have been no Anarchy, at least as we know it, without him.

---

[183] *Regesta* iii. no. 272: "sicut filium et heredem meum...manutenebo" (the Westminster charter of November or December 1153); *The Peterborough Chronicle*, 59; Henry of Huntingdon (1996), 770–1; Patterson, "Anarchy in England," 189–200; Holt, "1153: The Treaty of Winchester," 294, but also 291–316; Leedom, "The English Settlement of 1153," 251–63; Crouch, *Reign of King Stephen*, 269–78.
[184] *HN* (1998), 106–7.
[185] "Letter 196," *The Letters of John of Salisbury* ii. 278–9. King, *HN* (1998), xxxiii–xxxiv, esp. xciv; Crouch, *Reign of King Stephen*, 34–5.

# Bibliography

## I. MANUSCRIPTS

Aberystwyth, NLW, Penrice & Margam Estate Record no. 20
Berkeley, BCM, Select Charters nos. 14, 15
Bristol, BA: 01248; 5138 (448), 5139 (78), 5139 (139), 5139 (175), 5139 (238), 5139 (448), 5139 (449), 5139 (487), 5139 (488), AC/D.13/1; DC/E/45; MS 36074/32 (c)
Caen. AD du Calvados, H.1; 2.H.2, fol. 139r (mod. fol.), nos. 766–7; fol. 185 (mod. fol.), no. 859. H.6510, no. 90, fol. 22b (mod. fol.); H.7824
    Musée des Beaux-Arts, Collection Mancel 303 (VI), fol. 27r
Cambridge. Trinity College, The Wren Library, MSS 0.2.4; R.7.1; R.7.10
Dublin, TCD, MS 507
Gloucester. GRO D.471/T.1/1–2
Hereford. Hereford Cathedral Library MS 0.iv.14
Kew, PRO/NA, C.66/580; C.47/45/388a; C.56/98; C.132; E.132/2/13; E.164/1; E.164/1/15LH; PRO 31, 8/140B, pts. 1–3
London. BL, Additional Charter 20120; Harley Charter 75.A.31; Stowe Charters 158, 159; Additional MSS 5937, 28206; 28207; 36985; 38129; Arundel MS 161; Cotton MSS Claudius A.vi; C.vii; D.ii; D.x; E.i; Cleopatra A.vii; C.iii; C.vii; Julius A.xi; D.ii; Nero D.i; Otho B.xiv; D.iii; Tiberius E.vi?; Vitellius A.x.; MSS Harley 3601; Lansdowne 398; Royal 13 B.xix; 13 D.ii; D.v; Sloane 1301; Rolls: Harley A.3; Sloan xxxi.4
    Lambeth Palace, MS 138
Oxford. All Souls College MS 35
    Bodl., MSS Bodley 712; Dodsworth 38; 97; 102; Douce 287; Lat. Misc.b.2 (R); Laud misc. 548; Lyell 5; Tanner 3; Top. Glouc. d. 2; Wood empt. 1; Douce Charters a.l, no. 37
    Queens College: MSS 88, 152
    St. John's College Archives, MUN XXI(1)
Paris, BN, MSS latins nouvelles acquisitions 1020, 1022–3
Swansea, WGAS, GBO216 A/N 1
Torpoint, Antony House MS PG/B2/6 ("Book of Evidences"/"Pole's Charters")
Trowbridge. Wiltshire Record Office, 192/154/12, no.1
Winchester, Winchester Cathedral Library, MS XXB

## II. DISSERTATIONS

Abbott, Mary, "The Gant Family in England 1066–1191," Ph.D. Thesis Cambridge University, 1973.
Allen, Richard, 'The Norman Episcopate 989–1110,' Ph.D. Dissertation. University of Glasgow, 2009.
Patterson, Robert B., "Robert Fitz Roy, Earl of Gloucester: A Study of a Baron c.1093–1147," Ph.D. Dissertation. The Johns Hopkins University, 1962.
Ponsford, M. W., "Bristol Castle: Archaeology and History of a Royal Fortress." M.Litt. thesis. University of Bristol, 1979.
Solan, Edward William, "A Study of the Life and Works of Serlo of Wilton," Ph.D. Dissertation. Indiana University, 1973; University Microfilms, 1981.

## III. PRINTED SOURCES

"Abbreviatio Amalarii," ed. R. W. Pfaff, in *Recherches de théologie ancienne et médiévale* 48 (1981): 128–71.

*Accounts of the Constables of Bristol Castle*, ed. Margaret Sharp. Bristol Record Society xxxiv (1982).

*Les Actes de Guillaume le Conquérant et de la reine Mathilde pour les abbayes caennaises*, ed. Lucien Musset. *MSAN* xxxvii (1967).

*Adami de Domerham Historia de Rebus Gestis Glastoniensibus*, ed. Thomas Hearne. 2 vols. London, 1727.

Ailred of Rievaulx, *Genealogia Regum Anglorum*, in *PL* 2nd ser. cxcv, cols. 711–38.

—— "Relatio Venerabilis Aelredi, Abbatis Rievallensis, De Standardo," ed. Richard Howlett in *Chronicles*: 181–99.

*Ancient Charters*, ed. John Horace Round. PRS x (1888).

"The Anglo-Norman *Description of England*: An Edition," ed. Alexander Bell. *Anglo-Norman Anniversary Essays*, ed. Ian Short. Anglo-Norman Text Society, Occasional Publication Series, ii, London, 1993, 31–47.

*The Anglo-Saxon Chronicle*, ed. Dorothy Whitelock, David C. Douglas, and Susie I. Tucker. London, 1961.

"Annales Anglosaxonici breves auctt. monachis ecclesiae Christi Cantuariensis; cum continuatione Latina a. 925–1202," in *Ungedruckte Anglo-Normannische Geschichtsquellen*, 1–8.

*Annales Cambriae*, ed. John Williams ab Ithel. London, 1860.

"Annales Dorenses," in *Monumenta Germaniae Historiae. Scriptores*. xxvii, ed. F. Liebermann and R. Pauli. Hanover, 1885, 514–31.

"Annales monasterii de Bello," in *Ungedruckte Anglo-Normannische Geschichtsquellen*, 50–5.

"Annales Plymptonienses," in *Ungedruckte Anglo-Normannische Geschichtsquellen*, 25–30.

"Annales Wintonienses cum contin. S. Augustini Cantuar.," in *Ungedruckte Anglo-Normannishe Geschichtsquellen*, 56–83.

"Ann. Bermondsey"="Annales Monasterii de Bermundseia," in *Ann. Mon.* iii. 423–87.

"Ann. Burton"="Annales de Burton," in *Ann. Mon.* i. 183–500.

"Ann. Dunstaple"="Annales Prioratus de Dunstaplia," in *Ann. Mon.* iii. 1–420.

"Ann. Margam"="Annales de Margan," in *Ann. Mon.* i. 3–40.

*Ann. Mon.*=*Annales Monastici*, ed. H. R. Luard. 5 vols. London, 1864–9.

"Ann. Oseney"="Annales Monasterii de Oseneia," in *Ann. Mon.* iv. 3–352.

"Ann. Tewkesbury"="Annales de Theokesberia," in *Ann. Mon.* i. 43–80.

"Ann. Waverley"="Annales Monasterii de Waverleia," in *Ann. Mon.* ii. 129–411.

"Ann. Winchcombe"="The Winchcombe Annals," ed. R. R. Darlington in *A Medieval Miscellany for Doris Mary Stenton*. PRS n.s. xxxvi (1962): 111–37.

"Ann. Winchester"="Annales Monasterii de Wintonia," in *Ann. Mon.* ii. 3–125.

"Ann. Worcester"="Annales Prioratus de Wigornia," in *Ann. Mon.* iv. 355–564.

*ASS*=*Acta Sanctorum*, ed. J. Bolland et al. Antwerp, Paris, Rome, Brussels. 1643–.

*Basset Charters*, ed. William T. Reedy. PRS lxxxviii, n.s. l (1989–91).

*BF*=*The Book of Fees Commonly Called the Testa de Nevill*. PRO. 3 vols. London, 1920–31.

*Bristol Charters 1155–1373*, ed. W. Dermott Harding. BRS i (1930).

*Bristol Charters 1378–1499*, ed. H. A. Cronne. BRS xi (1945).

*Brut Y Tywysogyon or The Chronicle of the Princes*, ed. and transl. Thomas Jones. Board of Celtic Studies, University of Wales History and Law Series xi. Cardiff, 1952.

*BS*=*Sir Christopher Hatton's Book of Seals*, ed. Lewis C. Loyd and Doris Mary Stenton. Oxford, 1950.

*Calendar of Charter Rolls*. ii: *Henry III–Edward* I. London, 1906.
*C* & *S*=*Councils & Synods with Other Documents Relating to the English Church*, ed. D. Whitelock, M. Brett, and C. N. L. Brooke. 2 vols. Oxford, 1981.
*Canterbury Professions*, ed. Michael Richter. Canterbury and York Society lxvii (1973).
*Cart. Abingdon*=*Two Cartularies of Abingdon Abbey*, ed. C. F. Slade and Gabrielle Lambrick. Oxford Historical Society n.s. xxxii (1990), xxxiii (1992).
*The Cartae Antiquae Rolls 1–10*, ed. Lionel Landon. PRS n.s. xvii (1939).
*The Cartae Antiquae Rolls 11–20*, ed. J. Conway Davies. PRS n.s. xxxiii (1957).
*Cart. Bath*=*Two Cartularies of St. Peter at Bath*, ed. William Hunt. SRS vii (1893).
*Cart. Bayeux*=*Antiquus Cartularius Ecclesiae Baiocensis*, ed. V. Bourienne. 2 vols. Paris and Rouen, 1902–3.
*Cart. Beauchamp*=*The Beauchamp Cartulary Charters 1100–1268*, ed. Emma Mason. PRS lxxxi. n.s. xliii (1971–3).
*Cart. Bristol*=*The Cartulary of St. Augustine's Abbey, Bristol*, ed. David Walker. Bristol and Gloucestershire Archaeological Society: Gloucestershire Record Series xi (1997?).
*Cart. Bruton*=*Two Cartularies of the Augustinian Priory of Bruton and the Cluniac Priory of Montacute*, ed. the Council. SRS viii (1894).
*Cart. Canonsleigh*=*The Cartulary of Canonsleigh Abbey (Harleian MS. 3660)*, ed. Vera C. M. London. Devon and Cornwall Record Society, n.s. viii (1965).
*Cart. Cirencester*=*The Cartulary of Cirencester Abbey Gloucestershire*. i–ii, ed. C. D. Ross. iii, ed. Mary Devine. Oxford, 1964–77.
*Cart. Clerkenwell*=*The Cartulary of St. Mary, Clerkenwell*, ed. W. O. Hassal. Camden Society, 3rd ser. lxxi (1929).
*Cart. Colchester*=*Cartularium monasterii sancti Johannis Baptiste de Colecestria*, ed. S. A. Moore. 2 vols. Roxburghe Club, 1897.
*Cart. Forde*=*The Cartulary of Forde Abbey*, ed. Steven Hobbs. SRS lxxxv (1998).
*Cart. Glastonbury*=*The Great Chartulary of Glastonbury*, ed. Dom Aelred Watkin. 3 vols. SRS lix, lxiii, lxiv (1944–56).
*Cart. Gloucester*=*Historia et Cartularium Monasterii Sancti Petri de Gloucestria*, ed. W. H. Hart. 3 vols. Oxford, 1863–7.
*Cart. Langley*=*The Langley Cartulary*, ed. Peter Coss. Dugdale Society xxxii (1980).
*Cart. Launceston*=*The Cartulary of Launceston Priory*, ed. and introd. P. L. Hull. Devon & Cornwall Record Society, n.s. xxx (1987).
*Cart. Montacute*=*Two Cartularies of the Augustinian Priory of Bruton and the Cluniac Priory of Montacute…*, ed. Members of the Council. SRS viii (1894).
*Cart. Oseney*=*The Cartulary of Oseney Abbey*, ed. H. E. Salter. 6 vols. Oxford, 1929–36.
*Cart. Ramsey*=*Cartularium Monasterii de Rameseia*, ed. William Henry Hart and Ponsonby A. Lyons. 3 vols. London, 1884–93; reprn. edn. Wiesbaden, 1965.
*Cart. Reading*=*Reading Abbey Cartularies*, ed. B. Kemp. 2 vols. Camden Society. 4th ser., xxxi, xxxiii (1986–7).
*Cart. Shrewsbury*=*The Cartulary of Shrewsbury Abbey*, ed. Una Rees. 2 vols. Aberystwyth: The National Library of Wales, 1975.
*Cart. Thame*=The Thame Cartulary, ed. H. E. Salter. Oxford Historical Society xxv (1947).
*Cartulaire de l'abbaye de Saint-Père de Chartres*, ed. M. Guérard. *Collection des documents inédits sur l'histoire de France: collection des cartulaires de France* i–ii. Paris, 1840.
"Cartularium Prioratus S. Johannis Evang. De Brecon," *Archaeologia Cambrensis* 4th ser. xiii (1882): 275–308; xiv (1883): 18–48, 137–68; 221–36; 274–301.
*The Cartulary of Holy Trinity, Aldgate*, ed. G. A. J. Hodgett. London Record Society vii (1971).

*Cart. Warwick*=*The Newburgh Earldom of Warwick and its Charters*, ed. David Crouch. Introduction and Appendix by Richard Dace. Dugdale Society xlviii (2015).
*Cart. Worcester*=*The Cartulary of Worcester Cathedral Priory*, ed. R. R. Darlington. PRS n.s. xxxviii (1962–3).
*Catalogue of Ancient Deeds in the Public Record Office*. iii. London, 1900.
*CDF*=*Calendar of Documents Preserved in France, Illustrative of the History of Great Britain and Ireland*, ed. J. H. Round. vol. 1: *918–1206*. London, 1899.
*Chart. Basset*=*Basset Charters c.1120 to 1250*, ed. William T. Reedy. PRS n.s. l (1989–91).
*Chart. Chester*=*Charters of the Anglo-Norman Earls of Chester, c.1071–1237*, ed. Geoffrey Barraclough. Record Society of Lancashire and Cheshire cxxvi (1988).
*Charters and Custumals of the Abbey of Holy Trinity Caen*, pt. 2: *The French Estates*, ed. John Wamsley. *Records of Social and Economic History*, n.s. xxii (1994).
*Charters of the Honour of Mowbray 1107–1191*, ed. D. E. Greenway. Records of Social and Economic History. n.s. i (London, 1972).
"Charters of the Redvers Family and the Earldom of Devon, 1090–1217: An addendum," ed. Robert Bearman, *The Devonshire Association for the Advancement of Science, Literature, and the Arts* cxlii (2010): 73–96.
*Chartes Anciennes du prieuré de Monmouth en Angleterre*, ed. Paul Marchegay (Les Roches-Baritand, Vendée, 1879).
*Chartes de l'abbaye de Jumièges*, ed. J. J. Vernier. 2 vols. Rouen, 1916.
*Chart. Hereford*=*Charters of the Earldom of Hereford, 1095–1201*, ed. David Walker. *Camden Miscellany* xxii (1964), 1–75.
*Chronica Monasterii de Melsa*, ed. Edward A. Bond. 3 vols. London, 1866–8.
*The Chronicle of Battle Abbey*, ed. and transl. Eleanor Searle. Oxford, 1980.
*Chronicles*=*Chronicles of the Reigns of Stephen, Henry II, and Richard I*, ed. Richard Howlett. 4 vols. London, 1884–9; reprn. edn. Wiesbaden, 1964.
*Chronicon Abbatiae Rameseiensis*, ed. W. Dunn Macray. London, 1886.
*Chronicon Monasterii de Abingdon*, ed. J. Stevenson. 2 vols. London, 1858.
"Chronicon S. Stephani Cadomensis," *RHG* xii (Paris, 1731), 779–80.
*Chronicon Valassense*, ed. F. Sommènil. Rouen, 1868.
*Chronicon Vulgo Dictum Thomae Wykes*, ed. Henry Richards Luard in *Ann. Mon.* iv. 6–319.
*Chroniques anglo-normandes*, ed. Francisque Michel. 3 vols. Rouen, 1836–40.
*Chroniques des comtes d'Anjou et des seigneurs d'Amboise*, ed. Louis Halphen and René Poupardin. Paris, 1913.
*CIPM*=*Calendar of Inquisitions Post Mortem*. i. London, 1904; iii. London, 1912.
Clark, *Cartae et alia*=*Cartae et alia Munimenta quae ad Dominium de Glamorgancia pertinent*, ed. G. T. Clark. 6 vols. Cardiff, 1910.
*Concilia Rotomagensis Provinciae*, ed. G. Bessin. ii. Rouen, 1717.
"Constitutio Domus Regis," ed. and transl. S. D. Church. in *Dialogus de Scaccario*, 195–215.
"Cont. Wace,"="Extrait de la continuation de Brut d'Angleterre de Wace, par un anonyme," in *Chroniques anglo-normandes*, ed. Francisque Michel. i (Rouen, 1835), 65–117.
*Cornwall Feet of Fines I*, ed. Joseph Hambley Rowe. Devon and Cornwall Record Society, 1914.
*Coutumiers de Normandie*, ed. Ernest-Joseph Tardif. i: *Très Ancien Coutumier de Normandie*. Société de l'Histoire de Normandie xii. Rouen, 1881.
*CPR*=*Calendar of Patent Rolls*: *Henry IV* iii. London, 1907; reprn. edn. Nendeln, 1971; *Henry VII* ii. London, 1916; reprn. edn. Nendeln, 1970.

*Crown Pleas of the Devon Eyre of 1238*, ed. Henry Sommerson. Devon and Cornwall Record Society n.s. xxviii (1985).
*CRR=Curia Regis Rolls*. i. London, 1922; iv. London, 1924; reprn edn. 1971; x. London, 1949; xi. London, 1955; xii. London, 1957.
*DB=Domesday Book.*
*De Expugnatione Lyxbonensi: The Conquest of Lisbon*, ed. Charles Wendell David. New York, 1936.
Delisle-Berger=*Recueil des actes de Henri II roi d'Angleterre et duc de Normandie*, ed. Léopold Delisle and Élie Berger. 3 vols. in 4. Paris, 1909–27.
*De Nugis Curialium=Walter Map De Nugis Curialium: Courtiers' Trifles*, ed. M. R. James; rev. edn. by C. N. L. Brooke and R. A. B. Mynors. Oxford, 1983.
*Département de la Manche: archives ecclésiastiques. Serie H*. i, pt.1, ed. M. Dubosc (St-Lô, 1866).
*Dialogus de Scaccario=Dialogus de Scaccario; Constitutio Domus Regis*, ed. and transl. Emily Amt and S. D. Church, reprn. edn. Oxford, 2013.
*DNB=The Dictionary of National Biography*, reprn. edn. Oxford, 1921–2.
*Documents and Extracts Illustrating the Honour of Dunster*, ed. H. C. Maxwell-Lyte. Somerset Record Society xxxiii (1917–18).
*Domesday Book seu Liber Censualis Willelmi Primi Regis Angliae*, ed. A. Farley and H. Ellis. 4 vols. London, 1783–1816.
*Domesday Book*, Phillimore Edition. vols. by counties. Chichester, 1983–.
*The Domesday Monachorum of Christ Church Canterbury*, ed. David C. Douglas. London, 1944.
Eadmer=*Eadmeri Historia Novorum in Anglia*, ed. Martin Rule. London, 1884; reprn. edn. Wiesbaden, 1965.
*EEA=English Episcopal Acta.*
*EEA* i: *Lincoln 1067–1185*, ed. David M. Smith. Oxford, 1980.
*EEA* v: *York 1070–1154*, ed. Janet E. Burton. Oxford, 1988.
*EEA* vi: *Norwich 1070–1214*, ed. Christopher Harper-Bill. London, 1990.
*EEA* vii: *Hereford 1079–1234*, ed. Julia Barrow. Oxford, 1993.
*EEA* viii: *Winchester 1070–1204*, ed. M. J. Franklin. Oxford, 1993.
*EEA* x: *Bath and Wells 1061–1205*, ed. Frances M. R. Ramsey. Oxford, 1995.
*EEA* xi, xii: *Exeter 1046–1184, 1186–1257*, ed. Frank Barlow. 2 vols. Oxford, 1996.
*EEA* xv: *London 1076–1187*, ed. Falko Neininger. Oxford, 1999.
*EEA* xxxiii: *Worcester 1062–1185*, ed. Mary Cheney, David Smith, Christopher Brooke, and Philippa Hoskin. Oxford, 2007.
*EHD* ii=*English Historical Documents 1042–1189*, ed. David C. Douglas and George W. Greenaway. ii. London, 1968.
*English Lawsuits from William I to Richard I*, ed. R. C. van Caenegem. Selden Society. cvi (1990).
*Episcopal Acts and Cognate Documents Relating to Welsh Dioceses*, ed. James Conway Davies. 2 vols. Cardiff, 1948.
"Ex Brevi Chronico Ducum Normanniae," in *RHG* xii. 786–8.
"Ex Brevi Chronico Gemeticensi," in *RHG* xii. 775.
"Extrait de la continuation du Brut d'Angleterre de Wace par un anonyme," in *Chroniques anglo-normandes*, ed. Francisque Michel i. Rouen, 1835, 65–117.
*Extraits des chartes et autres actes normands ou anglo-normands qui se trouvent dans les archives du Calvados*, ed. Lechaudé D'Anisy. *MSAN* vii–viii. Rouen, 1833–4.

*Eynsham Cartualry*, ed. H. E. Salter. i. Oxford, 1907.
*Facsimiles of English Royal Writs to A.D. 1100*, ed. T. A. M. Bishop and P(ierre) Chaplais. Oxford, 1957.
Gaimar, *Lestorie des Engles*, ed. Thomas Duffus Hardy and C. Trice Martin. 2 vols. London, 1888–9.
——— *L'Estoire des Engleis*, ed. Alexander Bell. Anglo-Norman Text Society, xiv–xvi; reprn. edn., New York and London, 1971.
*Gallia Christiana in Provincias Ecclesiasticas Distributa*, ed. P. Piolin. xi. Paris, 1759; reprn. edn., Farnborough, 1970.
*Geffrei Gaimar Estoire des Engleis, History of the English*, ed. and transl. Ian Short. Oxford, 2009.
Gerald of Wales, *Itinerarium=Geraldi Cambrensis Itinerarium Kambriae et Descriptio Kambriae*, ed. James F. Dimock. London, 1868; reprn. edn. Wiesbaden, 1964.
Gervase of Canterbury=*Chronica Gervasii* in *The Historical Works of Gervase of Canterbury*, ed. William Stubbs. i. London, 1879; reprn. edn., Wiesbaden, 1965.
*Die Gesetze der Angelsachsen*, ed. Felix Liebermann. 3 vols. Halle, 1903–16.
*Gesta Abbatum Monasterii Sancti Albani*, ed. H. T. Riley. 3 vols. Oxford, 1867–9.
*Gesta Regis Henrici Secundi Benedicti Abbatis. The Chronicle of the Reigns of Henry II and Richard I*, ed. William Stubbs. 2 vols. London, 1867.
Glanville=*Tractatus de Legibus et Consuetudinibus Regni Anglie*, ed. and transl. G. D. G. Hall. Edinburgh, 1965.
*GND=The Gesta Normannorum Ducum of William of Jumièges, Orderic Vitalis, and Robert of Torigni*, ed. and transl. Elizabeth M. C. Van Houts. 2 vols. Oxford, 1992–5.
*GP=William of Malmesbury Gesta Pontificum Anglorum*, ed. and transl. M. Winterbottom with assistance of R. M. Thomson. Oxford, 2007.
*GR=William of Malmesbury, Gesta Regum Anglorum* i, ed. and transl. R. A. B. Mynors, R. M. Thomson, and M. Winterbottom. Oxford, 1998. ii: *General Introduction and Commentary*, by R. M. Thomson. Oxford, 1999.
*GS=Gesta Stephani*, ed. K. R. Potter and R. H. C. Davis; reprn. edn. Oxford, 2004.
Henry of Huntingdon (1996)=*Henry, Archdeacon of Huntingdon, Historia Anglorum*, ed. and transl. Diana Greenway. Oxford, 1996.
*L'Histoire de Guillaume le maréchal*, ed. Paul Meyer. i. Paris, 1891.
*Histoire des ducs de Normandie et des rois d'Angleterre*, ed. Francisque Michel; reprn. edn. New York, 1964.
"Historia Gaufridi ducis Normannorum et comitis Andegavorum," in *Chroniques des comtes d'Anjou et des seigneurs d'Amboise*, ed. Louis Halphen and René Poupardin. Paris, 1913.
*Historia Monasterii S. Augustini Cantuariensis*, ed. Charles Hardwick. London, 1858.
*The Historia Pontificalis of John of Salisbury*, ed. Marjorie Chibnall. Oxford, 1986.
*The Historia Regum Britannie of Geoffrey of Monmouth* v, ed. Neil Wright. Cambridge, 1984.
*History of William Marshal*, ed. A. J. Holden, S. Gregory, and D. Crouch. Anglo-Norman Text Society, Occasional Publications Series iv (2002).
*The History of William Marshal*, transl. Nigel Bryant. Woodbridge, 2016.
*HN* (1998)=*William of Malmesbury Historia Novella: The Contemporary History*, ed. Edmund King and transl. K. R. Potter. Oxford, 1998.
Howden=*Chronicon Magistri Rogeri de Hovedene*, ed. William Stubbs, 4 vols. London, 1868–71.
*HRB=Geoffrey of Monmouth, The History of the Kings of Britain (Historia Regum Britanniae)*, ed. Michael D. Reeve; transl. Neil Wright. Woodbridge, 2007.

Hugh the Chanter, *The History of the Church of York*, ed. and transl. Charles Johnson. London, 1961; rev. edn. ed. M. Brett, C. N. L. Brooke, and M. Winterbottom, Oxford 1990.
"Inquest of 1133," in *Extraits des chartes* ii. 426–31.
"Inquest of 1133," in *RBE* ii. 645–7.
"Inquest of 1133," in *RHG* xxiii. 699–702.
"Institutio Cnuti Aliorumque Regum Anglorum," in *Die Gesetze der Angelsachsen* i. 612–16.
"Inventio S. Nectani Martyris," in "Vie de S. Rumon, Vie, Invention et Miracles de S. Nectan," ed. Paul Grosjean. *Analecta Bollandiana* lxxi (1953): 359–414.
*The Itinerary of John Leland the Antiquary*, ed. Thomas Hearne. vi–vii. Oxford, 1769.
John of Ford, *The Life of Wulfric of Haselbury*, ed. M. Bell. SRS xlvii (1933).
John of Hexham, "Historia Johannis Prioris Hagustaldensis Ecclesiae xxv. Annorum," in *Symeonis Monachi Opera Omnia*, ed. Thomas Arnold. London, 1865; reprn. edn. Wiesbaden, 1965, ii. 284–332.
John of Marmoutier, "Vita Gaufridi Ducis Normannorum et Comitis Andegavorum," in *Chroniques des comtes d'Anjou et des seigneurs d'Amboise*, 172–238.
John of Salisbury, *Historia Pontificalis*, ed. Marjorie Chibnall. Edinburgh, London, Paris, and New York, 1956.
*Journal de Verdun*. October, 1760, p. 276.
*JW* iii= *The Chronicle of John of Worcester* iii: *The Annals from 1067 to 1140 with the Gloucester Interpolations and Continuation to 1141*, ed. and transl. P(atrick) McGurk. Oxford, 1998.
*The Kalendar of Abbot Samson of Bury St. Edmunds and Related Documents*, ed. R. H. C. Davis. Camden Society 3rd ser. lxxxiv (1954).
*Kirby's Quest for Somerset and Nomina Villarum for Somerset of the 16th Year of Edward 3rd*, ed. F. H. Dickinson. SRS iii (1889).
*LCGF= The Letters and Charters of Gilbert Foliot*, ed. Adrian Morey and C. N. L. Brooke. Cambridge, 1967.
*LE=Liber Eliensis*, ed. E. O. Blake. Camden Society, 3rd ser. xcii (1962).
*LEA=Llandaff Episcopal Acta 1140–1287*, ed. David Crouch. Cardiff, 1988.
"Leges Edwardi Confessoris," in *Die Gesetze der Angelsachsen* i. 627–72.
*Leges Henrici Primi*, ed. and transl. L. J. Downer. Oxford, 1972.
*Leland's Itinerary in England and Wales*, ed. Lucy Toulmin Smith. iv (1964).
*The Letters of Arnulf of Lisieux*, ed. Frank Barlow. Camden Society, 3rd ser. lxi (1939).
*The Letters of John of Salisbury*, ed. W. J. Millor and C. N. L. Brooke. ii. Oxford, 1979.
*The Letters of Peter the Venerable*, ed. Giles Constable. 2 vols. Cambridge, MA, 1967.
*Liber Landavensis= The Text of the Book of Llan Dâv*, ed. J. Gwenoguryn Evans and John Rhys. Oxford, 1893.
*Liber Niger Scaccarii*, ed. Thomas Hearne. 2 vols. London, 1774.
Liebermann, Felix, "The Text of Henry I's Coronation Charter," *TRHS* n.s. viii (1894): 21–49.
*The Lincolnshire Domesday and the Lindsey Survey*, ed. C. W. Foster and Thomas Langley, with introd. by F. M. Stenton. *Lincoln Record Society* xix (1924).
*The Lincolnshire Survey*, ed. James Greenstreet. London, 1884.
*The Little Red Book of Bristol*, ed. Francis B. Bickley. Bristol and London, 1900.
*LW*="Liber Winton," in *Winchester*, 32–141.
*Magni Rotuli Scaccarii Normanniae sub Regibus Angliae*, ed. Thomas Stapleton. 2 vols. London, 1840–4.
*The Maire of Bristowe Is Kalendar by Robert Ricart Town Clerk of Bristol 15 Edward IV*, ed. Lucy Toulmin Smith. Camden Society n.s. v (1872).

Mansi, Joannes, *Sacrorum Conciliorum Nova et Amplissima Collectio. Editio Novissima*. xxii. Paris, 1903.

Matthew Paris, *Chronica Majora=Matthaei Parisiensis, Monachi Sancti Albani, Chronica Majora*, ed. Henry Richards Luard. ii. London, 1874; reprn. edn., Wiesbaden, 1964.

—— *Flores Historiarum*, ed. Henry Richards Luard. 2 vols. London, 1890; reprn. edn. Wiesbaden, 1965.

*A Medieval Miscellany for Doris Mary Stenton*. PRS n.s. xxxvi (1962): 111–37.

Merrick, Rice, *A Booke of Glamorganshires Antiquities*, ed. James Andrew Corbett. London, 1887.

*The Metrical Chronicle of Robert of Gloucester*, ed. William Aldis Wright. 2 vols. London, 1887.

*MHTB=Materials for the History of Thomas Becket, Archbishop of Canterbury*, ed. J. C. Robertson. 7 vols. London, 1875–85.

*Mon. Angl.*=William Dugdale, *Monasticon Anglicanum*, ed. John Caley, Henry Ellis, and Bulkeley Bandinell. 6 vols. London, 1817–30.

*Neustria Pia*, ed. Arthur Du Monstier. Rouen, 1663.

"The Northamptonshire Survey," ed. J. H. Round in *VCH Northamptonshire* i. 365–89.

*OASPG=The Original Acta of St. Peter's Abbey Gloucester c.1122 to 1263*, ed. Robert B. Patterson. The Bristol and Gloucestershire Archaeological Society. Gloucestershire Record Series xi (1998).

Orderic Vitalis, "Interpolations," in William of Jumièges, *Gesta Normannorum Ducum*, ed. Jean Marx. Rouen and Paris, 1914, 151–98.

*OV=The Ecclesiastical History of Orderic Vitalis*, ed. Marjorie Chibnall. 6 vols. Oxford, 1969–80.

*Papsturkunden in Frankreich* ii, ed. Johannes Ramackers. Göttingen, 1937.

Patterson, *EGC =Earldom of Gloucester Charters: The Charters and Scribes of the Earls and Countesses of Gloucester to A. D. 1217*, ed. Robert B. Patterson. Oxford, 1973.

*The Peterborough Chronicle 1070–1154*, ed. Cecily Clark. 2nd edn. Oxford, 1970.

*Pipe Rolls of the Exchequer of Normandy for the Reign of Henry II 1180 and 1184*, ed. Vincent Moss. PRS xci n.s. liii (2004).

*PL=Patrologiae Cursus Completus*, ed. J. P. Migne. Series Latina. 221 vols. Paris, 1844–55.

*PR 2, 3, 4 Henry II=The Great Rolls of the Pipe for the Second, Third, and Fourth Years of the Reign of King Henry the Second, A.D. 1155, 1156, 1157, 1158*, ed. Joseph Hunter. London, 1844.

*PR 31 Henry I=Magnum Rotulum Scaccarii vel Magnum Rotulum Pipae de Anno Tricesimo-primo Regni Henrici Primi*, ed. J. Hunter. Record Commission. London, 1833.

*PR 31 Henry I* (Green)=*The Great Roll of the Pipe for the Thirty First Year of the Reign of King Henry I: Michaelmas 1130*, ed. and transl. Judith A. Green. PRS xcv, n.s. lvii (2012).

*PR 31 Henry II=The Great Roll of the Pipe for the Thirty-First Year of the Reign of King Henry II*, ed. J. H. Round. PRS xxxiv (1913).

*PR 32 Henry II=The Great Roll of the Pipe for the Thirty-Second Year of the Reign of King Henry II*, ed. J. H. Round. PRS xxxvi (1914).

*PR 33 Henry II*, PRS xxxvii (1915).

*PR 34 Henry II*, PRS xxxviii (1925).

*PR 3–4 Richard I*, ed. Doris M. Stenton. PRS n.s. ii (1926).

*PR 5 Richard I*, ed. Doris M. Stenton. PRS n.s. iii (1927).

*PR 6 Richard I*, ed. Doris M. Stenton. PRS n.s. v (1928).

*PR 1 John*, ed. Doris M. Stenton. PRS n.s. x (1933).

*PR 2 John*, ed. Doris M. Stenton. PRS n.s. xii (1934).

*PR 3 John*, ed. Doris M. Stenton. PRS n.s. xiv (1936).
*PR 4 John*, ed. Doris M. Stenton. PRS xv (1937).
*PR 5 John*, ed. Doris M. Stenton. PRS xvi (1938).
*RADN=Recueil des actes des ducs de Normandie (911–1066)*, ed. Marie Fauroux. *MSAN* xxxvi (1961).
*Radulfi Nigri Chronica: The Chronicles of Ralph Niger*, ed. Robert Anstruther. Caxton Society xiii (1851); reprn. edn. New York, 1967.
Ralph de Diceto=*Radulfi De Diceto Deaconi Lundoniensis Opera Historica*, ed. William Stubbs. 2 vols. London, 1876; reprn. edn. Wiesbaden, 1965.
*RBE=The Red Book of the Exchequer*, ed. Hubert Hall. 3 vols. London, 1896; reprn. edn. Wiesbaden, 1965.
*Records of the Templars in England in the Twelfth Century*, ed. Beatrice A. Lees. London, 1935.
*Recueil des actes de Henri II roi d'Angleterre et duc de Normandie*, ed. Léopold Delisle and Élie Berger. 3 vols. in 4. Paris, 1909–27.
*The Red Book of Worcester*, ed. Marjorie Hollins. Worcestershire Historical Society. London, 1950.
*Redvers Charters=Charters of the Redvers Family and the Earldom of Devon*, ed. Robert Bearman. Devon & Cornwall Record Society, n.s. xxxvii (1994).
*Regesta* i–iv=*Regesta Regum Anglo-Normannorum 1066-1154*, i: *1066–1100*, ed. H. W. C. Davis. Oxford, 1913; ii: *1100–1135*, ed. Charles Johnson and H. A. Cronne. Oxford, 1956; iii–iv: *1135–1154*, ed. H. A. Cronne and R. H. C. Davis. 2 vols. Oxford, 1968–9.
*Regesta* i. (1998)=*Regesta Regum Anglo-Normannorum: The Acta of William I (1066–1087)*, ed. David Bates. Oxford, 1998.
*Regesta Pontificum Romanorum ab condita ecclesia ad annum post Christum natum MCXCVIII*, ed. P. Jaffé. 2 vols. Leipzig, 1885–8.
*Regesta Regum Scottorum* i: *The Acts of Malcolm IV King of Scots 1153–1165*, ed. G. W. S. Barrow. Edinburgh, 1960.
*Registrum Roffense*, ed. J. Thorpe. ii. London, 1769.
*RHG=Recueil des historiens des Gaules et de la France*, ed. M. Bouquet et al. 24 vols. Paris, 1869–1904.
Richard of Hexham, "De Gestis Regis Stephani et de Bello Standardii," in *Chronicles*, iii. 139–78.
Robert of Torigny, "Chronica," in *Chronicles* iv. 81–315.
—— "Interpolations," in William of Jumièges, *Gesta Normannorum Ducum*, ed. Jean Marx. Rouen and Paris, 1914, 199–334.
Roger of Howden, *Chronica Magistri Rogeri De Houedene*, ed. William Stubbs. 2 vols. London, 1868; reprn. edn. Wiesbaden, 1964.
Roger of Wendover, *Rogeri De Wendover Chronica, Sive Flores Historiarum*, ed. H. O. Cox. ii. London, 1841.
*Rotuli Chartarum in Turri Londinensi Asservati*, i, pt. 1: *1199–1216*, ed. Thomas Duffus Hardy. London, 1837.
*Rotuli de Dominabus et Pueris et Puellis de Donatione Regis in xii Comitatibus (1185)*, ed. John Horace Round. PRS xxxv (1913).
*Rotuli Normanniae in Turri Londinensi asservati*. i: *1199–1216*, ed. Thomas Duffus Hardy. London, 1835.
*S. Anselmi Cantuariensis Archiepiscopi Opera Omnia*, ed. F. S. Schmitt. iv. Edinburgh, 1902.

*Sarum Charters and Documents*, ed. W. Rich-Jones and W. Dunn Macray. Oxford, 1891.

Scott, John, *The Early History of Glastonbury: An Edition, Translation and Study of William of Malmesbury's De Antiquitate Glastonie Ecclesie*. Woodbridge, 1981.

*Select Charters and Other Illustrations of English Constitutional History*, ed. William Stubbs. Oxford, 1900.

*Select Documents of the English Lands of Bec*, ed. Marjorie Chibnall. Camden Society. 3rd ser. lxxiii (1951).

*Serlon de Wilton: Poèmes latins*, ed. Jan Öberg. Stockholm, 1965.

*Sir Christopher Hatton's Book of Seals*, ed. Lewis C. Loyd and Doris Mary Stenton. Oxford, 1950.

*Somerset Pleas from the Rolls of the Itinerant Justices* iv, pt. 1, ed. Lionel Landon SRS xliv (1929).

Suger, *Vie de Louis VI le Gros*, ed. and transl. Henri Waquet. Paris, 1964.

—— *The Deeds of Louis the Fat*. transl. and ed. Richard Cusimano and John Moorhead. Washington DC, 1984.

Symeon of Durham=*Historia Regum* in *Symeonis Monachi Opera Omnia* ii, ed. Thomas Arnold. London, 1865; reprn. edn. Wiesbaden, 1965.

—— *Libellus de Exordio atque Processu Istius hoc est Dunhelmensis Ecclesie*, ed. and transl. David Rollason. Oxford, 2000.

*The Thame Cartulary*, ed. H. E. Salter. Oxford Record Society xxv (1947).

*Ungedruckte Anglo-Normannische Geschichtsquellen*, ed. F. Lieberbann; reprn. edn. Ridgewood, NJ, 1966.

"Vita S. Bernardi Abbatis de Tiron," *ASS* April ii. 220–54.

*The Vita Wulfstani of William of Malmesbury*, ed. R. R. Darlington. Camden Society 3rd ser. xl (1928).

Wace, *Le Roman de Rou de Wace*, ed. A. J. Holden. 3 vols. Paris, 1970.

—— *The History of the Norman People: Wace's Roman de Rou*, transl. G. S. Burgess; rev. edn. Woodbridge, 2004.

*The Warenne (Hyde) Chronicle*, ed. Elizabeth M. C. Van Houts and Rosalind C. Love. Oxford, 2013.

Warner & Ellis=*Facsimiles of Royal and Other Charters in the British Museum* i, ed. George F. Warner and Henry J. Ellis. London, 1903.

*Westminster Abbey Charters*, ed. Emma Mason. London Record Society xxv (1988).

*The White Book of Peterborough*, ed. Sandra Raban; transcr. by Claire de Trafford and Sandra Raban. Northamptonshire Record Society. xli (2001).

William fitz Stephen, "Vita S. Thomae," in *MHTB* iii. 1–154.

William of Malmesbury, *GR*=*Willelmi Malmesbiriensis Monachi De Gestis Regum Anglorum; Historiae Novellae*, ed. William Stubbs. 2 vols. London, 1887; reprn. edn. Wiesbaden, 1964.

—— *HN*=*The Historia Novella*, ed. and transl. K. R. Potter; discussion of texts by R. A. Mynors. London and Edinburgh, 1955.

William of Newburgh=*The Historia Rerum Anglicarum of William of Newburgh*, ed. Richard Howlett, in *Chronicles* i; ii. 415–500.

William of Poitiers=*The Gesta Guillelmi of William of Poitiers*, ed. and transl. R. H. C. Davis and Marjorie Chibnall. Oxford, 1998.

*William Worcester: Itineraries*, ed. John H. Harvey. Oxford, 1969.

*William Worcester: The Topography of Medieval Bristol*, ed. Frances Neal. BRS li (2000).

*Wulfric of Haselbury by John Abbot of Ford*, ed. Dom Maurice Bell SRS xlvii (1933).

## IV. MODERN WORKS

Aird, William M., *Robert Curthose Duke of Normandy (c.1050–1134)*. Woodbridge, 2008.
Amt, Emilie, *The Accession of Henry II in England*. Woodbridge, 1993.
*The Anarchy of King Stephen's Reign*, ed. Edmund King. Oxford, 1994.
*Anglo-Norman Literature: A Guide to Texts and Manuscripts*, ed. Ruth J. Dean with collaboration of Maureen B. M. Boulton. Anglo-Norman Text Society. London, 1999.
*Anglo-Norman Political Culture and the Twelfth-Century Renaissance*. Proceedings of the Borchard Conference on Anglo-Norman History, 1995, ed. C. Warren Hollister. Woodbridge, 1997.
Anon., "The Lovels of Castle Cary," *Notes and Queries for Somerset and Dorset*, ed. G. W. Saunders and R. G. Bartelot, 17 (1925): 173–6.
Appleby John T., "Richard of Devizes and the Annals of Winchester," *BIHR* 36 (1963): 70–5.
—— *The Troubled Reign of King Stephen*. London, 1969.
Archibald, Marion, "The Lion Coinage of Robert Earl of Gloucester and William Earl of Gloucester," *BNJ* 61 (2001): 71–86 & plates.
Babcock, Robert S., "Rhys ap Tewdwr, King of Deheubarth," *ANS* 16 (1994): 21–35.
Baker, Derek, "Ailred of Rievaulx and Walter Espec," *HSJ* 1(1989): 91–8.
Barber, Richard, "When is a Knight not a Knight?," *Medieval Knighthood V: Papers from the Sixth Strawberry Hill Conference 1994*, ed. Stephen Church and Ruth Harvey. Woodbridge, 1995, 1–17.
Barker, Lynn K., "Ivo of Chartres and the Anglo-Norman Cultural Tradition," *ANS* 13 (1990): 15–33.
Barkly, G. M., "The Earlier House of Berkeley," *BGAST* 8 (1893–94): 193–223.
Barlow, Frank, *The English Church 1066–1154*. London and New York, 1979.
—— *William Rufus*. Berkeley and Los Angeles, 1983.
—— *Thomas Becket*. Berkeley and Los Angeles, 1986.
—— "Corbeil, William de," *ODNB* xiii. 382–5.
Barraclough, Geoffrey, "The Earldom and County Palatine of Chester," reprn. Oxford, 1963.
Barrett, William, *The History and Antiquities of the City of Bristol*. Bristol, 1789; reprn. edn. Stroud, 1982.
Barrow, G. W. S., "The Charters of David I," *ANS* 14 (1991): 25–37.
—— "The Scots and the North of England," in *The Anarchy of King Stephen's Reign*, 231–53.
—— "David I," *ODNB* xv. 285–8.
Bartlett, Robert, *England under the Norman and Angevin Kings 1075–1225*. Oxford, 2000.
Bates, David, "The Character and Career of Odo, Bishop of Bayeux (1049/50–1097)," *Speculum* l (1975): 1–20.
—— "The Origins of the Justiciarship," *ANS* 4 (1981): 1–12.
—— *Normandy before 1066*. London and New York, 1982.
—— "The Earliest Norman Writs," *EHR* 100 (1985): 266–84.
—— "The Prosopographical Study of Anglo-Norman Royal Charters," in Keats-Rohan, *Family Trees and the Roots of Politics*, 89–101.
—— *William the Conqueror*. Stroud, 2001.
—— "The Conqueror's Adolescence," *ANS* 25 (2002): 1–18.
—— "Address and Delivery in Anglo-Norman Royal Charters," in *Charters and Charter Scholarship*, 32–52.

Bates, David, "Robert of Torigny and the *Historia Anglorum*," in *The English and their Legacy, 900–1200: Essays in Honour of Ann Williams*, ed. David Roffe. Woodbridge, 2012, 175–84.

—— *The Normans and Empire*. Oxford, 2013.

Bearman, Robert, "Baldwin de Redvers: Some Aspects of a Baronial Career in the Reign of King Stephen," *ANS* 18 (1996): 19–46.

—— "Mohun, William de, Earl of Somerset," *ODNB* xxxviii. 515–16.

Beeler, John, *Warfare in England 1066–1189*. Ithaca, NY, 1966.

Beresford, Maurice, *New Towns of the Middle Ages*. London, 1967.

Berry V. G., "The Second Crusade," in *A History of the Crusades* i, ed. Marshall W. Baldwin (Philadelphia, PA, 1955), 463–512.

Bethell, Denis, "William of Corbeil and the Canterbury York —— Dispute," *Journal of Ecclesiastical History* 19 (1968): 145–59.

—— "The Making of a Twelfth-Century Relic Collection," *Studies in Church History* 8 (1972): 61–72.

Beziers, Michel, *Histoire sommaire de la ville de Bayeux*. Caen, 1773.

Biddle, Martin, "Seasonal Festivals and Residence: Winchester, Westminster and Gloucester in the Tenth to Twelfth Centuries," *ANS* 8 (1985): 51–72.

—— and Keane, D. J., "Winchester in the Eleventh and Twelfth Centuries," in *Winchester*, 241–448.

Birch, *Margam Abbey*=Birch, Walter De Gray, *A History of Margam Abbey*. London, 1897.

—— *A History of Neath Abbey*. London, 1902.

Bishop, T. A. M., *Scriptores Regis*. Oxford, 1960.

Bisson, Thomas N., *The Crisis of the Twelfth Century: Power, Lordship, and the Origins of European Government*. Princeton, NJ, and Oxford, 2009.

Blackburn, Mark, "Coinage and Currency under Henry I: A Review," *ANS* 13 (1990): 49–81.

—— "Coinage and Currency," in *The Anarchy of King Stephen's Reign*, 145–205.

Bloch, Herbert, "The Schism of Anaclitus and the Glanfeuil Forgeries of Peter the Deacon," *Traditio* 8 (1952): 159–264.

Bloch, Mark, *Feudal Society*, transl. L. A. Manyon. 2nd edn. London, 1962.

Boase, T. S. R., *English Art 1100–1216*. Oxford, 1963.

Boone, George C., *Coins of the Anarchy, 1135–54*. National Museum of Wales. Cardiff, 1988.

Böuard, Michel, *Le Château de Caen*. Centre des Recherches Archéologiques et Historiques Anciennes et Médiévales, Caen, 1979.

Boulton, D'A. J. D., "Classic Knighthood as Nobiliary Dignity: The Knighting of Counts and Kings' Sons in England 1066–1272," in *Medieval Knighthood V: Papers from the Sixth Strawberry Hill Conference 1994*, ed. Stephen Church and Ruth Harvey. Woodbridge, 1995, 41–100.

Boussard, Jacques, *Le Gouvernement d'Henri II Plantegenêt*. Paris, 1956.

Bowles, Charles, *A Short Account of the Hundred of Pentwith in the County of Cornwall*. Shaftesbury, 1805.

Bradbury, Jim, "Battles in England and Normandy, 1066–1154," *ANS* 6 (1983): 1–12; also in *Anglo-Norman Warfare*, 182–93.

—— "The Early Years of the Reign of Stephen, 1135–39," in *England in the Twelfth Century*: 17–30.

—— "Geoffrey V of Anjou, Count and Knight," in *The Ideal and Practice of Medieval Knighthood* iii, ed. Christopher Harper-Bill and Ruth Harvey, Woodbridge, 1990, 21–38.

—— *Stephen and Matilda: The Civil War of 1139–53*. Stroud, 1996.

Brett, M(artin), *The English Church under Henry I*. Oxford, 1975.

—— "John of Worcester and his Contemporaries," in *The Writing of History in the Middle Ages*, 101–26.
*Bristol*, M. D. Lobel and E. M. Carus-Wilson. Historic Towns. London, 1975.
Brooke, Christopher N. L., *The Twelfth Century Renaissance*. London and New York, 1969.
—— *Medieval Church and Society*. London, 1971.
—— "St. Peter of Gloucester and St. Cadog of Llancarfan," in *The Church and the Welsh Border in the Central Middle Ages*, by Christopher N. L. Brooke, ed. D. N. Dumville and C. N. L. Brooke. Woodbridge, 1986, 50–94.
—— "Geoffrey of Monmouth as a Historian," in *The Church and the Welsh Border*, 95–106.
—— *The Medieval Idea of Marriage*. Oxford, 1989.
—— "Foliot, Gilbert," *ODNB* xx. 218–21.
—— and Keir, Gillian, *London 800–1216: The Shaping of a City*. London, 1975.
Brooke, Z. N., *The English Church and the Papacy*. reprn. edn., with new foreword by Christopher N. L. Brooke. Cambridge, 1968.
—— and Brooke, C. N. L., "Henry II Duke of Normandy and Aquitaine," *EHR* 61 (1946): 81–9.
Brown, R. Allen, *Origins of English Feudalism*. London and New York, 1973.
—— *English Castles*. 3rd rev. edn. London, 1976.
—— "The Status of the Norman Knight," in *War and Government in the Middle Ages*, 18–32; also in *Anglo-Norman Warfare*, ed. Strickland, 128–42.
Brown, Stewart, "Excavations at Temple Church, Bristol: A Report on the Excavations by Andrew Saunders," *BGAST* 126 (2008): 113–29.
Burnett, Charles, "The Education of Henry II," in Burnett, *The Introduction of Arabic Learning into England*. London, 1997, 31–60.
—— "Bath, Adelard of," *ODNB* iv. 339–41.
Burton, Janet, "Thurstan," *ODNB* liv. 723–7.
Butler, Lawrence, "The Foundation Charter of Neath Abbey, Glamorgan," *Archaeologia Cambrensis* 148 (1999): 214–16.
Calthrop, M. M. C., "Priory of Cranborne," *VCH Gloucestershire* ii. 74–5.
Campbell, James, "The Significance of the Anglo-Norman State in the Administrative History of Western Europe," *TRHS* 5th ser. 25 (1975): 39–54; also in James Campbell, *Essays in Anglo-Saxon History*. London and Ronceverte, 1986, 155–70.
Carus-Wilson, E. M., "Origins," in *Bristol*, 2–3.
—— "The Norman Town," in *Bristol*, 3–6.
*Catalogue of the Collection of Medieval Manuscripts Bequeathed to the Bodleian Library, Oxford by James P. R. Lyell*, ed. Albinia De La Mare. Oxford, 1971.
Chaplais, Pierre, "The Original Charters of Herbert and Gervase, Abbots of Westminster (1121–1157)," in *A Medieval Miscellany for Doris Mary Stenton*, 89–110; also in Chaplais, *Essays in Medieval Diplomacy and Administration*, XVIII, with Addendum.
—— "The Authenticity of the Royal Anglo-Saxon Diplomas of Exeter," *BIHR* 39 (1966): 1–34; also in Chaplais, *Essays in Medieval Diplomacy and Administration*: XV.
—— *English Royal Documents*. Oxford, 1971.
—— *Essays in Medieval Diplomacy and Administration*. London, 1981.
*Charters and Charter Scholarship in Britain and Ireland*, ed. Marie Therese Flanagan and Judith A. Green. Basingstoke and New York, 2005.
Chartrou, Josèphe, *L'Anjou de 1104 à 1151*. Paris, 1928.
Cheney, C. R., *English Bishops' Chanceries*. Manchester, 1950.
Cheney, Mary, "William fitz Stephen and his Life of Archbishop Thomas," in *Church and Government in the Middle Ages*, ed. C. N. L. Brooke, D. E. Luscombe, G. H. Martin, and Dorothy Owen. Cambridge, 1976, 139–56.

Cheney, Mary, *Roger, Bishop of Worcester, 1164–1179*. Oxford, 1980.
Chew, Helena M., *The English Ecclesiastical Tenants-in-Chief and Knight Service*. Oxford, 1932.
Chibnall, Marjorie, "*Mercenaries* and the *Familia Regis* under Henry I," *History* 62 (1977): 15–23; also in *Anglo-Norman Warfare*, ed. Strickland, 84–92.
—— *The World of Orderic Vitalis*. Oxford, 1984.
—— *Anglo-Norman England*. Oxford, 1986.
—— *The Empress Matilda: Queen Consort, Queen Mother and Lady of the English*. Oxford and Cambridge, MA, 1991.
—— "Normandy," in *The Anarchy of King Stephen's Reign*, 93–115.
—— "The Charters of the Empress Matilda," in *Law and Government*, 276–98.
—— "The Empress Matilda as a Subject for Biography," in *Writing Medieval Biography*, 185–94.
—— "Introduction," in *King Stephen's Reign*, 1–9.
Christelow [also Mooers], Stephanie Mooers, "Chancellors and Curial Bishops: Ecclesiastical Promotions and Power in Anglo-Norman England," *ANS* 22 (1999): 49–69.
—— "The Fiscal Management of England under Henry I," in *Henry I and the Anglo-Norman World: Studies in Memory of C. Warren Hollister*, ed. Donald F. Fleming and Janet M. Pope. *HSJ* 17 (2006): 158–82.
Clanchy, M. T., *From Memory to Written Record*. 2nd edn. Oxford and Cambridge, MA, 1993.
Clapham, Alfred, "The Form of the Early Choir of Tewkesbury and its Significance," *Archaeological Journal* 106 (for 1959; Supplement, 1952): 10–15.
Clark, Howard B., "Those Five Knights which you Owe in Respect of your Abbacy. Organizing Military Service after the Norman Conquest: Evesham and Beyond," *HSJ* 24 (2013): 1–39.
Clay, C. T. and Greenway, D., *Early Yorkshire Families*. Yorkshire Archaeological Society. Wakefield, 1973.
Colvin, H. M., "A List of the Archbishop of Canterbury's Tenants by Knight-Service in the Reign of Henry II," in *Documents Illustrative of Medieval Kentish Society*. Kent Archaeological Society xviii. Ashford, 1964, 1–40.
Constable, Giles, "The Second Crusade as Seen by Contemporaries," *Traditio* 9 (1953): 213–79.
—— "Peter the Venerable, the Lateran Council of 1139, and the Case between King Stephen and the Empress Matilda," *The Letters and Charters of Peter the Venerable*. Cambridge, MA, 1966, 252–56.
Coplestone-Crow, B., "Payn Fitz John and Ludlow Castle," *Transactions of the Shropshire Archaeological and Historical Society* 70 (1995): 171–83.
Coss, P(eter) R., "Bastard Feudalism Revised," *Past and Present* 125 (1989): 27–64.
Coulson, Charles, "The Castles of the Anarchy," in *The Anarchy of King Stephen's Reign*, 67–92.
Cowley, F. G., "The Church in Medieval Glamorgan," in *GCH* iii. 87–166.
—— *The Monastic Order in South Wales, 1066–1349*. Cardiff, 1977.
Cownie, Emma, *Religious Patronage in Anglo-Norman England 1066–1135*. Royal Historical Society. Woodbridge, 1998.
Cox, D. C., "Two Unpublished Charters of King Stephen for Wenlock Priory," *Transactions of the Shropshire Archaeological and Historical Society* 66 (1989): 56–9.
CP=*The Complete Peerage of England, Scotland, Ireland Great Britain and the United Kingdom* by G. E. C(ockayne), ed. Vicary Gibbs et al. 12 vols. London, 1910–50.

Crick, *Summary Catalogue*=Crick, Julia C., *The Historia Regum Britannie of Geoffrey of Monmouth.* iii: *A Summary Catalogue of the Manuscripts.* Cambridge, 1989.

Crick Julia C., and Walsham, Alexandra, *The Uses of Script and Print.* Cambridge and New York, 2004.

Cronne H. A., "Ranulf de Gernons, Earl of Chester 1129–1153," *TRHS* 4th ser., 20 (1937): 103–34.

Crosby, Everett U., "The Organization of the English Episcopate under Henry I," in *Studies in Medieval and Renaissance History* iv, ed. William M. Bowsky. Lincoln, NE, 1967, 1–88.

Crouch, David, *The Reign of Stephen: Anarchy in England.* London, 1970.

—— "Geoffrey de Clinton and Roger, Earl of Warwick: New Men and Magnates in the Reign of Henry I," *BIHR* 55 (1982): 113–24.

—— "Oddities in the Early History of the Marcher Lordship of Gower, 1107–66," *The Bulletin of the Board of Celtic Studies* 31 (1984): 133–41.

—— "Robert of Gloucester and the Daughter of Zelophehad," *Journal of Medieval History* 11 (1985): 227–43.

—— "The Slow Death of Kingship in Glamorgan, 1067–1158," *Morgannwg* 29 (1985): 20–41.

—— *The Beaumont Twins: The Roots and Branches of Power in the Twelfth Century.* Cambridge, 1986.

—— "Earl William of Gloucester and the End of the Anarchy: New Evidence Relating to the Honor of Eudo Dapifer," *EHR* 103 (1988): 69–75.

—— "Urban, First Bishop of Llandaff, 1107–37," *The Journal of Welsh Ecclesiastical History* 6 (1989): 1–15.

—— *William Marshal: Court, Career and Chivalry in the Angevin Empire 1147–1219.* Harlow, 1990.

—— "Administration of the Norman Earldom," in *Earldom of Chester and its Charters*, 69–95.

—— "Debate: Bastard Feudalism Revised," *Past and Present* 131 (1991): 165–77.

—— *The Image of Aristocracy in Britain.* London, 1992.

—— "The March and the Welsh Kings," in *The Anarchy of King Stephen's Reign*, 255–89.

—— "Normans and Anglo-Normans: A Divided Aristocracy," in *England and Normandy in the Middle Ages*, 51–67.

—— "Robert of Gloucester's Mother and Sexual Politics in Norman Oxfordshire," *HR* 72 (1999): 323–35.

—— *The Reign of King Stephen 1135–1154.* Harlow, 2000.

—— "A Norman *Conventio* and Bonds of Lordship in the Middle Ages," in *Law and Government*, 299–324.

—— *The Normans: The History of a Dynasty.* London and New York, 2002.

—— "Marshal, John," *ODNB* xxxvi. 811–12.

—— "Waleran Count of Meulan and Earl of Worcester (1104–1166)," *ODNB* lvi. 789–90.

—— *The Birth of Nobility.* Harlow, 2005.

—— "The Transformation of Medieval Gwent," in *Gwent County History* ii, ed. Ralph A. Griffiths, Tony Hopkins, and Ray Howell. Cardiff, 2008, 1–45.

—— "Between Three Realms: The Acts of Waleran II, Count of Meulan and Worcester," in *Records, Administration and Aristocratic Society in the Anglo-Norman Realm*, 75–87.

Crouch, David, *The English Aristocracy 1070–1272: A Social Transformation.* New Haven, CT, and London, 2011.

―― and de Trafford, Claire., "The Forgotten Family in Twelfth-Century England," *HSJ* 13 (1999): 41–63.

Dalton, Paul, "Aiming at the Impossible: Ranulf II Earl of Chester and Lincolnshire in the Reign of King Stephen," in *Earldom of Chester and its Charters*, 119–34.

―― "*In Neutro Latere*: The Armed Neutrality of Ranulf II Earl of Chester in King Stephen's Reign," *ANS* 14 (1991): 39–59.

―― *Conquest, Anarchy and Lordship: Yorkshire, 1066–1154*. Cambridge, 1994.

―― "Eustace Fitz John and the Politics of Anglo-Norman England: The Rise and Survival of a Twelfth-Century Royal Servant," *Speculum* 71 (1996): 358–83.

―― "Churchmen and the Promotion of Peace in King Stephen's Reign," *Viator* 31 (2000): 79–119.

―― "Espec, Walter," *ODNB* xviii. 602–3.

Damian-Grint, Peter, *The New Historians of the Twelfth-Century Renaissance*. Woodbridge, 1999.

D'Anisi, Léchaudé, "Notice historique sur la baronnie et sur l'église de Than," *MSAN* 2nd ser. ii (1841): 105–16.

Darlington, R(eginald) R(alph), *The Anglo-Norman Historians*. London, 1947.

David, Charles Wendell, *Robert Curthose: Duke of Normandy*. Cambridge, MA, 1920.

―― "The Claim of King Henry I to Be Called Learned," in *Anniversary Essays in Mediaeval History by Students of Charles Homer Haskins*, ed. C. H. Taylor and J. L. LaMonte. Boston, MA, and New York, 1929.

Davies, Kerrith, "The Count of the Cotentin: Western Normandy, William of Mortain, and the Career of Henry I," *HSJ* 22 (2010): 123–40.

Davies, R. R., "The Law of the March," *The Welsh History Review* 5 (1970–1): 1–30.

―― "Kings, Lords, and Liberties in the March of Wales, 1066–1272," *TRHS* 5th ser. 29 (1979): 41–61.

―― "Henry I and Wales," in *Studies in Medieval History Presented to R. H. C. Davis*, ed. Henry Mayr-Harting and R. I. Moore. London, 1985, 133–47.

―― *Conquest, Coexistence, and Change: Wales 1063–1415*. Oxford, 1987.

Davies, Wendy, *The Llandaff Charters*. Aberystwyth, 1979.

Davis, H. W. C., "The Anarchy of Stephen's Reign," *EHR* 72 (1903): 630–41.

―― "Henry of Blois and Brian Fitz Count," *EHR* 98 (1910): 297–303.

―― "Some Documents of the Anarchy," in *Essays in History Presented to Reginald Lane Poole*, ed. H. W. C. Davis. Oxford, 1927, 168–89.

―― "London Lands and Liberties of St. Paul's 1066–1135," in *Essays in Medieval History Presented to Thomas Frederick Tout*, ed. A. G. Little and F. M. Powicke; reprn. edn. London, 1967, 45–59.

Davis, R. H. C., "King Stephen and the Earl of Chester Revised," *EHR* 75 (1960): 654–60.

―― "Treaty between William Earl of Gloucester and Roger Earl of Hereford," in *A Medieval Miscellany for Doris Mary Stenton*, ed. Patricia M. Barnes and C. F. Slade. PRS n.s. 36 (1960): 139–46.

―― "What Happened in Stephen's Reign, 1135–54," *History* 49 (1964): 1–12.

―― *King Stephen*. 3rd edn. London, 1990.

―― "Authorship," in *GS* (2004): xviii–xl.

De La Rue, Gervais, *Essais Historiques sur la ville de Caen et son arrondissement*. 2 vols. Caen, 1820.

*Descriptive Catalogue of Derbyshire Charters*, ed. Isaac Herbert Jeayes. London, 1906.

*Descriptive Catalogue of the Charters and Muniments in the Possession of the Rt. Hon. Lord Fitz Harding at Bristol Castle*, ed. I. H. Jeayes. Bristol, 1892.

*A Descriptive Catalogue of the Medieval Manuscripts in Worcester Cathedral Library*, ed. R. M. Thomson, with a contribution on bindings by Michael Gullick. Cambridge, 2001.

*Design and Distribution of Late Medieval Manuscripts in England*, ed. Margaret Connolly and Linne R. Mooney. York, 2008.

Deville, Étienne, *Notices sur quelques manuscrits normands conservés à la bibliothèque Sainte-Geneviève*. iv: *Analyse d'un ancien cartulaire de l'abbaye de Saint-Étienne de Caen*. Évreux, 1905.

Dickinson, J. C., "The Origins of St. Augustine's, Bristol," in *Essays in Bristol and Gloucestershire History*, 109–26.

*The Domesday Geography of South-West England*, ed. H. C. Darby and R. Weldon Finn. Cambridge, 1967.

Douglas, Audrey C., "Frankalmoin and Jurisdictional Immunity: Maitland Revisited," *Speculum* 53 (1978): 26–48.

Douglas, David C., *William the Conqueror*. London, 1964.

—— "Bristol under the Normans," in *Essays in Bristol and Gloucestershire History*, 101–8.

Dowdeswell, E. R., "Some Ancient Deeds Illustrating the Devolution of an Estate in the Manor of Walton Cardiff, near Tewkesbury, between the Years A. D. 1166 and 1833," *BGAST* 32 (1909): 165–76.

Duby, Georges, *The Chivalrous Society*. transl. Cynthia Postan. Berkeley and Los Angeles, 1977.

—— "Youth in Aristocratic Society," in Duby, *The Chivalrous Society*, 112–22.

—— *Medieval Marriage: Two Models from Twelfth-Century France*, transl. Elsborg Forster. Baltimore, MD, 1978.

Du Cange, Charles Du Fresne., *Glossarium Mediae et Infimae Latinitatis*. reprn. edn. 6 vols. in 5. Graz, 1954.

Du Motey, Henri R., *Origines de la Normandie et du duché d'Alençon de l'an 850 à l'an 1085*. Paris, 1920.

Dumville, David, "An Early Text of Geoffrey of Monmouth's *Historia Regum Britanniae* and the Circulation of Some Latin Histories in Twelfth-Century Normandy," *Arthurian Literature* 4 (1985): 1–36.

Dutton, Kathryn, "*Ad Erudiendum Tradidit*: The Upbringing of Angevin Comital Children," *ANS* 32 (2009): 24–39.

Dyer, Christopher, *Lords and Peasants in a Changing Society: The Estates of the Bishopric of Worcester 680–1540*. Cambridge, 1980.

Eales, Richard, "Local Loyalties in Norman England: Kent in Stephen's Reign," *ANS* 8 (1985): 88–108.

*Earldom of Chester and its Charters: A Tribute to Geoffrey Barraclough*, ed. A. T. Thacker. *Journal of the Chester Archaeological Society* 71 (1991).

Edwards, J. G., "The Normans and the Welsh March," *Proceedings of the British Academy* 42 (1956): 155–77.

Ellis, Henry (ed.), *A General Introduction to Domesday Book*. ii. reprn. edn. London, 1971.

*England and Normandy in the Middle Ages*, ed. David Bates and Anne Curry. London and Rio Grande, OH, 1994.

*England in the Twelfth Century*. Proceedings of the 1988 Harlaxton Symposium, ed. Daniel Williams. Woodbridge, 1990.

English, Barbara, *The Lords of Holderness*. Oxford, 1979.

*English Romanesque Art 1066–1200*, eds. George Zarnecki, Janet Holt, and Tristram Holland. London, 1984.

Esmein, Adhémar, *Le Mariage en droit canonique*. i. Paris, 1891.

*Essays in Bristol and Gloucestershire History*, eds. P. McGrath and J. Cannon. Bristol, 1976.

*Essays in History Presented to Reginald Lane Poole*, ed. H. W. C. Davis. Oxford, 1927; reprn. edn. Freeport, NY, 1967.

Evans, A. Leslie, "The Lords of Afan," *Transactions of the Port Talbot Historical Society* 2 (1974): 193–200.

Eyton, R. W., *Antiquities of Shropshire*. 6 vols. London, 1854–60.

—— *Court, Household and Itinerary of King Henry II*. reprn. edn. Hildesheim and New York, 1974.

Farmer, Hugh, "William of Malmesbury's Commentary on Lamentations," *Studia Monastica* 4 (1962): 283–311.

—— "William of Malmesbury's Life and Works," *Journal of Ecclesiastical History* 13 (1962): 39–54.

Farrell, Jennifer, "History, Prophecy, and the Arthur of the Normans: The Question of Audience and Motivation behind Geoffrey of Monmouth's *Historia Regum Britanniae*," *ANS* 37 (2014): 99–114.

Farrer, William, *Honors and Knights' Fees*. ii–iii. London, 1924–5.

Fenton, Kirsten A., *Gender, Nation and Conquest in the Works of William of Malmesbury*. Woodbridge, 2008.

Fernie, Eric, *The Architecture of Norman England*. Oxford, 2000.

*Feudalism and Liberty: Articles and Addresses of Sidney Painter*, ed. Fred A. Cazel Jr. Baltimore, MD, 1961.

Finberg, H. P. R. (ed.), *Gloucestershire Studies*. Leicester, 1957.

—— *Lucerna: Studies of Some Problems in the Early History of England*. London, 1964.

Fleming, Robin, "Christchurch's Sisters and Brothers: Canterbury Obituary Lists," in *The Culture of Christendom: Essays in Medieval History in Commemoration of Denis L. T. Bethell*, ed. Marc Anthony Mayer. London, 1993, 6–153.

Flori, Jean, "Les Origines de l'adoubement chevaleresque: étude des remis d'armes et du vocabulaire qui les exprime dans les sources historiques latines jusqu'au début du XIII$^e$ siècle," *Traditio* 35 (1970): 209–72.

Foulds, Trevor, "The Lindsey Survey and an Unknown Precept of King Henry I," *BIHR* 59 (1986): 212–15.

Freeman, Edward A., *The History of the Norman Conquest of England*. 6 vols. Oxford, 1867–79.

Galbraith, V. H., "Royal Charters to Winchester," *EHR* 35 (1920): 385–400.

—— "The Literacy of Medieval English Kings," *Proceedings of the British Academy* 21 (1935): 201–38.

—— *Historical Research in Medieval England*. London, 1951.

Gameson, Richard, *The Manuscripts of Early Norman England*. The British Academy. Oxford, 1999.

Garnett, George S., "'Ducal' Succession in Early Normandy," in *Law and Government*, 80–110.

—— *Conquered England: Kingship, Succession, and Tenure, 1066–1166*. Oxford, 2007.

Gazeau, Véronique, *Normannia Monastica: Princes normands et abbés bénédictins; Prosopographie des abbés bénédictins*. 2 vols. Caen, 2007.

*GCH=Glamorgan County History*, iii, ed. T. B. Pugh. Cardiff, 1971.

*GFAL=Gilbert Foliot and his Letters*, ed. Adrian Morey and C. N. L. Brooke. Cambridge, 1965.

Gillingham, John, "The Context and Purposes of Geoffrey of Monmouth's *History of the Kings of Britain*," *ANS* 13 (1990): 99–118.

—— "1066 and the Introduction of Chivalry into England," in *Law and Government*, 31–55; also rev. in *The English in the Twelfth Century*, 209–31.

—— "Kingship, Chivalry and Love. Political and Cultural Values in the Earliest History Written in French: Geoffrey Gaimar's *Estoire des Engleis*," in *Anglo-Norman Political Culture and the Twelfth-Century Renaissance*, 33–58.

—— "Conquering the Barbarians: War and Chivalry in Twelfth-Century Britain,' in Gillingham, *The English in the Twelfth Century*, 41–58.

—— *The English in the Twelfth Century*. Woodbridge, 2000.

Given-Wilson, Chris, and Curteis, Alice, *The Royal Bastards of Medieval England*. London, 1984.

Gleason, Sarell Everett, *An Ecclesiastical Barony of the Middle Ages*. Cambridge, MA, 1936.

GOE=Judith Green, *The Government of England under Henry I*. Cambridge, 1986.

Golding, Brian, "Anglo-Norman Knightly Burials," in *The Ideals and Practices of Medieval Knighthood: Papers from the First and Second Strawberry Hill Conference*, ed. Christopher Harper-Bill and Ruth Harvey. Woodbridge, 1986, 35–48.

Graham, Rose, "Abbey of Tewkesbury," in *VCH Gloucestershire* ii. 61–6.

—— "Priory of St. James, Bristol," in *VCH Gloucestershire* ii. 74–5.

—— "Priory of Lanthony by Gloucester," in *VCH Gloucestershire* ii. 87–91.

Gransden, *Historical Writing* i=Gransden, Antonia, *Historical Writing in England c.550–c.1307*. London, 1974.

Gransden, *Historical Writing* ii=Gransden, Antonia, *Historical Writing in England ii.: c.1307 to the Early Sixteenth Century*. London and Henley, 1982.

Gransden, Antonia, "Prologues in the Historiography of Twelfth-Century England," in *England in the Twelfth Century*, 55–81.

Grant, John P., *Cardiff Castle: Its History and Architecture*. Cardiff, 1923.

Grant, Lindy, "Architectural Relationships between England and Normandy, 1100–1204," in *England and Normandy in the Middle Ages*, 117–29.

Green, Judith A., "William Rufus, Henry I and the Royal Demesne," *History* 64 (1979): 337–52.

—— "Lords of the Norman Vexin," in *War and Government in the Middle Ages*, 47–61.

—— "King Henry I and the Aristocracy of Normandy," in *La France anglaise au Moyen Âge: actes du III[e] Congrès des Sociétés Savantes*. Paris, 1988, 161–73.

—— "Unity and Disunity in the Anglo-Norman State," *HR* 62 (1989): 114–34.

—— "Aristocratic Loyalties on the Northern Frontier of England, c.1100–1174," in *England in the Twelfth Century*, 83–100.

—— *English Sheriffs to 1154*. London, 1990.

—— "Earl Ranulf of Chester and Lancashire," in *Earldom of Chester and its Charters*, 97–108.

—— "Financing Stephen's War," *ANS* 14 (1991): 91–114.

—— *The Aristocracy of Norman England*. Cambridge, 1997.

—— "Aristocratic Women in Early Twelfth-Century England," in *Anglo-Norman Political Culture*, 59–82.

—— "Family Matters: Family and the Formation of the Empress's Party in South-West England," in Keats-Rohan, *Family Trees*, 147–64.

—— "The Piety and Patronage of Henry I," *HSJ* 12 (2001): 1–16.

—— "Le Gouvernement d'Henri Ier Beauclerc en Normandie," in *La Normandie et l'Angleterre au Moyen Âge*, ed. Pierre Bouet and Véronique Gazeau. Centre de Recherches Archéologiques et Historiques Médiévales. Caen, 2003, 61–73.

—— "Robert fitz Haimon," *ODNB* xlvii. 117–19.

—— "A Lasting Memorial: The Charter of Liberties of Henry I," in *Charters and Charter Scholarship*, 53–69.

Green, Judith, *Henry I: King of England and Duke of Normandy*. Cambridge, 2006.
Griffiths, Ralph A., "The Medieval Boroughs of Glamorgan and Medieval Swansea," in *GCH*, 333–77.
Gross, Charles, *The Gild Merchant*. ii. reprn. edn. Cambridge, MA, 1927.
Gullick, Michael, "How Fast Did Scribes Write? Evidence from Romanesque Manuscripts," in *Making the Medieval Book: Techniques of Production*, ed. Linda L. Brownrigg. Los Altos Hills, CA, 1995, 39–58.
Hagger, Mark, "A Pipe Roll for 25 Henry I," *EHR* 122 (2007): 133–40.
Hague, D. B., "The Castles of Glamorgan and Gower," in *GCH*, 417–48.
Hamilton, Bernard, *The Latin Church in the Crusader States: The Secular Church*. London, 1980.
*Handbook of Dates for Students of English History*, ed. C. R. Cheney. London, 1961.
Harper-Bill, C., "The Piety of the Anglo-Norman Knightly Class," *ANS* 2 (1979): 63–77.
Harvey, Barbara, *Westminster Abbey and its Estates in the Middle Ages*. Oxford, 1977.
Harvey, P. D. A., and McGuinness, Andrew, *A Guide to British Mediaeval Seals*. Toronto and Buffalo, NY, 1996.
Haskins, Charles Homer, "Adelard of Bath and Henry Plantagenet," *EHR* 28 (1913): 515–16.
—— "Henry II as a Patron of Literature," in *Essays in Medieval History Presented to T. F. Tout*, ed. A. G. Little and F. M. Powicke. Manchester, 1925, 71–7.
—— *The Renaissance of the Twelfth Century*. reprn. edn. New York, 1957.
—— *Norman Institutions*. reprn. New York and London, 1960.
Hayward, Paul Anthony, "The Importance of Being Ambiguous: Innuendo and Legerdemain in William of Malmesbury's *Gesta Pontificum Anglorum*," *ANS* 33 (2010): 75–102.
Helmerichs, Robert, "King Stephen's Norman Itinerary," *HSJ* 5 (1995): 89–97.
Herbert, Nicholas, *Medieval Gloucester* (Gloucester, 1993); reprn. from *VCH Gloucestershire* iv. London, 1988.
Hicks, Michael, *Bastard Feudalism*. London and New York, 1995.
—— "The Early Lords: Robert Fitz Hamon to the Clares," in *Tewkesbury Abbey: History, Art, and Architecture*, 11–18.
Hicks, Sandy Burton, "The Anglo-Papal Bargain of 1125: The Legatine Mission of John of Crema," *Albion* 8 (1976): 301–10.
Hill, Rosalind, "The Battle of Stockbridge," in *Studies in Medieval History Presented to R. Allen Brown*, 173–7.
Hillaby, Joe, and Sermon, Richard, "Jacob's Well, Bristol: Mikveh or Bet Tohorah?" *BGAST* 122 (2004): 127–52.
Hindle, Brian Paul, *Medieval Roads*. Aylesbury, 1982.
Holdsworth, Christopher, "The Church," in *The Anarchy of King Stephen's Reign*, 207–29.
Hollister, C. Warren, *The Military Organization of Norman England*. Oxford, 1965.
—— "The Anglo-Norman Civil War: 1101," *EHR* 88 (1973): 315–34; also in *MMI*, 77–96.
—— "Magnates and 'Curiales' in Early Norman England," *Viator* 4 (1973): 115–22; also in *MMI*, 97–115.
—— "The Misfortunes of the Mandevilles," *History* 58 (1973): 18–28; also in *MMI*, 117–27.
—— "The Strange Death of William Rufus," *Speculum* 48 (1973): 637–53; also in *MMI*, 59–75.

—— "The Anglo-Norman Succession Debate of 1126: Prelude to Stephen's Anarchy," *Journal of Medieval History* 1 (1975): 19–39; also in *MMI*, 145–69.

—— "The Taming of a Turbulent Earl: Henry I and William of Warenne," *Réflexions Historiques* 3 (1976): 83–91; also in *MMI*, 137–44.

—— "The Origins of the English Treasury," *EHR* 93 (1978): 262–75; also in *MMI*, 209–22.

—— "The Rise of Administrative Kingship: Henry I," *American Historical Review* 83 (1978): 867–905; also in *MMI*, 223–45.

—— "War and Diplomacy in the Anglo-Norman World: The Reign of Henry I," *ANS* 6 (1983): 72–88; also in *MMI*, 273–89.

—— "The Greater Domesday Tenants-in-Chief," in *Domesday Studies*, ed. J. C. Holt, reprn. edn. Woodbridge, 1990, 219–48.

—— "The Aristocracy," in King, *The Anarchy of King Stephen's Reign*, 37–66.

—— "Anglo-Norman Political Culture and the Twelfth-Century Renaissance," in *Anglo-Norman Political Culture*, 1–16.

—— *Henry I*, ed. Amanda Clark Frost. New Haven, CT, and London, 2001.

—— "William (called William Clito; 1102–1128)," *ODNB* lix. 35–7.

—— and Thomas K. Keefe, "The Making of the Angevin Empire," *Journal of British Studies* 12 (1973): 1–25; also in *MMI*: 247–71.

Holt, Sir James C., "Politics and Property in Early Medieval England," *Past and Present* 57 (1972): 3–52.

—— "Feudal Society and the Family in Early Medieval England: I. The Revolution of 1066," *TRHS* 5th ser. 32 (1982): 193–212. II. "Notions of Patrimony," *TRHS* 5th ser. 33 (1983): 193–220. III. "Patronage and Politics," *TRHS* 5th ser. 34 (1984): 1–26. IV. "The Heiress and the Alien," *TRHS* 5th ser. 35 (1985): 1–28.

—— "The Introduction of Knight Service in England," *ANS* 6 (1983): 89–106; also in *Anglo-Norman Warfare*, 41–58.

—— *Magna Carta*. 2nd edn. Cambridge, 1992.

—— "1153: The Treaty of Winchester," in *The Anarchy of King Stephen's Reign*, 291–316.

Houth, Émile (ed.), "Galeran II Comte de Meulan. Catalogue de ses actes, précédé d'une étude biographique," in *Bulletin philologique et historique (jusquà 1610) du Comité des travaux historiques et scientifiques*. 1960, pt. 2. Paris, 1960, 627–82.

Hoyt, Robert S., *The Royal Demesne in English Constitutional History: 1066–1272*. Ithaca, NY, 1950.

Hudson, John, "Diplomatic and Legal Aspects of the Charters," in *Earldom of Chester and its Charters*, 153–78.

—— "Anglo-Norman Land Law and the Origins of Property," in *Law and Government*, 198–222.

—— *Land, Law, and Lordship in Anglo-Norman England*. Oxford, 1994.

—— *The Formation of the English Common Law*. Edinburgh and New York, 1996.

—— "Henry I and Counsel," in *The Medieval State: Essays Presented to James Campbell*, ed. J. R. Maddicott and D. M. Palliser. London, 2000, 109–26.

Hulsey, Richard, "Tewkesbury Abbey: Some Recent Observations," in *Medieval Art and Architecture at Gloucester and Tewkesbury*, 16–35.

Hurnard, Naomi, "The Anglo-Norman Franchises," *EHR* 64 (1949): 289–327; 433–60.

Huws, Daniel, "The Making of *Liber Landavensis*," *The National Library of Wales Journal* 25 (1987): 133–60 and plates.

Jackson, Reg, et al. (eds.), *Excavations at St. James's Priory, Bristol*. Oxford, 2006.

Jameson, Catherine, "Great Gransden," in *VCH Hundingdonshire* ii. 296–302.
Johnson, Lesley, "The Anglo-Norman *Description of England*: An Introduction," *Anglo-Norman Anniversary Essays*, ed. Ian Short. Anglo-Norman Text Society, Occasional Publication Series ii. London, 1993, 11–30.
Jones, S. R., "The Borough of Tewkesbury," in *VCH Gloucestershire* viii. 110–69.
*Journal de Verdun* (October, 1760).
Karn, Nicholas, "Robert de Sigillo: An Unruly Head of the Royal Scriptorium in the 1120s and 1130s," *EHR* 123 (2008): 539–53.
—— "QUADRIPARTITUS, LEGES HENRICI PRIMI and the Scholarship of English Law in the Early Twelfth Century," *ANS* 37 (2014): 149–60.
Kealey, Edward J., *Roger of Salisbury: Viceroy of England*. Berkeley, Los Angeles, and London, 1972.
Keats-Rohan, K. S. B., "The Devolution of the Honour of Wallingford, 1066–1148," *Oxoniensia* 55 (1989): 311–18.
—— "The Bretons and Normans in England 1066–1154," *Nottingham Medieval Studies* 36 (1992): 42–78.
—— "Aspects of Robert of Torigny's Genealogies Revisited," *Nottingham Medieval Studies* 37 (1993): 21–7.
—— (ed.), *Family Trees and the Roots of Politics*. Woodbridge, 1997.
—— (ed.), *Domesday People* i: *Domesday Book*. Woodbridge, 1999.
—— (ed.), *Domesday Descendants*. Woodbridge, 2002.
Keefe, Thomas K., *Feudal Assessments and the Political Community under Henry II and his Sons*. Berkeley, Los Angeles, and London, 1983.
—— "Counting those who Count: A Computer-Assisted Analysis of Charter Witness-Lists and the Itinerant Court in the First Year of the Reign of King Richard I," *HSJ* 1 (1989): 135–45.
Keen, Maurice, *Chivalry*. New Haven, CT, and London, 1984.
Kemp, B(rian) R., "Bohun, Jocelin de," *ODNB* vi. 445–7.
Kern, Fritz, *Kingship and Law in the Middle Ages*, transl. S. B. Chrimes. Oxford, 1956.
Kidson, Peter, "The Abbey Church of St. Mary at Tewkesbury in the Eleventh and Twelfth Centuries," in *Medieval Art and Architecture at Gloucester and Tewkesbury*, 6–15.
King, D. J. Cathcart, *Castellarium Anglicanum*. 2 vols. Millwood, NY, 1983.
King, Edmund, "The Origins of the Wake Family: The Early History of the Barony of Bourne in Lincolnshire," *Northamptonshire Past and Present* 5 (1973): 166–76.
—— *Peterborough Abbey*. Cambridge, 1973.
—— "King Stephen and the Anglo-Norman Aristocracy," *History* 59 (1974): 180–94.
—— "The Anarchy of King Stephen's Reign," *TRHS* 5th ser. 34 (1984): 133–53.
—— "Waleran, Count of Meulan, Earl of Worcester (1104–1166)," in *Essays in Honour of Marjorie Chibnall*, ed. Diana Greenway et al. Cambridge, 1985, 165–81.
—— "The Knights of Peterborough Abbey," *Journal of the Peterborough Museum Society* 2 (1986): 36–50.
—— "Dispute Settlement in Anglo-Norman England," *ANS* 14 (1991): 115–30.
—— "Introduction," in *The Anarchy of King Stephen's Reign*, 1–36.
—— "The Memory of Brian Fitz Count," *HSJ* 13 (1999): 75–98.
—— "Stephen of Blois, Count of Mortain and Boulogne," *EHR* 115 (2000): 271–96.
—— "Brian fitz Count," *ODNB* vii. 538–40.
—— "Stephen (c.1092–1154), King of England," *ODNB* lii. 408–16.
—— "The *Gesta Stephani*," in *Writing Medieval Biography*, 195–206.
—— *King Stephen*. New Haven, CT, and London, 2010.

—— "Henry of Winchester: The Bishop, the City, and the Wider World," *ANS* 37 (2014): 1–23.
*King Stephen's Reign (1135–1154)*, eds. Paul Dalton and Graeme J. White. Woodbridge, 2008.
Knowles, David, *The Episcopal Colleagues of Archbishop Thomas Becket*. Cambridge, 1951.
Knowles, *HRH=The Heads of Religious Houses England and Wales 940–1216*, ed. David Knowles, C. N. L. Brooke, and Vera C. M. London. Cambridge, 1972.
Knowles, *MOE=The Monastic Order in England*, Dom David Knowles. Cambridge, 1950.
Könsgen, Ewald, "Zwei unbekannte Briefe zu den *Gesta Regum Anglorum* des Wilhelm von Malmesbury," *Deutsches Archiv für Erforschung des Mittelalters* 31 (1975): 204–14.
*Language and Culture in Medieval Britain*, ed. Jocelyn Wogan-Browne. Woodbridge, 2009.
Latham, R. E. (ed.), *Revised Medieval Latin Word-List*. London, 1965.
Latimer, Paul, "Grants of 'Totus Comitatus' in Twelfth-Century England: Their Origins and Meaning," *BIHR* 59 (1986): 137–45.
—— "Estate Management and Inflation: The Honor of Gloucester, 1183–1263," *Albion* 34 (2002): 187–212.
*Law and Government=Law and Government in Medieval England and Normandy: Essays in Honour of Sir James Holt*, eds. George Garnett and John Hudson. Cambridge, 1994.
Leblond, Bernard, *L'Accession des Normands de Neustrie a la culture occidentale ($X^{ème}$–$XI^{ème}$ siècles)*. Paris, 1966.
Leckie, R. William Jr., *The Passage of Dominion: Geoffrey of Monmouth and the Periodization of Insular History in the Twelfth Century*. Toronto, Buffalo, NY, and London, 1981.
Leech, Robert, *The Topography of Medieval and Early Modern Bristol*. BRS xlviii. Bristol, 1997.
Leedom, J. W., "William of Malmesbury and Robert of Gloucester Reconsidered," *Albion* 6 (1974): 347–64.
—— "The English Settlement of 1153," *History* 65 (1980): 347–64.
Legge, M. Dominica, *Anglo-Norman Literature and its Background*. Oxford, 1963.
——"L'Influence littéraire de la cour d'Henri Beauclerc," in *Mélanges offerts à Rita Lejeune*. Gembloux, 1969, 679–87.
Le Goff, Jacques, *Time, Work, & Culture in the Middle Ages*, transl., Arthur Goldhammer. Chicago and London, 1980.
Lennard, Reginald, *Rural England 1086–1135*. Oxford, 1959.
Le Patourel, John, "The Anglo-Norman Succession 996–1135," *EHR* 86 (1971): 225–50.
—— *The Norman Empire*. Oxford, 1976.
Lewis, C. P., *Feudal Empires Norman and Plantagenet*, ed. Michael Jones. London, 1984.
—— "Norman Barons," in *Feudal Empires* vi: 3–32.
—— "Normandy and England 1066–1144," in *Feudal Empires* vii. 3–38.
—— "The King and Eye: A Study in Anglo-Norman Politics," *EHR* 112 (1989): 569–89.
—— "The Early Earls of Norman England," *ANS* 13 (1990): 207–23.
—— "Formation of the Honor of Chester," in *Earldom of Chester and its Charters*, 37–68.
Leyser, Karl, "England and the Empire in the Early Twelfth Century," *TRHS* 5th ser. 10 (1960): 61–83.
—— "Frederick Barbarossa, Henry II and the Hand of St. James," *EHR* 90 (1975): 481–506.
—— "The Crisis of Medieval Germany," *Proceedings of the British Academy* 69 (1983): 409–43.
—— "The Anglo-Norman Succession 1120–1125," *ANS* 13 (1990): 225–41.

Liebermann, Felix, "On the Instituta Cnuti Aliorumque Regum Anglorum," *TRHS* n.s. 7 (1893): 77–107.

Lloyd, John Edward, *A History of Wales*. ii. 3rd edn., new imp. London, 1967.

LoPrete, Kimberly A., "Adela of Blois and Ivo of Chartres: Piety, Politics, and the Peace in the Diocese of Chartres," *ANS* 4 (1991): 131–52.

—— "Adela of Blois: Familial Alliances and Female Lordship," in *Aristocratic Women in Medieval France*, ed. Theodore Evergates. Philadelphia, PA, 1999, 7–43.

—— *Adela of Blois Countess and Lord (c.1067–1137)*. Dublin, 2007.

Loyd, Lewis C., *The Origins of Some Anglo-Norman Families*, ed. Charles Travis Clay and David C. Douglas. *Publications of the Harleian Society* ciii (1951).

Luscombe, David, "Hugh," *ODNB* xxviii. 618–19.

Luxford, Julian M., "The Founders' Book," in *Tewkesbury Abbey: History, Art, and Architecture*, 53–64.

—— "'Secundum Originale Examinatum': The Refashioning of a Benedictine Historical Manuscript," in *Design and Distribution of Late Medieval Manuscripts in England*, 161–79.

McAleer, J. Philip, "Tewkesbury Abbey in the Later Twelfth Century," *BGAST* 110 (1992): 77–86.

McFarlane, K. B., "Bastard Feudalism," in *England in the Fifteenth Century*, ed. G. L. Harris. London, 1981, 23–43.

Mack, R. P., "Stephen and the Anarchy 1135–1154," *BNJ* 35 (1966): 38–112.

Magnus, Leonard A., "Camberwell," in *VCH Surrey* iv. 24–36.

Maitland, F. W., "William Stubbs, Bishop of Oxford." *EHR* 16 (1901): 417–26.

Marshall, Kenneth, "Excavations in the City of Bristol, 1948–51," *BGAST* 70 (1951): 5–50.

Martindale, Pamela, "Some London Moneyers and Reflections on the Organization of English Mints in the Eleventh and Twelfth Centuries," *Numismatic Chronicle* 162 (1982): 34–50.

Mason, J. F. A., "Barons and their Officials in the Later Eleventh Century," *ANS* 13 (1990): 243–62.

—— "William (William Æthelin, William Adelinus, William Adelingus)," *ODNB* lix. 37–8.

Mayer, Hans Eberhard, *The Crusades*. 2nd edn. Oxford, 1990.

*Medieval Art and Architecture at Gloucester and Tewkesbury*, ed. T. A. Heslop and V. A. Sekules. *British Archaeological Association Confereence Transactions* 7 (1985).

*Medieval Cartularies of Great Britain*, ed. G. R. C. Davis. London, New York, and Toronto, 1958.

*A Medieval Cornish Miscellany*, ed. Oliver Padel. Chichester, 2000.

*Medieval Humanism and Other Studies*, ed. R. W. Southern. New York, 1970.

*A Medieval Miscellany for Doris Mary Stenton*, ed. Patricia M. Barnes and C. F. Slade. PRS n.s. xxxvi (1962).

Megaw, Isabel, "The Ecclesiastical Policy of Stephen: A Reintrepretation," in *Essays in British and Irish History in Honour of James Eadie Todd*, ed. H. A. Cronne, T. W. Moody, and D. B. Quinn. London, 1949, 24–46.

Miller, Edward and Hatcher, John, *Medieval England: Rural Society and Economic Change 1086–1348*. London and New York, 1978.

—————— *Medieval England: Towns, Commerce and Crafts 1086–1348*. London and New York, 1995.

Milsom, S. F. C., *The Legal Framework of English Feudalism*. Cambridge, 1976.

Mitchell, Sidney Knox, *Taxation in Medieval England*, ed. Sidney Painter. reprn. edn. Hamden, CT, 1971.

*MLGB=Medieval Libraries of Great Britain*, ed. N.R. Ker. 2nd edn. Oxford, 1964.

*MMI=Monarchy, Magnates and Institutions in the Anglo-Norman World*, C. Warren Hollister. London and Ronceverte, 1986.

Mooers, Stephanie L. (see also Christelow, Stephanie Mooers), "Familial Clout and Financial Gain in Henry I's Reign," *Albion* 14 (1982): 267–92.

—— "Networks of Power in Anglo-Norman England," *Medieval Prosopography* 7 (1982): 25–52.

—— "Patronage in the Pipe Roll of 1130," *Speculum* 59 (1984): 282–307.

—— "A Reevaluation of Royal Justice under Henry I of England," *American Historical Review* 93 (1988): 340–58.

Moore, John S., "'The Evesham MSS' and 'Evesham K'," in *Domesday Book: Gloucester*. G1–4.

Morey, Adrian, and Brooke, C. N. L., "The Cerne Letters of Gilbert Foliot and the Legation of Imar of Tusculum," *EHR* 63 (1948): 523–7.

Morillo, Stephen, *Warfare under the Anglo-Norman Kings 1066–1135*. Woodbridge, 1994.

Morris, William Alfred, *The Medieval English Sheriff to 1300*. reprn. edn. New York, 1968.

Musset, Lucien, "La Contribution de Fécamp à la reconquête de la Basse-Normandie (990–1066)," in *L'Abbaye bénédictine de Fécamp: ouvrage scientifique du XIII[e] centenaire 658–1958*. i. Fécamp, 1959, 57–79.

—— "Actes inédits du xie siècle vi: l'abbé de Saint-Ouen de Rouen et la ville de Caen," *BSAN* 58 (1965–6): 119–26.

—— *Normandie Romane* i. Yonne, 1967.

—— "Naissance de la Normandie," in *Histoire de la Normandie*, ed. Michel de Böuard. Toulouse, 1970, 75–130.

—— "Aux origines d'une classe dirigeante: les Tosny, grand barons normands du Xe au XIIIe siècle," *Francia* 5 (1977): 45–80.

Navel, H(enri), "L'Enquête de 1133 sur les fiefs de l'évêché de Bayeux," *BSAN* 42 (1934): 5–80.

—— "Recherches sur les institutions féodales en Normandie," *BSAN* 51 (1948–51): 5–175.

Nelson, Lynn H., *The Normans in South Wales, 1070–1171*. Austin, TX, and London, 1966.

Newman, Charlotte A., *The Anglo-Norman Nobility in the Reign of Henry I*. Philadelphia, PA, 1988.

Nicholl, Donald, *Thurstan, Archbishop of York (1114–1140)*. York, 1964.

Nicholl, Lewis D., *The Normans in Glamorgan, Gower and Kidweli*. Cardiff, 1936.

*Ninth Report of the Royal Commission on Historical Manuscripts*. Part i: *Report and Appendix*. London, 1883.

Norgate, Kate, "Robert, Earl of Gloucester," *DNB* xvi. reprn. edn. Oxford, 1949–50, 1242–4.

—— *England under the Angevin Kings*. i. London, 1887; reprn. edn., New York, 1969.

North, Christine, "The Arundell Archive," *The Royal Institution of Cornwall*, pt. 1 (1991): 47–57.

O'Brien, Bruce, *God's Peace and King's Peace: The Laws of Edward the Confessor*. Philadelphia, PA, 1999.

—— "The Instituta Cnuti and the Translation of English Law," *ANS* 25 (2003): 177–97.

O'Brien, Bruce, "Legal Treatises as Perceptions of Law in Stephen's Reign," in *King Stephen's Reign*, 182–95.

*ODNB*= *The Oxford Dictionary of National Biography*. 20 vols. Oxford, 2004.

Orme, Nicholas, *From Childhood to Chivalry*. London and New York, 1984.

Painter, *Feudal Barony*=Painter, Sidney, *Studies in the History of the English Feudal Barony*. Baltimore, MD, 1943.

Painter, Sidney, "The Rout of Winchester," *Speculum* 7 (1932): 70–5; also in *Feudalism and Liberty*, 157–64.

—— *French Chivalry*. reprn. edn. Ithaca, NY, 1957.

—— "Castle-Guard," in *Feudalism and Liberty*, 144–56.

—— "Family and the Feudal System in Twelfth-Century England," in *Feudalism and Liberty*, 195–219.

Parker, Thomas W., *The Knights Templars in England*. Tucson, AZ, 1963.

Patterson, "Anarchy in England"= Patterson, Robert B., "Anarchy in England, 1135–54: The Theory of the Constitution," *Albion* 6 (1974): 189–200.

Patterson, Robert B., "William of Malmesbury's Robert of Gloucester: A Re-Evaluation of the Historia Novella," *American Historical Review* 70 (1965): 983–97.

—— "Stephen's Shaftesbury Charter: Another Case against William of Malmesbury," *Speculum* 43 (1968): 487–92.

—— "Vassals and the Norman Earldom of Gloucester's Scriptorium," *The National Library of Wales Journal* 20 (1978): 342–4 & Plate.

—— "Robert Fitz Harding of Bristol: Profile of an Early Angevin Burgess-Baron Patrician and his Family's Urban Involvement," *HSJ* 1 (1989): 109–22.

—— "Bristol: An Angevin Baronial Capital under Royal Siege," *HSJ* 3 (1991): 171–81.

—— "The Ducal and Royal *Acta* of Henry Fitz Empress," *BGAST* 109 (1991): 117–37.

—— "The Author of the 'Margam Annals': Early Thirteenth-Century Margam Abbey's Compleat Scribe," *ANS* 14 (1992): 197–210.

—— *The Scriptorium of Margam Abbey and the Scribes of Early Angevin Glamorgan: Secretarial Administration in a Welsh Marcher Barony c.1150–c.1225*. Woodbridge, 2002.

—— "Isabella Countess of Gloucester," *ODNB* xxix. 416–17.

—— "William, Second Earl of Gloucester," *ODNB* lix. 39–40.

Payling, Simon, *Political Society in Lancastrian England*. Oxford, 1991.

Peirce, Ian, "The Knight, his Arms and Armour in the Eleventh and Twelfth Centuries," in *The Ideals and Practice of Medieval Knighthood: Papers from the First and Second Strawberry Hill Conference*, ed. Christopher Harper-Bill and Ruth Harvey. Woodbridge, 1986, 152–64.

Perkins, Clarence, "The Knights Templars in the British Isles," *EHR* 25 (1910): 209–30.

Pettifer, Adrian, *English Castles*. Woodbridge, 1995.

Pevsner, Nikolaus, *North Somerset and Bristol*. reprn. edn. London, 1973.

Pezet, R. A. L., "Les Barons de Creully," *Bulletin de la Société d'Agriculture, Sciences, Arts, et Belles-lettres de Bayeux* 6 (1854): 253–509.

Pfaff, Richard, "The 'Abbreviatio Amalarii' of William of Malmesbury," *Recherches de théologie ancienne et médiévale* 47 (1980): 77–113.

Picken, W. M. M., "The Descent of the Devonshire Family of Willington from Robert Earl of Gloucester," in *Medieval Cornish Miscellany*, 92–112.

—— "The Feudality of Pendrim Manor," in *Medieval Cornish Miscellany*, 125–34.

Pohl, Benjamin, "When Did Robert of Torigni First Receive Henry of Huntingdon's *Historia Anglorum*, and Why Does it Matter?," *HSJ* 26 (2014): 143–67.

Pollock, Sir Frederick and Maitland, Frederick William, *The History of English Law before the Time of Edward I*. 2nd edn. reprn. 2 vols. Cambridge, 1911.
Poole, A. L., "Henry Plantagenet's Early Visits to England," *EHR* 47 (1932): 447–51.
Poole, Reginald L(ane), *The Exchequer in the Twelfth Century*. Oxford, 1912.
Postan, M. M., *The Medieval Economy and Society*. London, 1972.
Postles, Dave, "Religious Houses and the Laity in Eleventh to Thirteenth-Century England: An Overview," *HSJ* 12 (2002): 1–13.
Pounds, Norman John Greville, *The Medieval Castle in England and Wales*. Cambridge, 1990.
Power, Daniel, *The Norman Frontier in the Twelfth and Early Thirteenth Centuries*. Cambridge, 2004.
—— "Guérin de Glapion, Seneschal of Normandy (1200–1): Service and Ambition under the Plantagenet and Capetian Kings," in *Records, Administration and Aristocratic Society in the Anglo-Norman Realm*, 153–92.
Powicke, Sir Maurice, *The Loss of Normandy 1189–1204*. 2nd reprn. edn. Manchester, 1963.
—— and Millican, P., rev. Janice Gordon-Kelter, "Norgate, Kate," *ODNB* xli. 9–10.
Prestwich, J. O., "War and Finance in the Anglo-Norman State," *TRHS* 5th ser. 4 (1954): 19–43; also in *Anglo-Norman Warfare*, ed. Strickland, 59–83.
—— "The Military Household of the Norman Kings," *EHR* 96 (1981): 1–37; also in *Anglo-Norman Warfare*, ed. Strickland, 93–127.
—— "Military Intelligence under the Norman and Angevin Kings," in *Law and Government*, 1–30.
*Records, Administration and Aristocratic Society in the Anglo-Norman Realm*, ed. Nicholas Vincent. Woodbridge, 2009.
Reedy, William T., Jr., "The Origin of the General Eyre in the Reign of Henry I," *Speculum* 41 (1966): 688–724.
—— "The First Two Bassets of Weldon," *Northamptonshire Past & Present* 4 (1966–72): 241–5, 295–8.
Renn, Derek, *Norman Castles in Britain*. 2nd edn. New York, 1973.
Reynolds, Susan, "The Rulers of London in the Twelfth Century," *History* 57 (1972): 337–57.
—— *An Introduction to the History of English Medieval Towns*. Oxford, 1977.
Richardson, H. G. and Sales, G. O., *The Governance of Medieval England from the Conquest to Magna Carta*. Edinburgh, 1963.
Rigg, A. G., "Serlo of Wilton: Biographical Notes," *Medium Aevum* 65 (1996): 96–101.
Roffe, David, "From Thegnage to Barony: Sake and Soke, Title, and Tenants-in-Chief," *ANS* 12 (1989): 157–76.
Round, John Horace, *Geoffrey de Mandeville*. London, 1892.
—— "The Rout of Winchester," in Round, *Geoffrey de Mandeville*, 123–35.
—— "King Stephen and the Earl of Chester," *EHR* 10 (1895): 87–91.
—— "Bernard, the King's Scribe," *EHR* 14 (1899): 417–30.
—— *The Commune of London*. Westminster, 1899.
—— *Studies in Peerage and Family History*. London, 1901; reprn. edn., Baltimore, MD, 1970.
—— "Castle-Guard," *Archaeological Journal* 59 (1902): 144–59.
—— *Feudal England*. London, 1909.
—— "The Lindsey Survey (1115–18)," in Round, *Feudal England*, 181–95.
—— "The Northamptonshire Survey," in Round, *Feudal England*, 215–24.

Round, John Horace, "The Knight-Service of Malmesbury Abbey," *EHR* 32 (1917): 249–52.

—— "The Bayeux Inquest of 1133," in Round, *Family Origins*, 201–16.

—— "'Burh-bot' and 'Brig-bot'," in Round, *Family Origins*, 252–65.

—— "The Granvilles and the Monks," in Round, *Family Origins*, 130–69.

—— "The Prise of Wine," in Round, *Family Origins*, 237–51.

—— *Family Origins*. London, 1930; reprn. edn. Baltimore, MD, 1970.

—— "Introduction to the Northamptonshire Survey," in *VCH Northamptonshire* i. 257–98.

Rowlands, I. W., "The Making of the March: Aspects of the Norman Settlement in Dyfed," *ANS* 3 (1980): 142–57.

Runciman, Steven, *A History of the Crusades* i. Cambridge, 1957.

Saltman, Avrom, *Theobald, Archbishop of Canterbury*. London, 1956.

Sanders, I. J., *English Baronies*. Oxford, 1960.

Schramm, Percy Ernst, *A History of the English Coronation*, transl. Leopold G. Wickham Legg. Oxford, 1937.

Schütt, Marie, "The Literary Forms of William of Malmesbury's 'Gesta Regum'," *EHR* 46 (1931): 255–60.

Searle, Eleanor, "Seignorial Control of Women's Marriage: The Antecedents and Function of Merchet in England," *Past & Present* 82 (1979): 3–43.

Sharpe, Richard, "Address and Delivery in Anglo-Norman Royal Charters," in *Charters and Charter Scholarship*, 32–52.

—— (ed.), *A Handlist of Latin Writers of Great Britain before 1540*. Turnhout, 1997. *Additions and Corrections*. Turnhout, 2001.

—— "1088–William II and the Rebels," *ANS* 24 (2004): 139–57.

—— "Norman Rule in Cumbria 1092–1136," Cumberland and Westmorland Antiquarian and Archaeological Society, Tract Ser. xxi (2006), 5–78.

Sheppard, Jennifer M., "The Twelfth-Century Library and Scriptorium at Buildwas: Assessing the Evidence," in *England in the Twelfth Century*, 193–204.

Short, Ian, "Patrons and Polyglots: French Literature in Twelfth-Century England," *ANS* 14 (1991): 229–49.

—— "Gaimar's Epilogue and Geoffrey of Monmouth's *Liber Vetustissimus*," *Speculum* 69 (1994): 323–43.

Smalley, Beryl, *Historians in the Middle Ages*. London, 1974.

Smith, David M., "Alexander," *ODNB* i. 645–8.

Smith, J. Beverly, "The Kingdom of Morgannwg and the Norman Conquest of Glamorgan," in *Glamorgan County History* iii. 1–43.

Southern, R. W., "The Place of Henry I in English History," *Proceedings of the British Academy* 48 (1962): 127–69; also as "Henry I" in *Medieval Humanism*, 206–33.

—— *Saint Anselm and his Biographer*. Cambridge, 1963.

—— *Medieval Humanism*. Oxford, 1970.

—— "The Place of England in the Twelfth-Century Renaissance," in *Medieval Humanism*, 158–80.

—— "Aspects of the European Tradition of Historical Writing, iv. The Sense of the Past," *TRHS* 5th ser. 23 (1973): 243–63.

Spear, David S., "Une Famille ecclésiastique anglo-normande," *Études Normandes*. Association d'Études Normandes. iii (1986): 21–7.

—— "William Bona Anima, Abbot of St. Stephen's of Caen, 1070–79," *HSJ* 1 (1989): 51–60.

—— "Geoffrey Brito, Archbishop of Rouen (1111–28)," *HSJ* 2 (1990): 123–37.

—— "The School of Caen Revisited," *HSJ* 4 (1993): 55–66.
—— *The Personnel of the Norman Cathedrals during the Ducal Period, 911–1204*. Institute of Historical Research, London: 2006.
Stacy, N. E., "Henry of Blois and the Lordship of Glastonbury," *EHR* 114 (1999): 1–33.
Stenton, *English Feudalism*=Stenton, Frank, *The First Century of English Feudalism 1066–1166*. Oxford, 1961.
Stenton, Frank, *Anglo-Saxon England*, 2nd edn. reprn. Oxford, 1955.
—— "The Road System of Medieval England," in *Preparatory to Anglo-Saxon England*, ed. Doris Mary Stenton. Oxford, 1970.
Stephenson, Carl, "The Aids of the English Boroughs," *EHR* 24 (1919): 457–75.
—— *Borough and Town*. Cambridge, MA, 1933.
Strevett, Neil, "The Anglo-Norman Civil War of 1101 Reconsidered," *ANS* 26 (2003): 159–75.
Strickland, Matthew, "Securing the North: Invasion and the Strategy of Defense in Twelfth-Century Anglo-Scottish Warfare," *ANS* 12 (1989): 177–98; also in *Anglo-Norman Warfare*, ed. Strickland, 208–29.
—— (ed.), *Anglo-Norman Warfare: Studies in Late Anglo-Saxon and Anglo-Norman Military Organization and Warfare*. Woodbridge, 1992.
—— "Against the Lord's Anointed: Aspects of Warfare and Baronial Rebellion in England and Normandy, 1075–1265," in *Law and Government*, 56–79.
—— *War and Chivalry: The Conduct and Perception of War in England and Normandy, 1066–1217*. Cambridge, 1996.
Stringer, Keith J., *The Reign of Stephen: Kingship Warfare and Government in Twelfth-Century England*. London and New York, 1993.
*Studies in Medieval History Presented to R. Allen Brown*, ed. Christopher Harper-Bill, Christopher Holdsworth, and Janet I. Nelson. Woodbridge, 1989.
Tabuteau, Emily Zack, *Transfers of Property in Eleventh-Century Norman Law*. Chapel Hill, NC, 1988.
—— "The Role of Law in the Succession to Normandy and England, 1087," *HSJ* 3 (1992): 141–69.
Tait, James, *The Medieval English Borough*. Manchester, 1936.
*Tewkesbury Abbey: History, Art and Architecture*, ed. Richard K. Morris and Ron Shoesmith. Woonton, Almeley, 2003.
Thomas, Hugh M., "Lay Piety in England from 1066 to 1215," *ANS* 29 (2006): 179–92.
—— "Violent Disorder in Stephen's England: A Maximum Argument," in *King Stephen's Reign*, 139–70.
Thompson, James Westfall, *The Literacy of the Laity in the Middle Ages*. Berkeley, CA, 1939.
Thompson, Kathleen, "Family and Influence to the South of Normandy in the Eleventh Century: The Lordship of Bellême," *Journal of Medieval History* 11 (1985): 215–26.
—— "Robert of Bellême Reconsidered," *ANS* 13 (1990/1991): 263–86.
—— "William Talvas, Count of Ponthieu, and the Politics of the Anglo-Norman Realm," in *England and Normandy in the Middle Ages*, 169–84.
—— "The Lords of Laigle: Ambition and Insecurity on the Borders of Normandy," *ANS* 18 (1995): 177–99.
—— "Dowery aand Inheritance Patterns: Some Examples from the Descendants of King Henry I of England," *Medieval Prosopography* 17 (1996): 45–61.
—— "The Formation of the County of Perche: The Rise and Fall of the House of Gouet," in Keats-Rohan, *Family Trees*, 299–314.

Thompson, Kathleen, *Power and Border Lordship in Medieval France: The County of Perche, 1000–1226*. Royal Historical Society. Woodbridge, 2002.

—— "Affairs of State: The Illegitimate Children of Henry I," *Journal of Medieval History* 29 (2003): 129–51.

—— "From the Thames to Tinchebray: The Role of Normandy in the Early Career of Henry I," in *Henry I and the Anglo-Norman World: Studies in Memory of C. Warren Hollister*, ed. Donald F. Fleming and Janet M. Pope. *HSJ* 17 (2006): 16–26.

—— "The First Hundred Years of the Abbey of Tiron: Institutionalizing the Reform of the Forest Hermits," *ANS* 31 (2009): 104–17.

Thomson, *GR ii*=Thomson, R. M. in collaboration with Winterbottom, M., William of Malmesbury, *Gesta Regum Anglorum* ii: *General Introduction and Commentary*. Oxford, 1999.

Thomson, R. M., "Serlo of Wilton and the Schools of Oxford," *Medium Aevum* 68 (1999): 1–12.

—— *William of Malmesbury*. rev. edn. Woodbridge, 2003.

Thurlby, Malcolm, "Romanesque Sculpture at Tewkesbury Abbey," *BGAST* 98 (1980): 89–94.

—— "The Elevations of the Romanesque Abbey Churches of St. Mary at Tewkesbury and St. Peter at Gloucester," in *Medieval Art and Architecture at Gloucester and Tewkesbury*, 36–51.

—— "The Norman Church," in *Tewkesbury Abbey, History, Art and Architecture*, 89–108.

Truax, Jean A., "From Bede to Orderic Vitalis: Changing Perspectives on the Role of Women in Anglo-Saxon and Anglo-Norman Churches," *HSJ* 3 (1991): 35–51.

Turner, Ralph V., *Men Raised from the Dust: Administrative Service and Upward Mobility in Angevin England*. Philadelphia, PA, 1988.

Tyerman, Christopher, *England and the Crusades 1095–1588*. Chicago and London, 1988.

Urry, William, "The Normans in Canterbury," *Annales de Normandie* 8 (1958): 119–38.

—— *Canterbury under the Angevin Kings*. London, 1967.

Van Caenegem, R. C., *Royal Writs in England from the Conquest to Glanvill*. Publications of the Selden Society lvii. London, 1959.

Van Houts, Elizabeth M. C., "Robert of Torigni as Genealogist," in *Studies in Medieval History Presented to R. Allen Brown*, 215–33.

—— "Wace as Historian," in Keats-Rohan, *Family Trees*, 104–32.

—— "The Warenne View of the Past 1066–1203," *ANS* 26 (2004): 103–21.

—— "The Fate of Priests' Sons in Normandy with Special Reference to Serlo of Bayeux," *HSJ* 25 (2014): 57–105.

Vaughan, Richard, *Matthew Paris*. Cambridge, 1958.

Vaughn, Sally, "Robert of Meulan and Raison d'État in the Anglo-Norman State," *Albion* 10 (1978): 352–73.

—— *Anselm of Bec and Robert of Meulan: The Innocence of the Dove and the Wisdom of the Serpent*. Berkeley, CA, 1987.

*VCH*=*Victoria History of the Counties of England*.

Venables, Edmund (as E.V.), "Alexander," *DNB* i. (Oxford, 1921); reprn. edn.: 267–71.

Vincent, Nicholas, *The Acta of Henry II and Richard I*, ed. J. C. Holt and Richard Mortimer. List and Index Society. Special Series xxi, 1986.

—— "The Early Years of Keynsham Abbey," *BGAST* 111 (1993): 95–113.

—— "The Borough of Chipping Sodbury and the Fat Men of France (1130–1270)," *BGAST* 116 (1998): 141–59.

―― "Hugh de Gundeville (fl. 1147–81)," in *Records, Administration and Aristocratic Society in the Anglo-Norman Realm*, 125–45.
Voss, Lena, *Heinrich von Blois Bischof von Winchester (1129–71)*. Berlin, 1929; reprn. edn. Vaduz, 1965.
Waldman, Thomas G., "Hugh of Amiens, Archbishop of Rouen (1130–64), the Norman Abbots, and the Papacy: The Foundation of a 'Textual Community'," *HSJ* 2 (1990): 139–53.
Walker, David, "Miles of Gloucester, Earl of Hereford," *BGAST* 77 (1958): 66–84.
―― "The 'Honours' of the Earls of Hereford in the Twelfth Century," *BGAST* 79 (1960): 174–211.
―― "The Medieval Bishops of Llandaff," *Morgannwg* 6 (1962): 5–32.
―― *Bristol in the Early Middle Ages*. Bristol Branch of the Historical Association. Bristol, 1971.
―― "The Norman Settlement in Wales," *ANS* 1 (1978): 131–43.
―― "Cardiff," in *The Boroughs of Medieval Wales*, ed. R. A. Griffiths. Cardiff, 1978, 103–28.
―― "Gloucester, Miles of," *ODNB* xxii. 481–3.
*War and Government in the Middle Ages: Essays in Honour of J. O. Prestwich*, ed. John Gillingham and J. C. Holt. Woodbridge, 1984.
Ward, J., "Fashions in Monastic Endowment," *Journal of Ecclesiastical History* 32 (1981): 428–37.
Wareham, Andres, "The Motives and Politics of the Bigod Family, c.1066–1177," *ANS* 16 (1995): 223–42.
Warren, W. L., *Henry II*. London, 1973.
Webber, Teresa, "The Handwriting of the Original Charters," in Thacker, *Earldom of Chester and its Charters*, 137–77.
Weiler, Björn, "William of Malmesbury, King Henry I, and the *Gesta Regum Anglorum*," *ANS* 31 (2009): 157–76.
West, F. J., *The Justiciarship in England 1066–1232*. Cambridge, 1966.
White, G. H., "The Sisters and Nieces of Gunnor, Duchess of Normandy," *The Genealogist* n.s. 37 pt. 2 (1920): 57–65; pt. 3 (1921): 128–32.
―― "Constables under the Norman Kings," *The Genealogist*. n.s. 38, pt. i (1921): 113–27.
―― "Financial Administration under Henry I," *TRHS* 4th ser. 8 (1925): 56–78.
―― "King Stephen's Earldoms," *TRHS* 4th ser. 13 (1930): 51–82.
―― "The Career of Waleran, Count of Meulan and Earl of Worcester (1104–66)," *TRHS* 4th ser. 17 (1934): 19–48.
―― "The Household of the Norman Kings," *TRHS* 4th ser. 30 (1948): 127–55.
―― "War and Finance in the Anglo-Norman State," *TRHS* 5th ser. 4 (1954): 19–43.
White, Graeme, "King Stephen, Duke Henry, and Ranulf de Gernons," *EHR* 91(1976): 555–65.
―― "Were the Midlands 'Wasted' during Stephen's Reign," *Midland History* 10 (1985): 26–46.
―― "Continuity in Government," in *The Anarchy of King Stephen's Reign*, 117–43.
―― "The Myth of the Anarchy," *ANS* 22 (1999): 323–37.
―― "Earls and Earldoms in Stephen's Reign," in *War and Society in Medieval and Early Modern Britain*, ed. D. E. S. Dunn. Liverpool, 2000.
―― "Ranulf (II), Fourth Earl of Chester," *ODNB* xlvi. 53–6.

White, Graeme, "Royal Income and Regional Trends," in *King Stephen's Reign*, 27–43.
Wightman, W. E., *The Lacy Family in England and Normandy 1066–1194*. Oxford, 1966.
Wilcox, Michael, "The Foundation Charter of Neath Abbey," *Annual Report of the Glamorgan Archivist 1990*, 1, 17–18.
Williams, Ann, *The English and the Norman Conquest*. Woodbridge, 1995.
—— "A West-Country Magnate of the Eleventh Century: The Family, Estates and Patronage of Beorhtric Son of Ælfgar," in Keats-Rohan, *Family Trees*, 41–68.
Williams, David H., *The Welsh Cistercians*. 2 vols. Cyhoeddiadau Sistersiaidd (Caldey Island, Tenby), 1984.
Williams, L. F. Rushbrook, "William the Chamberlain and Luton Church," *EHR* 28 (1913): 719–30.
*Winchester*=*Winchester in the Early Middle Ages: An Edition and Discussion of the Winton Domesday*, ed. Frank Barlow, Martin Biddle, Olof von Feilitzen, and D. J. Keene. *Winchester Studies* i, gen. ed. Martin Biddle. Oxford, 1976.
Wogan-Browne, Jocelyn, "General Introduction: What's in a Name: The 'French' of England," in *Language and Culture in Medieval Britain*, 1–13.
*Writing Medieval Biography 750–1250: Essays in Honour of Professor Frank Barlow*, ed. David Bates, Julia Crick, and Sarah Hamilton. Woodbridge, 2006.
*The Writing of History in the Middle Ages: Essays Presented to Richard William Southern*, ed. R. H. C. Davis and J. M. Wallace-Hadrill. Oxford, 1981.
Yoshitake, K., "The Arrest of the Bishops in 1139 and its Consequences," *Journal of Medieval History* 14 (1988): 97–114.
—— "The Exchequer in the Reign of King Stephen," *EHR* 103 (1988): 150–9.
Yver, Jean, "Les Châteaux-forts en Normandie jusqu'au milieu du xiie siècle: contribution à l'étude du pouvoir ducal," *BSAN* 53 (1955–6): 28–115.
Zarnecki, George, *Romanesque Art*. London, 1971.

# Maps

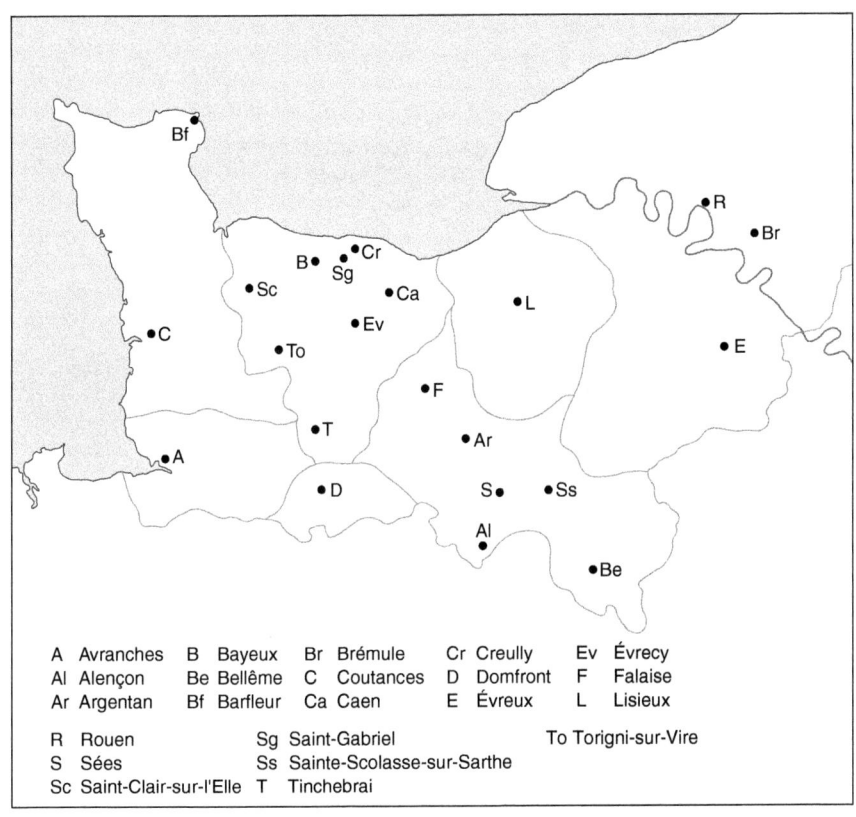

Map 1. Robert earl of Gloucester and Normandy.

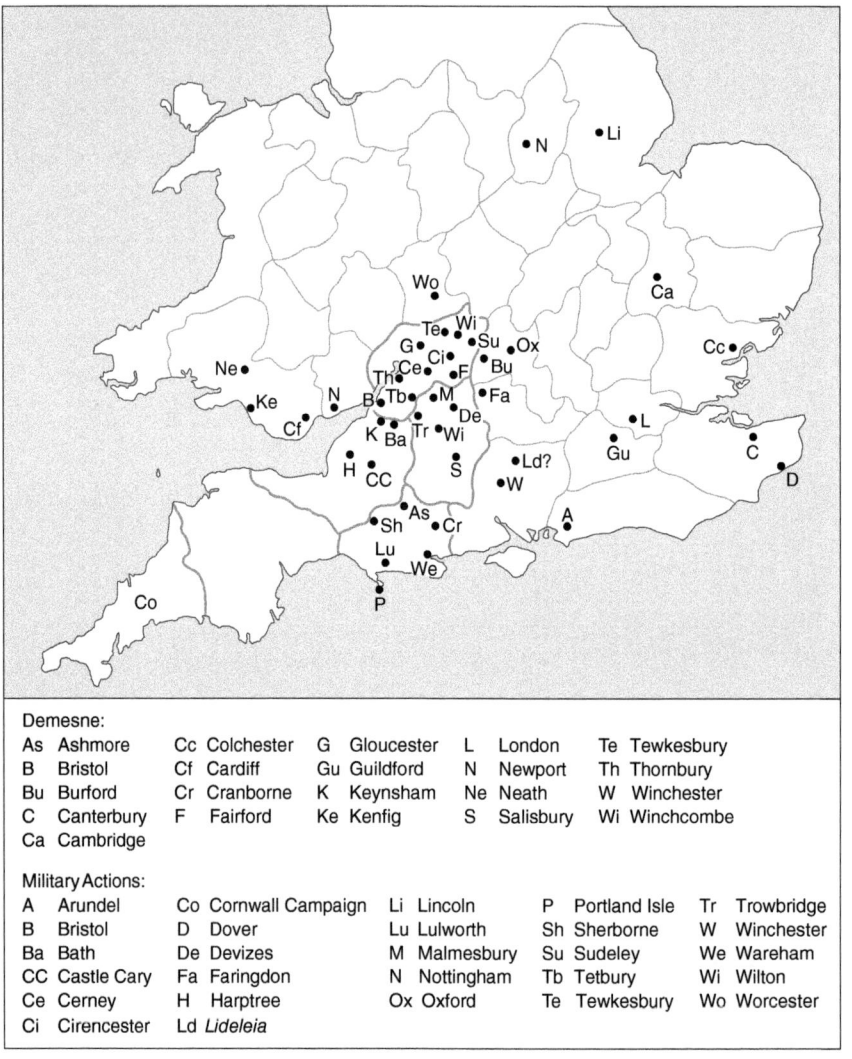

**Map 2.** Significant Anglo-Welsh Demesne and Military Actions Involving Earl Robert of Gloucester.

# Index

Note: Figures are indicated by *f* after the page number.

Abergavenny (Gwent) 31, 139, 147
Abingdon (Berks.) 167
  Abbey 3, 52
Acquigny (Eure) 15
Adam of Ely 93, 108, 112
Addington Parva (Northants) 66
Adela, countess of Blois xxi, 1n.1, 38, 40, 129
Adelaide, Queen 42
Adelard of Bath xx, 166, 178
  *Quaestiones Naturales* 178
Adeliza of Louvain, Queen of England xxi, 14–15, 28–9, 40, 54, 68n.89, 143–5, 180
Adeliza, mother of Walter, sheriff of Gloucestershire 117
affinity xix, 3–4, 139, 141–2, 170–3
Afon Cynffig river (Kenfig,) 77, 95
Ailred, abbot of Rievaulx 50
Aisthorpe (Lincs.) 19, 66–7
Aiulphus a Foro 63n.41
Alan, count of Brittany, lord of Richmond 145, 155
Aldreth (Cambs) 145
Alençon (Orne) 130, 239
Alexander, bishop of Lincoln 36, 37n.50, 49, 55, 145, 157, 180
Alfred fitz Judhael 141
Alfred of Lincoln 140, 145
Alice of Berkeley 105
Alton (Surrey) 8, 15
  invasion of 17
  Treaty of 6, 19, 40
Alverton (Corn.) 65n.59
Amaury IV de Montfort, count of Évreux 15, 26, 34, 40
Ambrières (Mayenne) 42
amercements/fines 34, 39, 46, 48, 94
Anacletus II, Pope (Peter Pierleone) 38
Anarchy xv–xviii, 3–4, 88, 91, 97, 104, 114n.207, 117, 123, 143, 189, 193, 195, 202, 204–5, *see also* civil war
Angevin
  alliance/allies 27–8, 171, 174
  civil war xv, 64, 85, 89, 123, 128, 156, 162, 169, 171, 174, 205
  dynasty 1, 131, 138, 165, 201n.159, 202, 205
  heir 166–7, 176, 205
  leaders 138, 148, 157, 159–61, 185
  marriage 41, 43, 184

  party/supporters/allies 1, 45, 88, 91–2, 99, 118, 129, 132, 135–40, 142, 145–50, 153, 155–8, 162–3, 164, 166–9, 171, 173–5, 185–6, 193–4, 197, 203, 205
  succession/cause xv, 119, 150–1, 174, 177, 179, 197, 202, 206
  *see also* Robert earl of Gloucester, leadership of the Angevin party
Anglo-Norman
  colonial conquests in South Wales 74–8, 103, 122, 134, 180
  earls 28, 33–4, 36–7, 50, 52–4, 89, 110, 174, 191, 204
  Francophone elite 9
  French xix, 4, 4n.24, 9, 98, 180
  period xv–xvii, xix–xx, 100
  realm ii, 1, 3, 8, 16, 25, 36, 50, 60, 70, 117, 179, 183
  succession xvi, xvii, 2, 40–1, 44, 105, 126, 129, 131, 135, 138, 143, 183–4, 206
  verse chronicle 4
Anglo-Saxon
  burghal predecessors 101
  *burh* 69, 95
  earls 33, 33n.26, 77
  *Instituta Cnuti* 8
  kings 4
  legal terms 49
  period 44
  thane 3
*Anglo-Saxon Chronicle* 192, 203
Anjou 16, 25, 41–2, 61, 128, 166, 184
Anselm, archbishop of Canterbury (St. Anselm) 7–8, 17, 121, 181, 193–4
Ansfrida 2n.8, 3
appanages xix, 3, 65, 79, 82, 84–7, 89
Apulia (Italy) 8
Arabic science and philosophy xx, 178
Arganchy (Calvados) 22
Argentan (Orne) 42, 128, 136, 239
aristocracy xix, 5, 17, 33, 36n.39, 57, 65, 82, 90, 105, 126, 175, 191
  boys 9
  families 9, 24, 84
  family surnames 6
  *iuvenes* 24
  *see also* bastards/bastardy/illegitimacy; *cognatus*; education; inheritance; knights; literacy; *miles litteratus*

armies xix, 8, 13, 16–17, 26, 50, 128, 131,
    133, 135–6, 139, 145–7, 154–5, 159,
    161, 168–9, 173–4, 176, 186, 192, 195
Arnulf, bishop of Lisieux 175
Arnulf of Chocques 9
Arreville (Manche) 58
Arthur, King 13, 49
    legend xx, 180
Arundel (Sussex) 80, 143–7, 191, 240
Asceline Peverel 110
Ascelin de Waterville 109
Ashley (Glos.) 85, 108
Ashmore (Dors.) 65, 94, 240
Asnières (Calvados) 58–9
Asselina a Foro 63n.41
Aubrey de Vere 56, 84n.13, 96
Audoin, bishop of Évreux 32, 36, 55, 126–7
Aunay Priory (Calvados) 3
*auxilium civitatis* (city aids) 46, 48, 68–9, 73,
    80–1, 94n.83, 100, *see also* city aids
Avon rivers 71, 96–7, 99, 103, 105, 107
Avranches (Manche) 4, 23, 60, 112, 239
Avranchin 4, 62, 165
Axminster (Devon) 170

bailiffs 52, 94, 117
Baldwin I, King of the Latin Kingdom of
    Jerusalem 175
Baldwin II, King of the Latin Kingdom of
    Jerusalem 42, 43n.77
Baldwin VII, count of Flanders 20–1, 25, 40
Baldwin de Redvers, earl of Devon 74, 91, 131,
    133–4, 138, 141, 143, 146, 148, 154,
    160, 175, 195
Baldwin fitz Gilbert de Clare 11, 139–40, 155
Bamburgh (Nthmb.) 140
Bampton (Oxon.) 158
Barfleur (Manche) 27, 146, 239
baronage xix–xx, 57–62, 64–9, 74–7, 82
    curial 21, 79
    honorial 60, 69n.90, 72n.112, 100, 104–6,
        115, 141
    *see also* landlords; magnates; Marcher lords;
        subinfeudation; tenants-in-chief
barons of the exchequer 23n.133, 32n.22, 115
Barrow Gurney (Som.) 66
Barton Regis/the earl's barton (Bristol,
    Glos.) 65, 69, 71, 94, 97, 101, 115
Barton Seagrave (Northants.) 66
bastards/bastardy/illegitimacy xv, 1–2, 5, 7–9,
    12, 15–18, 21, 28, 32, 38, 42, 62, 72,
    83n.12, 84, 86–7, 135, 189, 193, 204
Bath (Som.) 71, 141, 152, 172, 174, 199, 240
battles
    Alençon 26, 239
    Bath 97, 123, 151, 176, 240
    Bourgthéroulde 35, 40, 61
    Brémule 25–6, 239
    Hastings 16

Lincoln 151, 154, 158, 162, 186, 188–90,
    200, 202, 240
Ramla 1n.1
of the Standard 50, 140
Tinchebrai 6, 17, 20–1, 40, 239
Wilton 170, 240
Bayeux (Calvados) 12, 20, 39, 48, 59n.23,
    60–4, 86, 88, 90, 135, 142, 239
    Cathedral of Sainte-Marie 12, 58, 86
Bazenville (Calvados) 58, 119n.251
Beaumont-le-Vicomte (Sarthe) 128
Bec Abbey (Eure) 21, 61, 179n.4
Bede 180
    *Ecclesiastical History* 183
Bedford castle 175
Bedminster (Som.) 65, 97, 99, 105, 107, 119
Bellême (Orne) 239
Benedeit
    *The Voyage of St. Brendan* 180
Benedict, abbot of Tewkesbury 97
benefices 85, 86, 108, 120
Benefrei 93, 107
Beorhtric fitz Algar 64
Berkeley (Glos) 91, 104n.136, 105, 174
    castle 105
Berkeley Hernesse (Glos.) 14
Bernard, abbot of Clairvaux 38, 119, 123–4,
    175, 205
Bernard, bishop of St. David's 157
Bernard of Neufmarché 75
Bessin 4n.27, 12, 17, 20, 48, 60, 62–3, 89–90,
    104, 119, 127, 132, 142, 165, 176, 205
Bickmarsh (War.) 67
Bilswick (Bristol) 97, 99, 105
Binnerton (Corn.) 65, 108
Bletchingdon (Oxon.) 109n.170
Bonneville (Calvados) 127
*Book of Llandaff* 122
*Book of Numbers* 150, 193
Bordesley Abbey (Worcs.) 52n.131, 90n.54,
    138n.70
boroughs xix, 28, 65, 70–1, 76–7, 94–6,
    98–105, 115, 133, 138, 143, 167, 171
    burgages 97, 101, 103–4, 108
    burgesses xix, 54, 59, 63–4, 71, 94, 97,
        100–1, 103–5, 110, 127n.6, 130, 155,
        158–9
    castle boroughs 28, 65, 77, 95, 143
    charters of liberty 101, 111n.186, 201n.160
Boulogne, county of 40, 126, 129
Bourn (Cambs.) 110
Box hoard 171
Brasted (Kent) 68
Breage (Corn.) 65, 108
Brecon 31, 75, 139, 147
Brémule (Eure) 239
    battle of 25–6
Breteuil (Eure) 15, 26–7, 61, 129
Bretinghurst (Surrey) 61n.29, 141

Bretons 17, 141
Brian fitz Count 13–14, 23–4, 30–1, 41, 43–4, 46, 49, 55, 74, 139, 147–8, 150, 153–4, 157, 159–63, 173–6, 185, 193, 205
Bridgend (Glam.) 119n.250
Briquessart (Calvados) 62, 165
Brislington (Som.) 71, 94
Bristol xviiin.20, xix, 4, 14, 16, 18, 28, 44, 58, 65, 69–72, 74–6, 84–5, 88, 92–8, 100–5, 107–8, 110–12, 114–15, 117, 119, 124, 134, 139–4, 146–51, 156–7, 163, 169, 171, 172*f*, 173–4, 176, 178, 180, 191, 194, 198–9, 204, 240
  castle 84, 96n.89, 108, 115, 141, 166
Bristol Channel 74
Briton Ferry (Glam.) 77, 119
Brittany 5
Brotonne (Eure-Seine-Inférieure) 61
Bruges, county of Flanders 42
*Brut y Tywysogyon* 75
Brycheiniog (Brecon) 75
Burford (Oxon.) 66, 69–1, 93, 101–2, 138, 190, 240
Bushley (Worcs.) 64, 72, 73n.118

Caen (Calvados) 2, 4, 12, 17, 20, 31, 35, 39, 57–8, 63–4, 86, 96, 98, 115, 119, 126–7, 132, 135, 142, 165, 195, 239
Calixtus II, Pope 27, 37, 40, 110, 122
Calne (Wilts.) 147
Camberwell (Surrey) 61n.29, 69, 108n.162
Cambridge 80, 150, 240
Canon Law 181, 190n.89, 194
Canterbury (Kent) xxiii, 44, 47, 68, 70, 80, 122, 130, 142, 194
  castle 44, 47, 68
Caradog ap Gruffydd 75
Caradog, son of Iestyn ap Gwrgant 78
Cardiff (Glam.) 4, 16, 74–7, 92–3, 95, 102–3, 110, 118, 171, 180
  castle 44n.82, 76, 115, 240
  church and priory of St. Mary 76
Carlisle (Cumb.) 131, 150
Carron river 103
Carworgie (Corn.) 65n.55
Castle Cary (Som.) 141–2, 240
Castle Combe (Wilts.) 171
Castle Hedingham (Essex) 96
Castle Rising (Norf.) 96
castles 4–5, 20, 25, 35, 42, 44, 47, 49, 52, 68n.89, 69n.90, 75–6, 82, 89–90, 95–6, 105, 114–15, 128–9, 131, 135, 137n.63, 140, 145, 147, 149, 151, 156, 160–1, 165, 168, 170, 173–4, 176, 186, 191, 199, 202
Caux (Hérault) 127
Cecilia, abbess of Caen, daughter of King William I xxi, 9
Cecilia of Shaftsbury 67n.81

Celtic culture 179
Cerne (Dors.) 124
Cerney (Glos.) 147, 240
Chaddesley Corbet (Worcs.) 66
chamberlains 23, 31n.10, 45, 67n.72, 70, 104, 106, 108, 110, 111n.181, 129
Channel (English) 2, 51, 86n.25, 124, 132, 140, 165, 170
chaplains 10, 12, 23–4, 30, 65n.60, 86, 108, 111–12, 115, 140
Charles the Good, count of Flanders 25, 40, 42
Châtillon-sur-Colmont (Mayenne) 42
Chellington (Beds.) 50
Chepstow (Monm.) 72, 109, 139
Cherbourg (Manche) 58
Chester 60, 71, 75, 77, 83n.13, 90, 111n.187, 112, 124, 154, 205
Chipping Campden (Glos.) 90, 115
chivalry xvi, 11, 13–14, 146
Chouain (Calvados) 58
Christianity 9–10, 181, 183
*Chronicon Monasterii de Abingdon* 2n.8
*Chronicon Thomas Wykes* 137n.63
Church (Latin) xv, 39, 90, 97, 120–1, 124–5, 132, 157, 183, 190, 205
Cicero 11, 180–1
Cirencester (Glos.) xxiii, 71, 87, 156, 158, 167–8
Cistercians 14, 38, 50, 95, 119, 175, 177, 205
Cîteaux (Côte d'Or)
city aids 46–7, 70, see also *auxilium civitatis*
Claybrook (Leics.) 154
Clayhanger (Som.) 109n.169
clerks 9, 12, 14, 84, 93, 104, 108, 111–13, 115, 158, 198
Cluny, abbey (Saone-et-Loire) 38, 194
  abbots/houses xx, 38, 117
  see also Reading Abbey
codex xviii, 187, 198, 200–1
Codford Farleigh (Som.) 65n.55
Coety (Glam.) 76
Cogan (Glam.) 106
*cognatus* 3–4, 89n.47, 141
coins/pennies xix, 10n.57, 33–4, 52–3, 75, 96–7, 102, 142, 170–1, 172*f*, 200,
  see also money/moneyers/mints
Colchester (Essex) 69–70, 80, 96, 240
Combe (Glos.) 107
*comes* 10n.57, 33–4, 200, see also Anglo-Norman/Anglo-Saxon, earls
*comitatus* 53, 68n.89, 77, 122
*compositio* 123–4, 170
Compostella (Galicia) 22
Conches (Eure) 15
*confederatio amoris* 114
*coniuratio* 127, 132n.35, 144, 152, 195
Connerton (Corn.) 65, 85, 91n.56
Conquest (Norman) xix–xx, 4, 9, 33, 54, 64, 66, 73–4, 77, 79, 101, 104, 139, 152

constables xix, 24, 31, 33, 52–4, 71, 77–8, 93, 108, 114–15, 133–4, 143–4, 147–9, 153, 160, 164, 167, 173, 188
Constance de Grainville 92, 118
*Constitutio domus Regis* 49
*Consuetudines et Iusticie* 116
*consul* 10n.57, 34, 200, *see also* Anglo-Norman, earls
*conventio/ conventiones* 36, 45, 48, 59, 62, 78, 83, 87, 91n.60, 92, 109, 111n.186, 115, 120–1, 123–4, 131–6, 140, 143–4, 148, 157, 164–5, 186, 196
Corbon (Calvados) 30
Corbonnais 15
Corfe castle (Dors.) 145
Cornard (Suff.) 67
Cotentin 4–6, 8, 20, 34, 60, 89, 131–2, 136, 138, 165
Cotswolds 66, 96, 175
councils 7, 22–4, 27, 29, 34, 36–7, 38n.50, 39, 42–3, 89, 92, 122, 127–8, 131, 143, 145, 155–6, 158, 159, 163, 166, 184, 190–1, 193
  Lillebonne 39
  Oxford 190–1, 240
  Rheims 27, 122
  Winchester 159, 240
counselors xviii, 1, 29, 54, 173, 186, see also *curiales, familiares*
courts, *curia regis,* king's court xviii, xx, 11, 17, 21–5, 28–9, 30n.5, 30–3, 35–9, 41–2, 43–6, 48, 92, 94, 122, 126, 129–30, 132, 134–6, 145, 148, 150, 157, 159, 163–4, 174, 176, 180, 185, 191, 195, 197
  Gloucester honorial courts xix, 48, 71, 76–7, 83, 89–90, 92, 94, 101, 103, 105, 109–10, 111n.187, 114–16, 122–3, 141
  protocol 22, 33, 35, 41–2, 43n.79, 47, 130, 132, 148
Coutances (Manche) 4, 58, 65–6, 239
Cranborne (Dors.) 65, 71, 84, 92–4, 114, 170, 240
Cranford (Northants.) 66
Creully (Calvados) 16n.89, 48, 57–9, 64, 83n.10, 88–90, 120–1, 169, 239
Cricklade (Wilts.) 87, 173–4, 176
Crowan (Corn.) 65, 108
Crusades/Crusaders 1n.1, 8–9, 174
  First Crusade 6, 175
  Second Crusade 88, 127n.6, 174–5
Cumberland 131, 150
*curialis/curiales* 11, 22–3, 30, 31n.10, 32nn.15, 20, 35n.33, 36–8, 45–7, 50, 54, 70, 108, 129, 135, 164

Damerham (Wilts.) 170
danegeld 44n.84, 46–8, 73, 80, 85, 94n.83
Danvou (Calvados) 30

*dapifer* xxi, 16, 44, 47–8, 57n.3, 67–9, 73n.120, 74n.124, 85n.22, 88n.40, 89–90, 93, 96, 108–10, 116, 123, 158, 169, 175, *see also* stewards
Dartford (Kent) 138, 190
David, King of Scotland xxi, 35, 41, 43, 45, 67n.72, 131, 139, 143, 150, 159–60, 162, 183, 185
  invasion of England 131, 140
Devizes (Wilts.) 123, 145, 152–3, 161, 163–4, 166, 176, 240
  castle 43, 151, 205
Devon 65–6, 71–2, 77, 80, 91, 94, 107, 127n.6, 131, 133–4, 141, 174–5
Ditton (Kent) 115, 116
Domesday Survey 45, 50, 60, 65, 67nn.71–2, 68–9, 71, 73n.118, 74, 90, 93, 97, 99, 101, 103, 109, 141
Domfront (Orne) 5, 42, 128, 143, 239
Dorchester (Dors.) 71
Dover (Kent) 68, 96, 110, 130, 140–1, 240
  castle 44, 47, 60, 61n.29, 68–9, 141–2
Droitwich (Worcs.) 52
Dublin (Ireland) 28, 99
Ducy-Sainte-Margarite (Calvados) 58
Dudley (Worcs.) 140, 142
Durham (Durham) 131
Dursley (Glos.) 91

Eadric, son of Chetel 53
Easton (Glos.) 65, 115
Ecajeul (Calvados) 58
Écrammeville (Calvados) 58, 108n.163
Edessa, county of 175
Edith/Matilda 1, 7, 184, *see also* Matilda II
Edith of Greystoke 157
Edward the Confessor, King of England 3, 7, 75
*Eigenkloster* 28, 38, 71, 77, 92, 95, 97, 104, 117
Eldersfield (Worcs.) 67, 71, 73n.118, 93–4, 99, 107
Eleanor of Aquitaine, Queen of England 87, 112, 206
Elias Oriescuilz 72, 106
Ellesmere (Salop.) 140
Eltham (Kent) 68
Ely (Cambs.) 49n.111, 145
Ely river 120, 123
Engelran de Bohun 193
Engeram de Spineto 60
Epaignes (Eure) 61
Erlestoke (Wilts.) 131
Ernulf de Hesding 142
Esterville (Calvados) 58
Eu (Seine-Maritime) 25, 33
Eudo *Dapifer* 69n.91, 85n.22, 88n.40, 96, 123, 169
Eugenius III, Pope 62, 119, 123–4, 176, 205
  *Quantum predecessors* 175
Eustace III, count of Boulogne 175

Eustace IV, count of Boulogne, son of King Stephen xxi, 135, 159, 163, 205
Eustace de Pacy xxi, 15, 26–7, 129
Eustace fitz John 56, 140, 171
Évrecy (Calvados) 16n.89, 57–8, 89, 93, 116, 120, 123–4, 239
Évreux (Eure) 15, 33–4, 135, 239
Ewenny Priory (Glam.) 117–19
Ewias Harold (Herefs.) 75
Exchequer 23, 31–2, 39, 45–7, 59, 63, 69, 73–4, 80, 93, 97, 111–12, 115
excommunication 119, 123–4, 158–9, 163, 176, 205
Exeter, siege of 133, 195
Exmes (Orne) 16, 42, 128
Exton (Hants.) 115
Eye (Suff.) 40, 73n.120, 136

Fairford (Glos.) 64, 71, 84, 93–4, 107, 240
Falaise (Calvados) 82, 89, 239
  castle 48, 126, 131
  siege of 17, 64, 142
  surrender of 202
  treasury 48, 127
*familia regis* 24–6, 35, *see also* mercenaries
*familiaris/familiares* 15, 23–4, 28, 30–1, 36, 41, 43, 46–9, 54, 61, 75, 100, 104, 115, 136, 148, 160, 188–9
Faringdon (Oxon.) 72, 167, 174, 203, 240
Farthegn (moneyer) 96, 171, 172f
fealty xvi, xviii, 15, 21, 25, 41, 43, 53, 61, 79, 88, 121, 128, 137–8, 141, 144, 147, 154, 157, 159, 184–5, 195, 196n.125, *see also* homage
Fécamp Abbey (Seine-Maritime) 48, 59, 120–1
fees xix, 4–6, 19, 30, 39, 42, 45, 48, 50, 52, 54, 57n.5, 58–62, 69n.90, 72, 73n.120, 74n.126, 76–8, 85n.22, 86–91, 95, 97, 99, 103–8, 110–11, 115, 119–21, 123–4, 131–2, 141, 144, 159, 169
Finmere (Oxon.) 66
Flanders/Flemings xx, 25, 27, 42, 130, 135–7, 152, 162, 173, 192, 195
Fontevrault Abbey (Maine-et-Loire) 36
Fossdyke canal 154
Fosse Way 154
Framlingham (Suff.) 60
France 5, 8, 20, 25, 40, 42, 60–1, 129, 152, 175
Frome river 65, 96–9
Frome St. Quintin (Dors.) 65
Fulk V, count of Anjou 20–1, 25–6, 34, 40–2, 129–30
Fulk fitz Warin 93, 105, 114
Fyfield (Oxon.) 66

Geoffrey I de Clinton 45, 48, 56
Geoffrey II de Clinton 148
Geoffrey I de Traillí 50
Geoffrey, bishop of Coutances 50, 65–6, 95, 102

Geoffrey Brito, archbishop of Rouen 23, 30, 39
Geoffrey V, count of Anjou/ le Bel xxi, 42–3, 123, 128–9, 131, 135–6, 156, 164, 186, 199, 202, 204
Geoffrey, count of Mortagne 16
Geoffrey de Mandeville 158, 200
Geoffrey de Waterville 34, 48n.110, 109, 117, 163–4
Geoffrey fitz Payn 55
Geoffrey Gaimar
  *Estoire des Engleis* xx, 50, 178–9
Geoffrey of Monmouth xx, 13, 27, 51
  *Historia Regum Britanniae* (*De gestis Britonum*) 11, 49–50, 178–9, 179n.4, 180, 182, 187f, 189, 198, 201–2
Geoffrey Rufus 30, 46–7, 55, 70
Geoffrey Talbot 141–2, 151, 153
Gerald of Wales 54
Germany 44, 97
Germoe (Corn.) 65n.55, 108
Gervase of Canterbury 177
  *Chronica* 202
*Gesta Stephani* 1, 84, 91, 96, 100, 130, 132–3, 146, 162, 166–70, 172, 174, 192, 204
Gilbert Becket 104
Gilbert D'Almary 109
Gilbert de Gant 67n.72
Gilbert de Lacy of Weobly 123, 141, 153
Gilbert de Turberville 119
Gilbert de Umfraville 72, 76, 100, 105–6, 109n.170, 164
Gilbert fitz Gilbert, earl of Pembroke 109, 110n.174, 139, 142
Gilbert Foliot, abbot of St. Peter's Gloucester xx, 91n.60, 124–5, 149–50, 157, 170, 193
Gilbert Maminot, bishop of Lisieux 61n.29, 141
gilds 101–2
Gisors (Eure) 27, 42
Glamorgan xix–xx, 16, 38, 45, 49, 57, 64, 74, 76–7, 95, 106, 110, 115–17, 120–3, 134, 177
  Shire Fee 76–8, 95, 106, 119, 121
Gloucester xix, 16, 28, 53, 57–8, 61, 64–6, 68–9, 72, 74, 79–80, 85, 93, 102, 104–6, 109, 111, 114–15, 119, 141, 149, 240
  castle xix, 33, 48, 53–4, 132, 143, 148
Gloucester Chronicle 3
Godfrey VII, count of Lorraine 29
Godfrey of Jumièges, abbot of Malmesbury (Wilts.) 181
Gorron (Mayenne) 42
Gower (Glam.) 45
Great Gransden (Hunts.) 66
Greensted (Essex) 69
Greenwich, West (Kent) 141
Gregory de Turri 107
Grimsby (Lincs.) 175

# 246  Index

Gruffudd ap Ivor 84n.13
Gruffudd ap Rhys ap Tewdwr 78
Guigan Algason 128
Guildford (Surrey) 70, 80, 240
Gwent (Gwent) 41, 74–6, 134, 154
Gwithian (Corn.) 65, 108
Gwynllŵg, lordship of (Monm.) 16, 57, 64, 74, 76, 78, 84, 95, 106, 110, 116, 134, 141

Haimo I xxi, 16, 69
Haimo II xxi, 16, 44, 47–8, 57, 67–8, 73n.120, 74n.124, 104, 174–5
Haimo Dentatus ("The Toothed") of Torigni 16n.89, 104, 121
Haimo fitz Earl xxi, 83–4, 87, 92
Halberton (Devon) 107
Haliwell (Mx) 108n.162
Hambledon (Bucks.) 109n.170
Hanley (Worcs.) 72, 93
Hanley Castle (Worcs.) 64, 71, 73n.118, 94, 99
Harescombe (Glos.) 53
Harold Godwinson, King of England 143, 184
Harptree (Som.) 142, 240
  castle 151
Hartwell (Northants.) 61n.29, 141
Hawisia de Redvers 83n.13, 85n.22, 91–2, 140n.81, 141, 148, 205
Hawkesbury (Glos.) 107
Helias de Saint-Saens 20
Helmsley (Yorks.) 50
Henry I, King of England xv, xviii, xxi, 1, 3–6, 8, 12–13, 16, 19–24, 27, 30, 34–5, 37–9, 41–2, 44–5, 47–8, 52–3, 61–8, 73, 86, 88n.40, 90, 95–6, 104, 109n.170, 120, 126, 129, 133, 150, 169, 181
  acknowledgment of son Robert 13
  administration 6, 11–13, 22–3, 31, 36, 75, 145, *see also* courts, *curia regis*; exchequer; treasury; Nigel bishop of Ely; *familiaris/familiares*
  Angevin marriage 40–1, 42–3
  Anglo-Norman civil war 2–3, 6, 8, 15–17, 19–20
  coronation 7
  Coronation Charter 17–18
  creation of careers for son Robert 1, 9, 13–14, 18; Chapt.2
  death 32, 43, 50, 78, 126–8, 190–1, 196
  deathbed designation of successor 192
  education 10
  fiscal patronage 41, 46–8, 51, 80–1, 130
  grant of the earldom of Gloucester to Robert 28
  funeral 132
  legitimate children, *see* Matilda, Empress; William Aetheling
  literate court xx, 49, 180
  marriages 15, 28, 29, 40, *see also* Matilda II, Adeliza of Louvain

Norman count 4–6
Norman wars 6, 20–1, 25–7, 34–5, 43
Oaths to Matilda's succession 39–41, 43
White Ship disaster 27
Henry V, Emperor xxi, 8, 28, 40, 41n.67
Henry, bishop of Llandaff 28, 114
Henry Caldy 173
Henry de Beaumont, earl of Warwick 52–3
Henry de Pomeroy 30–1, 35
Henry de Port 60
Henry de Tracy 142, 174
Henry fitz Empress/ Henry II King of England xix, xxi, 43n.80, 57n.5, 63, 74, 83n.11, 84–6, 88n.39, 89, 96, 102, 105, 107, 111–12, 115, 166, 176, 184, 188n.70, 199, 204–6
Henry fitz Nest 160
Henry of Blois, abbot of Glastonbury, bishop of Winchester xxi, 30n.6, 38, 46–7, 49, 55, 70, 111, 129, 145, 148, 150n.141, 160–1, 167, 176, 191, 197
Henry of Huntingdon 11, 26, 28, 45, 64, 137n.63, 139n.77, 155, 174, 179n.4, 180, 190, 201, 204
*Historia Anglorum* 49, 201
Henry Tusard 93, 112
Herbert D'Almary 109
Herbert de Lucy 167
Herbert de St. Quintin 76
Hereford (Herefs.) 28, 54, 75, 86, 99, 122, 141, 148, 205
  siege of 153
High Wycombe (Bucks.) 72
Hinganus 93, 107
Holm Hill (Tewkesbury) 99
Holy Trinity Church Bristol 93
homage xvi, xviii, 8, 20, 27, 53, 79, 121, 131–3, 135, 139, 141, 144, 148, 185, 189, 192, 196, 199, 202, *see also* fealty
Honorius II, Pope 38, 123
Honors, *see* Évrecy, Glamorgan; Gloucester
Hospitallers 88, 118
Houndstreet (Marksbury, Som.) 111
Hubert de Pierrepont 109, 115, 140
Hugh II de Montfort 60
Hugh IV de Montfort 61
Hugh Bigod 30, 55, 130, 155
Hugh de Chateauneuf-en-Thimerais 34
Hugh de Crèvecoeur 60, 69n.90
Hugh de Gournay 127, 136, 192
Hugh de Gundeville 90n.54, 93, 114, 140
Hugh de Loges 85n.22
Hugh de Montfort 34, 61
Hugh de Walterville 109
Hugh Maminot 60–1
Hugh of Amiens, archbishop of Rouen 32, 38, 55, 87, 88n.39, 126–7, 136, 156, 185, 190, 192
Hugh of Avranches, earl of Chester 4, 12, 20, 74, 77, 90, 123

Humber river 174
Humphrey I de Bohun 56
Humphrey II de Bohun 30, 56, 144, 147, 151, 171
Humphrey fitz Odo 144n.107
hunting 6, 9, 16, 48, 71, 93–4, 107, 126, 149, 169
Huntingdon 33, 131

Iddisleigh (Devon) 64
Iestyn ap Gwrgant 76, 78
Ifor ap Meurig 78
Ilchester (Som.) 108n.163
inheritance 6–7, 16, 20, 25, 27, 44, 57, 60, 66n.65, 69, 75, 83, 87, 93, 95, 101, 103–4, 111, 116–17, 128, 150, 164, 175, 183, 193, see also *iure uxoris*
Innocent II, Pope (Gregory of St. Angelo) 38, 87, 130, 143, 190, 193
Iordan (moneyer) 96, 171, 172*f*
Iowerth ap Owain 78, 134, 154
Ireland 17, 96
Isabel, countess of Gloucester xxi, 74, 93, 101n.122, 107n.153
Isabelle de Douvres xxi, 4, 12, 86
Isidore of Seville
  *Etymologies* 34
*iure uxoris* 17, 20, 57, 67, 74, 97, 104, 143
Ivo of Chartres 181, 190n.89

Jeanne de Montferrat 42
Jerusalem 10, 43n.77, 175
Jocelin de Bohun, bishop of Salisbury 3n.21, 4, 124, 205
John, bishop of Lisieux 23, 30–1, 36, 39, 41, 55
John, bishop of Sées 32, 36, 39, 55
John, bishop of Worcester 87n.37
John, count of Mortain /King of England xxi, 93, 101, 107n.153, 116n.223, 118n.239
John fitz Gilbert 149, 152–3, 160, 163, 171
John fitz Harold 149
John Fleming 76
John of Crema 37
John of Hexham 201n.159
John of Marmoutier 128n.14, 136, 192
  *Historia Gaufridi Ducis* 193
John of Salisbury 206
John of Worcester 3, 29, 132, 144–5, 159n.189, 160n.191, 182, 201
John the Marshal 161
John Scotus Erigena 181
Jordan de Chambernowne 83n.13
Juliana, daughter of King Henry I xxi, 2, 15, 27
justices 31, 39, 63, 87n.30

Kemerton (Glos.) 66
Kenfig (Glam.) 77, 95, 240
Kent 16, 24, 44, 57n.3, 60, 62, 67–70, 80, 138, 142, 144, 158, 162, 190

Keynsham (Som.) 67, 71, 85, 94, 240
  Abbey 85n.24, 109n.170
Kibur forest (Glam.) 93
Kidwelly (Carm.)31 45
Kilkhampton (Corn.) 66
King's Barton (Glos.) 143
Kingsholm (Glos.) 143
king's peace 34, 39, 46, 145
Kingston-Buci (Sussex) 66
Kingswood, abbey (Glos,) 107
Kirkham Priory (Yorks.) 50
knights xx, 1–2, 13–14, 24–6, 35, 44–5, 48–50, 57, 60, 62–3, 68, 73–6, 82, 88, 89, 91, 97, 105–7, 110–11, 114, 123, 127, 141, 145–7, 154–5, 165–7, 170, 173, 180, 186, 190, 194
  bachelors 2, 87
  fees xix, 45, 60–2, 72, 74n.126, 88–9, 91, 104, 106, 123
  knight-service xix, 100, 106–7, 111

Laleu (Orne) 39
Lambeth (Surrey) 7, 108
Lancaster 40, 73n.120
landlords/lords xix, 3, 17, 46, 54, 57, 59–60, 66, 68–73, 79n.149, 82, 84–5, 93–5, 97, 100–1, 108, 110, 118, 121, 133, 169n.222, 175–6, see also magnates; super-magnates
  demesnes xix, xxiii, 3, 28, 44, 46, 50, 57–9, 65–6, 68–73, 74n.124, 75–8, 81, 83–5, 92–6, 99–100, 104–5, 108, 114, 119–20, 134, 138, 143, 151, 170–2, 180, 190
  endowments 17n.93, 64, 66, 77, 95, 98, 119, 124
  enfeoffement 57, 60, 68, 72–3, 76, 93, 106–7, 114–15
  rents/revenues xix, 32–3, 36, 44, 52–3, 59, 68, 76, 82, 93–4, 97–103, 106–8, 110–11, 116–21, 162, 170
  subinfeudation 57, 69, 72, 82, 85, 98–100, 105–6, 138, 141
  tenants xix–xx, 3nn.19,21, 14, 23, 30, 45, 50, 54n.142, 59–61, 66–8, 70–2, 76–7, 82–3, 94, 99–100, 102–5, 108–11, 115–18, 120–2, 133, 139, 141–2, 159, 164, 170, 176, 178
  tenants-in-chief 17, 21–2, 24, 35, 44, 57, 66, 68–9, 73, 79, 88, 90, 105–7, 131, 157
  vassals xix, 4–6, 8, 10, 16–17, 27, 33–4, 45, 53–4, 59n.19, 60, 68, 72, 75–7, 87n.37, 88, 90n.54, 93, 95, 105, 111n.187, 114, 118–20, 122–3, 132–3, 134, 141–2, 147–9, 151, 164–6, 171, 175, 188, see also bsiliffs, courts, fees, knights
Lanfranc, archbishop of Canterbury 10, 181
Lanthony Priory (Glouc.) 54, 118–19
Lateran Councils 143, 193

Latin xix–xx, 8–11, 30, 108, 122
L'Aumône Abbey (Val-d'Oise) 14
Laws of King Edward 159
Leckwith (Glam.) 76
Leeds (Yorks.) 69, 142
  Priory 68n.86
legatine councils 37
*Leges Edwardi Confessoris* 33, 159
Le Grand Andely (Eure) 25–6
Leland, John 99, 177n.245
Le Mans (Sarthe) 43
Le Neubourg (Eure) 128
Les Loges (Seine-Maritime) 30
Lewin fitz Ailric of Brislington 104, 110–11
*Lidelea* (unident.) 176, 205–6
Liège (Indre-et-Loire) 12
Lillebonne (Seine-Maritime) 129
Lincoln (Lincs.) 36, 155, 240
  battle of 150–1, 154, 158, 162, 186, 188–90, 199–200, 202
  castle 150, 175
Lindsey Survey 19, 66
Lisbon (Portugal) 127n.6
Lisieux (Calvados) 128, 135, 239
Littleham (Devon) 64
Little Marlow (Bucks.) 65n.57
Little Wigborough (Essex) 69
Livarot (Calvados) 136, 192, 193
Llandaff (Glam.) 28, 37, 99, 110, 120, 122–3
Llandeilo-Talypont (Glam.) 77n.143, 119n.250
Llandough (Glam.) 106
Llandow (Glam.) 106
Llanthony Priory, Prima (Monm.) 54
Llantrithyd (Glam.) 106, 110n.177
Llantwit (Glam.) 76
London (Mx) 37, 41, 44, 69–70, 72, 80, 94, 100, 104, 108, 114, 127n.6, 130, 156, 158–9, 161, 171, 174, 197, 240
  White Tower 96
Louis VI, King of France 8, 20–1, 25–7, 38, 40, 42, 61, 129–30, 135
Louis VII, King of France 89, 152, 175
Ludgershall (Wilts.) 149, 161
Lulworth (Dors.) 240
  castle 167
Luton (Beds.) 67, 109, 139
Lyons-la-Forêt (Eure) 48, 126–7

Mabel de Bellême xxi, 59
Mabel fitz Hamon, countess of Gloucester xix, xxi, 4n.24, 16–19, 44, 47, 57–8, 62, 64–5, 67, 69, 71, 82–4, 87–90, 91n.60, 92–3, 95, 97, 113–14, 116, 118, 146, 162–4, 189, 191, 194, 198–200
*magistri* 97, 108, 111–12
magnates 5, 16–17, 19, 24, 29, 31, 33, 36, 41, 91–2, 108, 111, 121, 126–7, 136, 160, 164, 177, 186, 189, 192, *see also* super-magnates
Magneville (Manche) 131

Maine, county of 20, 25, 42, 59, 128
Malcolm III, King of Scotland xxi, 1, 7
Malmesbury 66, 72, 145, 167, 172–4, 240
  Abbey 46, 178, 181, 183, 201
  castle 152
Malpas Priory (Monm.) 116–18
Malvern (Worcs.) 19n.103, 64, 72, 73n.118, 99
Malvern Chase (Worcs.) 71, 93–4
Manche 5, 27, 30, 57–60, 62, 88n.40, 131, 165n.209
Mangotsfield (Glos.) 65
Mapledurham (Hants.) 65
Marcher lords, xix, 16, 31, 75, 122, 139, 147
Marcigny (Saône-et-Loire) 38
Margam Abbey (Glam.) xviii, 77–8, 93, 95, 105, 112, 118–19, 124, 177–8, 179f, 187, 198–201, 201n.157, 203–4
  codex 187f, 198–201
  Scribe 24
  Annals of Margam Abbey xvin.12, 203
Margaret, Queen of Scotland xxi, 7
Marholm (Northants.) 109
Marksbury (Som.) 111
Marlborough (Wilts.) 71, 149, 171
  castle 152
Marshfield (Glos.) 66
Marston (Lincs.) 67
Master Elias 112
Master Herveus 112
Master Matthew 84, 166
Master Picard 84, 108, 112
Master William 9
Mathieu (Calvados) 58, 88
Matilda, countess of Boulogne, Queen of England xxi, 142, 152, 158–9, 161–2, 205
Matilda, daughter of King Henry I xxi, 2, 15–16, 27
Matilda, daughter of King Stephen xxi, 137, 137n.66
Matilda, Empress xvi–xxi, 1–2, 6, 29, 38, 40, 43, 45, 79, 97, 123, 126, 128–9, 131, 137, 143–6, 152, 154, 156–60, 162, 177, 178, 182n.23, 183–4
  invasion plan for invasion of England involving Robert earl of Gloucester 143–6
  *see also* Henry I, Angevin marriage, Oaths to Matilda's succession
Mabel/Matilda, daughter of Earl Robert, countess of Chester xxi, 90, 154, 189
Matilda of Anjou 25
Matilda of Flanders, duchess of Normandy, Queen of England xxi, 3, 63, 65, 103
Matilda of Wallingford 148
Matilda II, Queen of England xxi, 7, 22, 28, 32, 180
Matthew Paris xvi, 203
  *Chronica Majora* 202
  *Flores Historiarum* 202

## Index

Maupertuis (Manche)  58
Maurice de Londres  45, 76n.134, 119
Meaux (Seine-et-Marne)  129
Melisende, Queen of the Latin Kingdom of Jerusalem  42, 43n.77
Mendips  96
mercenaries  xx, 24, 74, 106, 127, 135–7, 152, 158, 161, 168, 169, 173, 176, 195,
see also *familia regis*
Merlin  27, 49, 180
Merrick, Rice (Rhys)  76, 95n.86, 110n.179
Merthyr Mawr (Glam.)  120
Mesnilbuye (Calvados)  58
Meulan (Seine-et-Oise)  61
Mézidon (Calvados)  58
Midlands  66, 90, 92, 150
*miles litteratus*  xx, 180
Miles of Gloucester, earl of Hereford  31, 48, 53–4, 56, 72, 83, 104, 114, 117–19, 121, 132–3, 139, 143–4, 147–9, 151, 153–5, 157, 159–60, 162–6, 168–70, 172–3, 185, 205
Milton (Kent)  68
monasteries/nunneries  4, 7, 9, 11, 17, 30, 37–8, 49n., 50, 52, 59n., 78, 93–5, 98, 103, 108n.163, 111, 117–19, 121, 132, 157–9, 168, 177, 180–1, 183, 204–5
money/moneyers/mints  xix, 34, 64, 75, 95–7, 102–4, 142, 170–1, 172f, 176, 195,
see also coins/pennies
Montacute Priory (Som.)  94, 110n.177, 119
Montaigu (possibly a. location at Caen)  58
Montfort-sur-Risle (Eure)  34–5
Mont Saint-Michel (Manche)  4–5, 9
Morcar, earl  67
Morgan ap Owain  78, 134, 141
Morgannwg, kingdom (Glam.)  74, 76–8, 95, 120–1, 134
Mortagne (Orne)  156
Mortain (Manche)  33, 40, 129, 159, 165
murder fines  46, 48

Neath (Glam.)  76–8, 95, 103, 106, 240
  Abbey  10, 77, 78n.146, 92, 109n.168, 114, 116, 118–19
Newark (Notts.)  145
New Forest (Hants.)  6
Newport (Monm.)  16, 74, 78, 93–5, 134, 240
Nigel, bishop of Ely  34n.26, 49, 55, 145, 149, 157
Nigel d'Aubigny  19n.104, 23, 34, 66n.71
Nigel d'Oilli  31
Nigel fitz Arthur  107
Nigel fitz William  4
Nivard, brother of Bernard of Clairvaux  38, 124
Norbertine canons  117
Normans  26, 38, 77n.138, 110, 128, 136, 192
Northallerton (Yorks.)  140
Northamptonshire  20, 43, 54, 66, 70, 80, 109, 141

Notre Dame du Voeu (Cherbourg, Manche)  58
Nottingham (Notts.)  152–3, 240
Noyon-sur-Andelle (Eure)  26

oaths  xvi, xviii, 8, 11, 32, 41–4, 83, 121, 127, 131, 132n.35, 136–7, 144, 147, 156, 159, 183–6, 188–95, 200–2, 205
Odo, bishop of Bayeux  5, 12, 65–8, 74
Odo Borleng  35
Odo Sor  72, 164
Ogmore river  76–7, 95
Okehampton (Devon)  91, 133
Oliver St. John  76
Orderic Vitalis  1, 4–5, 14, 16–17, 19, 26, 27n.156, 30, 33, 64, 105, 127, 128n.14, 131–2, 135, 139, 145n.114, 147, 155, 192–3, 204
  *Historia Ecclesiastica*  3, 25, 35
Osbern Pentecost  75
Osbert Eightpence  xix, 69, 100, 104, 158–9, 164
Othuer  12
Owain Wan  75, 78
Oxenton (Glos.)  67, 107
Oxford (Oxon.)  xvi, 14, 66, 72, 101, 132, 145, 157–9, 163–4, 166–8, 173–4, 240
  castle  31, 148, 160
Oximin  142

Pain de Turberville  76
papal legates  37, 145, 148, 152, 157–8, 190–1,
see also Lateran Councils
pardons  41n.70, 44n.84, 46–7, 68–70, 73, 80, 94n.83, 100, 106n.146
Paris (France)  14, 85
Paschal II, Pope  8
Paschasius Radbertus  181
Passais (Orne)  128
Paul the deacon  181
Pawlett (Som.)  85
Paygrove (Glos.)  119
Payn fitz John  54, 56, 141n.87
Penarth (Glam.)  106
Pendoylan (Glam.)  76n.134, 106
Penllyn (Glam.)  110
Peterborough Abbey (Northants)  36, 109
Peter of Porto  190
Peter Sor  76
Peter the Venerable, abbot of Cluny  38, 192–4
Pevensey (Sussex)  6
Philip de Creully  58
Philip de Harcourt, bishop of Bayeux  62, 87, 90, 104, 123–4, 145, 176, 205
Philip fitz Earl  xxi, 4, 4n.23, 84, 87–8, 88n.39, 89, 91, 152, 168n.217, 169, 169n.221, 174–6, 206
Philip Gay  3–4
Philippe de Thaon
  *Bestiaire*  180
Phillack (Corn.)  65, 108
Pimperne (Dors.)  115

Plympton Priory (Devon) 145
Pont-Audemer (Eure) 127, 135–6
Portchester (Hants.) 173
Portes (Eure) 15
Portland Isle (Dors.) 167, 240
Portsmouth (Hants.) 8, 135
prévôts 63, 116n.224, 117
Puddleton (Dorss.) 91
Purton (Wilts.) 176

Quarr Abbey (Isle of Wight) 91
Queen Hill (Worcs.) 73n.118, 107, 110n.177

Rabanus Maurus 181
Rabel de Tancarville 56, 129, 135
Radcot (Oxon.) 158
Ralph the monk 9
Ralph, sheriff of Cardiff 122
Ralph Basset 14, 23
Ralph Caldy 173, 174n.235
Ralph de Diceto
 *Abbreviationes Chronicorum* 201
Ralph d'Escures, archbishop of Canterbury 24, 29
Ralph de Gael 15n.82, 26
Ralph de Pîtres 54
Ralph III de Tosny and Conches 15
Ralph fitz Gilbert 178
Ralph Lovel of Castle Cary 141
Ralph of Mantes, earl of Hereford 75
Ralph Paynel 140, 152
Ramsey Abbey (Hunts) 18n.95
Ranulf II, earl of Chester xxi, 34–5, 39, 44n.83, 56, 62, 74, 90, 111, 127, 150–1, 154, 160, 164–5, 170, 173n.232, 174–5, 186
Ranulf III, earl of Chester, grandson of Earl Robert xxi, 90
Raymond de Sully 76
Reading (Berks.) 22, 126, 157, 190
 Abbey 38, 52n.130, 98, 127, 132, 162
Redland (Glos.) 108
Reginald de Cahagnes 164
Reginald de Dunstanville, son of King Henry I, earl of Cornwall xxi, 34n.28, 91, 131, 138, 148, 153, 157, 160, 176, 186
Reginald de Grancey 15
Reginald Gay 3n.19
Reginald of Saint-Valéry 136, 192
Reginald Poinz 108
Renaissance of the Twelfth Century xx, 9
Rhymney river 76
Rhys ap Tewdwr 75, 78
Richard II, duke of Normandy xxi, 9
Richard, son of King Henry I xxi, 2, 2n.10, 11, 15n.82, 21–2, 22n.125, 24–7
Richard II fitz Samson, bishop of Bayeux 39, 48, 56, 61–2, 86, 123
Richard Basset 14, 56
Richard III, bishop of Bayeux, fitz Earl xxi, 2, 12, 32, 38, 63, 84, 87, 117n.238, 119, 123, 135, 137, 149n.138

Richard Butler/*Pincerna* 85, 85n.22
Richard de Capella 30
Richard de Grainville 10, 76–7, 92, 109n.168, 114, 118, 134, 164
Richard de Redvers 5, 20, 154
Richard de St. Quintin 72, 76n.134, 100, 105–6, 164
Richard fitz Count, son of Earl Robert xxi, 59n.19, 83, 88, 91n.58
Richard fitz Nigel 33n.26, 119
Richard fitz Scrob 75
Richard Foliot xix, 72, 100, 105, 111n.187
Richard Guuiz 72, 106
Richard of Avranches, earl of Chester 60
Richard of Clare 74
Richard of Hexham 201n.160
Richard of Ilchester 22, 46n.96, 97, 112, 149
Richard Seward 76
Richer II de Laigle 129, 135
Richer of Eldersfield 71
Rievaulx Abbey (Yorks.) 50
Ringwood (Hants.) 71
Risle Valley 61
Roath (Glam.) 76
Robert I the Frisian, count of Flanders xxi, 135
Robert II, count of Flanders xxi, 25
Robert II, earl of Leicester xxi, 9, 13–14, 24, 35, 92, 111, 126, 129, 136, 156, 171, 205
Robert Bloet, bishop of Lincoln 11, 23
Robert de Beaumont, count of Meulan, earl of Leicester xxi, 15, 20, 24, 24n.142, 31–2, 33, 33n.24, 39, 61, 101, 111, *see also* Robert II earl of Leicester, Waleran count of Meulan
Robert Curthose, Duke of Normandy xxi, 3–10, 15, 17, 19–20, 27, 40–1, 43–5, 63–4
Robert D'Almary 109
Robert de Bellême xxi, 5, 16–17, 20, 21n.113, 27, 128
Robert de Béthune 54
Robert de Clavill 106
Robert de Courcy 31, 56
Robert de Crèvecoeur 44n.84, 67, 69
Robert de Gurnay 72, 106
Robert de la Haye 30–1, 36–7, 39, 56, 76, 110n.177
Robert de Mauduit 117
Robert de Meisi 106
Robert de Melun 85
Robert de Montfort 59n.20, 91n.58
Robert de Mowbray 50, 65
Robert de Neubourg 61
Robert de Saint-Remi-des-Landes 63–4
Robert de Sigillo 30–1, 47, 55
Robert de St. Quintin 76
Robert de Vere 56
Robert d'Oilli 148, 157, 160
Robert, earl of Gloucester xv–xvii, xx–xxi, 6, 8, 10*f*, 13, 19, 22, 25–6, 28, 31, 33, 38–9,

# Index

41–3, 45, 49, 52–3, 66, 90–1, 95, 105, 109, 111, 113*f*, 114, 128, 163, 172*f*, 179*f*, 184, 197
administrative system xviii, 94, 108–17, 171
abandonment of Matilda's cause 126–31
birth and bastardy xv, 2–8, 12, 86–8
burghal and burgess patron 69, 95–7, 100–5
career changes 27, 35, 50, 127
*conventio* with King Stephen 132–5
curial assignments and functions 21–3, 29, 33, 36–9, 44, 46, 48
curial relationships 23–4, 30–2, 36–8; Chapt. 2; Appendix 2.2
decline in fortunes and death 174–7, 204–6
demesne landlord and developer 73, 80–1, 92–7
*diffidatio* and rationales 136–8, 198
earl of Gloucester 28, 33–4, Chapt. 2, Appendix 2.1
*familiaris* and *curialis* 21–4, 28–33, 35–6, 45–7, 55–6, 80–1
family xxi, 83–92, *see also* Mabel fitz Hamon, William earl of Gloucester, Robert fitz Earl, Haimo fitz Earl, Richard fitz Count, Roger bishop of Worcester, Matilda/Mabel countess of Chester, Philip fitz Earl, Richard III, bishop of Bayeux
leadership of the Angevin party xv, xix, 1, 64, 88, 91, 124, 139–43, 145–9, 155–6, 159–60, 162–4, 167–8, 171, 185–6, 194
literacy, education, and other influences xx, 9–12, 10*f*, 14, 21–4, 30, 34, 48–50, 78–9, 85, 94, 178, 180
literary patron xvii–xx, 1, 9, 11–12, 49–50, 57, 156, 160, 162, 178–80, 179*f*, 180–4, 186–8, 190–2, 194–8, 206
  as possible contributor to the Historia Novella 191–3, 200
marriage 14–15, 21, 57, 82, 100, 204
military activities 138, 151–8, 160–2, 165–9, 173–4, 176
pro-Angevin inner circle 39–44
subinfeudations 106–8, 141
super-magnate xix, 14, 57–9, 64–9, 72–4, 76–7, 137
viceregal functions/powers xix, 18, 22n.125, 148, 188
Robert fitz Earl xxi, 73n.118, 83, 83n.11, 84–5, 85n.22, 90–1, 91n.56, 92
Robert fitz Edith, son of King Henry I xxi, 157, 160–1
Robert fitz Ernesius 58, 119n.251
Robert fitz Hamon xxi, 16–17, 19–20, 50, 60, 62n.35, 65–7, 70, 72, 74–6, 99, 101, 103, 106n.147, 109, 110n.177, 120–1
Robert fitz Harding xix, 85, 97, 98n.100, 99, 104–5, 107, 165–6
Robert fitz Harold 140

Robert fitz Henry 9
Robert fitz Hildebrand 168, 173
Robert fitz Hubert 152–3, 195
Robert fitz Martin 118
Robert fitz Richard Foliot 149
Robert, son of Earl William of Gloucester xxi, 89n.47, 91n.56
Robert Norreys 110
Robert of Bampton 133n.42
Robert of Ferrers, earl of Derby 140n.85, 142
Robert of Lincoln 140n.81, 145
Robert of Mortain 74
Robert of Rouen 69, 108
Robert of Torigny 7, 19n.101, 83, 87, 95, 128, 136, 137n.63, 144, 146, 147n.123, 165, 192, 201–2
Robert Ridel 14
Robert Sor 76, 106
Rochester (Kent) 24, 163
  castle 162
Rodbert (moneyer) 96, 104, 113
Roger I Bigod 60
Roger III of Berkeley 53, 88, 91, 107, 174
Roger, abbot of Fécamp 36, 48, 59, 91n.60, 111n.186, 115, 120–1
Roger, abbot of Tewkesbury 120, 157
Roger, bishop of Salisbury 18, 23, 30–2, 41, 44–6, 55, 70, 72–3, 130, 145, 151, 183, 188, 191, 205
Roger, earl of Hereford 92, 173
Roger de Beaumont, earl of Warwick 45, 53, 152, 160, 174
Roger II de Montgomery, earl of Shrewsbury xxi, 59, 74, 83n.12
Roger, son of Earl Robert, bishop of Worcester xxi, 84, 88n.39, 166, 198–201
Roger de Creully 58
Roger de Nonant 160
Roger de Tosny 129, 135
Roger fitz Mauger 106
Roger le Poer 145, 151
Roger Malfilastre 60
Roger of Bergvalle 106
Roger of Berkerole 76, 106
Roger of Saint-Sauveur 60
Roger of Wendover
  *Flores Historiarum* 202
Roger Suhard 60
Roger Waspail 72
Roger Witeng 72
Rome (Italy) 37, 38n.50
Romsey (Hants.) 7
Roscelin of Maine 128
Rotherhithe (Surrey) 69
Rotrou, count of Mortagne-Perche xxi, 15–16, 126, 135, 156
Rouen 2, 8, 19, 22, 34, 36–8, 43, 48, 126–8, 156, 195, 239
  Treaty of 5, 7

Round, John Horace 19, 39n.58, 59, 69n.90, 83n.12, 107n.151, 132n.35, 157
 *Geoffrey de Mandeville* xvii, 204
Rout of Wilton 169
Rout of Winchester 83, 151n.148, 161, 163, 186, 189, 190, 201n.160, 202
Rowberrow (Som.) 85
Rumney (Monm.) 78, 84, 134, 141

St. Albans (Herts.) xvi, 37n.50, 158, 202
St. Anselm, *see* Anselm, archbishop of Canterbury
St. Athan, lordship of (Glam.) 106
St. Augustine 181
St. Augustine, abbey of (Bristol) 98n.100, 105, 166
St. David's (Pembs.) 37, 75, 106, 122
Saint-Clair-sur-l'Elle (Manche) 59, 88, 239
Saint-Étienne, abbey of (Caen) 12, 58, 63, 119, 127, 132
Saint-Évroul, abbey of (Eure) 19, 21, 33
Saint-Gabriel, priory of (Calvados) xxii, 48, 59, 111n.186, 115–16, 120–1
Saint-Germain-la-Blanche-Herbe, church of (Calvados) 109
Saint-Lô, abbey of (Coutances, Manche) 58
Saint-Martin d'Aubigny (Manche) 30
Saint-Martin de Troarn, abbey of (Calvados) 57n.5, 58, 59nn.19, 21
Saint-Martin-du-Bosc (Eure) 31n.10
Saint-Sauveur (Manche) 62
Sainte-Marie Ardenne, priory of (Calvados) 58n.13, 63, 83n.11, 87, 109, 119
Sainte-Marie de Longues, abbey of (Calvados) 58
Sainte-Scolasse-sur-Sarthe (Orne) xxii, 59
Sainte-Trinité, abbey of (Caen) 58, 63, 64n.51
Salisbury (Wilts.) 70–1, 80, 145, 168, 171, 240
Samson de Douvres, bishop of Worcester 12, 86
Sancreed (Corn.) 65, 108
Savenay (Loire-Atlantique) 30
Savigny, abbey of (Manche) 58, 117, 119
Sées (Orne) 23–4, 31n.11, 59n.21, 239
Seffrid, bishop of Chichester 157
Selles (Eure) 61
Senghennydd (Glam.) 78
Serlo of Wilton xx, 11, 14, 178, 180, 204
*servitium debitum* 57, 107, *see also* landlords, tenants-in-chief
Seulles (Calvados) 120
Severn river/valley 16, 64, 70–2, 74–6, 79, 94, 99, 103, 124, 139, 157, 170–1
Shelswell (Oxon.) 66
Sherborne (Dors.) 114n.207, 170, 240
 castle 145, 169–70
sheriffs xix, 16, 31, 33, 44–6, 50, 52–4, 57n.3, 60, 66–8, 70, 72, 76–7, 104, 109n.170, 110, 115–16, 122–3, 132–4, 140, 143–4, 148–9, 158, 163

Shrewsbury (Salop.) 75, 140, 142
Sibyl fitz Hamon/de Montgomery xxi, 17–18, 59, 66, 82
Sibyl of Anjou 40
Sibyl of Conversano xxi, 8
Sibyl, daughter of King Henry I 2
Simon of Northampton 155
Simon, bishop of Worcester 53, 97
Somme river 130
Southampton (Hants.) 71
South Cerney (Glos.) 147, 153
South Wales xx, 16, 30, 57, 74–5, 101, 122, 134, 171, 180, *see also* Wales
Southwick (Sussex) 66
Sowton (Devon) 66
Stambourne (Essex) 69
Standish (Glos.) 53
Stapleton (Glos.) 65, 98
Stephen de Beauchamp 85n.22
Stephen de Mandeville, lord of Erlestoke 131, 141, 175
Stephen Gay 3–4
Stephen-Henry, Count of Blois xxi, 1n.1, 129, *see also* xxi and Stephen (of Blois), King
Stephen of Aumâle 26
Stephen (of Blois), King xv–xviii, xxi, 1, 13–14, 24, 29, 33, 35–6, 40–1, 44, 47–8, 50–1, 52n.123, 56, 61–4, 68, 73, 73n.118, 78–9, 85, 87–8, 91, 104–5, 118, 123–4, 126, 129–47, 149–53, 157–71, 173–6, 178, 183–6, 188–96, 199, 202–3
 Beaumont alliance 61, 92, 135, 137, 137n.68, 138, 189
 coup d'état and coronation 130–1, 184
 death 206
 family xxi, 40, 129–30, 137, 137n.69, 205
 Henry I's patronage 13–14, 40, 47
 lordships 40, 123, 126, 169
 papal recognition 130, 143, 193–4, 205
 status in court protocol 35–6, 36n.37, 41–2, 47, 47n.103, 56, 73, 88, 88n.40, 184
 treaty of Winchester 205–6
Stephen lord of Richmond, count of Brittany 74
stewards 31, 34, 36, 39, 56, 60, 88n.40, 93, 108–10, 116–17, 163–4, 169, see also *dapifer*
St. Ewen, church of (Bristol) 4, 98
St. James of Compostella, cathedral of (Galicia) 22
St. James, priory of (Bristol) xviii, 44, 58, 85, 97–9, 117–19, 176, 204
St. Jerome 181
St. Leonard, Newcastle, church of (Glam.) 120
St. Mary, church of, Kirklington (Oxon) 3
St. Mary, abbey of (Nunnaminster), Winchester 157
St. Mary, priory of, Worcester 52
St. Mary, Malling, abbey of (Kent) 67

*Index* 253

Stockbridge (Hants) 161–2
St. Peter, abbey of Gloucester xx, 44n.82, 53, 54, 71, 109, 116–19, 124, 141, 149, 157, 193
St. Swithun, Old Minster of, (Winchester) 177
Stubbs, William xvi, 183n.25, 187n.59, 197n.133, 198, 203–4
Sudbury (Suff.) 67, 93
Sudeley (Glos.) 149, 151, 153, 240
Suger, abbot of Saint-Denis 27, 38
super-magnates 40, 57, 65, 69, 72, 130, *see also* landlords/lords, magnates
Swilgate river 103

Taddington (Glos.) 52
Taff river 75–6, 103, 120, 123
Tailleville (Calvados) 59n.19
Talyfan (Glam.) 76, 106
Tarrant Gunville (Dors.) 115
Templars 99, 118–19, 175
Test river 161–2
Tetbury (Glos.) 173, 240
Tetsworth (Oxon.) 72
Tewkesbury (Glos.) 64, 65n.60, 69–70, 72, 84, 99–100, 102–3, 107, 111n.186, 118, 120, 138, 153, 157, 203, 240
  Abbey 17–19, 28, 58, 59n.19, 71, 76, 82, 87n.37, 92–4, 97, 103, 109n.170, 117–19, 133, 176–7, 182, 191, 204
Thames river and valley 147, 158, 161, 168
Thaon (Calvados) 88, 169n.222
Theobald, archbishop of Canterbury 124–5, 152, 157–8, 163, 170, 199, 205
Theobald IV, count of Blois xxi, 20, 27, 38, 40, 127–31, 135, 152, 156
Theulf, bishop of Worcester 28, 53
Thomas Becket, archbishop of Canterbury 83n.12, 85, 123n.269, 199
Thomas de Douvres, archbishop of York 12, 86
Thornbury (Glos.) 64, 71, 93–4, 240
Thurstan (priest) 98, 108
Thurstan, archbishop of York 24, 37, 48, 55, 101
Tinchebrai (Orne) 239
  battle of 6, 17, 20, 40
Tiron Abbey (Perche) xviiin.20, 117–18
Toppesfield (Essex) 69
Torigni-sur-Vire (Manche) 34, 57–8, 64, 88–9, 93, 95, 131–2, 239
Tosny (Eure) 15
Totnes (Devon) 141
*totus comitatus* 77
Toulouse (Haute-Garonne) 87
trans-Channel
  attributes 36, 39
  barons/barony xx, 6, 21, 57, 92, 105, 131
  landed interests 31, 156
  magnates 5, 17
  realm 22
  super-magnates 130
Treasury 23, 32, 44–6, 48, 70, 127

treaties xx, 5–8, 19, 25, 40–1, 92, 104–5, 110, 131–2, 150, 172, 180, 186, 200, 205–6
  Alton 6, 19, 40
  Durham I 131, 150
  Durham II 140
  Rouen 5, 7
  Winchester 205–6
Trent river 154
*Très Ancien Coutumier* 116
Trevalga (Corn.) 65, 108
Trowbridge (Wilts.) 144, 147, 151, 171, 240
Truce of God ordinance 39
Turstin de Creully 59n.19

Urban, bishop of Llandaff 28, 45, 77, 99, 110, 114–15, 121, 123
Usk (Monm.) and river 75–6, 134, 141
Uthred, bishop of Llandaff 120, 122–3
Uxbridge (Mx) 72

Vexin, Norman (Andelle to Epte rivers)/French (Epte to the Oise) 20, 25, 42, 61
viceroys 32–3, 186
villeins 100, 103
Villiers (Manche) 88
Virgil 180–1
  *Aeneid* 11, 190
Vitalis, abbot of Bernay 59n.19, 120

Wace, canon of Bayeux 17, 57, 63–4
  *Roman de Rou* 63
Walchelin Maminot 60–1, 69, 140–2
Waleran, count of Meulan xviii, 9, 13–14, 24, 34–5, 43, 52, 61, 72, 91n.58, 92, 99, 126, 129, 135–8, 145–7, 153, 155–6, 163, 189, 191, 205
Wales/Welsh xix, xx, xxiii, 31, 50, 53–4, 57, 64, 73n, 74–5, 76–8, 92, 106, 110n.177, 111, 119, 133, 139–40, 173, 178, 180, *see also* South Wales
Wallingford 41, 132, 147, 153, 166–8, 173, 175
Walter Clavill 72
Walter de Chesney 110
Walter de Pinkney 173–4
Walter Espec 50, 178
Walter fitz Richard de Clare 72
Walter Map 11, 49, 204
Walter of Hereford 174
Walter of Salisbury 72
Walter, sheriff of Gloucestershire 53, 109n.170, 114, *see also* Adeliza, mother of Walter sheriff of Gloucestershire
Walter Tirel 6
Waltheof, earl of Northampton and Huntingdon 15
Wardon Abbey (Beds.) 50
Wareham (Dors.) 71, 88, 92, 112, 140, 142–3, 145, 165–8, 170–1, 240
Wark (Nthmb) 50

Watling Street 154
Wentloog (Monm.) 106
Weobly (Herefs.) 141, 153
Westbourne (Sussex) 22
Westminster (Mx) 22, 36, 42n.71, 132, 158
  Abbey 7, 130, 159
Wherwell (Hants.) 157
  Abbey 161
White Ship 27, 28n.160, 129
William I, duke of Normandy, King of
    England xv, xxi, 2–3, 6, 9–10, 13, 16,
    48, 65, 75–6, 88n.40, 101, 120, 191
William I of Eynsford 117
William II, *see* William Rufus, King of England
William II de Warenne, earl of Surrey 31, 39,
    55, 126–7, 162
William III de Warenne, earl of Surrey 155, 175
William Aetheling xxi, 8, 12, 21–9, 32, 41,
    129, 137, 184
William Clito xxi, 6, 8, 20–1, 25–6, 28–9,
    34–5, 40–2, 61, 129, 130
William, count of Évreux 15, 20, 33
William, count of Mortain, earl of Cornwall,
    son of King William I's half-brother,
    Robert. count of Mortain 17, 19–20, 65
William Crassus 109, 116
William Crassus II 58
William Crassus III 59
William Crispin 26
William d'Aubigny 30, 56, 96, 143–5
William de Beauchamp 52, 163–4
William de Bosco 107
William de Cahagnes 155
William de Eynesford 66, 68, 117
William de Harcourt 35
William de la Mare 72, 106
William de Londres 76
William de Magny-le-Freûle 58
William de Mohun of Dunster 109, 115, 140,
    142, 160, 172n.232, 174
William de Pacy 129
William de Pont de l'Arche 30, 56, 70, 173
William de Roumare 127, 136, 150, 154
William de Saint-Clair 88, 169
William de Tancarville 23
William de Tracy 2
William d'Ypres 135–8, 142, 152, 155, 158,
    161–2, 185, 189, 192–3
William, earl of Gloucester xxi, 3, 58, 77n.138,
    85, 89, 90n.54, 91n.60, 92, 106,
    108nn.162–3, 109n.170, 110–14, 116,
    172n.230, 201, 206
William Esterling 76
William fitz Alan 140, 142, 160
William fitz Baldwin 106
William fitz John of Harptree 72, 106, 141, 151
William fitz Odo of Torrington 31, 56, 72,
    139n.77, 141–2
William fitz Osbern 15n.83, 75
William fitz Otto 100

William fitz Stephen 83n.12, 84n.16, 199
William Ghot 39
William Lovel of Bréval 34
William Martel 72, 158, 169, 170
William Mauduit I 66
William Mauduit II 31n.10, 66
William of Aumâle 155
William of Berkeley 107
William of Blois, brother of King Stephen xxi,
    129
William of Breteuil 15
William of Corbeil, archbishop of
    Canterbury 37, 55, 130, 184
William of Glastonbury 31, 37, 56, 167
William of Jumièges 7n.41, 184
William of Malmesbury xvi–xviii, xx, 1, 4, 11,
    11n.60, 13–14, 17n, 18, 23, 27, 32, 35,
    41, 41n.67, 42, 53, 57, 64, 96, 131–2,
    134, 136–7, 139, 145, 148–9, 151, 154,
    156, 158–60, 162–3, 165–7, Chapter 6
  *De Antiquitate Glastonie Ecclesie* 181
  *Gesta Pontificum Anglorum* 181
  *Gesta Regum Anglorum* 11, 35, 178, 181,
    187*f*, 202
  *Historia Novella* xvi–xviii, 1, 11, 18, 41,
    41n.67, 53, 166, 179*f*, 182–7, 187*f*,
    187–91, 194–8, 203, *see also* Robert,
    Earl Of Gloucester, Literary Patron
  *Historia Pontificalis* 181
William of Poitiers 184
William of Salisbury 168–9, 171
William Peverel of Dover 68, 140, 173–5
William, Peverel of Nottingham 152
William Rufus (William II, King of England)
    xxi, 2–3, 5, 8–9, 13, 16, 20, 23, 50,
    57n.3, 64–5, 67, 69, 74–5, 88n.40
William Scotus, abbot of Cerne (Dors.) 124–5
William, sheriff of Cardiff 110, 122
  probably the William de Cardiff of 107,
    110n.177, 123
William, sheriff of Warwickshire 52
William Talvas 128–9
William Turniant 19, 66–7
Wilton (Wilts.) 7, 124, 142, 157, 168–70,
    173, 203, 240
  Priory 169
Winchcombe (Glos.) 70, 80, 94, 149, 153, 240
  castle 173–4
Winchester (Hants.) 8, 19, 23, 32, 36, 44,
    46–7, 70–1, 80, 83, 94, 145, 158–61,
    163, 169, 177, 186, 189, 190, 197,
    199, 202, 205, 240
  Cathedral 157
*Winchester Annals* xvin.12, 203
Windsor (Berks.) 41
Wingfield (Winkfield) (Wilts.) 66, 109n.170
Winkleigh (Devon) 65
Winterborne (Dors.) 66
Wissant (Pas-de-Calais) 130
Witham river 154

Woodstock (Oxon.) 34, 36, 37n.46, 45, 110, 122, 157–8
Wootton St. Mary's (Glos.) 119
Worcester 18n.96, 71, 86, 99, 138, 153, 176, 201, 240
Worcestre, William 96n.89
Wotton-under-Edge (Glos.) 107
Wye Valley 75

Yelden (Beds.) 50